The Constitutional Boundaries of European Fiscal Federalism

This book bridges the study of European constitutionalism with the study of 'fiscal federalism' – the subfield of public economics concerned with structuring public finances between different levels of government in federal states. On one axis, this book delves into European Union and Member State constitutional law from all EU Member States in order to investigate and identify the existence of permanent constitutional boundaries that will impinge upon the selection of proposed models for EU fiscal federalism. On the second axis, this book engages the study of fiscal federalism in order to determine which institutional configurations known to that field remain legally and economically implementable within those boundaries. It provides a far-reaching investigation of which models of fiscal federalism are compatible with the constitutional boundaries of the European legal order.

Brady Gordon is an Adjunct Professor at the University of British Columbia, and a barrister and solicitor at Blake, Cassels & Graydon LLP in Canada. He obtained his PhD from Trinity College, the University of Dublin, where he was an Irish Research Council postdoctoral scholar at the School of Law.

Cambridge Studies in European Law and Policy

The focus of this series is European law broadly understood. It aims to publish original monographs in all fields of European law, from work focusing on the institutions of the EU and the Council of Europe to books examining substantive fields of European law as well as examining the relationship between European law and domestic, regional and international legal orders. The series publishes works adopting a wide variety of methods: comparative, doctrinal, theoretical and inter-disciplinary approaches to European law are equally welcome, as are works looking at the historical and political facets of the development of European law and policy. The main criterion is excellence i.e. the publication of innovative work, which will help to shape the legal, political and scholarly debate on the future of European law.

Books in the Series

The Constitutional Boundaries of European Fiscal Federalism

Brady Gordon
The University of British Columbia
Blake, Cassels & Graydon LLP

CAMBRIDGE
UNIVERSITY PRESS

CAMBRIDGE
UNIVERSITY PRESS

University Printing House, Cambridge CB2 8BS, United Kingdom

One Liberty Plaza, 20th Floor, New York, NY 10006, USA

477 Williamstown Road, Port Melbourne, VIC 3207, Australia

314–321, 3rd Floor, Plot 3, Splendor Forum, Jasola District Centre, New Delhi – 110025, India

103 Penang Road, #05–06/07, Visioncrest Commercial, Singapore 238467

Cambridge University Press is part of the University of Cambridge.

It furthers the University's mission by disseminating knowledge in the pursuit of education, learning, and research at the highest international levels of excellence.

www.cambridge.org
Information on this title: www.cambridge.org/9781108830096
DOI: 10.1017/9781108909037

© Brady Gordon 2022

First published 2022

A catalogue record for this publication is available from the British Library.

Library of Congress Cataloging-in-Publication Data
Names: Gordon, Brady, editor.
Title: The constitutional boundaries of European fiscal federalism / [edited by] Brady Gordon, Cassels & Graydon LLP.
Description: Cambridge, United Kingdom ; New York, NY : Cambridge University Press, 2022. | Series: Cambridge studies in European law and policy | Includes bibliographical references and index.
Identifiers: LCCN 2021024119 | ISBN 9781108830096 (hardback) | ISBN 9781108909037 (ebook)
Subjects: LCSH: Finance, Public – Law and legislation – European Union countries. | Fiscal policy – European Union countries. | Intergovernmental fiscal relations – European Union countries. | Monetary unions – European Union countries. | Economic integration – European Union countries. | Constitutional law – European Union countries. | Treaty on European Union (1992 February 7)
Classification: LCC KJE7050 .C67 2021 | DDC 343.24/034–dc23
LC record available at https://lccn.loc.gov/2021024119

ISBN 978-1-108-83009-6 Hardback

Basic Table of Contents

Detailed Table of Contents

Figures

Acknowledgements

This book began as a PhD thesis at Trinity College, the University of Dublin in 2013, and was finished a few months after the birth of my first child in 2020 while teaching at the University of British Columbia and enjoying generous leave from Blake, Cassels & Graydon LLP. It could not have been completed without the support, inspiration and input I received from my family, friends and colleagues in the law on both sides of the Atlantic.

At the outset, this study would not have been possible without generous doctoral funding and support from the Irish Research Council and the School of Law at Trinity College, the University of Dublin. Nor would it have been possible to convert it into a book without the partners at Blake, Cassels & Graydon LLP, who supported me without equivocation and asked nothing in return save that some day it might end (a sometimes dubious prospect). Thank you for making it possible for me to pursue my research and to write this book.

I am grateful to my colleagues and friends at Trinity College, who honed my research through innumerable insights and discussions over many years. In particular, I am grateful to Professors Diarmuid Rossa Phelan, Caoimhín MacMaoláin, Catherine Donnelly, Neville Cox, Alex Schuster and Stuart MacLennan for their confidence, their advice and their insight. A special thank you to Kelley McCabe, Catherine Finnegan and all the staff and faculty who made my many years researching at the School of Law smooth and joyful.

I am grateful to the anonymous peer reviewers at Cambridge University Press, as well as my external and internal examiners, Professors Damian Chalmers and David Fennelly, who challenged my research at every turn and provided innumerable improvements to my approach, all of which have greatly benefitted this book.

Thank you to the editors and staff of the Cambridge Studies in European Law and Policy Series, Tom Randall, Gemma Smith, Professor Mark Dawson, Professor Laurence Gormley, and Professor Jo Shaw, for allowing me to update and publish my work with their series, and ultimately for guiding me smoothly through the process.

Importantly, thank you to my mum for being the sort of mum that always worries and always calls. Thank you to my dad, for being the sort of dad who coaches at fifteen and proofreads at thirty. Thank you to my sister, for her friendship despite my many years abroad. Thank you to my grandparents, for inspiration.

Most of all, thank you to my wife Allie. At times my surrogate supervisor, at times my benefactor, but always my best friend and the love of my life, I started this project for me, but I finished it for her.

Table of Cases

General Court of the European Union

Austria

Belgium

Bulgaria

Canada

Croatia

Denmark

Estonia

Finland

Germany

rs202005052bvr085915, *Bundesverfassungsgericht* (Constitutional Court), available in English at: www.bundesverfassungsgericht.de accessed 22 July 2020

Weiss v. *Bundestag and Federal Government (Order for Reference) (Germany)* (Cases 2 BvR 859/15, 2 BvR 1651/15, 2 BvR 2006/15, 2 BvR 980/16); ECLI: DE:BVerfG:2017:rs201707182bvr085915 *Bundesverfassungsgericht* (Constitutional Court), available in English at: www .bundesverfassungsgericht.de accessed 22 July 2020

Greece

Athens Paper SA (Greece), Decision 161/2010, ECLI:EL: COS:2010:0115A16101E3166, Συμβούλιο της Επικρατείας (Council of State)

Athens Water Supply and Sewerage Company S.A. (Greece), Decision 2906/ 2014; ECLI:EL:COS:2014: 0523A190612E4344 Συμβούλιο της Επικρατείας (Council of State)

Banana Market (Greece), Case 815/1984 in Oppenheimer, *The Cases* (Vol I) 576, Συμβούλιο της Επικρατείας (Council of State)

Jus Soli (Greece), Decision 260/2013; ECLI:EL: COS:2013:0204A46010E6342, Συμβούλιο της Επικρατείας (Council of State)

Karella v. *Minister of Industry (Greece)*, Case 3312/1989 in Oppenheimer, *The Cases* (Vol I) 584, Συμβούλιο της Επικρατείας (Council of State)

Katsarou v. *DI.KATSA (Greece)*, Case 3458/1998) in Oppenheimer, *The Cases* (Vol II) 300, Συμβούλιο της Επικρατείας (Council of State)

Michaniki (Greece), Decision 3470/2011; ECLI:EL: COS:2011:1104A347002E7710, Συμβούλιο της Επικρατείας (Council of State)

Mineral Rights Discrimination (Greece), Case 2152/1986 in Oppenheimer, *The Cases* (Vol I) 581, Συμβούλιο της Επικρατείας (Council of State)

Real Property Acquisition (Greece), Case 43/1990 in Oppenheimer, *The Cases* (Vol I) 589, Συμβούλιο της Επικρατείας (Council of State)

Hungary

Agricultural Surplus Stocks (Hungary) Decision 17/2004 (V(25) ABIV1 *Magyarország Alkotmánybírósága* (Constitutional Court) English version available at: www.mkab.hu accessed 3 June 2015

Italy

Latvia

Lithuania

Luxembourg

Malta

Netherlands

Bosch GmbH and Another v. *De Geus en Uitdenbogerd (Netherlands)*, Case 13/61 [1965] NILR 318 Hoge Raad (Supreme Court) in Oppenheimer, *The Cases* (Vol I) 672

Metten v. *Minister van Financiën (Netherlands)* [1995] NJB-katern 545 (7 July 1996) *Afdeling Gschillen van Besturr Raad van State* (Administrative Disputes Division, Council of State) in Oppenheimer, *The Cases* (Vol 2) 401

Poland

Brussels Regulation (Poland), SK 45/09 (6 November 2011) in Biblioteka Trybunału Konstytucyjnego, *Selected Rulings* (Vol LI) 247 *Trybunał Konstytucyjny* (Constitutional Tribunal)

Constitutional Tribunal Act (Poland), K 39/16 (11 August 2016) *Trybunał Konstytucyjny* (Constitutional Tribunal)

Constitutionality of the Accession Treaty (Poland), K 18/04 (11 May 2005) in Biblioteka Trybunału Konstytucyjnego, *Selected Rulings* (Vol LI) *Trybunał Konstytucyjny* (Constitutional Tribunal)

European Arrest Warrant (Poland), P 1/05 (27 April 2005) in Biblioteka Trybunału Konstytucyjnego, *Selected Rulings* (Vol LI) 41 *Trybunał Konstytucyjny* (Constitutional Tribunal)

Excise Duties (Poland), P 37/05 (19 December 2006) in Biblioteka Trybunału Konstytucyjnego, *Selected Rulings* (Vol LI) 80 *Trybunał Konstytucyjny* (Constitutional Tribunal)

Lisbon Treaty (Poland), K 32/09 (24 November 2010) in Biblioteka Trybunału Konstytucyjnego, *Selected Rulings* (Vol LI) 80 *Trybunał Konstytucyjny* (Constitutional Tribunal)

Ratification of European Council Decision 2011/199/EU (Poland), K 33/12 (27 June 2013) in Biblioteka Trybunału Konstytucyjnego, *Selected Rulings* (Vol LI) 295 *Trybunał Konstytucyjny* (Constitutional Tribunal)

Representation in the European Council, Kpt 2/08 (20 May 2009) in Biblioteka Trybunału Konstytucyjnego, *Selected Rulings* (Vol LI) 122 *Trybunał Konstytucyjny* (Constitutional Tribunal)

Portugal

40 Hour Work Week (Portugal), Cases 935/12 and 962/13 (Judgment 794/ 2013) *Tribunal Constitucional* (Constitutional Court)

Romania

Slovak Republic

Switzerland

United Kingdom

United States

Table of Legislation, Treaties and Conventions

Intergovernmental Treaties, Agreements, Conventions, Charters and Protocols

Agreement of 9 February 1970 Setting up a System of Short-term Monetary Support Among the Central Banks of the Member States of the EEC, in *Compendium of Community Monetary Texts* (Monetary Committee, 1986) 55

Agreement of 10 April 1972 between the Central Banks of the Member States of the EEC on the narrowing of the margins of fluctuation between Community currencies (Basel Accord), in *Compendium of Community Monetary Texts* (Monetary Committee, 1974) [1974] EC Bulletin Supplement

Agreement of 13 March 1979 between the central banks of the Member States of the EEC laying down the operating procedures for the European Monetary System, in *Compendium of Community Monetary Texts* (Monetary Committee of the EC, 1986) 47

EFSF Consolidated Articles of Association (23 April 2014) www .efsf.europa.eu/attachments/EFSFStatusCoordonnes23AVRL2014.pdf accessed 31 December 2014

EFSF Framework Agreement (2014) www.efsf.europa.eu/attachments/2 0111019efsf_frameworkagreementen.pdf accessed 31 December 2014

EFSF, 'Amendment Agreement Relating to the Loan Facility Agreement' (EFSF, 26 June 2013)

EFSF, 'Master Financial Assistance Facility Agreement' (22 December 2010) www.efsf.europa.eu/attachments/Master%20FFA %20Ireland.pdf accessed 25 February 2015

Primary EU Law

EU Secondary Legislation

Council Directives

Council Directive 77/91/EEC of 13 December 1976 on co-ordination of safeguards in respect of the formation of public limited liability companies and the maintenance and alteration of their capital, with a view to making such safeguards equivalent [1977] OJ L 26/1

Council Directive 89/106/EEC of 21 December 1988 on the approximation of laws, regulations and administrative provisions of the Member States relating to construction products [1989] OJ L 40/12

Council Directive 93/6/EEC on the capital adequacy of investments firms and credit institutions [1993] OJ L 141/1

Council Directive 2011/85/EU of 8 November 2011 on requirements for budgetary frameworks of the Member States [2011] OJ L 306/41

Council Regulations

Council Regulation (EC) No 1466/97 of 7 July 1997 on the strengthening of the surveillance of budgetary positions and the surveillance and co-ordination of economic policies [1997] OJ L 209/1

Council Regulation (EC) No 1467/97 of 7 July 1997 on the speeding up and clarifying the implementation of the excessive deficit procedure [1997] OJ L 209/6

Council Regulation (EC) No 1055/2005 of 27 June 2005 amending Regulation No 1466/97 on the strengthening of the surveillance of budgetary positions and the surveillance and co-ordination of economic policies [2005] OJ L 174/1

Council Regulation (EC) No 1056/05 on speeding up and clarifying the implementation of the excessive deficit procedure [2005] OJ L 174/5

Council Regulation (EU) No 407/2010 of 11 May 2010 establishing a European financial stabilisation mechanism [2010] OJ L 118/1

Council Regulation (EU) No 1173/2011 of the European Parliament and of the Council of 16 November 2011 on the effective enforcement of budgetary surveillance in the euro area [2011] OJ L 306/1

Council Regulation (EU) No 1175/2011 of the European Parliament and of the Council of 16 November 2011 amending Council Regulation (EC) No 1466/97 on the strengthening of the surveillance of budgetary

Council Decisions

Council Implementing Decisions

Council Recommendations

European Parliament Resolutions

Commission Communications

European Commission, 'Common principles on national fiscal correction mechanisms' (Communication) COM(2012) 342 final

European Commission, 'A blueprint for a deep and genuine economic and monetary union' (Communication) COM(2012) 777 final

European Commission, Alert Mechanism Report COM(2012) 68 final

European Commission, 'Strengthening the Social Dimension of the Economic and Monetary Union' COM(2013) 690 final.

European Commission, Alert Mechanism Report 2014 COM(2013) 790 final

European Commission, Economic Governance Review: Report on the application of Regulations (EU) no 1173/2011, 1174/2011, 1175/2011, 1176/2011, 1177/2011, 472/2013 and 473/2013 COM(2014) 905 final

European Commission, 'Making the Best Use of the Flexibility within the Existing Rules of the Stability and Growth Pact' COM(2015) 12 final

European Commission, Annual Growth Survey 2016 COM(2015) 690 final

European Commission, Reflection paper on the Deepening of the Economic and Monetary Union COM(2017) 291 final

European Commission, 'New Budgetary instruments for a Stable Euro Area' COM(2017) 822 final

European Commission, 'Proposal for a Council Directive laying down provision for strengthening fiscal responsibility and the medium-term budgetary orientation in the Member States' COM(2017) 824 final

European Commission, 'Proposal for a Council Regulation on the establishment of the European Monetary Fund' COM(2017) 827 final

European Commission, 'Opinion of 21.11.2018 on the revised Draft Budgetary plan of Italy' COM(2018) 8028 final

European Commission, 'Opinion of 23.10.2018 on the Draft Budgetary Plan of Italy' COM(2018) 7510 final

European Commission, 'Alert Mechanism Report 2019 Statistical Annex' COM(2018) 758 final

European Commission, 'Economic governance review: Report on the application of Regulations (EU) no 1173/2011, 1174/2011, 1175/2011, 1176/2011, 1177/2011, 472/2013 and 473/2013' COM(2020) 55 final

European Commission, 'Report from the Commission: France' COM (2020) 538 final 1

Commission Recommendations and Decisions

Commission Decision (EU) 2015/1937 of 21 October 2015 establishing an independent advisory European Fiscal Board [2015] OJ L 282/37

Commission Recommendation for a Council Decision giving notice to France, in accordance with Art. 104(9) of the EC Treaty, to take measures for the deficit reduction judged necessary in order to remedy the situation of excessive deficit (Recommendation) SEC (2003) 1121 final

Commission Recommendation for a Council Decision giving notice to Germany, in accordance with Art. 104(9) of the EC Treaty, to take measures for the deficit reduction judged necessary in order to remedy the situation of excessive deficit (Recommendation) SEC (2003) 1317 final

Commission Recommendation for a Council Recommendation on the 2014 National Reform Programme of Ireland and delivering a Council opinion on the 2015 Stability Programme of Ireland COM(2014) 408 final

National Legislation

Austria

Federal Constitutional Law on the Accession of Austria (Federal Law Gazette 1994/744)

Austrian Federal Constitutional Law (version dated 1 January 2010) English version available at: www.ris.bka.gv.at/ accessed 6 June 2019

Belgium

Constitution of the Kingdom of Belgium, as updated following the constitutional revision of 22 April 2019 (Belgian Official Gazette of 2 May 2019 (Belgian House of Representatives, 2020), English version accessible at: www.dekamer.be/kvvcr/pdf_sections/publications/con stitution/GrondwetUK.pdf accessed 2 November 2020

Bulgaria

Constitution of the Republic of Bulgaria, Prom SG 56/13 JUL 1991, Amend. SG 85/26 Sep 2003, SG 18/25 Feb 2005, SG 27/31 Mar 2006, SG 78/26 Sep 2006 – Constitutional Court Judgment No.7/2006, SG 12/6 Feb 2007, SG 100/18 Dec 2015, English version accessible at: www .parliament.bg/en/const/ accesed 5 July 2020

Canada

Constitution Act, 1982, being Schedule B to the Canada Act 1982 (UK), 1982 c. 11 (UK)

Balanced Budget Act, C.Q.L.R. 2001 c. E-12.00001 (Quebec)

Balanced Budget and Ministerial Accountability Act, S.B.C. 2001, c. 28 (British Columbia)

Bank of Canada Act, R.S.C. 1985 c. B-2 (Canada)

British North America Act 1867 (UK) 30 & 31 Vict, c. 3 [1985] RSC App II, No 5 (UK)

Budget Transparency and Accountability Act, S.B.C. 2000, c. 23 (British Columbia)

Federal-Provincial Fiscal Arrangements Act, R.S.C. 1985 c. F-8 (Canada)

Finance Act, S.N.S. 2010, c. 2 (Nova Scotia)

Fiscal Planning and Transparency Act, S.A. 2015, c. F-14.7 (Alberta)

The Fiscal Responsibility and Taxpayer Protection Act, C.C.S.M. 2018 c. F84 (Manitoba)

Fiscal Sustainability, Transparency and Accountability Act, S.O. 2019, c. 7 (Ontario)

Fiscal Transparency and Accountability Act, S.N.B. 2014, c. 63 9 (New Brunswick)

The Growth and Financial Security Act, S.S. 2008, c. G-81 (Saskatchewan)

Croatia

The Constitution of the Republic of Croatia (Consolidated Text) English translation accessible at: www.sabor.hr/files/uploads/CONSTITUTIO N_CROATIA.pdf accessed 15 June 2020

Cyprus

The Fifth Amendment of the Constitution, Law 127(I) of 2006 (English Translation, Office of the Law Commissioner) ΓΕΝ (A) – L.94

Constitution of the Republic of Cyprus (Πρόεδρος της Κυπριακής Δημοκρατίας, President of the Republic of Cyprus, 2019)

Czech Republic

Constitution of the Czech Republic of 16 December 1992, Amended by Act No. 347/1997 Coll., Act No. 300/2000 Coll., Act No. 448/2001 Coll., Act No. 395/2001 Coll., Act No. 515/2002 Coll., English translation available at: www.psp.cz/en/docs/laws/1993/1.html.org/ accessed 9 July 2019

Denmark

The Constitutional Act of Denmark (*Folketinget*, 2011) English translation available at: www.thedanishparliament.dk/ accessed 6 June 2019.

Estonia

The Constitution of the Republic of Estonia Amendment Act RT I 2003, 64, 429

Constitution of the Republic of Estonia of 28 June 1992, RT 1992, 26, 349 (as amended to 13.08.2015 – RT I, 15.05.2015, 1) English translation available at: www.president.ee/en/republic-of-estonia/the-constitution/index.html accessed 12 December 2019

Finland

Act 1540/94 of the Statutes of Finland (Act of Accession of Finland to the EU)

The Constitution of Finland 11 June 1999 (731/1999, as amended to 8172/2018) (Unofficial translation, Ministry of Justice Finland, 2018)

France

Constitution of October 4, 1958 (France) (Amendments to Constitutional Act no. 2008–78 of 23 July 2008, Assemblée Nationale, 2008)

Declaration of the Rights of Man and the Citizen of 26 August 1789 (France), English translation available at: www.refworld.org/docid/3a e6b52410.html accessed 21 July 2020

Germany

Basic Law for the Federal Republic of Germany (Deutscher Bundestag, 2019), English translation available at: www.btg-bestellservice.de/pdf/ 80201000.pdf accessed 5 October 2020

Greece

The Constitution of Greece (As revised by the parliamentary resolution of May 27th 2008 of the VIIIth Revisionary Parliament, Hellenic Parliament, 2019), accessible at: www.hellenicparliament.gr/en/Voul i-ton-Ellinon/To-Politevma/Syntagma

Hungary

The Fundamental Law of Hungary (25 April 2011) (courtesy translation effective as of 1 January 2019, Ministry of Justice, 2019) accessible at: https://njt.hu/translated/doc/TheFundamentalLawofHungar y_20190101_FIN.pdf

Ireland

Constitution of Ireland (Department of the Taoiseach, Government Publications, 2020)
European Communities Act 1972 No 27/1972 (Ireland)
Euro Area Loan Facility Act 2010, No 7 of 2010 (Ireland)
European Communities Act 1972 No 27/1972 (Ireland)

Italy

Constitution of the Italian Republic (Senato Della Repubblica, 2019), unofficial English translation available at: www.senato.it/ accessed 6 June 2019

Latvia

On International Treaties of the Republic of Latvia, Latvian journal, 2009, 205 (Text consolidated by *Valsts valodas centrs* (State Language Centre) with amending laws of: 26 February 2004; 17 December 2009; 13 June 2013)
The Constitution of the Republic of Latvia (*Latvijas Republikas Saeima,* 2014), English translation available at: www.saeima.lv/en/legislation/ constitution accessed 2 July 2019
Constitutional Court Law (Text consolidated by *Valsts valodas centrs* (State Language Centre) with amending laws of: 11 September 1997 to 12 September 2013)

Lithuania

Constitution of the Republic of Lithuania of 25 October 1992, *Lieutovos Respublikos Seimas* official translation, 2015, accessible at: http://euro pam.eu/data/mechanisms/COI/COI%20Laws/Lithuania/Lithuania_Con stitution_1992,%20 amended%20in%202003.pdf
Constitutional Act On Membership of the Republic of Lithuania in the European Union of 13 July 2004 (Lithuania), English version accessible at: www.lrs.lt accessed 14 June 2020

Luxembourg

Constitution of Luxembourg of 1868, Texte coordonné à jour au 20 Octobre 2016, Ministère d'État.- Service Central de Législation, accessible at: www.legilux.lu accessed 12 January 2019

Malta

European Union Act of 2003, Act V of 2003, as amended by Act III of 2006; Legal notice 427 of 2007 and Act VII of 2012, Chap. 460 of the Laws of Malta

Constitution of Malta (Ministry for Justice, Culture and Local Government, 2020) English translation accessible at: https://legisla tion.mt/eli/const/eng/pdf. accessed 9 July 2020

Netherlands

The Constitution of the Kingdom of the Netherlands (Ministry of the Interior and Kingdom Relations, 2019) English version available at: www.government.nl/ accessed 6 December2019.

Poland

The Constitution of the Republic of Poland of 2nd April 1997, as pulished in *Dziennik Ustaw* No. 79, item 483 (as amended), English translation available at: www.sejm.gov.pl/prawo/konst/angielski/kon se.htm accessed 3 June 2019

Portugal

Resolution No 22/85 of 19 July 1985 of the Parliament of the Republic (*Suplemento ao Diário da República*, Series I, No 215), English translation available in: Andrew Oppenheimer (ed), *The Relationship between European Community law and National Law: The Cases* (Cambridge University Press, 1996), 686

Constitution of the Portuguese Republic (7th Revision, *Tribunal Constitucional*, 2005) available in English at: www .tribunalconstitucional.pt accessed 6 June 2018

Romania

Constitution of Romania, Official Gazette of Romania, Part I No 233 of 21 November 1991 (as amended) English translation acccessible at: www.cdep.ro/pls/dic/site.page?id=371 accessed 20 June 2020

Slovak Republic

Constitution of the Slovak Republic, 460/1992 Coll (inclusive of amendments to 1 July 2019), English translation available at: < www .ustavnysud.sk/en/ustava-slovenskej-republiky> accessed 1 January 2020

Slovenia

Constitution of Slovenia (Official Gazette of the Republic of Slovenia Nos. 33/91-I, 42/97, 66/2000, 24/03, 69/04, 68/06, and 47/13) available in English at: www.us-rs.si accessed 10 July 2019

Spain

The Spanish Constitution of 1978 (*Agencia Estatal Boletín Oficial del Estado*, 2019), English translation available at: www.boe.es/legislacion/docu mentos/ConstitucionINGLES.pdf accessed 10 July 2020
Ley Orgánica 10/1985 on Authorization for the Accession of Spain to the European Communites (2 August 1985)

Sweden

Act concerning the accession of Sweden to the European Union, Swedish Code of Statutes (*Svensk Författningssamling*) 1994 No 1500.
The Constitution of Sweden: The Fundamental Laws and the Rikstag Act (*Sveriges Rikstag*, 2016), English translation accessible at: www .riksdagen.se/globalassets/07.-dokument–lagar/the-constitution-of-sweden-160628.pdf accessed 12 January 2020

Switzerland

Federal Constitution of the Swiss Confederation of 18 April 1999 (Status as of 1 January 2020), English translation available at: www.admin.ch accessed 2 January 2020

United Kingdom

Bank of England Act, 1998 c. 11
European Communities Act, 1972 c. 68
European Union Act 2011, 2011 c. 1
European Union (Withdrawal) Act, 2018 c. 16
European Union (Withdrawal Agreement) Act, 2020 c. 1

United States

American Recovery and Reinvestment Act of 2009 (ARRA), Pub L 111–5; 122 Stat 115

The Constitution of the United States of America, National Archives Record Group 11: General Records of the United States Government, 1778–2006

Federal Reserve Act of 1913, ch 6, 38 Stat. 251, codified at 12 USC. ch. 3

Abbreviations

AAA	Act on the Accession of Austria to the European Union
ACIR	Advisory Commission on Inter-governmental Relations
AG	Advocate General
AGS	Annual Growth Survey
AMR	Alert Mechanism Report
APP	Asset Purchase Programme
ARRA	American Recovery and Reinvestment Act
AT	Austria
BBR	balanced-budget rule
BE	Belgium
BEPS	broad economic policy guidelines
BG	Bulgaria
BGLF	Bilateral Greek Loan Facility
BIS	Bank for International Settlements
BL	(German) Basic Law
BNA Act	British North America Act
BoG	(ESM) Board of Governors
BoP	balance of payments
bps	basis points
BVerfG	Bundesverfassungsgericht (German Federal Constitutional Court)
CAC	Collective Action Clause
CAP	Corrective Action Plan
CAR	Capital Adequacy Ratio
CEAA	Constitution of the Republic of Estonia Amendment Act
CEPS	Centre for European Policy Studies
CHT	Canada Health Transfer
CJEU	Court of Justice of the European Union

CRD	Capital Adequacy Directive
CST	Canada Social Transfer
CY	Cyprus
CZ	Czechia/Czech Republic
DG	Directorate-General (of the EU Commission)
DK	Denmark
ECCL	Enhanced conditions credit line
ECFIN	Directorate-General for Economic and Financial Affairs
ECJ	European Court of Justice
ECOFIN	Economic and Financial Affairs Council
ECSC	European Coal and Steel Community
ECU	European Currency Unit
EDP	Excessive Deficit Procedure
EE	Estonia
EESC	European Economic and Social Committee
EFB	European Fiscal Board
ESRI	Economic and Social Research Institute
EFSF	European Financial Stability Facility
EFSM	European Financial Stabilisation Mechanism
EIB	European Investment Bank
EIP	Excessive Imbalance Procedure
EL	Greece
EMCF	European Monetary Cooperation Fund
EMS	European Monetary System
EMU	(European) Economic and Monetary Union
EPP	Economic Partnership Programme
EPU	European Payments Union
ERM	Exchange Rate Mechanism
ES	Spain
ESA	European System of Accounts
ESDRF	European Sovereign Debt Restructuring Framework
ESM	European Stability Mechanism
ESRB	European Systemic Risk Board
EURIBOR	Euro InterBank Offered Rate
FGFF	First Generation Fiscal Federalism
FI	Finland
FPT	Federal-Provincial Territorial Collaboration
FR	France
FRSI	Fiscal Rule Strength Index
FSP	Fiscal Stabilization Program

GDP	Gross Domestic Product
HR	Croatia
HTS	Harmonized Technical Standard
HU	Hungary
IADB	Inter-American Development Bank
IDR	In-depth Review
IGC	(Maastricht) Inter-governmental Conference
IE	Ireland
IEO	(IMF) Independent Evaluation Office
IFI	Independent fiscal institution
IMF	International Monetary Fund
ISB	Independent Standards Body
IT	Italy
LiA	Lending into Arrears
LT	Lithuania
LU	Luxembourg
LV	Latvia
MIP	Macroeconomics Imbalance Procedure
MLSA	Minimum linear structural adjustment
MoU	Memorandum of Understanding
MSP	Multilateral Surveillance Procedure
MT	Malta
MTO	Medium-Term Objective
NASBO	National Association of State Budget Officers
NBER	National Bureau of Economic Research
NEER	Nominal Effective Exchange Rate
NL	Netherlands
NRP	National Reform Programme
NSI	National Statistical Institute
OCA	Optimum Currency Area (theory)
OECD	Organisation for Economic Co-operation and Development
OJ	Official Journal (of the European Union)
OMC	Open Method of Coordination
OMT	Outright Monetary Transactions
PCCL	Precautionary credit line
PIIGS	Portugal, Ireland, Italy, Greece, Spain
PL	Poland
PPP	Public-private partnership
pps	Percentage points

PSPP	Public Sector Purchase Programme
PT	Portugal
QMV	Qualified Majority Vote
REER	Real Effective Exchange Rate
RO	Romania
RWA	Risk-Weighted Assets
S&P	Standard & Poor's
SCPs	Stability and Convergence Programmes
SE	Sweden
SGFF	Second Generation Fiscal Federalism
SGP	Stability and Growth Pact
SI	Slovenia
SK	Slovakia
SMP	Securities Markets Programmes
SPV	Special-purpose vehicle
SSHD	Secretary of State for the Home Department
SST	Secretary of State for Transport
TEU	Treaty on European Union
TFP	Total Factor Productivity
TFEU	Treaty on the Functioning of the European Union
TSCG	Treaty on Stability, Coordination and Governance
UK	United Kingdom
US	United States
VfGH	Verfassungsgerichtshof (Austrian Constitutional Court)

Part I

Methods and Introduction

The European Union (EU) has struggled with the meaning of fiscal federalism in Europe since the Treaty on European Union and the creation of the Economic and Monetary Union (EMU). The model of fiscal federalism inscribed in the Treaty at Maastricht conceived of national governments as distinct, miniature sovereign borrowers which retained the necessary fiscal competencies to manage sovereign economies. Central to the Maastricht model is a prohibition on financial assistance (Article 125 TFEU, ex Article 103 TEC) that enshrines a constitutional consensus on fiscal sovereignty and exposes Member States to market discipline and hard budget constraints.[1] This follows a formula for federal equilibrium that is well-established in theory and well-evidenced in history, visible in the autonomous credit ratings of Swiss cantons, Canadian provinces and American states.[2]

That model has been vitiated by the (now-realized) sovereign bailout expectation.[3] The European bailouts, the (now permanent) European Stability Mechanism (ESM), and a new Article 136(3) TFEU have

---

[1] On these concepts, see below, at nn 62–63 and Chapter 2, Sections 2.2.4 and 2.3.

[2] See Sections 8.2.2, 8.2.3, 8.2.4 for Switzerland, the United States and Canada. As Jens Weidmann, 'Crisis Management' (Walter Eucken Lecture, Freiburg, 2 November 2013), observes, 'The framework of monetary union was quite coherent, it reflected well-established regulatory policy principles, and the attempt was made to learn the lessons and not to repeat the errors of the past.' See also Jürgen Stark, 'Lessons from the European Crisis' (2013) 33 Cato J 541, 544–545, 'Historical examples show that the aforementioned principles and rules are essential for the smooth functioning of a monetary union.'

[3] Edoardo Chiti and Gustavo Teixeira Pedro, 'The Constitutional Implications of the European Responses to the Financial and Public Debt Crisis' (2013) 50 CMLR 683, 698–699; R Daniel Kelemen, 'Law, Fiscal Federalism, and Austerity' (2015) 22 Ind J Global Stud 379, 388; Hans-Werner Sinn, *The Euro Trap: On Bursting Bubbles, Budgets and Beliefs* (Oxford University Press, 2014), 6: 'This destroyed the basic pillars of the Maastricht Treaty.'

institutionalized a joint liability group.[4] In the wake of the sovereign debt crisis, successive reforms have incrementally supplanted the decentralized architecture of fiscal federalism in the Treaties with mechanisms more commonly seen in unitary states: financial transfers and centralized governance of Member State fiscal policy. Fiscal federalism in the EU is now the subject of piecemeal renegotiation that increasingly exceeds the limits of the Maastricht model: a European Monetary Fund, direct tax harmonization, binding budget contracts and a concomitant power to rewrite national budgets were all the objects of recent EU initiatives. A new model is emerging, yet there is no consensus on what elements of 'fiscal union' are necessary to achieve equilibrium in the new model, and no consensus on what is permissible within the constitutional boundaries of the EU legal order. Where individual measures have inched beyond the boundaries of fiscal sovereignty contemplated by national legal orders, the result has been stirrings of legal revolt and revolution: legal challenges,[5] political upheaval[6] and divergent national appetites to deepen or repatriate European powers.[7] The EU must not only redefine its model of fiscal federalism, but ensure that it is anchored within deeper constitutional boundaries underlying the European legal order as a whole.

In order to remain stable and permanent as a matter of law and economics, the model chosen for EU fiscal federalism must do two things: it must, first, be compatible with the constitutional boundaries of the EU legal order; and, second, it must 'work' – that is, it must not be economically unstable. In that respect, the EMU has now spent over half its life in a state of crisis.[8] Some economists estimate that Europe's GDP

---

[4] On the problem of EU joint liability, see Chapter 3 Sections 3.1.1–3.1.2 (and sources cited).

[5] Case C-370/12 *Pringle* v. *Ireland* EU:C:2012:756; *Gauweiler* v. *Bundestag (Germany)* (2 BvR 2728-2731/13, 2 BvE 13/13); ECLI:DE:BVerfG:2016:rs201606212b-vr272813; Joined Cases C-8-10/15 P *Ledra et al.* v. *Commission and ECB* EU:C:2016:701; Joined Cases 105–109/15 P *Mallis* v. *Commission and ECB* EU:C:2016:702; Case C-41/15 *Dowling et al.* v. *Minister for Finance* EU:C:2016:836; Case C-493/17 *Weiss* EU:C:2018:1000; *Weiss* v. *Bundestag and Federal Government (Germany)* (2 BvR 859/15, 2 BvR 1651/15, 2 BvR 2006/15, 2 BvR 980/16); ECLI:DE: BVerfG:2020:rs202005052bvr085915.

[6] Jorge Valero, 'EU Puts "Ever Closer Union" on Hold' *EurActiv.com* (11 October 2016) www .euractiv.com/section/future-eu/news/eu-puts-ever-closer-union-on-hold/ accessed 11 October 2016.

[7] Editorial, 'Some Thoughts Concerning the Draft Treaty on a Reinforced Economic Union' (2012) 49 CMLR 1; Charlemagne, 'Europe à l'Hollandaise' *The Economist* (London, 9 February 2013) 27.

[8] See Chapter 3, nn 2, 4.

is now as much as 18% lower than if the EMU had never been invented at all.[9] From its inception, the EMU precipitated unthinkable macroeconomic imbalances that were unprecedented in over thirty years of economic data.[10] Now over a decade since the European sovereign debt crisis emerged, the cycle of macroeconomic imbalances which led to the crisis in the first place is repeating: EMU current account imbalances are widening, not narrowing;[11] interest rate spreads on sovereign bonds are near non-existent[12] and general government debt ratios remain far above those levels which triggered the sovereign debt crisis in the first place.[13]

And yet, a glance at the fiscal federalism literature should give pause. Comparative federations such as the United States, Switzerland and Canada – with no federal oversight of state budgets and no economic coordination whatsoever – have long since recovered from the global financial crisis. The United States, the very progenitor of the 2008 global financial crisis, declared its 'Great Recession' over in June 2009.[14] Its largest trading partner, Canada – another decentralized federation with comparable debt dispersion characteristics to the EU – suffered just seven months of recession.[15] The Swiss Confederation, whose two

---

[9] EMU GDP is 18% lower than if it had continued to grow at the modest pace before the euro was created: Joseph Stiglitz, *The Euro: How a Common Currency Threatens the Future of Europe* (Norton 2016), 72–73. It provided no boost to growth when it was supposedly working well: Stefan Kawalec, Ernest Pytlarczyk and Kamil Kamiński, *The Economic Consequences of the Euro* (Routledge 2020), 25–27; Paul De Grauwe, *Economics of Monetary Union* (13th ed., Oxford University Press, 2020), 64–65.

[10] See Chapter 3, Section 3.2.2, Figure 3.10.

[11] IMF, 'Current Account Balance, % GDP' (*IMF WEO Database*, 2020) www.imf.org/external/datamapper/BCA_NGDPD@WEO/OEMDC/ADVEC/WEOWORLD accessed 10 September 2020. EMU current account imbalances narrowed as a result of the crisis between 2008 and 2015, and have been growing again since 2016.

[12] Anna Hirtenstein, 'Europe's Riskiest Countries Find Debt Markets Wide Open' (*Wall Street Journal*, 2020) www.wsj.com/articles/europes-riskiest-countries-find-debt-markets-wide-open-11603191613 accessed 30 October 2020.

[13] EMU debt as a percentage of GDP in 2019 was 84.1%, compared with 70% in 2008. Among periphery countries, it was 117% (2019) compared to 74.7% (2008). Eurostat, 'Government Consolidated Gross Debt (gov_10dd_3dpt1)' (*Eurostat*, 2020) http://epp.eurostat.ec.europa.eu accessed 2 January 2020.

[14] NBER, 'Business Cycle Dating Committee' (*NBER*, 20 September 2010) www.nber.org/cycles/sept2010.html accessed 12 September 2016.

[15] OECD, 'Quarterly GDP' (*OECD*, 2018) https://data.oecd.org/gdp/quarterly-gdp.htm accessed 12 October 2018 ; Jean Boivin, 'The "Great" Recession in Canada: Perception vs Reality' *Bank of Canada* (Montreal, 28 March 2011) www.bankofcanada.ca/2011/03/great-recession-canada-perception-reality/ accessed 14 August 2020.

largest banks were highly exposed to the US subprime crisis, was out of negative growth within three quarters.[16]

The European Union now faces a choice between two well-worn paths in the history of constitutional law and economics in federal states: centralization under a single fiscal authority, or decentralization to the level of national constitutional authority. At stake in this debate is nothing less than the economic welfare of millions of people and the integrity of the EU legal order as a whole.

This book is intended to bridge the study of European constitutionalism and the study of 'fiscal federalism' – the subfield of public economics concerned with the structuring of public finance incentives in federal states. On one axis, this book delves deeply into European constitutional law in order to identify permanent boundaries integral to the stability of the European legal order as a whole.[17] On the second axis, it engages fiscal federalism to determine which models known to that field remain theoretically and empirically implementable within the European legal order. This approach is vital because the incumbent political prescriptions for 'fiscal union' set out in the EU *Five Presidents' Report* and Commission proposals enunciate blueprints that are, by their own admission, manifestly beyond the limits of the EU Treaties.[18] Furthermore, as Wyplosz points out, these catalogues of proposals to establish federal fiscal union 'do not even mention at all fiscal federalism principles [. . .] It is worrying to note that they seem unaware of the principles of fiscal federalism.'[19]

The central argument of this book is that the limits of the EU legal order in fiscal policy are circumscribed by unconferrable constitutional principles typically referred to as the limits of 'constitutional

---

[16] OECD, 'Quarterly GDP'.

[17] Unless otherwise specified, in this book the term 'European legal order' encompasses both Member State and EU legal orders as a contiguous interacting whole, including the constitutional bases for conferral outside the EU legal order, and national implementations of EU law within the EU legal order. 'EU legal order' refers to that part of the European legal order that is derived from the EU Treaties and that applies within the EU legal order. 'Member State' or 'national' legal orders and constitutional law refer to that part of the European legal order that does not derive from the EU Treaties and is Member State law.

[18] European Commission, 'A Blueprint for a Deep and Genuine Economic and Monetary Union' (Communication) COM(2012) 777 final, 26; Jean-Claude Juncker et al., *Completing Europe's Economic and Monetary Union (Five Presidents' Report)* (European Commission, 2015), 5.

[19] Charles Wyplosz, 'The Centralization-Decentralization Issue' (2015) European Economy Discussion Papers No 14, 23.

identity' – inviolable, immutable powers or principles so integral to the twenty-seven constitutional democracies at the basis of the European legal order that they can never be impinged or disposed-of without abrogating the constitutive identity of the state.[20] This book examines how this curtails the selection of available models of fiscal federalism in the EU and, among those remaining, which would result in a stable economic equilibrium based on available economic data. The thesis of this book is as follows.

First, Member State fiscal sovereignty is a permanent constitutional constraint upon the application of fiscal federalism theory in the EU. That constraint is implicitly but plainly impressed upon the allocation of competences in economic policy (Articles 2(3) and 5(1) TFEU) and the substantive provisions governing public finance in Articles 121–126 TFEU.[21] Under those articles, the Union competence for economic policy is one of 'mere coordination',[22] limited to providing 'a framework to coordinate these policies to a certain degree'.[23] The EU has no power to determine the content and composition of government revenues and expenditures, dictate structural reforms, or determine social allocations at national level.[24] This is not a mere reflection of good administration under the principle of subsidiarity. Under Articles 4(1), and 5(1)–(2) TEU, the Union can have no powers

---

[20] See Chapter 1, Section 1.2.2.

[21] Hereafter, unless otherwise specified, this book follows EU policy documents in using both 'economic policy' and 'fiscal policy' interchangeably to describe those competences over the use of government revenue, debt or expenditure to influence the economy. Cf: Kaarlo Tuori and Klaus Tuori, *The Eurozone Crisis: A Constitutional Analysis* (Cambridge University Press, 2014), 31 on the distinction between economic and fiscal policy.

[22] Federico Fabbrini, 'The Fiscal Compact, the "Golden Rule" and the Paradox of European Federalism' (2013) 36 BC Intl & Comp L Rev 1, 5.

[23] Alicia Hinarejos, 'The Euro Area Crisis and Constitutional Limits to Fiscal Integration' (2014) 14 CYELS 243.

[24] *Pringle* v. *Ireland* [64]: 'arts 2(2) and 5(1) TFEU restrict the role of the Union in the area of economic policy to the adoption of coordinating measures.' *Brunner* v. *EU Treaty (Germany)* (2 BvR 2134/92 & 2159/92) BVerfGE 89, 155, [1994] 1 CMLR 57 (*Bundesverfassungsgericht*) [64], [91]; *Gauweiler Order for Reference (Germany)* (2 BvR 2728/13); ECLI:DE:BVerfG:2014:rs201401142bvr272813, [39]: 'In this field of economic policy, the European Union is [...] essentially limited to a coordination of Member States economic policies.' *Weiss* v. *Bundestag and Federal Government (Order for Reference) (Germany)* (2 BvR 859/15, 2 BvR 1651/15, 2 BvR 2006/15, 2 BvR 980/16); ECLI:DE:BVerfG:2017: rs201707182bvr085915, [65]; *Weiss Decision (Germany)* [163]: 'the competence of the European Union in economic policy matters is essentially limited to coordinating the polices of the Member States [...] it is not, however, authorised to pursue its own economic policy agenda.'

other than what the Member States have given it, and *nemo plus iuris transfere (ad alium) potest quam ipse habet*, what the Member States have given it is limited by their own constitutional identities.[25] This marks

[25] For judicial statements to that effect, see: Germany: *R v. Oberlandesgericht (Germany)* (2 BvR 2735/14); ELCI:DE:BVerfG:2015:rs201512152bvr273514; [2017] 2 CMLR 2, [41] excerpted below, Section 1.2.2.1, at n 287. Spain: *Constitutional Treaty (Spain)* Opinion 1/ 2004; ECLI:ES:TC:2004:1D, [3] excerpted below, Section 1.2.2.1 at n 297; *Maastricht (Spain)* DTC 1/1992; ECLI:ES:TC:1992:1, [4] excerpted below, Section 1.2.1.1, at n 99. Poland: *Lisbon Treaty (Poland)* K 32/09 (24 November 2010) in Biblioteka Trybunału Konstytucyjnego, *Selected Rulings* (Vol LI) 80, [2.1], excerpted below, Section 1.2.2.1, n 338; *Ratification of European Council Decision 2011/199/EU (Poland)*, K 33/12 (27 June 2013) in Biblioteka Trybunału Konstytucyjnego, *Selected Rulings* (Vol LI) 295, [6.3.1]: Art. 90 of the Polish Constitution cannot 'constitute a basis of conferring … competence to enact legal acts or take decisions that would be inconsistent with the Constitution'. Denmark: *Carlsen v. Rasmussen* (Case I 361/1997); [1999] 3 CMLR 854 (*Højesteret*) [13] 'the authorities of the realm have themselves no such power'. Ireland: *Crotty v. An Taoiseach (Ireland)* [1987] IESC 4; [1987] IR 713, 783 (further excerpted below, Section 1.2.2.2, n 372), 'If it is now desired to qualify, curtail or inhibit the existing sovereign power […] it is not within the power of the Government itself to do so.' Belgium: *European School v. Hermans-Jacobs and Heuvelmans-van Iersel*, Case 12/94 (*Cour d'arbitrage*), in Oppenheimer, *The Cases* (Vol II) 155, [B.4] (further excerpted in Chapter 1, nn 98, 118), 'no rule of international law, which is the creation of States […] gives the power to States to conclude treaties which are contrary to their Constitutions.' *TSCG (Belgium)*, Case 62/2016 (28 April 2016) (*Cour constitutionnel*) [B.8.5], 'When assenting to a treaty, the legislator cannot undermine the guarantees provided for by the Constitution.' Czech Republic: *Treaty of Lisbon I (Czech Republic)* Pl ÚS 19/08 (26 November 2008) (*Ústavní Soud*) [145] excerpted below, Section 1.2.1.1, n 98. Lithuania: *On Amending Article 125 of the Constitution (Lithuania)*, Case 22/2013 (24 January 2014) English version at: www.lrkt.lt/lt accessed 4 June 2020 (*Konstitucinis Teismas*) [4]–[6.1] 'the fundamental constitutional values – the independence of the state, democracy and the republic […] must not be negated under any circumstances'. Croatia: *Referendum on Auxiliary Activities in the Public Sector (Croatia)* U-VIIR-1159/2015 (8 April 2015) (*Ustavni sud*) [33.4]; *Notification on Referendum on Definition of Marriage (Croatia)* SUS – 1/2013 (14 November 2013) (*Ustavni sud*) [6] excerpted below, Section 1.2.2.1 at nn 320–321. Latvia: *Lisbon (Latvia)*, Case 2008–35-01 (7 April 2009), English version at: www.satv.tiesa.gov.lv accessed 17 July 2016 (*Satversmes tiesa*) [11.1], [14],[15], [17], [18.3]. Slovakia: *Constitutional Treaty (Slovakia)* II ÚS 171/05 (27 February 2008) (*Ústavný Súd*), 36. Romania: *Decision 80/2014 on the proposal to amend the Constitution (Romania)*, Monitorul Oficial No. 246 of 7 April 2014 (*Curtea Constituțională*) [450]–[460] excerpted below, Section 1.2.2.1, n 319. Bulgaria: *Decision 7/2018 on Mixed EU Treaties (Bulgaria)*, SG No 36 of 27 April 2018 (Конституционен съд) excerpted below, Section 1.2.2.1 at n 322. Slovenia: *Vatican Agreement (Slovenia)* Rm-1/02, UL 118/2003; ECLI:SI:USRS:2003:Rm102, [22]–[24] and cases cited below, Section 1.2.2.1 at nn 325–326. UK: *Thoburn v. Sunderland City Council (UK)* [2002] EWHC 195 (Admin); [2003] QB 151, [69] excerpted below, Section 1.2.2.1, n 300 and cases cited in Section 1.2.2.1, nn 126–127, and Section 1.2.2.2, nn 300–302. Greece: *Katsarou v. DI.KATSA (Greece)*, Case 3458/ 1998 (Συμβούλιο της Επικρατείας) in Oppenheimer, *The Cases* (Vol II), 300 [5], [16]; *Karella v. Minister of Industry (Greece)*, Case 3312/1989 (Συμβούλιο της Επικρατείας) in Oppenheimer, *The Cases* (Vol I) 584, 586 [10]. Portugal: *Special Sustainability Contribution (Portugal)* (Case 819/2014) Judgment 575/2014 (*Tribunal Constitucional*) [25] excerpted below, Section 1.2.2.1 at n 308; *European Regional Development Fund (ERDF) (Portugal)* (Case 184/89)

METHODS AND INTRODUCTION 9

an immutable boundary of the EU legal order. Not only has fiscal policy not been conferred on the Union but, according to the 'constitutional identity' jurisprudence of the German Constitutional Court (BVerfG), it cannot ever be so conferred without infringing the 'eternity clause' (Article 79(3)) of the German Basic Law (BL).[26] Numerous other constitutional courts have drawn similar boundaries around their own constitutional formulas for democratic legitimation of fiscal policy.[27] Chapter 1 extracts three constitutional tests that constrain the application of fiscal federalism theory in the European legal order: [1.3.1.2] no unlawful *restrictions* on fiscal sovereignty;[28] [1.3.1.3] no unlawful *conferral* or delegation of fiscal sovereignty;[29] and [1.3.1.4] no structural *impairments* of fiscal sovereignty through finite financial dispositions of structural significance to budgetary autonomy.[30]

The second thesis of this book is that, as a matter of fiscal federalism theory, hard budget constraints and market discipline are indispensable for the fundamental guiding principles of price stability, sound public finances and a sustainable balance of payments (Article 119(3) TFEU) in EMU. Chapter 8 concludes with five institutional determinates necessary for fiscal federalism to 'work' in a large, decentralized economic and monetary union bound by the fiscal sovereignty of its Member States: [8.1.1] market discipline; [8.1.2] hard budget constraints; [8.1.3] fiscal

---

Judgment 184/89 (*Tribunal Constitucional*) in Oppenheimer, *The Cases* (Vol 1), 687–688 excerpted below, Section 1.2.1.1, at n 130. France: *Treaty of Maastricht I (France)* Decision no 1992-308 DC; [1993] 3 CMLR 345 (*Conseil Constitutionnel*) [14], [49]; CETA *(France)* Decision No 2017-749; ECLI:FR:CC:2017:2017749DC, [10]–[11] excerpted below, Section 1.2.2.1, at n 294. Estonia: *ESM (Estonia)*, Case 3-4-1-6-12 (12 July 2012) (*Riigikohus Üldkogu*) [222] excerpted below, Section 1.2.1.1, at n 146. Hungary: *Lisbon (Hungary)* Decision 143/2010 (VII14) (*Magyarország Alkotmánybírósága*) available at: www.mkab.hu accessed 3 June 2015, [I]V.2(3).

[26] See Section 1.3.1, in particular, sources cited in n 459.

[27] See Section 1.3.1, nn 459–480, and Section 1.3.1.1, nn 482–484.

[28] A restriction on budgetary sovereignty must not 'fetter the budget legislature to such an extent that the principle of democracy is violated', that is, 'with the effect that it or a future Parliament can no longer exercise the right to decide the budget on its own'. See cases cited below, Chapter 1, Section 1.3.1.1, n 482, and Section 1.3.1.2.

[29] A delegation or conferral of budgetary decision-making must not compromise the principle that 'the [national] Parliament remains the place in which autonomous decisions on revenue and expenditure are made'. See cases cited below, Chapter 1, Section 1.3.1.1, n 483, and Section 1.3.1.3.

[30] Finite financial dispositions must not be of structural significance to the Parliament's right to decide on the budget such that it causes an irreversible prejudice to future majority decisions and cannot be reversed by an equivalent action by the Parliament in the future. See cases cited below, Chapter 1, Section 1.3.1.1, n 484, and Section 1.3.1.4.

symmetry; [8.1.4] decentralized fiscal autonomy; and [8.1.5] appropriately designed fiscal rules.

In sum, any model of European fiscal federalism must, first, preserve the fiscal sovereignty of its constitutional democracies; and, second, it must have market discipline under hard budget constraints. As for the selection of appropriate models for EU fiscal federalism, this book proposes that the three constitutional tests identified in Chapter 1,[31] as well as the five principles identified in Chapter 8,[32] provide an intersecting set of criteria to guide the determination of which models are implementable within the constitutional boundaries of the European legal order.

The procedure of this book is divided into two parts, each according to its two research aims.

Overview of Part I

Part I pursues the first principal aim of this study: to investigate the existence of permanent constitutional boundaries of European fiscal federalism that are integral to the stability of the EU as a whole.[33] Rules which limit the integration of EU law in national legal orders are a necessity that derives from the nature of European constitutionalism.[34] The EU is different from other advanced federations that presuppose the existence of a single 'constitutional demos'.[35] EU constitutionalism is characterized by opposing forces of perennial disquiet, possessed of a top-down hierarchy of greater legal supremacy than any individual expression of Member State sovereignty on one hand, yet on the other hand derived from the confederate authority of national orders which sanction its reach.[36] Where EU

---

[31] Listed in Chapter 1, Section 1.3.1.1, at nn 482–484 and Section 1.4, at nn 574–576. For discussion, see Sections 1.3.1.1–1.3.1.5.

[32] See Chapter 8, Sections 8.1.1–8.1.5, listed at Section 8.1.6.

[33] Part I (Chapters 1–4) employs a grounded-theory approach, by which the analysis pursues hypotheses implicit in the data. This is appropriate because, while this book begins with the notion that there are indeed constitutional boundaries of the EU legal order, it does not begin with a supposition of what those boundaries might be. A grounded-theory approach is necessary to extract them before they can be subjected to classical positivist methodologies in Part II. See the general framework in Kathy Charmaz, *Constructing Grounded Theory* (Sage Publications, 2006).

[34] DR Phelan, *Revolt or Revolution: The Constitutional Boundaries of the European Community* (Sweet and Maxwell, 1997).

[35] JHH Weiler, 'In Defence of the Status Quo: Europe's Constitutional *Sonderweg*' in JHH Weiler and Marlene Wind (eds), *European Constitutionalism Beyond the State* (Cambridge University Press, 2003), 7.

[36] Weiler, '*Sonderweg*', 9.

law overreaches this boundary and demands a court dis-apply a constitutional commitment, the result must either be a repudiation by the national court (which may result in the withdrawal of a Member State),[37] or a revolution wherein either legal order must reconstitute itself to accommodate the other.[38] Blind advancement of legal instruments without identifying the constitutional limits which must underpin them risks more than individual instruments – it destabilizes the EU legal order as a whole.

Many aspects of fiscal union have already stumbled on the limits of the EU legal order. The European Financial Stabilisation Mechanism (EFSM), for example, was tacitly acknowledged by the European Council and the ECJ as wanting a proper legal basis before being folded into the ESM and anchored in a new Article 136(3) TFEU.[39] The latter instrument has been the subject of legal challenges in numerous countries, and is broadly criticized in the economic and legal literature as exceeding the bounds of the Treaties.[40] Following a string of 2011 rulings by the constitutional courts of Germany, Ireland, Austria, Poland, Estonia, Slovenia and the Finnish Constitution Committee, certain 'capital call' provisions of the ESM Treaty (TESM) remain subject to quantitative caps that clearly curtail the unlimited joint and several

---

[37] For judicial statements to that effect, see: *Treaty of Lisbon (Germany)* (2 BvE 2/08): BVerfGE 123, 267; [2010] 3 CMLR 13 (*Bundesverfassungsgericht*) [217] 'The ultra vires review as well as the identity review may result in Community law or, in future, Union law being declared inapplicable in Germany [...] [240] and in the worst case to refuse further participation in the European Union.' *MAS and MB (Taricco II Order for Reference) (Italy)* Order 24/2017 (23 November 2016) (*Corte costituzionale*) [2]; *Talamucci* v. *Minister of Health (Italy)*, Case 1512/98 (*Corte di Cassazione*) in Oppenheimer, *The Cases* (Vol II) 388, 393: if the EU evolves such 'that the Treaty itself is in conflict with the Constitution', this will justify 'the radical and disruptive remedy of the withdrawal from the European Union'. *Constitutionality of the Accession Treaty (Poland)* K 18/04 (11 May 2005) in Biblioteka Trybunału Konstytucyjnego, *Selected Rulings* (Vol LI), [13] 'In such an event the Nation as the sovereign, or a State authority organ authorised by the Constitution [...] would need to decide [...] ultimately, on Poland's withdrawal from the European Union.' *Brussels Regulation (Poland)* SK 45/09 (6 November 2011) in Biblioteka Trybunału Konstytucyjnego, *Selected Rulings* (Vol LI) 247, [2.7]; *Crotty (Ireland)*, 759 excerpted below, Section 1.2.1.1, at n 142; *Sugar Quotas III (Czech Republic)* Pl ÚS 50/04; [2006] 3 CMLR 15 (*Ústavní Soud*) [109] excerpted below, Section 1.2.2.1, at n 311; *Constitutional Treaty (Spain)* [3] referring to 'sovereignty recoverable by means of the "voluntary withdrawal"'.

[38] On revolutions in law see Phelan, *Revolt or Revolution*, 10; Matthias Kumm, 'The Jurisprudence of Constitutional Conflict: Constitutional Supremacy in Europe before and after the Constitutional Treaty' (2005) 11 ELJ 262, 270; Daniele Gallo, 'Challenging EU Constitutional Law' (2019) 25 ELJ 433, 434.

[39] See Chapter 6, Section 6.1.4, at nn 40–41.

[40] See Chapter 6, Section 6.3, and sources cited.

liability sanctioned by the ECJ in *Pringle* v. *Ireland*.[41] Actualization of that constraint on callable capital in a crisis would vitiate the credibility of the EMU's financial backstop and trigger a collapse of the euro.[42] ECB asset purchase programmes,[43] financial memorandums of understanding with EU institutions[44] and Council Decisions setting economic policies provide numerous other instances of fomenting constitutional turmoil.[45] The BVerfG has explicitly stated since its *Maastricht* decision that it will stage a legal revolt if the constitutional principles of the '*Stabilitätsgemeinschaft*' (Stability Community) in Articles 119–127 TFEU are not observed,[46] and in the recent *Gauweiler* v. *Bundestag* and *Weiss* v. *Bundestag* litigations, it appeared prepared to do so.[47]

At the outset, this increasing contact by the EU's emerging fiscal architecture with Member State fiscal sovereignty appears unlike constitutional conflicts seen with the expansion of EU law in past decades. This is so for three reasons.

First, the boundaries of 'constitutional identity' jurisprudence examined in this book curtail the range of institutions that can be built not (merely) because of their normative superiority over EU law (though national courts assert this also),[48] but from an inability to confer them in the first place.[49]

Second, these constraints are inviolable; they concern core constitutional structures that simply cannot be released by the legislator or even (in many cases) by constitutional amendment. Under Articles 79(3) and 20 of the German Basic Law, for example, any amendment affecting the

---

[41] In those countries, the constitutionality of the TESM was predicated on the interpretation that financial commitments were capped to the extent of parliamentary authorization, and so did not entail an unconstitutional disposition of fiscal sovereignty. See cases cited below, Chapter 1, Section 1.3.1, nn 473–479. Cf: *Pringle* v. *Ireland* [144]–[146].

[42] Christian Bauer and Bernhard Herz, 'Reforming the European Stability Mechanism' (2020) 58 JCMS 636, 636–637; European Economic Advisory Group (EEAG) Report on the European Economy (*CESifo*, 2011), 33: 'In this case, the ESM and the euro area would probably be on the verge of collapse.'

[43] *Weiss Decision (Germany)*; *Gauweiler Decision (Germany)*.

[44] *Ledra* v. *Commission*; Case C-64/16 *Associação Sindical dos Juízes Portugueses* v. *Tribunal de Contas* EU:C:2018:117; Case C-258/14 *Florescu et al.* v. *Romania* EU:C:2017:488 and cases cited below, Chapter 7, Section 7.5, nn 305–306, 310.

[45] See cases cited in Section 7.5, in particular nn 307, 385.

[46] *Brunner (Germany)* [90]; *Gauweiler Reference (Germany)* [41]; *Aid Measures for Greece and the Euro Rescue Package (Germany)* (2 BvR 987/10, 1485/10 & 1099/10) BVerfGE 129,124, English version at: www.bundesverfassungsgericht.de/ accessed 23 July 2020 [129], [137]; *Weiss Reference (Germany)* [68], [103].

[47] *Gauweiler Decision (Germany)* [174], [205]–[207], [220]; *Weiss Decision (Germany)* discussed below, Section 1.2.1.3 at nn 240–241 and Section 6.1.7 at nn 90–98.

[48] See Sections 1.2.1.2 and 1.2.2.2 and sources cited.

[49] See sources cited above, n 25, and discussion below, Section 1.2.1.1.

basic principles of the democratic, social and federal state is unconstitutional.[50] In that democratic state, the competence to prepare the budget 'lies solely with the legislature',[51] and the 'transfer of the right of the *Bundestag* to adopt the budget and control its implementation by the government [would] violate the principle of democracy and the right to elect the German *Bundestag* in its essential content'.[52] The only way this constitutional lock may be changed is by enacting a new constitution upon a free decision of the German people under Article 146 BL (against which lies a right to resist the abolishment of the constitutional order under Article 20(4) BL).[53]

Third, even if such boundaries could one day be traduced, fiscal federalism is a field uniquely entwined with such things as temperamental bond markets, financial expectations, and the politico-economic incentives of restive electorates. Given that is so, it is hard to dispute that the legal boundaries pursued here are probably an unsafe place to install critical pieces of any model of fiscal federalism that requires those pieces to work smoothly – particularly if there are perfectly good models that do not involve treading on the inviolable core of fiscal sovereignty at all.

To that end, Part I delves into constitutional jurisprudence from all Member States to identify where in European constitutional law these boundaries may be found, how they work, and which models of fiscal federalism they impair. It proceeds as follows.

Chapter 1 begins by analysing the *Kompetenz-Kompetenz* and 'constitutional identity' jurisprudence of the CJEU and Europe's constitutional courts in order to identify the legal principles which constrain the expansion of EU law in the field of public economics.[54] It identifies two constitutional boundaries pursued through the remainder of the book:

The first is fiscal sovereignty. According to Member State constitutional identity and *Kompetenz-Kompetenz* jurisprudence, an incursion on fiscal sovereignty would require Member States to repudiate the advance

---

[50] *Lisbon (Germany)* [192]–[194].

[51] *Euro Rescue Package (Germany)* [122].

[52] *Lisbon (Germany)* [232].

[53] *Lisbon (Germany)* [155]; Christian Calleiss, 'Constitutional Identity in Germany: One for Three or Three in One?' in Christian Calleiss and Gerhard Van der Schyff (eds), *Constitutional Identity in a Europe of Multilevel Constitutionalism* (Cambridge University Press 2020), 162–163.

[54] By 'constitutional court' this study refers to the court or court(s) in each Member State with the jurisdiction to interpret or apply the constitution. This may be a constitutional court, a supreme court, or ordinary courts of jurisdiction in countries with decentralized constitutional review. For Finland, which has no constitutional court, the term instead includes the *Perustuslakivaliokunnan* (Constitution Committee).

(refusing to apply the offending EU law) or withdraw from the Union altogether.[55] Section 1.3.1 extracts three judicial tests for fiscal sovereignty from this jurisprudence, and highlights some room for manoeuvre through permissible limitations on fiscal sovereignty under these tests.[56]

The second constitutional boundary is comprised of the guiding principles of price stability, sound public finances and a sustainable balance of payments set forth in the mandate for EMU itself under Article 119(3) TFEU. It is the achievement of these principles which informs the entire legal architecture of Articles 119–127 (Economic and Monetary Policy) of the TFEU, and it is by these principles that that architecture is defined and delimited.[57] This, too, reflects a (national) constitutional boundary of the EU legal order: According to the BVerfG, the fundamental principles of the *Stabilitätsgemeinschaft* (Stability Community) underlying Articles 119–127 TFEU are 'the basis and subject-matter of the German Act of Accession'.[58] A development contrary to that constitutional framework would violate the conditions subject to which monetary policy was conferred,[59] and these limits of conferral are in turn underpinned by deeper boundaries of constitutional identity.[60] In particular, the BVerfG has warned that the principles of *Stabilitätsgemeinschaft* safeguard the parliament's 'national budgetary responsibility', and Germany's constitutional identity would be violated if EMU should become a 'liability community' through the 'direct or indirect communitarisation of state debts'.[61]

Chapter 2 moves from the constitutional foundations of the EU legal order to the architecture of fiscal federalism constructed atop them. It investigates where the constitutional principles identified in Chapter 1 inhere in

---

[55] See cases cited above, n 37.

[56] See Section 1.3.1, in particular Section 1.3.1.1 and nn 482–484.

[57] *Pringle* v. *Ireland* [48], [51], [55], [77], [92], [135].

[58] *Brunner (Germany)* [90] and cases cited below, Section 1.3.2, nn 547–552.

[59] *Weiss Decision (Germany)* [234]: such an act 'does not participate in the precedence of application of EU law [. . .] is not to be applied in Germany, and has no binding effect in relation to German constitutional organs, administrative authorities and courts'.

[60] *ESM Treaty and Fiscal Compact I (Germany)* (2 BvR 1390/12); [2013] 2 CMLR 3, [203]–[204] and cases below, n 61.

[61] *ESM I (Germany)* [203]; *ESM Treaty and Fiscal Compact II (Germany)* (2 BvR 1390/12); [2014] 2 CMLR 42, [167]–[171]. See also *Euro Rescue Package (Germany)* [129], [137]; *Weiss Decision (Germany)* [225]–[227]; *Weiss Reference (Germany)* [129]–[131]; *Gauweiler Reference (Germany)* [41]: 'independence of national budgets, which opposes the direct or indirect common liability of the Member States for government debts, is constituent for the design of the monetary union'.

the legal architecture of EMU under Articles 2(3), 5(1) and 119–127 TFEU, and explains the basic principles of economic theory inscribed for their attainment. By those provisions, the model of fiscal federalism inscribed in the Treaties since Maastricht is shown to rest upon two principles:

Fiscal sovereignty: Under Articles 2(3), 5(1), and 119–126 TFEU, the EU has no competence in economic policy. Member States have complete fiscal sovereignty, left to their devices outside the EU legal order and responsible for their own budgetary policies; and

Market discipline under hard budget constraints. Under Articles 121–126 TFEU, Member States are exposed to 'market discipline' and 'hard budget constraints' for the guiding principles of sound public finances and a sustainable balance of payments. 'Market discipline' refers to the condition in which each country's economic performance is assessed across a range of indicators and priced into interest rates by market actors, resulting in differentiated interest rates (even within a monetary union).[62] A 'hard budget constraint' refers to the condition where expenditures are limited by the inter-temporal budget constraint, meaning that Member States are limited by their own solvency condition and won't be bailed out when this limit is exceeded.[63] Importantly, Chapter 2 explains that a legal basis for conditional financial assistance proposed under Articles 104–104a of a 1990 Commission draft treaty for monetary union was rejected at Maastricht.

The hypothesis extracted from Chapters 1–2 is that hard budget constraints and market discipline are fundamental requirements for sound public finances and a sustainable balance of payments in an EMU bound by the fiscal sovereignty of its Member States.

In order to test that hypothesis and establish economic criteria for EU fiscal federalism, Chapter 3 investigates the collapse of the Maastricht architecture in the European sovereign debt crisis. It applies a grounded-theory law and economics approach to public accounts statistics and the economic literature concerning the period from 1992 to 2012 – up to and including the sovereign debt crisis – when the Maastricht architecture should have been operating as intended.[64]

---

[62] Timothy Lane, 'Market Discipline' (1993) IMF Staff Papers No 53. See Chapter 2, Section 2.2.4 and Chapter 8, Section 8.1.1.

[63] See below, Section 2.2.4 and Section 8.1.2.

[64] On law and economics see Robert Cooter and Thomas Ulen, *Law and Economics* (3rd ed., Addison-Wesley, 2000), 3–4; Guido Galabresi, *The Future of Law & Economics* (Yale University Press, 2016).

The analysis finds that the *causa sine qua non* of the Euro Crisis is a severe mispricing of private and public debt caused by a failure of Articles 121–126 TFEU to induce markets to differentiate between sovereign borrowers under a (now-realized) bailout expectation.

This challenges the incumbent prescriptions for European fiscal federalism. In the EU, the crisis is commonly described as a sovereign debt crisis.[65] In particular, it is described in terms of the inability of crisis-hit periphery countries (pejoratively acronymed the 'PIIGS') to run a sustainable fiscal policy. Yet the official characterization of the crisis is 'given the lie' by a simple glance at government finance statistics – the Euro Crisis was a private debt crisis, not a public one.[66] The dysfunction at the heart of the euro is the disconnection of EMU credit prices from economic fundamentals prevailing at national level – not the accumulation of sovereign debt.

Chapter 4 concludes for Part I by setting out two criteria for EU fiscal federalism which emerge from Chapters 1–3. These criteria are tested and applied as the thesis of this book throughout Part II:

First, any model of EU fiscal federalism must preserve the fiscal sovereignty of the twenty-seven constituent constitutional democracies at the base of its legal order; and

Second, hard budget constraints and market discipline are indispensable requirements for price stability, sound public finances and a sustainable balance of payments in an EMU bound by the fiscal sovereignty of its Member States.

Overview of Part II

Part II pursues the second undertaking of this book: to determine which models of fiscal federalism remain empirically and theoretically implementable within the constitutional boundaries of the EU legal order and, among those remaining, which would result in a stable economic equilibrium based on available economic data.

The choice of which model should be pursued, and what each model requires to 'work' in a given legal system, is the principal object of the

---

[65] Federico Fabbrini, *Economic Governance in Europe* (Oxford University Press, 2016), 2.

[66] Thanos Skouras, 'The Euro Crisis and Its Lessons from a Greek Perspective' (2013) 35 Econ Soc 51. See below, Chapter 3, Figure 3.3 and Figures 3.12–3.18. For an accessible summary: The Economist, 'The Euro Crisis was not a Government Debt Crisis' *The Economist* (23 November 2015) 12.

subfield of public economics known as 'fiscal federalism'.[67] This literature is applied in-depth in Chapter 8, but it suffices to state that the appropriate architecture of a given federal model depends on where it sits on the spectrum between 'centralization' or 'surveillance' models of fiscal union,[68] and the 'classical' model of decentralized fiscal federalism, (known as 'ideal-type' federalism, 'market-preserving federalism' or 'self-preserving federalism' in the literature).[69] Occupying one end of the spectrum, highly centralized fiscal federations such as Germany exhibit the 'centralization' or 'surveillance' model, in which the central government exerts 'such a degree of fiscal control that credit distinctions between the constituent states are almost non-existent'.[70] Occupying the other end of the spectrum lie highly decentralized 'classical' or 'ideal-type' fiscal federations such as the United States, Switzerland, and Canada, which exercise no federal oversight of state-level finances, and in which states govern their own finances under differentiated interest rates depending on their own macroeconomic circumstances.[71]

---

[67] As Wyplosz, 'Centralization-Decentralization', 3 notes, 'The make-up of the EU institutions, and their evolution, should explicitly be based on accepted federalism principles.' Similarly: Marek Dabrowski, 'Monetary Union and Fiscal and Macroeconomic Governance' (2015) European Economy Discussion Papers No 13, 27: 'Thus, the question of how much fiscal and political integration is needed must be answered [...] by the theory of fiscal federalism.'

[68] Teresa Ter-Minassian and Jon Craig, 'Control of Subnational Government Borrowing' in Teresa Ter-Minassian (ed.), *Fiscal Federalism in Theory and Practice* (International Monetary Fund 1997), 157; Alicia Hinarejos, *The Euro Area Crisis in Constitutional Perspective* (Oxford University Press, 2015), 181–183.

[69] Barry R Weingast, 'The Economic Role of Political Institutions: Market-Preserving Federalism and Economic Development' (1995) 10 JL Econ & Org 1; Yinyi Qian and Barry R Weingast, 'Federalism as a Commitment to Preserving Market Incentives' (1997) 11 J Econ Persp 83; Ronald McKinnon, 'Market-Preserving Fiscal Federalism in the American Monetary Union' in Mario I Bleier and Teresa Ter-Minassian (eds), *Macroeconomic Dimensions of Public Finance* (Routledge, 1997), 71; Jonathan Rodden and Gunnar Eskeland, 'Lessons and Conclusions' in Jonathan Rodden, Gunnar Eskeland and Jennie Litvack (eds), *Decentralization and the Challenge of Hard Budget Constraints* (MIT Press 2003), 432–433; Rui De Figueiredo and Barry R Weingast, 'Self-Enforcing Federalism' (2005) 21 JL Econ & Org 103; Raji Singh and Alexander Plekhanov, 'How Should Subnational Government Borrowing Be Regulated?' (2007) 53 IMF Staff Papers 426, 6–8; Wallace Oates, 'Towards a Second-Generation Theory of Fiscal Federalism' (2005) 12 Int Tax Pub Finan 349, 368; Dietmar Braun, 'How to Make German Fiscal Federalism Self-Enforcing: A Comparative Analysis' (2007) 5 ZSE 235; Wallace Oates, 'On the Evolution of Fiscal Federalism: Theory and Institutions' (2008) 62 Nat Tax J 313; Barry R Weingast, 'Second Generation Fiscal Federalism: The Implications of Fiscal Incentives' (2009) 65 J Urban Econ 279, 281.

[70] Graham Bishop, Dirk Damrau and Michelle Miller, *Market Discipline CAN Work in the EC Monetary Union* (Salomon Brothers, 1989), 2. See below, Section 8.2.1 and sources cited.

[71] See Sections 8.2.2, 8.2.3, 8.2.4 for Switzerland, the United States and Canada.

Chapter 5 opens for Part II with the task of taxonomy, classifying the emergent post-crisis European fiscal architecture from the perspective of fiscal federalism theory in order to determine what it demands from the EU legal order to 'work'. Chapter 5 finds that, from the perspective of fiscal federalism theory, the EU has sunk the cornerstones of an institutional configuration that is far more apt to unitary states than any of the other federations touched upon in this book.[72] At its core, the new model supplants a legal pillar of fiscal sovereignty and market discipline (an entrenched 'no bailout' law) with a legal feature of unitary states: centralized financial assistance and legal governance of fiscal policy. In order to stem the dysfunctional cost incentives entailed with this shift and make the new model 'work', it now depends, for its effective operation, on intensified governance regimes that bear no relation to the legislative competences of the Union. The new legal framework effects economic outcomes through a complex and beguiling quasi-legislative legal framework which has stretched athwart the gap between legal orders and injected binding interlinkages directly into Member State budgetary frameworks and constitutional law.[73] 'Fiscal union', as it is used in the Commission Blueprint and the EU *Five Presidents' Report*, does not refer to the existence of independent *federal* tax and spending competences (which model the EU already has). It refers to the centralization of *Member State* tax and spending competences in the Union – or, as the Commission so puts it, to 'a means to imposing budgetary and economic decisions on its members'.[74]

Chapter 6 examines whether the instruments of conditional financial assistance enacted since the crisis are genuinely reconcilable with the boundaries of EMU inscribed in the Treaties as a matter of EU law. This is necessary because the text of the Treaty is but the litmus paper for determining whether a legal instrument coheres with much deeper constitutional boundaries underlying the EU legal order.[75] Chapter 6 concludes, unavoidably, that conditional financial assistance is simply not reconcilable with the Treaties according to the analytical framework set down by

---

[72] See also Fabbrini, 'Paradox', 56 excerpted below, Section 7.3.2, at n 169; Dabrowski, 'Fiscal and Macroeconomic Governance', 7; Mark Dawson, *New Governance and the Transformation of European Law* (Cambridge University Press, 2011); Wyplosz, 'Centralization-Decentralization', 17 excerpted below, Section 5.1, at n 45.

[73] Those mechanisms are examined in Sections 7.2–7.5 of this book.

[74] Commission Blueprint, 31.

[75] *Lisbon (Germany)* [210]; *Carlsen (Denmark)* [13]–[15]; *Decision 2011/199/EU (Poland)* [6.3.1]; Tuori and Tuori, *Eurozone Crisis*, 9 excerpted below, Section 2.2.3, n 74.

the ECJ in *Pringle* v. *Ireland, Gauweiler* v. *Bundestag*, and *Weiss*.[76] This emerges from an analysis of the allocation of competences (within which the ESM, EFSM, EFSF and OMT do not together sit) and the substantive provisions of Articles 121–126 TFEU (to which they do not adhere). By restoring a permissive interpretation of the 'no bailout' rule that had been rejected under Articles 104–104a of the Commission's 1990 draft treaty at Maastricht, the ECJ in *Pringle* v. *Ireland* would seem to have reached back through history, brushed aside the stated will of the Treaty drafters, plucked a (rejected) Commission draft treaty from the floor of Maastricht, and christened it as primary EU law.[77] This provides the first testable indication that the emerging new model is incompatible with much deeper boundaries underlying the EU legal order.

  Chapter 7 examines the new architecture of EU economic and fiscal governance against the deeper constitutional boundaries of Member State fiscal sovereignty underlying the EU legal order as a whole. It conducts a piece-by-piece deconstruction of the European governance framework to identify instruments which explicitly, or *a fortiori* implicitly, trespass on *ultra vires* and constitutional identity rulings of national constitutional courts. It examines: [7.2] EU legislation governing budgetary frameworks; [7.3] the architecture of EU fiscal governance; [7.4] the architecture of EU economic governance; and [7.5] the EU architecture governing conditional financial assistance. Chapter 7 concludes that the new model of EU fiscal federalism is comprehensively dependent, for its stable functioning, on multiple instruments which are manifestly beyond the boundaries of the EU legal order and may perhaps exist only in so far as they are not actually enforced. By restricting fiscal autonomy and providing bailouts, the EU has sunk the cornerstones of a unitary model that is manifestly incompatible with the constitutional jurisprudence of the twenty-eight Member States catalogued in this book. This is not merely legally unsound; it is economically ineffective and inimical to good principles of fiscal federalism.

  Chapter 8 seeks to extract principles of fiscal federalism for the EU and determine what models of fiscal federalism will 'work' in the context of the constitutional boundaries of the European legal order. The first part of Chapter 8 extracts a number of institutional determinants of fiscal discipline in a decentralized federal system: [8.1.1] market discipline;

---

[76] *Pringle* v. *Ireland*; C-62/14 *Gauweiler* v. *Bundestag* EU:C:2015:400; *Weiss (CJEU)*.
[77] See Chapter 2, Section 2.3.1.4 on the draft treaty, and Chapter 6 Section 6.3.1 on the interpretation of the ECJ.

[8.1.2] hard budget constraints; [8.1.3] fiscal symmetry; [8.1.4] expenditure and revenue autonomy; and [8.1.5] specific characteristics for credibly designed fiscal rules. The second part of Chapter 8 then tests those
determinates in operation through a comparative analysis of five federations selected using a 'most similar cases' and a 'prototypical cases'
methodology: [8.2.1] the Federal Republic of Germany, [8.2.2] the Swiss
Confederation, [8.2.3] the United States of America, [8.2.4] Canada, and
[8.2.5] the European Economic and Monetary Union.[78]

Chapter 8 finds that the incumbent prescriptions for centralized EU
'fiscal union' are, quite simply and profoundly, wrong. [79] The essential
premise of the emerging EU fiscal union is that centralized legal governance can ensure fiscal discipline in a federated monetary union with an
established bailout precedent and institutionalized financial assistance.
This is the essence of the *ratio decidendi* in *Pringle* v. *Ireland*,[80] and incumbent

---

[78] On the comparative methodologies applied for case selection, see Section 8.2, n 192.

[79] Dirk Foremny, 'Sub-National Deficits in European Countries: The Impact of Fiscal Rules and
Tax Autonomy' (2014) 34 Europ J Polit Economy 86, 86: 'Only deficits in unitary countries
can be avoided by tying the government's hands with fiscal rules [. . .] they are ineffective in
federations.' Teresa Ter-Minassian, 'Fiscal Rules for Subnational Governments: Can they
Promote Fiscal Discipline?' (2007) 6 OECD Journal on Budgeting 1, 8: fiscal rules 'are neither
necessary nor sufficient to ensure fiscal discipline at the subnational level'. Lili Liu and
Stephen Webb, 'Laws for Fiscal Responsibility for Subnational Discipline' (2011) World
Bank Policy Research Working Papers No 5587: 'Evidence shows that fiscal responsibility
laws [. . .] are not a substitute for commitment and should not be viewed as ends in
themselves.' See also: Luc Eyraud and Raquel Gomez Sirera, 'Constraints on Sub-National
Fiscal Policy' in Carlo Cottarelli and Martine Guerguil (eds), *Designing a European Fiscal Union:
Lessons from the Experience of Thirteen Federations*(Routledge, 2014), 96 and 108 excerpted
below, Chapter 8, n 114; R Daniel Kelemen and Terence K Teo, 'Law, Focal Points, and Fiscal
Discipline in the United States and the European Union' (2014) 108 Am Polit Sci Rev 355,
356–357, 381 excerpted below, Section 8.1.1, at n 73; Richard Bird and Almos Tassonyi,
'Constraining Subnational Fiscal Behaviour in Canada – Different Approaches, Similar
Results?' in Rodden, Eskeland and Litvack (eds), *Challenge of Hard Budget Constraints*, 101
excerpted below, Section 8.2.4, at n 434; Wayne Simpson and Jared Wesley, 'Effective Tool
or Effectively Hollow? Balanced Budget Legislation in Western Canada' (2012) 38 Can Public
Pol'y 291; OECD, *Economic Surveys: Canada 2010* (OECD, 2010), 93; IMF, *Fiscal Rules – Anchoring
Expectations for Sustainable Public Finances* (IMF 2009), 15 excerpted below, Chapter 8, n 12;
C Randall Henning and Martin Kessler, 'Fiscal Federalism: US History for Architects of
Europe's Fiscal Union' (*Bruegel Essay and Lecture Series*, 2012); Charlotte Rommerskirchèn,
'Fiscal Rules, Fiscal Outcomes and Financial Market Behaviour' (2015) 54 Eur J Polit Res 836,
839–840 excerpted below, Section 8.1, n 45; Dietmar Braun and Philipp Trein, 'Federal
Dyanmics in Times of Economic and Financial Crisis' (2014) 53 EJPR 803, 808: 'Whatever
governance system with regard to borrowing country has developed (administrative regulation, cooperative rules, self-imposed rules or markets) opportunism may show up if there
is a belief that [the central authority] will be the "lender of last resort"'. See further
Chapter 8, Sections 8.1.1–8.1.2.

[80] *Pringle* v. *Ireland* [136]–[137] discussed below, Chapter 6.

proposals by the Five Presidents and the Commission endorse this premise.[81] In *Pringle* v. *Ireland* the ECJ duly sanctioned the abrogation of the 'no bailout' rule in Article 125 TFEU through the establishment of the ESM and the amendment of Article 136 TFEU, instead entrusting budgetary discipline to centralized fiscal rules under Articles 121 and 126 TFEU.[82] Yet the debt limits provided by those provisions are demonstrably lacking in credibility, having already been exceeded 97 times by 24 of the EU-27 countries by the time of the *Pringle* decision.[83] Centralized fiscal governance *never* works in a decentralized federation without market discipline,[84] and contemporary economists already find the new governance framework no more credible than its predecessors.[85] Empirical analyses find that the new 'centralized' EU model has not reduced structural sovereign debt; it has not improved implementation rates of EU policy recommendations (even over systems with no enforcement whatsoever); and it has not even been enforced under its own terms.[86] Allowing Member States a margin of error of 0.5% of GDP, this author counts 141 breaches of the 3% deficit limit by 24 countries between 1999 and 2018,[87] and 18 countries with multi-year periods in breach of the 60% debt limit.[88] Yet rule-breakers are far more likely to receive a bailout (which count stands at €500.07bn dispersed over eight separate bailout agreements for five Member States)

[81] Herman Van Rompuy, *Towards a Genuine Economic and Monetary Union* (EUCO 120/12, 2012), 8–9; Commission Blueprint, 30–31; Juncker et al., *Five Presidents' Report*, 14–15; European Commission, 'Reflection Paper on the Deepening of the Economic and Monetary Union' COM(2017) 291 final, 7, 15–17, 25; European Commission, 'New Budgetary Instruments for a Stable Euro Area' COM(2017) 822 final, 3–4, 13; European Commission, 'Proposal for a Council Regulation on the Establishment of the European Monetary Fund' COM(2017) 827 final, 4, 6–7, 11–12.

[82] *Pringle* v. *Ireland* [137]–[143].

[83] EEAG Report 2011, 71; Friedrich Groeteke and Karsten Mause, 'New Constitutional "Debt Brakes" for Euroland? A Question of Institutional Complementarity' (2012) 23 Const Polit Econ 279, 280.

[84] See the analysis in Section 8.1 and sources cited above, n 79.

[85] See Chapter 8, Section 8.2.5.4 and sources cited.

[86] See Chapter 8, Sections 8.1.5.2–8.1.5.4 and 8.2.5.4 (and sources cited). See further Dariusz Adamski, *Redefining European Economic Integration* (Cambridge University Press, 2018), 36–66.

[87] Only Estonia, Luxembourg, Sweden and Finland have maintained deficits smaller than −3.5% since 1999. Sweden reached −3.4% in 2007. Eurostat, 'Government Deficit/ Surplus, Debt and Associated Data (gov_10dd_edpt1)' (*Eurostat*, 2020) http://epp .eurostat.ec.europa.eu accessed 14 September 2020.

[88] Only the Czech Republic, Estonia, Latvia, Lithuania, Luxembourg, Poland, Romania and Slovenia have complied with the 60% debt limit since 1999. Denmark and Sweden have complied since 2000. Eurostat, 'Consolidated Gross Debt (gov_10dd_3dpt1)'.

than they are to face sanctions under EU law (which count stands at €0.00 in in fines levied).[89]

The EU's fiscal governance model does not work. Instead, it has institutionalized the dysfunctional credit mis-pricing at the root of the Euro Crisis. With a 'stagnant, unreformed economy',[90] Italy's gross debt (134.8% of GDP in 2019) is now larger than Greece's at the height of the crisis (126.7% of GDP in 2009),[91] but the yield on its ten-year bonds (1.19% in 2019) is less than AAA-rated American Treasuries (2.14%).[92] So are Portugal's (0.76%) and Spain's (0.66%).[93] Even Greece – a country the IMF has stated would be insolvent without debt relief[94] – borrowed at 4.95% in one of its first bond issues (compare this with AAA-rated New Zealand bonds, which were priced at 4.2%).[95] This is clearly at odds with the fundamental guiding principles of fiscal discipline binding on the mandate for EMU under Article 119(3) TFEU.

This book proposes a significant rethink of the incumbent political prescriptions for the structuring of public finance incentives in the EU. This book concludes that the inchoate configuration of EU 'fiscal union' is fundamentally incompatible with the constitutional boundaries of the EU, and anyways adherent to a formula for disequilibrium that is well-known in theory and well-evidenced in history. If Europe is not to continue further down this lonely, troubled path, the exceptionalist 'sui generis' myth of European integration must not become an excuse to ignore fundamental lessons of fiscal federalism, public economics and European constitutionalism.[96] The fiscal federalism literature is remarkably united

---

[89] This €500.07bn figure encompasses all EU bailouts from May 2010 and 31 December 2016, and excludes an additional €60.75 in BoP assistance to Romania, Latvia and Hungary. Greece I: €20.1bn (IMF) + €52.9bn. Greece II: €172.6bn (€28bn from IMF + €144.6bn from EFSF) (this included the remaining amount from Greece I, which was €110bn). Greece III: €86bn (ESM+IMF) from August 2015 to August 2018. Ireland: €68.2bn (€4.8bn bilateral + €22.5bn EFSM + €18.4bn EFSF). Portugal: €79bn (€26.5bn IMF + €24.3bn EFSM + €26bn EFSF). Spain: €43bn out of €100 ESM. Cyprus I: €2.5bn bilateral loans using ESM as disbursement vehicle. Cyprus II: €10b (€1bn IMF + €9bn ESM).

[90] Philippe Legrain, 'Investors are Ignoring Eurozone Risks' *Financial Times* (30 April 2014).

[91] Eurostat, 'Consolidated Gross Debt (gov_10dd_3dpt1)'.

[92] OECD, 'Long-Term Interest Rates' (*OECD*, 2020) https://stats.oecd.org accessed 16 November 2020.

[93] OECD, 'Long-Term Interest Rates' (2019 rates).

[94] Editorial, 'Endgame for the IMF-EU Feud over Greece's Debt' *Spiegel* (4 March 2016).

[95] OECD, 'Long-Term Interest Rates'; Eurostat, 'Maastricht Criterion Interest Rates (irt_lt_mcby_a)' (*Eurostat*, 2020) http://epp.eurostat.ec.europa.eu accessed 14 June 2020; Legrain, 'Ignoring Eurozone Risks'.

[96] Robert Schütze, *European Union Law* (Cambridge University Press, 2015), 44: 'The *sui generis* idea is not a theory. It is an *anti*-theory, for it refuses to search for commonalities, yet, theory must search for what is common among different entities.'

in its prescriptions,[97] and there is no mystery in where the EU's course leads.[98] Two-and-a-half centuries of history and data from 106 sub-federal government units in Germany, Canada, Switzerland and the United States admonish that the flaw at the heart of the euro is not the budgetary freedom of national electorates, nor their economic diversity, nor the small size of the EU budget. The fatal flaw at the heart of the euro is the pooling of risk and the over-centralization of economic governance.[99] Under this system, interest rates do not adapt to the economy,[100] electorates do not feel the costs of their own debts[101] and governments do not act.[102] When the credit market adjusts, the terms of reform are selected and enforced by the Union through its new governance architecture outside the constitutional authorization for fiscal policy – not the voters who must bear them. Systems of law which develop to enforce such conditions must then inevitably conflict with Member State 'constitutional identity' jurisprudence. This is manifestly incompatible with the integrity of the EU legal order.

This book proposes a different model, one that respects Member States' fiscal sovereignty and exposes them to differentiated interest rates under conditions of market discipline. It concludes by offering basic principles to guide the determination of which models of fiscal federalism are theoretically and empirically implementable within the constitutional boundaries of the European Union, and some thoughts on how to get there.

---

[97] 'The literature on the fiscal effects of fiscal institutions is well established, as is the underlying theory.' Lorenz Blume and Stefan Voigt, 'The Economic Effects of Constitutional Budget Institutions' (2013) 29 Eur J Polit Econ 236, 238. See also: Erik Wibbels, 'Bailouts, Budget Constraints and Leviathans' (2003) 36 Comp Polit Stud 475, 476: 'Scholars of comparative federalism [...] are increasingly united in their prescription for the economic complications of some federations.' Wyplosz, 'Centralization-Decentralization', 7: 'Federal institutions must be compatible with the theory's general principles.'

[98] For example, Michael Bordo, Lars Jonung and Agnieszka Markiewicz, 'A Fiscal Union for the Euro: Some Lessons from History' (2013) 59 CESifo Economic Studies 449 point to failures in the Argentinian, Brazilian and German models, and Sections 8.2.1, 8.2.3 and 8.2.4, below, point to the United States in 1842, Canada in 1936 and Germany from 1830 to 1918, 1920–1939 and 1955 to its 2020 debt brake. See also Sinn, *Euro Trap*, 6, excerpted in the Conclusion to this book, at n 9.

[99] See Chapter 3 (examining pre-crisis fiscal federalism) and Chapter 8 (examining post-crisis fiscal federalism).

[100] See Section 3.1.

[101] See Section 3.2.

[102] See Section 3.3.

1 The Constitutional Boundaries of European Fiscal Federalism

This chapter introduces and establishes the constitutional boundaries of European fiscal federalism which are the object of this book:

[1.3.1] The first constitutional boundary of European fiscal federalism studied in this book is Member State fiscal sovereignty. Fiscal sovereignty, broadly defined, refers to the exclusive competences of national legislative organs for economic and fiscal policy as they are charged with those competences by the *pouvoir constituent*. Economic and fiscal policy competences comprise the 'core of parliamentary rights in democracy' and a material limit of 'constitutional identity' in Europe's twenty-eight constitutional democracies.[1] According to European constitutional identity and *Kompetenz-Kompetenz* jurisprudence, a deprivation of fiscal sovereignty would require Member States to repudiate encroaching EU law (refusing to apply the offending EU instrument) or withdraw from the Union altogether.[2] This chapter tests the veracity of this constraint as a constitutional boundary of EU fiscal federalism and extracts three tests for evaluating whether a proposed legal model infringes Member State fiscal sovereignty. These are: no unlawful *restrictions* on fiscal sovereignty;[3] no unlawful *conferral* or delegations of fiscal sovereignty;[4] and no structural *impairments* of fiscal

---

[1] *Euro Rescue Package (Germany)* [101], [104].

[2] See *Lisbon (Germany)* [240]; *Gauweiler Decision (Germany)* [174], [205]–[211]; *Weiss Decision (Germany)* [101], [104], [115]–[119], [163], [227], [234] and cases cited above, in Methods and Introduction, n 37.

[3] See Section 1.3.1.1, n 482 and Section 1.3.1.2.

[4] See Section 1.3.1.1, n 483 and Section 1.3.1.3.

sovereignty through financial dispositions of structural significance to budgetary autonomy.[5]
[1.3.2] The second constitutional boundary is comprised of the fundamental guiding principles of price stability, sound public finances and a sustainable balance of payments enshrined in the mandate for EMU under Article 119(3) TFEU. It is these principles which form the basis of Member State (in particular, German) acts of accession, and it is these principles to which the entire legal architecture of EMU under Articles 119–127 TFEU is attuned.

However, before the constitutional boundaries which bear upon the field of fiscal federalism can be established, it must first be established that there are, indeed, constitutional boundaries which constrain the expansion of the EU legal order as a whole. This is so because, as a matter of pure EU law, the boundaries of the EU legal order are limitless in their potential. The scope of EU law is set out by the Treaties, and there are no substantive constraints on the amendment of those Treaties.[6] From the internal perspective of the EU legal order, any model of federalism is compatible with EU law *de lege ferenda* upon the flourish of twenty-seven (formerly twenty-eight) pens.

Then, once a competence has been conferred on the Union, the ECJ has, since *Costa* v. *ENEL* and *Internationale Handelsgesellschaft*, declared that EU law has absolute primacy over all constitutional laws and structures of the Member States.[7] National law must be interpreted in conformity with EU law,[8] and, where they are in conflict, EU law must prevail.[9] Secondary instruments such as regulations,[10] directives[11] or decisions[12] will prevail over national constitutional or statute law, even if the national law is later in time.[13] The CJEU is the sole arbiter of the legality

[5] See Section 1.3.1.1, n 484 and Section 1.3.1.4.
[6] Outside of the amending procedures, the CJEU has declined to review the substantive legality of Treaty amendments. See Case 43/75 *Defrenne* v. *Sabena* [1976] ECR 455 [58]; Case C-253/94 P *Roujansky* v. *Council* [1995] ECR 1-7; EU:C:1995:4, [11].
[7] Case 6/64 *Costa* v. *Enel* [1964] ECR 585; EU:C:1964:66; Case 11/70 *Internationale Handelsgesellschaft MbH* [1970] ECR 1125; EU:C:1970:114, 1135.
[8] Case 14/83 *Von Colson* v. *Land Nordrhein-Westfalen* [1984] ECR 1891; EU:C:1984:153; Case C-106/89 *Marleasing SA* [1990] ECR I-4135; EU:C:1990:395.
[9] Case 106/77 *Simmenthal SpA* [1978] ECR 629; EU:C:1978:49.
[10] Case 84/71 *Marimex* v. *Ministero delle Finanze* [1972] ECR 89; EU:C:1972:14.
[11] Case 158/80 *Rewe-Handelsgesellschaft Nord* v. *Kiel* [1981] ECR 1805; EU:C:1981:163.
[12] Case 130/78 *Salumificio de Cornuda* v. *Amminiztrazione delle Finanze dello Stato* [1979] ECR 867; EU:C:1979:60.
[13] Joined Cases C-46/93, C-48/93 *Brasserie du Pêcheur SA* v. *Germany and R* v. *SST, ex parte Factortame* [1996] ECR I-1029; EU:C:1996:79, [24]–[36].

of all EU measures, and it reserves for itself final authority to deliver binding rulings on the compatibility of EU law with fundamental rights and principles.[14] As Claes so puts it, EU law requires national courts 'to refrain from enforcing the constitutional provisions that they have a sword duty to uphold and protect, in favour of any act of Community law, whatever its rank or content'.[15]

Constituent within this supremacy claim is what is referred to in this study as the claim of 'absolute' supremacy: Not only does the CJEU determine the status and effect of EU law *within* its established competences (ordinary supremacy), but the CJEU is the final arbiter of the boundaries between Member State and EU competence (absolute supremacy).[16]

The question for the architects of EU fiscal federalism is whether this provides a true account of European constitutional law, or whether national legal orders are indeed capable of imposing constitutional constraints upon the selection of fiscal federalism models for the EU. In pursuit of that question, this chapter evaluates the competing claims of EU and Member State constitutionalism against three approaches to the validity of law in European legal theory:[17] Pure (Kelsenian) constitutional theory;[18] normative constitutional pluralism;[19] and (Hartian) legal positivism.[20]

---

[14] Joined Cases C-188 & 189/10 *Melki and Abdeli* [2010] ECR I-05667; EU:C:2010:206, [54]. Case C-399/11 *Melloni v. Ministerio Fiscal* EU:C:2013:107, [58]–[59].

[15] Monica Claes, *The National Courts' Mandate in the European Constitution* (Hart, 2006), 387.

[16] See, distinguishing between 'ordinary' and 'absolute' supremacy: *European Arrest Warrant (Czech Republic)* Pl ÚS 66/04; [2007] 3 CMLR 24 (*Ústavní Soud*) [53] 'refus[ing] to recognise the ECJ doctrine insofar as it claims absolute primacy of EC law'; *Lisbon (Germany)* [306]–[308], '[Germany] does not recognise an absolute primary of application of Union law'.

[17] On the use of legal theory to explain certain outcomes, see: DJ Galligan, 'Legal Theory and Empirical Research' in Peter Cane and Herbert Kritzer (eds), *The Oxford Handbook of Empirical Legal Research* (Oxford University Press, 2010), 981–982, 984–993.

[18] Hans Kelsen, *Pure Theory of Law* (2nd ed., Lawbook Exchange Ltd., 2002), 1–58, 70–101. For the application of pure law in comparative theory: Mark Tushnet, 'Comparative Constitutional Law' in Mathias Reimann and Reinhard Zimmerman (eds), *The Oxford Handbook of Comparative Law* (Oxford University Press, 2008), 1244–1246.

[19] This is necessary because the same normative claim may be valid in distinct systems despite different pure constitutional criteria for validity. See Tushnet, 'Comparative Constitutional Law', 1230; Neil MacCormick, 'Beyond the Sovereign State' (1993) 56 MLR 1, 8–9; Margaret Davies, 'Legal Pluralism' in Cane and Kritzer (eds), *Empirical Legal Research*, 805–825; and sources cited below, Section 1.1.3 in particular n 71.

[20] See HLA Hart, *The Concept of Law* (2 ed., Oxford University Press, 1994), 92–107 on 'rules of recognition', 'rules of change' and 'rules of adjudication'. An empirical approach to legal positivism seeks to determined which laws will apply, and when. See: Tushnet,

Section 1.1 begins by familiarizing the reader with European constitutional theory and the competing claims of Member State and EU constitutionalism. What is normatively at stake in this dispute is the locus of sovereignty and therefore the question of *Kompetenz-Kompetenz* – that is, who is the ultimate arbiter of which competences have and have not been conferred on the Union. The analysis seeks to inform the architects of fiscal federalism on where they should look for an authoritative description of what is and is not safe constitutional ground when selecting from models known to fiscal federalism theory. Section 1.1 sets out the background explaining why this book finds it necessary to look to both EU and Member State law in doing so.

Section 1.2 shows that national constitutional orders profess to impose two types of limitation on EU law: First, Member State courts profess that they have the jurisdiction to assert, through treaty ratification and *ultra vires* review, what powers they have and have not conferred on the Union – the so-called *Kompetenz-Kompetenz*. Second, Member State courts assert that their own state 'constitutional identities' determine the absolute limits of conferral and application of Union law – the so-called 'constitutional identity' review jurisdiction.[21] Section 1.2 evaluates the veracity of these claims as a matter of pure constitutional law, as normative legal principle, and as a positivist statement of law. It finds that, by all three approaches, these jurisdictions provide a valid description of the limits of the EU legal order for the purposes of this study. Of the twenty-eight Member States surveyed in this book, all assert *Kompetenz-Kompetenz* and twenty-four have developed a body of jurisprudence surrounding 'constitutional identity' – a set of constitutive principles so integral to the constitutive nature of the state that they are beyond the reach of the national (and European) legislator.

'Comparative Constitutional law', 1225, 1230–1234; David Law, 'Constitutions' in Cane and Kritzer (eds), *Empirical Legal Research*, 388. In the context of legal pluralism, see sources cited below, Section 1.1.3, n 76.

21 See also Hinarejos, 'Constitutional Limits', 263; Peter M Huber, 'The Rescue of the Euro and its Constitutionality' in Wolf-Georg Ringe and Peter M Huber (eds), *Legal Challenges in the Global Financial Crisis: Bail-outs, the Euro and Regulation* (Hart 2014), 11–14; Chiti and Pedro, 'Constitutional Implications', 698; Tobias Lock, 'Why the European Union Is Not a State' (2010) 5 EuConst 407; Mark Dawson and Floris de Witte, 'Constitutional Balance in the EU after the Euro-Crisis' (2013) 76 MLR 817; Ingolf Pernice, 'Domestic Courts, Constitutional Constraints and European Democracy: What Solution for the Crisis?' in Maurice Adams, Federico Fabbrini and Pierre Larouche (eds), *The Constitutionalization of European Budgetary Constraints* (Hart 2014), 297–318; Alina Kaczorowska, *European Union Law* (3rd ed., Routledge, 2013), 239.

Section 1.3 conducts the main task of this chapter: To identify those constitutional boundaries which bear upon the field of fiscal federalism. It sets out those principles and tests which constitutional courts (and this book) will apply to novel legal apparatus in the field of fiscal federalism.

1.1   An Introduction to European Constitutionalism

1.1.1   European Monist Federalism and the Principle of Supremacy

The European Union is founded on the principle of democracy.[22] An essential precept common to the legal heritage of the Member States is that the bearer of sovereignty is the people.[23] Under European 'social contract' theories of constitutionalism, the locus of sovereignty is indivisible.[24] At the base of every legal order is a historically first constitution – a revolutionary act – which is enacted by the *pouvoir constituent originaire* in a manner different from that prescribed by any prior constitution. This is Kelsen's 'basic norm' (or *Grundnorm*) which forms the basis for the legal system.[25] Under European constitutional theory a 'Union of States' must, therefore, either be a 'confederation' (under which participants retain their character as sovereign states) or a sovereign 'federal state' (under which powers are devolved by the central government).[26] In a conflict of norms, only one institution can have the ultimate claim to empowerment by the *pouvoir constituent*.[27] Schütze explains:

> Within this European tradition, 'federalism' came thus to refer to the constitutional devolution of power within a sovereign *nation*. A federation was a Federal State.[28]

Coloured by this tradition, European constitutionalism from the 1960s treated the residual existence of Member State sovereignty as

---

[22] Art. 10 TEU.

[23] See FH Hinsely, *Sovereignty* (2nd ed., Cambridge University Press, 1986), 37–41 on the *imperium populi Romani*. Seventeenth-century natural theory then led to 'social contract' theories of popular sovereignty which rejected the Roman distinction between the origins of sovereignty (in the people) and its exercise (by the state): Jean-Jacques Rousseau, *The Social Contract* (Penguin Classics, 1968); John Locke, *Two Treatises on Civil Government* (Routledge, 1884).

[24] Schütze, *EU Law* (2015), 50.

[25] Kelsen, *Pure Theory of Law*.

[26] Schütze, *EU Law* (2015), 52.

[27] Theodor Schilling, 'The Autonomy of the Community Legal Order: An Analysis of Possible Foundations' (1996) 37 Harv Int'l LJ 389', 391–393.

[28] Schütze, *EU Law* (2015), 50.

incompatible with EU federalism. The object of European law, namely, 'to substitute a common and uniform European law for the divergences and conflicts of national bodies of legislation',[29] required early European jurists to free it from the obvious criticism that there could be no such thing as an autonomous legal order superior to the Member States.[30] As Schütze so puts it, '[i]t became the task of European scholarship to make the "Federal State" look like its unitary sisters [. . .] through feats of legal "reasoning"'.[31]

In *Van Gend en Loos*, and *Costa* v. *ENEL*, the ECJ famously stated that through 'the establishment of institutions *endowed with sovereign rights*' the Community constituted an 'autonomous legal order' stemming from 'an independent source of law'.[32] By asserting that ratification of the Treaties was a constituent act, a historically-first basic norm for a 'constitutional charter based on the rule of law',[33] the ECJ fashioned a constitutional basis for a 'federal-type structure' in Europe.[34] From this 'federal type' constitution, the ECJ asserted itself to be the final arbiter of what powers have and have not been conferred on the Union.[35]

Under this 'absolute' conception of supremacy, Member State *Kompetenz-Kompetenz* has been criticized as an 'anachronistic idea' invoked under the 'guise of protecting democracy'.[36] Judge Schiemann, for example, has reduced the defence of Member State sovereignty to 'much the same instinctive defensive reactions as asking questions about a man's virility'.[37]According to scholars such as Habermas and Pernice, 'National Courts are not authorised to monitor

---

[29] Pierre Pescatore, 'International Law and Community Law – A Comparative Analysis' (1970) 7 CMLR 167, 170.

[30] Matthias Kumm, 'Who is the Final Arbiter of Constitutionality in Europe?' (1999) 36 CMLR 351, 355.

[31] Schütze, *EU Law* (2015), 51.

[32] Case 26/62 *Van Gend en Loos* [1963] ECR 1; EU:C:1963:1, 12 (emphasis added); *Costa* v. *ENEL*, 594.

[33] Case 294/83 *Parti ecologiste, 'Les Verts'* v. *European Parliament* [1986] ECR 1357; EU: C:1986:166, [23]; Case 1/91 *Opinion on the European Free Trade Agreement (EFTA)* [1991] I-06079; EU:C:1991:490, [21].

[34] Eric Stein, 'Lawyers, Judges and the Making of a Transnational Constitution' (1981) 75 Am J Comp L 1. Koen Lenaerts, 'The Basic Constitutional Charter of a Community Based on the Rule of Law' in Loïc Azoulay Miguel Poiares Maduro (ed.), *The Past and Future of EU Law* (Hart, 2010), 295.

[35] Case 314/85 *Foto-Frost* v. *Hauptzollamt Lübeck-Ost* [1987] ECR 4199; EU:C:1987:452, [15].

[36] Jo Murkens, '"We Want Our Identity Back" – The Review of National Sovereignty in the General Federal Constitutional Court's Decision on the Lisbon Treaty' (2010) 10 PL 530, 542.

[37] Konrad Schiemann, 'Europe and the Loss of Sovereignty' (2007) 56 Int'l & Comp LQ 475, 476.

the limits of the transfer of national sovereign rights to the European level'.[38] This is so 'even in the case of a conflict with the very substance of fundamental rights' and even if EU law is 'found to violate such fundamental rights or to be *ultra vires*'.[39]

There is no explicit Treaty basis for this doctrine. It is based on two doctrinal justifications in ECJ jurisprudence – one pure constitutional and one normative.

The first (pure constitutional) justification holds, in essence, that the conferral of powers by the '*peoples* of Europe' (Articles 1, 3(1) TEU) adds up to much the same thing as a single '*people* of Europe', and the supremacy of EU law now derives from an autonomous source of legitimation that supersedes the national impulse to clutch back disputed territory. This can be seen in the 'sovereignty building' cases since the 1960s, wherein the ECJ justified supremacy by a direct connection between the peoples and the Union.[40] The European Parliament now provides a direct connection between a constituent people and EU law, not intermediated by national authorities.[41] The supremacy of EU law is founded on 'a common decision of the *peoples* of the Member States' that cannot be questioned by national courts.[42]

The second justification for supremacy is a normative one: the effective and uniform application of EU law.[43] This is most forcefully expressed when it is couched in terms of the rule of law,[44] legal certainty,[45] or the coherence of the EU legal order.[46] On this teleology, a failure to secure the uniformity and effectiveness of any EU law is an existential threat to the entire EU legal order as a whole.[47] This concern

---

[38] Jürgen Habermas, *The Crisis of the European Union: A Response* (Polity Press, 2012), 25.

[39] Ingolf Pernice, 'Multilevel Constitutionalism and the Treaty of Amsterdam: European Constitution-Making Revisited?' (1999) 36 CMLR 703, 719.

[40] *Costa v. ENEL*, 593; *Van Gend en Loos*, 12; Opinion C-2/13 *Opinion on Accession of the EU to the ECHR* EU:C:2014:2454, [157].

[41] Pescatore, 'Comparative Analysis', 170; Armin von Bogdandy and Jurgen Bast, 'The European Union's Vertical Order of Competences: The Current Law and Proposals for its Reform' (2002) 39 CMLR 227, 237.

[42] Pernice, 'Multilevel Constitutionalism', 719 (emphasis added).

[43] *Simmenthal* [24]; Case 34/73 *Variola* [1973] ECR 992 [15].

[44] *Costa v. ENEL*, 594.

[45] *Foto-Frost* [15]–[19].

[46] Case 473/93 *Commission v. Luxembourg* [1996] ECR I-3207 [38].

[47] Pescatore, 'Comparative Analysis', 167, 181; Koen Lenaerts, 'Federalism: Essential Concepts in Evolution – the Case of the European Union' (1997) 21 Fordham Int'l Law J 746, 777; R Daniel Kelemen, 'The Uses and Abuses of Constitutional Pluralism' (2019) 21 CYELS 59, 62–63.

has animated ECJ jurisprudence since *Internationale Handelsgesellschaft*, where it held:

[T]he law stemming from the Treaty, an independent source of law, cannot [be] overridden by rules of national law, however framed [...] without the legal basis of the Community itself being called into question.[48]

1.1.2   The Federation of Sovereign States

In proclaiming autonomy and supremacy over all constitutional law, Europe's judges enunciated a form of 'federalism'. However, the inability to reconcile this with European constitutional theory meant, as Schütze writes, 'In the absence of a federal theory beyond the State, European thought invented a new word – supranationalism – and proudly announced the European Union to be *sui generis*.'[49]

Yet while this '*sui generis*' claim pretended to reconcile two separate, sovereign constitutional orders, the hierarchy it enunciated was, in fact, a unitary monist legal order.[50] This was so because the ECJ 'arrogated to itself the ultimate authority to draw the line between Community law and national law'.[51] By denying the *peoples* of the Member States the final say over which powers they had or had not conferred on the Union, it denied the sovereignty of those peoples and in fact subjugated them under a unitary legal order.[52] As the Italian *Corte constituzionale* noted, the ECJ 'certainly considers that the source of legal norms of the Community and that of each Member State are founded on a single system'.[53]

This led to irreconcilable tensions with persisting Member State sovereignty at the boundaries of EU law.

First, the declaration that the EU derived from its own autonomous *Grundnorm* didn't simply deprive the Member States of their own. EU constitutionalism had not emerged from an act of a European *people*, but from the acts of public authorities – 'governments, legislatures, courts(!)'.[54] Applying basic principles of constitutional theory, scholars found that it

---

[48] *Internationale Handelsgesellschaft* [3]; *Costa v. ENEL*, 594.
[49] Schütze, *EU Law* (2015), 44. E.g. *EU Accession to the ECHR* [157].
[50] Kumm, 'Final Arbiter', 353–362; Pernice, 'Multilevel Constitutionalism', 712; Henry Schermers and Denis Waelbroeck, *Judicial Protection in the European Union* (6th ed., Kluwer Law International 2001), 160–164.
[51] Stein, 'Transnational Constitution', 1.
[52] Neil MacCormick, 'The Maastricht-Urteil: Sovereignty Now' (1995) 1 ELJ 259, 263–264.
[53] *Granital SpA v. Amministrazione Finanziaria dello Stato (Italy)* Judgment 170/1984; [1984] I Giur It 1521, in Oppenheimer, *The Cases* (Vol 1) 643, 651.
[54] JHH Weiler, 'Does Europe Need a Constitution? Demos, Telos and the German Maastricht Decision' (1995) 1 ELJ 219, 220.

was 'difficult – if not impossible to accept that "the founding treaties as well as each amendment agreed upon by the governments" appear as the *direct expression* of the corresponding will of the peoples of the Union'.[55] National constitutional courts agreed.[56] The EU was not a sovereign federal state,[57] but a federation of sovereign states (*Staatenverbund*) to which sovereign powers are delegated.[58] The German,[59] French,[60] Italian[61] and Spanish[62] constitutional courts all denied the autonomous 'sovereignty'

[55] Schütze, *EU Law* (2015), 56.

[56] *Treaty Establishing a Constitutional Treaty (France)* Decision 2004-505 DC; ECLI:FR: CC:2004:2004505DC, [9]–[11]: the EU 'retains the nature of an international treaty' and 'has no effect upon the existence of the French Constitution and the place of the latter at the summit of the domestic order'. *Lisbon (Latvia)* [16.3]: 'exercise of power by the Union appears not as the will of a single sovereign'. *Accession Treaty (Poland)* [6], 'It is insufficiently justified to assert that [EU institutions] are "supranational organisations" – a category that the Polish Constitution, referring solely to an "international organisation," fails to envisage.' See also *Hausgaard (Denmark)* [32]; *Carlsen (Denmark)* [35]–[36]; *Ajos (Denmark)*, 442 excerpted below, Section 1.2.1.3, n 232; *Constitutional Treaty (Spain)* [3]–[4]; *Frontini (Italy)* [7]; *Taricco II Reference (Italy)* [2]; *ERDF (Portugal)*, 687–688; *European School v. Hermans-Jacobs and Heuvelmans-van Iersel (Belgium)*, Case 12/94 (*Cour d'arbitrage*), in Oppenheimer, *The Cases* (Vol II) 155, [B.4] excerpted below, Section 1.2.1.1, nn 98, 118 and above, in Methods and Introduction, n 25; *Thoburn v. Sunderland (UK)* [69] excerpted below, n 300; *Opinion on the Constitutional Treaty (Finland)*, PeVL 36/2006 vp (*Perustuslakivaliokunnan*); *Amending Article 125 (Lithuania)*, III [6.2.3]; *Lisbon I (Czech Republic)* [132], [139]; *Lisbon II (Czech Republic)* Pl ÚS 29/09 (3 November 2009) (*Ústavní Soud*) [136], [150], [170]; *Lisbon (Hungary)* [I]V.2(3); *Article E(2) of the Fundamental Law (Hungary)* Decision 22/2016 (XII 5) AB (*Magyarország Alkotmánybírósága*) English version at: www.mkab.hu accessed 3 June 2020, [32]; *ESM (Estonia)* [223]; *Auxiliary Activities in the Public Sector (Croatia)* [45] excerpted below, at n 167; *Data Retention (Slovakia)*, PL ÚS 4/09 (26 January 2011) (*Ústavný Súd*) [69] excerpted below, n 232; *Decision 80/2014 (Romania)* [450]–[456] excerpted below, n 319; *Decision 3/2004 EU Amendments (Bulgaria)*, [V.1] excerpted below, n 57; *Slovene National Holding Company Act (SNHCA) (Slovenia)* U-II-1/12, U-II-2/12; ECLI:SI: USRS:2012:UII112, (*Ustavno Sodišče*) [22]; *Crotty (Ireland)*, 758–759, 767 excerpted below, Section 1.2.1.1, nn 140–142; *Karella (Greece)* [10]; *Decision 2011/199/EU (Poland)* [6.3.3] excerpted below, Section 1.2.1, n 83.

[57] *Weiss Decision (Germany)* [111]: 'the EU has not evolved into a federal state'. *Constitutional Treaty (Slovakia)*, 35–38: the EU is not a 'state union'. *Lisbon I (Czech Republic)* [132]: 'if the Union does not have the competence-competence, it cannot be considered either a kind of federal state or special entity'. *Decision 3/2004 EU Amendments (Bulgaria)*, SG No 61 of 13 July 2004 (Конституционен съд) V.1. 'The European Union is neither a federation nor any other form of government.'

[58] *Lisbon (Germany)* [205]; *Hausgaard v. Prime Minister (Denmark)* (Case 199/2012); [2014] 3 CMLR 16 (*Højesteret*) [32] the EU is 'an organisation consisting of independent, mutually obliged States functioning based on powers delegated by each Member State'.

[59] *Brunner (Germany)* [43]–[46], [60].

[60] *Elections to the European Parliament (France)* Decision 76-71 [1978] 74 ILR 527; ECLI:FR: CC:1976:7671DC, [2]–[4].

[61] *Frontini v. Ministero delle Finanze (Italy)*, Judgment 183/1973; [1974] 2 CMLR 372.

[62] *Re Electoral Law (Spain)* DTC 28/1991; ECLI:ES:TC:1991:28, [4].

claim of the European Parliament in their earliest encounters with it. The EU (including its parliament) was not founded by a *pouvoir constituent originaire*, but bound within competences set by international treaty.[63]

Second, the institutions of the EU were not wholly supranational,[64] not wholly unknown to international law as claimed,[65] and those aspects which were supranational were not wholly democratic. The sole institution intended to embody a European people, the European Parliament, is bestowed with the weakest influence on the programme of legislation.[66] How could it be accepted that each EU norm is the direct expression of a European people, and yet, 'the Community legislator does not receive any direct electoral mandate'?[67]

Third, given the constitutional basis of conferral, 'nearly all of the appellate courts balk at the claim of the ECJ that the European Treaties are the constitutions of an autonomous legal order'.[68] As will be shown, all twenty-eight Member State courts have come to assert that EU law takes effect not as an autonomous constitutionalism, but as a normative principle of national constitutional law. The *Brunner (Germany)* decision is perhaps the best known in that regard:

Germany is one of the 'Masters of the Treaties', which have established their adherence to the Union Treaty [. . .] but could also ultimately revoke that adherence by a contrary act. The validity and application of European law in Germany depends on the application-of-law instruction of the Accession Act.[69]

This assertion deprived autonomous European unitarism of its descriptive power because, as Maduro admits, 'a different perspective is taken by national legal orders and national constitutions [requiring] a conception of the law which is no longer dependent upon a hierarchical construction'.[70]

---

[63] Maria Cahill, 'Subverting Sovereignty's Voluntarism: Pluralism and Subsidiarity in Cahoots' in Gareth Davies and Matej Avbelj (eds), *Research Handbook on Legal Pluralism and EU Law* (Elgar, 2018), 22, 28.

[64] Council and Commissioners hold their positions 'only by reference to the place they hold according to state-systems of law'. MacCormick, 'Maastricht-Urteil', 264.

[65] 'Law-making' treaties are not unknown to international law, and supremacy is a well-established principle of international law. Weiler, 'Demos', 220.

[66] Dieter Grimm, 'Does Europe Need a Constitution?' (1995) 1 ELJ 282, 294–296.

[67] Koen Lenaerts, 'Constitutionalism and the Many Faces of Federalism' (1990) 38 Am J Comp L 205, 231.

[68] Schilling, 'Autonomy', 397. See further sources below, nn 244–247.

[69] *Brunner (Germany)* [55].

[70] Miguel Poiares Maduro, 'Europe and the Constitution: What If This Is as Good as It Gets?' in Weiler and Wind (eds), *European Constitutionalism*, 95. See also: Weiler, '*Sonderweg*', 13.

1.1.3   Constitutional Pluralism

Constitutional pluralism may now be said to have several strands, but the central tenet is that it departs from the Kelsenian emphasis on the locus of sovereignty in exchange for a normative conception of overlapping and interacting heterarchical (not hierarchical) claims.[71] Constitutional pluralism accepts that neither authority – EU or Member State courts – can abandon the legal order they have been charged to protect.[72] The benefit is that, in allowing theorists to 'escape from the idea that all law must originate in a single power source',[73] it 'suggests that conflicts between the [ECJ] and national constitutional courts should be resolved through mutual accommodation rather than through uncompromising assertions of primacy'.[74]

While not all can agree that pluralism justifies the competing claims of European and national constitutionalism, there are few who disagree that it describes them.[75] The virtue of constitutional pluralism lies in its ability to describe what courts *will* do, rather than what they should do as a matter of doctrinal principle.

In that respect, constitutional pluralism contains an inextricable (but oft-unacknowledged) thread of (Hartian) legal positivism.[76] This is so because not all constitutional disputes will be resolved through normative dialogue and, eventually, an irreconcilable conflict will arise.[77] Where it does, the methods constitutional pluralism has devised to resolve conflicts of law become little more than normative criteria for

---

[71]   See: MacCormick, 'Maastricht-Urteil', 264; Neil Walker, 'The Idea of Constitutional Pluralism' (2002) 65 MLR 317; Miquel Poiares Maduro, 'Contrapunctual Law: Europe's Constitutional Pluralism in Action' in Neil Walker (ed.), *Sovereignty in Transition* (Hart, 2003), 501; Julio Baquero Cruz, 'The Legacy of the Maastricht-Urteil and the Pluralist Movement' (2008) 14 ELJ 389; Kumm, 'Constitutional Supremacy'; Pernice, 'Multilevel Constitutionalism'. See further the collections of papers in Gráinne De Búrca and JHH Weiler (eds), *The Worlds of European Constitutionalism* (Cambridge University Press, 2012); Matej Avbelj and Jan Komárek (eds), *Constitutional Pluralism in the European Union and Beyond* (Hart 2012); Davies and Avbelj (eds), *Handbook on Legal Pluralism*.

[72]   Neil MacCormick, *Questioning Sovereignty* (Oxford University Press, 1999), 118.

[73]   MacCormick, 'Beyond the Sovereign State', 8.

[74]   Kelemen, 'Uses and Abuses', 60.

[75]   Miguel Poiares Maduro, 'Three Claims of Constitutional Pluralism' in Avbelj and Komárek (eds), *Constitutional Pluralism*, 67, 70.

[76]   Mark Jones, 'The Legal Nature of the European Community: A Jurisprudential Analysis using HLA Hart's Model of Law and a Legal System' (1984) 17 Cornell Int'l LJ 1; MacCormick, 'Beyond the Sovereign State', 8–9; Schilling, 'Autonomy', 399–401; Pavlos Eleftheriadis, 'The EU's Relationship to International Law: Lessons from Brexit' in Davies and Avbelj (eds), *Handbook on Legal Pluralism*, 369.

[77]   Cahill, 'Subverting Voluntarism', 24.

identifying which rule will in fact be recognized and applied in the positivist sense.

In that regard, the reality that matters for this book is that, whether one adopts a Kelsenian, normative or Hartian approach, Member States will often have the 'final say' as arbiters of the boundaries of EU law.[78] When applying MacCormick's pluralist approach, 'what matters [...] is that a conflict rule must be valid from the vantage point of the norm taken as reference point of the legal system in order to be regarded as a rule of that legal system'.[79] On this approach, there are few jurists who would credibly argue that a declaration of invalidity by, say, the BVerfG with regard to the PSPP, or a European arrest warrant, would be ignored by German institutions, bound by the German constitution, for a normative claim by the CJEU that another rule should be applied.[80]

This now seems accepted by Europe's judges as an empirical matter, even if it is not admitted as a matter of doctrine. As Judge Maduro observes, while the doctrinal position is that EU law is the higher law, 'National law still holds a veto power over EU law, and that is important even when it is not used'.[81] Judge Lenaerts observes:

Day after day [...] the [ECJ] must win the trust of Member States and national supreme courts as the 'ultimate judicial umpire' of [Union] competences [...] The conceptual reason for this is rather straightforward: the Member States – and not the people as such – hold the *Kompetenz-Kompetenz* as makers of the constitution.[82]

1.2 The Constitutional Boundaries of the EU Legal Order

1.2.1 Member State Kompetenz-Kompetenz

The first limit imposed by national constitutional orders on EU law is that of competence. Member States profess to retain for themselves the competence to decide on competences – the so-called *Kompetenz-Kompetenz*.[83]

---

[78] Pernice, 'Multilevel Constitutionalism', 714; Schilling, 'Autonomy', 399–401; Bruno De Witte, 'Sovereignty and European Integration: The Weight of Legal Tradition' in JHH Weiler, Anne-Marie Slaughter and Alec Stone Sweet (eds), *The European Courts and National Courts: Doctrine and Jurisprudence* (Hart Publishing, 1998), 147.

[79] Arthur Dyevre, 'European Integration and National Courts: Defending Sovereignty under Institutional Constraints?' (2013) 9 EuConst 139, 147.

[80] Maduro, 'Europe and the Constitution', 96.

[81] Maduro, 'Europe and the Constitution', 95, 97–98.

[82] Lenaerts, 'Essential Concepts', 778, 787.

[83] See, for example: *Weiss Decision (Germany)* [102]: 'The Basic law [...] prohibits conferring upon the [EU] the competence to decide on its own competences (*Kompetenz-Kompetenz*).'

This is asserted in two ways: Through judicial *ultra vires* review by national courts (the judicial *Kompetenz-Kompetenz*), and through the act of treaty ratification itself (the so-called legislative *Kompetenz-Kompetenz*).[84]

Such *ultra vires* review jurisdictions are based on intuitive logic: Under Articles 4(1), 5(1) and 5(2) TEU the limits of Union competence are governed by the principle of conferral, and under Articles 48(4) TEU, 49 TEU, 54 TEU and 357 TFEU, the EU acquires its competences when the Treaties are 'ratified by the High Contracting parties *in accordance with their respective constitutional requirements.*'[85] This means that – supreme and legitimate within its bounds though it may be – there are nonetheless boundaries of the Union legal order beyond which the states are sovereign, and Member State constitutional law is the reference point for what those boundaries are.[86] Thus, Article 263 TFEU grants the CJEU jurisdiction to hear claims for lack of competence, but national courts have not-infrequently pointed-out that the same confederate foundations which constrain the EU legal order also apply to its court – the CJEU itself is a creature of the Treaties bound within its competences (and capable of acting *ultra vires*).[87] In *Brunner (Germany)*, the BVerfG held:

[I]f European institutions or agencies were to treat or develop the Union Treaty in a way that was no longer covered by the Treaty in the form that is the basis for the Act of Accession [. . .] German state organs would be prevented for constitutional reasons from applying them in Germany. Accordingly, the [BVerfG] will review legal instruments of European institutions and agencies to see whether

---

Lisbon I (Czech Republic) [132], [145]: 'the Union does not have competence-competence'. *Lisbon (Latvia)* [18.3]; *Decision 2011/199/EU (Poland)* [6.3.3] Member States 'maintain "the competence of competences"'. See further cases cited above, n 56.

[84] *Lisbon I (Czech Republic)* [132]: 'the legislative competence-competence remains with the member states'. See Jo Shaw, 'Europe's Constitutional Future' (2005) 1 PL 132, 142.

[85] Art. 48(4) TEU (ordinary revision procedure); Art. 49 TEU (accession procedure); Art. 54 TEU (TEU ratification); Art. 357 TFEU (TFEU ratification).

[86] Grimm, 'Need a Constitution?', 287–288.

[87] *Slovak Pensions XVII (Czech Republic)* PL ÚS 5/012 (*Ústavní Súd*) English version at: www.us oud.cz accessed 28 May 2019, 12–13; *Weiss Decision (Germany)* [116]–[119], [154]–[157], [163], [234]; *Carlsen (Denmark)* [33]; *Hausgaard (Denmark)* [32]-[40]; *Danski Industri (DI) (Ajos A/S) v. Estate of Rasmussen* (Case 15/2014); [2017] 2 CMLR 14 (*Højesteret*), 444; *MAS and MB (Taricco II Judgment) (Italy)* Judgment 115/2018 (31 May 2018) (*Corte constituzionale*) [9], [12]; *Decision 80/2014 (Romania)* [458]; *Pham v. SSHD (UK)* [2015] UKSC 19; [2015] 2 CMLR 1414, [58]; *Society for the Protection of Unborn Children Ltd. (SPUC) v. Grogan I* [1989] 1 IR 753 (Supreme Court), 765 and 770; *Melloni v. Ministerio Fiscal (Spain)* DTC 26/2014; ECLI:EC: TC:2014:26, [3]-[4]; *Constitutional Treaty (Spain)* [4]; *Lisbon (Latvia)* [18.3], [18.7]; *Accession Treaty (Poland)* [16], 'The interpretation of Community law performed by the ECJ should fall within the scope of functions and competences delegated to the Communities by its Member States.'

they remain within the limits of the sovereign rights conferred on them or transgress them.[88]

If that is so, the architects of EU fiscal federalism cannot rely on the authority of the ECJ alone to secure the good functioning of models that stretch the interpretation of EU competences, or depend on legal machineries placed beyond them.[89] As Irish Supreme Court Judge Charleton so puts it: 'Cleary, the issue of what powers have been transferred remains a matter of German law for which only German courts have competency.'[90] The purpose of this Section 1.2.1 is therefore to evaluate this claim as a valid constitutional, normative and positivist description of the limits of EU law for the purposes of this book.

1.2.1.1 Pure Constitutional Evaluation of Member State *Kompetenz-Kompetenz* Adjudication

As a matter of pure constitutional law, the EU acquires its competences when the Treaties are ratified by the Member States in accordance with their respective constitutional requirements.[91] The EU does not exist independently of the Treaties, and has no competences by right. The Union is 'thus *not* "national" – that is: sovereign – in scope'.[92] As the BVerfG has stated, 'sovereignty under international law and public law requires independence from an external will precisely for its constitutional foundations'.[93] Other constitutional courts (including, at times, the ECJ)[94] arrive at similar evaluations of EU 'sovereignty'.[95] As constitutional courts have been keen to assert, it is the Member States which are the 'Masters of the Treaties'.[96]

Without the limits of conferral, entering into the European Union would have been unconstitutional in all twenty-eight of Europe's constitutional

---

[88] *Brunner (Germany)* [49], [68].

[89] See, for example, *Weiss Decision (Germany)*, excerpted in Methods and Introduction, n 59; Section 1.2.1.1, at n 104; and Section 1.2.1.3, at n 241.

[90] Peter Charleton and Angelina Cox, 'Accepting the Judgements of the Court of Justice of the EU as Authoritative' (2016) 23 MJ 1, 207.

[91] Arts. 4(1), 5(1)–(2), 48(4), 49, 54 TEU; Art. 357 TFEU.

[92] Schütze, *EU Law* (2015), 61.

[93] *Lisbon (Germany)* [207].

[94] *EU Accession to the ECHR*, [156].

[95] See cases cited at nn 56, 96.

[96] *Brunner (Germany)* [55]; *Lisbon (Germany)* [207], [247], [274]; *Weiss Decision (Germany)* [111], [157]; *Lisbon I (Czech Republic)* [146]; *Lisbon (Poland)* [3.8]; *Maastricht (Spain)* [4]; *TCSG (Belgium)*, B.8.7; *Ajos (Denmark)*, 444.

democracies (with one qualification)[97] reviewed in this chapter. The EU's powers are carved-out from Member State constitutions and, *nemo plus iuris*, none of Europe's constitutional democracies allow the disposition of the constitutional amending power by conferring *Kompetenz-Kompetenz* on the Union.[98] *Maastricht (Spain)* is characteristic:

[T]he Spanish parliament can grant or transfer the exercise of 'powers derived from the Constitution', but cannot dispense with the Constitution itself, contravening or permitting the contradiction of its provisions. The possibility of amending the Constitution is not a 'power' whose exercise can be granted.[99]

In any event, Articles 48(4) TEU, 49 TEU, 54 TEU and 357 TFEU are quite clear on the manner of democratic legitimation for the acquisition of competence: the Treaties must be ratified by the Member States '*in accordance with their respective constitutional requirements*'. If supremacy is 'founded on a common decision' by a European *people*, then that 'common decision' was to resolve – by writing Articles 5 TEU, 48(4) TEU, 49 TEU, 54 TEU and 357 TFEU into the Treaties – that the EU cannot extend its own powers through any act not in accordance with Member State constitutional requirements. Thus, even if one accepts the pure

---

[97] In the Netherlands and Luxembourg courts are prohibited from reviewing the constitutionality of international treaties. This has led to a debate over whether EU law could apply outside the constitutional empowerment. See sources cited below, Section 1.2.1.1, at nn 174–181.

[98] See, for example, *Carlsen (Denmark)* [15]: the Danish Constitution 'precludes that it can be left to the international organisation to make its own specification of its powers'. *Lisbon (Poland)* [2.2]: 'Within the meaning of the Constitution, it is possible to confer competences "in relation to certain matters" which excludes conferral of competence to determine competences.' *Lisbon I (Czech Republic)* [145]: 'if the Union could change its competences at will, independently of the signatory countries, then by ratifying the [Lisbon Treaty] the Czech Republic would violate [. . .] the Constitution.' *European Schools (Belgium)* [B.4]: 'having forbidden the legislature to pass rules contrary to those referred to by [the] Constitution, may not be supposed to have authorised the same legislature to do so indirectly through the assent given to an international Treaty'. See further *Lisbon (Germany)*, excerpted below, Section 1.2.1.1, at n 182; *Crotty (Ireland)*, 783 excerpted below, Section 1.3.1, at n 462; *Elections to the EP (France)* [2]–[4]; *TCSG (Belgium)*, B.8.5 excerpted above, in Methods and Introduction, n 25; *Maastricht (Spain)* [4]; *Amending Article 125 (Lithuania)* [2]; *ESM (Estonia)* [223]; *Constitutional Treaty (Slovakia)*, 35–38; Ch 10§6 of Sweden's Instrument of Government, discussed below, Section 1.2.1.1, at nn 121–125 and Section 1.2.2.1 at nn 332–335; *Decision 80/2014 (Romania)* [456] excerpted below, n 319; *Decision 3/2004 EU Amendments (Bulgaria)* [V.1] discussed below, Section 1.2.1.1 at nn 151–153; *Fiscal Balance Act 2012 (Slovenia)* U-I-146/12; ECLI:SI:USRS:2013:UI14612, [32]–[33] excerpted below, at n 154; *HS2 Action Alliance Ltd. v. SST (UK)* [2014] UKSC 3; [2014] 1 WLR 324, [79]; *Constitutional Treaty (Finland)*, 3; *Karella (Greece)* [10] excerpted below, n 132; *ERDF (Portugal)*, 687–688; *Lisbon (Hungary)* [I]V.2(3).

[99] *Maastricht (Spain)* [3c], [4].

constitutional justification for supremacy – that the conferral of powers by the *'peoples'* of Europe' adds up to much the same thing as a single constitutional *'people* of Europe' – it remains that this legitimation can only ever flow *within* the limits of the EU's conferred powers.[100] As asserted by the Spanish *Tribunal Constitucional*:

> [T]he primacy set forth *according to the Treaty* [...] is reduced expressly to the exercise of competences attributed to the European Union [...] it is not a primacy with a general scope. [...] Therefore, the primacy operates with regard to the competences transferred to the Union by the sovereign will of the State [...] the competences whose exercise is transferred to the [EU] could not, *without a breakdown of the Treaty itself*, act as a foundation for the production of Community regulations whose content was contrary to the values, principles or fundamental rights of our Constitution.[101]

'Absolute' supremacy, however, implies something different. It implies that the Union may acquire competences other than in the manner provided by Articles 48(4), 49 and 54 TEU or 357 TFEU – that is, other than an act of ratification in accordance with constitutional law. This is because a well-meaning but erroneous ECJ *intra vires* ruling on an act outside EU law would effect a misappropriation of state power which nobody – neither the *'peoples'* nor a *'people* of Europe' – has voted to confer on the Union.[102] Moreover, because supremacy applies within the scope of EU competence, the misappropriation of this 'new' EU competence permanently switches the power to determine law in that area from the Member State to the Union.[103] As the BVerfG warned in *Weiss (Germany)*:

> If the Member States were to completely refrain from conducting any kind of ultra vires review, they would grant EU organs exclusive authority over the Treaties even in cases where the EU adopts a legal interpretation that would essentially amount to a treaty amendment or an expansion of its competences.[104]

For this reason, the German BVerfG has long held that it has an *ultra vires* review jurisdiction to decide whether the EU has stepped over the

---

[100] *Lisbon (Germany)* [216], [307]–[308]; *Constitutional Treaty (Spain)* [3]; *Elections to the EP (France)* [2]–[4].

[101] *Constitutional Treaty (Spain)* [3] (emphasis added).

[102] *Lisbon (Germany)* [214].

[103] Derrick Wyatt, 'Is the European Union an Organisation of Limited Powers?' in Catherine Barnard, Anthony Arnull, Michael Dougan and Eleanor Spaventa (eds), *A Constitutional Order of States?* (Hart, 2011), 5.

[104] *Weiss Decision (Germany)* [111].

boundaries given to it.[105] According to that Court, an act of EU law that is manifestly outside the scope of competences, or an expansive interpretation of EU law that is 'structurally significant' to the allocation of competences in a manner 'equivalent to an extension of the Treaty [. . .] would not produce any binding effects for Germany'.[106]

It is far from alone.

In **Italy**, the *Corte constituzionale* exercises *Kompetenz-Kompetenz* control over EU law under its '*controlimiti*' (counter-limits) doctrine.[107] EU law is not autonomous, but is 'founded upon [. . .] Article 11(2) of the Constitution'.[108] It is only '*within those areas in which the organs of the Community are competent*' that '*the Community rule takes precedence*' over any rule of national law.[109]

In **France**, the *Conseil Constitutionnel* exercises *a priori* constitutional control over acts of conferral,[110] and the *Conseil Constitutionnel*,[111] *Conseil d'État*[112] and *Cour de Cassation*[113] exercise *a posteriori* control of secondary law in excess of the constitutional authorization.[114] Article 54 of the

---

[105] *Brunner (Germany)* [49]; *Lisbon (Germany)* [314]; *Honeywell (Germany)* (2 BvR 2551/06): BVerfGE 126, 286; [2011] 1 CMLR 33, [32], [48]–[51]; *ESM I (Germany)* [193]; *ESM II (Germany)* [160]; *Gauweiler Reference (Germany)* [20]–[26]; *Gauweiler Decision (Germany)* [161]–[163]; *Weiss Decision (Germany)* [110–112].

[106] *Brunner (Germany)* [49]. *Manifestly* in violation of competences will be assessed by reference to CJEU case law on manifest and grave disregard for the limits of discretion: Case C-472/00 *Commission* v. *Fresh Marine* [2003] ECR I-7541; EU:C:2003:399, [26]. *Structurally significant* means 'highly significant in the structure of competences [with] regard to the principle of conferral'. *Euro Rescue Package (Germany)* [99]–[100].

[107] If EU law exceeds the *controlimiti*, it ceases to produce effects in the Italian legal order: *Talamucci (Italy)*, 393: *Frontini (Italy)* [3]; *Granital (Italy)* [7]; *Fragd* v. *Amministrazione Delle Finanze Dello Stato (Italy)*, Case 232/1989; [1990] 93 ILR 538, 657; *President of Council of Ministers* v. *Sardinian Region (Sardinian Taxes)* Judgment 102/2008 (13 April 2008) available at www.cortecostituzionale.it accessed 18 May 2016, [8.2.8.1] and cases cited below, n 291.

[108] *Frontini (Italy)* [7].

[109] *Frontini (Italy)* [8] (emphasis added).

[110] *Maastricht I (France)* [34], [44]–[50]; *Treaty of Lisbon (France)* Decision No 2007-560 DC; ECLI: FR:CC:2007560DC, [9]; *Constitutional Treaty (France)* [7], [24], [29].

[111] *Confidence in the Digital Economy (France)* Decision No 2004-496 DC; ECLI:FR: CC:2004:2004496DC, [7]; *Act on Electronic Communications (France)* Decision No 2004-497 DC; ECLI:FR:CC:2004:2004497DC, [18]; *Bioethics Act (France)* Decision No 2004-498; ECLI: FR:CC:2004:2004498DC, [4]; and cases cited below, n 294.

[112] *Nicolo (France)* [1989] RTDE 771; *Minister of the Interior* v. *Cohn-Bendit (France)* [1979] RGDIP 832; [1980] 1 CMLR 543; *Sarran, Levacher et autres (France)* [1998] RFDA 1081; *Arcelor Atlantique et Lorraine (France)* [2007] 2 CMLR 28. See Claudina Richards, 'Sarran et Levacher: Ranking Legal Norms in the French Republic' (2000) 25 EL Rev 192.

[113] *Administration des Douanes* v. *Cafes Jaques Vabre (France)* [1975] 2 CMLR 336, [4]; *Mlle Fraisse (France)* Decision No 99-60274; Dalloz 2000, 965 Note B.

[114] See further Claudina Richards, 'The Supremacy of Community Law before the French Constitutional Court' (2006) 31 EL Rev 499, 511; Stefan Theil, 'What Red Lines, if Any,

Constitution contains a *nemo plus iuris* rule,[115] pursuant to which EU law cannot run counter to an 'express contrary provision' of the Constitution, unless the constituting power consents thereto.[116] In **Belgium** the *Cour constitutionnelle* and *Conseil d'État* locate authority for the supremacy of EU law in Article 34 of the Belgian Constitution.[117] This does not allow the disposition of *Kompetenz-Kompetenz*, and there is no basis for the application of EU law outside the national constitutional empowerment.[118] In **Denmark**, an open-ended conferral, or the assumption of powers not specified in the Accession Act (including by judicial interpretation) would violate the Section 20 of the Constitutional act of Denmark.[119] The *Højesteret* (Supreme Court) retains a powerful *ultra vires* jurisdiction: CJEU interpretations 'must not result in the widening of the scope of Union powers' and 'it is for the Danish courts to decide whether EU acts exceed the limits for the surrender of sovereignty which has taken place by the Accession Act'.[120]

Do the Lisbon Judgments of the European Constitutional Courts Draw for Future EU Integration?' (2014) 15 German LJ 599, 612–613; Jans-Herman Reestman, 'The Franco-German Constitutional Divide: Reflections on National and Constitutional Identity' (2009) 5 EUConst 267, 390.

[115] *Treaty of Maastricht II (France)* Decision No 93-312 DC; ECLI:FR:CC:192:92312DC, [9]–[10].

[116] *Immigration, Integration and Nationality Act (France)* Decision No 2011-631 DC; ECLI:FR: CC:2011:2011631DC, [45] and sources cited above, n 111. Since *Société de l'information (France)* Decision No 2006-540 DC; ECLI:FR:CC:2006:2006540DC, [19], the *Conseil Constitutionnel* has held that Art. 88-1 grants consent for supremacy over ordinary constitutional provisions, save that EU law cannot 'run counter to a rule or principle inherent to the constitutional identity of France'. See also sources cited below, Section 1.2.2.1, nn 292–294. However, it remains that only in the absence of a constitutional conflict does it fall to the CJEU to resolve the conflict: *Confidence in the Digital Economy (France)* [7] and cases cited above, n 111.

[117] *European School (Belgium)* [B.4]; *Minister for Economic Affairs* v. *SA Fromagerie Franco-Suisse (Le Ski)* [1971] *Jornal des Tribunauz* 460; [1972] CMLR 330 (*Cour de Cassation*), 261; Case 62/922 *Orfinger* v. *Belgium (Minister for Civil Service)* [1997] *Journal des Tribunaux* 254 (*Conseil d'Etat*), in Oppenheimer, *The Cases* (Vol II) 162, 165–166, 188.

[118] *European School (Belgium)* [B.4]: 'Article 34 provides a constitutional basis for the institutional mechanism established by the Treaty [. . .] Nevertheless this provision determines neither those competences which may be transferred nor their limits.' *TCSG (Belgium)* [B.8.5], [B.8.7]. See Claes, *National Courts*, 199–204, 242–243, 490, 506–513, 639–645; Philippe Gérard and Willem Verrijdt, 'Belgian Constitutional Court Adopts National Identity Discourse' (2017) 13 Eur Const Law Rev 182, 187–189.

[119] *Carlsen (Denmark)* [33]; *Hausgaard (Denmark)* [32].

[120] *Hausgaard (Denmark)* [46], [41]. See also *Ajos (Denmark)*, 442; Ulla Neergaard and Karsten Engsig Sørensen, 'Activist Infighting among Courts and Breakdown of Mutual Trust?' (2017) 36 Yearb Eur Law 275, 296.

In **Sweden**, the *Högsta Domstolen* (Supreme Court) and *Högsta förvalt-ningsdomstolen* (Supreme Administrative Court) derive authority for the direct effect,[121] indirect effect[122] and supremacy of EU law[123] from Chapter 10§6 of the Instrument of Government – not autonomous EU constitutionalism.[124] As Lebeck explains, a 'legal act or decision from an EC/EU institution that exceeds the powers that have been delegated to the EC/EU would be *ultra vires* and hence not be valid law in the Swedish legal order'.[125]

In the **United Kingdom**, the permissible scope of application of EU law was a function of the interpretation of the European Communities Act 1972,[126] and the UK courts retained an *ultra vires* jurisdiction to determine 'whether the European Communities Act 1972 or any succes-sor statute conferred any authority on the Court of Justice to exercise [...] jurisdiction' over issues outside the scope of authority so provided.[127]

In **Spain**, the *Tribunal Constitucional* distinguishes between the *primacía* of EU law afforded by Section 93 of the Spanish Constitution (allowing EU law to supersede conflicting national law), and the *supremacía* of the Constitution itself (which both determines the status of EU law in the national order, and subjects it to integral constitutional guarantees).[128] In *Constitutional Treaty (Spain)* it held: 'the primacy set

---

[121] *VK (Church Tax) (Sweden)*, Case 2471/94; RA 1997 ref 56 (*Regeringsrätten*) available at: htt ps://lagennu/dom/ra/1997:6 accessed 4 July 2016.

[122] *Klippan Company (Sweden)*, Case 3356/94; RA 1996 ref 57 (*Regeringsrätten*) available at: h ttps://lagennu/dom/ra/1996:57 accessed 4 July 2016; *PH (Motor Vehicles Sales Tax) (Sweden)*, Case 329/99; RA 20000 ref 27 (*Regeringsrätten*) available at: https://lagennu/dom/ra/200 0:27 accessed 4 July 2016.

[123] *Lassagard (Sweden)*, Case 210/1997; RA 1997 ref 65 (*Högsta domstolen*) in Oppenheimer, *The Cases* (Vol I) 428; *SO Buss i Sollentuna AB (Sweden)*, Case 2195/95; RA 1997 ref 82 (*Regeringsrätten*) available at: https://lagennu/dom/ra/1997:82 accessed 4 July 2016.

[124] Ch 10§6 Instrument of Government. See also below, Section 1.2.2.1, at nn 332–336. See: Joakim Nergelius, 'The Constitution of Sweden and European Influences' in Anneli Albi and Samo Bardutzky (eds), *National Constitutions in European and Global Governance* (Springer 2019), 319–320.

[125] Carl Lebeck, 'Supranational Law in a Cold Climate: European Law in Scandanavia' (2010) 4 Sant'Anna Legal Studies 2, 13. See further sources cited below, Section 1.2.2.1, nn 332–336.

[126] *HS2 (UK)* [79] excerpted below, n 228; *R (Miller)* v. *Secretary of State for Exiting the EU* [2017] UKSC 5; [2018] AC 61, [65]–[67]. European Communities Act, 1972 c. 68, s. 2 and European Union Act, 2011 c. 12, s. 28 govern the supremacy of EU law. These were repealed by the European Union (Withdrawal) Act 2018, c. 16, though at the time of writing their effects had been saved by the European Union (Withdrawal Agreement) Act, 2020 c. 1.

[127] *G1* v. *SSHD (UK)* [2012] EWCA Civ 867; [2013] QB 1008, [43]; *Pham* v. *SSHD (UK)* [58].

[128] *Maastricht (Spain)* [3c], [4]; *Constitutional Treaty (Spain)* [2], [4].

forth for the Treaty and its resulting legislation [. . .] is reduced expressly to the exercise of the competences attributed to the European Union [. . .] by the sovereign will of the State'.[129]

In **Portugal**, the supremacy of EU law derives from Articles 7(6) and 8 (4) of the Portuguese Constitution, and the *Tribunal Constitucional* has held since *ERDF (Portugal)* that 'there can be no exercise of the regulatory power without some basis in a *lex anterior*'.[130]

In **Greece**, the Council of State (Συμβούλιο της Επικρατείας) locates constitutional authority for EU law in Article 28 of the Hellenic Constitution – not autonomous EU law.[131] In *Karella (Greece)*, the Council of State confirmed that the EU's powers are constrained by the act of conferral, and the act of conferral is constrained by the Constitution.[132]

In the **Czech Republic**, the *Ústavní Soud* (Constitutional Court) retains ultimate jurisdiction to determine 'whether an act of the Union has exceeded the limits [of powers] which the Czech Republic transferred to the EU under Art. 10a of the Constitution'.[133]

In **Poland**, Article 90(1) of the Constitution permits Poland to 'delegate' competences only 'in relation to certain matters', and the *Trybunał Konstytucyjny* (Constitutional Court) retains jurisdiction to 'assess whether or not, in issuing particular legal provisions, the Community legislative organs acted within the delegated competences'.[134] Should they exceed them, 'the principle of the precedence of Community law fails to apply with respect to such provisions'.[135]

In **Latvia**, EU competences are legitimated by Article 68 of the Constitution, which allows Latvia to 'delegate a part of its State

---

129 *Constitutional Treaty (Spain)* [3].
130 *ERDF (Portugal)*, 687–688. See also *Cadima (Portugal)*, Case 12 381-36 052 (*Tribunal de Relação de Coimbra*), in Oppenheimer, *The Cases* (Vol 1) 675, 679–680.
131 *Banana Market (Greece)*, Case 815/1984 in Oppenheimer, *The Cases* (Vol I) 576, 578; *Mineral Rights Discrimination (Greece)*, Case 2152/1986 in Oppenheimer, *The Cases* (Vol I) 581, 583; *Real Property Acquisition (Greece)*, Case 43/1990 in Oppenheimer, *The Cases* (Vol I) 589, 589; *Athens Paper SA (Greece)* Decision 161/2010, ECLI:EL:COS:2010:0115A16101E3166, [6]. See further below, Section 1.2.2.1, n 329.
132 *Karella (Greece)* [10], 'the primacy of the EEC Treaty [is] subject to certain conditions for the possibility of conferring [. . .] those powers provided for in the Constitution'.
133 *Lisbon I (Czech Republic)* [139]. See also *Lisbon II (Czech Republic)* [136], [150], [170]; *Sugar Quotas III (Czech Republic)* [106].
134 *Accession Treaty (Poland)* [15]. See also *Lisbon (Poland)* [2.2] excerpted above, n 98; *Decision 2011/199/EU (Poland)* [3.2], [6.3.1]; *Representation in the European Council (Poland)* Kpt 2/08 in Biblioteka Trybunału Konstytucyjnego, *Selected Rulings* (Vol LI) 122, [5.8]; *Brussels Regulation (Poland)* [1.5], [2.2] *et seq*; *European Arrest Warrant (Poland)* P 1/05 in Biblioteka Trybunału Konstytucyjnego, *Selected Rulings* (Vol LI) 41, [9].
135 *Accession Treaty (Poland)* [15].

institution competences',[136] and the *Satversmes tiesa* (Constitutional Court) denies EU *Kompetenz-Kompetenz*.[137]

In **Lithuania**, the *Konstitucinis Teismas* (Constitutional Court) denies EU *Kompetenz-Kompetenz*[138] and asserts its jurisdiction to 'guarantee the supremacy of the constitution in the legal system as well as constitutional legality' in the context of the EU.[139]

In **Ireland**, Article 29.4.6 of the Constitution grants constitutional supremacy to EU law within the scope of the act of ratification, but the Supreme Court holds that this is only so *provided* that future expansions or amendments of EU law 'did not alter the essential scope or objectives of the Union'.[140] Article 29.4.6 does not allow the state to dispose of *Kompetenz-Kompetenz*.[141] EU law 'has immunity but only if [the act of ratification] does not go outside the terms of the licence granted by [Article 29.4.6]', failing which 'such acts of the institutions of the Community as depend on [the act of ratification] for their

---

[136]   The 'ordinary' supremacy of EU law within its competences is accepted on this basis: *Convention on International Marine Traffic (Latvia)*, Case 2004-01-06 (7 July 2004) English version at: www.satv.tiesa.gov.lv accessed 17 July 2016, 10; *Riga Land Use Plan (Latvia)*, Case 2007-11-03 (17 January 2008), in *Selected Case-Law of the Constitutional Court of the Republic of Latvia: 1996-2017 (Satversmes tiesa*, 2018), [24.2].

[137]   *Lisbon (Latvia)* [11.1], 'the constitutional Court has the duty to ensure supremacy of the Satverseme', and [17–18.3] the constitution guarantees the people not only 'the right to the last word' but also the 'right to the first word' on competence. See: Tatjana Evas, *Judicial Application of European Union Law in Post-Communist Countries: The Cases of Estonia and Latvia* (Routledge 2016), 42; Kristīne Krūma and Sandijs Statkus, 'The Constitution of Latvia – a Bridge between Traditions and Modernity' in Albi and Bardutzky (eds), *National Constitutions*, 959–960.

[138]   *Amending Article 125 (Lithuania)* III [6.2.3]: '[T]he Constitutional Act of Membership [...] establishes, *inter alia*, the constitutional grounds of the membership in [...] the European Union. If such constitutional grounds were not consolidated in the Constitution, [Lithuania] would not be able to be a full member of the European Union.'

[139]   *On applying to the Court of Justice (Lithuania)*, Case 47/04 (8 May 2007) English version at: www.lrkt.lt/lt/en/ accessed 3 July 2016, [I.1] (see also [II.3]). See further cases cited below, n 318.

[140]   *Crotty (Ireland)*, 767. The European Communities Act 1972 (No 27/1972) (Ireland) is the 'conduit pipe' through which EU law enters Irish law: *Tate* v. *Minister for Social Welfare (Ireland)* [1995] 1 IR 418; [1995] 1 CMLR 825 (High Court), [41]. See further William Phelan, 'Can Ireland Legislate Contrary to European Community Law?' (2008) 33 EL Rev 530, 537.

[141]   *Crotty (Ireland)*, 767 'to construe [Article 29.4.6] as an open-ended authority to agree, without further amendment of the Constitution, to any amendment of the Treaties would be too broad'. See further DR Phelan and Anthony Whelan, 'National Constitutional Law and European Integration' (1997) 6 IJEL 24, 28; Phelan, *Revolt or Revolution*, 338–339.

status in domestic law would lose that status and would be of no effect in domestic law'.[142]

The position is similar in **Austria**, where the Constitutional Court (VfGH) derives authorization for the supremacy of EU law from the Act on Accession of Austria (AAA), enacted by the 'total revision' procedure under Article 44(3) of the Austrian Constitution in 1993.[143] However, the 1993 'total revision' does not cover future expansions of the EU legal order, and the EU does not have *Kompetenz-Kompetenz*.[144]

In **Estonia**, the Constitution of Estonia Amendment Act (CEAA) provides that the Constitution will be applied 'without prejudice to the rights and obligations arising from the Accession Treaty'.[145] However, as the *Riigikohus* (Supreme Court) has held, this applies only 'within the spheres' of EU competence,[146] and 'does not authorise the integration process of the [EU] to be legitimised or the competences of Estonia to be delegated to the [EU] to an unlimited extent'.[147] A 'more extensive delegation of the competence of Estonia to the European Union' requires further consent from the Estonian people (by referendum).[148]

In **Romania**, the *Curtea Constituțională* (Constitutional Court) distinguishes between the 'priority' or 'precedence' of EU law over legislation and the 'supremacy' of the Constitution (which both determines the

---

[142] *Crotty (Ireland)*, 758–759.

[143] *Natural Mineral Water (Austria)*, Case QZ V 136/94 in Oppenheimer, *The Cases* (Vol I) 133; *Tourism Promotion Tax (Austria)*, Case G 2/97 in Oppenheimer, *The Cases* (Vol I) 137, 142; *Telecom Control Commission (Austria)*, Case B 1625/98 (24 February 1999); *Tyrolian Provincial Allocation Office*, Case GZ-B 2477/05 in Oppenheimer, *The Cases* (Vol I) 135. See Art. 44(3) Austrian Federal Constitution (*Bundeskanzleramt*) English translation at:www.ris.bka.g v.at accessed 6 June 2015. Since 2008 lesser treaty amendments that do not affect the Constitution's Basic Principles have been possible with a 2/3 majority in both houses under Article 50 of the Constitution.

[144] Stefan Griller, 'Introduction to the Problems in the Austrian, the Finnish and the Swedish Constitutional Order' in Alfred E Kellermann, Jaap W de Zwaan and Jenö Czuczai (eds), *EU Enlargement: The Constitutional Impact at EU and National Level* (TMC Asser Press 2001), 148–150; Nigel Foster, *Austrian Legal System & Laws* (Cavendish 2003), 144; Christoph Grabenwarter, 'National Constitutional Law Relating to the EU' in Armin Von Bogdandy and Jürgen Bast (eds), *Principles of European Constitutional Law* (2nd ed., Hart, 2011), 85, 98; Claes, *National Courts*, 163; Nigel Foster, *Foster on EU Law* (4th ed., Oxford University Press 2013), 153.

[145] The Constitution of the Republic of Estonia Amendment Act RT I 2003, 64, 429, s. 2. *ESM (Estonia)* [223].

[146] *Interpretation of the Constitution (Estonia)*, Case 3-4-1-3-06 (11 May 2006) (*Riigikohus*) [16].

[147] *ESM (Estonia)* [222].

[148] *ESM (Estonia)* [223].

effect of EU law and prevails over it).[149] This precludes EU *Kompetenz-Kompetenz*. EU law is derived from Article 148 of the Constitution (which permits 'exercising' 'certain powers' with other states), and EU acts are 'norms interposed within the constitutionality control'.[150]

In **Bulgaria**, the Constitutional Court (Конституционен съд) holds that the supremacy of EU law is justified because 'the institutions of the European Communities act within their competences [which are] subject to ratification'.[151] Authorization for conferral is 'not unlimited',[152] and the EU can only acquire powers through acts of the people, 'at their own will, through the National Assembly elected by them'.[153]

In **Slovenia**, the *Ustavno Sodišče* (Constitutional Court) holds that EU law becomes 'internal constitutional principles that have the same binding effect as the Constitution' by virtue of Art. 3a of the Slovenian Constitution – it is neither autonomous nor constitutionally supreme.[154] In *SNHCA (Slovenia)*, the Court declined to endorse EU supremacy over the Constitution and described *Kompetenz-Kompetenz* as a permanent constraint on conferral.[155]

In **Slovakia**, the *Ústavný Súd* (Constitutional Court) holds that EU law has the status of international treaties under Article 7(2)[156] or 7(5)[157] of the Constitution (or both), meaning EU law does not have *Kompetenz-Kompetenz* and is subject to the Constitution.[158] In *Constitutional Treaty*

---

[149] *Decision 148/2003 On the legislative proposal to amend the Constitution (Romania)*, Monitorul Oficial al României No 317 of 16 April 2003: Member states 'agreed to situate the *acquis Communautaire* [. . .] on an intermediate position between the Constitution and other law'. See also *Decision 80/2014 (Romania)* [453]–[460] excerpted below, n 319.

[150] *Decision 80/2014 (Romania)* [453]–[460].

[151] *Decision 3/2004 EU Amendments (Bulgaria)* V.1.

[152] *Decision 7/2018 on Mixed EU Treaties (Bulgaria)* [3.1].

[153] *Decision 3/2004 EU Amendments (Bulgaria)* V.1.

[154] *Fiscal Balance Act 2012 (Slovenia)* [32]–[33]. *Electronic Communications Act (Slovenia)* U-I-65/13; ECLI:SI:USRS:2014:UI6513, [6]–[7]; *AA Company v. Maribor Higher Court Ruling (Slovenia)* U-I-186/04; ECLI:SI:USRS:2004:Up32804, [10].

[155] *SNHCA (Slovenia)* [20]–[23], [41]–[42], [53]. The constitution prevents the state from transferring sovereignty: *Vatican Agreement (Slovenia)* [22]–[24].

[156] *Health Insurance (Slovakia)* PL ÚS 3/09 (26 January 2011), V[3.4].

[157] *Data Retention (Slovakia)* [69] excerpted below, n 232.

[158] Art. 7(5) of the Constitution of the Slovak Republic (Verejny Ochranca Práv, 2016) gives human rights treaties primacy over 'laws', and Art. 7(2) states EU norms 'shall have precedence over laws of the Slovak Republik'. 'Laws' does not include the Constitution (Art. 84(4)) and laws are subject to constitutional review (Art. 125(1)(a)). See *Constitutional Treaty (Slovakia)*, 35–38; *Data Retention (Slovakia)* [62], [70]–[71]. See further Frank Hoffmeister, 'Constitutional Implications of EU Membership' (2007) 3 CYELP 59, 85–86.

(Slovakia), the Court denied the EU was a 'state union' with *Kompetenz-Kompetenz*.[159]

In **Finland**, constitutional review is exercised by the *Perustuslakivaliokunnan* (Constitutional Committee), which holds that neither the Act of Accession nor Sections 94–95 of the Constitution (the bases for conferral and application of EU law) can endanger the democratic foundations of the Constitution, in particular *Kompetenz-Kompetenz*.[160] As Ojanen observes, 'the Committee's message is that *Kompetenz-Kompetenz* remains – and should continue to remain, in the hands of Finland'.[161]

The Constitution of **Malta** states that Parliamentary legislation made in conformity with international/EU obligations are 'Subject to the provisions of [the Maltese] Constitution',[162] and an amendment to Malta's constitutional supremacy clause (Article 6) could not be achieved.[163] Thus, as Xuereb explains, because the authority for EU law must 'take the form of an Act of Parliament passed in virtue of the Constitution', the Constitutional Court (*Qorti Kostituzzjonali*) retains the 'final say' on the scope and effect of EU law within the constitutional system.[164]

---

[159] *Constitutional Treaty (Slovakia)*, 35–38.

[160] *Opinion 30/2001 on the Nice Treaty (Finland)*, PeVL 38/2001 vp; *Constitutional Treaty (Finland)*, 3; *Opinion on the ERM (Finland)*, PeVL 3/1996 vp. Act 1540/94 of the Statutes of Finland (Finland Act of Accession) (Suomen säädöskokoelma), provided for EU supremacy by derogation from the Constitution since *VAT Deduction Rights (Finland)* Decision of 31 December 1996 (*Korkein hallinto-oikeus*) in Oppenheimer, *The Cases* (Vol II) 193. However, as a dualist country, all constitutional acts must be given force through an act of ratification, and further transfers of power that contain provisions of a 'legislative nature' or are 'otherwise significant' occur by 2/3 majority under ss. 94–95 of the Constitution. See: Griller, 'Problems', 166–167; Tuomas Ojanen and Janne Salminen, 'Finland' in Albi and Bardutzky (eds), *National Constitutions*, 363–373 and below, Section 1.2.2.1, nn 357–360.

[161] Tuomas Ojanen, 'EU Law and the Response of the Constitutional Law Committee of the Finnish Parliament' (2007) 52 Scan Stud L 204, 219.

[162] Art. 65, Constitution of Malta (Ministry for Justice, 2020) accessible at: https://legisla tion.mt/eli/const/eng/pdf accessed 9 July 2020.

[163] Frank Hoffmeister, 'Constitutional Implications of EU Membership: A View from the Commission' (2007) CYELP 59, 67.

[164] Peter Xuereb, 'The Constitution of Malta' in Albi and Bardutzky (eds), *National Constitutions*, 145. Although the *Qorti Kostituzzjonali* has declared itself the 'guardian of the Constitution' (*Mintoff in the name of Alternattiva Demokratika v. Broadcasting Authority (Malta)* (31 July 1996)) and has jurisdiction declare 'the unconstitutionality of laws' (*Vasallo v. Prime Minister (Malta)* (27 February 1978)), unconstitutional laws remain valid until repealed by Parliament. Thus, Parliament may have the final say: John Stanton, 'The Constitution of Malta: Supremacy, Parliament and the Separation of Powers' (2019) 6 JICL 47.

In **Croatia**, the supremacy of EU law is derived from Articles 141–143 and 145 of the Croatian Constitution, not autonomous EU constitutionalism.[165] Under Article 2 of the Constitution, Croatia 'retain[s] its sovereign right to decide upon the powers to be so delegated',[166] and the *Ustavni sud* (Constitutional Court) holds that 'the Constitution is, by its legal nature, supreme to EU law'.[167]

In **Hungary**, the *Magyarország Alkotmánybírósága* (Constitutional Court) has asserted judicial *Kompetenz-Kompetenz* under the sovereignty provisions of both the 1989 Constitution and the 2011 Fundamental Law.[168]

In **Cyprus**, the *Ανώτατο Δικαστήριο* (Supreme Court) derives the supremacy of EU law from Article 1A of the Constitution,[169] a constitutional exceptive clause introduced in 2006 after the Supreme Court ruled EU law could not prevail over conflicting Constitutional provisions.[170] However, this does not confer *Kompetenz-Kompetenz*. Under the Cypriot Constitution, treaties 'shall only be operative and binding on the Republic when approved by a law made by the House of Representatives',[171] and the Constitution remains 'the supreme law of the Republic'.[172] Consequently, 'any delegation of transfer of competences is

---

[165] *Z et ors. (Croatia)*, Revt 249/14-2 (9 April 2015) *(Vrhovni sud)*. Art. 143 permits conferral by treaties 'concluded and ratified in accordance with the Constitution' once an association with the EU is passed by a 2/3 majority in Parliament and a referendum (Art. 142), whereupon they 'shall be a component of the domestic legal order', 'shall have primacy over domestic law' (Art. 141), and shall be 'equal to the exercise of rights under Croatian law' (Arts. 145).

[166] Art. 2 of the Constitution of the Republic of Croatia (Consolidated Text) English translation at: www.sabor.hr/files/uploads/CONSTITUTION_CROATIA.pdf accessed 15 June 2020. See Iris Goldner Lang, Zlata Đurđević and Mislav Mataija, 'Constitution of Croatia' in Albi and Bardutzky (eds), *National Constitutions*, 1147.

[167] *Auxiliary Activities in the Public Sector (Croatia)* [45]; *Referendum on Amendment to the Roads Act (Croatia)* U-VIIR-1158/2015 (21 April 2015), [60].

[168] Under the 1989 Constitution: *Lisbon (Hungary)* [2.2]–[2.5]; *The Europe Agreement* Decision 30/1998 (VI25) (English version at: www.mkab.hu/admin/data/file/672_17_2004.pdf accessed 3 June 2015, [V.3]. Under the 2011 Fundamental Law: *Article E(2) (Hungary)* [46], [54].

[169] *Michaelides v. AG (Cyprus)*, Civil Appeal 221/2013 (2 September 2013) *(Ανώτατο Δικαστήριο)* available at: www.cylaw.org accessed 18 July 2016; *President v. House of Representatives (Cyprus)* [2009] 3 CLR 648 *(Ανώτατο Δικαστήριο)*.

[170] *Attorney General v. Constantinou (Cyprus)* [2005] 1 CLR 1356; [2007] 3 CMLR 42.

[171] Art. 169 Constitution of the Republic of Cyprus (Πρόεδρος της Κυπριακής Δημοκρατίας, President of the Republic of Cyprus, 2015).

[172] Art. 179(1) of the Cypriot Constitution. The constitution also contains an expansive eternity clause (Art. 182(1)). In practice, the Supreme Court has tended to either interpret national implementing laws in conformity with the ECHR and the constitution, or ignore conflicting EU law altogether. See: *Koutselini-Ioannidou v. Cyprus*, Cases 740/2011-

understood as an expression of the will of the sovereign state and as a matter of choice'.[173] In **Luxembourg** and the **Netherlands**, national courts are prohibited from reviewing the constitutionality of acts ratifying international treaties, and international law prevails over constitutional law.[174] This has led to a debate over whether EU law would apply even if the constitutional bases for conferral were abolished – *idem est*, 'the Dutch constitution is entirely irrelevant in that regard'.[175] However, this would seem to be overstated. In both countries the constitutional supremacy of EU law cannot arise unless ratified by special majorities in accordance with the constitution.[176] Besselink, Claes and De Witte point out that the early decisions of the *Hoge Raad*[177] and *Raad van State*[178] derived authority to disapply national law from the Dutch Constitution, and there is little to have altered this position.[179] The position is similar in Luxembourg, where the special ratification

587/2012 (7 October 2014); *Alexandrou (Cyprus)* [2010] 1 CLR 17; *Charalambos v. Cyprus*, Cases 1480-1484/2011 et al. (11 June 2014). Cf: *Christodoulou (Cyprus)* [2013] 3 CLR 427, per Erotokriou.

[173] Constantinos Kombos and Stéphanie Laulhé Shaelou, 'The Cypriot Constitution under the Impact of EU Law: An Asymmetrical Formation' in Albi and Bardutzky (eds), *National Constitutions*, 1382, 1394, 1387-1389.

[174] Art. 120 of the Constitution of the Kingdom of the Netherlands (Ministry of the Interior and Kingdom Relations, 2008) available at: www.government.nl accessed 20 June 2016 prohibits judicial review of treaties, and unconstitutional treaties can be ratified by a 2/3 majority in the Houses of the States (Art. 91(3)). In Luxembourg, Art. 95ter of the Constitution prohibits judicial review of treaties, and international treaties have prevailed over national law since *Chambres des Métiers v. Pagani (Luxembourg)* [1954] *Pas Lux* 150 (*Cour de Cassation*) in Oppenheimer, *The Cases* (Vol 1) 671. See further Kaczorowska, *EU Law* (2013), 256; Claes, *National Courts*, 531-532, 243.

[175] Monica Claes and Bruno De Witte, 'Report on the Netherlands' in JHH Weiler, Anne-Marie Slaughter and Alec Stone Sweet (eds), *The European Courts and National Courts: Doctrine and Jurisprudence* (Hart 1998), 183.

[176] Arts. 9(1), (3) of the Dutch Constitution. Arts. 37, 49*bis*, 114(2) of the Luxembourg Constitution. See: Bruno De Witte, 'Direct Effect, Primacy and the Nature of the Legal Order' in Paul Craig and Gráinne de Búrca (eds), *The Evolution of EU law* (2 ed., Oxford University Press 2011), 199; Claes, *National Courts*, 206, 218-219.

[177] *Bosch GmbH v. De Geus en Uitdenbogerd (Netherlands)* (Case 13/61) [1965] NILR 318 in Oppenheimer, *The Cases* (Vol I) 672.

[178] *Metten v. Minister van Financiën (Netherlands)* [1995] NJB-katern 545 (7 July 1996) in Oppenheimer, *The Cases* (Vol 2) 401.

[179] Claes and De Witte, 'The Netherlands', 184-190; Leonard Besselink, 'Curing a "Childhood Sickness"? On Direct Effect, Internal Effect, Primacy and Derogation from Civil Rights' (1996) 3 MJ 165; Claes, *National Courts*, 206. See also, Franz Mayer, 'Multilevel Constitutional Jurisdiction' in Von Bogdandy and Bast (eds), *European Constitutional Law*, 85; Leonard Besselink and Monica Claes, 'The Netherlands' in Albi and Bardutzky (eds), *National Constitutions*, 189-193.

procedure in Article 114(2) of the Constitution was necessary to ensure the constitutionality of the Maastricht Treaty,[180] and 'the [Luxembourg] *Chambre* is clearly the holder of revision power'.[181]

In sum, as a matter of pure constitutional law, no Member State accepts the absolute supremacy of EU law over the *Kompetenz-Kompetenz*. In all Member States, EU acts not conferred in accordance with the constitution are, in principle, invalid in the national legal order without (at minimum) parliamentary ratification or constitutional amendment. As the BVerfG concludes:

> The 'Constitution of Europe', international treaty law or primary law, remains a derived fundamental order [...] according to the principle of conferral, without the possibility for the European Union of taking possession of *Kompetenz-Kompetenz*.[182]

1.2.1.2 Normative Evaluation of Member State *Kompetenz-Kompetenz* Adjudication

This section evaluates competing *normative* claims over *Kompetenz-Kompetenz* adjudication. This is necessary because 'absolute' EU supremacy over *Kompetenz-Kompetenz* adjudication also relies upon a normative claim: That is, even if national courts retain formal authority over the status of EU law under constitutional law, they must accept that the 'effectiveness and uniformity of EU law' is of such normative importance that the constitutional authorization for EU law will always outweigh *any* conflicting constitutional norms – even those which constrain the act of ratification.[183] Take, for example, the apocryphal statement of EU supremacy by Pernice:

> A residual control of the Court of Justice by national Constitutional courts in cases of *continuous and evident violations of fundamental rights or [ultra vires acts]* as an element of balance of powers is excluded, since [...] non-application of Community law in one Member State would jeopardize the status of legal equality of the Union citizens which is the foundation of its functioning.[184]

---

[180] Georges Friden, 'Ratification Processes of the Treaty on European Union: Luxembourg' (1993) 18 EL Rev 241. See also Claes, *National Courts*, 218–219.

[181] Jörg Gerkrath, 'The Constitution of Luxembourg in the Context of EU and International Law as "Higher Law"' in Albi and Bardutzky (eds), *National Constitutions*, 226–227.

[182] *Lisbon (Germany)* [207], [215].

[183] Stephen Weatherill, *Law and Integration in the European Union* (Oxford University Press, 1995), 106; Christiaan Timmermans, 'Publication Review: The Worlds of European Constitutionalism' (2014) 10 EuConst 349, 352.

[184] Pernice, 'Multilevel Constitutionalism', 727 (emphasis added).

Suffice it here to state that this normative claim is not accepted in any of the constitutional courts catalogued in this book.[185] When the Union acquires its competences upon ratification by the Member States 'in accordance with their respective constitutional requirements',[186] the supremacy of EU law is secured within the constitutional order because conferral cannot be done in such a way that it would violate or vitiate conflicting norms in the constitution. As the Spanish *Tribunal Constitucional* so puts it, 'public authorities are no less subject to the Constitution when they act in the international or supranational relations than when they exercise their competences *ad intra*'.[187] The principle that emerges here is that national courts cannot hold the 'effectiveness and uniformity' of EU law over the constitutional boundaries of conferral, because the EU is a derived legal order circumscribed by constitutional norms exerted on conferral itself.[188] From this common foundation, Member States evince three approaches to situating the normative supremacy of EU law within the constitution.[189]

In a first group of countries, consisting of France (to 2006),[190] Denmark,[191] Greece,[192] Spain,[193] the Czech Republic,[194] Poland,[195] Slovenia,[196] Slovakia,[197] Romania,[198] Bulgaria,[199] Latvia,[200] Malta,[201]

---

[185] See also Claes, *National Courts*, 261: 'None of the constitutional courts has accepted the unconditional supremacy of Community law,' and sources below, nn 244–247.

[186] Arts. 48(4), 49, 54 TEU and 357 TFEU.

[187] *Maastricht (Spain)* [1].

[188] See De Witte, 'Direct Effect', 201–202 and cases cited below, n 403.

[189] Grabenwarter, 'Constitutional Law', 85–91 similarly classifies the Member States by these three approaches (though several are classified differently).

[190] See sources cited above, nn 110–116 and below, nn 292–294.

[191] See Section 1.2.1.1, nn 119–120 on s. 20 of the Danish Constitution.

[192] See sources above, nn 131–132 and below, nn 327–329 on Art. 28 of the Hellenic Constitution.

[193] See Section 1.2.1.1, nn 128–129 on s. 93 of the Spanish Constitution.

[194] Arts. 10a (the basis for conferral) and 1(2) (observation of obligations resulting from international law) of the Constitution of the Czech Republic 1993 (English translation available at: www.constituteproject.org accessed 9 July 2016) grant supremacy over statutes, but not constitutional law: *Lisbon I (Czech Republic)* [85]; *EAW (Czech Republic)* [78]. See Zdenek Kühn, 'The Czech Republic' in Albi and Bardutzky (eds), *National Constitutions*, 798.

[195] Art. 91 of the Constitution grants EU law the same rank as international agreements: *Accession Treaty (Poland)* [5]–[6]; *Lisbon (Poland)* [2.1].

[196] See Section 1.2.1.1, nn 154–155 and Section 1.2.2.1, nn 325–326 on Art. 3a of the Slovene Constitution.

[197] See Section 1.2.1.1, nn 156–159.

[198] See Section 1.2.1.1, nn 149–150 and Section 1.2.2.1, n 319.

[199] See below, Section 1.2.2.1, nn 322–323.

[200] See above, Section 1.2.1.1, n 137.

[201] See above, Section 1.2.1.1, nn 162–164.

Croatia[202] and Lithuania,[203] the constitutional basis for EU law is subject to a *nemo plus iuris* rule which prevents the state from conferring the competence to exercise its powers in a manner contrary to the constitution. Provisions of the constitution in conflict with the treaty must be amended and, if they cannot be so amended, the treaty (or the application thereof) will be unconstitutional.[204]

In a second group of countries, consisting of Germany,[205] Italy,[206] France (from 2006),[207] the UK,[208] Ireland,[209] Portugal,[210] Austria,[211] Sweden,[212] Estonia,[213] Finland,[214] Belgium[215] and Hungary,[216] the constitutional empowerment for EU law *does* apply irrespective of conflicting constitutional law, either by derogation or by an extraordinary instrument that bestows heightened rank on EU law. However, EU law does not take effect autonomously, and the derogation does not apply to important constitutional principles which are either beyond the reach of the legislator, or anyways always of greater normative weight than the effectiveness of EU law. This model includes, for example,

---

[202] See above, Section 1.2.1.1, n 167.

[203] See above, Section 1.2.1.1, nn 138–139.

[204] For example, *Maastricht I (France)* [14]; *Maastricht (Spain)* [3](a)–(c), [4]; *Lisbon (Latvia)*, 53; *Vatican Agreement (Slovenia)* [23].

[205] See sources cited below, Section 1.3.1.1, in particular nn 509–511, on Art. 23 of the German Basic Law.

[206] See Section 1.2.1.1, nn 107–109 and Section 1.2.2.1, nn 289–291 on the 'controlimiti' doctrine.

[207] See *Société de l'information (France)* and annotation above, n 116. See further, Section 1.2.2.1 at nn 292–294.

[208] See Section 1.2.1.1, at nn 126–127 on the European Communities Act 1972 and Section 1.2.2.1, at nn 300–304 on parliamentary sovereignty.

[209] See Section 1.2.1.1, nn 140–142, and Section 1.2.2.1, nn 343–345 on Art. 29.4.6 of the Irish Constitution.

[210] See Section 1.2.2.1, nn 305–308, on Arts. 7(6), 8(4) and 288 of the Portuguese Constitution.

[211] See Section 1.2.1.1, nn 143–144 and Section 1.2.2.1, nn 349–351, on the AAA and Article 44(3) of the Austrian Constitution.

[212] See Section 1.2.1.1, nn 121–125 and Section 1.2.2.1, nn 332–336 on Ch 10§6 Instrument of Government.

[213] See Section 1.2.2.1, nn 346–348.

[214] See Section 1.2.1.1, nn 160–161, and Section 1.2.2.1, nn 357–360 on ss. 1, 94(3) of the Finnish Constitution.

[215] See Section 1.2.1.1, nn 117–118 and Section 1.2.2.1, nn 309–310 on Art. 34 of the Belgian Constitution.

[216] See Section 1.2.2.1, nn 340–341 on the 'Europe Clauses' of the 1989 and 2011 constitutions.

British parliamentary sovereignty,[217] the Italian *controlimiti* doctrine[218] and the German 'eternity clause'.[219] This model can be seen at work in such cases as *Grogan (Ireland)*,[220] or *Taricco II (Italy)*,[221] where normatively important constitutional principles trounced the imperative of the 'effectiveness and uniformity' of EU law.

In a third group of countries, consisting of the Netherlands, Luxembourg and Cyprus, EU law is normatively supreme over the constitution because judicial review of the EU Treaties is precluded by the constitution. However, even then it seems EU law is not normatively supreme over democracy: The EU can have no powers without a legislative act of conferral made in accordance with the constitution.[222]

Whatever group they fall into, all of these jurisdictions have two features in common. First, no Member State accepts that the 'uniformity and effectiveness' of EU law is of such normative importance that it prevails over constitutional control of *Kompetenz-Kompetenz*. As Member State courts have been keen to point out, the 'effectiveness and uniformity' of EU law *within* its competences cannot depend on the appropriation of national powers *outside* them.[223] For this reason, according to the BVerfG, *ultra vires* review does not 'factually contradict' supremacy,[224] and 'a substantial risk to the uniform application of [EU] law does not result'.[225]

The second thing they have in common is that acts of conferral are made of the same fabric as the constitution from which they have been

---

[217] See below, Section 1.2.2.1, nn 300–304.

[218] See Section 1.2.1.1, nn 107–109 and Section 1.2.2.1, nn 289–291.

[219] See Section 1.2.2.1, n 287 and Section 1.3.1.1.

[220] *Grogan I (Ireland)*, 765 excerpted below, Section 1.2.2.2 at n 401.

[221] *Taricco II Reference (Italy)* [4]: 'EU law and the judgments of the Court of Justice [. . .] for the purposes of its uniform application cannot be interpreted as requiring a Member State to give up the supreme principles of its constitutional order.' See also *Taricco II Judgment (Italy)* [5] excerpted further below, Section 1.2.2.3, at n 447.

[222] See sources cited above, Section 1.2.2.1, at nn 169–181.

[223] *Taricco II Reference (Italy)* [4]: 'there is no requirement whatsoever for uniformity across European legal systems regarding [supreme principles of national law] which [do] not directly affect either the competences of the Union or the provisions of EU law'. *Weiss Decision (Germany)* [113]: 'If the CJEU crosses the limit [of competence], its actions are no longer covered by the mandate conferred in Art. 19(1) TEU in conjunction with the domestic Act of approval.' *Constitutional Treaty (Spain)* [4]: '*supremacía* [of the constitution] and *primacía* [of EU law] are categories which are developed in differentiated orders'. See also *Accession Treaty (Poland)* [17]; *Lisbon (Poland)* [2.1]–[2.2] *et seq*; *Re Lisbon (France)* [8]–[9]; *Sugar Quotas III (Czech Republic)*, 486–486 (at [A-3B]); and sources cited below, nn 395–398.

[224] *Lisbon (Germany)* [216], [316].

[225] *R v. Oberlandesgericht (Germany)* [46].

cut – they can have no 'extra-constitutional' properties other than those ascribed by the constitution.[226] In virtually all Member States, a conflict between EU law and the constitution from whence it has been carved is either 'infra-constitutional' – that is, the EU law is not of constitutional rank at all;[227] or 'intra-constitutional' – a clash between two national constitutional provisions: the one authorizing EU law and whatever one is in conflict with it.[228] The EU provision is given a higher or lower normative weight in a conflict depending on which country and which values are concerned, but in all instances the consequence of EU law spilling over into conflict with another constitutional provision is, as the Spanish Court puts it, 'a fact which must be considered as established from the perspective of [national] law',[229] and a matter of 'the selection of the rule to be applied'.[230]

1.2.1.3 Positivist Evaluation of Member State *Kompetenz-Kompetenz* Adjudication

This brings us to a positivist consideration of *Kompetenz-Kompetenz* adjudication. If the absolute supremacy of EU acts, as interpreted by the ECJ,

---

[226] *Solange II (Germany)* (2 BvR 197/83): BVerfGE 73, 339 *(Bundesverfassungsgericht)* [I]I(1)(b); *Crotty (Ireland)*, 783 excerpted below, n 372; *Constitutional Treaty (Spain)* [3] excerpted below, Section 1.2.2.1 at n 297.

[227] See, for example: *Accession Treaty (Poland)* [1] 'The norms of the Constitution, being the supreme act which is an expression of the National's will, would not lose their binding force [. . .] by the mere fact of an irreconcilable inconsistency [with] any Community provision.' *On limitation of rights of ownership (Lithuania)*, Cases 17/02, 24/02, 06/03, 22/04 (14 March 2006) English version at: www.lrkt.lt/lt/en/ accessed 3 July 2016 *(Konstitucinis Teismas)* [9.4] 'In the event of collision of legal norms, [EU law] shall have supremacy over laws and other legal acts [. . .] save the Constitution itself.' See also *Decision 148/ 2003 (Romania)* excerpted above, n 149; *Belmonte* v. *Fels Werker SA (Spain)* DTC 41/2001; ECLI:EC:TC:2002:41, [2]; *Amendment to the Roads Act (Croatia)* [60] excerpted above, at n 167; *Lisbon (Latvia)* [11.1] excerpted above, Section 1.2.1.1, n 138.

[228] *HS2 (UK)* [79]: 'the supremacy of EU law [is not determinative in a conflict with another statute] since the application of that doctrine in our law itself depends on the 1979 Act [. . .] a conflict between a constitutional principle [and EU law] has to be resolved by our courts [. . .] under the constitutional law of the United Kingdom'. See also *SNHCA (Slovenia)* [3]–[6], [20]–[22], [51]–[54]; *Grogan I (Ireland)*, 765 excerpted below, Section 1.2.2.2 at n 401; *Société de l'information (France)* [19]; *Sugar Quotas III (Czech Republic)* [106]; *Taricco II Reference (Italy)* [4]; *Michaniki (Greece)* Decision 3470/2011; ECLI:EL: COS:2011:1104A347002E7710, [9] and sources cited below, n 329.

[229] *Canary Islands Customs Regulation (Spain)*, DTC 4524/1989 in Oppenheimer, The Cases (Vol I) 694, 697.

[230] *Electoral Law (Spain)* [5]. This is so even in Luxembourg, Netherlands and Cyprus where the Treaties are not reviewable because of *national constitutional law*: Claes, *National Courts*, 159, 206; Xavier Groussot, 'Supr[i]macy *à la Française*: Another French Exception' (2008) 27 YEL 89, 99 at footnote 47.

is to be accepted as the rule of recognition for identifying which models of fiscal federalism are implementable in the EU, it must *in fact* provide an authoritative and reliable account of what is and is not safe constitutional ground to install legal instruments of public economics. This is particularly so when dealing with such things as temperamental bond markets and the politico-economic incentives of restive electorates. Certainty, expansive *intra vires* rulings of the ECJ over such instruments cannot be so constitutionally fraught that they risk destabilizing the entire fiscal architecture each time they are issued.

In that regard it must be recalled that, in all Member States, the constitutional authorization for the application of EU law is a legislative instrument enacted under a specific constitutional window.[231] Debates about whether it is legitimate for national courts to conduct *ultra vires* review are, first and foremost, debates about national constitutions.[232] Given this is so, a coercive approach to imposing supremacy in areas considered outside the boundaries of conferral is, with certainty, counterproductive to the goal of effectiveness and uniformity in the EU legal order.[233] As Kumm notes, 'The likelihood that all laws will in fact be applied throughout the community will decrease as the probability that a particular law will be struck down on constitutional grounds by a national court increases.'[234] Judge Maduro concurs:

A hierarchical alternative imposing a monist authority of European law and its judicial institutions over national law would be difficult to impose in practical terms and could undermine the legitimacy basis on which European law has developed.[235]

---

[231] Grabenwarter, 'Constitutional Law', 94; Monica Claes, 'The "European Clauses" in the National Constitutions: Evolution and Typology' (2005) 24 YEL 81.

[232] *Ajos (Denmark)*, 442, 'The question of whether a rule of EU law can be given direct effect in Danish law, as required under EU law, turns first and foremost on the Law on accession by which Denmark acceded to the European Union.' *Data Retention (Slovakia)* [69] 'The position of the founding EU Treaties in the Slovak legal order is governed by Art. 1(2) and Art. 7(5) of the Constitution.' See also *HS2 (UK)* [79] excerpted above n 228; *RSI Residency Requirement (Portugal)* (Case 136/2014) Judgment 141/2015 (*Tribunal Constitucional*), [6]; *Amending Article 125 (Lithuania)* III [6.2.3] excerpted above, n 138. For this point: Mattias Kumm, 'Rethinking Constitutional Authority' in Avbelj and Komárek (eds), *Constitutional Pluralism*, 50.

[233] Damian Chalmers, 'Judicial Preferences and the Community Legal Order' (1997) 60 MLR 165, 180; Albi, 'Supremacy of EC Law', 29.

[234] Kumm, 'Final Arbiter', 359.

[235] Maduro, 'Europe and the Constitution', 97. Similarly: Koen Lenaerts, 'The Principle of Democracy in the Case Law of the European Court of Justice' (2013) 62 ICLQ 271, 280.

Such admissions align with statements of law from the Member States – 'absolute' supremacy cannot be applied as the rule governing the validity of contested acts without jeopardizing the integrity of the Union itself.[236] The BVerfG states:

[I]t is not enough simply to speak of the 'precedence' of Community law over national constitutional law in order to justify the conclusion that Community law must always prevail over national constitutional law because, otherwise, the Community would be put in question.[237]

For the architects of fiscal federalism, it would be foolish to proceed on the cheerful basis that Member States daren't apply the jurisdictions they have set out, just to preserve the good functioning of some ideal model that impinges the boundaries of competence. Attempts to assert 'absolute' supremacy over *Kompetenz-Kompetenz* adjudication have provoked several of these jurisdictions – with immediate and deleterious effects on the uniformity and effectiveness of EU law.

Perhaps most recently, in *Ajos (Denmark)*, the *Højesteret* refused to disapply national employment legislation as directed by the ECJ in *Ajos (CJEU)*,[238] holding that ECJ case law on age discrimination was itself *ultra vires* the Danish act of accession.[239] In *Gauweiler (Germany)* the BVerfG inveighed against a permissive interpretation of ECB competence by the ECJ and placed six conditions on the operation of a (technically supreme) EU law bond-buying programme.[240] In *Weiss (Germany)* the BVerfG held that the ECJ's permissive interpretation of the same competence in *Weiss (CJEU)* 'manifestly exceeded the judicial mandate conferred upon the CJEU in Art. 19(1) TEU' such that 'the CJEU Judgment itself constitutes an *ultra vires* act and thus has no binding effect [in Germany]'.[241]

Even where such outright conflicts are avoided through subtler shades of interpretive disobedience, the jurisprudence cited in this chapter is replete with examples of EU law bending around constitutional guarantees at the margins of competence.[242] As the BVerfG

---

[236] *Constitutional Treaty (Spain)* [3] excerpted above, Section 1.2.1.1 at n 101; *Taricco II Reference (Italy)* [6] excerpted below, Section 1.2.2.1 at n 368.

[237] *Internationale Handelsgesellschaft MbH (Solange I) (Germany)* (2 BvL 52/71) BVerfGE 37, 272; [1974] 2 CMLR 540, [21].

[238] Case C-441/14 *Danski Industri (DI) (Ajos A/S)* v. *Estate of Rasmussen* EU:C:2016:278, [25], [37].

[239] *Ajos (Denmark)*, 443–444.

[240] *Gauweiler Decision (Germany)* [205]–[207].

[241] *Weiss Decision (Germany)* [143], [116]–[119], [146], [154]–[157], [163], [234].

[242] See examples cited below, nn 411–430. See further House of Lords European Union Committee 6th Report of Session 2003–2004: The Future Role of the European Court of Justice (2004 HL 47), [65] per Paul Craig.

observed in *R* v. *Oberlandsgeright (Germany)* (citing 27 judgments from ten countries):

The overwhelming majority of the constitutional and supreme courts of other Member States shares for their respective sectors in the view of the [BVerfG] that the (application) primacy of Union law is not unlimited, but that are drawn to it by the national (constitutional) limits.[243]

Legal scholars trawling the case law make similar observations. Woods and Watson find that 'all the constitutional courts of the Member States regard themselves as having the power to review the boundary of EU competence'.[244] Surveys by Grabenwarter,[245] Claes,[246] Kumm and others reach similar conclusions: 'National Constitutional Supremacy is a legal rule that governs practice as a matter of fact, and that is all there is to it.'[247]

1.2.2 Member State Constitutional Identity

The second constitutional boundary imposed on the EU legal order is an absolute one: Not only have some powers not been conferred on the EU, but some constitutional powers or principles can *never* be transferred to the Union or vitiated by conflicting EU law. These are typically referred to as the limits of 'constitutional identity' – inalienable, inviolable structures or principles so integral to the constitutional order that they either cannot be formally altered by the amending power at all; or otherwise impose material constraints that cannot be released without effecting a 'total revision' or legal revolution that would result in a different constitutional system – a different constitutional identity.[248] Constitutional identity principles ensure that amendments and evolutions of constitutional law remain within

---

[243] *R* v. *Oberlandesgericht (Germany)* [I](2)(c). See also: *Sugar Quotas III (Czech Republic)*, VI(A) (citing 7 judgments from 4 countries); *Article E(2) (Hungary)* [34] (citing 28 judgments from 11 countries).

[244] Lorna Woods and Philippa Watson, *Steiner & Woods EU Law* (12th ed., Oxford University Press 2012), 103.

[245] Grabenwarter, 'Constitutional Law', 94.

[246] Monica Claes, 'The Primacy of EU Law in European and National Law' in Anthony Arnull and Damian Chalmers (eds), *The Oxford Handbook of European Union Law* (Oxford University Press, 2015), 178, 198–199.

[247] Kumm, 'Constitutional Supremacy', 269. See also, Kaczorowska, *EU Law* (2013), 256; Dyevre, 'Defending Sovereignty?', 147; Denis Preshova, 'Battleground or Meeting Point? Respect for National Identities in the European Union – Article 4(2) of the Treaty on European Union' (2012) 8 CYELP 267, 280.

[248] 'Constitutional identity' may derive from unamendable or material constraints. The doctrine of unwritten material constraints is often traced to *Kesavandanda Bharati* v.

the framework of the constitution and consistent with its foundational principles. They may often be recognized apart from 'ordinary' constitutional principles by their various functions: preserving popular or state sovereignty,[249] safeguarding the distinction between constitution-making and constitution-amending authority[250] and setting limits on the disposal of state competences and the supremacy of EU law.[251]

The unamendable 'eternity clause' in the 1949 German Basic Law is the most notorious in this respect, but many other constitutional courts and committees have also asserted some 'inviolable core' integral to the constitution. The Belgian *Cour constitutionnelle*,[252] the Bulgarian Конституционен съд (Constitutional Court),[253] the Croatian *Ustavni Sud*,[254] the Czech *Ústavní Soud*,[255] the Danish *Højesteret*,[256] the Estonian *Riigikohus*,[257] the Finnish *Perustuslakivaliokunnan*,[258] the Austrian *Verfassungsgerichtshof*,[259] the French *Conseil Constitutionnel*,[260] the Greek Συμβούλιο της Επικρατείας (Council of State),[261] the Hungarian

---

Kerala (India) AIR 1973 SC 1461 (Supreme Court), at [208] and [159], where the constitutional amending power was found not to include the 'basic structure' of the constitution. The doctrine is now widespread in constitutional democracies. See Richard Albert, 'Constitutional Handcuffs' (2010) 42 Ariz St L J 663; Yaniv Roznai, 'Unconstitutional Constitutional Amendments – The Migration and Success of a Constitutional Idea' (2013) 61 Am J Comp L 657; Richard Albert, 'The Expressive Function of Constitutional Amendment Rules' (2013) 59 McGill LJ 225; Yaniv Roznai, *Unconstitutional Constitutional Amendments* (Oxford University Press 2017), 8–9, 151.

[249] Sources *ibid* and Josê Martín Y Pérez de Nanclares, 'Constitutional Identity in Spain' in Calleiss and Van der Schyff (eds), *Constitutional Identity*, 272.

[250] Roznai, 'Migration and Success', 664; Kriszta Kovács, 'Changing Constitutional Identity via Amendment' in Paul Blokker (ed.), *Constitutional Acceleration within the European Union and Beyond* (Routledge, 2018), 197, 201–202.

[251] Constitutional identity may perform some of these functions, and not others. See Kriszta Kovács, 'The Rise of an Ethnocultural Constitutional Identity in the Jurisprudence of the East Central European Courts' (2017) 18 German LJ 1703, 1706–1707 on Hungary, which has been unable to erect material identity constraints against predations by the state through formal amendments.

[252] See below, Section 1.2.2.1 at nn 309–310.

[253] See below, Section 1.2.2.1 at nn 322–324.

[254] See below, Section 1.2.2.1 at n 321.

[255] See below, Section 1.2.2.1 at nn 311–312.

[256] See below, Section 1.2.2.1 at n 298.

[257] See below, Section 1.2.2.1 at n 348.

[258] See below, Section 1.2.2.1 at nn 357–360.

[259] See below, Section 1.2.2.1 at nn 349–351 on Art. 44(3) and the fundamental principles of the Austrian Constitution.

[260] See below, Section 1.2.2.1 at nn 292–294.

[261] See below, Section 1.2.2.1 at nn 327–331.

Magyarország Alkotmánybírósága,[262] the Irish Supreme Court,[263] the Italian *Corte constituzionale,*[264] the Latvian *Satversmes Tiesa,*[265] the Lithuanian *Konstitucinis Teismas,*[266] the Polish *Trybunał Konstytucyjny,*[267] the Portuguese *Tribunal Constitucional,*[268] the Romanian *Curtea Constituțională,*[269] the Slovak *Ústavný Súd,*[270] the Slovenian *Ustavno Sodišče,*[271] the Spanish *Tribunal Constitucional,*[272] the Swedish *Konstitutionsutskottet,*[273] the UK Supreme Court[274] and the German BVerfG[275] have all asserted that some constitutional powers or principles cannot be disposed-of under the national constitution or vitiated by conflicting EU law, either *de lege lata* or at all.[276]

The 2010 Polish *Trybunał Konstytucyjny* encapsulates the jurisprudence thusly:

> Constitutional identity is a concept which determines the scope of excluding – from the competence to confer competences – the matters which constitute [. . .] 'the heart of the matter', i.e., are fundamental to the political system of a given state.[277]

For the architects of European fiscal federalism, this presents a dilemma. This is so because, under Article 4(2) TEU, the Union itself is under a duty to 'respect the national identities of its Member States', and the ECJ disavows the interpretation that this allows constitutional

---

[262] See below, Section 1.2.2.1 at nn 341–342 under the 1989 Constitution and 2011 Fundamental Law.
[263] See below, Section 1.2.2.1 at nn 343–345.
[264] See Section 1.2.1.1 at n 107 and Section 1.2.2.1 at nn 289–291.
[265] See below, Section 1.2.2.1, nn 313–315.
[266] See below, Section 1.2.2.1, nn 316–318.
[267] See below, Section 1.2.2.1, nn 337–338.
[268] See below, Section 1.2.2.1, nn 305–308.
[269] See below, Section 1.2.2.1, n 319.
[270] See below, Section 1.2.2.1 at nn 353–356.
[271] See below, Section 1.2.2.1 at nn 325–326.
[272] See below, Section 1.2.2.1 at nn 295–297.
[273] See below, Section 1.2.2.1 at nn 332–336.
[274] See below, Section 1.2.2.1 at nn 301–304.
[275] See below, Section 1.2.2.1 at n 287 and Section 1.3.1.1. on Arts. 79(3) and 23 of the German Basic Law.
[276] In the remaining countries, the Netherlands, Luxembourg, Cyprus and Malta, the author did not identify sufficient case law to establish constitutional identity reserves against EU law for the purposes of this book. However, the Cypriot constitution contains unamendability provisions which reflect its bi-communal identity, and although the Netherlands and Luxembourg are not generally thought to have substantive reserves which cannot be conferred, it is clear that both states retain *Kompetenz-Kompetenz.*
[277] *Lisbon (Poland)* [2.1].

identities to limit the scope of EU law.[278] As Judge Lenaerts has written, 'There simply is no nucleus of sovereignty that the Member States can invoke, as such, against the Community' – even when the Treaty 'expressly acknowledges the existence of residual powers for the Member States'.[279] Instead, the ECJ has interpreted *national identity* under Article 4(2) as encompassing an open-ended list of cultural, social or legal values not common enough to be 'general principles' on their own right into a single principle that Lenaerts calls 'value diversity' – over which the CJEU then has jurisdiction.[280] 'National identity' includes 'constitutional identity'.[281] In the eyes of EU law, national identity is no different than other 'legitimate aims' whose purpose is, as stated in *Cassis*, 'not to reserve certain matters to the exclusive jurisdiction of the Member States' but to restrict derogations to the extent justified against the objectives of EU law.[282] On this reading, Article 4(2) TEU does not brace the containment walls of EU competence – it subsumes those boundaries within the EU legal order and gives the ECJ jurisdiction to examine their merit.

Member State *constitutional identity* and CJEU *national identity* jurisdictions therefore profess to govern the same thing, but draw very different red lines around the contours of EU competence. What the architects of fiscal federalism must determine is whether – as the ECJ maintains – it is the sole and final arbiter of what is or is not an infringement of constitutional identity, capable of 'ousting' the jurisdictions of national courts;[283] or whether it is national courts that will determine what the ultimate boundaries of the EU legal order (and EU fiscal federalism) will be.

1.2.2.1   Pure Constitutional Evaluation of Constitutional Identity Review

The first task must be to compare the pure constitutional authority for these jurisdictions. The constitutional basis for the CJEU's *national*

---

[278] See Armin Von Bogdandy and Stephan Schill, 'Overcoming Absolute Primacy: Respect for National Identity under the Lisbon Treaty' (2011) 48 CMLR 1417, 1441; Elke Cloots, *National Identity in EU Law* (Oxford University Press, 2015), 190–191; and sources cited cases below, nn 386–389.

[279] Lenaerts, 'Many Faces', 220–221.

[280] Koen Lenaerts, 'How the ECJ Thinks: A Study on Legitimacy' (2013) 36 Forham Int'l LJ 1302, 1327.

[281] Case C-213/07 *Michaniki* EU:C:2008:544 (Opinion of AG Maduro), [31].

[282] Case 120/78 Rewe-Zentral AG v. *Bundesmonopolverwaltung für Branntwein* (Cassis de Dijon) [1979] ECR 649, [5]. See: *Michaniki (AG Maduro)* [32].

[283] Case C-409/06 *Winner Wetten* [2010] ECR I-08015; EU:C:2010:503, [67].

identity jurisdiction is Article 4(2) TEU – a provision of EU law. Introduced at Maastricht to reassert 'that the external limit on the exercise of the Union's conferred powers are the fundamental constitutional structures of the Member States',[284] it reads:

> The Union shall respect the equality of Member States before the Treaties as well as their national identities, inherent in their fundamental structures, political and constitutional, inclusive of regional and local self-government.[285]

Member State *constitutional identity* jurisdictions, by contrast, derive from constitutional provisions and principles which bind acts of conferral *outside* the EU legal order *before* they become EU law, and therefore define what may never be conferred on the Union and is therefore outside the EU legal order altogether.[286]

In **Germany**, the precedence of EU law is 'limited by the Basic Law's constitutional identity that, according to Art. 23(1) in conjunction with Art. 79(3) [BL] is neither open to constitutional amendments nor to European integration'.[287] Those articles, the so-called 'eternity clause' (Article 79(3) BL) and the constitutional safeguard clause (Article 23(1) BL), entrench the highest principles of the German state from constitutional change by amendment or conferral.[288]

In **Italy**, the *Corte costituzionale* has held since 1973 that 'fundamental principles of the Italian Constitution' impose *controlimiti* (counterlimits) to the entry of EU law, and that the Italian Court would 'always control the continuing compatibility of the Treaty with fundamental principles'.[289] A violation of these principles by EU law will result in its

---

[284] Preshova, 'Battleground or Meeting', 274–276. See also, Von Bogdandy and Schill, 'Absolute Primacy', 1425; Reestman, 'Franco-German Divide', 269.

[285] Ex Art. F(1), *Treaty on European Union* [1992] OJ C 191/1 read: 'The Union shall respect the national identities of its Member States, whose systems of government are founded on the principles of democracy.'

[286] See, for example, *Taricco II Reference (Italy)* [8], excerpted below, at n 398; *Taricco II Judgment (Italy)* [8]: 'the constitutional identity of the Republic of Italy [...] falls outside the substantive scope of EU law'.

[287] *R v. Oberlandesgericht (Germany)* [41]. See also *Solange I (Germany)* [22]; *Brunner (Germany)* [52]; *Lisbon (Germany)* [194], [216], [221], [306]-[308]; *Honeywell (Germany)* [40]; *Euro Rescue Package (Germany)* [99]-[101]; *ESM I (Germany)* [150], [193]; *Anti-terror Database (Germany)* [91]; *Gauweiler Reference (Germany)* [25]-[27]; *Gauweiler Decision (Germany)* [120]; *Weiss Decision (Germany)* [101], [104], [115], [117], [163], [227].

[288] See below, Section 1.3.1.1, and cases cited.

[289] *Frontini (Italy)* [21]. See also, *Granital (Italy)* [7]; *Fragd (Italy)*, 545 excerpted below, Section 1.2.2.2, at n 400; *Sardinian Taxes Reference (Italy)* Order 103/2008 (13 February 2008) www .cortecostituzionale.it accessed 18 May 2016, [6]-[7], [8.2.8.1]; *GP et al. v. Avellino and Leonforte (Direct Effect of the ECHR) (Italy)* Judgment 349/2007 English version at:

invalidity,[290] or, if the Treaty is itself is in conflict with the Constitution, 'the radical and disruptive remedy of withdrawal from the European Union'.[291]

In **France**, the '*identité constitutionnelle de la France*' is assimilated to the '*conditions essentielles d'exercise de la souveraineté*',[292] and the '*structures constitutionnelles*' of the indivisible, secular, democratic and social Republic.[293] The 'ordinary' supremacy of EU law is derived from Articles 55, 88-1 and 88-2 of the Constitution, but the French Constitution remains 'at the pinnacle of the national legal order' and does not permit ratification of EU law that 'calls into question the rights and freedoms guaranteed by the Constitution or runs contrary to the essential conditions for the exercise of national sovereignty'.[294]

In **Spain**, the *Tribunal Constitucional* recognizes an 'essential nucleus of powers',[295] which impose 'material limits imposed on the transfer [to the EU] itself'.[296] Said material limits are understood as 'the sovereignty of the State, or our basic constitutional structures and of the system of fundamental principles and values set forth in our Constitution, [including] fundamental rights'.[297]

---

www.cortecostituzionale.it accessed 22 April 2016, [6.1]; *UN Convention (Italy)* Judgment 238/2014 English version at: www.cortecostituzionale.it accessed 22 June 2016, [3.2]; *Taricco II Reference (Italy)* [2].

[290] See cases cited above, Section 1.2.1.1, n 107.

[291] *Talamucci (Italy)*, 393. See also *Taricco II Reference (Italy)* [2].

[292] *Liberté d'association (France)* Decision No 71-44 DC; ECLI:FR:CC:1971:7144DC; *Elections to the EP (France)* [2]–[4].

[293] *Constitutional Treaty (France)* [1]–[7], [10], [18]–[22], [24]. For a full account, see François-Xavier Millet, 'Constitutional Identity in France: Vices and – Above All – Virtues' in Calleiss and Van der Schyff (eds), *Constitutional Identity*, 134.

[294] *CETA (France)* [10]–[11]. See further *Société de l'information (France)* [19]; *Immigration, Integration and Nationality Act (France)* [44]–[45]; *Genetically Modified Organisms (GMOs) (France)* Decision No 2008-564 DC; ECLI:FR:CC:2008:2008564DC, [42]–[44]; *Betting and Gambling Sector (France)* Decision No 2010-605 DC; ECLI:FR:CC:2010:2010605DC, [17]–[19] *Personal Data Protection Law (2018) (France)* Decision No 2018-765 DC; ECLI:FR: CC:2018:2018765DC, [3].

[295] *Maastricht (Spain)* [3c].

[296] *Constitutional Treaty (Spain)* [3]. See further *Asepesco (Spain)* DTC 64/1991; ECLI:ES: TC:1991:74, [4]; *Rudolfo et al. v. FOGASA (Spain)* Decision 180/1993 in Oppenheimer, *The Cases* (Vol I) 707; *Belmonte v. Fels Werker (Spain)* [2]; *Resolution of Catalonia 1/XI (Spain)* DTC 259/2015; ECLI:ES:TC:2015:259, [5]–[7]; *Catalonia Referendum Act (Spain)* DTC 114/2017; ECLI:ES:TC:2017:114, [5]. For a full account, see Fernando Castillo de la Torre, 'Opinion 1/2004 on the Treaty Establishing a Constitution for Europe' (2005) 42 CMLR 1169, 1186; Pérez de Nanclares, 'Spain'.

[297] *Constitutional Treaty (Spain)* [3]–[4]. See also, *Melloni (Spain)* [3].

In **Denmark**, the *Højesteret* has held since *Carlsen (Denmark)* that 'no transfer of powers can take place to such an extent that Denmark can no longer be considered an independent state' or undermine the 'democratic system of government',[298] and the *Højesteret* rejects the claim that EU supremacy ousts the 'Danish court's testing of the constitutionality of acts and EU Acts'.[299]

In the **United Kingdom**, constitutional identity inheres in the doctrines of parliamentary sovereignty,[300] the rule of law, legality and constitutional statutes.[301] The supremacy of EU law was effected by treating the European Communities Act 1972 as one such constitutional statute, but parliamentary sovereignty is 'fundamental to the United Kingdom's constitutional arrangements' and 'EU law can only enjoy a status in domestic law which that principle allows'.[302] ECJ rulings were not to be interpreted so as to 'question the identity of the national constitutional order',[303] or exert jurisdiction over 'issues integral to the identity of the nation state'.[304]

In **Portugal**, the fundamental principles of the Portuguese Constitution are entrenched by an unamendability clause (Article 288), and Articles 7(6) and 8(4) of the Constitution contain constitutional safeguard clauses that condition EU law on 'respect for the fundamental principles of a democratic state based on the rule of law'.[305] The *Tribunal Constitucional* 'has never accepted the supremacy of EU law over the Constitution', and the prevailing view is that Articles 7(6) and

---

[298] *Carlsen (Denmark)* [35]–[36]. See also, *Hausgaard (Denmark)* [32]; *Ajos (Denmark)*, 442 excerpted above, n 232.

[299] *Hausgaard (Denmark)* [42]. See further Helle Krunke, 'The Danish Lisbon Judgment' (2014) 10 EuConst 542, 556–558; Oliver Garner, 'Editorial: The Borders of European Integration on Trial in the Member States' (2017) 9 Eur J Legal Stud 1, 7.

[300] *Thoburn* v. *Sunderland (UK)* [69]: 'There is nothing [...] which allows the [ECJ] or any other institutions of the EU, to touch or qualify the conditions of Parliament's legislative supremacy in the United Kingdom. [...] The British Parliament has not the authority to authorise any such thing [...] it cannot abandon its sovereignty.'

[301] Paul Craig, 'Constitutional Identity in the United Kingdom' in Calleiss and Van der Schyff (eds), *Constitutional Identity*, 288–298, 297–298. Legislation is read subject to a principle of legality which cannot be impliedly overridden: *R* v. *SSHD, ex parte Simms (UK)* [2000] 2 AC 115. Constitutional statutes may not be impliedly repealed or amended without an express enactment by parliament: *Thoburn* v. *Sunderland (UK)* [62]–[63]. Parliament may not have authorized the abrogation of these principles by the European Communities Act: *HS2 (UK)* [207].

[302] *Miller (UK)* [67].

[303] *HS2 (UK)* [110]–[111], [201]–[209].

[304] *Pham* v. *SSHD (UK)* [58]; *G1* v. *SSHD (UK)* [43].

[305] Constitution of the Portuguese Republic (7th Revision, *Tribunal Constitucional*, 2005) English version at: www.tribunalconstitucional.pt accessed 6 June 2020.

8(4) provide a basis to review EU law against its fundamental principles.[306] Most recently, in its conditionality case law, the *Tribunal Constitutional* identified a 'hard core' of the rule of law and annulled measures it considered were 'binding on the Portuguese State [as] legal instruments [of] European Union law',[307] holding:

> [B]inding or not [...] in a multilevel Constitutional system, in which several legal orders interact, internal legal norms cannot breach the Constitution [...] European Union law itself establishes that the Union respects the national identity of its Member States, reflected in the fundamental political and constitutional structures of each of them (see Article 4(2) TEU).[308]

In **Belgium**, the *Cour constitutionnelle* holds that the Constitution 'does not allow a discriminating derogation to the national identity inherent in the fundamental structures, political and constitutional, or to the basic values of protection offered by the Constitution'.[309] As Gérard and Verrijdt encapsulate: the Court 'forbids attributions of powers to the EU, and the application thereof by the EU organs, insofar as they encroach upon Belgian national identity or the basic values of constitutional rights protection'.[310]

In the **Czech Republic**, the *Ústavní Soud* has held since *Sugar Quotas* that 'the essential attributes of a democratic state governed by the rule of law [...] remain beyond the reach of the Constituent Assembly itself' and that 'should developments in the EC, or the EU, threaten the very essence of state sovereignty of the Czech Republic or the essential attributes of a democratic state governed by the rule of law, it will be necessary to insist that these powers be once again taken up by the Czech Republic's state bodies'.[311] In the event of a lesser but clear

---

[306] Francisco Pereira Coutinho and Nuno Piçarra, 'Portugal: The Impact of European Integration and the Economic Crisis on the Identity of the Constitution' in Albi and Bardutzky (eds), *National Constitutions*, 601–602, 624.

[307] *State Budget 2012 (Portugal)* (Case 40/12) Judgment 353/2012, [3] and cases cited below, Chapter 7, Section 7.5, n 320.

[308] *Special Sustainability Contribution (Portugal)* [25]; *Pay Cuts 2014-2018 (Portugal)* (Case 818/14) Judgment 574/2014, [12].

[309] *TCSG (Belgium)*, B.8.7.

[310] Gérard and Verrijdt, 'National Identity Discourse', 189. See also Elke Cloots, 'Constitutional Identity in Belgium' in Calleiss and Van der Schyff (eds), *Constitutional Identity*, 65.

[311] *Sugar Quotas III (Czech Republic)* [A-3B]. On the attributes of the democratic state governed by the rule of law (Arts. 1 and 9(2) of the Constitution) see: *Act on the Lawlessness of the Communist Regime (Czech Republic)*, Pl ÚS 19/93 (*Ústavný Súd*) English version at: www.us oud.cz accessed 12 July 2019; *Euro-amendment (Czech Republic)*, Pl ÚS 36/01 (*Ústavný Súd*) available at: www.usoud.cz accessed 12 July 2019; *Melčák (Czech Republic)*, Pl ÚS 27/09 (10

conflict with EU law, 'the constitutional order of the Czech Republic, in particular, its material core, must take precedence'.[312]

In **Latvia**, the *Satversmes tiesa* holds that 'National identity of the Member States is an essential basis of the EU',[313] and the fundamental principles of the *Satversme* (Constitution) place an ultimate stop on the conferral and application of EU law – including the duty of conforming interpretation.[314] The fundamental principles of the *Satversme* 'cannot be infringed by introducing amendments to the Satversme' and delegation of competencies to the EU 'cannot exceed the rule of law and the basis of an independent, sovereign and democratic republic based on the basic rights'.[315]

In **Lithuania**, Article 1 of the Constitutional Act on Membership (Lithuania) allows Lithuania to 'share with or entrust' state competences, but only with a Union that 'respects the national identity and constitutional traditions of its Member States'.[316] As interpreted by the *Konstitucinis Teismas*, the Lithuanian constitutional identity comprises the independent democratic republic, encompassing the independence of the state, democracy, the republic, innate human rights and freedoms,[317] and the supremacy of the constitution over EU law itself.[318]

September 2009) (*Ústavný Súd*); *Lisbon II (Czech Republic)* [111]–[113], [136], [150]; David Kosar and Ladislav Vyhnánek, 'Constitutional Identity in the Czech Republic' in Calleiss and Van der Schyff (eds), *Constitutional Identity*, 28.

[312] *Lisbon I (Czech Republic)* [85].

[313] *Lisbon (Latvia)* [14], [16.3].

[314] *Riga Land Use Plan (Latvia)* [24.2], [25.4]: 'Latvian law must be interpreted so as to avoid any conflicts with the obligations of Latvia towards the European Union, *unless the fundamental principles incorporated in the Satverseme are affected.*' (Emphasis added) See also *On Prevention of Money Laundering (Latvia)*, Case 2008-47-01 (28 May 2009) English version at: www.satv.tiesa.gov.lv/wp-content/uploads/2008/11/2008-47-01_Spriedums_ENG.pd f accessed 13 June 2020, [15.2]. On the fundamental principles entrenched by Article 77 of the Latvian Constituion, see: Krüma and Statkus, 'Constitution of Latvia', 951.

[315] *Lisbon (Latvia)* [17].

[316] Arts. 1–2, Constitutional Act on Membership of the Republic of Lithuania in the European Union of 13 July 2004 (Lithuania) English version accessible at: www.lrs.lt accessed 14 June 2020. See Irmantas Jarukaitis and Gintaras Švedas, 'The Constitutional Experience of Lithuania in the Context of European and Global Governance Challenges' in Albi and Bardutzky (eds), *National Constitutions*, 1005–1007.

[317] *Amending Article 125 (Lithuania)* III [2], [4], [6.1]–[6.4].

[318] *On organising and calling referendums*, Case 16-29/2004 (11 July 2014) English version at: www.lrkt.lt/lt/en/ accessed 3 July 2016, [2.4]; *On limitation of rights of ownership (Lithuania)* [9.4]; *On the status of the national broadcaster (Lithuania)*, Case 30/03 (21 December 2006) English version at: www.lrkt.lt/lt/en/ accessed 3 July 2016, [IV], [1.1]; *On elections to the European Parliament (Lithuania)*, Case 26/2009 (9 November 2010) English version at: www.lrkt.lt/lt/en/ accessed 3 July 2016, [III]; *On measures to enhance the financial stability of*

In **Romania**, the *Curtea Constituțională* holds that the 'supreme values' of the Constitution entrenched by its unamendability clause (Article 152), in particular the rule of law and the supremacy of the Constitution, impose permanent constraints on the supremacy of EU law.[319]

In **Croatia**, the *Ustavni sud* holds that 'the Constitution is, by its legal nature, supreme to EU law',[320] and amendments to the constitution by referendum cannot alter 'the structural characteristics of the Croatian constitutional state, or in other words, of its *constitutional identity*, including the highest values of the constitutional order of the Republic of Croatia (Article 1 and Article 3 of the Constitution)'.[321]

The Constitutional Court of **Bulgaria** (Конституционен съд) holds that EU law becomes part of Bulgarian law only in so far as it is 'in compliance with the provided conditions' of the Constitution, and that Bulgaria's 'constitutional identity is preserved' in participation in the EU.[322] Constitutional identity finds *locus* in Article 158 of the Constitution, the onerous 'Grand National Chamber' revision procedure that entrenches 'the people's sovereignty, supremacy of the Constitution, political pluralism, separation of powers, rule of law and judicial independence' from amendment.[323] In particular, under the

banks (Lithuania), Cases 2/2012, 9/2012, 12/2012 (5 July 2013) English version at: www.lrkt.lt/lt/en/ accessed 3 July 2016; and cases above, nn 138–139.

[319] *Decision 80/2014 (Romania)* [453]–[460]: the Romanian Court is the 'guarantor for the supremacy of the Constitution' and 'the Constitution is the expression of the will of the people and cannot lose its binding force only by the existence of a discrepancy between its provisions and those of Europe [...] accession to the European Union cannot affect the supremacy of the Constitution'. See also: *Decision 148/2003 (Romania)* excerpted above n 149; *Decision 871/2010 (Romania) Monitorul Oficial al României* No 871 of 25 June 2010; *Decision 668/2011 (Romania) Monitorul Oficial al României* No 487 of 8 July 2011; *Decision 137/2010 (Romania) Monitorul Oficial al României* No 182 of 22 March 2010; *Decision 1249/2010 (Romania) Monitorul Oficial al României* No 764 of 16 November 2010. See further Viorica Vita, 'The Romanian Constitutional Court and the Principle of Primacy' (2019) 16 German LJ 1623, 1655–1657.

[320] *Auxiliary Activities in the Public Sector (Croatia)* [45]; *Amendment to the Roads Act (Croatia)* [60].

[321] *Auxiliary Activities in the Public Sector (Croatia)* [33.4]; *Referendum on Definition of Marriage (Croatia)*, U-VIIR-164/2014 (13 January 2014) (*Vrhovni sud*), [10]; *Notification on Definition of Marriage (Croatia)* [6]. See: Jurij Toplak and Djordje Gardasevic, 'Concepts of National and Constitutional Identity in Croatian Constitutional Law' (2017) 42 RCEEL 263; Lang et al., 'Constitution of Croatia', 1147.

[322] *Decision 7/2018 on Mixed EU Treaties (Bulgaria)* [3.1].

[323] Decision 3/2004 EU Amendments (Bulgaria), IV, V.I. See also Decision 3/2003 Form of State Structure and Government (Bulgaria), SG No 36 of 18 April 2013, [1]–[3]; Decision 8/2005 Amendments Affecting the Judiciary (Bulgaria), SG No 74 of 13 September 2005. See further Martin Belov, 'Constitutional Courts as Ultimate Players in Multilevel

'democratic constitutional model' of Bulgaria, the National Assembly must retain the 'basic powers [...] assigned by the Constitution'.[324]

In **Slovenia**, EU law is given an equivalent (but not superior) rank to the Constitution,[325] and both sovereignty and the *pravna država* (state governed by the rule of law) limit the permissible transfer of powers under Article 3a of the Constitution (the basis for conferral).[326]

In **Greece**, acts of conferral are constrained by both a constitutional safeguard clause (Article 28(3)) and an unamendability clause (Article 110(1)) which place the Parliamentary Republic, the powers of the state and basic civil and political rights beyond amendment or conferral.[327] The Council of State has sometimes been at pains to interpret the Hellenic Constitution in conformity with EU law,[328] but it has also formally denied the supremacy of EU law over it.[329] In *DI.KATSA (Greece)* the Council of State resolved a conflict with EU law in favour of the Constitution, concluding that it was 'clearly necessary for the preservation of the national identity',[330] and in *Jus Soli (Greece)* it asserted that Article 4(2) TEU guaranteed respect for national identity in Article 1 (3) of the Constitution (as interpreted by the Council of State).[331]

In **Sweden**, Chapter 10§6 of the Instrument of Government states that conferral must not affect the Basic Principles of the Form of Government, and that EU membership is presupposed on an equivalent level of fundamental rights protection to the Swedish Constitution and the ECHR.[332] The clause was modelled after Germany's 'constitutional

---

Constituent Power Games: The Bulgarian Case' in Martin Belov (ed.), Courts, Politics and Constitutional Law (Routledge, 2020), 165–169.

[324] *Decision 3/2004 EU Amendments (Bulgaria)*, V.1.

[325] *European Communities Association Agreement (Slovenia)*, RM-1/97; ECLI:SI:USRS:1997: Rm197, [12] and cases above, n 154.

[326] *SNHCA (Slovenia)* [20]–[22], [41]–[42], [49], [51]–[54]; *Vatican Agreement (Slovenia)* [22]–[24]. See further Samo Bardutzky, 'The Future Mandate of the Constitution of Slovenia: A Potent Tradition Under Strain' in Albi and Bardutzky (eds), *National Constitutions*, 701–703 and 892–894.

[327] Art. 28 of the Constitution is read as an implicit rejection of absolute supremacy. See Grabenwarter, 'Constitutional Law', 91; Panos Kapotas, 'Greek Council of State Judgment 3470/2011' (2014) 10 Eur Const Law Rev 162, 168–171. See further Xenophon Contiades, Charalambos Papacharalambous and Christos Papastyliano, 'The Constitution of Greece: EU Membership Persectives' in Albi and Bardutzky (eds), *National Constitutions*, 663.

[328] *Michaniki (Greece)* [9].

[329] *DI.KATSA (Greece)* [4]–[16]; *Karella (Greece)* [10]. *Athens Paper (Greece)* [11].

[330] *DI.KATSA (Greece)* [16].

[331] *Jus Soli (Greece)* Decision 260/2013; ECLI:EL:COS:2013:0204A46010E6342, [6].

[332] Ch 10§6, the Constitution of Sweden: The Fundamental Laws and the Rikstag Act (*Sveriges Rikstag*, 2016). The Basic Principles (Ch 1 Instrument of Government) include

identity' jurisprudence,[333] and 'implies a serious reservation against the principle of supremacy'.[334] According to the Constitution Committee (*Konstitutionsutskottet*), law-making powers conferred on the EU cannot modify fundamental principles of Sweden's constitutional system.[335] The *Högsta Domstolen* has not openly invalidated EU law on this basis, but it has treated national implementations of EU law as purely internal law and interpreted them in conformity with basic principles, even though this has appeared *prima facie* contrary to EU law.[336]

In **Poland**, the *Trybunał Konstytucyjny* has long asserted an 'untouchable material core' inherent in the Polish constitutional identity.[337] In *Lisbon (Poland)*, it held:

The Constitutional Tribunal shares the view expressed in the doctrine that the competences, under the prohibition of conferral, manifest about a constitutional identity [...] the following should be included among the matters under the complete prohibition of conferral: decisions specifying the fundamental principles of the Constitution and decisions concerning the rights of the individual which determine the identity of the state, including, in particular [...] human dignity and constitutional rights [...] statehood [...] democratic governance [...] the rule [of] law [...] social justice [...] and the prohibition to confer the power to amend the Constitution and the competence to determine competences.[338]

Although long asserted against external predations by international law, since 2015 executive reforms aimed at undermining the Polish judiciary under the guise of a political 'constitutional identity' narrative have instead appeared to work 'in violation of clear constitutional standards and in conflict with their interpretation laid down in the

---

popular sovereignty, parliamentary government, the rule of law, equality, liberty, freedom of expression, Rikstag competences over state funds and Monarchy. For a full account: Nergelius, 'Constitution of Sweden', 324.

[333] Nergelius, 'Constitution of Sweden', 319.

[334] Griller, 'Problems', 173.

[335] *Konstitutionsutskottet, Constitutional amendments before swedish membership of the European Union* (Report 1993/94 KU21 available at: wwwriksdagense/sv/dokument-lagar/arende/betankande/grundlagsandringar-infor-ett-svenskt-medlemskap-i_GH01KU21 1993).

[336] *AA v. Strix Television et al. (Sweden)*, Case 33134/00; NJA 2002 314, available at: https://lagennu/dom/nja/2002s314 accessed 4 July 2016. Cf: *Ne bis in idem I (Sweden)*, Case B4946-12; NJA 2013 502, available at: https://lagennu/dom/nja/2013s502 accessed 4 July 2016. See Angelica Ericsson, 'The Swedish De Bis in Idem Saga – Painting a Multi-Layered Picture' (2014) 17 Europarättslig tidskrift 54.

[337] *Accession Treaty (Poland)* [1], [2.1], [8], [12]–[14], [18]; *Decision 2011/199/EU (Poland)* [3.2], [6.3.1] excerpted above, in Methods and Introduction, n 25.

[338] *Lisbon (Poland)* [2.1].

case law of the Constitutional Tribunal, the Supreme Court and the legal doctrine that has developed since the adoption of the 1997 Constitution of the Republic of Poland'.[339]

In **Hungary**, the *Magyarország Alkotmánybírósága* enunciated a material form of constitutional identity constraint under the 'European clauses' of both the 1989 Constitution (Article 2/A)[340] and the 2011 Fundamental Law (Article E (2)).[341] However, the absence of any procedural entrenchment provisions in the Constitution (all constitutional provisions are formally amendable with the same 2/3 majority) has left it comparatively defenceless against internal predations by the Hungarian executive.[342]

In **Ireland**, the Supreme Court holds that Article 29.4.6 of the Constitution (the basis for conferral) does not bestow a power on state institutions to dispose of their own competences or 'qualify, curtail or inhibit the existing sovereign power',[343] and in *Grogan (Ireland)*, the Court rejected the supremacy of EU law over fundamental constitutional guarantees.[344] As Cahill concludes: The Supreme Court will

---

[339] Małgorzata Gersdorf, 'Opinion on the White Paper on the Reform of the Polish Judiciary' (*First President of the Supreme Court of Poland*, 2018) https://archiwumosiatynskiego.pl/images/2018/04/Supreme-Court-Opinion-on-the-white-paper-on-the-Reform-of-the-Polish-Judiciar y.pdf accessed 12 June 2020. See also, *Constitutional Tribunal Act (Poland)*, K 39/16 (11 August 2016) (*Trybunał Konstytucyjny*). See further Laurent Pech and Kim Land Scheppele, 'Illiberalism Within: Rule of Law Backsliding in the EU' (2017) 19 CYELS 3; Wojciech Sadurski, 'Polish Constitutional Tribunal under PiS: From an Activist Court, to a Paralysed Tribunal, to a Government Enabler' (2019) 11 Hague J Rule Law 63, 75.

[340] Under the 1989 Constitution, the *Magyarország Alkotmánybírósága* held Article 2/A could not be interpreted in a way that would 'deprive the sovereignty and rule of law of their substance' and implied a *nemo plus iuris* rule that prevented conferral unless Hungarian constitutional guarantees were respected: *Lisbon (Hungary)* [V.2.3]; *Europe Agreement (Hungary)* [V.3] excerpted further above, n 168; *Agricultural Surplus Stocks (Hungary)* Decision 17/2004 (V 25) ABIV1 English version at: www.mkab.hu accessed 3 June 2015, [IV.1], [IV.4]. See: Wojciech Sadurski, '"Solange, Chapter 3": Constitutional Courts in Central Europe' (2014) 14 ELJ 1, 10.

[341] *Article E(2) (Hungary)* [46]-[49], [54], [59]-[69]. See: Gábor Halmai, 'Abuse of Constitutional Identity. The Hungarian Constitutional Court on Interpretation of Article E (2) of the Fundamental Law' (2018) 43 RCEEL 23; Timea Drincóczi and Agnieszka Bień-Kacała, 'Illiberal Constitutionalism: The Case of Hungary and Poland' (2019) 20 German LJ 1140, 1153-1158.

[342] The *Magyarország Alkotmánybírósága* enunciated a material jurisdiction over amendments to the basic structure of the Constitution in *Transitional Provisions of the Fundamental Law (Hungary)* Decision 45/2012 (XII 29) accessible at: https://hunconcour thu/uploads/sites/3/2017/11/en_0045_2012.pdf accessed 11 June 2019, III [6], IV [7], but this was undone by a retaliatory amendment that prohibited review of amendments on substantive grounds. See: Kovács, 'Changing Constitutional Identity'.

[343] *Crotty (Ireland)*, 783.

[344] *Grogan I (Ireland)*, 695-770, excerpted below, in Section 1.2.2.2 at nn 399, 401. See further *Attorney General* v. *X (Ireland)* [1992] IESC 1; [1992] 1 IR 1; *Minister for Justice* v. *Tobin*

'defend the Irish constitutional legal order on almost exactly the same terms as the constitutional courts in other Member States'.[345]

In **Estonia**, the CEAA grants supremacy over Estonian law,[346] including constitutional law,[347] but this is only so 'provided that the fundamental principles of [the Constitution] are respected'.[348]

In **Austria**, the Basic Principles of the Austrian Constitution (democracy, the Republic, the federal state and the rule of law) 'are considered to form a constitutional core that may not be limited by EU law' and 'present limitations to European integration'.[349] If EU law is in conflict with Basic Principles, the VfGH 'has to [...] declare that the relevant rules of EU law are not applicable in Austria [...] [t]hey have to be regarded as void acts'.[350] ESM (Austria) and TSCG (Austria) indicate that a conferral of economic competences on EU institutions would contradict the Basic Principles.[351]

In **Slovakia**, Articles 7(2) and 7(5) of the Constitution grant EU supremacy over 'laws',[352] but amendments to grant supremacy over 'constitutional law' or the 'transfer a part of the exercise of its

---

(No 1) (Ireland) [2008] IESC 3; [2008] 4 IR 42; Minister for Justice v. Tobin (No 2) (Ireland) [2012] IESC 37; [2012] IR 147.

[345] Maria Cahill, 'Constitutional Exclusion Clauses, Article 29.4.6, and the Constitutional Reception of European Law' (2011) 34 DULJ 74, 95.

[346] Ministry of Agriculture Tax Notice, Case 3-3-1-74-05 (25 April 2006) (Riigikohus Halduskolleegium) [12]; Constitutionality of the Local Government Council Election Act, Case 3-4-1-1-05 (19 April 2005) (Riigikohus põhiseaduslikkuse järelevalve kolleegium) [49]; Hadleri Toidulisandite AS, Case 3-3-1-33-06 (5 October 2006) (Riigikohus Halduskolleegium).

[347] Interpretation of the Constitution (Estonia) [15]–[16] (cf: Kõve J [2]–[3], Kergandberg J [2]–[3]).

[348] ESM (Estonia) [222]. See also, Makkar (Estonia), Case 3-2-1-71-14 (15 December 2015) (Riigikohus) [81]. The fundamental principles include sovereignty, human dignity, democracy, the rule of law, the social state and the Estonian identity. See: Madis Ernits et al., 'The Constitution of Estonia: The Unexpected Challenges of Unlimited Primacy of EU Law' in Albi and Bardutzky (eds), National Constitutions, 887.

[349] Georg Lienbacher and Matthias Lukan, 'Constitutional Identity in Austria' in Calliess and Van der Schyff (eds), Constitutional Identity, 43–44, 56. See further Grabenwarter, 'Constitutional Law', 85; Konrad Lachmayer, 'The Constitution of Austria in International Constitutional Networks' in Albi and Bardutzky (eds), National Constitutions, 1274–1276; Foster, Austrian Legal System, 144; and sources cited above, n 144.

[350] Lienbacher and Lukan, 'Austria', 57–58.

[351] In ESM (Austria), Case SV 2/12; ECLI:AT:VFGH:2013:SV2.2012 the VfGH upheld ratification of the TESM under Art. 9(2) (ratification of non-EU treaties not affecting the Basic Principles) as being sufficiently 'specific and limited' because it provided for a capped amount of financial contribution. A contrario, an open-ended transfer of the power over financial dispositions would affect the Basic Principles. See further, Section 7.3.2.4, at nn 182–186, on TSCG (Austria), Case SV 1/13; ECLI:AT:VFGH:2013:SV1.2013.

[352] See above, n 158.

sovereignty' were rejected.[353] The *Ústavný Súd* has held that Slovakia 'can only enter into a state union [. . .] in which there is no violation of [the Constitution], in particular Art. 1 [the sovereign democratic state governed by the rule of law]',[354] and that 'the referential framework of constitutional review remains limited to the norms of the Slovak constitutional order' even after accession to the EU.[355] As Kovacs concludes, it is clear that Court 'has the power to review EU law if this is indispensable to protect the constitutional identity of the country'.[356]

In **Finland**, the *Perustuslakivaliokunnan* holds that EU law cannot affect the democratic foundations of the sovereign republic under Section 1 of the Constitution,[357] and Section 94(3) now contains a constitutional safeguard clause that constitutionalizes this interpretation.[358] Under this constraint, the *Perustuslakivaliokunnan* has found that Finland cannot confer its competence for controlling financial liabilities on an international body voting by QMV,[359] and EU law cannot weaken domestic standards of fundamental rights.[360]

From this tour it is clear that, as a matter of pure constitutional law, the CJEU's 'national identity' jurisdiction under Article 4(2) TEU does not, and could not, grant jurisdiction over the grounds for constitutional identity review that bind acts of conferral in any of these countries. For Member State constitutional courts, therefore, Article 4(2) TEU is merely ratificatory of 'the thrust of the jurisprudence of numerous

---

[353] Zuzana Vikarská and Michal Bobek, 'Slovakia: Between Euro-Optimism and Euro-Concerns' in Albi and Bardutzky (eds), *National Constitutions*, 845, 880.

[354] *Constitutional Treaty (Slovakia)*, 35–38.

[355] *Data Retention (Slovakia)* [76] and [62]. See also: *Tax Office Košice IV (Slovakia)*, II ÙS 501/2010-94, [20].

[356] Kovács, 'Ethnocultural Identity', 1711.

[357] *Opinion on the ESM (Finland)*, PeVL 13/2012 vp – HE 34/2012 vp; *Opinion on the Treaty of Lisbon (Finland)*, PeVL 13/2008 vp; *Constitutional Treaty (Finland)*. See further above, Section 1.2.1.1, n 160 and Niilo Jääskinen, 'The Application of Community Law in Finland: 1995–1998' (1999) 36 CMLR 407.

[358] Section 94(3) states that 'An international obligation shall not endanger the democratic foundations of the Constitution.' See further Griller, 'Problems', 149, 166–168; Ojanen and Salminen, 'Finland', 280.

[359] *Opinion on the ESM (Finland)*, PeVL 1/2011 vp – U 6/2011 vp; *Opinion on the ESM (Finland)*, PeVL 22/2011 vp – U 27/2011 vp; *Opinion on the ESM (Finland)*, PeVL 25/2011 vp; *Opinion 13/ 2012 on the ESM (Finland)*. See: Päivi Leino and Janne Salminen, 'The Euro Crisis and Its Constitutional Consequences for Finland: Is There Room for National Politics in EU Decision-Making?' (2013) 9 Eur Const Law Rev 451.

[360] *Opinion on the EU's Future (Finland)*, PeVL 25/2001 vp – E 27/2001 vp. See Ojanen and Salminen, 'Finland', 397; Juha Lavapuro, Tuomas Ojanen and Martin Scheinin, 'Rights-Based Constitutionalism in Finland and the Development of Pluralist Constitutional Review' (2011) 9 I Con 505, 515.

domestic constitutional courts on the relationship between EU law and national constitutional law'.[361] The Spanish *Tribunal Constitucional*, for example, has stated that 'the limits referred to by the reservations of said constitutional justifications now appear proclaimed unmistakeably by the Treaty'.[362] Numerous other courts have cited Article 4(2) TEU as though it was merely ratificatory of their own constitutional identity jurisdictions.[363]

This is so because the interpretation of constitutional identity involves the interpretation of national constitutional laws, and the CJEU lacks jurisdiction to do so under Article 19 TEU.[364] As a matter of law, it is blind to the 'identities' which it professes to define respect for. Indeed, the ECJ has itself accepted (though not always)[365] that only national courts can define what comprises national identity.[366] Yet, as Preshova points out, this is not enough: it remains that when deciding the weight of such claims in a conflict with EU law, the ECJ will still 'enter into a forbidden zone of determining the content and scope of the constitutional identity of a Member State. This is in essence contrary to Article 19 TFEU and also contrary to its duty to respect Article 4(2) TEU'.[367] As the *Corte costituzionale* has emphasized:

There would be no respect if the requirements of unity demand the cancellation of the very core of values on which the Member State is founded. [...] Otherwise, the European Treaties would seek, in a contradictory fashion, to undermine the very constitutional foundation of which they were born by the wishes of the Member States. [...] It is therefore reasonable to expect that [...] the European court will [leave] to the national authorities the ultimate assessment concerning compliance with the supreme principles of the national order.[368]

[361] Von Bogdandy and Schill, 'Absolute Primacy', 1419.
[362] *Constitutional Treaty (Spain)* [3].
[363] *Lisbon (Poland)* [2.1]; *Lisbon (Germany)* [216]–[217]; *Taricco II Judgment (Italy)* [11]; *Taricco II Reference (Italy)* [6]; *Special Sustainability Contribution (Portugal)* [25] and *Pay Cuts 2014-2018 (Portugl)* [12]; *Jus Soli (Greece)* [6]; *Lisbon (Latvia)* [16.3]–[17].
[364] Case 27/74 *Demag v. Finanzamt Duisburg-Sud* [1974] ECR 1037; EU:C:1974:104, [8]; Case C-177/94 *Perfili* [1996] ECR I-161, [9]; Case C-515/08 *Dos Santos Palhota & Others* [2010] ECR I-9133; EU:C:2010:589, [18].
[365] Case C-393/10 *O'Brien v. Ministry of Justice* EU:C:2012:110, [49]; Case C-58/13 *Torresi v. Ordine degli Avvocati di Macerata* EU:C:2014:2088, [58]; Case C-399/11 *Melloni v. Ministerio Fiscal* EU:C:2012:600 (Opinion of AG Bot), [140]–[141].
[366] Case C-36/02 *Omega Spielhallen-und Automatenaufstellungs-GmbH v. Bonn* [2004] ECR I-9509; EU:C:2004:614, [31]; Case C-53/04 *Marrosu and Sardino v. Aziedna ospidaliera Ospedale* [2006] ECR I-7213 (Opinion of AG Maduro), [40].
[367] Preshova, 'Battleground or Meeting', 296.
[368] *Taricco II Reference (Italy)* [6].

The interpretation of national identity under Article 4(2) TEU therefore does not provide an authoritative description of the boundaries of constitutional identity for the purpose of this study. The CJEU has no pure legal authority to interpret or loosen the bounds of constitutional identity by extra-constitutional interpretation.[369] Whatever authority the CJEU has under Articles 19 and 4(2) TEU, it can only ever be derived authority from constitutional organs which themselves are subject to constitutional identity constraints on their conferring power.[370]

1.2.2.2   Normative Evaluation of Constitutional Identity Review

Pure constitutional claims aside, EU and national law also field competing normative descriptions of what values constitute constitutional identity, and subsequently what weight should be ascribed to them when they are in conflict with EU law. Normative disputes most frequently arise where the EU discovers itself to possess principles mirroring constitutional identity principles in national law, but these are interpreted differently, with a different rank, standard or content to the equivalent norm in national law. In particular, EU iterations of such norms can be subserviated to competing objectives of EU law – typically, the 'effectiveness' and 'uniformity' that justifies the supremacy of otherwise mundane acts of EU law. Member State constitutional identities cannot.

In that respect, although heterogeneous in specificity and entrenchment, Member State constitutional identities show a 'remarkable convergence' on two core normative principles:[371]

> **Constitutional Democracy**, sometimes derived from popular sovereignty and sometimes from parliamentary or national sovereignty, is the basic principle of all Member State constitutions. The primary condition is that state law-making institutions remain accountable by election to the people in the manner specified in the constitution. Under all constitutional identity jurisdictions in this book, no state institution may validate an exercise of public power that is not democratically legitimated in the manner *specified in the constitution*. All, including the most basic among them, preclude a disposition of the *Kompetenz-Kompetenz*. The most developed, such as the German 'eternity'

---

[369] *Lisbon (Germany)* [155].
[370] Ernits et al., 'Constitution of Estonia', 941.
[371] Von Bogdandy and Schill, 'Absolute Primacy', 1432. See also Giovanni Piccirilli, 'The "Taricco Saga": The Italian Constitutional Court Continues Its European Journey' (2018) 14 ECL Rev 814, 826.

clause, entrench a specific formula for democracy: they require, in essence, that *x* powers can only be exercised by *y* institutions according to *z* formula, and these components themselves are not amendable.

The Rule of Law requires that constitutional organs comply with substantive limits on state power inscribed in the constitution. This means that legislative and executive organs cannot transfer the power to act free from the constitution to the Union, because they are not empowered to act free from the constitution themselves.[372]

That these two principles can be essentially encapsulated as the definition of constitutional democracy is perhaps not surprising. And yet, the tension that arises whenever the ECJ interprets 'national identity' under Article 4(2) as having a different normative content or weight than national law seems to be a continuous source of surprise for Europe's jurists. Indeed, some judges and scholars have poured scorn on the notion that the shape of the Union's competences is constrained by the shape of national constitutional identities.[373] The ECJ itself is under the duty to 'respect' national identities but has, by many accounts, made a hash of it.[374] The ECJ has often refused to weigh constitutional identity considerations, even when flagged by AG Opinions,[375] or the Member States themselves,[376] and has sometimes dismissed or flatly ignored assertions from governments – and even constitutional courts – that some principle or other is part of the national identity.[377] Despite several AG Opinions, Article 4(2) TEU was not cited in a single ECJ decision from its introduction in 1992 until after the rejection of the Constitutional

---

[372] *Crotty (Ireland)*, 783: 'It is not within the competence of the Government, or indeed of the Oireachtas, to free themselves from the constraints of the Constitution [. . .] [t]hey are both creatures of the Constitution and are not empowered to act free from the restraints of the Constitution.'

[373] Pescatore, 'Comparative Analysis', 181; Case C-62/14 *Gauweiler v. Bundestag* EU:C:2015:7 (Opinion of AG Cruz-Villalón), [59]–[60] excerpted below, at n 392 and sources cited above, Section 1.1.1, nn 36–39.

[374] See, for example, *Melloni (Spain)* [3]: 'equivalence and sufficiency in [constitutional] protection [. . .] only becomes clear [. . .] when there is an underlying legitimate trust in Community institutions and other Member States.' See also Murkens, 'Want Our Identity Back', 532.

[375] Case C-160/03 *Kingdom of Spain v. Eurojust* [2005] ECR I-2077; EU:C:2004:817 (Opinion of AG Maduro), [24]; *Marrosu and Sardino* [40]; Case C-135/08 *Rottman v. Freistaat Bayern* EU:C:2009:58 (Opinion of AG Maduro), [23]–[25]. See Leonard Besselink, 'National and Constitutional Identity Before and After Lisbon' (2010) 6 Utrecht L Rev 36, 41.

[376] Case C-364/10 *Hungary v. Slovakia* EU:C:2012:630; *Italy v. Commission* EU:C:2013:116.

[377] Case C-42/17 *MAS and MB (Taricco II) (Opinion of AG Bot)* EU:C:2017:564, [169]–[187]; Case C-42/17 *MAS and MB (Taricco II)* EU:C:2017:936 (no mention of constitutional identity in judgment); *Gauweiler (CJEU)* (constitutional identity concerns raised by the BVerfG in its preliminary reference unaddressed) and cases cited above, n 365.

Treaty in 2008.[378] In the entire history of EU integration, just once has the ECJ found that a conflict between a fundamental constitutional right and an EU law compatible with the Charter could be decided in favour of the former.[379] As Judge Pescatore has written, the teleology of CJEU interpretation is integration:

[T]he interpretation of Community Law depends not on the idea of maintaining an equilibrium which has been reached but on the vision of a European unity which is to be built.[380]

Accordingly, the EU courts are seen to have 'laboured in the field of doctrine to extend the Community's competences',[381] to have 'stretch[ed] their competences to the outermost limits [to] bring home the reality of European integration',[382] and to evince a school of thought that 'no opportunity should be missed of moving the Community caravan forward, if necessary by night marches'.[383] Criticisms of a 'dialogue among the deaf' and a 'lack of respect for the constitutional traditions of the Member States' have been levelled against the ECJ where integral constitutional principles have been placed faithfully before it.[384]

Under Article 4(2) TEU, there is no recognition of inalienable constitutional reserves of sovereignty outside the legal order which can be invoked against the expansion of EU law.[385] In all cases, 'identity' claims will be assimilated as 'legitimate aims' pursuant to a recognized EU derogation (and then subserviated to EU legislation under the proportionality test);[386] or they will be assimilated as indistinguishable from

---

[378] Preshova, 'Battleground or Meeting', 284.
[379] Clara Rauchegger, 'National Constitutional Rights and the Primacy of EU Law: M.A.S.' (2018) 55 CMLR 1521.
[380] Pescatore, 'Comparative Analysis', 174.
[381] Kumm, 'Final Arbiter', 359.
[382] Wyatt, 'Limited Powers?', 20.
[383] Alan Dashwood, 'The Limits of European Community Powers' (1996) 21 EL Rev 113. See also JHH Weiler, 'The Transformation of Europe' (1990–1991) 100 Yale LJ 2403, 2434–2435.
[384] Leonard Besselink, 'The Parameters of Constitutional Conflict after Melloni' (2014) 39 EL Rev 531, 549; Elke Cloots, 'Germs of Pluralist Judicial Adjudication' (2010) 47 CMLR 645, 663.
[385] Lenaerts, 'Many Faces', 220–221.
[386] *Case 473/93 Commission v. Luxembourg* [35]; Case C-213/07 *Michaniki AE* EU:C:2008:731, [61]; *Omega* [36]; Case C-341/05 *Laval un Partneri Ltd. v. Svenska Byggnadsarbetareförbundet* [2007] ECR I-11767; EU:C:2007:809, [87], [91]–[92]; C-438/05 *Viking Line ABP* [2007] ECR I-10779; EU:C:2007:772, [85]–[90]; Case C-208/09 *Sayn-Wittgenstein v. Landeshauptmann von Wien* [2010] ECR I-13693; EU:C:2010:806, [93]; Case C-391/09 *Runevič-Vardyn* [2011] ECR I-03787, [83]–[96]; Case C-202/11 *Anton Las* v. *PSA Antwe.rp* (Opinion of AG Jääskinen), [58]–[61].

EU norms – such as the protection of language or other fundamental values of the *Union* (and then interpreted in conformity with the EU law iteration).[387] So, for example, in *Melloni*, it was accepted that the right to a fair trial under the Spanish Constitution could constitute national identity, but it was denied that it could be given a stricter interpretation than under the EU Charter.[388] In *Michaniki*, AG Maduro explained:

[N]ational constitutional rules can be taken into consideration to the extent that they fall within the discretion available to the Member States [. . .] *within the limits fixed by the principle and the [instrument of EU legislation] itself.*[389]

In short, constitutional identity is limited by the objectives of EU law, not the other way around.

The case for accepting this privileging of EU law over constitutional identity is normative: Member States must privilege the 'uniformity and effectiveness' of EU law over 'constitutional identity' claims, else the EU legal order will break down.[390] The danger is what Kumm refers to as the 'Cassandra scenario' – constitutional identity review would cast the EU into inter-statal anarchy, threatening over sixty-eight years of peace and cooperation.[391] In *Gauweiler* v. *Bundestag*, AG Cruz-Villalón opined:

[I]t seems to me an all impossible task to preserve *this* Union, as we know it today, if it is to be made subject to an absolute reservation, ill-defined and virtually at the discretion of each of the Member States, which takes the form of a category described as 'constitutional identity' [. . .] Such a 'reservation of identity', independently formed by the competent – often judicial – bodies of the Member States would very probably leave the EU legal order in a subordinate position.[392]

With respect, however, it is difficult to see why this is so, and virtually no constitutional court has accepted this normative justification over constitutional identity. For two reasons.

---

[387] *Sayn-Wittgenstein* [84]; *Omega* [33]–[34]; *Anton Las (AG Jääskinen)* [58]–[59]; Case C-556/10 *Italy* v. *Commission* EU:C:2012:528 (Opinion of AG Kokott), [87]; *Runevič-Vardyn* [83]–[96]. See also: Brady Gordon, 'A Sceptical Analysis of the Enforcement of ISDS Awards in the EU Following the Decision of the CJEU on CETA' (2020) 5(1) EILA Rev 92, 130.

[388] *Melloni (AG Bot)* [139]–[142]. *Melloni* [58]–[59]; Gordon, 'A Sceptical Analysis', 130.

[389] *Michaniki (AG Maduro)* [33] (emphases added). See also *Michaniki* [63].

[390] *Costa* v. *ENEL*, 594; *Internationale Handelsgesellschaft* [3] excerpted above, Section 1.1.1, at n 48.

[391] Kumm, 'Final Arbiter', 375. See, for example, Groussot, 'Supr[i]macy', 103; Pescatore, 'Comparative Analysis', 170–176.

[392] *Gauweiler (AG Cruz-Villalón)* [59]–[60].

First, as Judge Kõve of the *Riigikohus* so puts it, 'absolute' supremacy would appear to 'overestimate the theory'.[393] Participation in *this* Union as we know it today simply does not entail 'supranational "access" to the Member States' legal orders' outside its competences – particularly when no such authorization is even possible under many constitutions.[394] That sort of 'in for a penny, in for a pound' argument has been dismissed as disingenuous and undemocratic.[395] As the *Trybunał Konstytucyjny* has pointed out, 'it is impossible in a democratic state ruled by law to create presumed competences'.[396] The BVerfG agrees: 'integration into a free community neither requires submission removed from constitutional limitation and control nor the forgoing one's own identity'.[397] The *Corte constituzionale* explains:

[W]hilst the aim of the [*Corte constituzionale*] is to preserve the constitutional identity of the Republic of Italy, it does not however compromise the require-ments of uniform application of EU law [because it] does not result from an alternative interpretation of EU law, but exclusively from the fact, which in itself *falls outside the substantive scope of EU law*, that the Italian legal system [. . .] subjects [criminal offences] to the principle of legality.[398]

Second, constitutional courts anyway doubt the normative superiority of a principle of legal ordering where the only inviolable principle is the effectiveness of executive-made law.[399] In *Fragd*, for example, the *Corte constituzionale* stated that compared to the infringement of a fundamen-tal principle, 'concerns of uniform application of Community law and

---

[393] *Interpretation of the Constitution (Estonia)* per Kõve J, [3].
[394] *Lisbon (Germany)* [318] and [204], [239].
[395] *Vatican Agreement (Slovenia)* [23]–[24]; *Taricco II Reference (Italy)* [4]–[6] excerpted above, nn 221, 223; *Ajos (Denmark)*, 442–444, excerpted above, n 232; *Amending Article 125 (Lithuania)*, III [2], [4], [6]–[6.2.3]; *Weiss Decision (Germany)* [111]; *Constitutional Treaty (Slovakia)*, 35–36; *Decision 3/2004 EU Amendments (Bulgaria)*, V.1; *Thoburn v. Sunderland (UK)* [69] excerpted above, n 300; *HS2 (UK)* [110]–[111], [201]–[207] and [78]–[79], excerpted above n 228; *Crotty (Ireland)*, 767 and 758–759 excerpted above, n 372 and in Methods and Introduction, n 25; *Constitutional Treaty (Spain)* [3]; *Asepesco (Spain)* [4]; *Elections to the EP (France)* [2]–[4]; *Melloni (Spain)* [3], [4], [7].
[396] *Lisbon (Poland)*, ground 2.4.
[397] *Lisbon (Germany)* [204].
[398] *Taricco II Judgment (Italy)* [8] (emphasis added). See also *Taricco II Reference (Italy)* [8] 'the primacy of EU law is not called into question because [constitutional identity] is extraneous to EU law'.
[399] *Grogan I (Ireland)*, 769: 'it cannot be one of the objectives of the [EC] that a member state should be obliged to permit activities which are clearly designed to set at nought the constitutional guarantees for the protection within the State of a fundamental human right'. See, similarly: *Taricco II Judgment (Italy)* [5] below, excerpted below, Section 1.2.2.3, at n 447.

legal certainty did not have any overriding force'.[400] Likewise, in *Grogan (Ireland)* the Irish Supreme Court stated:

Where an injunction is sought to protect a constitutional right, the only matter which could properly be capable of being weighed in a balance against it would be another constitutional right [...] there can be no question of a possible or putative right which might exist in European law as a corollary to a right to travel so as to avail of services, counterbalancing [that right] as a matter of convenience.[401]

Simply put, Member State constitutional courts do not weigh EU laws and constitutional identity norms in accordance with the normative weight the ECJ ascribes to them.[402] The architects of EU fiscal federalism can place no stock in the claim that the 'effectiveness and uniformity' of EU law will impel constitutional courts to accept intrusions on constitutional identity in order to accommodate some ideal institutional model. They are not authorized to decide that EU objectives should persist while national constitutional guarantees should perish.[403]

1.2.2.3   Positivist Evaluation of Constitutional Identity Review

Finally, the merits for accepting the absolute supremacy of EU law as a positivist statement of the law governing the boundaries of 'constitutional identity' are dubious. This was demonstrated in recent cases such as *Weiss (Germany)*,[404] *Slovak Pensions XVII (Czech Republic)*,[405] *R v.*

---

[400] *Fragd (Italy)* 653–662.
[401] *Grogan I (Ireland)*, 765 (see also n 399).
[402] De Witte, 'Direct Effect', 201–202 and sources above, nn 244–247.
[403] See, for example, *Lisbon (Germany)*, [217] 'the finding of a violation of constitutional identity is incumbent on the federal Constitutional Court alone'. *UN Convention (Italy)* [3.2]: 'The examination [of constitutionality] is a task of the constitutional judge alone [...] any different solution goes against the exclusive competence given by the Constitution to this Court.' *Special Sustainability Contribution (Portugal)* [25]: 'it is an undeniable task of the Portuguese Constitutional Court to exercise the competence that Art. 221 of the Constitution confers on it.' *Decision 3/2004 EU Amendments (Bulgaria)*: EU accession cannot affect the 'democratic constitutional model' including the 'functions assigned by the Constitution to the [...] Constitutional Court'. See also *Decision 80/2014 (Romania)* [456] excerpted above, Section 1.2.2.1, at n 319; *HS2 (UK)* [201]–[209], [110]–[111]; *Grogan I (Ireland)*, 765; *Re Lisbon (France)* [7]–[9]; *Melloni (Spain)* [3]; *Constitutional Treaty (Spain)* [4]; *Amendment to the Roads Act (Croatia)* [60]; *Data Retention (Slovakia)* [62] excerpted above, Section 1.2.2.1, at n 355.
[404] *Weiss Decision (Germany)* [118].
[405] *Slovak Pensions XVII (Czech Republic)* excerpted below, at n 451.

Oberlandesgericht (Germany),[406] *Ajos (Denmark)*,[407] *Taricco II (Italy)*,[408] and *HS2 (UK)*,[409] where national courts *in fact* invalidated or disapplied ECJ rulings, and these decisions were *in fact* taken as an authoritative statement of law by the legal system.

Indeed nearly every constitutional court – even the most communautaire among them – has invalidated or interpreted EU law in conformity with the boundaries of national constitutional identities, rather than the other way around. If this has averted newsworthy open conflicts most of the time, it has nonetheless led to a diffusive realm of 'parallel' interpretations where EU law is nonetheless invalidated or warped against the shape of constitutional identities. This can be seen in, *inter alia*, *Constitutional Treaty (France)*,[410] *EM Eritrea (UK)*,[411] *Gauweiler (Germany)*,[412] *HS2(UK)*,[413] *Anti-terror Database (Germany)*,[414] *Pham v. SSHD (UK)*,[415] *AAA v. Strix (Sweden)*,[416] *Constantinou (Cyprus)*,[417] the Portuguese financial conditionality cases,[418] *Grogan (Ireland)*,[419] *ESM (Estonia)*,[420]

---

[406] *R v. Oberlandesgericht (Germany)* excerpted above, Section 1.2.2.1, at n 287.
[407] *Ajos (Denmark)*, 441: 'it is not possible to interpret para 2.a(3) of the Law on salaried employees as then in force in accordance with the Employment Directive [. . .] as interpreted by the Court of Justice.'
[408] *Taricco II Judgment (Italy)* [5], [8], [12] excerpted below, Section 1.2.2.3, at n 447.
[409] *HS2 (UK)* [78]–[79], [110]–[111], [201]–[207]. See also *Pham v. SSHD (UK)* [58].
[410] *Constitutional Treaty (France)* [16], [18] (interpreting the EU Charter in conformity with, *inter alia*, French secularity). See: Millet, 'Constitutional Identity in France', 149.
[411] *R (EM (Eritrea)) v. SSHD (UK)* [2014] UKSC 12; [2014] 2 WLR 409, interpreting Joined Cases C-411/10, C-493/10 *R (NS (Afghanistan)) v. SSHD* EU:C:2011:865, on Art. 4 of the EU Charter in conformity with the ECHR and Human Rights Act 1998, rather than the other way around.
[412] *Gauweiler Decision (Germany)* [205]–[207] (placing six conditions on the application of the ECB's OMT programme).
[413] *HS2 (UK)* [110]–[111], [201]–[209] (refusing to submit a preliminary reference on the compatibility of a hybrid bill process with EU law and reading ECJ jurisprudence in conformity with a constitutional statute, rather than the other way around).
[414] *Anti-terror Database (Germany)* [91].
[415] *Pham v. SSHD (UK)* [54]–[55] (treating the ECJ's *Rottman* decision as *ultra vires* and reading it in conformity with respect for national constitutional identity, rather than the other way around).
[416] *AA v. Strix (Sweden)* (declining to submit a preliminary reference and treating an EU norm in conflict with freedom of expression as purely national law).
[417] *Constantinou (Cyprus)* (implementation of EAW Framework Decision unconstitutional).
[418] *Special Sustainability Contribution (Portugal)* [25] excerpted above, Section 1.2.2.1, at n 308 and cases cited below, Chapter 7, Section 7.5, n 320.
[419] *Grogan I (Ireland)*, 765 excerpted above, Section 1.2.2.2, at nn 399 and 401.
[420] Although not an EU institution, in *ESM (Estonia)* the *Riigikohus* considered the ESM a creature of the EU for the purposes of constitutional law and nonetheless read limits into the capital call provisions of the ESM which were not read by the ECJ.

Sugar Quotas III (Czech Republic),[421] *EAW (Poland)*,[422] *Riga Land Use (Latvia)*,[423] *Data Retention (Romania)*,[424] *Telecommunications Market Act (Finland)*,[425] *Money Laundering (Belgium)*,[426] *DI.KATSA (Greece)*,[427] *Auxiliary Activities in the Public Sector (Croatia)*,[428] *Agricultural Surplus Stocks (Hungary)*,[429] and *Taricco II (Italy)*,[430] where courts exercised a sort of 'reverse-Simmenthal' supremacy or studiously ignored conflicting interpretations of EU law entirely.

Article 4(2) TEU may therefore be said to constitute a 'material' (merely persuasive) competence to blunt an EU measure before it protrudes over the boundaries of the EU legal order into constitutional identities, but it is clear it does not have 'formal' authority – Member States do not accept the supremacy of the ECJ's assessment over their own.[431] To the contrary, where the CJEU has asserted itself over constitutional identity adjudication, the jurisdiction has proven so constitutionally fraught that its very use is prejudicial the integrity of the European legal order (it should not be forgotten that it was precisely that phenomenon in *Internationale Handelsgesellschaft* which provoked the birth of 'constitutional identity' jurisprudence in the first place).[432]

---

[421] *Sugar Quotas III (Czech Republic)* excerpted above, Section 1.2.2.1, at n 311.

[422] *EAW (Poland)* (invalidating the national implementation of the EAW Framework Decision).

[423] *Riga Land Use Plan (Latvia)* excerpted above, n 314.

[424] *Decision 1258/2009 Data Retention I (Romania) Monitorul Oficial al României* No 798 of 23 November 2009 (*Curtea Constituțională*) English translation available at: www.legi-inte rnet.ro accessed 5 July 2016 (Directive 2004/24/EC declared unconstitutional without addressing validity under EU law). Similarly: *Procurement Complaints (Romania)* Decision No 569 of 17 May 2008 (*Curtea Constituțională*) English translation available at: www .legi-internet.ro accessed 5 July 2016. See Vita, 'Romanian Constitutional Court', 1649.

[425] *Opinion on the Telecommunications Market Act (Finland)*, PeVL 5/2001 vp – HE 73/2000 vp, 2–3.

[426] *Money Laundering (Belgium)*, Case 10/2008 (23 January 2008) (*Cour constitutionelle*). See also, *Bressol (Belgium)*, Case 89/2011 (31 May 2011) (*Cour constitutionelle*). For comment: Patricia Popelier and Catherine Van de heyning, 'The Belgian Constitution' in Albi and Bardutzky (eds), *National Constitutions*, 1233.

[427] *DI.KATSA (Greece)* [10] (interpreting Directive 89/48 in conformity with respect for Art. 16(5) of the Constitution).

[428] *Auxiliary Activities in the Public Sector (Croatia)* [45] and *Amendment to the Roads Act (Croatia)* [60], declining to consider compatibility of measures with EU law because 'the Constitution is, by its legal nature, supreme to EU law'.

[429] *Agricultural Surplus Stocks (Hungary)*, treating the implementation EU law as purely national law and interpreting it in conformity with constitutional guarantees. See Sadurski, 'Solange, Chapter 3' for comment.

[430] *Taricco II Reference (Italy)*, excerpted below, at n 446.

[431] Schilling, 'Autonomy', 407.

[432] Groussot, 'Supr[i]macy', 99.

Most recently, the rather transparent attempt to absorb constitutional identities into the EU legal order under Article 4(2) TEU is credited with provoking the emergence of new 'constitutional identity' jurisprudence in Belgium,[433] and the recentralization of overlapping EU Charter/constitutional claims in the Constitutional Courts of Italy and Austria.[434] In Austria, the VfGH recently asserted that the interpretation of EU rights 'must heed the constitutional traditions of the Member States and therefore the distinct characteristics of the rule of law in the Member States'.[435] In Italy, the *Corte constituzionale* recently reasserted its jurisdiction to 'ensure that the rights [under the EU Charter] are interpreted in a way consistent with constitutional traditions'.[436]

Prior to that, the straight assertion of supremacy over constitutional identity in *Akerberg Fransson (CJEU)*[437] and *Melloni (CJEU)*[438] provoked a broader rebellion to EU supremacy in *Melloni (Spain)*,[439] *Taricco II (Italy)*,[440] *R v. Oberlandesgericht (Germany)*,[441] *Anti-terror Database (Germany)*[442] and *HS2 (UK)*,[443] where constitutional courts attacked the ECJ's reasoning and reasserted their own supreme constitutional principles over EU law.[444]

In *R v. Oberlandesgericht (Germany)*, the BVerfG explicitly rebuffed *Melloni* under its *Solange I (Germany)* jurisdiction, overturning a decision of a lower court even though 'the [lower] Court's decision is determined by Union law' and the ECJ had 'specifically ruled' that execution of a

---

[433] Gérard and Verrijdt, 'National Identity Discourse', 192–193; Cloots, 'Constitutional Identity in Belgium', 70–71.

[434] S Giuseppe Martinico and Giorgio Repetto, 'Fundamental Rights and Constitutional Duels in Europe: An Italian Perspective on Case 269/2017 of the Italian Constitutional Court and Its Aftermath' (2019) 15(4) Eur Const Law Rev 731, 732 and 746; Gallo, 'Challenging EU Constitutional Law'.

[435] *Fengije and Jie (Austria)*, Cases U466/11–18, U1836/11–13; ECLI:AT:VFGH:2012: U466.2011, [7.3.3], English version at: www.vfgh.gv.at/downloads/VfGH_U_466-11__U _1836-11_Grundrechtecharta_english.pdf accessed 12 June 2020, [59].

[436] *Supervisory Authority for Competition and the Market (AGCM) (Italy)* Judgment 269/2017 (9 June 2019), English version at: www.cortecostituzionale.it/documenti/download/doc/ recent_judgments/S_269_2017_EN.pdf accessed 13 December 2020, [5.2].

[437] *Akerberg Fransson* [20]–[21].

[438] *Melloni* [58]–[59]; *Melloni (Opinion of AG Bot)* [140]–[141].

[439] *Melloni (Spain)* [3] (refuting supremacy over the 'material limits' of constitutional identity and reasserting its right to a higher level of protection higher than the Charter, *contra Melloni*). See further Besselink, 'Parameters of Constitutional Conflict', 531.

[440] *Taricco II Reference (Italy)* [8]–[9].

[441] *R v. Oberlandesgericht (Germany)* [78]–[84] above, Section 1.2.2.1 at n 287.

[442] *Anti-terror Database (Germany)* [88]–[89], [91].

[443] *HS2 (UK)* [110]–[111] (see also [201]–[209]).

[444] See Valsamis Mitsilegas, 'Trust' (2020) 21 German LJ, 69.

warrant could not be conditional on compliance with constitutional law.[445]

Melloni also received a drubbing under the *controlimiti* doctrine in *Taricco II (Italy)*, forcing the CJEU into a *volte-face* after the *Corte constituzionale* held, again *contra Melloni*, that 'the Italian Constitution construes the principle of legality in criminal matters more broadly than European law',[446] and an ECJ interpretation of the TFEU contrary to that standard 'therefore may not be permitted, even in light of the primacy of EU law'.[447]

Similarly, in *Anti-terror Database (Germany)*, the BVerfG refused to submit a preliminary reference as obliged by the ECJ's *Akerberg Fransson* decision (seen by some as an extension of EU competence) and appeared to state that *Akerberg Fransson* was itself *ultra vires* and inapplicable in Germany:

> The ECJ's decision in the case *Akerberg Fransson* [. . .] must not be read in a way that would view it as an apparent *ultra vires* act [. . .] in a way that questioned the identity of the Basic Law's constitutional order.[448]

The UK Supreme Court followed suit in *HS2 (UK)*, where it refused to submit a reference on the compatibility of a 'Hybrid Bill' process with EU law, and held that 'a decision of the [ECJ] should not be read by a national court in a way that places in question the identity of the national constitutional order'.[449]

More recently, in *Ajos (Denmark)*, a unanimous decision of the Højesteret refused to disapply a provision of domestic legislation as directed by the ECJ because to apply the principle of age discrimination 'as interpreted by the EU Court of Justice' would be *contra legem*.[450]

In 2012, the straight application of supremacy to Czechoslovakian dissolution arrangements in *Landtová v. Česká správa socialního zabezpečení* provoked a constitutional identity ruling by the *Ústavní Soud* so vociferous it bears full repetition here:

> [The *Ústavní Soud*] expected that [. . .] the ECJ would familiarize itself with the [. . .] constitutional identity of the Czech Republic, which it draws from the common

[445] R v. *Oberlandesgericht (Germany)* [76], [82].
[446] *Taricco II Reference (Italy)* [2], [8].
[447] *Taricco II Judgment (Italy)* [5].
[448] *Anti-terror Database (Germany)* (Case 1 BvR 1215/07) ECLI:DE:BVerfG:2013:
rs201304241bvr121507, English version at www.bundesverfassungsgericht.de
accessed 18 June 2020, [88]–[89], [91].
[449] *HS2 (UK)* [110]–[111] (see also [201]–[209]).
[450] *Ajos (Denmark)*, 441.

constitutional tradition with the Slovak Republic [*idem est*] a completely idiosyncratic and historically-created situation that has no parallel in Europe. [...]

The failure to distinguish legal relationships arising from the dissolution of a state with a uniform social security system from legal relationships arising from the free movement of persons in the European Communities [...] is a failure to respect European history; it is comparing matters that are not comparable. For this reason it is not possible to apply European law [...] it is not possible to do otherwise than to find [...] that an act *ultra vires* has occurred.[451]

As the European Law Journal editors wryly point out, EU primacy vis-à-vis the national *pouvoir(s) constituant(s)* grants the ECJ 'a power that perhaps can only exist as long as it is not made use of'.[452]

A power that can 'perhaps exist as long as it is not made use of' cannot offer an authoritative statement of law for the purposes of this study. Constitutional courts have stated (and demonstrated) that legal architectures will be invalidated if they exceed EU competence or intrude on constitutional identities, and this study must take them at their word. Member State *Kompetenz-Kompetenz* and constitutional identity jurisprudence provides a valid constitutional, normative and positivist descriptions of the limits of the EU legal order for the purposes of this study on fiscal federalism.

1.3   The Constitutional Boundaries of European Fiscal Federalism

The conclusion that Member State *Kompetenz-Kompetenz* and constitutional identity jurisprudence provides a valid description of the constitutional boundaries of the EU legal order means the architects of fiscal federalism cannot look solely to EU law, as interpreted by the CJEU, as the ultimate constraint on European fiscal federalism. Member State constitutional courts impose constraints not only on the current boundaries of EU law *lex lata*, but also on potential expansions of EU law and revisions of the EU Treaties *de lege ferenda*.[453] The question of whether a specific fiscal federalism model might 'work' in the EU must heed these

---

[451] *Slovak Pensions XVII (Czech Republic)*, 12–13. See Case C-399/09 *Landtová* v. *Česká správa sociálního zabezpečení* [2011] ECR I-05573; EU:C:2011:415.

[452] Agustín José Menéndez, 'Editorial: A European Union in Constitutional Mutation' (2014) 20 ELJ 127, 133.

[453] Pernice, 'Domestic Courts', 298, 303.

fundamental constitutional limits of European integration in national constitutional law. That being so, the remainder of this chapter will attempt to specify the precise substantive boundaries which will impinge upon the selection of fiscal federalism systems in the EU.

1.3.1 Fiscal Sovereignty

The first boundary is Member State fiscal sovereignty. This principle is implicitly but plainly impressed upon the allocation of competences in economic policy (Articles 2(3) and 5(1) TFEU) and the substantive provisions governing public finance (Articles 121–126 TFEU). Under those articles, the EU has no competence in economic and fiscal policy.[454] The Union competence under these articles is 'mere coordination',[455] limited to providing 'a framework to coordinate these policies to a certain degree'.[456] This is not a mere reflection of good administration under the principle of subsidiarity (though it undoubtedly coheres with that principle).[457] As the BVerfG so puts it, fundamental decisions on public finance and expenditure are 'a fundamental part of the ability of a constitutional state to democratically shape itself', 'the core of parliamentary rights in democracy' and 'an essential manifestation of constitutional democracy'.[458]

This marks an immutable boundary of the EU legal order. Not only has economic and fiscal policy not been conferred on the Union, but, according to the BVerfG, it cannot ever be so conferred without abrogating the national constitutional identity and violating the 'eternity clause' (Article 79(3)) of the 1949 German Basic Law.[459] In Lisbon (Germany), it held:

A transfer of the right of the Bundestag to adopt the budget and control its implementation by the government [would] violate the principle of democracy [...] in its essential content.[460]

Numerous other courts have drawn similar boundaries around national fiscal sovereignty. In Lisbon (Poland) the Trybunał Konstytucyjny held that the conduct of 'independent financial, budget and fiscal policies' is one

---

[454] See above, Methods and Introduction at n 24.
[455] Fabbrini, 'Paradox', 5.
[456] Hinarejos, 'Constitutional Limits', 244.
[457] European Commission, 'Towards a Stability Pact' (Note for the Monetary Committee) II/011/96-EN, 10 January 1996, 14, excerpted below, Chapter 2, Section 2.2.4, at n 100.
[458] Euro Rescue Package (Germany) [107], [127].
[459] Lisbon (Germany) [228], [232]; Euro Rescue Package (Germany) [121]–[127]; ESM I (Germany) [195]–[196]; ESM II (Germany) [161]–[165]; Gauweiler Reference (Germany) [28]; Gauweiler Decision (Germany) [211]–[214]; Weiss Decision (Germany) [101], [104], [115], [117], [163], [227].
[460] Lisbon (Germany) [228].

of the 'attributes of sovereignty' comprising Poland's constitutional identity.[461] In *Crotty (Ireland)* the Irish Supreme Court stated that the freedom to form economic policy 'is just as much a mark of sovereignty' as the freedom to legislate itself, such that the desire to 'qualify, curtail or inhibit the existing sovereign power [...] is not within the power of the Government itself'.[462] In *Collins (Ireland)* the High Court held that 'Budgetary allocation is a fundamental responsibility which [the] Constitution cast upon the Daíl [...] This constitutional responsibility may under no circumstances be abrogated, whether by statute, parliamentary practice or otherwise.'[463] In *TSCG (France)* the *Conseil Constitutionnel* held that Articles 120–126 TFEU did not 'infringe the essential conditions for the exercise of national sovereignty' because they did 'not result in the transfer of any powers over economic or fiscal policy'.[464] In *TSCG (Belgium)*, the *Cour constitutionnelle* held that public finance measures belong to the 'democratically elected legislative assembly, solely competent for this purpose' and '[i]t is therefore up to the respective parliaments to exercise this budgetary competence'.[465] The Spanish *Tribunal Constitucional* holds that budgetary autonomy is the essence of 'the ability to self-government, expressed especially in the possibility of developing [a region's] own policies or matters within their range of competence'.[466] In Sweden, parliamentary fiscal competences are listed among the Basic Principles in Chapter 1 of the Instrument of Government excluded from conferral under Chapter 10§6.[467] In Lithuania the *Konstitucinis Teismas* holds that decisions concerning state loans and liabilities 'may be adopted by the Seimas only [...] an institution [which] may neither transfer nor waive these powers. Such powers may neither be changed nor limited by law'.[468]

---

[461] *Lisbon (Poland)*, 200. See also: *Decision 2011/199/EU (Poland)*, 4.1.3 and 7.3.

[462] *Crotty (Ireland)*, 783.

[463] *Collins* v. *Minister for Finance* [2013] IEHC 530, [95]–[98].

[464] *Treaty on Stability, Coordination and Governance (TSCG) (France)* Decision No 2012-653 DC; ECLI:FR:CC:2012:2012652DC, [16], [30]–[31].

[465] *TCSG (Belgium)* [B.8.3]. In that case the court found that the TSCG did not infringe the budgetary competences of the legislator because [B.6.6.] it does not impinge on 'the substantive choices that the respective authorities can make in the political fields assigned to them' and [B.8.8] 'do[es] not [...] obligate the contracting states, which may freely choose their corrective measures'.

[466] *Parliament of Catalonia* v. *State Solicitor (Law 18/2001) (Spain)*, DTC 134/2011; ECLI:ES: TC:2011:134, [8](a).

[467] Ch 1§4: 'The Rikstag enacts the laws, determines State taxes and decides how State funds are to be employed.' See Section 1.2.2.1 at nn 332–336 on Ch 10§6 and the Basic Principles.

[468] *On the reorganisation of joint stock companies (Lithuania)*, Cases 29/98-16/99-3/2000 (18 October 2000), IV[7].

In *EFSF (Slovenia)*, the *Ustavno Sodišče* held that 'the fundamental power of the National Assembly [...] to decide on state revenue and expenditure' fell under the 'principle of a state governed by the rule of law and the principle of the legality of the operation of the state administration' (Slovene constitutional identity) and so could not be delegated to another institution, including the executive.[469] In Latvia the *Satversmes tiesa* holds that, 'the law on the state budget is an important function of the *Saeima*, which it fulfils as an institution directly responsible to the people of Latvia'[470] and 'solely the legislator can take decisions concerning the state budget' under the basic principles of the democratic state.[471] In Croatia, the *Ustavni sud* holds that 'the exclusive authorities of the Government and the Croatian Parliament concerning issues relevant for the State Budget' are part of the 'constitutional identity' beyond the reach of amendment by referendum.[472]

In a string of 2011 rulings on the constitutionality of the EFSF/ESM legal frameworks before the Irish Supreme Court,[473] the German BVerfG,[474] the Austrian VfGH,[475] the Finnish *Perustuslakivaliokunnan*,[476] the Polish *Trybunał Konstytucyjny*,[477] the

---

[469] *EFSF (Slovenia)* U-I-178/10, UL 12/2011; ECLI:SI:USRS:2011:UI17810, [24]–[25].

[470] *2011 State Budget Subprogram 23.00.00 (Latvia)*, Case 2011-11-01 (3 February 2012) English version at www.satv.tiesa.gov.lv/wp-content/uploads/2011/05/2011-11-01_Spriedums_ENGpdf accessed 13 June 2020, [10].

[471] *Judges' Remuneration (Latvia)*, Case 2009-11-01 in *Selected Case-Law of the Constitutional Court of the Republic of Latvia: 1996-2017 (Satversmes tiesa*, 2018), [8.1]. See also: *Old Age Pension (Latvia)*, Case 2009-43-01 in *Selected Case-Law of the Constitutional Court of the Republic of Latvia: 1996-2017 (Satversmes tiesa*, 2018), [30.1]: International commitments cannot 'replace the rights [...] and also the duty [on the *Saeima*] to decide on all substantial matters' relating to loans and financial dispositions – such issues 'had to be decided by the legislator itself'.

[472] *Auxiliary Activities in the Public Sector (Croatia)* [33.4]; *Amendment to the Roads Act (Croatia)*.

[473] *Pringle v. Government of Ireland (Ireland)* [2012] IESC 47; [2012] 7 JIC 3101, [8.14]: Spending obligations 'must come from funds already committed by Ireland (with the approval of the Dáil)'.

[474] *ESM I (Germany)* [211]–[222]; *ESM II (Germany)* [161]–[162] excerpted below, Section 1.3.1.2, at n 516.

[475] *ESM (Austria)* [3.5.3], 'the National Council decided that the Republic of Austria should accede to the Treaty and therefore assume obligations which are defined and limited', and [4.4.3] the TESM does not 'set out an unlimited liability for making supplementary payments'.

[476] *Opinion 25/2011 on the ESM (Finland)*; *Opinion 13/2012 on the ESM (Finland)*: Art. 3 of the Constitution ('the legislative powers are exercised by the Parliament, which shall also decide on State finances') is within the 'democratic foundations of the Constitution' which EU obligations cannot endanger under Art. 94 of the Constitution.

[477] *Decision 2011/199/EU (Poland)* [4.1.3], [6.3.1]–[6.3.3], [7.3].

Estonian *Riigikohus*[478] and the Slovenian *Ustavno Sodišče*,[479] the legality of the EFSF or ESM were predicated on the conclusion that financial commitments were capped to the extent of the parliamentary authorization, so the agreements did not entail an open-ended transfer of fiscal sovereignty. In *ESM (Estonia)* the *Riigikohus* explained:

> The sovereignty of the people gives rise to the sovereignty of the state and thereby all state institutions obtain their legitimation from the people. [...] One element of the state's sovereignty is its financial sovereignty, which contains taking decisions on budgetary matters and on the assumption of financial obligations for the state.[480]

In all countries which have had occasion to pronounce on the matter in the context of EU integration, parliamentary control over fiscal policy is what separates a (constitutional) exercise of sovereignty from an (unconstitutional) abrogation of constitutional identity.[481]

1.3.1.1   Three Tests for Fiscal Sovereignty

This book extracts three tests for evaluating whether a proposed legal arrangement coheres with the limits of Member State fiscal sovereignty under European constitutional identity case law:

[1.3.1.2] A *restriction* on budgetary sovereignty must not 'fetter the budget legislature to such an extent that the principle of democracy is violated', i.e., 'with the effect that it or a future Parliament can no longer exercise the right to decide the budget on its own';[482]

---

[478] *ESM (Estonia)* [105]–[106], [144]: 'the maximum limit of Estonia's [budgetary] obligations [...] cannot be changed without the consent of Estonia and without amending the Treaty'.

[479] *EFSF (Slovenia)* [24]–[25]: 'The constitutional requirement for the adoption of a law on the basis of which the state may borrow needs to be understood as a requirement that (future) obligations be precise or at least determinable [...] a decision on borrowing is always adopted by the National Assembly itself and [it] does not transfer this decision with general and unlimited authority'.

[480] *ESM (Estonia)* [127].

[481] Tuori and Tuori, *Eurozone Crisis*, 195 notes: 'Fiscal competences [...] have historically lain at the very core of the parliamentary regime and [...] constituted the vital pillars of representative democracy and parliamentary control over government.'

[482] *Euro Rescue Package (Germany)* [104]. See also, *ESM I (Germany)* [195]; *Lisbon (Poland)* [2.1]; *Joint stock companies (Lithuania)* IV[7] excerpted above, at n 468; *TCSG (Belgium)* [B.6.6] and [B.6.8.] excerpted above, at n 465; *Auxiliary Activities in the Public Sector (Croatia)* [33.4] (constitutional referendum bill unconstitutionally constrains legislative competences in issues relevant for the State Budget); *TSCG (France)* [30]–[31] (economic programmes under TSCG do not violate national sovereignty because 'such a programme does not have any binding consequences under national law'); *Crotty (Ireland)*, 783: fiscal policy is one of the areas of sovereignty where 'the State's organs

[1.3.1.3] A *delegation* of budgetary decision-making must not compromise the principle that 'the [national] Parliament remains the place in which autonomous decisions on revenue and expenditure are made';[483] and

[1.3.1.4] A finite financial *disposition* must not be of structural significance to the Parliament's right to decide on the budget such that it causes an irreversible prejudice to future majority decisions and cannot be reversed by an equivalent action by the Parliament in the future. The test applied is that 'the democratic process remains open and that legal re-evaluations may occur on the basis of other majority decisions and that an irreversible legal prejudice to future generations is avoided'.[484]

Although the burgeoning Member State case law on these principles appears remarkably convergent thus far, it must be said that these tests are quarried, first and foremost, from the leading German jurisprudence, and it is that jurisprudence which this section will expound upon to explain these tests. This is so for two reasons.

cannot contract to exercise in a particular procedure their policy-making roles or in any way to fetter powers bestowed unfettered by the Constitution' (further excerpted above, at n 462).

[483] *Euro Rescue Package (Germany)* [124]. See also, *TCSG (Belgium)* [B.8.3.] excerpted above, at n 465; *Pringle v. Ireland (Ireland)* [8.14] excerpted above, n 473; *Collins (Ireland)* excerpted above, at n 463; *TSCG (France)* excerpted above, at n 464; *Lisbon (Poland)* [2.1]; *Decision 2011/199/EU (Poland)* [4.1.3] and [7.3]; *Joint stock companies (Lithuania)* IV[7] excerpted above, at n 468; *EFSF (Slovenia)* [24]-[25]; *Judges' Remuneration (Latvia)* [8.1] and cases excerpted above, at nn 470-471; *Auxiliary Activities in the Public Sector (Croatia)* [33.4]; *ESM (Austria)* [104]-[105] excerpted above, n 475; *Opinion 13/2012 on the ESM (Finland)* excerpted above, n 476; *Opinion on the Six Pack (Finland)*, SuVL 11/2010 vp (Article 126 TFEU not an adequate legal basis for economic policies with a significant impact on Parliament's budgetary powers); *ESM (Estonia)* [127] excerpted above, at n 480; *EFSF (Slovenia)* [24]-[25] (further excerpted above, Section 1.3.1 at n 479) 'the fundamental power of the National Assembly [. . .] to decide on state revenue and expenditure' cannot be delegated – 'a decision on borrowing is always adopted by the National Assembly itself'.

[484] *ESM II (Germany)* [173]. See also *Pringle v. Ireland (Ireland)* [8.14] excerpted above, n 473; *Opinion 25/2011 on the ESM (Finland)*; *Opinion 13/2012 on the ESM (Finland)*; *ESM (Estonia)* [105]-[106], [144] excerpted above, n 478; *ESM (Austria)* excerpted above, n 475; *TCSG (Belgium)* [B.6.6.], 'Annual approval of the budget does not prevent parliaments from entering into multi-year commitments, provided these commitments are considered each year in the estimation and authorisation.' *EFSF (Slovenia)* [24]-[25]: the competence for state revenue and expenditure implies 'an upper limit that, despite the absence of an explicit constitutional provisions on a borrowing ceiling' means the legislature may not deplete or pledge the financial resource 'to a degree it would jeopardise the democratic life of the state'.

First, much of the legal architecture at issue in this book derives directly from German constitutional constraints. Price stability (Article 127(1) TFEU), the prohibition on monetary financing (Article 123 TFEU), the 'no bailout' rule (Article 125 TFEU) and the fiscal governance rules (Articles 121–126 TFEU) are 'parallel provisions' to the German Basic Law, and 'permanent constitutional requirements of German participation in the monetary union'.[485]

Second, the 'eternity clause' that grounds the German 'constitutional identity' jurisdiction is unusually strong and well-defined compared to other 'identity' provisions in Europe. It is the high-water mark of constitutional identity in Europe – and it is unamendable. While novel instruments proposed for EU fiscal federalism may trespass on constitutional identity in any number of countries, they will most likely cross the limits of Article 79(3) BL first. Article 79(3) states:

Amendments of this Constitution affecting the division of the Federation into *Länder*, their participation in principle in the legislative process, or the basic principles laid down in Articles 1 [Human Dignity] and 20 [Democratic and Social Federal State] shall be inadmissible.

This provision is a permanent feature of German – and European – constitutional heritage. It is, according to the BVerfG, an indelible consequence of history – 'a reaction to the historical experience of a creeping or abrupt erosion of the free substance of a democratic fundamental order'.[486] It permanently shields the highest constitutional principles of the German state – human dignity (Article 1 BL)[487] and the basic principles of the democratic social and federal State (Article 20 BL)[488] – from constitutional change.

Fiscal sovereignty falls primarily within the protection of the basic principles of the democratic and social federal state under Article 20. Article 20 states, in part:

(1) The Federal Republic of Germany is a democratic and social federal state.

---

[485] *ESM I (Germany)* [203].
[486] *ESM I (Germany)* [203].
[487] *Solange I (Germany)* [4]: 'The part of the Basic Law dealing with fundamental rights is an inalienable, essential feature of the valid Basic Law.'
[488] *Lisbon (Germany)* [192]: 'The principle of democracy may not be weighed against other legal interests; it is inviolable.'

(2) All state authority emanates from the people. It is exercised by the people through elections and voting and by specific organs of the legislature, the executive power and the judiciary.[489]

The principles of popular sovereignty and constitutional democracy in Article 20(2) secure the constitutional link between the act of voting in elections and the exercise of state power. As stated by the BVerfG: 'Article 20(2) sentence 2 guarantees in conjunction with art.79(3) that the exercise of state duties and the exercise of state powers can be traced back to the people of the state and are accounted for *vis-à-vis* the people.'[490]

This is in turn given substance by the right to vote in Article 38.[491] Article 38 states, in part:

(1) The deputies to the German House of Representatives [*Bundestag*] are elected in general, direct, free, equal and secret elections. They are representatives of the whole people not bound by orders and instructions, and subject only to their conscience.

(2) Anyone who has attained the age of eighteen years is entitled to vote; anyone who has attained majority is eligible for election.

The right to elect the *Bundestag* under Article 38(1) is a right to elect a parliament that remains accountable to the people which elect it.[492] This precludes legal commitments entered into by treaty 'if the result of this is that the people's democratic self-government is permanently restricted in such a way that central political decisions can no longer be made independently'.[493] In *ESM (Germany)*, the Court held:

A necessary condition for the safeguarding of political latitude in the sense of the core of identity of the constitution (art.20(1)-(2), art.79(3) BL) is that the budget legislature makes its decisions on revenue and expenditure free of other-directedness on the part of the bodies and of other Member States of the European Union and remains permanently 'the master of its decisions'.[494]

---

[489] Basic Law for the Federal Republic of Germany (Deutscher Bundestag, 2019) English translation available at: www.btg-bestellservice.de/pdf/80201000.pdf accessed 5 October 2020.

[490] *ESM II (Germany)* [234]. See also, *Weiss Decision (Germany)* [99].

[491] *Euro Rescue Package (Germany)* [120]; *Lisbon (Germany)* [151], [184]-[187]; *Weiss Decision (Germany)* [99].

[492] *Parliamentary Rights to Information (ESM and Euro Plus Pact) (Germany)* (2 BvE 4/11): BVerfGE 131, 151, English version at: www.bundesverfassungsgericht.de accessed 24 May 2020, [113]; *Brunner (Germany)* [35]; *Weiss Decision (Germany)* [99].

[493] *Euro Rescue Package (Germany)* [98], [101].

[494] *ESM I (Germany)* [197].

Any break in the 'chain of legitimation' between the right to vote under Article 38(2) and the exercise of state power under Article 20 will *prima facie* constitute an infringement of German constitutional identity under Article 79(3). If voters are no longer able to exercise the right to vote under Article 38(2) BL; if the right to vote is to be exercised by a method of voting other than the formula described in Article 38(1); if votes are no longer connected to the autonomous *Bundestag* in Article 38 (1); or if the *Bundestag* no longer possesses the substance of the power to rule through conferral or 'other-directedness' (Article 20(2) BL) – then the chain of legitimation will be broken.[495] What is guaranteed under the German Constitution is not just 'democracy' in an openly defined or purely formal sense.[496] It is 'self-determination in the exercise of public power' through a *specific* democratic formula.[497] It is the *substance of the power to rule*:

Article 38 [BL] protects the citizens with a right to elect the *Bundestag* from a loss of *substance of their power to rule*, which is fundamental to the structure of a constitutional state, by far-reaching or even comprehensive transfers of duties and powers of the *Bundestag,* above all to supranational institutions.[498]

Under Article 79(3) BL, the basic principles and constituent structures of the democratic social and federal state are inviolable.[499] They may not be weighed against any other legal interests (including the mandate of peace and integration and the constitutional principle of the openness towards EU law);[500] they cannot be narrowed or disposed of by constitutional amendment;[501] and they cannot be weighed against the 'constructive force of the mechanism of integration'.[502] They cannot be transcended in the name of public good under a Schmittian state of exception,[503] and so cannot be interpreted in the light of *effet utile* or *ultima ratio* justifications seen to underlie recent EU crisis measures – no

---

[495] *Brunner (Germany)* [4]–[5], [172], [341]; *Euro Rescue Package (Germany)* [98], [102], [120]; *ESM II (Germany)* [224], [230], [235]; *Lisbon (Germany)* [225]–[228]; *Weiss Decision (Germany)* [98]–[99].

[496] *Weiss Decision (Germany)* [99].

[497] *ESM I (Germany)* [192].

[498] *Brunner (Germany)* [4]–[5].

[499] *Lisbon (Germany)* [192]–[194].

[500] *Brunner (Germany)* [182]; *Lisbon (Germany)* [192]–[193].

[501] *Euro Rescue Package (Germany)* [101]; *ESM II (Germany)* [159].

[502] *Lisbon (Germany)* [214].

[503] Carl Schmitt, Political Theology: Four Chapters on the Concept of Sovereignty (MIT Press 1985), 5.

matter how meritorious.[504] As the BVerfG has stated, Article 79(3) does not require 'cases of imminent totalitarian seizure of power' for it to be exceeded.[505] Indeed, it is precisely that argument which Article 79(3) is meant to guard against.[506] In *Lisbon (Germany)*, the BVerfG held:

> The principle of democracy may not be weighed against other legal interests; it is inviolable. The constituent power of the Germans which gave itself the Basic Law wanted to set an insurmountable boundary to any future political development. Amendments to the Basic Law affecting the principles laid down in art.1 and art.20 of the Basic Law shall be inadmissible (art.79.3 of the Basic Law).[507]

How, then, is EU legislation to be squared with that formula? EU Parliamentary elections are not taken in the general, direct, free and equal manner prescribed by Article 38(1) BL; it is not the German people in Article 38(2) BL which exercise state power through the *Bundestag* in Article 38(1); and the European Parliament, the Council and the Commission are not the legislature and executive in Article 20(2) BL.[508]

The answer is that, within the context of the EU, constitutional identity is safeguarded by Article 23(1) BL. It states:

> To realize a unified Europe, Germany participates in the development of the European Union which is bound to democratic, rule of law, social, and federal principles as well as the principle of subsidiarity and provides a protection of fundamental rights essentially equivalent to that of this Constitution. The federation can, for this purpose and with the consent of the Senate [*Bundesrat*], delegate sovereign powers. Article 79(1) & (3) is applicable for the foundation of the European Union as well as for changes in its contractual bases and comparable regulations by which the content of this Constitution is changed or amended or by which such changes or amendments are authorized.[509]

This constitutional safeguard clause creates an 'exception' for democratic opinion-forming in ways different to that envisioned under Article 38 BL, but this only 'applies as far as the limit of the inviolable constitutional identity' of which Article 20 and its machinery (Article

---

[504] Paul Craig, 'Economic Governance and the Euro Crisis: Constitutional Architecture and Constitutional Implications' in Adams, Fabbrini and Larouche (eds), *Constitutionalization of European Budgetary Constraints*, 27.

[505] *Euro Rescue Package (Germany)* [10].

[506] Weiler, 'Demos', 236: 'Is it not just a little bit like the Weimer elections which democratically approved a non-democratic regime? Is it not the task of a constitutional court to be a counter balance to such self-defeating democratization?'

[507] *Lisbon (Germany)* [192].

[508] *Parliamentary Information (ESM & EPP) (Germany)* [96].

[509] German Basic Law (Deutscher Bundestag, 2019).

38) are a part.[510] In short, powers conferred on the union can be conferred up to the hilt of Article 79(3), but no further. In *Lisbon (Germany)*, the BVerfG explained:

The empowerment to embark on European integration permits a different shaping of political opinion-forming than the one determined by the Basic law for the Constitutional order. This applies *as far as the limit of the inviolable constitutional identity* (art.79.3). [...] The minimum standard protected by art.79.3 of the Basic Law must not fail to be achieved even by Germany's integration into supranational structures.[511]

In *Lisbon (Germany)*, the BVerfG enumerated a list of inalienable, essential powers so 'particularly sensitive for the ability of a constitutional state to democratically shape itself' that they comprise the substance of self-government and fall under the umbrella of the eternity clause.[512] These included fiscal competences, criminal law, monopoly of force, social living conditions, and decisions of cultural importance, such as family, education and religion.[513] Fiscal policy was among the most important of those powers. The BVerfG held:

Particularly sensitive for the ability of a constitutional state to democratically shape itself are [...] fundamental fiscal decisions on public revenue and public expenditure. [...] A transfer of the right of the Bundestag to adopt the budget and control its implementation by the government [would] violate the principle of democracy and the right to elect the German *Bundestag* in its essential content if the determination of the type and amount of the levies imposed on the citizen were supranationalised to a considerable extent. The German Bundestag must decide, in an accountable manner vis-à-vis the people, on the total amount of the burdens placed on citizens. The same applies correspondingly to essential state expenditure. In this area, the responsibility concerning social policy in particular is subject to the democratic decision-making process, which citizens want to influence through free and equal elections. [...] What is decisive, however, is that the overall responsibility, with sufficient political discretion regarding revenue and expenditure, can still rest with the German Bundestag.[514]

From this and the case law which follows, this book extracts three ways by which fiscal sovereignty may be denuded in violation of Articles 38, 20 and 79(3) BL.

---

[510] *Lisbon (Germany)* [195]–[196].
[511] *Lisbon (Germany)* [205], [225].
[512] *Lisbon (Germany)* [225]–[228].
[513] *Lisbon (Germany)* [225]–[228].
[514] *Lisbon (Germany)* [228]–[232].

1.3.1.2   Unlawful Restrictions on Fiscal Sovereignty

The first way in which the principle of democracy might be denuded is through formal *restrictions* on parliamentary budgetary powers, 'with the effect that it or a future *Bundestag* can no longer exercise the right to decide the budget on its own'.[515] As representatives of the people under Article 38(1), not bound by any orders or instructions, the *Bundestag* 'must retain control of fundamental budgetary decisions even in a system of intergovernmental administration'.[516] If the German *Bundestag* were to find itself in the role of 'mere subsequent enforcement', it could 'no longer exercise its overall budgetary responsibility'.[517] In *Euro Rescue Package*, the BVerfG stated:

> [F]undamental decisions on public revenue and public expenditure are part of the core of parliamentary rights in democracy. Article 38.1 excludes the possibility of depleting the legitimation of state authority and the influence on the exercise of that authority provided by the election by fettering the budget legislature to such an extent that the principle of democracy is violated.[518]

It should be emphasized that it is not, from the outset, undemocratic for the budget-setting executive to be fettered by a particular fiscal policy. In *ESM II*, the BVerfG accepted that a commitment to a particular fiscal policy may be made through agreeing corresponding obligations under international law.[519] The test for evaluating whether a fetter on budgetary autonomy amounts to an unconstitutional deprivation of sovereignty is whether control over that policy is relinquished, such that the fetter is not reversible by an equivalent act of the *Bundestag* in the future.[520] The test applied is that 'the democratic process remains open and that legal re-evaluations may occur on the basis of other majority decisions and that an irreversible legal prejudice to future generations is avoided'.[521]

1.3.1.3   Unlawful Conferral of Fiscal Sovereignty

The second way the substance of the power to rule might be depleted is through delegation or conferral of the powers of the parliament

---

[515] *ESM I (Germany)* [195]. See also, *ESM II (Germany)* [161]; *Weiss Decision (Germany)* [101].
[516] *ESM II (Germany)* [162].
[517] *ESM I (Germany)* [195]; *ESM II (Germany)* [161]–[162].
[518] *Euro Rescue Package (Germany)* [104].
[519] *ESM II (Germany)* [168]–[170].
[520] *Euro Rescue Package (Germany)* [124], [127].
[521] *ESM II (Germany)* [173].

itself.[522] The budgetary powers still exercised by the parliament must not be depleted to such a degree that the right to make legal re-evaluations of budgetary policy under Articles 38 and 20 BL is rendered meaningless.[523] The test in that regard is the same: A violation of the principle of democracy will occur 'if the German *Bundestag* relinquishes is parliamentary budget responsibility with the effect that it or a future *Bundestag* can no longer exercise the right to decide on the budget on its own responsibility'.[524] In *Euro Rescue Package*, the BVerfG held:

> The relevant factor for adherence to the principles of democracy is whether the German Bundestag remains the place in which autonomous decisions on revenue and expenditure are made, even with regard to international and European commitments.[525]

First and most obviously, this means the parliament cannot confer its competence in budgetary policy. A violation of the principle of democracy would occur if 'the type and amount of the levies imposed on the citizen were supranationalised to a considerable extent and thus the *Bundestag* would be deprived of its right of disposal'.[526]

Second, Articles 38 and 20 BL cannot simply be got-around by signing over the common finances of the citizenry by blank cheque. The *Bundestag* may not transfer its budgetary responsibility through 'imprecise authorisations' or mechanisms with 'incalculable burdens' that are tantamount to accepting liability for decisions by free will of other states.[527] The BVerfG has explicitly precluded the 'transfer union' or 'liability community' and instruments of loss-sharing in which budgetary dispositions are no longer determined by the autonomous exercise of the free will of the *Bundestag* in the manner required by Article 38 BL.[528] In *Euro Rescue Package*, the Court held:

> The *Bundestag* may not transfer its budgetary responsibility to other actors by means of imprecise budgetary authorisations. In particular it may not, even by statute, deliver itself up to any mechanisms with financial effect which [...] may result in incalculable burdens with budget relevance without prior mandatory consent, whether these are expenses or losses of revenue. [...] The *Bundestag*

---

[522] *ESM I (Germany)* [195]; *ESM II (Germany)* [161]–[165]; *Weiss Reference (Germany)* [129]; *Weiss Decision (Germany)* [101], [104].
[523] *Lisbon (Germany)* [151], [186].
[524] *Euro Rescue Package (Germany)* [121].
[525] *Euro Rescue Package (Germany)* [124].
[526] *Euro Rescue Package (Germany)* [126]. See also, *Weiss Reference (Germany)* [129].
[527] *ESM I (Germany)* [196]; *ESM II (Germany)* [163]; *Weiss Decision (Germany)* [227].
[528] See cases cited in Methods and Introduction, n 61.

must specifically approve every large-scale measure [...] involving public expenditure on the international or European level.[529]

1.3.1.4   Unlawful Impairments of Fiscal Sovereignty

Finally, even a finite disposition must not be so large that the *Bundestag* is no longer able to conduct economic policy on its own responsibility.[530] The right to vote under Article 38 would be as equally meaningless if the *Bundestag* elected to give over the entire endowment of the citizenry, in one lump sum, as it would be if it signed up to open-ended authorizations.

However, on this limb, the BVerfG exercises a high degree of curial deference where finite dispositions are concerned. The test applied to finite dispositions is a 'manifest overstepping of ultimate limits'[531] – that is, whether the amount of the disposition is 'of structural significance for parliament's right to decide on the budget, for example by giving guarantees the honouring of which may endanger budget autonomy'.[532]

In monetary terms, the Court has refrained from putting a number on this 'ultimate limit', but it seems nothing short of over half the federal budget will do. In *Euro Rescue Package (Germany)*, the pledging of a sum 'far greater than the largest federal budget item' and 'substantially exceeding half of the federal budget' did not deprive the *Bundestag* of its autonomy.[533] In *ESM I*, budget commitments of €190,024,800,000 (approximately 50% of all central government expenditure) did not exceed the legislature's margin of appreciation, so long as it did not constitute an open-ended commitment and did not deprive the parliament of the ability to shape the economic and social life of the state.[534]

There is a ceiling to this, however. In *Weiss (Germany)*, the BVerfG held that risk-sharing through the PSPP, 'which amounts to more than EUR 2 trillion [...] would affect the limits set by the overall budgetary responsibility of the German *Bundestag* [...] and be incompatible with Art. 79(3)'.[535]

---

[529] *Euro Rescue Package (Germany)* [125]–[128].
[530] *Euro Rescue Package (Germany)* [107]; *Weiss Decision (Germany)*, [227].
[531] *Euro Rescue Package (Germany)* [131]; *ESM II (Germany)* [174].
[532] *ESM I (Germany)* [198].
[533] *Euro Rescue Package (Germany)* [135].
[534] *ESM I (Germany)* [200], [240]; *ESM II (Germany)* [185].
[535] *Weiss Decision (Germany)* [227].

1.3.1.5 Permissible Limitations on Fiscal Sovereignty

From this case law, this book extracts the above-noted three tests (listed at the start of Section 1.3.1.1) for determining whether fiscal sovereignty is infringed under the leading German constitutional identity jurisprudence. This does not mean that the contours of other countries' jurisdictions are not lurking just behind.[536] However, given that the German tests are likely to remain the leading tests in this area, it is useful to highlight some room for manoeuvre through permissible limitations on fiscal sovereignty under these tests. Contrary to how Article 79(3) BL is sometimes perceived, 'constitutional identity' does not mean that all the core constitutional powers are absolutely and forever entombed at national level, with no capacity for delegation. There are three limits on the jurisdiction.

First, the words 'particularly sensitive' in *Lisbon (Germany)* indicate that not all 'state-founding elements' are included in the list of competences listed in that decision, and not all intrusions to that list will violate Article 79(3).[537] It is only if the competence is both particularly sensitive *and* the formula for democratic legitimation specified in the constitution is structurally compromised that constitutional identity is infringed.[538] For example, the expansion of QMV under the Lisbon Treaty did not infringe constitutional identity because the scope of conferral was controlled under Article 23 BL, and the essential powers under the umbrella of Article 20 were still exercised in accordance with Article 38 BL.[539]

Second, the enumeration of constitutional identity competences in *Lisbon (Germany)* does not mean that those core competences can never be delegated; it means that they cannot be conferred or delegated in a manner which breaks the chain of legitimation under the German constitution. There is a difference. For example, automatic budgetary liability under the 'capital calls' provisions of the ESM Treaty did not violate Article 38 BL, because the voting formula gave Germany an effective veto over each new disposition to the ESM. Similarly, monetary policy is lawfully conferred on the ECB because the conditions which apply to the ECB under Article

---

[536] It is clear the principles of budgetary autonomy 'should essentially have a very similar substance throughout the 28 Member States of the EU'. Ernits et al., 'Constitution of Estonia', 939.
[537] Preshova, 'Battleground or Meeting', 283.
[538] *Lisbon (Germany)* [242]–[245], [327].
[539] *Lisbon (Germany)* [250]–[253].

127 TFEU are the same as those that apply to the *Bundesbank* under Article 88 BL, so no usurpation of fiscal competence could occur.[540] The essential staple is that delegation is permitted, as long as this does not change the substance of the guarantee itself.[541]

Third, not all encroachments on 'state founding' powers will constitute a violation of democracy in its essential content.[542] For fiscal policy, this will only occur where a fiscal policy decision is not reversible by an equivalent action by the *Bundestag* and the degree of the infringement is of structural significance to Parliament's right to decide on the budget.[543] So, for example, we know from *Weiss (Germany)* that €2 trillion is too much, but in *ESM (Germany)*, the Court applied a test of proportionality and a margin of discretion to huge sums – approximately 50% of all central government expenditure – without this constituting a complete failure of budgetary autonomy.

1.3.2   Price Stability and Fiscal Discipline

The second constitutional boundary of European fiscal federalism pursued in this book is comprised of the fundamental guiding principles of price stability, sound public finances and a sustainable balance of payments binding on the mandate for EMU under Article 119(3) TFEU. These are the principles of the '*Stabilitätsgemeinschaft*' or 'Stability Community,' which limit the mandate for monetary union and define the decentralized model of fiscal federalism inscribed in the Treaties. Article 119(3) TFEU reads:

These activities [economic and monetary policy] of the Member States and the Union shall entail compliance with the following guiding principles: stable prices, sound public finances and monetary conditions and a sustainable balance of payments.

The first principle is price stability. Price stability is the first constitutional principle of EMU and the sole objective of EU monetary policy competence.[544]

---

[540] *Brunner (Germany)* [96]; *Weiss Reference (Germany)* [126]; *Weiss Decision (Germany)* [143].

[541] The same approach applies to human rights: *Solange II (Germany)*; *Banana Market (Germany)* (2 BvL 1/97) BVerfGE 102, 147 English version at www.bundesverfassungsgericht.de accessed 18 June 2014.

[542] Dieter Grimm, 'Defending Sovereign Statehood against Transforming the Union Into a State' (2009) 5 EuConst 369. See, for example, *Honeywell (Germany)* [50].

[543] *ESM II (Germany)* [235].

[544] See Chapter 2, Section 2.2.1 and sources cited.

The second and third guiding principles, sound public finances and sustainable balance of payments, are principles of fiscal and economic policy – competences of the Member States. Sound public finances means that Member States must run a sound fiscal policy that avoids excessive public debts or sovereign defaults with adverse spillovers on monetary policy.

Sustainable balance of payments means they must run a sound economic policy so that the external deficit of the country as a whole does not become unsustainable, impoverishing the country and leading to the same result.

Hereafter, this book generally refers to these two principles together under the single term 'fiscal discipline'.[545]

These principles, price stability and fiscal discipline, inform the entire legal architecture of fiscal federalism under Articles 119–127 TFEU. The design of this architecture is discussed in Chapter 2, but it is sufficient to remark here that the principles of the *Stabilitätsgemeinschaft* are a constitutional stipulation of the EU's conferred competence in monetary policy and economic coordination. As stated in *Brunner (Germany)*:

Article [119 TFEU] sets up the guiding principles for member-States' activities the maintenance of price stability, sound public finances and monetary conditions, and a sustainable balance of payments. [. . .] This conception of the currency union as a community based on stability *is the basis and subject-matter of the German Act of Accession.* If the monetary union should not be able to develop on a continuing basis [. . .] within the meaning of the agreed mandate for stabilization, it would be abandoning the Treaty conception.[546]

The fundamental principles of the *Stabilitätsgemeinschaft* have been linked by the BVerfG to the independence of the ECB,[547] price stability,[548] the prohibition on monetary financing,[549] the 'no bailout' clause[550] and the Stability and Growth Pact.[551] In particular, the BVerfG has warned that the principles of *Stabilitätsgemeinschaft* would be violated – in turn

---

[545] As noted in Methods and Introduction, n 21, this book follows the approach of EU policy documents in using the terms 'economic' and 'fiscal' policy interchangeably to describe the use of government revenue, debt or expenditure to influence the economy.

[546] *Brunner (Germany)* [89]–[90] (emphasis added).

[547] Art. 130 TFEU. *ESM I (Germany)* [203]; *Weiss Reference (Germany)* [103].

[548] Art. 127 TFEU. *Brunner (Germany)* [89]–[90].

[549] Art. 123 TFEU. *Gauweiler Reference (Germany)* [32]; *Weiss Reference (Germany)* [68], [78].

[550] Art. 125 TFEU. *Euro Rescue Package (Germany)* [129].

[551] Art. 121, 126 TFEU. *ESM I (Germany)* [203].

violating Articles 20 and 79(3) of Germany's constitutional identity – if the Union should become a 'liability community' through the 'direct or indirect communitarisation of state debts'.[552]

This section will explain how these principles reflect deeper constitutional boundaries underlying the EU legal order as a whole.

1.3.2.1   Price Stability

Under Articles 3(1)(c), 119(2) and 127 TFEU, and Articles 2–3 and 17 to 24 of the Statute of the ESCB, the ECB's monetary policy competence and all of the ECB's instruments are bound to the primary objective of price stability (defined as 2% inflation by the ECB Governing Council). Subject to that objective, it may also 'support' economic policies which contribute to the aims of the Union, but it can pursue none of its own.[553]

This, too, is a restriction carved directly from the German Basic Law.[554] Article 88 BL states:

The Federation establishes a note-issuing currency bank as the *Bundesbank*. Its tasks and powers can, in the context of the European Union, be transferred to the European Central Bank which is independent and primarily bound by the purpose of securing stability of prices.[555]

Article 88 permits conferral of monetary competence on the ECB only in *so far as* it remains independent and bound to price stability. Unlike the Bank of Canada,[556] the Bank of England[557] or the United States Federal Reserve,[558] for example, the ECB can have no mandate for financial stability. Not because the EU legislator would not allow it, but because the German Basic Law does not allow the German legislator to confer it.

Since *Brunner* v. *EU Treaty (Germany)*, the primacy of price stability has been central to the constitutionality of Germany's ongoing participation in the EMU under Article 79(3)BL.[559] The BVerfG has held, for instance, that 'The Union Treaty governs the monetary union as a community

---

[552] *ESM I (Germany)* [203] and cases cited above, in Methods and Introduction, n 61.
[553] Tolek Petch, 'The Compatibility of Outright Monetary Transactions with EU Law' (2013) 7 LFMR 13, 14.
[554] *Brunner (Germany)* [85]; *Gauweiler Reference (Germany)* [32]; *Weiss Decision (Germany)* [143].
[555] German Basic Law (Deutscher Bundestag, 2019).
[556] *Bank of Canada Act*, R.S.C. 1985 c.B-2, preamble and s. 11.
[557] Bank of England Act 1998 c. 11, s. 11.
[558] Federal Reserve Act of 1913, ch 6, 38 Stat. 251, codified at 12 USC. ch 3, s. 2A
[559] *Brunner (Germany)* [85].

which is *permanently obliged* to maintain stability and, in particular, to *guarantee* the stability of the value of the currency.'[560] A development contrary to that mandate would violate the conditions subject to which monetary policy was conferred, mandating 'withdrawal from the Community in the event of the community based on stability failing to materialise'.[561]

Article 88 BL is not, in and of itself, part of the German constitutional identity shielded by the eternity clause in Article 79(3) BL. Article 88 could be amended and it would pose no further constraint on conferral. An ordinary breach of that provision will first fall to BVerfG's *ultra vires* review jurisdiction, under which the BVerfG will afford a margin of appreciation to an *ultra vires* act unless it is 'structurally significant' to the division of competences.[562]

However, Article 88 does shield other constitutional provisions which *are* linked to Article 79(3) BL. These are, specifically, the right to property under Article 14 (protected by Article 1 BL), which guards against the expropriation of value from money-holders through inflation; and the basic principles of the democratic state under Article 20 BL, which protects the constituent power against unauthorized or open-ended financial dispositions.[563]

The reason Article 88 shields these principles is that, unlike federal banks in Canada, the United States or Switzerland, the funding structure of the ECB has the potential to circumvent parliamentary control of budgetary policy. This is because the ECB is financed by all EMU Member States in accordance with the ESCB capital key. This is unlike the Bank of Canada, the United States Federal Reserve and the Swiss National Bank, which are not financed by the contributions of their provinces, states or cantons. When the United States Federal Reserve conducts bond purchase operations, for example, it purchases the bonds of a separate *federal* treasury, independently of state treasuries. The bonds are not guaranteed by any state governments, and so 'The Fed is not bailing out a cash-strapped country [and] distributing risks among the taxpayers with an excellent credit rating.'[564] In the United

---

[560] *Brunner (Germany)* [89] (emphasis added).
[561] *Brunner (Germany)* [89].
[562] See above, n 106.
[563] *Weiss Decision (Germany)* [98]–[115], [222]–[228]. Pernice, 'Multilevel Constitutionalism', 721.
[564] Editorial, 'Bundesbank President on ECB Bond Purchases: Too Close to State Financing Via the Money Press' *Der Spiegel* (29 August 2012).

States, 'the printing presses cannot be used to provide particular states or regions with credit at below-market interest rates',[565] and purchases of public sector securities 'do not lead to redistributional effects among the individual states of the US'.[566]

In the EU, by contrast, deliberately targeting the bonds of, say, Greece would use taxpayer contributions from all countries to assume risks incurred by one country and, as the *Bundesbank* states: 'Monetary policymakers have no authorisation to redistribute such risks or burdens among the taxpayers of various euro-area countries.'[567] Because the *Bundestag* backstops the *Bundesbank*, an expenditure campaign by the ECB for an economic objective – like bond market stability or staving off state defaults – would commit parliamentary funds to an economic policy without a parliamentary vote. For this reason, a violation of Articles 123 or 127 TFEU will not only be *ultra vires* Article 88 BL, but may constitute a structurally significant infringement of constitutional identity.[568]

1.3.2.2 Fiscal Discipline: Sound Budgetary Policies and a Sustainable Balance of Payments

In the field of economic policy, the principles of 'fiscal discipline' – sound budgetary policy and a sustainable balance of payments – manifest in the legal architecture under Articles 119–126 TFEU. That architecture is examined in Chapter 2, however it suffices to state here that the model entrenches independent financial liability and the budgetary autonomy of national parliaments. For this reason, these provisions are also constitutional stipulations of Germany's participation in EMU. As stated in *Weiss Reference (Germany)*:

The current European integration agenda is based on an understanding of the monetary union as a community of stability; for [Germany], this is an essential prerequisite for its membership in the monetary union. Most notably, this safeguards the German *Bundestag's* overall responsibility for the budget.[569]

---

[565] Sinn, *Euro Trap*, 5–6.
[566] Dietrich Murswiek, 'ECB, ECJ, Democracy and the Federal Constitutional Court' (2014) 15 German LJ 147, 150.
[567] Deutsche Bundesbank, 'Monthly Report: August 2011' (2011) 63 Deutsche Bundesbank Monthly Report 165.
[568] *Gauweiler Reference (Germany)* [43]; *Gauweiler Decision (Germany)* [188]; *Weiss Decision (Germany)* [98]–[99], [110], [116], [157]–[159].
[569] *Weiss Reference (Germany)* [68], [103].

It should be emphasized here, too, that while fiscal discipline and Articles 121–126 TFEU safeguard the German constitutional identity, 'not every single manifestation of the stability community is guaranteed by [Article 20 BL] in conjunction with art.79(3)'.[570] Violations are first and foremost a matter of *ultra vires* review, not constitutional identity, unless it *also* violates one of the tests set out in Section 1.3.1 of this book.

In practice, however, it may make no difference how many lines are crossed since a violation of the *Stabilitätsgemeinschaft* that results in automatic financial liability or deprives parliamentary control over fiscal policy will also lead to a violation of Articles 38, 20 and 79(3) BL, and the consequences of both *ultra vires* and identity review are invalidity.[571] So, for example, as a matter of economics, a failure to achieve budgetary discipline implies monetary financing or debt mutualization, and this offends the right to property (Article 14 BL) and the right to vote (Article 38 BL), which *are* part of the constitutional identity in conjunction with Article 1 BL (Human Dignity) and Article 20 BL (Basic Principles), and are *not* amendable under Article 79(3) BL. Hence, even if no individual act of fiscal indiscipline will vitiate the *Stabilitätsgemeinschaft*, the overall system of fiscal federalism chosen for the EMU must be based on fiscal discipline and individual financial responsibility if it is to ultimately remain within its constitutional boundaries. However, unless the three tests set out in Section 1.3.1 are also met, the test applied here is different: It is whether the Union violated the 'community based on stability (*Stabilitätsgemeinschaft*) [that] is the basis and subject-matter of the German Act of Accession [. . .] within the meaning of the agreed mandate for stabilisation'.[572]

1.4   Conclusions: Permanent Constraints on European Fiscal Federalism

The constitutional boundaries extracted in this chapter are real, they are permanent, and they exert real positive force on the boundaries of EU law. Constitutional courts have stated (and demonstrated) that nascent machineries of fiscal federalism will be invalidated if they trespass

---

[570] *ESM I (Germany)* [204].
[571] *ESM I (Germany)* [203]–[205]; *Weiss Decision (Germany)* [116]–[119], [154]–[157], [163], [234].
[572] *Brunner (Germany)* [90].

on constitutional fiscal sovereignty or exceed the boundaries of conferral, and this study must take them at their word. This conclusion derives from three cumulative analyses.

[1.1] First, the EU is a 'federation of states', possessed of a top-down federal hierarchy with a legal supremacy greater than any individual expression of Member State sovereignty on one hand, yet on the other hand derived from the confederate authority of national orders which sanction its reach. However, the reality that concerns this book is that, whether one adopts a Kelsenian, normative or positivist approach, national constitutions (as interpreted by national constitutional courts) remain the reference point for validity of law in Member State legal systems.

[1.2] In the EU, national constitutional orders profess to impose two limits on the EU's conferred powers: First, that they have the jurisdiction to assert, through Treaty ratification and *ultra vires* review, what powers they have and have not conferred on the Union – the so-called *Kompetenz-Kompetenz*. Second, that their own 'constitutional identity' principles determine the absolute limits of Union law. These assertions pose a valid constitutional, normative and positivist description of the limits of the EU legal order.

[1.3] Under these jurisdictions, two substantive constitutional boundaries will bear upon any model of European fiscal federalism. [1.3.1] The first is Member State fiscal sovereignty. Not only have parliamentary competences in economic and fiscal policy not been conferred on the Union, but, according to the BVerfG, they cannot ever be so conferred without abrogating the 'Basic Principles' of the 'Democratic State' (Article 20) and violating the 'eternity clause' (Article 79(3)) of the 1949 German Basic Law. Numerous other constitutional courts have drawn similar boundaries around fiscal sovereignty.[573] The tests applied by this book in that regard are:

> [1.3.1.2] No unlawful *restrictions* of fiscal sovereignty: A restriction on budgetary sovereignty must not 'fetter the budget legislature to such an extent that the principle of democracy is violated', that is, 'with the effect that it or a future Parliament can no longer exercise the right to decide the budget on its own';[574]

---

[573] See above, Section 1.3.1, nn 459–480, Section 1.3.1.1, nn 482–484.

[574] *Euro Rescue Package (Germany)* [104] and sources cited above, Section 1.3.1.1, n 482.

[1.3.1.3] No unlawful *conferral* of fiscal sovereignty: A delegation or conferral of financial competences must not compromise the principle that 'the [national] Parliament remains the place in which autonomous decisions on revenue and expenditure are made';[575] and

[1.3.1.5] No structural *impairments* of fiscal sovereignty: even a finite financial disposition must not structurally impair the parliament's right to decide on the budget and shape the economic and social life of the state in the future.[576]

[1.3.2] The second constitutional boundary is comprised of the fundamental guiding principles of price stability and fiscal discipline (sound budgetary policy and sustainable balance of payments) impressed upon the architecture in Articles 119–127 TFEU. Articles 119–127 TFEU are not in themselves part of Member State 'constitutional identity'; however, the architecture of the *Stabilitätsgemeinschaft* indirectly shields basic principles of the democratic state (Article 20 BL) and human dignity (Article 1 BL), which *are* part of the constitutional identity shielded by the German 'eternity clause' and are *not* amendable, *lex lata* or *de lege ferenda*.

Having identified these principles underlying the boundaries of the EU legal order in economic and monetary policy, Chapter 2 will seek to examine how they inhere in the legal architecture inscribed in the EU Treaties as a matter of EU law.

---

[575] *Euro Rescue Package (Germany)* [124] and sources cited above, Section 1.3.1.1, n 483.
[576] *ESM II (Germany)* [173] and sources cited above, Section 1.3.1.1, n 484.

2 The Maastricht Architecture of European Fiscal Federalism

Chapter 1 identified two constitutional boundaries underlying Economic and Monetary Union (EMU): Fiscal sovereignty, which binds acts of conferral at the base of the EU legal order; and the fundamental principles of price stability and fiscal discipline, which bind the mandate for EMU under Article 119(3) TFEU itself. This chapter identifies how these constitutional boundaries inhere in the legal design of EMU, and explains the basic principles of fiscal federalism theory inscribed in Title VIII (Economic and Monetary Policy) of Part III of the TFEU for their attainment.

Section 2.1 begins by outlining the teleology of EMU and familiarizing the reader with the main technical inputs for the *travaux préparatoires* at Maastricht.

Section 2.2 conducts the task of identifying where the constitutional boundaries pursued in this book underlie the construction of EMU in Articles 119–127 TFEU. That construction follows a blueprint for a 'classical model' or 'market-preserving' model of fiscal federalism that is well-established in theory and well-evidenced in history. By those provisions, EMU rests on four principles:

[2.2.1] Price stability – under Articles 119(2), 127(1) TFEU, and Articles 2–3 and 17 to 24 of the Statute of the ESCB, EU monetary institutions and all of their instruments are bound to the objective of price stability, without competence in economic policy;

[2.2.2] Fiscal discipline – the fundamental guiding principles of budgetary discipline and a sustainable balance of payments under Article 119(3) TFEU are necessary to ensure financial stability in a decentralized EMU;

106

[2.2.3] Fiscal sovereignty – under Articles 2(3), 5(1), and 120–126 TFEU, the EU has no competence in economic policy. Member States have complete fiscal sovereignty, left to their devices outside the EU legal order and responsible for their own budgetary policies;[1] and

[2.2.4] Market discipline – under Articles 121–126 TFEU, Member States are subject to hard budget constraints and exposed to market discipline for the achievement of these principles.[2]

Of these principles, it is the latter two which define the architecture of European fiscal federalism in Articles 121–126 of Chapter 1 (Economic Policy) of Title VIII, Part III of the TFEU.

Section 2.3 examines that technical model of fiscal federalism inscribed in the Treaties since Maastricht. It explains that Articles 121–126 TFEU are based on three criteria for establishing 'market discipline' in a federal system bound by the fiscal sovereignty of its Member States: Hard budget constraints, full information on Member States' liabilities and creditworthiness, and policy correction. Articles 121–126 TFEU comprise three interlocking mechanisms for market discipline:

[2.3.1] **The Prohibition on Financial Assistance** (Articles 122–125 TFEU, ex 100–103 TEC) prohibits Member States from obtaining privileged financing from financial institutions (Article 124 TFEU), from the ECB (Article 123 TFEU), and from each other or the Union (Article 125 TFEU). The effect of this interlocking framework is that Member States are subject to hard budget constraints and unable to access finance other than under conditions of market discipline.

[2.3.2] **The Multilateral Surveillance Procedure (MSP)** (Article 121 TFEU, ex 99 TEC), or the 'preventative arm' of the Stability and Growth Pact (SGP),[3] institutionalizes the surveillance system established for convergence under a non-binding 'soft law' method of

---

[1] Dariusz Adamski, 'Europe's (Misguided) Constitution of Economic Propserity' (2013) 50 CMLR 47, 62: fiscal sovereignty is the 'implicit crux' of the European economic constitution.

[2] *Gauweiler (AG Cruz-Villalón)* [131], [191]; *Pringle v. Ireland* [135]. See Section 2.2.4 and Chapter 8, Section 8.1.1 on 'market discipline' and Section 2.3 and Chapter 8, Section 8.1.2 on 'hard budget constraints' as a requirement for market discipline.

[3] Amendments to the SGP in 2005 and 2011 are discussed in Chapters 3 and 6. This chapter is concerned with the SGP as originally enacted by Council Regulation (EC) No 1466/97 of 7 July 1997 on the strengthening of the surveillance of budgetary positions and the surveillance and coordination of economic policies [1997] OJ L 209/1; Council Regulation (EC) No 1467/97 of 7 July 1997 on the speeding up and clarifying the implementation of the excessive deficit procedure [1997] OJ L 209/6.

coordination known as the Open Method of Coordination (OMC).[4] It is designed to support market discipline by ensuring that imbalances do not accrue hidden to markets, electorates and stakeholders.[5]

[2.3.3] **The Excessive Deficit Procedure (EDP)** (Article 126 TFEU, ex 104 TEC), now the 'corrective arm' of the SGP, provides a multilateral sanctioning framework by which EMU governments can sanction 'excessive deficits' exceeding 3% of GDP or 'excessive debts exceeding 60% of GDP.[6] According to the Commission, by levying fines and promulgating recommendations, the EDP is designed to 'result in an increasing market pressure on this country (market asks a higher price on its debt) to adopt corrective measures in favour of fiscal discipline'.[7]

2.1   The Teleology of European Economic and Monetary Union

Since the late nineteenth century, successive generations of European liberal economists have argued for the achievement of two conditions for the optimal allocation of production factors in Europe, one economic and one monetary – the removal of economic barriers to trade and currency convertibility.[8]

The removal of economic barriers to trade began in 1951 with the Treaty of Paris and the establishment of the European Coal and Steel Community (ECSC),[9] followed by the Treaty of Rome in 1957

---

[4] See Dermot Hodson and Imelda Maher, 'The Open Method as a New Mode of Governance' (2001) 39 JCMS 719; Mark Dawson, 'The Ambiguity of Social Europe in the Open Method of Coordination' (2009) 34 EL Rev 55; Dermot Hodson, *Governing the Euro Area in Good Times and Bad* (Oxford University Press, 2011), 78–94.

[5] See Section 2.3, nn 101–109, and Sections 2.3.2 and 2.3.3.

[6] Art. 126(11) TFEU.

[7] European Commission, 'A Stability Pact to Ensure Budgetary Discipline in EMU (Note for the Monetary Committee) II/163/96-EN, 18 March 1996, 15–16.

[8] Andreas Predöhl, 'The Theory of Location in Its Relation to General Economics' (1928) 36 JPE 371; Friedrich Hayek, 'The Economic Conditions of Interstate Federalism' in Friedrich Hayek (ed.), *Individualism & Economic Order* (University of Chicago Press, 1948), 255–272; Gottfried Haberler, 'Economic Aspects of a European Customs Union' (1949) 11 World Politics 431; Wilhelm Röpke, *International Order and Economic Integration* (D Reidel Publishing Company, 1959); Andreas Grotewold, 'West Germany's Economic Growth' (1973) 63 Ann Assoc Am Geogr 353, 354. See John Gillingham, *European Integration* (Cambridge University Press, 2003), 6–16.

[9] Treaty Instituting the European Coal and Steel Community, Paris, 18 April 1951, 261 UNTS 140. For a detailed history: John Gillingham, *Coal, Steel, and the Rebirth of Europe, 1945–1955* (Cambridge University Press, 1991).

and the establishment of the European Economic Community (EEC).[10] European officialdom often describes monetary union as 'implicit' in these initial stages of integration.[11] The Commission has, since 1962, repeated the refrain that economic integration 'would be incomplete, and therefore possibly ineffective, if no comparable action were undertaken in the field of monetary policy'.[12]

However, until the Single European Act (1985),[13] the refrain that a single currency was somehow necessary for a common market was generally seen by EEC central bankers as 'a stretch'.[14] The Treaty of Rome establishing the common market did not give the EEC any competence in monetary policy. At the time the EEC was born, monetary union seemed 'as utopian as unnecessary' – and possibly harmful.[15] In 1988, *Bundesbank* President Karl Otto Pöhl warned, presciently:

In a monetary union with irreversibly fixed exchange rates the weak would become ever weaker and the strong ever stronger. We would thus experience great tensions in the real economy of Europe.[16]

The reason for this is a principle of monetary economics and Optimum Currency Area (OCA) theory known as the 'Mundell-Fleming trilemma' or the 'impossible trinity'.[17] There is no doubt that fluctuating exchange rates divide national economies and distort the optimal location of

---

[10] Treaty Establishing the European Economic Community (Treaty of Rome), 25 March 1957, 298 UNTS 250.

[11] See Gillingham, *European Integration*, 271 (quoting Tommaso Padoa-Schioppa).

[12] Commission of the EEC, Memorandum of 24 October 1962 on the action programme of the Community for the second stage (Memorandum) COM(62) 300, para 127.

[13] See below, n 36.

[14] Harold James, *Making the European Monetary Union* (Princeton University Press, 2014), 42.

[15] Robert Schütze, *European Union Law* (Cambridge University Press, 2018), 776. See Gillingham, *European Integration*, 269–275.

[16] James, *Making EMU*, 232. See also Ferdinand Protzman, 'Germany's Top Banker Gives Europe a Warning' New York Times (20 March 1991) www.nytimes.com/1991/03/20/b usiness/germany-s-top-banker-gives-europe-a-warning.html accessed 22 August 2016.

[17] This was developed in three seminal papers: Marcus Fleming, 'Domestic Financial Policies Under Fixed and Under Floating Exchange Rates' (1962) 9 IMF Staff Papers 369; Robert Mundell, 'The Monetary Dynamics of International Adjustment under Fixed and Flexible Exchange Rates' (1960) 75 QJ Econ 227; Robert Mundell, 'Capital Mobility and Stabilization Policy under Fixed and Flexible Exchange Rates' (1963) 29 Can J Econ Polit Sci 475. For an accessible summary: The Economist, 'The Mundell-Fleming Trilemma' (27 August 2016) www.economist.com/schools-brief/2016/08/27/two-out-of-three-aint-bad accessed 22 November 2020.

economic factors.[18] A manufacturer seeking to source inputs from across a border cannot compare prices or contract to pay in the vendor's currency if it is fluctuating wildly. It must not be missed, however, that what is required for a single market is not a single currency.[19] What is required is currency convertibility. Currency convertibility in turn requires exchange rate stability, and exchange rate stability between heterogeneous economies requires independent monetary policies.

This is the impossible trinity. Unless countries meet the conditions of an 'optimum currency area' (which it is widely accepted the EU does not),[20] independent states with heterogeneous economic characteristics cannot have fixed exchange rates, independent monetary policies and free capital flows simultaneously. They can only ever have two out of the three. This is because maintaining cross-border price stability is only tenable where central banks are capable of affecting the value of currency so as to keep it on a level plane with other countries with different economic characteristics. There are two main mechanisms for doing so: (1) the interest rate set by the central bank for borrowing by eligible deposit-taking institutions (known as the interest rate channel) and (2) the quantity of base money.[21] Neither will work if using one causes investors to rush inwards or outwards from the country with their money. Therefore, in order to (1) maintain a fixed exchange rate, the central bank must be able to (2) affect the quantity of base money and the cost of credit through the adjustment of interest rates, and (3) control the money supply through capital controls if necessary. It is impossible to have fixed exchange rates without independent interest rates *and* capital controls. As will become relevant in Chapter 3, in the absence of capital controls, an increase in the interest rate intended to absorb money in the system may have the opposite effect: as capital

[18] Commission of the EC, *One Market, One Money* (European Economy No 44, 1990), 87–100; Miroslav Jovanović, *European Economic Integration: Limits and Prospects* (Taylor & Francis, 2002), 43–44, 52–53; De Grauwe, *Economics of Monetary Union*, 56–59, 61–67.

[19] Jacques Delors, *Report on Economic and Monetary Union in the European Community (The Delors Report)* (Committee for the Study of Economic and Monetary Union, 1989), para 23.

[20] De Grauwe, *Economics of Monetary Union*, 72–99. On OCA theory see below, n 59.

[21] Base money consists of the quantity of currency in circulation and held in commercial bank reserves (which includes sight deposits and accounts deposited with the central bank). The interest rate channel is the effect of the interest rate on the cost of capital. Through the credit channel, an increase in the money supply to banks increases the supply of loans to the economy. Karl Brunner and Allan Meltzer, 'Money Supply' in Benjamin Friedman and Frank Hahn (eds), *Handbook of Monetary Economics* (Elsevier, 1990), 357; Benjamin M Friedman and Kenneth N Kuttner, 'Implementation of Monetary Policy: How Do Central Banks Set Interest Rates?' in Benjamin M Friedman and Michael Woodford (eds), *Handbook of Monetary Economics* (Elsevier, 2010), 1345.

moves in order to seek greater returns, capital inflows may actually increase the money supply in an area that is already experiencing high inflation.[22] The same is true in reverse: attempting to decrease the value of currency through lower interest rates may trigger an outflow of capital as it flees for a higher rate of return.

In short, independent monetary policies are required for exchange rate stability between countries with heterogeneous economic characteristics.

For this reason, until 1992, monetary cooperation took place entirely outside the European legal order. Until 1971, Bretton Woods required each country to maintain fixed parities (±1%) using the dollar pegged to gold at $35 per ounce,[23] and the European currency 'Snake' (1972–1979)[24] and European Monetary System (EMS) (1979–1992) required European central banks to maintain the value of their currencies within a ±2.25% band (±6% for some).[25] Each of these fulfilled the theoretical requisites of economic integration, and none occurred within the EEC legal order.[26] The impossible trinity was preserved. A 1985 Federal Reserve study parsing the stability of the EMS, for example, found that EEC exchange rate stability was dependent on capital controls.[27]

Throughout these decades, the Commission continued to push its thesis that the single market required monetary union. In 1962 it asserted that monetary union was necessary for the 'cohesion of the Common Market'.[28] In 1969 the Commission issued the *Barre Report*

---

[22] Jovanović, *Economic Integration*, 62; James, *Making EMU*, 325.

[23] This made European monetary integration unnecessary: Ungerer, *A Concise History of European Monetary Ingegration: From EPU to EMU* (Quorum Books, 1997), 46; Gillingham, *European Integration*, 59.

[24] Agreement of 10 April 1972 between the Central Banks of the Member States of the EEC on the narrowing of the margins of fluctuation between Community currencies (Basel Accord), [1974] EC Bulletin Supplement.

[25] The EMS band was assessed on a Parity Grid of bilateral rates evaluated in European Currency Units (ECUs). See Agreement of 13 March 1979 between the central banks of the Member States of the EEC, in *Compendium of Community Monetary Texts* (Monetary Committee, 1986) 47. See Jacques Van Ypersele and Jean-Claude Koeune, *The European Monetary System* (European Communities, 1985).

[26] These and the European Payments Union (EPU) (1951–1958) are often credited with the post-WWII growth patterns on which subsequent EC treaties would be based. See Barry Eichengreen, *The European Economy since 1945* (Princeton University Press, 2007), 84–85; Wilhelm Nölling, *Monetary Policy in Europe After Maastricht* (Palgrave Macmillan, 1993), 38–41, 46–56; Gillingham, *European Integration*, 39–40, 53; James, *Making EMU*, 36–43, and sources cited above, n 23.

[27] Kenneth Rogoff, 'Can Exchange Rate Predictability Be Achieved without Monetary Convergence: Evidence from the EMS' (1985) 28 Eur Econ Rev 93. See James, *Making EMU*, 206-207.

[28] Commission, Memorandum of 24 October 1962, paras 127–130.

charting full monetary union.[29] In 1970, the *Werner Report* proposed a complete monetary union with centralized control over national budgets and extensive fiscal transfers.[30] In 1971, the Commission endorsed the *Werner Report* and submitted its own proposals for EMU.[31] When that failed, new proposals were promulgated in 1975, 1977 and 1978.[32]

None of these proposals led to monetary union. In 1964, side meetings at the BIS between EEC Central bankers were institutionalized as the 'Committee of Governors of the Central Banks of the EEC' (Committee of Governors), but this remained an appendage of the Bretton Woods monetary system, 'not an EEC institution'.[33] In 1978 the EMS was promulgated by a Council Resolution, but in legal terms it remained another 'soft law' agreement between central banks, outside the EEC legal order.[34] At no point had any of the intergovernmental monetary arrangements constituted a 'monetary embodiment of the EEC'.[35]

Such was the state of affairs until 1985, when Commission President Jacques Delors launched the '1992' programme with the humble aim of completing the internal market, resulting in the Single European Act (SEA) in 1986.[36] On its face, the SEA 'was not very ambitious' and asked little in the way of transfers of sovereignty.[37] It contained a 'hidden agenda', however.[38] This was so because at the heart of the SEA was complete capital liberalization.[39] As noted above, a 1985 Federal Reserve

---

[29] Commission of the EEC, 'Memorandum to the Council on the Coordination of Economic Policies and Monetary Cooperation Within the Community' (Memorandum) (Barre Report I) COM(69) 150; Commission of the EEC, 'Memorandum and Proposals to the Council on the Establishment by Stages of Economic and Monetary Union' (Memorandum) (Barre Report III) COM(70) 1250.

[30] Pierre Werner, *Report on the Realization by Stages of Economic and Monetary Union in the Community (Werner Report)* (EC Bulletin 11 supplement, 1970), 19.

[31] Commission of the EEC, '*Communication et propositions de la Commission au Conseil relatives à l'institution par eetapes de l'union économique et monétaire* [1970] OJ C 140/20.

[32] James, *Making EMU*, 146–150; Loukas Tsoukalis, *The Politics and Economics of European Monetary Integration* (George Allen & Unwin, 1977), 159–168; Report of the Study Group 'Economic and Monetary Union 1980' [1975] II/675/3/74 – E fin; Commission of the EEC, *Report on European Union* COM(75) 400; Roy Jenkins, *Memorandum for the European Council* (Copenhagen, 7–8 April, 1978).

[33] James, *Making EMU*, 53, 56–58.

[34] It was a 'non-act' adopted by a 'non-body': David Edward and Robert Lane, *Edward and Lane on European Union Law* (Edward Elgar, 2013), 845.

[35] James, *Making EMU*, 109.

[36] Commission of the EC, 'Completing the Internal Market' (White Paper) COM(85) 310 final; Single European Act [1987] OJ L 169/1.

[37] Alina Kaczorowska, *European Union Law* (2nd ed., Routledge, 2011), 16.

[38] Kaczorowska, *EU Law* (2011), 19.

[39] Art. 26(2) TFEU, ex Art. 14(2) EC.

study had concluded that the EMS (the basis for price stability on the common market) was held together by capital controls.[40] Abolishing them, therefore, would invoke the 'impossible trinity' and 'might endanger the whole system'.[41] According to ECB historian Harold James, Delors was aware of this.[42] Shortly after the SEA was signed, Delors commissioned the *Padoa-Schioppa Report* spelling out the implications of capital liberalization – the impossible trinity had been set in effect. It read:

> In a quite fundamental way, capital mobility and exchange rate fixity together leave no room for independent monetary policies. In these conditions, it is pertinent to consider afresh the case for a strengthened organisation of monetary coordination or institutional advances in this field [...] There are serious risks of aggravated regional imbalance in the course of market liberalisation.[43]

Perhaps appropriately, the EMS collapsed in 1992, the year for which the 1985 programme was named.

Following the *Padoa-Schioppa Report*, the European Council commissioned a report on EMU by the 'Delors Committee' under the leadership of Jacques Delors.[44] The resultant *Delors Report* was accepted by the European Council in 1989 and is often credited as the blueprint for EMU. In broad strokes this is true; however, it should be noted that Delors eschewed comment from academic economists and accelerated the work of the Committee beyond its own research inputs.[45] Much of the technical design of EMU instead fell to four bodies tasked by the European Council with carrying out the preparatory work for the Maastricht Intergovernmental Conference (IGC):[46] The Commission,[47] the Committee of

---

[40] James, *Making EMU*, 206–207. See: Rogoff, 'Evidence from the EMS'.

[41] James, *Making EMU*, 206–207 (see also 213–214); Charles Wyplosz, 'Monetary Union and Fiscal Policy Discipline' (1991) European Economy Special Edition No 1 165, 3–4; Charles Wyplosz, 'EMU: Why and How It might Happen' (1997) 11 J Econ Persp 3, 3–4.

[42] Art. 20 SEA contained an apparently idle reference to EMU which Delors called his 'little white pebble' leading to monetary union. See James, *Making EMU*, 206–207.

[43] Tommaso Padoa-Schioppa, *Efficiency, Stability, and Equity: A Strategy for the Evolution of the Economic System of the European Community (Padoa-Schioppa Report)* (Oxford University Press, 1987), 4.

[44] European Council, 'European Council Hanover Summit of 27–28 June' (1988) Bull EC 6/1988.

[45] Charles Wyplosz, 'European Monetary Union: The Dark Sides of a Major Success' (2006) 21 Econ Policy 208–211.

[46] European Council, 'Conclusions of the European Council in Madrid, 26–27 June 1989' (1989) 254/2/89 SN, 11.

[47] The Commission's main contribution, Commission of the EC, *Intergovernmental Conferences: Contributions by the Commission* (Bulletin of the European Communities,

Governors,[48] and the ECOFIN Monetary Committee alternates.[49] The European Parliament also made technical contributions.[50] The remainder of this chapter relies heavily on the *travaux préparatoires* of these committees and academic commentary from and about this period.

2.2 The Principles of Economic and Monetary Union

This section moves from the teleology behind the creation of EMU as a whole to the foundational constitutional principles underlying the design of EMU itself.

2.2.1 Price Stability

The first principle of EMU is price stability. Price stability is the '*sine qua non* for economic and monetary union' – the principle for which the entire chapter on monetary policy (Articles 127–133 TFEU) is drafted.[51] Article 127(1) TFEU and Article 2 of the ESCB statute state:

The primary objective of the [ESCB] shall be to maintain price stability. Without prejudice to the objective of price stability, [the ESCB] shall support the general economic policies of the Union with a view to contributing to the Achievement of the objectives of the Union as laid down in [Article 3] of the [TEU].

The instatement of price stability over other historical objectives for monetary policy, such as full employment or growth, has both a distinct economic and legal pedigree. As a matter of legal pedigree, as shown in Chapter 1, price stability derives from the constitutional imperatives of the German Basic Law. Conferral of monetary policy on the ESCB is only compatible with German constitutional law if the ESCB only has competence for price stability and cannot pursue economic policy.[52] For this

---

supplement 2/91, 1990) contained a draft treaty that formed the starting point for the conference.

[48] The Committee of Governors was responsible for drafting the statutes ESCB and ECB. See: James, *Making EMU*, 265–324.

[49] The Monetary Committee was the main chamber for technical negotiations on economic governance. See Monetary Committee, 'Economic and Monetary Union Beyond Stage I: Orientations for the preparation of the intergovernmental conference' [1990] Europe Documents No 1609 (3 April 1990).

[50] Fernand Herman, *Report of the Committee on Economic and Monetary Affairs and Industrial Policy on Economic and Monetary Union* (A3-223/90/A-B, 1990).

[51] Commission, *Contributions by the Commission*, 17. European Council, 'Conclusions of the Presidency of European Council in Madrid, 15–16 December 1995' (1995) Bull EC 12-1995, 24.

[52] See Section 1.3.2.1.

reason, the EU Treaty 'makes price stability the very essence, the *raison d'être* of EMU, a pre-eminence unparalleled in legal history'.[53]

But price stability also has its own economic pedigree: As a matter of economics, the European Parliamentary report to the Maastricht IGC marked a pan-institutional consensus that price stability had proved, over the preceding fifteen years, to be 'more effective' than competing policies at fostering cross-border investment, growth and employment.[54] Price stability was therefore the uncontested starting point at Maastricht.[55] The Committee of Governors, the Monetary Committee and European Parliament reports at Maastricht were clear: 'the first priority and objective in the Community should be price stability'.[56]

2.2.2   Fiscal Discipline

The economic counterpart to price stability is fiscal discipline. Fiscal discipline – sound public finances and a sustainable balance of payments – is the principle for which the entire chapter on economic policy (Articles 120–126 TFEU) is drafted.[57] No other fiscal policy objectives (such as high levels of public service, welfare, equal growth, high employment, low taxes, etc.) appear, implicitly or otherwise, in Chapter 1 (Economic Policy) of Title VIII in Part III TFEU.

This so because, as a matter of economics, fiscal discipline is a condition precedent to price stability in a federated monetary union. As Bishop et al. explain:

In purely economic terms, there are probably two principal requirements for such a [monetary] union to be credible and permanent: Fiscal prudence – to guard against inflation; and Internal balance – to prevent weaker countries from becoming impoverished.[58]

---

[53] Matthias Herdegen, 'Price Stability and Budgetary Restraints in the Economic and Monetary Union: The Law as Guardian of Economic Wisdom' (1998) 35 CMLR 9, 12–16.

[54] Herman, *Herman Report*, 22.

[55] Rory O'Donnell and Patrick Honohan (eds), *Economic and Monetary Union* (Institute of European Affairs 1991), 19; Wayne Sandholtz, 'Monetary Bargains: The Treaty on EMU' in Alan Cafruny and Glenda Rosenthal (eds), *The State of the European Community: The Maastricht Debates and Beyond* (Lynne Rienner Publishers Inc., 1994), 126.

[56] Committee of Governors, *Report by the Chairmain to the Informal ECOFIN Meeting on EMU Beyond Stage One* (26 March, 1990), 3. See also, Monetary Committee, EMU Beyond Stage I (1990) [16]; Herman, *Herman Report*, 22.

[57] For judicial interpretations of this framework: *Pringle* v. *Ireland* [135]–[137]; *Gauweiler (CJEU)*, [100]; *Weiss (CJEU)*, [107]; *Gauweiler (AG Cruz-Villalón)*, [131], [191].

[58] Bishop et al., *Market Discipline*. See also, European Commission, 'Ensuring Budgetary Discipline in Stage Three of EMU' (Note for the Monetary Committee) II/409/96-EN, 19 July 1996, 6.

According to OCA theory, a currency union must have certain mechanisms in place if it is to remain stable and permanent.[59] One of these is a fiscal stabilization capacity to stabilize asymmetric shocks and ensure the solvency of the state during balance of payments (BoP) imbalances.[60] This is necessary because vital macroeconomic tools which allow a state to remain solvent during BoP deficits – the interest rate, capital controls, and the tax base – are beyond the control of Member States in a monetary union with full capital liberalization.[61] The result is that the burden of adjustment must fall onto economic and fiscal policy if the state is to remain solvent.[62]

Proponents of EU fiscal union regularly seize on this prescription to argue for the centralization of fiscal policy in the Union.[63] In reality, however, centralization is not necessarily entailed by OCA theory.[64] What is required by OCA theory is that an adequate fiscal buffer be maintained to safeguard solvency and stabilize the economy in periods of adjustment – regardless of whether this is at federal or at state level.[65]

[59] Robert Mundell, 'A Theory of Optimum Currency Areas' (1961) 51 Am Econ Rev 509; Ronald McKinnon, 'Optimum Currency Areas' (1963) 53 Am Econ Rev 717; Peter B Kenan, 'The Theory of Optimum Currency Areas: An Eclectic View' in Robert Mundell and Alexander K Swoboda (eds), Monetary Problems of the International Economy (University of Chicago Press, 1969) 41; Harris Dellas and George S Tavlas, 'An Optimum-Currency-Area Odyssey' (2009) 28 J Int Money Financ 1117.

[60] The other key factors are factor mobility and real price and wage flexibility.

[61] See Alberto Giovannini and Luigi Spaventa, 'Fiscal Rules in the Monetary Union: A No-Entry Clause' in Alberto Giovannini (ed.), The Debate on Money in Europe (MIT Press, 1995), 244–245 and below, Section 3.3.3 in particular n 208.

[62] Wyplosz, 'Fiscal Policy Discipline'; Paul De Grauwe, 'Fiscal Discipline in Monetary Unions' (1992) 6 Int Econ 101 and sources cited in Chapter 3, Section 3.3.3, n 208.

[63] Giulio Peroni, 'The Crisis of the Euro and the New Role of the European Central Bank' in De Witte, Héritier and Trechel (eds), The Euro Crisis and the State of European Democracy (European University Institute, 2013), 186; Commission Blueprint, 31; Guntram Wolff, 'A Budget for Europe's Monetary Union' (2012) 22 Breugel Policy Contribution 1; Commission Reflection Paper (2017), 25–26; De Grauwe, Economics of Monetary Union (2020), 221.

[64] Mundell's OCA theory emphasized factor mobility, but did not call for a centralized fiscal capacity. It was only later that Kenan argued that a large 'federal' spending capacity could help a great deal in offsetting symmetric shocks. Neither argued centralization was required (see above n 59). For this point: Marek Dabrowski, 'Fiscal or Bailout Union: Where is the EU/EMU's Fiscal Integration Heading?' (2013) 2014/1 Revue de l'OFCE No 132; Dabrowski, 'Fiscal and Macroeconomic Governance', 8; Charles Wyplosz, 'Fiscal Discipline in a Monetary Union without Fiscal Union' in L'udovít Ódor (ed.), Rethinking Fiscal Policy after the Crisis (Cambridge University Press, 2017) 167.

[65] See sources cited above, n 59. See also, Tamim Bayoumi and Barry Eichengreen, 'Restraining Yourself: The Implications of Fiscal Rules for Economic Stabilization' (1995) 4 IMF Staff Papers 32.

In short, governments must have enough money saved up to deal with adverse economic circumstances.[66] What is absolutely necessary, therefore, is fiscal discipline.

If fiscal discipline is not maintained, there are a number of spillover mechanisms which jeopardize price stability.[67] This first is monetary financing: the central bank may be pressured to 'bail out' governments by buying government debt and lowering risk premia, or simply by diluting the value of the currency.[68] The second is default risk: higher borrowing costs may spread to other countries through their own exposures to the defaulting state, in turn affecting their stability.[69] The third is currency risk: the more government debt grows, the more currency markets will view it as a possible source of currency depreciation, increasing the cost of EMU-denominated debt.[70]

Near-identical conclusions were expressed by the Commission,[71] the Monetary Committee[72] and the Committee of Governors: 'Sound budgetary policies are indispensable and complementary to stability-oriented monetary policies.'[73] The question was how to achieve this in an EMU bound by the fiscal sovereignty of its Member States.

2.2.3 Fiscal Sovereignty

The most fundamental principle of EMU, Member State fiscal sovereignty, is not written in Article 119 TFEU or any provision of the Treaties. It does not derive from EU law. It constrains the foundations of the EU legal order as a whole, visible only by impression on the

---

[66] Commission, 'Ensuring Budgetary Discipline in Stage Three', 6.
[67] Willem Buiter, Giancarlo Corsetti and Nouriel Roubini, 'Excessive Deficits: Sense and Nonsense in the Treaty of Maastricht' (1993) 8 Econ Policy 57, 693–705; Claudio Borio, *Macro-fiscal poliy coordination in an EMU* (6 July 1989) accessible at: wwwecbeuropaeu/ecb/access_to_documents/archives/delors/html/indexenhtml accessed 8 August 2020, 1989), 7–8; De Grauwe, *Economics of Monetary Union* (2020), 228–236.
[68] A Lans Bovenberg, Jeroen Kremers and Paul Maason, 'Economic and Monetary Union in Europe and Constraints on National Budgetary Policies' (1991) 38 IMF Staff Papers 374, 380; Giovannini and Spaventa, 'No-Entry Clause', 249–252.
[69] Wyplosz, 'Dark sides', 225. This is compounded by a free-riding risk in economic unions: Jürgen von Hagen and Ian Harden, 'National Budget Processes and Fiscal Performance' (1994) 3 European Economy 311.
[70] Marco Buti, 'Monetary and Fiscal Rules for Public Debt Sustainability' (1990) Economic Papers No 84; Bovenberg et al., 'EMU in Europe', 379–383; Wyplosz, 'Dark sides', 227.
[71] Commission, *One Market, One Money*, 168; Commission, *Contributions by the Commission*, 24.
[72] Monetary Committee of the EC, 'Result of the discussion in the Committee on 24 April' (Meeting Minutes) [1990] II/185/90-EN.
[73] Committee of Governors, *Report of 26 March 1990*, 2.

allocation of competences for economic policy under Articles 2(3), 5(1), and 120–126 TFEU.

It is nonetheless a foundational principle of EMU.[74] Not only must the model chosen to secure fiscal discipline 'work', but it must remain within the containment walls of Europe's constitutional boundaries. So, for example, the Committee of Governors rejected proposals for a legal constraint on budgetary powers,[75] and the Monetary Committee insisted that 'the Member States must remain masters of the main aspects of budgetary policy'.[76] Centralized fiscal governance, legally binding fiscal rules and centralized finance mechanisms were ruled out of court – 'politically unacceptable just as much [as] legally inadmissible'.[77]

To date, under Articles 2(3), 5(1), 121 and 126 TFEU, the Union has no competence in economic policy. Indeed, the EU's famed 'economic coordination' competence is something of a misnomer: Articles 2(3) and 5(1) TFEU state that it is for the '*Member States* [to] coordinate their economic policies'.[78] The Union's competence is confined to establishing 'arrangements' for them to do so.[79] Articles 2(3) and 5(1) TFEU are listed separately from Articles 2(1) and 3 TFEU (exclusive EU competences) and Articles 2(2) and 4 TFEU (shared EU competences), and there is no provision for the approximation or harmonization of Member States' laws, as often accompanies areas of Member State competence (like direct taxation).[80]

---

[74] Tuori and Tuori, *Eurozone Crisis*, 9: 'Member States' national fiscal sovereignty is a principle of both European and national constitutional law and encroachments on this sovereignty hint at a crisis of both European and national constitutions.'

[75] Committee of Governors, *Report of 26 March 1990*, 3; Minutes of the 245th Meeting of the Committee of Governors of the Central Banks of the Member States of the EEC (Basle, 15 May 1990), 36.

[76] Monetary Committee, EMU Beyond Stage I (1990), para 2.

[77] Hugo Hahn, 'The Stability Pact for European Monetary Union: Compliance with Deficit Limit as a Constant Legal Duty' (1998) 35 CMLR 77, 85.

[78] Arts. 2(3), 5(1) TFEU.

[79] Arts. 2(3), 5(1) TFEU.

[80] Ranier Palmstorfer, 'To Bail Out or Not to Bail Out? The Current Framework of Financial Assistance for Euro Area Member States Measured against the Requirements of EU Primary Law' (2012) 37 EL Rev 771 773–774; Dominique Servais and Rodolphe Ruggeri, 'The EU Constitution: Its Impact on Economic and Monetary Union and Economic Governance', *Legal Aspects of the European System of Central Banks* (ECB, 2005), 49–50; Rose Maria Lastra, *Legal Foundations of International Monetary Stability* (Oxford University Press, 2006), 249.

2.2.4   Market Discipline

The task for the architects of EMU was therefore to select a model of fiscal federalism that would ensure fiscal discipline while remaining outside the boundaries imposed by Member State fiscal sovereignty. Unlike the price-stability mandate of the ECB, as Joerges points out, fiscal policies simply 'cannot be enforced by conventional legal techniques' as to do so would 'disrespect the democratic legitimacy of national institutions, in particular the budgetary powers of parliaments'.[81] With no constitutional power of legal compulsion in economic policy, whether Member States act in accordance with fiscal discipline therefore depends on the balance of incentives which play on elected legislators with exclusive competence in economic policy.[82] The achievement of price stability, a creature of monetary economics, is therefore predicated on the field of public economics known as fiscal federalism, and it is here where we cross into that field.

Fiscal federalism is concerned with the structuring of financial relationships and incentives between governmental units in a federal system.[83] That literature is applied extensively in Chapter 8; however it suffices to state here that the appropriate construction of a given federal model depends on its placement on a continuum between 'centralization' or 'surveillance' models of fiscal union, and 'classical' or 'ideal type' models of decentralized fiscal federalism (sometimes known as 'market-preserving federalism', 'self-preserving federalism' or 'competitive federalism').[84]

Occupying one end of the spectrum lie highly decentralized 'market-preserving' federations such as the United States, Switzerland and Canada.[85] In these countries there is no debt mutualization and no federal oversight of state-level expenditure, revenue or debt. For the Delors Committee, the main technical input examining these federations was a 1989 paper submitted by BIS Director Alexandre Lamfalussy.[86] The

---

[81] Christian Joerges, 'The European Economic Constitution and Its Transformation through the Financial Crisis' in Dennis Patterson and Anna Söderstn (eds), *A Companion to European union Law and International Law* (Wiley-Blackwell, 2013) 242.

[82] Jörn Pipkorn, 'Legal Arrangements in the Treaty of Maastricht for the Effectiveness of the Economic and Monetary Union' (1994) 31 CMLR 263, 272.

[83] See Chapter 8, Section 8.1 and sources cited for an overview.

[84] See Methods and Introduction, nn 68–69, and Chapter 5, Section 5.2.

[85] See Chapter 8, Sections 8.2.2–8.2.4.

[86] Alexandre Lamfalussy, 'Macro-Coordination of Fiscal Policies in an Economic and Monetary Union in Europe', *Collection of papers submitted to the Delors Committee* (1989), 168.

Lamfalussy paper noted that, with no mechanisms of economic coordination, and 'no *federally imposed* constraints on regional government borrowing', none of these federations have 'experienced serious problems with, or been much concerned about' fiscal imbalances.[87]

In these federations, fiscal discipline is enforced by market discipline. As defined in a seminal IMF staff paper in 1992, 'Market discipline means that financial markets provide signals that lead borrowers to behave in a manner consistent with their *solvency*.'[88] Under conditions of market discipline, each country's economic performance is assessed across a range of indicators by market actors, resulting in differentiated interest rates on government debt (even within a monetary union). If investors know that each state/canton/province is 'on its own' in relation to its liabilities (with no possibility of a bailout), markets closely monitor sub-federal finances and price default risk into government debt. A government which borrows against a fixed envelope of resources will face rising credit risk premiums as they approach their inter-temporal budget constraint (otherwise known as the solvency condition).[89] Eventually, it becomes cheaper to cut expenditure or raise money through taxation than to continue borrowing, and governments change their behaviour.[90]

Occupying the other end of the spectrum lie highly centralized federations, such as Germany or Australia. These states exhibit what is referred-to as the 'centralization' or 'surveillance' model, characterized by extensive fiscal transfers and centralized oversight of sub-federal budgetary policies. In these federations, the federal government exerts 'such a degree of fiscal control that credit distinctions between the constituent states are almost non-existent'.[91] So, for example, all sixteen German *Länder* enjoy credit ratings in the highest rating category, despite wildly different base risk, and despite the fact that some (e.g. Bremen and Saarland) have been so in excesses of the solvency condition in recent decades that their default would have become immediately necessary without constant infusions of financial assistance.[92]

---

[87] Lamfalussy, 'Macro-Coordination' 102–106 (emphasis in original). See also, Borio, *Macro-Fiscal Policy Coordination*, 11.

[88] Lane, 'Market Discipline', 55.

[89] Lane, 'Market Discipline', 54.

[90] See Mark Hallerberg, 'Fiscal Federalism Reforms in the European Union and the Greek crisis' (2010) 12 Eur Union Polit 127, 130.

[91] Bishop et al., *Market Discipline*, 2.

[92] See: Chapter 8, Section 8.2.1.

According to the 1989 Lamfalussy paper, three characteristics deter-mined whether fiscal discipline was found in a fiscal federation: (1) No bailouts, (2) complete spending and revenue autonomy and (3) 'no *federally imposed* constraints on regional government borrowing'.[93] Indeed, Lamfalussy found that where fiscal discipline did break down, such failure was often *caused* by some attempt 'to enforce restraint on state governments'.[94] The paper concluded:

A key aspect of all the federal systems considered is the denial (or strict limita-tion) of access to central bank financing to regional governments in an attempt to subject them to the discipline of the market.

Federally-decided limits on the borrowing of regional governments exist only in Australia [and] except for Australia [. . .] no country appears to have experiences serious problems with, or been much concerned about, medium-term control over sub-federal budgetary positions. [. . .] This centralization has meant that financial markets have not been encouraged to differentiate between the debts of the various government units, in sharp contrast to the Canadian Case. Some concern would also seem to exist in Germany, where tax powers are highly centralized and there are a number of institutional, albeit mainly consultative, arrangements for coordination.[95]

The lesson left to the drafting committees was clear: Market discipline was not just more effective than centralized fiscal rules, but governing state fiscal policies could introduce moral hazard by signalling that Member States are not 'on their own' in relation to their debts, ultimately under-mining fiscal discipline.[96] The Monetary Committee IGC report stated: 'Measures should be taken to reinforce market discipline over budget deficits.'[97] The first memorandum of the Delors Committee observed:

In nations with a federal structure, in which there is one currency and once central bank, no formal constraint is in general imposed by the federal author-ities on the budgetary decisions of local governments. It is clear from experiences of highly centralised administrations that, in the interests of both democracy and efficiency, the principle of decentralization should be espoused.[98]

---

[93] Lamfalussy, 'Macro-Coordination', 102 (emphasis in original).
[94] Lamfalussy, 'Macro-Coordination', 102.
[95] Lamfalussy, 'Macro-Coordination', 98, 102–106.
[96] Tommaso Padoa-Schioppa, *The Road to Monetary Union in Europe* (Clarendon Press, 1994), 142–145.
[97] Monetary Committee, EMU Beyond Stage I (1990) [4] (ii).
[98] Economic and Monetary Union: The Main Issues (1 September 1988, CSEMU/2/88), 4. See also, Maurice Doyle, 'Regional Policy and European Economic Integration',

Yet more than that, for the architects of EMU at Maastricht, a 'market-preserving' model of fiscal decentralization was not merely the optimal economic choice,[99] it was a constitutional stipulation of fiscal sovereignty. As stated by the Commission:

In the end achieving stable public finances will depend on the successful self-discipline of Member States [...] There are sensitive issues concerning parliamentary sovereignty over budgetary policy, and in any case no single model would be appropriate given the diversity of historical and constitutional backgrounds.[100]

2.3   The Legal Architecture of European Fiscal Federalism

There are three requirements for market discipline to be effective in fiscal federalism theory, and it is these requirements which the technical architecture in the Maastricht Treaty is based upon.[101]

The first condition is a hard budget constraint under a credible 'no bailout' rule, accompanied by 'a strict prohibition on monetary and compulsory financing of public deficits or privileged market access for public authorities'.[102] A hard budget constraint refers to the condition where a state's expenditures are limited by the inter-temporal budget constraint (or the solvency condition – the notion that present liabilities must be compensated by future surpluses and international investment gains) and will not be bailed-out when this constraint is exceeded.[103] The preparatory committees were unanimous on this requirement. The

   Collection of papers submitted to the Committee for the Study of Economic and Monetary Union (Delors Committee) (1989), 78.

[99]   Commission, *Contributions by the Commission*, 22: 'There does not need to be a single economic policy in the same way as for monetary policy [...] [e]ven in mature federations economic policy is made up of different functions and is conducted at different levels of government [...] this has not only a theoretical but also a solid empirical foundation.'

[100]   Commission, 'Towards a Stability Pact', 14. See also, Padoa-Schioppa, *Padoa-Schioppa Report*, 9.

[101]   Monetary Committee, EMU Beyond Stage I (1990) [4] (ii); Committee of Governors, '245th Meeting Minutes'; European Council, Conclusions of the European Council in Rome, 27–28 October 1990, 11; Commission of the EEC, 'Economic and Monetary Union' SEC (90) 1659, 24; Commission, 'A Stability Pact', 15–16; Commission, *Contributions by the Commission*, 15; and sources cited above, nn 95–100. On the three conditions, see Bishop et al., *Market Discipline*, 1; Lane, 'Market Discipline', 62; Eyraud and Gomez Sirera, 'Constraints', 97.

[102]   Monetary Committee, EMU Beyond Stage I (1990) [4]; Committee of Governors, *Report of 26 March 1990*, 2.

[103]   Charles Wyplosz, 'Theory to Practice', *Independent Fiscal Institutions in the EU Fiscal Framework* (European Union, 2019), 9. See further, Pablo D'Erasmo, Enrique Mendoza and Jing Zhang, 'What is a Sustainable Public Debt?' in John Taylor and Harold Uhlig (eds), *Handbook of Macroeconomics*, vol. 2 (Elsevier, 2015) 2493.

Committee of Governors recorded 'consensus on two rules, namely no monetary financing of budget deficits and no bailout or unconditional Community guarantee'.[104] The European Council concluded that EMU could only occur after 'the monetary financing of budget deficits has been prohibited and any responsibility on the part of the Community or its Member States for one Member State's debt precluded'.[105] The July 1990 Monetary Committee Report stated:

> It must be clear that neither the Community nor the other Member States stand behind a Member State's debts. The 'no bail-out' rule would ensure that the financial markets exercise a degree of discipline on any Member State pursuing unsound budgetary policies, by imposing differential terms on its paper and ultimately by refusing to lend.[106]

The second condition for market discipline to work is that full information on the borrowers' creditworthiness must be available to market participants, creditors and stakeholders in order for costs and pressure on governments to arise.[107] Markets and voters will not penalize risk if they do not know what risks they are exposed to. An obvious remedy is to 'improve the quality of information and disseminate it to the markets' through some sort of multilateral surveillance framework.[108] To this end, the preparatory committees recommended a second mechanism: 'appropriate procedures to monitor budgetary policies and identify slippages which may occur'.[109]

The third condition is policy correction: Governments must not be inure to market sanctions – they must actually undertake fiscal policy adjustment.[110] In the *travaux préparatoires*, this condition is expressed as 'the avoidance of excessive deficits'.[111] In a democratic market economy, this condition is typically ensured by electorates and creditors: as the cost of debt becomes increasingly unsustainable and spending priorities are curtailed, stakeholders are forced to resolve internal 'wars of attrition' over the costs of adjustment.[112] However, a government

---

[104] Committee of Governors, '245th Meeting Minutes'. See also, Commission, 'Economic and Monetary Union' SEC (90) 1659, 24.
[105] Meeting of 27–28 October 1990 (Rome), 11.
[106] Monetary Committee, EMU Beyond Stage I (1990), 2.
[107] Bishop et al., *Market Discipline*, 1; Lane, 'Market Discipline', 62; Eyraud and Gomez Sirera, 'Constraints', 97.
[108] Lane, 'Market Discipline'. Bishop et al., *Market Discipline*, 19.
[109] Committee of Governors, *Report of 26 March 1990*, 2.
[110] See sources cited above, n 107.
[111] Committee of Governors, *Report of 26 March 1990*, 2.
[112] Lars Feld and Christoph Schaltegger, 'Are Fiscal Adjustments Less Successful in Decentralized Governments?' (2009) 25 Europ J Polit Economy 115.

which is rewarded for rising debts, for instance because the costs are shared with the wider federation, will be slower to respond. For this reason, the preparatory committees recommended 'a second direction of policies' to support market discipline.[113] The Commission explained that a multilateral sanctioning mechanism 'could be expected to impact on public opinion in the country concerned. It would certainly influence market perceptions leading to a downgrading in the credit rating of the Member State in question'.[114]

In accordance with these criteria, the fiscal federalism architecture inscribed in the Maastricht Treaty consists of three pillars described in the following sections of this chapter:

[2.3.1] The prohibition on financial assistance under Articles 123–125 TFEU;

[2.3.2] The Multilateral Surveillance Procedure under Article 121 TFEU; and

[2.3.3] The Excessive Deficit Procedure under Article 126 TFEU.

2.3.1   Articles 123–125 TFEU: The Prohibition on Financial Assistance

Central to European fiscal federalism since Maastricht has been an interlocking prohibition on financial assistance under Articles 123–125 TFEU (ex Articles 101–103 TEC). The undoubted keystone of this structure is the 'no bailout' rule (Article 125 TFEU) with which it has become synonymous. However, the 'no bailout' rule is merely the 'final piece' of an integrative structure which functions to cut off access to all non-market public finance under Articles 122–125 TFEU.[115] Article 123 prohibits monetary financing of public debt by the ESCB; Article 124 prohibits privileged financing from captured financial institutions; and Article 125 prohibits bailouts by the Union or the Member States. The only exception to this integrated structure is Article 122(2) TFEU, which

---

[113] Tommaso Padoa-Schioppa, *Proceeding by Steps* (Committee of Governors, 17 November, 1988): 'To the maximum possible extent adjustment should occur by market mechanisms. *A first direction of policy*, therefore, should aim at making such mechanisms more effective. [. . .] However [. . .] *a second direction of policies* will be necessary to supplement them.'

[114] Commission, 'Towards a Stability Pact', 9–10. See also Commission, *Contributions by the Commission*, 31.

[115] Vestert Borger, 'The ESM and the European Court's Predicament in *Pringle*' (2013) 14 German LJ 113, 119. See also, Rene Smits, 'The Crisis Response in Europe's Economic and Monetary Union: Overview of Legal Developments' (2015) 38 Fordham Int'l Law J 1135, 1141.

permits *Union* financial assistance in the event of natural disasters or exceptional occurrences beyond the control of a Member State. There is nothing in the way of a financial umbrella to protect EMU Member States against insolvency.[116] As the Commission states, the Treaty 'is designed to dispel any investor's doubt, or hope, about the risk they run in financing governments that incur excessive deficits'.[117]As interpreted by AG Cruz-Villalón:

Articles 123-125 TFEU [. . .] lay down strict prohibitions of the financing of States, whether by means of monetary financing measures or by means of transfers between Member States. Those prohibitions confirm that monetary union [. . .] seeks to maintain financial stability, for which purpose it is based on a principle of fiscal discipline and the principle that there is no shared financial liability (the 'no-bailout' rule).[118]

This interlocking purpose of these provisions is referenced explicitly in primary and secondary law,[119] and is described clearly throughout the *travaux préparatoires* of the Monetary Committee,[120] the Committee of Governors[121] and the Commission.[122]

Yet more than this, Articles 123–125 TFEU also entrench the fiscal sovereignty of the Member States. The 'no bailout' rule is, beyond its literal wording, 'the expression of the responsibility of each Member State for its own public finance'.[123] As Bishop explains:

---

[116] Franz-Christoph Zeitler, 'The European Public Debt Crisis and the Institutional Framework of the Monetary Union: Experience and Adjustments' in Ringe and Huber (eds), *Bail-outs, the Euro and Regulation*, 246.

[117] Commission, 'A Stability Pact', 15–16.

[118] *Gauweiler (AG Cruz-Villalón)*, [131], [191]. See also, *Pringle v. Ireland* [135].

[119] Council Regulation (EC) no 3603/93 of 13 December 1993 specifying definitions for the application of the prohibitions referred to in Articles 104 and 104b(1) of the Treaty [1993] OJ L 332/1 refers to Article 123 TFEU as 'an essential element of the submission of the public sector in its financing operations to the discipline of the market mechanism [that] so makes a contribution to the strengthening of budgetary discipline'. Article 125(2) TFEU ties these provisions together, referring to 'the *prohibitions* referred to in Articles 123, 124 *and* [125]'.

[120] Monetary Committee, EMU Beyond Stage I (1990), 2, excerpted above, Section 2.3 at n 106.

[121] Committee of Governors, *Report of 26 March 1990*, 2.

[122] Commission, *Contributions by the Commission*, 15; Commission of the EC, 'Economic and Monetary Union: The Economic Rationale and Design of the System'(Brussels 22 March 1990) http://europa.eu/rapid/press-release_IP-90-231_en.htm accessed 10 February 2014; Commission, 'A Stability Pact', 15–16,

[123] Jean-Victor Louis, 'Guest Editorial: The No-Bailout Clause and Rescue Packages' (2010) 47 CMLR 971, 978.

The purpose of the [no bailout] rule is clear: it is the circuit breaker between monetary union and the back-door creation of a 'United States of Europe'. When you look at the creation of monetary unions and federations in the past [. . .] you see all too often that when one of the members of the club got into financial difficulties, the other members of the club had an interest in helping that member and in doing so, they take control over their spending. Finally and inexorably there was a centralisation of political power.[124]

2.3.1.1   Article 125 TFEU: The 'No Bailout' Rule

Article 125(1) contains two identical sentences, one addressed to the Union and one addressed to the Member States. They state:

[The Union/A Member State] shall not be liable for or assume the commitments of central governments, regional, local or other public authorities, other bodies governed by public law, or public undertakings of any Member State, without prejudice to mutual financial guarantees for the joint execution of a specific project.

The interpretation of this article by the ECJ is assessed in Chapter 6 (see Section 6.3); however, it suffices to remark here that the teleology of this provision is not fiscal discipline by any means. Price stability requires fiscal discipline, but the Treaty drafters did not inscribe just any model for this purpose. According to the ECJ: 'The prohibition laid down in art.125 TFEU *ensures that the Member States remain subject to the logic of the market* when they enter into debt, since that ought to prompt them to maintain budgetary discipline.'[125]

2.3.1.2   Article 123 TFEU: The No Monetary Financing Rule

Article 123 TFEU, the 'no monetary financing' rule, prohibits the ESCB from financing Member States directly, through primary market bond purchases (which are prohibited outright), or indirectly, through secondary market instruments which have the effect of monetary financing.[126] Article 123 states:

Overdraft facilities or any other type of credit facility with the European Central Bank or with the central banks of the Member States in favour of Union

---

[124] Graham Bishop, 'The Financial Market Alternative' in Harry Cowie (ed.), *Towards Fiscal Federalism: Federal Trust Conference Report* (Federal Trust for Education and Research, 1992).

[125] *Pringle v. Ireland* [135] (emphasis added).

[126] Art. 123 TFEU is read together with Reg 3603/03 which states in its preamble that 'purchases on the secondary market must not be used to circumvent the objective of Article 123'.

institutions, bodies, offices or agencies, central governments, regional, local or other public authorities, other bodies governed by public law, or public undertakings of Member States shall be prohibited, as shall the purchase directly from them by the European Central Bank or national central banks of debt instruments.[127]

According to the *travaux préparatoires*, this serves three purposes: to prohibit monetary financing of government debt; to safeguard the independence of the ECB; and to expose Member States to market discipline.[128] Article 123 is interpreted purposively.[129] It prohibits *any* operations on the secondary market with the effect of circumventing the prohibition by having the effect of monetary financing.[130] According to the ECJ, 'Article 123(1) TFEU prohibits *all financial assistance* from the ESCB to a Member State.'[131] It is, in short, a 'no bailout' rule tailored to the ECB.[132]

2.3.1.3   Article 124 TFEU: No Privileged Access to Private Finance

Article 124 fills the gap between these two rules by preventing governments from capturing, colluding or inducing financial institutions to lend to them at below-market rates.[133] Article 124 TFEU reads:

Any measure, not based on prudential considerations, establishing privileged access by Union institutions, bodies, offices or agencies, central governments, regional, local or other public authorities, other bodies governed by public law, or public undertakings of Member States to financial institutions, shall be prohibited.

2.3.1.4   Article 122 TFEU: (No) Conditional Financial Assistance

Perhaps the truest cornerstone of this architecture, however, is present by its absence: Nothing vaguely related to conditional financial assistance in the event of a threat to economic or monetary stability appears

---

[127] See also, Art. 21.1 of the Protocol (No 4) on the Statute of the ESCB and of the ECB [2012] OJ C 326/320.

[128] Committee of Governors, *Monetary Financing of Budget Deficits in Stage Three* (19 June, 1991) 2–4.

[129] *Gauweiler Reference (Germany)*, [86]; *Gauweiler (AG Cruz-Villalón)* [227]; *Gauweiler (CJEU)* [94]–[95].

[130] ECB, *ECB Monthly Bulletin October 2012* (ECB, 2012), 7.

[131] *Gauweiler (CJEU)* [94]–[95] (emphasis added).

[132] René Smits, *The European Central Bank: Institutional Aspects* (Kluwer Law International, 1997), 77; Samo Bardutzky and Elaine Fahey, 'Who Got to Adjudicate the EU's Financial Crisis and Why?' in Adams, Fabbrini and Larouche (eds), *European Budgetary Constraints*, 356.

[133] Monetary Committee, *EMU Beyond Stage I* (1990), 2; Monetary Committee, *Results of the Meeting of 24 April 1990*, 2; Committee of Governors, *Report of 26 March 1990*, 2–3.

in the Treaty, except those provisions which expressly preclude such a mechanism. Instead, Article 108 EEC – which has afforded the protection of 'mutual financial assistance' since the Community's founding Treaty – was removed from the title on EMU at Maastricht.

This was a clear drafting choice. After being rejected by the technical committees in 1989–1990,[134] the Commission attempted to reintroduce conditional financial assistance by inserting two articles into the draft treaty that would form the *de facto* starting point for the Maastricht IGC.[135] Articles 104 and 104a of that treaty provided a legal basis for a financial stability mechanism that would prove remarkably prescient of the ESM enacted two decades later in 2012. Article 104a presaged the 'narrow' interpretation of the 'no bailout' rule later to be adopted in *Pringle* v. *Ireland* (see Section 6.3)[136] by narrowing the scope of the rule from a prohibition on all types of bailouts to a mere prohibition on '*unconditional guarantees* in respect of the public debt of a Member State'.[137] Article 104 then watered-down the substance of the 'no bailout' principle itself into a 'conditional bailouts' principle.[138]

Conditional financial assistance had already been rejected by the technical committees in 1989–1990,[139] it was given 'rough treatment' by ECOFIN,[140] and it was excluded from the mandates for the IGC by the European Council in Rome.[141] Instead, 'mutual financial assistance' under the existing Article 108 EEC was stripped from the title on EMU

---

[134] Monetary Committee, EMU Beyond Stage I (1990), 2; Committee of Governors, *Report of 26 March 1990*, 2.

[135] Commission, *Contributions by the Commission*.

[136] See Chapter 6, Section 6.3.

[137] Art. 104a of the draft Treaty read: 'The following shall be recognised as incompatible with the economic and monetary union and shall accordingly be prohibited: [. . .] (b) the granting by the Community or the Member States *of an unconditional guarantee* in respect of the public debt of a Member State.'

[138] Art. 104 read: 'Where a Member State is in difficulties or is seriously threatened with difficulties [. . .] subject to certain conditions, the Member State concerned [may] be granted Community financial assistance which may take the form of a support programme accompanied by budgetary intervention or special loans.'

[139] See sources cited above, n 134.

[140] Peter Ludlow, '"Reshaping Europe:" The Origins of the Intergovernmental Conferences and the Emergence of a New European Political Architecture', *The Annual Review of European Community Affairs* (CEPS, Brassy's 1991), 398.

[141] Where the Conclusions of the Meeting of 27–28 October 1990 (Rome), 9 and European Council, European Council in Rome, 14–15 December 1990 [1990] EC Bull 12 lists agreement for the preparatory work, conditional financial assistance is not among them.

and, to ensure such a mechanism never arose again, 'the Monetary Committee [wrote] itself out of the future of the European design'.[142] As will become important later in this book, the Treaty drafters simply did not trust the Union's integrationist institutions to enforce its own criteria for fiscal discipline in a debt crisis.[143] In the Monetary Committee, it was predicted that 'Country conditionality would be watered down by politics, including by interventions by the Commission'.[144] As ECB Historian James encapsulates, '[t]he history of EC conditionality was a saga of softness and failure'.[145] According to Padoa-Schioppa (who sat on the Monetary Committee and Committee of Governors), it was seen as 'essential that traps of this sort be avoided in the design of the European Monetary Union'.[146]

The only exception to the prohibition on financial assistance in the Treaties is Article 122(2) TFEU. It reads:

Where a Member State is in difficulties or is seriously threatened with severe difficulties caused by natural disasters or exceptional occurrences beyond its control, the Council, on a proposal from the Commission, may grant, under certain conditions, Union financial assistance to the Member State concerned.

Two features of this article are of note. First, the occurrence justifying financial assistance has to be exceptional and out of control of the Member State – a limitation that does not apply under 143 TFEU (ex 108 EEC) to Member States outside the EMU.[147] It is 'a true crisis clause',[148] which narrowness only serves to emphasize the 'limited scope for exercising financial solidarity'.[149]

Second, Article 122(2) TFEU is different from Article 143 TFEU, which allows for 'mutual financial assistance' to be granted to a non-EU Member State experiencing BoP difficulties.[150] As there is no 'no bailout' rule applying outside EMU, Article 143 is not subject to any external restrictions on its activation. It is a self-contained legal basis to give financial assistance where

---

[142] James, *Making EMU*, 280.
[143] Committee of Governors, '245th Meeting Minutes', 10; Monetary Committee, EMU Beyond Stage I (1990), 4.
[144] James, *Making EMU*, 279–280.
[145] James, *Making EMU*, 279.
[146] Padoa-Schioppa, *Road to Monetary Union*, 150.
[147] Louis, 'Guest Editorial', 981.
[148] Louis, 'Guest Editorial', 983.
[149] Lastra, *Legal Foundations*, 253.
[150] Art. 143 TFEU (ex 108 TEC).

its internal criteria are met. Article 122(2) is not.[151] It was drafted as a *lex specialis*, 'a kind of escape clause', to the 'no bailout' rule.[152] It is only if financial assistance meets the terms of Article 122(2) *and* does not amount to a financial bailout under Article 125 that it is permitted.[153]

2.3.2 Article 121 TFEU: The Multilateral Surveillance Procedure (MSP)

The Multilateral Surveillance Procedure under Article 121 TFEU (ex 99 TEC) supports the second criteria for market discipline by ensuring that financial risks do not accrue hidden to markets, electorates and stakeholders. The MSP originated as the economic surveillance and coordination system for convergence during Stage I of preparing for EMU,[154] and in 1997 was operationalized as the 'preventative arm' of the Stability and Growth Pact (SGP) with the purpose of monitoring 'the full range of economic developments in each of the Member States' and to give warning when economic policies are going off track.[155] The MSP outlined a surveillance/coordination cycle with three stages:

> First, the Council, on a recommendation from the Commission, formulates Broad Economic Policy Guidelines (BEPGs) for the Member States and the Union under Article 121(2) TFEU.
>
> Second, under Article 121(3) TEU, Member States submit annual Stability and Convergence Programmes (SCP's) outlining their planned fiscal policies.[156] At the centre of these programmes is the 'medium-term objective' (MTO) legislated under the SGP, a three-year target for the budgetary balance set at 'close to balance or in surplus' (initially interpreted as −0.5% of GDP).[157]

---

[151] Art. 122(1) TFEU declares itself to be 'without prejudice to any other procedures provided for in the Treaties' (including Art. 125). Art. 122(2) contains no such language.

[152] Louis, 'Guest Editorial', 981; Pipkorn, 'Legal Arrangements', 273.

[153] Declaration No 6 on Article 100 of the TEC [2001] OJ C 80/78 refers to 'decisions regarding financial assistance, such as are provided for in Article [122 TFEU] *and* are compatible with the "no bail-out" rule laid down in Article [125 TFEU]'. See further Section 6.3.1, below, at nn 215–238.

[154] Council Decision 90/141/EEC of 12 March 1990 on the attainment of progressive convergence of economic policies and performance during stage one of EMU [1990] OJ L 78/33.

[155] Reg 1466/97, rec 6.

[156] Arts. 3(1), 4, 7(1), 8 Reg 1467/97.

[157] Art. 3(2)(a), Reg 1467/97. The 2005 reform amended this to MTOs of up to −1.0% of GDP. See Chapter 3, Section 3.3.4, n 237.

Third, under Article 121(4) TFEU, should the Council identify 'actual or expected significant divergence' from the MTO or the adjustment path towards it, the Council (on a recommendation of the Commission) would issue a warning to the Member State to 'take the necessary adjustment measures'.[158]

Article 121 TFEU contained, and still contains, no legal or financial penalty for deviation from the MTO. Neither the concept of the MTO nor an obligation of compliance with it is inscribed anywhere in primary Treaty law.

2.3.3   Article 126 TFEU: The Excessive Deficit Procedure (EDP)

The Excessive Deficit Procedure, or the 'corrective arm' of the SGP, supports the third criteria for market discipline: policy correction. Its purpose is to 'deter excessive general government deficits and, if they occur, to further their prompt correction'.[159]

As originally designed, the EDP is triggered by a Commission report finding that a Member State budget exceeds the 3% or 60% of GDP reference values in Protocol No 12, unless the ratio has declined 'substantially and continuously' and is 'close to the reference value', or if the deficit is 'exceptional and temporary'.[160] If a Member State fails to take corrective action following 'notice' of non-compliance with Council recommendations to correct the excessive deficit,[161] Article 126(11) TFEU provides a selection of penalties to be visited on profligate Member States by the Council voting by QMV, including additional information on debt issuances, restrictions on EIB credit and sanctions of up to 0.5% of GDP.[162]

Two points must be emphasized about this framework.

First, as stated by the French *Conseil Constitutionnel*, Articles 120–126 TFEU do 'not result in the transfer of any powers over economic or fiscal policy and do not authorise any such transfers'.[163] Neither Article 121 nor 126 TFEU give the EU any competence in economic policy. The SGP raises the political and financial cost of running a deficit over 3% of GDP,

---

[158]   Art. 6(1), 10(1), Reg 1466/97.
[159]   Rec 1, Art. 1, Reg 1467/97.
[160]   Art. 126(3)-(5) TFEU; Art. 3(2) Reg 1467/97. 'Substantially and continuously', 'close to the reference value' and 'temporary' are undefined, leaving discretion to the Council. An 'exceptional' situation is an annual fall or real GDP of >2% or a particularly abrupt and severe downturn in output: Art. 2(2)(3) Reg 1467/97.
[161]   Arts. 126(5)-(9) TFEU; Arts. 2(3)-(4), 4(1)-(2) Reg 1467/97.
[162]   Arts. 6, 12, Reg 1467/97.
[163]   *TSCG (France)* [16].

just as markets do, but excessive deficits are *not* banned as a matter of law. Article 126(10) TFEU makes clear that infringement proceedings may not be brought against a Member State for refusing to abide by the 3% or 60% debt limits.[164] There is no *legal* power of compulsion. As the Commission describes it, the SGP is a 'voluntary commitment' to respecting the 3% deficit limit in the Treaty.[165] This was confirmed in *Commission v. Council*, where the ECJ held that there could be no infringement proceedings for failing to apply fines even when the conditions are met.[166]

Second, the SGP emerged as a 'second direction' of policy to support – not replace – market discipline.[167] Never was it thought that fiscal rules could replace market discipline to ensure fiscal discipline. As Moris et al. explain, 'Fiscal rules *supplement* the monitoring of fiscal policy by voters and by financial markets [. . .] The adoption of a fiscal rule per se is not [. . .] a sufficient condition for improving fiscal outcomes.'[168] The Commission proposal introducing the SGP described it not as an independent system for fiscal governance, but as a mechanism that would 'reinforce the role of market pressure in favour of fiscal discipline' alongside the 'no bailout' and monetary financing rules.[169] By levying fines and issuing recommendations, the EDP 'would result in an increasing market pressure on [a] country (market asks a higher price on its debt) to adopt corrective measures in favour of fiscal discipline'.[170]

Indeed, at the time the Maastricht Treaty was signed, there were no centralized fiscal rules governing Member States who gained entry to EMU at all. It might be recalled that the Lamfalussy paper found that indiscipline was more often *caused* by some attempt 'to enforce restraint on state governments'.[171] As observed by the UK Treasury Department in 1989:

Fixed exchange rate regimes have in the past operated successfully without such rules, as do the overwhelming majority of federal states today. Market pressures and multilateral surveillance will prevent deficits becoming unsustainable or

---

[164] Art. 126(10) TFEU states: The rights to bring actions provided for in Articles 258 and 259 may not be exercised within the framework of paragraphs 1 to 9 of this Article.

[165] Commission, 'Towards a Stability Pact', 3.

[166] Case C-27/04 *Commission v. Council* [2004] ECR I-6649; EU:C:2004:436, [81]–[86].

[167] Padoa-Schioppa, *Proceeding by Steps*, excerpted above, n 113. See also Commission, *Contributions by the Commission*, 27, 31, 36.

[168] R Morris, H Ongena and L Schuknecht, 'The Reform and Implementation of the Stability and Growth Pact' (2006) ECB Occasional Paper Series No 47, 8.

[169] Commission, 'A Stability Pact', 15–16.

[170] Commission, 'A Stability Pact', 15–16.

[171] Lamfalussy, 'Macro-Coordination', 102.

unneighbourly. Binding Community rules are undesirable because, being unnecessary, they infringe the principle of subsidiarity [and are] quite likely to have undesirable effects including the introduction of a degree of moral hazard.[172]

The only penalty for fiscal profligacy was to be non-admission to EMU for those outside it, and the cold winds of the markets for those within it.[173] Crawford observes:

> In the end, there was a good deal of agreement with the UK position, but the risk that a country with an incipient insolvency problem might enter the EMU nest was considered serious enough to warrant conditions concerning fiscal discipline, if only because [...] the risk that the Eurofed, or other EC governments, might be obliged to bail such a country out, were unpredictable.[174]

Articles 121 and 126 TFEU therefore began life not as a legal basis for centralized fiscal governance in EMU, but as 'no-entry' clause and a legal basis for convergence criteria.[175] They reflected a political compromise wherein completion of EMU would begin on a set date (1 January 1999) and in return binding convergence criteria – including binding limits on government debt – would be inscribed in the Treaty.[176] For the criteria of this mechanism, the *travaux préparatoires* settled on a debt ceiling of 60% of GDP (approximating the community average) and a deficit of 3% of GDP (considered consistent with the 60% benchmark assuming a 5% long-term growth rate in nominal GDP).[177] The final convergence criteria were fixed in Protocol (No 12) on the EDP and Protocol (No 13) on the Convergence

---

[172] HM Treasury, *An Evolutionary Approach to Economic and Monetary Union* (HM Treasury, 1989) (emphasis added).

[173] Malcolm Crawford, *One Money for Europe? The Economics and Politics of EMU* (Macmillan Press, 1996), 150, 289–290; Colette Mazzucelli, *France and Germany at Maastricht: Politics and Negotiations to Create the European Union* (Garland Publishing, 1997), 67–70.

[174] Crawford, *One Money?*, 150.

[175] Giovannini and Spaventa, 'No-Entry Clause' 255. For example, the first mention of the 3% deficit limit and attempts to define 'excessive deficits' occurred in the context of moving from Stage 1 to Stage 2: Monetary Committee, EMU Beyond Stage I (1990), 3; James, *Making EMU*, 251.

[176] On the 'economist' and 'monetarist' negotiations on whether economic convergence should precede monetary union, see: Andrew Moravcsik, *Choice for Europe* (Cornell University, 1999), 241–291, 379–472; Kenneth HF Dyson and Kevin Featherstone, *The Road to Maastricht: Negotiating Economic and Monetary Union* (Oxford University Press, 1999); James, *Making EMU*, 70–77, 210–323.

[177] O'Donnell and Honohan (eds), '*Economic and Monetary Union* 37; orenzo Bini Smaghi, Tommaso Padoa-Schioppa and Francesco Papadia, 'The Transition to EMU in the Maastricht Treaty' (1994) Essays in International Finance No 194, 28–30.

Criteria, which stipulated, *inter alia*, that a Member State must not be 'the subject of an "excessive deficit procedure"' in order to enter EMU.[178]

Yet as early as mid-1991, the Commission warned that progress towards convergence was 'faltering' and 'worrying', and by 1996, it was clear that only seven countries would have deficits below 3% of GDP.[179] Fully aware that the 'no entry' clause would prove to be no such thing (Italy, Belgium and Greece all acceded to the euro with debt-to-GDP ratios well above 60%)[180] the Council began to consider the need to ensure budgetary discipline even inside EMU,[181] and by 1996 the main features of the 'Stability and Growth Pact' to be adopted under Articles 121 and 126 were agreed.[182]

Articles 121 and 126 TFEU therefore do not derive from any conviction of the Treaty drafters that centralized fiscal rules should, or could, safeguard fiscal discipline in a federated EMU. Indeed, when proposals for a stability pact to ensure budgetary discipline *within* EMU were introduced a half-decade after Maastricht, there was no agreement even on 'how a stability pact could be implemented within existing Treaty arrangements under Article 103 and 104c'.[183] The SGP arises from an *ex post* scramble to compensate for the non-credibility of convergence criteria inscribed in primary EU law.

2.4   Conclusions: The Maastricht Architecture

The Maastricht architecture for fiscal federalism in Articles 121–126 TFEU follows a blueprint for a 'classical model' or 'market-preserving' model of fiscal federalism that is well-established in theory and well-evidenced in history. In the European Union, however, it is not a mere

---

[178] Art. 2 Protocol (No 13) on the Convergence Criteria [2008] OJ L 115/281; Art. 1 Protocol (No 12) on the excessive deficit procedure [1992] OJ C 224/35.

[179] Commission of the EC, 'Resuming Progress Towards Convergence of Economic Policies and Performances in the Community' (Communication) SEC(91) 1291 final, 1, 3. See also, Council Recommendation (EC) No 95/326/EC of 10 July 1995 on the broad guidelines of the economic policies of the Member States and of the Community [1995] OJ L 191/24, 26.

[180] Skouras, 'Lessons', 54.

[181] European Council Conclusions of 15–16 December 1995, 11.

[182] European Council, 'Conclusions of the European Council in Dublin, 13–14 December 1996' (1996) DOC 96/8. See further Lastra, *Legal Foundations*, 260–273; Martin Heipertz and Amy Vedun, *Ruling Europe: The Politics of the Stability and Growth Pact* (Cambridge University Press, 2010).

[183] Commission, 'Towards a Stability Pact', 8.

reflection of good economics; it is a function of the constitutional boundaries identified in Chapter 1 of this book.

Section 2.1 began this chapter by explaining the economic teleology of price stability that impelled the creation of monetary union itself, and Section 2.2 examined where the constitutional boundaries pursued in this book inhere in the basic principles underlying EMU. The legal architecture of fiscal federalism in Chapter 1 (Economic Policy) of Title VIII, Part III TFEU rests upon two principles:

Fiscal sovereignty – Under Articles 2(3) and 5(1) TFEU, the EU has no competence in economic policy. European fiscal federalism 'rests on the principle that Member States are responsible for their own budgets';[184] and

Market discipline – Articles 121–126 TFEU expose Member States to hard budget constraints and market discipline, internalizing the costs of poor economic decisions and so safeguarding the fundamental guiding principles of price stability and fiscal discipline binding on the mandate for EMU under Article 119(3) TFEU.

Section 2.3 examined the technical architecture of fiscal federalism inscribed in Articles 121–126 TFEU for the achievement of these principles. That architecture fulfils three criteria for establishing 'market discipline' in a federal system:

[2.3.1] The prohibition on financial assistance (Articles 123–125 TFEU) ensures that financial markets 'exercise a degree of discipline on any Member State pursuing unsound budgetary policies, by imposing differential terms on its paper and ultimately by refusing to lend,'[185] and is, beyond its literal wording, 'the expression of the responsibility of each Member State for its own public finance'.[186]
[2.3.2] The MSP (Article 121 TFEU) ensures that imbalances do not accrue hidden to markets, electorates and stakeholders, by 'monitor[ing] the full range of economic developments in each of the Member States' and giving warning when economic policies are going off track.[187]

---

[184] Alberto de Gregorio Merino, 'Legal Developments in the Economic and Monetary Union during the Debt Crisis: The Mechanisms of Financial Assistance' (2012) 49 CMLR 1613, 1626. See also, Borger, 'Predicament in *Pringle*', 118.
[185] Monetary Committee, EMU Beyond Stage I (1990), 2.
[186] Louis, 'Guest Editorial', 978.
[187] Reg 1466/97, r 6.

[2.3.3] The EDP (Article 126 TFEU) 'reinforce[s] the role of market pressure in favour of fiscal discipline'[188] by 'deter[ring] excessive general government deficits and, if they occur, [by] further[ing] their prompt correction'.[189]

The truest cornerstone of this architecture, however, is present by its absence: A legal basis for conditional financial assistance was rejected by the technical committees in 1989–1990 and excluded from the mandates for Maastricht by the Rome European Council. Instead, Article 108 EEC – which afforded the protection of 'mutual financial assistance' since the Community's founding Treaty – was written out of the title on EMU.

From this, this book extracts the hypothesis that hard budget constraints and market discipline are fundamental requirements for price stability, sound public finances and a sustainable balance of payments in an EMU bound by the fiscal sovereignty of its Member States. Chapters 1 and 2 therefore yield two testable constitutional criteria for EU fiscal federalism examined in the following chapters:

First, fiscal sovereignty is a permanent constitutional constraint upon the application of fiscal federalism theory in the EU. Any machineries of public economics which trespass on the tests for democratic legitimation in Member State legal orders may not be legally enforceable against the Member States under EU law, and will not be compatible with the European legal order, *de lege lata* or *de lege ferenda*.

Second, market discipline and hard budget constraints are indispensable requirements for price stability, sound public finances and a sustainable balance of payments under Article 119 TFEU. *Eo ipso*, systems of centralized legal governance and mutualization of risk are not compatible with these principles, and will not be compatible with the architecture for EMU inscribed in Chapter 1 (Economic Policy) of Title VIII, Part III TFEU.

---

[188] Commission, 'A Stability Pact'.
[189] Rec 1, Art. 1, Reg 1467/97.

3 The Failure and Abrogation of the Maastricht Model

The economic hypothesis obtained from the preceding chapters of this book is that hard budget constraints and market discipline are indispensable requirements for price stability and fiscal discipline in an EMU bound by the fiscal sovereignty of its Member States. In order to test that hypothesis and extract economic criteria for European fiscal federalism, this chapter analyzes public accounts statistics and the economic literature surrounding the period of 1992 to 2012 – up to and including the sovereign debt crisis – when the legal architecture in Articles 121–126 TFEU should have been operating as intended.[1] The analysis seeks to identify the stylized facts of the 2008 sovereign debt crisis in order to provide an uncontroversial basis for legal study in Part II of this book.

A legal analysis of fiscal federalism in the EU cannot be conducted independently of its economic implications. Stable prices, sound public finances and a sustainable balance of payments are fundamental principles binding on the construction of the EMU under Article 119(3) TFEU, and the constellation of provisions in Articles 121–126 TFEU are legal implements of public economics. The constitutional limits pursued in this book are written not only in law, but in economics.

In order to remain stable and permanent as a matter of law and economics, EU fiscal federalism must not only remain within its constitutional boundaries, but it must 'work'. In that regard, the EMU has now spent over

---

[1] After this period, EMU was given a new fiscal architecture and entered into a long period of relative stagnation, which is considered in Part II of this book. On grounded theory and law and economics approaches, see Methods and Introduction, nn 33 and 64.

half its life in a state of crisis.[2] Some economists estimate that Europe's GDP is now as much as 18% lower than if the euro had never been invented at all.[3] As Europe lurches into its next economic crisis, it has not recovered from the global financial crisis that arrived over a decade ago.[4]

And yet, comparative federations such as the United States and Canada – with no federal oversight of state budgets and no economic coordination – have long-since recovered from the global financial crisis. The United States, the epicentre of the 2008 financial crisis, declared its 'Great Recession' over in June 2009,[5] and its closest trading partner, Canada – another heterogeneous federation with comparable debt dispersion characteristics to the EU – suffered just seven months of recession.[6]

This chapter concludes that the 'fatal flaw' at the heart of the euro is not sovereign debt; it is not caused by public-sector governance failure; and it is not due to the inability of the EU to control the public finances of its Member States. The analysis finds that the *causa sine qua non* of the crisis is a severe mispricing of private and public debt caused by a failure of Articles 121–126 TFEU to induce markets to differentiate between sovereign borrowers under a (now-realized) bailout expectation.

This radically changes the incumbent prescription for European fiscal federalism. In the EU, the crisis is commonly described as a sovereign debt crisis. In particular, it is described in terms of the inability of crisis-hit periphery countries Portugal, Ireland, Italy, Greece and Spain (pejoratively acronymed the 'PIIGS') to run a sustainable fiscal policy.[7] All of the amendments examined in the second half of this book have been informed by the search for a legal solution to this problem.

This official characterization of the crisis is 'given the lie' by a simple glance at government finance statistics.[8] Of the common macroeconomic denominators which bind the periphery countries and

[2] The euro entered into circulation on 1 January 1999. The global financial crisis arrived in Europe in August 2007, when BNP Paribas froze redemptions on some of its structured products: Sebastian Boyd, 'BNP Paribas Freezes Funds as Loan Losses Roil Markets' *Bloomberg* (New York 9 August 2007)www.bloomberg.com/apps/news?pid=newsarchiv e&sid=aW1wj5i.vyOg accessed 20 June 2014.

[3] See sources cited in Methods and Introduction, n 9.

[4] Commission Reflection Paper (2017), 11; European Commission, 'Economic Governance Review' COM(2020) 55 final, 5.

[5] NBER, 'Business Cycle Dating Committee'.

[6] See Methods and Introduction, n 15.

[7] On this orthodoxy: Jean Pisani-Ferry, *The Euro Crisis and its Aftermath* (Oxford University Press, 2011) x; Economist, 'The PIIGS that Won't Fly' *The Economist* (18 May 2010) www .economist.com/node/15838029 accessed 7 August 2014.

[8] Skouras, 'Lessons', 55.

differentiate them from the core, excessive deficits are simply not among them.[9] The Euro Crisis was a private debt crisis, not a public one.[10] As De Grauwe and Je observe:

The surprising thing about this emerging new governance of the budgetary processes in the Eurozone is that there is so little evidence that the fiscal crisis that erupted after 2008 was the result of government profligacy prior to that date.[11]

To demonstrate this, this chapter follows the approach familiar to the literature by dividing the original twelve EMU countries on the basis of real interest and inflation rates prevailing when the decision to create EMU was taken. The 'Periphery' group consists of high-inflation, crisis-hit countries Portugal, Ireland, Italy, Greece and Spain. The 'Core' group consists of low-inflation 'responsible' countries Germany, the Netherlands, Austria, Belgium, France, Finland and Luxembourg.

The analysis follows a chain of macroeconomic indicators that describe a pattern of causality running from nominal interest-rate convergence to the sovereign debt crisis. This chapter examines: [3.1.1] nominal interest rates against key macroeconomic risk indicators; [3.1.2] structural determinants of sovereign bond yields; [3.1.3] real interest rates; [3.1.4] private-sector domestic credit; [3.2.1] cross-border credit flows and consolidated banking claims; [3.2.2] current account imbalances and external debt; [3.2.3] real effective exchange rates (REER); [3.3.1] public- and private-sector debt; [3.3.2] the sovereign-bank feedback loop; and [3.3.3] the (non) effect of fiscal policy on private-sector imbalances.

The analysis is structured in three parts, in order to trace the chain of causality through each of the three pillars of the Maastricht architecture described in Chapter 2: the prohibition on financial assistance (Articles 123–125 TFEU); the MSP (Article 121 TFEU); and the EDP (Article 126 TFEU).

Section 3.1, 'Sovereign Bond Yields and the Failure of the Prohibition on Financial Assistance', finds that the introduction of the euro precipitated unprecedented nominal interest-rate convergence which belied marked and persistent variations in underlying indicators of

---

[9] See Figure 3.3 in Section 3.1.1 at nn 31–32 and Figures 3.12–3.18 in Section 3.3.1. See also Lane, 'Sovereign Debt Crisis', 50, 55; Fagan and Gaspar, 'Adjusting to the Euro', 14: 'fiscal balances were remarkably similar across the two groups of countries'.

[10] See below, Section 3.3.1 and sources cited. For an accessible summary: The Economist, 'Not a Government Debt Crisis'.

[11] Paul De Grauwe and Uemi Ji, 'How Much Fiscal Discipline in a Monetary Union?' (2014) 39 J Macroecon 348, 349.

macroeconomic risk.[12] Markets failed to apply differentiated default risk to sovereign bonds because markets (correctly) perceived the EMU as a joint-liability group and (correctly) guessed that the EU would sooner re-interpret the Treaties than allow a Member State to default.[13] Nominal convergence meant that real interest rates in the Periphery were low or better than nil – debt was effectively subsidized by inflation.[14] Low real interest rates precipitated a rate of domestic credit expansion that was, on average, 20% of GDP higher than the next eight comparable advanced-country credit cycles in history.[15]

Section 3.2, 'Macroeconomic Imbalances and the Failure of the MSP', finds that nominal interest-rate convergence meant that unprecedented capital flows entered Periphery economies with no liquidity or inflation-risk premium,[16] fuelling current account imbalances which are unprecedented in over thirty years of economic data.[17] It concludes that the failure of the MSP to prevent – or even detect – historically unprecedented imbalances is attributable to information asymmetry problems that are well known to fiscal federalism theory.[18] Put simply, in an environment of unresponsive credit prices, all the symptoms of future insolvency are local phenomena spread across regional banks and myriad European boroughs that simply cannot be supervised or governed from the centre.[19]

Section 3.3, 'The European Sovereign Debt Crisis and the Failure of the EDP', finds that compliance with the EDP does not, and cannot, change the pattern of causality in this chapter because the 'sovereign debt crisis' is merely the final symptom of deeply rooted imbalances caused by the disconnection of real interest rates and private-sector credit from underlying economic conditions.[20] A brief counterfactual demonstrates that causality is incapable of running

---

[12] See Section 3.1.1.
[13] See Section 3.1.2.
[14] See Section 3.1.3.
[15] See Section 3.1.4. IMF, *Euro Area Policies: 2013 Article IV Consultation* (IMF Country Report No 13/232, 2013), 60.
[16] See Section 3.2.1.
[17] See Section 3.2.2 and 3.2.3.
[18] See Section 3.2.4.
[19] See Section 3.2.4 and sources cited.
[20] See Sections 3.3.1–3.3.2.

in reverse: Real interest rates are, in fact, 'a monetary phenomenon' – not a fiscal one – and no optimal fiscal policy is shown to
be capable of causing, or preventing, the crisis.[21] The EDP anyways
failed to function under its own terms. By 2011, the SGP debt/deficit
rules had been exceeded ninety-seven times, and no sanctions for
violation had ever been imposed.[22]

By proceeding through these three analyses, this chapter finds that
the prevailing view emergent from the economic literature is rather
robust: The dysfunction at the heart of the euro is the disconnection
of euro-area credit prices from economic fundamentals prevailing at
national level – not sovereign debt.[23]

3.1 Sovereign Debt Yields and the Failure of the Prohibition on Financial Assistance

3.1.1 Nominal Interest-Rate Convergence

Prior to the introduction of the euro, ten-year government bonds were
subject to individuated market pricing. In 1992, the year the Maastricht
Treaty was signed, Germany borrowed at 7.84%, Italy borrowed at nearly
double that rate, at 13.28%, and Greece borrowed at nearly double that, at
24.13% (Figure 3.1).

These interest rates reflected individuated market assessments of
the variety of fundamentals which constitute aggregate risk in each
country. From a theoretical perspective, the price of debt may be

---

[21] See Section 3.3.3. David E Rapach and Mark E Wohar, 'Regime Changes in International Real Interest Rates: Are They a Monetary Phenomenon?' (2005) 37 J Money Credit Bank 887.

[22] See Section 3.3.4. EEAG Report 2011, 94.

[23] For established tenets of the crisis, see: Richard Baldwin and Francesco Giavazzi, *The Eurozone Crisis: A Consensus View of the Causes and a Few Possible Solutions* (CEPR Press, 2015); Philip Lane, 'The European Sovereign Debt Crisis' (2012) 26 J Econ Persp 49; Gabriel Fagan and Vitor Gaspar, 'Macroeconomic Adjustment to Monetary Union' (2008) ECB Working Paper Series No 946; Gabriel Fagan and Vitor Gaspar, 'Adjusting to the Euro' (2007) ECB Working Paper Series No 716, 11–12; Francesco Giavazzi and Eleanor Spaventa, 'The Current Account in a Monetary Union' in Miroslav Beblavy, David Cobham and L'udovit Ódor (eds), *The Euro Area and the Financial Crisis* (Cambridge University Press, 2011), 199; Philip Lane, 'Capital Flows in the Euro Area' (2013) European Economy Economic Papers No 497; George Chouliarakis and Sophia Lazaretou, 'Deja vu? The Greek Crisis Experience, 2010's versus the 1930's.' (2010) Bank of Greece Working Papers No 176; Sebastian Barnes, Philip Lane and Artur Radziwill, 'Minimising Risks from Imbalances in European Banking' (2010) OECD Economics Department Working Papers No 828; EEAG Report 2011.

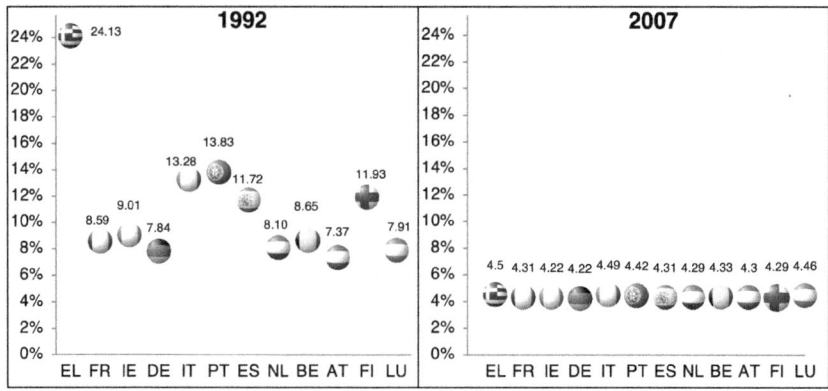

Figure 3.1 Interest rates on ten-year government bonds (per cent per annum)[24]

decomposed into two components: Risk endogenous to the invest-ment and risk in the macroeconomic environment. To account for the latter component, markets set a basic price for debt through a variety of fundamentals which indicate the economic well-being of the country.[25] The basic price on a riskless asset is a calculated insurance premium against risks inherent in the macroeconomic environment.

This basic price is typically represented in sovereign bond yields. Sovereign bond yields are important because they typically constitute the 'floor' for funding conditions in the private sector.[26] All other investments in the country are exposed to the credit and currency risk of the sovereign, but the sovereign is not typically exposed to the credit risk of individual firms. For example, a country unable to pay its debt may instead choose to monetize the debt, inducing the central bank to increase the money supply and using devalued currency to pay back debtors in nominal terms. This manages default risk by increasing currency risk: An investor may be paid back in nominal terms, but the

---

[24] Eurostat, 'Maastricht Criterion Interest Rates (irt_lt_mcby_a)'.

[25] For key factors see Jürgen von Hagen, Ludger Schuknecht and Guido Wolswijk, 'Government Bond Risk Premiums in the EU Revisited: The Impact of the Financial Crisis' (2011) 27 Eur J Polit Econ 36; Kerstin Bernoth, Jürgen von Hagen and Ludger Schuknecht, 'Sovereign Risk Premiums in the European Government Bond Market' (2012) 31 J Int Money Financ 975 and sources cited below, Section 3.1.1, nn 30–36.

[26] Jean-Claude Trichet, 'The ECB's Response to the Recent Tensions in Financial Markets' (38th Economic Conference of the *Oesterreichische Nationalbank*, Vienna, 31 May 2010).

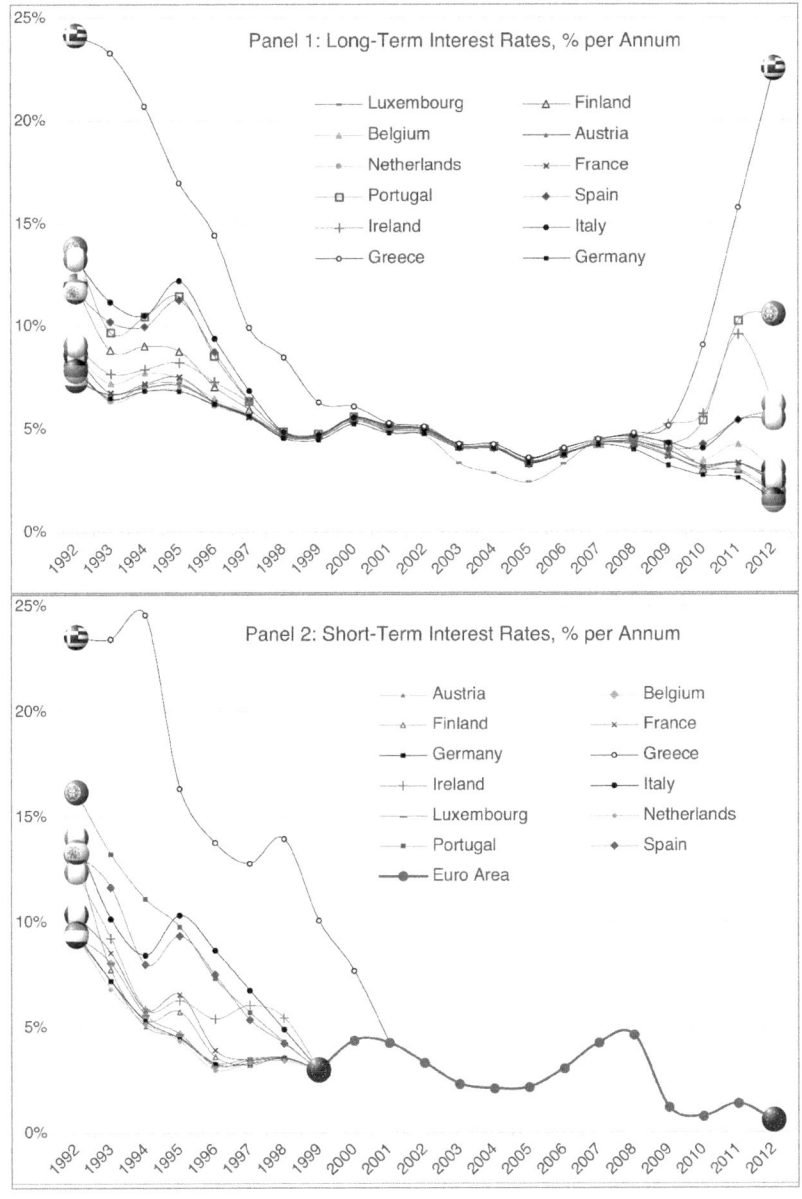

Figure 3.2 Nominal interest rates 1992–2012 (per cent per annum)[27]

[27] Panel 1: Interest rates on ten-year government bonds. Eurostat, 'Maastricht Criterion Interest Rates (irt_lt_mcby_a)'. Panel 2: Interest rates on three-year government bonds. Large, bold 'EU' nodules represent the dates under when the national bonds fell under the single interest rate policy of the ECB. Eurostat, 'Money-market interest rates – annual data; 3-month rates (irt_lt_mcby_a; MAT_M03)' (*Eurostat*, 25 April 2016) http://epp .eurostat.ec.europa.eu accessed 14 September 2016.

return on the investment is proportionally diminished. As this affects all debts denominated in that currency, this risk raises the basic price of credit across the entire economy.[28] A private borrower seeking to price a loan will therefore borrow at the rate of the sovereign, plus its own individuated default risk.

Sovereign bond yields can themselves be decomposed into two main components: Default risk (or credit risk) and currency risk (also known as inflation risk or exchange rate risk).[29] Default risk is the assessment of the probability of a sovereign default itself: The more likely it is that the creditor may not be paid back, the more they demand in the way of interest to compensate them for the risk. Currency risk represents the cost imposed by inflation over the period of a loan. This is important because inflation dilutes the value of a loan: if an investor anticipates a 10% return on an investment, a 10% depreciation in the value of the currency would reduce that return to zero.

Prior to the introduction of the euro, the differences in macroeconomic fundamentals between countries led to starkly differentiated yields on long-term government debt. In 1992, long-term interest rates ranged from a high of 24.13% (Greece) to a low of 7.37% (Austria). From 1999, however – the year the euro was introduced – spreads between government bonds had been reduced to zero. The markets considered government bonds to be near-perfect substitutes, with bond yields converging at a mean of 4.35% (±0.14%) (Figures 3.1 and 3.2).

This unprecedented nominal interest-rate convergence belied marked and persistent variations in underlying macroeconomic fundamentals of risk. Figure 3.3, for example, shows general government debt and general government deficits as a percentage of GDP. Traditionally, both measures are prime indicators of risk: They comprise over 50% of fiscal risk assessments by rating agencies, and both are Maastricht convergence criteria.[30] Yet the data reveals marked and persistent divergences over the period of 1993–2008. Greece, Italy and Belgium never come close to complying with the 60% of GDP gross debt

---

[28] Thomas Laubach, 'New Evidence on the Interest Rate Effects of Budget Deficits and Debt' (2009) 7 JEEA 858; Wyplosz, 'Dark sides', 225.

[29] Alberto Alesina et al., 'Default Risk on Government Debt in OECD Countries' (1992) 7 Econ Policy 427; De Grauwe, *Economics of Monetary Union* (2020), 231.

[30] Moody's, *Rating Methodology: Sovereign Bond Ratings* (Moody's, 2013); Standard and Poor's, *Sovereign Government Rating Methodology and Assumptions* (Standard & Poor's, 2013).

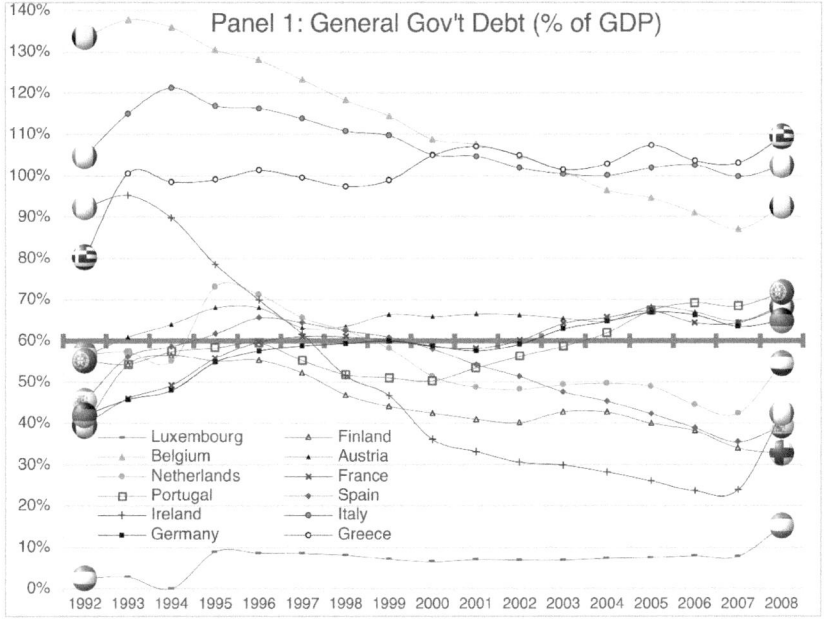

Figure 3.3 Consolidated gross government debt[31] and general government deficit[32] (percentage of GDP)

limit; Greece and Portugal breach the 3% of GDP deficit limit for the entire period of EMU; and Germany and France remain in breach from 2001–2006, and 2002–2005, respectively. There is no pattern of convergence similar to that of nominal interest rates.

---

[31] Panel 1: Maastricht indicator = 60% of GDP. Eurostat, 'Consolidated Gross Debt (gov_10dd_3dpt1)'. Data to 1994 (to 1995 for Ireland) from IMF, 'General government gross debt (percentage of GDP)' (*IMF World Economic Outlook*, 2016) www.imf.org/exter nal/pubs/ft/weo/2016/01/weodata/index.aspx accessed 14 September 2016. 1994 data unavailable for Luxembourg.

[32] Panel 2: Maastricht indicator = –3% GDP. Eurostat, 'Deficit/surplus (gov_10dd_edpt1)'. Data to 1994 from IMF, 'General Government Net Lending/Borrowing (percentage of GDP)' (*IMF World Economic Outlook*, April 2016) www.imf.org/external/pubs/ft/weo/2016/ 01/weodata/weoselser.aspx accessed 14 September 2016. Luxembourg, Ireland data to 1994 from World Bank, 'Surplus/Deficit (% of GDP) (GC.BAL.CASH.GD.ZS)' (*World Bank*, 2016) www.data.worldbank.org accessed 13 September 2016.

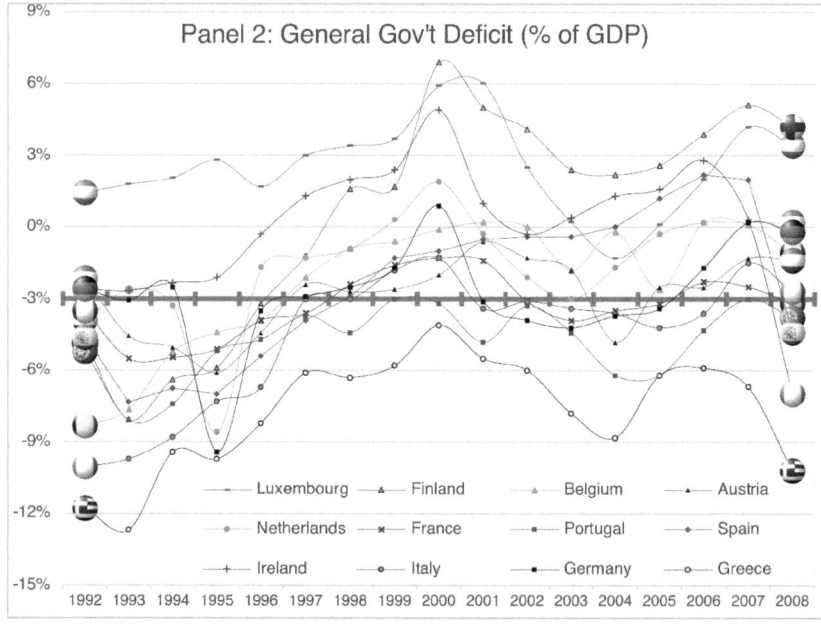

Figure 3.3 (cont.)

A similar disconnect can be observed against a miscellany of keystone components of risk. Figure 3.4 divides the EMU countries into their Core and Periphery groups. It compares national wealth (typically accounting for at least 25% of a country's economic strength rating);[33] debt affordability (approximately 50% of a country's fiscal strength rating);[34] inflation (25% of a country's institutional strength rating); competitiveness (about 17% of a country's economic strength rating);[35] and the current account balance (a 'max risk indicator' for credit ratings).[36] It shows that, while long-term interest rates converge, economic risk indicators do not.

Other studies find a similar convergence in bond yields all across the yield spectrum, indicating that markets failed to react to idiosyncratic risk

[33] Standard and Poor's, *Rating Methodology*, 3; Moody's, *Rating Methodology*.
[34] Moody's, *Rating Methodology*; Bernoth et al., 'Sovereign Risk Premiums'.
[35] Moody's, *Rating Methodology*, 3.
[36] A max risk indicator is capable of overriding all countervailing factors of any weight: Moody's, *Rating Methodology*, 3; Standard and Poor's, *Rating Methodology*.

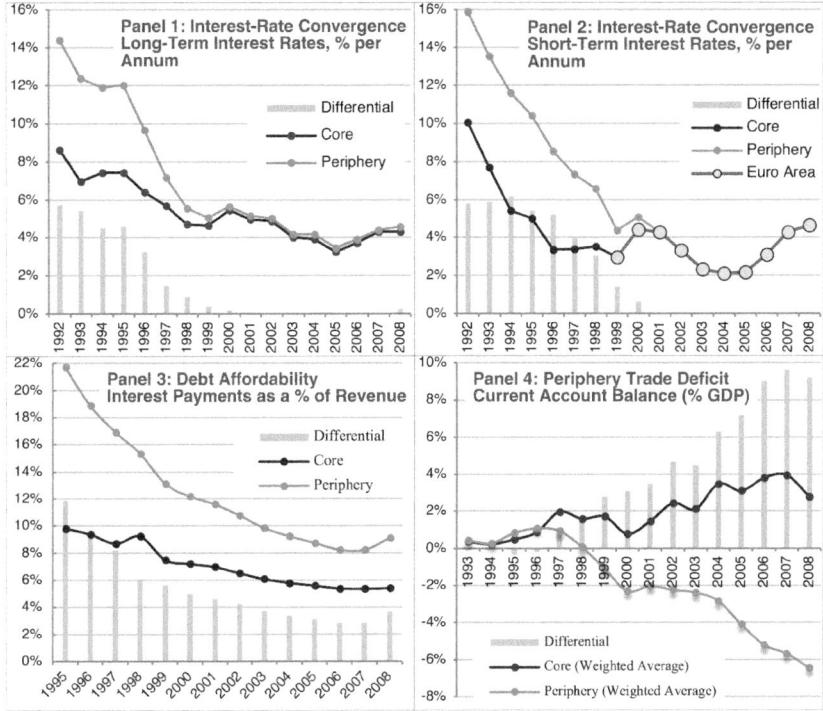

Figure 3.4 Nominal interest-rate convergence and macroeconomic risk divergence[37]

---

[37] All series calculated as unweighted averages unless otherwise noted. Panel 1: Interest rates on ten-year gov't bonds, Eurostat, 'Maastricht Criterion Interest Rates (irt_lt_mcby_a)'. Panel 2: Interest rates on three-month gov't bonds. The 'Euro Area' data series indicates the period under which short-term bonds are determined under ECB monetary policy. Eurostat, '3-month interest rates (irt_lt_mcby_a; MAT_M03)'. Panel 3: World Bank, 'Interest Payments as a % of Revenue (GC. XPN.INTP.RV.ZS)' (World Bank, 2015) data.worldbank.org accessed 26 November 2015. Core group average from 1995–1998 excludes Luxembourg due to data unavailability. Panel 4: Percentage of GDP calculated as the percentage of each individual country's GDP. IMF, 'Current Account Balance, % GDP' (IMF World Economic Outlook, 2016) www.imf.org/external/pubs/ft/weo/2016/01/weodata/index .aspx accessed 17 September 2016. Panel 5: World Bank, 'Real Effective Exchange Rate (PX.REX.REER)' (World Bank, 2014) www.data.worldbank.org accessed 26 November 2014. Panel 6: World Bank, 'GDP Per Capita (Current LCU)' (World Bank, 2014) www.data.worldbank.org accessed 26 November 2014. Panels 7–8: World Bank, 'Inflation by GDP Deflator (NY.GDP.DEFL.KD.ZG)' (World Bank, 2016) www.data.worldbank.org accessed 15 September 2016.

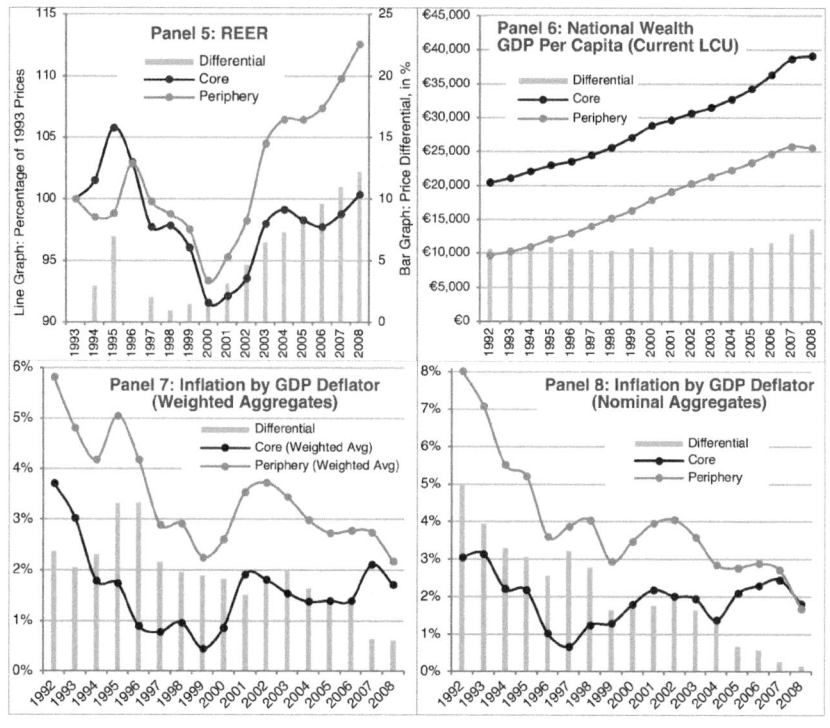

Figure 3.4 (cont.)

even where this entailed breaches of the SGP.[38] This is so despite the fact that business cycles did not become more aligned after EMU,[39] and nominal convergence did not eliminate country-specific shocks.[40]

[38] António Afonso and Rolf Strauch, 'Fiscal Policy Events and Interest Rate Swap Spreads: Evidence from the EU' (2007) 17 Int Fin Markets, Inst and Money 261; Fabrizio Balassone, Daniele Franco and Raffaela Giordano, 'Market-Induced Fiscal Discipline', Public Debt (Banca d'Italia, 2004), 394–395; Lieven Baele et al., 'Measuring Financial Integration in the Euro Area' (2004) 20 Oxford Rev Econ Policy 509, 516; Lorenzo Codogno et al., 'Yield Spreads on EMU Government Bonds' (2008) 18 Econ Policy 505; Luc Everaert, 'Euro Area Sovereign Risk During the Crisis' (2009) IMF Working Paper 222; Carlo Favero, Marco Pagano and Ernst-Ludwig von Thadden, 'How Does Liquidity Affect Government Bond Yields?' (2010) 45 J Financ Quant Anal 107; Heather Gibson, Stephen Hall and George Tavlas, 'The Greek Financial Crisis: Growing Imbalances and Sovereign Spreads' (2012) 31 J Int Money Financ 498 and sources cited below, n 207.

[39] Fabio Canova, Matteo Ciccarelli and Eva Ortega, 'Similarities and Convergence in G-7 Cycles' (2007) 54 J Monetary Econ 580.

[40] Michael Ehrmann et al., 'Convergence and Anchoring of Yield Curves in the Euro Area' (2011) 93 Rev Econ Stat 350, 358.

Ehrmann et al.'s study of high-frequency bond yields (which should be highly reactive to small idiosyncratic shocks) is typical:

> There is not a single day after 1999 on which the two-year yield on government notes was noticeably different in one of the countries compared to the others.[41]

3.1.2   The Interest Rate Channel and the Bailout Expectation

In the EMU, the complete elimination of interest rate spreads is the product of three mechanisms. First, the ECB accepted all government bonds on equal terms regardless of credit and inflation risk.[42] Second, under Directive 93/6/EEC on capital adequacy (CRD), any and all European sovereign bonds were assigned a default 0% risk weight, allowing banks to purchase unlimited amounts of government debt without holding any Tier 1 capital against it.[43] Ordinarily, investments in risky bonds or 'risk-weighted assets' (RWA), must be offset by burdensome capital-adequacy ratios that hinder leverage. But with a single face value set for all bonds by the ECB, and a universal 0% risk weight, commercial banks could purchase higher-yield bonds that had, shortly ago, been Baa3 outside the euro area (e.g. Greece, before entry to EMU), and then deposit them at the ECB 'as collateral for freshly-printed money' on equal terms as AAA bonds.[44] The effect was an immediate increase in cross-border banking claims as banks surged to lend to Periphery countries in order to accrue extra basis points.[45] As the OECD admonishes, 'the zero-risk weighting for sovereign debt in regulatory capital requirements does not accurately reflect risks'.[46] The Commission offers a similar conclusion:

> [C]onferring upon [sovereign bonds] the top-quality status required for central bank collateral [resulted in] strong yield convergence, considerably limiting market discipline, despite differences in national budgetary performances.[47]

Third – and most importantly for this book – markets ceased to price individuated credit risk along the maturity spectrum of sovereign bonds

---

[41] Ehrmann et al., 'Yield Curves', 358.

[42] EEAG Report 2011, 72; Trichet, 'ECB's Response'.

[43] Council Directive 93/6/EEC on the capital adequacy of investments firms and credit institutions [1993] OJ L 141/1.

[44] Peter Boone and Simon Johnson, 'The Next Global Problem: Portugal' *The New York Times* (New York 15 April 2010). http://economix.blogs.nytimes.com/2010/04/15/the-next-global-problem-portugal/ accessed 13 October 2016. EEAG Report 2011, 80.

[45] George Soros, 'Remarks at the Festival of Economics' (Festival of Economics, Trento, Italy, 2 June 2012).

[46] OECD, *Economic Surveys: Euro Area 2012* (OECD Publishing, 2012), 52.

[47] Commission Blueprint, 3.

because markets (correctly) perceived the EMU as a joint-liability group and (correctly) assessed that the legal 'no bailout' rule in Article 125 TFEU was not credible.[48] As explained by the President of the Federal Association of German Banks:

The markets never believed in the so-called 'no- bailout' clause of the Maastricht Treaty . . . [they] were confident that 'in an emergency, the strong countries would support the weak ones', a view based on European politicians' lax treatment of their own rules early in the game. Those who bought Greek bonds on a large scale at the time were betting that Europe's statesmen would break their rules if a crisis came along.[49]

Markets and ratings agencies were quite open about the reason for failing to price individuated credit risk into periphery bonds. In 1993, for example, Moody's had assigned Greece a Baa3 credit rating (one notch above junk).[50] In December 1996, this was raised to Baa1 – despite worsening external debt – due to 'the likelihood that the government's efforts would eventually qualify the country to join the European Monetary Union'.[51] Then, in 1997, Greece's drachma-denominated credit rating was upgraded to A2,[52] and its foreign-currency-denominated ratings followed suit in 1999.[53] The final rating stated:

[I]n *recognition of the high likelihood that Greece will soon qualify to join the* [. . .] *European Monetary Union* [. . .] Baa1-rated foreign-currency bonds issued by the Hellenic Republic and by the Bank of Greece are upgraded to A2. *In*

[48] Palmstorfer, 'To Bail Out', 777; Maurice Adams, Federico Fabbrini and Pierre Larouche, 'The Constitutionalization of European Budgetary Constraints' in Adams, Fabbrini and Larouche (eds), *Constitutionalization of European Budgetary Constraints*, 2; Jonathan Rodden, 'Can Market Discipline Survive in the US Federation?' in Paul E Peterson and Daniel Nadler (eds), *The Global Debt Crisis: Haunting US and European Federalism* (Brookings Institution Press, 2014), 45.

[49] Spiegel, 'The Ticking Euro Bomb: How a Good Idea Became a Tragedy' *Spiegel* (5 October 2011) www.spiegel.de/international/europe/the-ticking-euro-bomb-how-a-g ood-idea-became-a-tragedy-a-790138.html accessed 24 July 2015.

[50] Moody's, 'Moody's Assigns Long- and Short-term Sovereign Ceilings' (*Moody's*, 2 October 1995) www.moodys.com/research accessed 21 September 2016.

[51] Moody's, 'Moody's Upgrades Sovereign Ceiling Ratings of Greece to Baa1' (Moody's, 23 December 1996) www.moodys.com/credit-ratings/Greece-Government-of-credit-rating-348330 accessed 15 August 2020 see explanation in: Moody's, 'Moody's Will Review for Possible Downgrade to Greece's Long-Term Foreign Currency Country Ceilings' (*Moody's*, 20 February 1998) www.moodys.com/research accessed 21 September 2016.

[52] Moody's, 'Moody's Assigns A2 Rating to Drachma Denominated Bond of the Government of Greece' (*Moody's*, 28 January 1997) www.moodys.com/research accessed 18 September 2016.

[53] Moody's, 'Greece's Foreign Currency Rating Outlook Changed to Positive' (*Moody's*, 10 February 1999) www.moodys.com/research accessed 21 September 2016.

accordance with Moody's methodology on the ratings of current EMU member governments, Greece's probable entrance into the currency union indicates that the foreign- and domestic-currency government bond ratings should be merged at the level of the current A2 domestic currency rating.

The EMU was a joint-liability group.[54] As Gaillard observes, Fitch, Moody's and S&P 'were convinced that the Eurozone was a *default-free monetary union* and therefore upgraded most countries that were not already in the AAA rating category at the beginning of the period'.[55] Even before the euro was issued, there was empirical evidence by the early 1990s that 'Membership in the EC itself is associated with a perceived increase in the probability of a bailout.'[56] This explained why, for instance, Greek membership in the EC allowed it to maintain comparable debt levels to those which caused financial crises in Mexico and Turkey.[57] Throughout the life of the euro, sovereign bond yields ceased to be driven by idiosyncratic default risk factors,[58] and market spreads showed more sensitivity to debt in countries outside the euro area than within it, signalling a widespread bailout expectation.[59] Californian bonds, for example, experienced a greater differential from the United States average than Greek bonds did from the EMU average, despite California enjoying a far better economic position relative to its fellows.[60] Five years into the life of the euro, the *Financial Times* reported:

In theory, the founding Maastricht treaty is clear that countries that cannot keep their public finances in order cannot expect to be bailed out by others or by the ECB. In practice, however [...] there has been little differentiation in a market that has tended to believe that there is an implicit guarantee of all euro-zone government debt.[61]

---

[54] Riccardo Faini, 'Fiscal Policy and Interest Rates in Europe' (2006) 47 Econ Policy 443; Martin Feldstein, 'The Euro and the Stability Pact' (2005) 27 J Policy Model 421, 422.

[55] Norbert Gaillard, 'How and Why Credit Rating Agencies Missed the Eurozone Debt Crisis' (2014) 9 Cap Mark Law J 1, 1 (emphasis added).

[56] Lane, 'Market Discipline', 64. See also Bovenberg et al., 'EMU in Europe', 379–382.

[57] Miranda Xafa, 'EMU and Greece: Issues and Prospects for Membership' in Mario Baldassarri and Robert Mundell (eds), *Building the New Europe Volume I: The Single Market and Monetary Unification* (Palgrave Macmillan, 1990).

[58] See sources cited above, n 38.

[59] Barry Eichengreen, 'The Breakup of the Euro Area' in Alberto Alesina and Francesco Giavazzi (eds), *Europe and the Euro* (University of Chicago Press, 2010), 51.

[60] Jacques Mélitz, 'How To Save the Euro? Lessons from the US' in Beblavy, Cobham and Ódor (eds), *Euro Area and Financial Crisis*, 342.

[61] Editorial, 'ECB Shows its Hand' *Financial Times* (London 10 November 2005) www.ft.com /intl/cms/s/0/9a4c8a78-518e-11da-ac3b-0000779e2340.html#axzz3VDieCPOQ accessed 23 March 2015.

3.1.3   Low and Negative Real Interest Rates

Nominal interest-rate convergence resulted in a significant mispricing of the real cost of credit. This chapter selects the *ex post* real interest rate measure to indicate the real cost of debt.[62] The real *ex post* interest rate indicates the real yield (and real cost) of debt by factoring the impact of inflation on returns.[63] This is denoted by the Fisher equation ($i = r+\pi$), which states that the real cost of money (r) is approximately the nominal interest rate (i), minus inflation (π), or: ($r = i\text{-}\pi$).[64] If, for example, a firm can borrow at 4% (i), and the inflation rate is 3% (π), then the real cost of credit for that firm is 1% (r) or: ($4_i\text{-}3_\pi = 1_r$).

According to the 'Taylor rule', nominal interest rates must be set higher than inflation in order to turn a profit: A negative real interest-rate of -1% means that the lender issues €100 in order to receive €99 at maturity. Below-Taylor-rule interest rates are associated with a litany of distortive macroeconomic consequences.[65] This was the essence of the (in)famous 'Walters Critique', which informed the UK's decision to remain outside EMU:[66] A single interest rate would result in a damaging feedback cycle of low real interest rates in countries with above-average inflation, inducing credit expansion in those countries, which further increases inflation, which further discounts real interest rates, which further increases credit expansion, and so on.

---

[62] On use of the *ex post* measure in this context see Sebastian Barnes, 'Resolving and Avoiding Unsustainable Imbalances in the Euro Area' (2010) OECD Economics Department Working Papers No 827, 14–15. For criticism: ECB, *Monetary Policy and Inflation Differentials in a Heterogenous Currency Area* (ECB Monthly Bulletin May 2005), 69–70.

[63] Contrary to early theories, lenders do not always adequately account for inflation when pricing loans *ex ante*, so inflation cuts into yields *ex post*. Steven Leuthold, 'Interest Rates, Inflation and Deflation' (1981) 37 FAJ 28; Robert Mundell, 'Inflation and Real Interest' (1963) 71 JPE 280; Frederic Mishkin, 'The Real Interest Rate: A Multi-Country Empirical Study' (1984) 17 Can J Econ 283; Cf: Eugene Fama and Michael Gibbons, 'Inflation, Real Returns and Capital Investment' (1982) 9 J Monetary Econ 297.

[64] Where *i* denotes the nominal interest rate, *r* denotes the real interest rate, and *π* denotes the inflation rate. See further: Irving Fisher, *The Rate of Interest* (Macmillan, 1907); Irving Fisher, *The Theory of Interest* (Macmillan, 1930).

[65] John Taylor, 'Discretion versus Policy Rules in Practice' (1993) 39 Carnegie-Rochester Conference Series on Public Policy 195; John Taylor, 'The Financial Crisis and the Policy Responses: An Empirical Analysis of What Went Wrong' (2009) NBER Working Papers No 14631; André Perold, 'Negative Real Interest Rates: The Conundrum for Investment and Spending Policies' (2012) 69 FAJ 6; Rudiger Ahrend, 'Monetary Ease: A Factor behind Financial Crisis? Some Evidence from OECD Countries' (2010) 4 Economics 1.

[66] Alan Walters, *Sterling in Danger: The Economic Consequences of Pegged Exchange Rates* (Institute of Economic Affairs, 1990) predicted the EMS would prove unstable with the removal of capital controls.

Figures 3.5 to 3.7 show *ex post* real interest rates for the Periphery and Core groups from 1993–2007. In 1993, the year of the Maastricht Treaty, there was a substantial country-risk premium included in the price of credit, resulting in above-Taylor-rule rates ($i = r+\pi$).[67] So, for example, in Ireland in 1993, inflation (π) was 5.2%, and the short-term interest rate (i) was 9.6%, ensuring a real return (r) of 4.4% ($9.6\%_i - 5.2\%_\pi = 4.5\%_r$).[68]

As predicted by the Walters Critique, nominal interest-rate convergence reverses this trend. The nominal interest rate no longer accounts for the cost of inflation in the Periphery, and the real price of credit falls. Periphery real long-term rates move significantly lower than the Core group beginning in 1996 and never rise above 2%. Average short-term rates turn *negative* within two years of entry into EMU and never rise above zero until 2006. For much of the life of the euro between 1999 and 2007, the real cost of short-term credit in the Periphery group was better than free – debt was subsidized by inflation.

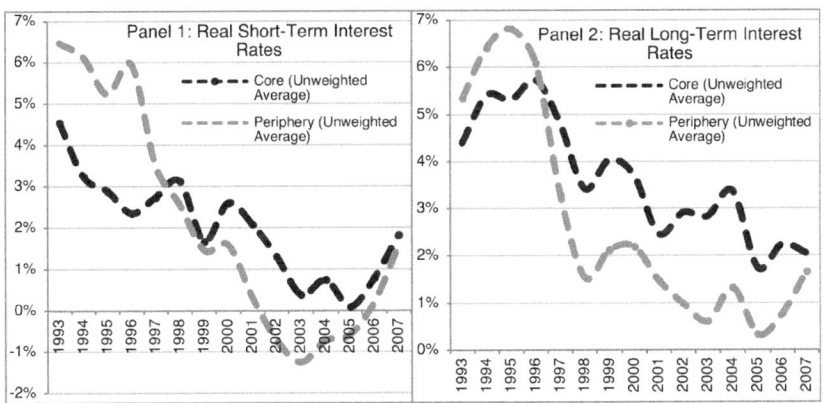

Figure 3.5 Real interest rates, 1993–2007 (per cent per annum): Core and Periphery[69]

---

67 Philip Lane, 'The Irish Crisis' in Beblavy, Cobham and Ódor (eds), *Euro Area and Financial Crisis*, 75.
68 World Bank, 'Inflation by GDP Deflator (NY.GDP.DEFL.KD.ZG)'; Eurostat, '3-month interest rates (irt_lt_mcby_a; MAT_M03)'.
69 OECD, 'Short-Term Interest Rates, Per cent per annum' (*OECD Monthly Monetary and Financial Statistics (MEI)*), http://stats.oecd.org accessed 15 September 2016, adjusted for inflation by GDP Deflator: World Bank, 'Inflation by GDP Deflator (NY.GDP.DEFL.KD.ZG)'.

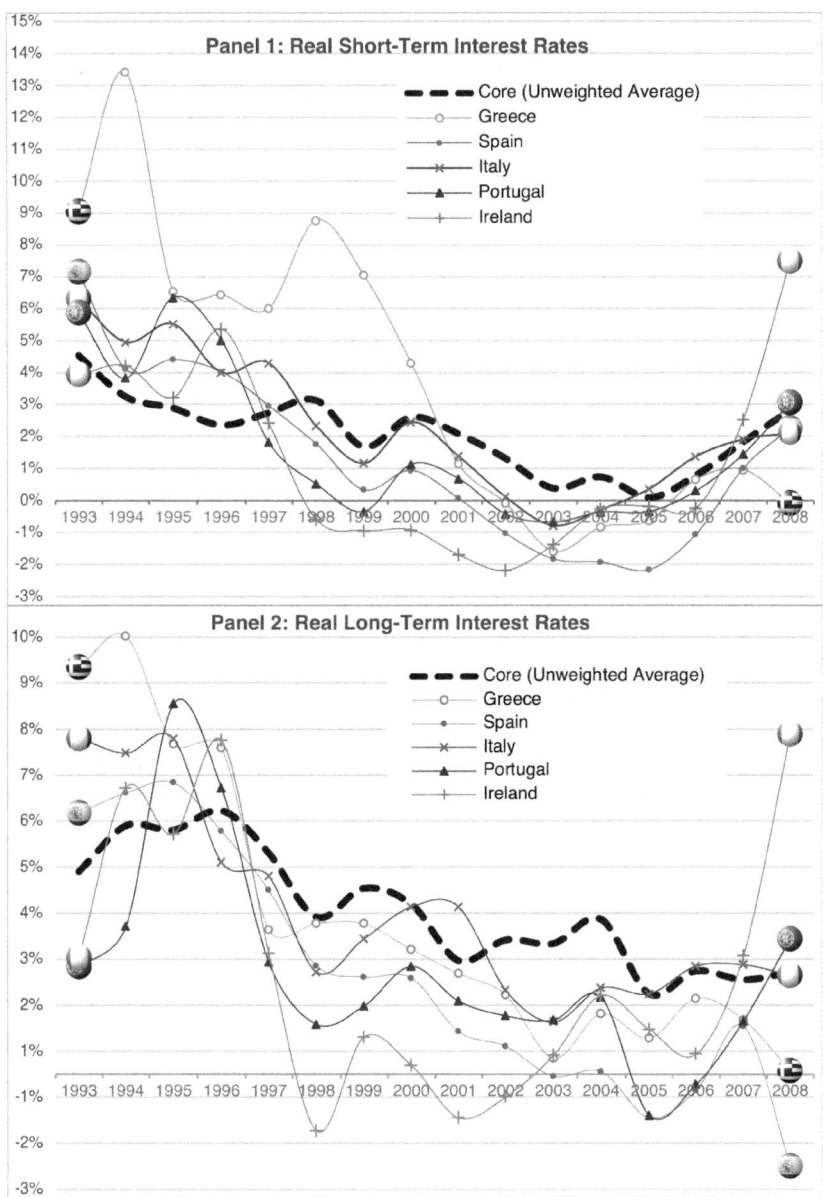

Figure 3.6 Real interest rates, 1993–2008 (percent per annum): Periphery countries[70]

[70] OECD, 'Short-Term Interest Rates' adjusted by GDP deflator: World Bank, 'Inflation by GDP Deflator (NY.GDP.DEFL.KD.ZG)'.

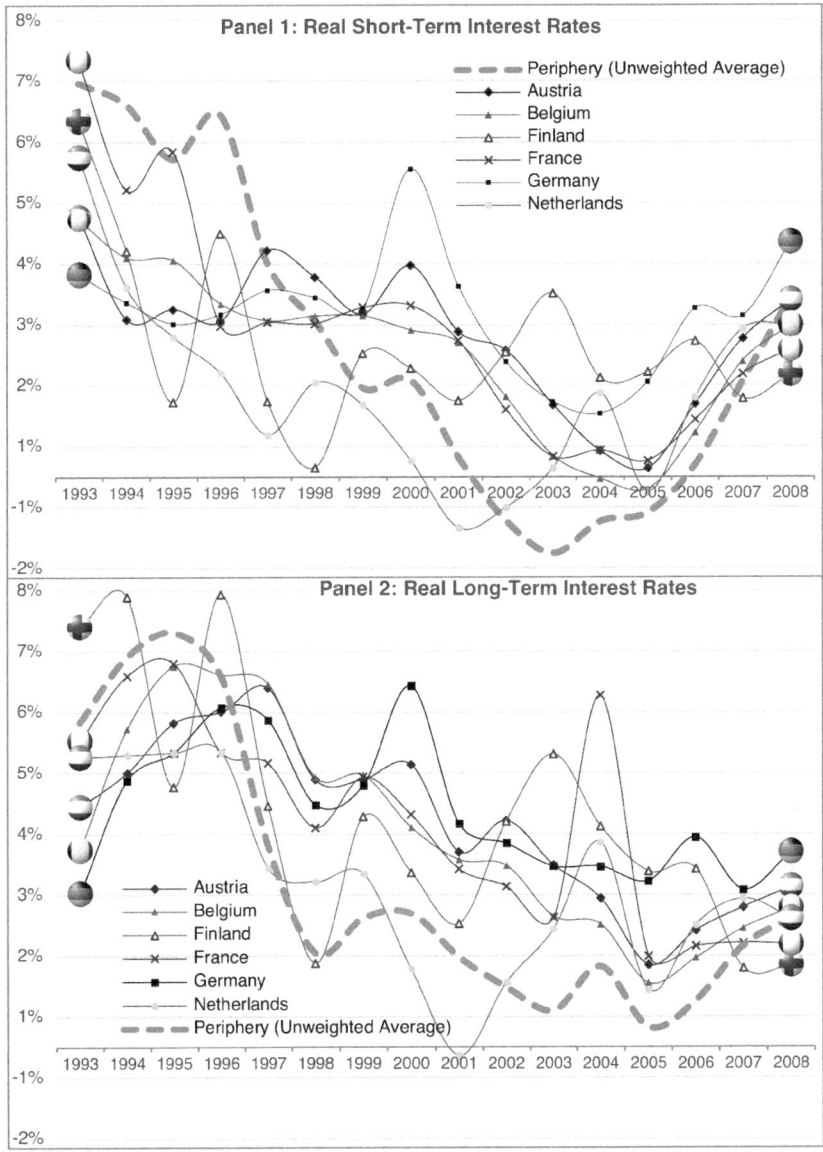

Figure 3.7 Real interest rates, 1993–2008 (per cent per annum): Core countries[71]

---

[71] OECD, 'Short-Term Interest Rates' adjusted by GDP deflator: World Bank, 'Inflation by GDP Deflator (NY.GDP.DEFL.KD.ZG)'.

3.1.4   Private-Sector Credit Expansion

The result was an unprecedented credit boom. According to the IMF, the increase in household indebtedness in the Periphery was, on average, 20 percentage points of GDP higher than the next eight comparable advanced-country credit cycles in history.[72] The creation of EMU was itself an asymmetric shock. The drop in interest rates in Periphery countries meant that households, firms and governments in the Periphery countries faced a permanent reduction in the cost of capital, triggering expenditure booms in those countries.[73]

Figure 3.8 shows an unprecedented acceleration of private-sector credit growth in all of the crisis-hit Periphery countries. In Ireland, the level of private credit increased over 165% from 1998 to 2009 (from 87.24% of GDP to 232%). Its total increase in private-sector domestic credit from 1993 (the year of the Maastricht Treaty) to 2007 (the last year before the crisis hit) was a whopping 368%. In Spain the level of private credit rose by nearly 150% from 1998 to 2009 (from 85.18% of GDP to 212.39%), and in Portugal it more than doubled (from 89.24% to 186.78%). The total increase in private-sector domestic credit between 1993 and 2007 for Spain and Portugal was 145% and 188%, respectively. Greece started slightly later due to its 2001 entry, but finished with the second-highest overall credit growth (114% – from 47.4% to 94.28% between 2000 and 2009). Its total percentage increase in private-sector domestic credit from 1993 to 2007 was 236%. Italy's credit growth occurred in two stages depending on whether it was experiencing Periphery or Core group real interest rates. From 1997 to 2004, Italy experienced lower-than-Core or negative real interest rates and its credit growth (55%) is in line with the Periphery cohort over that period (see Figure 3.6 and Figure 3.8). Then in 2005, Italy's inflation fell to the level of the Core (implying positive real interest rates), and its rate of credit growth tracks the average Core rate (of 25% from 2005 to 2009). The result is an overall increase of 66% (1997–2009), more than double the average Core increase (19.7%), but less than half the average Periphery increase (200%). Its total increase of domestic credit to private sector between 1993 and 2007 was 67%. As Italy demonstrates, low real interest rates operate as something of an on/off switch for credit expansion.

---

[72] IMF, *2013 Article IV Consultation (Euro Area)*.
[73] Lane, 'Irish Crisis', 74–75; Commission Blueprint, 3.

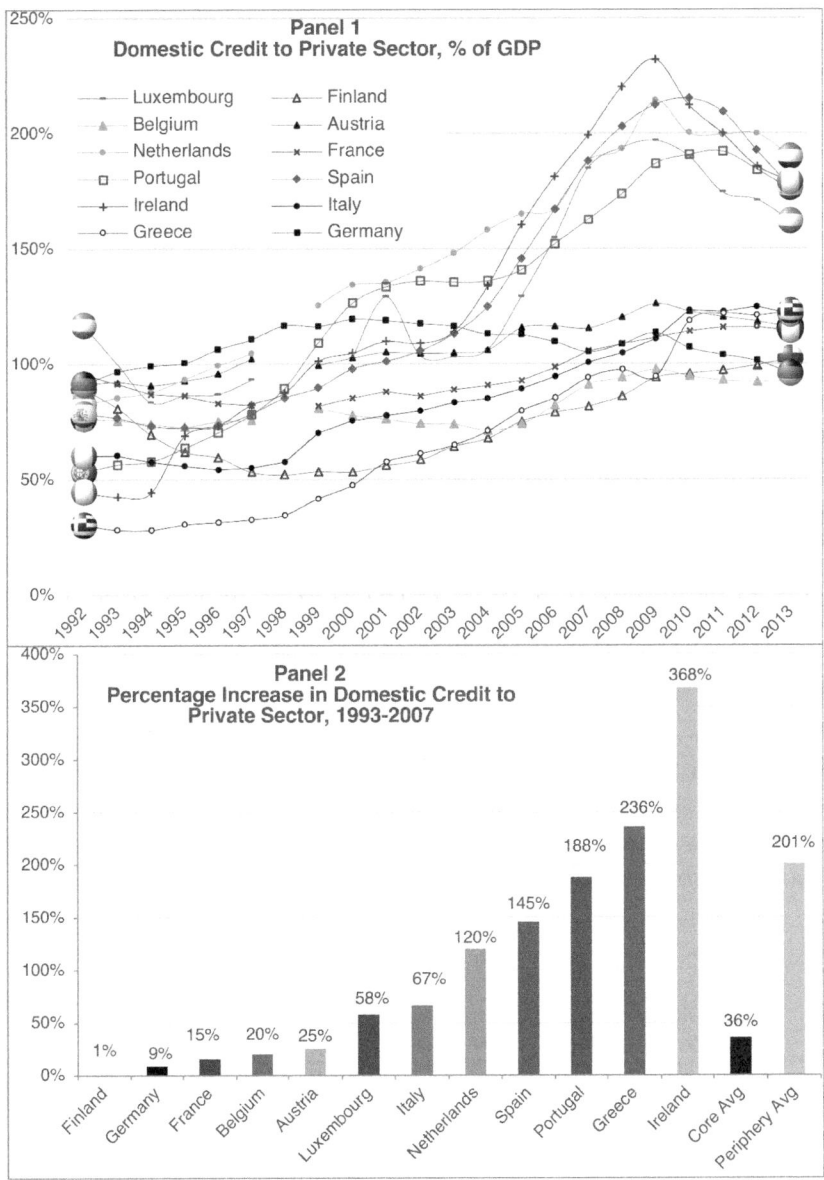

Figure 3.8 Private-sector credit expansion[74]

---

[74] World Bank, 'Domestic Credit to Private Sector (percentage of GDP) (FS.AST.PRVT.GD.
ZS)' (World Bank, 2014) www.data.worldbank.org accessed 26 November 2014. Panel 1
excludes: Luxembourg, Netherlands for 1998, and France, Austria and Belgium for 1999
due to data unavailability. Panel 2: Percentage increase in domestic credit to private
sector is relative to GDP. Core and Periphery averages are unweighted.

3.1.5 Analysis: The Failure of the Prohibition on Financial Assistance

The root of the chain of causality in this section is the failure of Article 125 TFEU. As shown in Chapter 2, the 'no bailout' rule was 'designed to dispel any investor's doubt, or hope, about the risk they run in financing governments that incur excessive deficits',[75] and so ensure that 'the financial markets exercise a degree of discipline on any Member State by imposing differential terms on its paper and ultimately by refusing to lend'.[76] It failed. Markets (correctly) assessed that the 'no bailout' rule was non-credible, and (correctly) guessed that the EU would sooner re-interpret the Treaties than allow a Member State to default. The EEAG concludes:

> What is the main deficiency of Europe's current economic constitution? To put it simply, markets found ample reason to disregard government defaults as a real possibility.[77]

The literature points to two reasons for this failure. First, the 'no bailout' rule suffered from a time-inconsistency problem.[78] As early as 1991, IMF staffers argued that EMU would lead to cross-border spillovers, exposing domestic investors to foreign debt and creating pressure to bail out those investments *ex post*.[79] This is exactly what occurred.[80] Germany, for example, pushed hard for a 'no bailout' rule at Maastricht. Yet by 2008, German banks had invested nearly 50% of German GDP in claims on EMU-12 banks (see Figure 3.9).[81] If Greece, Ireland, Portugal and Spain left EMU, Germany would be left with around $704bn in debts resulting from those loans alone – an amount exceeding German banks' entire aggregate capital.[82] As Hallerberg quips: 'Explicit bans on bailouts usually appear in

---

[75] Commission, 'A Stability Pact', 15–16.

[76] Monetary Committee, EMU Beyond Stage I (1990), 2.

[77] EEAG Report 2011, 80.

[78] Céline Allard et al., 'Lessons from the Crisis: Minimal Elements for a Fiscal Union in the Euro Area' in Cottarelli and Guerguil (eds), *Designing European Fiscal Union*, 227–229.

[79] Bovenberg et al., 'EMU in Europe', 379–382.

[80] Federico Steinberg and Mattias Vermeiren, 'Germany's Institutional Power and the EMU Regime after the Crisis: Towards a Germanized Euro Area?' (2015) 54 JCMS 388.

[81] See Figure 3.9, in Section 3.2.1.

[82] See: Bloomberg Editorial Board, 'Hey, Germany: You Got a Bailout Too' *Bloomberg* (New York 23 May 2012) www.bloombergview.com/articles/2012-05-23/merkel-should-know-her-country-has-been-bailed-out-too accessed 6 December 2014; Gregor Kirchhof, 'Debt Limits in Constitutional Law: The "Debt Brake"' in Ringe and Huber (eds), *Bail-outs, the Euro and Regulation*, 54.

places where a "no-bailout clause" is not credible in the first place'.[83]

But this points to a second, more important, failure. It is trite to say that economic spillovers will always pull in favour of a bailout for those involved. Yet it is not as though this danger was overlooked in the Treaty. Article 125 TFEU is inscribed in EU constitutional law and, unlike the SGP, its enforcement is left to the EU Court – not a political mechanism. The 'no bailout' rule was not a choice; it was European constitutional law. However, as noted in Chapter 1, EU institutions – including its court – are widely seen to be pulled by a strong integrationist teleology.[84] It was for this reason that Article 108 EEC was stripped from the Treaty in 1991 and replaced with a 'no bailout' rule in the first place.[85]

The problem with Article 125 TFEU was not ultimately that Member State executives amended the rule to allow bailouts – they didn't.[86] The problem was that it was re-interpreted by the European Court of Justice to permit bailouts.[87] The enforcement of EU law by EU institutions was itself not credible.

Markets (correctly) bet that the institutions of the EU would violate the EU's own rules rather than allow a state default, and this is precisely what occurred. In May 2010 the Commission and Eurogroup announced a €110bn bilateral loan package to Greece, outside of EU law, with no legal justification save that 'market access for Greece is not sufficient and that providing a loan is warranted to safeguard financial stability in the euro area as a whole'.[88] This was followed shortly by the €440bn EFSF and €60bn EFSM,[89] which were later recognized by the European Council and ECJ as wanting a proper legal basis before being folded into the €705bn

[83] Hallerberg, 'Fiscal Federalism Reforms', 132.
[84] See sources cited in Section 1.2.2.2, at nn 374–389.
[85] See Section 2.3.1.4.
[86] As will be discussed in Section 6.1.4, they couldn't re-write the Treaty, because an amendment which altered the essential scope of the Union or permitted large-scale fiscal transfers would come up against boundaries set by, *inter alia*, the German and Irish constitutional identity jurisprudence.
[87] See Section 6.3.
[88] Eurogroup, 'Statement by the Eurogroup' (*Brussels*, 2 May 2010) www.consilium.europa .eu/uedocs/cmsUpload/100502-%20Eurogroup_statement-sn02492.en10.pdf accessed 13 May 2014.
[89] Council of the EU, 'Press Release 9696/10: Extraordinary Council Meeting, Economic and Financial Affairs'(Brussels 9–10 May 2010); Council Regulation (EU) No 407/2010 of 11 May 2010 establishing a European financial stabilisation mechanism [2010] OJ L 118/ 1. See below, Chapter 5, nn 2–3

ESM.[90] The ESM then entered into force *before* the Treaty amendment that was effected to provide it sufficient legal cover,[91] and, when this was challenged in *Pringle* v. *Ireland*, the ECJ upheld the ESM by adopting a teleological interpretation of the Treaty which - as shown in Sections 2.3.1.4 and 6.2.1 of this book - was specifically precluded at Maastricht.[92]

As Adams et al. so aptly put it, the EU's model did not fail because it 'placed too much faith in markets', rather, it placed too much faith in the naivety of markets to 'accept the no-bailout clause at face value'.[93]

3.2   Macroeconomic Imbalances and the Failure of the MSP

The second phase in the chain of causality is the failure of the MSP to apprehend unprecedented macroeconomic imbalances stemming from systemic credit mispricing. This phase has four components: [3.2.1] Cross-border capital flows precipitated by low real interest rates [3.2.2] current account imbalances in the Periphery; [3.2.3] competitive divergence; and [3.2.4] information asymmetries built into the MSP itself.

3.2.1   Cross-Border Credit Flows

The effect of low real interest rates on credit flows is well established in the literature. On the demand side, a drop in borrowing costs reduces the cost of inputs, increases the amount of productive capital available to firms, increases firm market values and raises output expectations.[94] Put simply, borrowers who can borrow cheaply appear more valuable to investors. Boris et al., for example, find that EMU caused a 17.1% increase in Q-ratios in the Periphery.[95]

---

[90] See Chapter 6, Section 6.1.4, nn 40–41.

[91] *Pringle* v. *Ireland* [116].

[92] See Chapter 2, Section 2.3.1.4 and Chapter 6, Section 6.3.1.

[93] Adams et al., 'European Budgetary Constraints', 2. See also Pisani-Ferry, *Aftermath*, 69.

[94] Olivier Blanchard and Francesco Giavazzi, 'Current Account Deficits in the Euro Area: The End of the Feldstein-Horioka Puzzle?' (2002) 2 Brookings Papers on Economic Activity 147; Philip Lane and Barbara Pels, 'Current Account Imbalances in Europe' (2012) IIIS Discussion Paper No 397.

[95] A Q-ratio is a method for evaluating the value of a company, consisting of the market value of a company divided by the replacement value of the firm's assets. Based on the hypothesis that the value of all companies should be approximately equal to their replacement costs, a Q-ratio above 1 implies a firm's stock is overvalued. Arturo Bris,

At country level, more access to finance increases investment in capital, and investment in capital increases anticipated growth trajectories.[96] This raises the optimum amount of investment for international investors. Convergence or 'catching up' theory predicts a trajectory of growth based on the distance between actual and potential output levels.[97] A drop in financing costs allows poorer countries to purchase more productive capital than they could previously afford, thus allowing them to 'catch up' to rich countries. According to the so-called 'Rose effect', financing will flow from wealthy countries to poor countries where the rates of return are now higher as a result of steeper potential output trajectories.[98]

In the EMU, where there is no inflation- or liquidity-risk premia built into the cost of credit, this process is amplified through the balance-sheet channel and the bank-lending channel.[99] The balance-sheet channel is the mechanism by which interest rates affect the net worth of borrowers: As external credit premia are inversely related to a borrower's net worth, a higher net worth from lower financing costs accelerates borrowing and investment decisions.[100] The bank-lending channel is this function applied to banks: An increase in the supply of bank funding increases the amount of loans a bank can make. If that funding is international, this permits a departure from the banking sector's traditional role. In their traditional role, banks collect savings through deposits and then transform those deposits into loans to match the needs and risks of that economy.[101] In that role, banks are subject to the national liquidity constraint: They are simply unable to lend significantly more than they take in in deposits and revenues within the country. However, the introduction of a massive open capital market vastly increases the amount

Yrjö Koskinen and Mattias Nilsson, 'The Euro and Corporate Valuations' (2009) 22 Rev Financ Stud 3171.

[96] Thorsten Beck, Ross Levine and Norman Loayza, 'Finance and the Sources of Growth' (2000) 58 J Financ Econ 261; Julie Byrne, 'Ireland and the Global Financial Crisis: Growth, Volatility and Financial Development' (2010) 39 JSSISI 166.

[97] Robert Barro and Xavier Sala-i-Martin, *Economic Growth* (2nd ed., MIT Press, 2003) 12, 17, 117–118, 462–463; Blanchard and Giavazzi, 'Current Account Deficits', 149; Giavazzi and Spaventa, 'Current Account', 201–203.

[98] Andrew Rose, 'One Money, One Market: The Effect of Common Currencies on Trade' (2000) 15 Econ Policy 9.

[99] On these mechanisms, see: Ben Bernanke and Mark Gertler, 'Inside the Black Box: The Credit Channel of Monetary Policy Transmission' (1995) 9 J Econ Persp 27.

[100] Ben Bernanke, Mark Gertler and Simon Gilchrist, 'The Financial Accelerator and the Flight to Quality' (1996) 87 Rev Econ Stat 1.

[101] Alfredo Martin-Oliver, 'Financial Integration and Structural Changes in Spanish Banks During the Pre-Crisis Period' (2012) 24 Establidad Financiera 111, 113.

of funding available.[102] In EMU, this occurred at a time when negative interest rates also made Periphery banks more profitable investments for foreign banks. Periphery banks ceased relying on deposits, as foreign capital from the Core flowed into them.[103] In Ireland, for example, the Nyberg Report found that rapid loan growth in the banking sector could not have been financed by domestic deposits – it was financed on international wholesale markets.[104] Figure 3.9 shows that between 1999-Q2 and peak, consolidated banking claims on Periphery country banks from EMU-12 countries increased by approximately 283% in Ireland, 217% in Spain, 166% in Greece, 187% in Portugal and 127% in Italy.[105]

Negative real interest rates add a perverse acceleration to this cycle. This is so because financial institutions typically spend about 5% of endowment assets per year, and so they must make 5% in earnings after inflation.[106] But in an environment of negative real interest rates 'safe' investments lose purchasing power: A negative real interest rate of −1% means that the lender knowingly issues €100 in order to receive €99 at maturity. As a result, fixed-income investments and other safe assets actually detract from annual returns.[107] So, Periphery banks increase their exposure to risk because they are required to do so in order to make a profit. The growth rate of the balance sheet of Anglo Irish bank, for example, exceeded 20% in eight of nine years between 1998 and 2007, with an annual growth rate of 36% (growth rates of 20% or more are usually a trigger for regulatory scrutiny).[108] Across the Union, the leverage ratios of the ten largest EU banks increased from

---

[102] Barnes et al., 'Minimising Risks', 11–12; Emine Boz and Enrique G Mendoza, 'Financial Innovation, the Discovery of Risk and the US Credit Crisis' (2014) 62 J Monetary Econ 1.

[103] Jamie Caruana and Stefan Avdjiev, 'Sovereign Creditworthiness and Financial Stability: An International Perspective' (2012) Banque de France Financial Stability Review No 16, 75–79; Mary Everett and John Kelly, 'Financial Liberalisation and Economic Growth in Ireland' (2004) Central Bank of Ireland Quarterly Bulletin Autumn, 95–101.

[104] Peter Nyberg, *Misjudging Risk: Causes of the Systemic Banking Crises in Ireland: Report of the Commission of Investigation into the Banking Sector in Ireland* (Stationary Office, 2011), ii.

[105] See Figure 3.9.

[106] Perold, 'Negative Real Rates', 6.

[107] William Gibson, 'Interest Rates and Monetary Policy' (1970) 78 J Polit Econ 431, 434; Laurence Weiss, 'The Effects of Money Supply on Economic Welfare in the Steady State' (1980) 48 Econometrica 565, 566.

[108] Patrick Honohan, 'Resolving Ireland's Banking Crisis' (2009) 40 Econ Soc Rev 207, 217.

28% to nearly 45% between 1994 and 2006.[109] Cross-border inter-bank loans leaped from 22% of total interbank loans in 2000 to 34% in 2008, and short-term interbank funding increased 2,800% – from 0.1% to 2.9%.[110] Numerous studies point to a decline in lending standards and increased risk exposures following financial liberalization.[111]

In sum, low real interest rates subsidize the optimal amount of debt (for borrowers) and leverage (for creditors). Exposure to inflated assets increases the bank book values, which increases wholesale financing, in turn feeding back into rising asset values, and so on.[112] This increases inflation, further discounting real inter-est rates, and fuels the inflationary spiral predicted by the Walters Critique.

Excessive capital flows and credit growth are leading predictors of financial and sovereign debt crises.[113] Numerous studies find a correlation between the severity of the financial crisis and the pace and scale of credit expansion in the preceding period.[114]

---

[109] Barnes et al., 'Minimising Risks', 6–7. See also Philip Lane and Peter McQuade, 'Domestic Credit Growth and International Capital Flows' (2013) ECB Working Paper Series No 1566, 2.

[110] Barnes et al., 'Minimising Risks', 12.

[111] Barnes et al., 'Minimising Risks', 6; Hannah Hempell and Christoffer Kok Sørensen, 'The Impact of Supply Constraints on Bank Lending in the Euro Area: Crisis Induced Crunching?' (2010) ECB Working Paper Series No 1262; Giovanni Dell'Ariccia and Robert Marquez, 'Lending Booms and Lending Standards' (2006) 51 J Finance 2511; Angela Maddaloni and José-Luis Peydró, 'Bank Risk-taking, Securitization, Supervision, and Low Interest Rates' (2011) 24 Rev Financ Stud 2121; Cillian Ryan, 'The Euro Crisis and Crisis Management: Big Lessons from a Small Island' (2011) 8 Int Econ Policy 31.

[112] Blanchard and Giavazzi, 'Current Account Deficits', 149–150: 'Thus [. . .] borrower countries will want to borrow more. And, by a symmetric argument, lender countries will want to lend more.'

[113] Carmen Reinhard and Kenneth Rogoff, 'From Financial Crash to Debt Crisis' (2011) 101 Am Econ Rev 1676; Carmen Reinhart, Vincent Reinhart and Christoph Trebesch, 'Global Cycles: Capital Flows, Commodities and Sovereign Defaults, 1815-2015' (2016) 106 Am Econ Rev 574.

[114] Moritz Schularick and Alan M Taylor, 'Credit Booms Gone Bust: Monetary Policy, Leverage Cycles and Financial Crises' (2012) 102 Am Econ Rev 1029; Pierre-Oliver Gourinchas and Maurice Obstfeld, 'Stories of the Twentieth Century for the Twenty-First' (2012) 4 Am Econ J 227; Rosa Lastra and Geoffrey Wood, 'The Crisis of 2007–2009: Nature, Causes, and Reactions' 13 J Int'l Econ L 531; César Calderón and Megumi Kubota, 'Gross Capital Inflows Gone Wild: Gross Capital Inflows, Credit Booms and Crises' (2012) World Bank Policy Research Working Papers No 7270.

Figure 3.9 investigates growth in cross-border consolidated banking claims on an immediate-borrower basis from EMU-12 banks (excluding Luxembourg) on the five Periphery country banking sectors, plus their largest Core creditors (Germany, France and the Netherlands).[115] Consolidated banking claims represent exposures of banks by nationality, according to the residence of a bank's head office.[116] The cumulative bars represent the total value of claims on each host state (credit inflows), while the triangle markers represent the sum of claims by the state on EMU-12 banks (credit outflows). So, for example, if a German bank purchases a bond from an Irish bank, the value of this claim as a percentage of Irish GDP will add to the cumulative bar in Germany's assigned colour pattern in 'Panel 1: Ireland'; and its value as a percentage of German GDP will be represented in the height of the triangle marker in 'Panel 7: Germany'. Countries appear in each bar in the order they appear in the legend.

The scale of credit flows from Core to Periphery banks in the EMU is staggering. By the onset of the crisis, the banking sectors of France and Germany alone had flooded Irish banks with claims worth 130% of Ireland's entire GDP by 2008-Q2. Greek, Portuguese and Spanish banking sectors were all subject to foreign claims accounting for over 70% of their respective GDP. Total outflows from the Core were proportionally immense: German, French and Dutch foreign claims amounted to over 40%, 60% and 130% of their GDP, respectively.[117] As a Bloomberg editorial observes:

[I]rresponsible borrowers can't exist without irresponsible lenders [...] By December 2009, German banks had amassed claims of $704 billion on Greece, Ireland, Italy, Portugal and Spain, much more than the German banks' aggregate capital. In other words, they lent more than they could afford.[118]

---

[115] Luxembourg is excluded from the comparison due to data unavailability.

[116] This captures both the domestic operations of national banks, as well as the foreign subsidiaries of domestically owned national banks. They exclude intragroup positions, and so do not show international transactions within a bank of a single nationality. It captures only exposures to unaffiliated counterparties from other countries. See: BIS, 'Consolidated Banking Statistics: Foreign Claims by Nationality of Reporting Banks, Immediate Borrower Basis' (BIS, 2014) www.bis.org/statistics/consstats.htm accessed 27 November 2014.

[117] Barnes, 'Unsustainable Imbalances', 7.

[118] Bloomberg Editorial Board, 'Hey, Germany'.

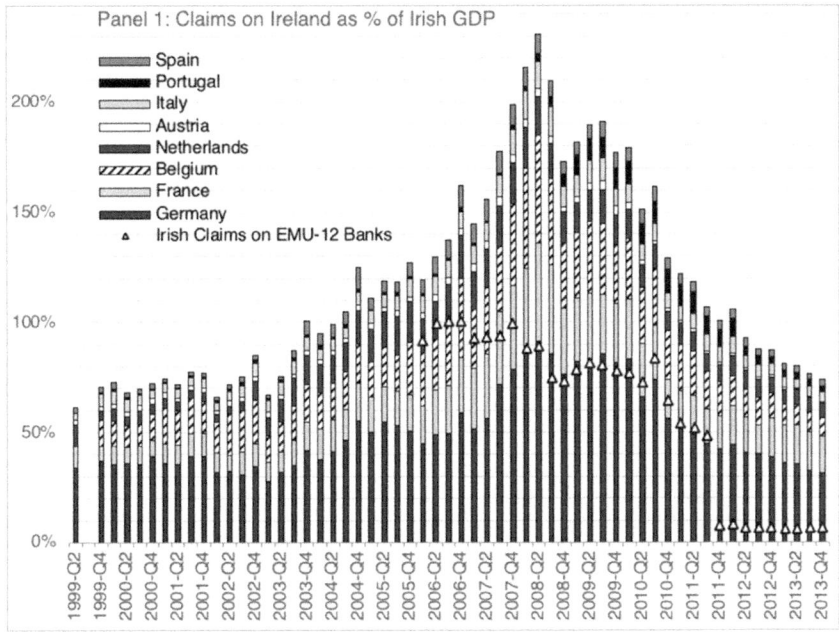

Figure 3.9 Consolidated banking claims by country on immediate borrower basis, as percentage of national GDP[119]

[119] Countries appear in each column in the order presented in the legend. All panels exclude Luxembourg due to data unavailability. All panels exclude 1999-Q3 due to data unavailability. All panels exclude claims from Ireland to 2006 due to data unavailability. Panel 1: Greece, Finland, excluded as all amounts = <1%. Irish claims on foreign banks exclude the following due to unavailability: Finland (all periods) and Greece and Portugal from 2006Q1-2006Q4. Panel 2: Austria, Finland and Greece excluded as all amounts = <1%. Panel 3: Finland excluded as all amounts = <1%. Panel 4: Greece and Finland excluded as all amounts = <1%. Panel 4: Finland, Greece excluded as all amounts = <1%. Panel 5: Italian Claims on EMU-12 banks exclude the following due to data unavailability: Austria 2001Q4-2004Q4; Finland 2001Q4; Greece 2001Q4-2007Q2; Netherlands 2001Q4-2005Q1; Portugal 2001Q4-2002Q1. Panel 6: Finland, Greece excluded as all amounts = <1%. Panel 7: Finland, Greece, Portugal excluded as all amounts = <1%. Panel 8: Austria, Finland, Greece, Portugal and Ireland excluded as excluded as all amounts = <1.3%. Bank for International Settlements, 'Consolidated banking statistics, immediate borrower basis'.

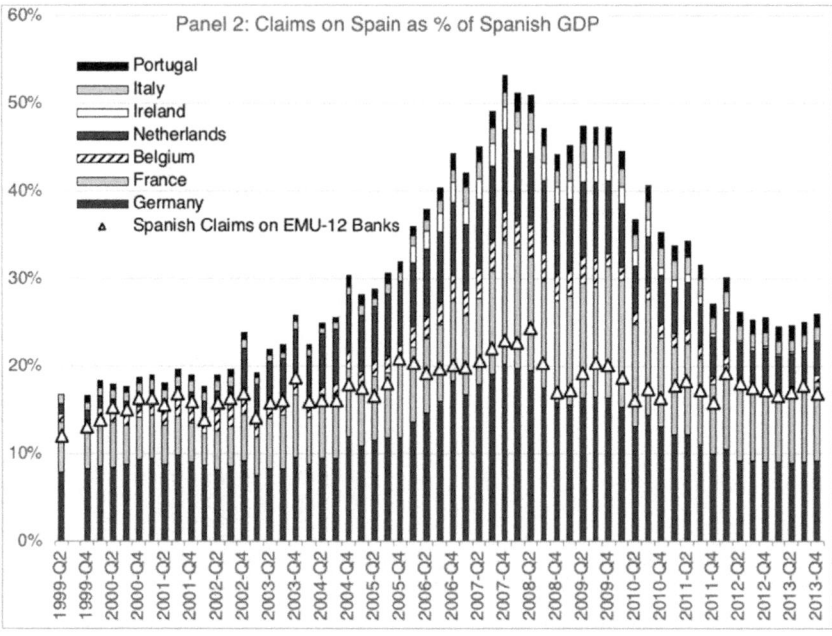

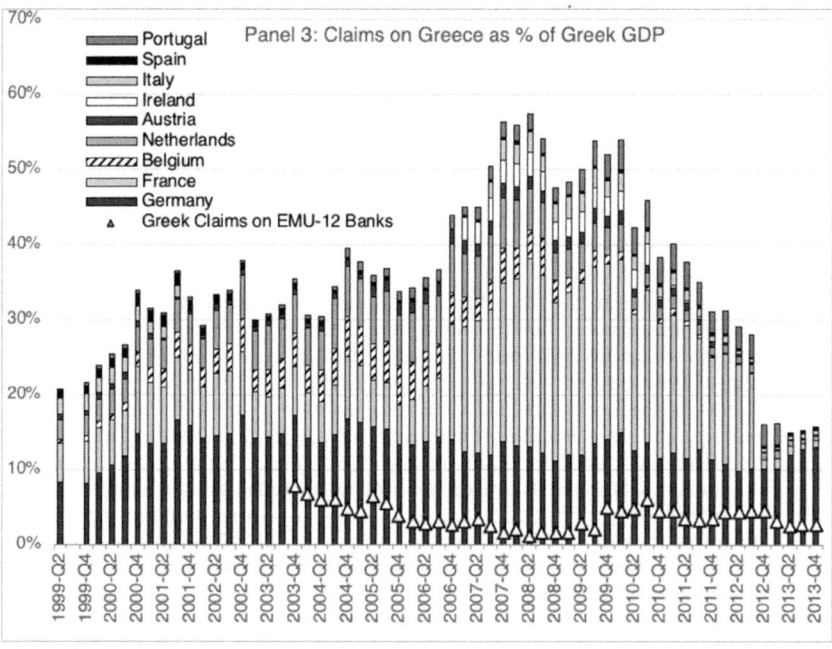

Figure 3.9 (cont.)

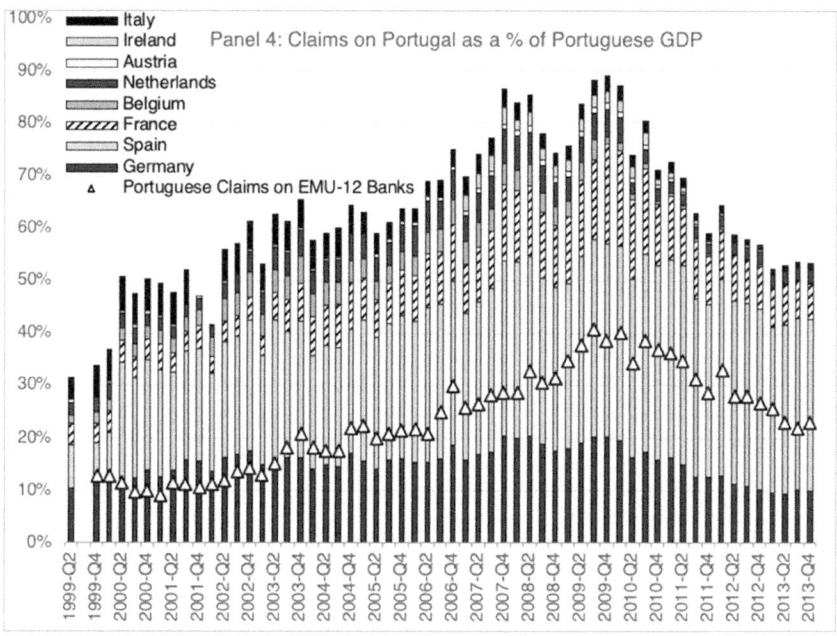

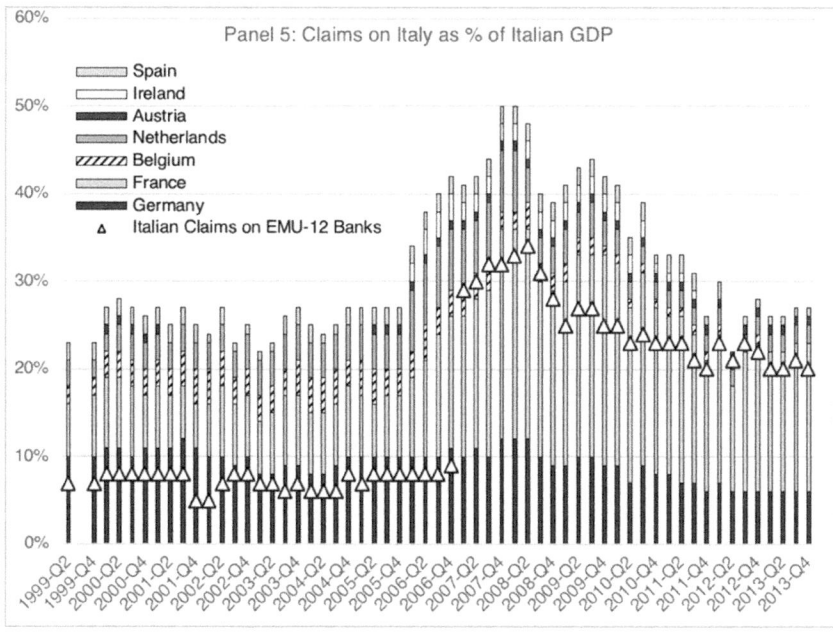

Figure 3.9 (cont.)

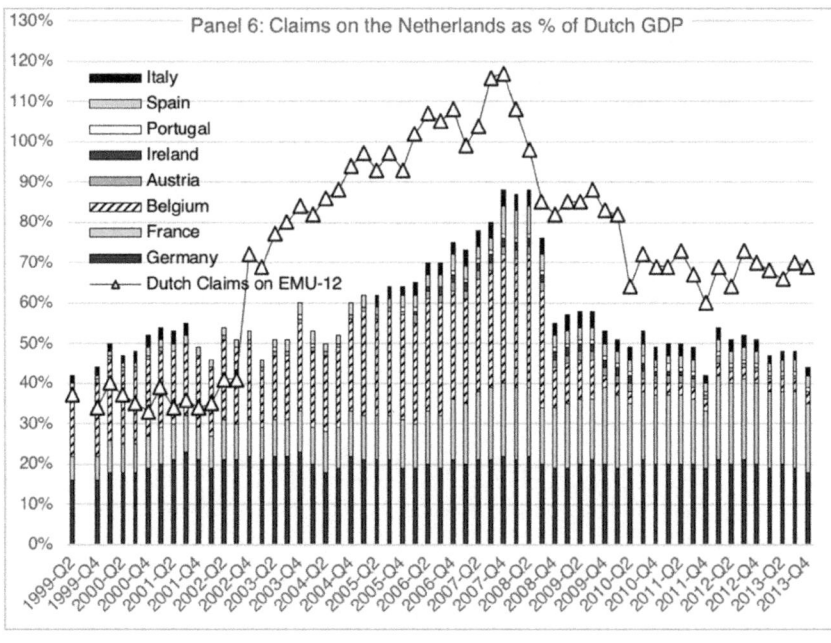

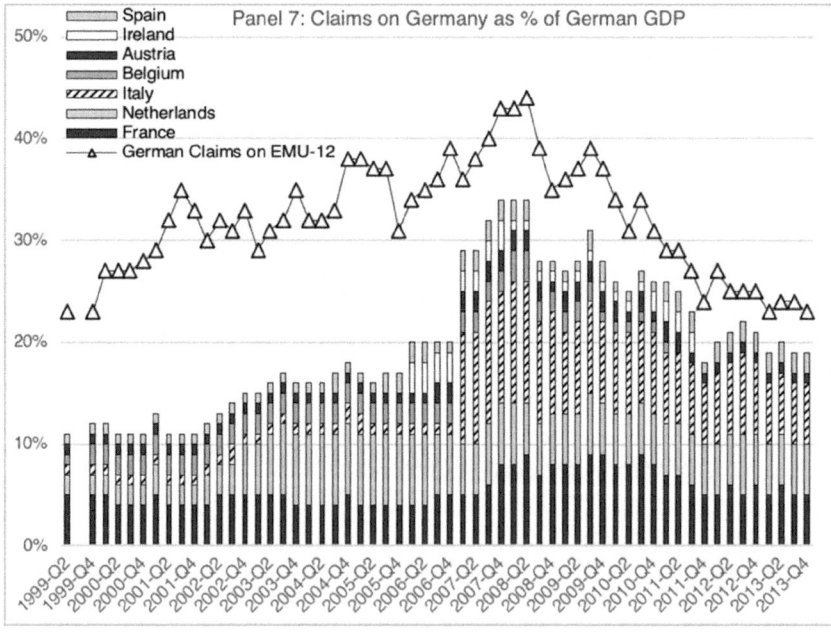

Figure 3.9 (cont.)

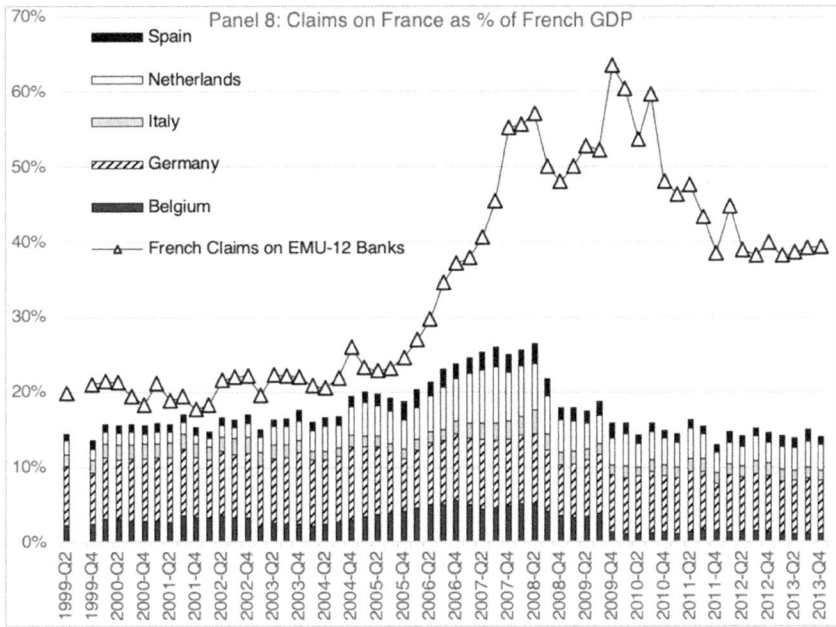

Figure 3.9 (cont.)

3.2.2   Current Account Imbalances and Net External Indebtedness

The distortionary effect of credit expansion on periphery economies is difficult to overstate. Figure 3.10 shows the evolution of current account balances in EMU countries as a percentage of GDP.[120] The gulf which emerged between Core and Periphery under the euro is unprecedented in over thirty years of economic data. Beginning in 1993, the year of the Maastricht Treaty, the current accounts of both Core and Periphery groups were roughly in balance: Neither group sold nor borrowed significantly more than the other, and both groups were, on average, net exporters to the world. As real interest rates fell in the Periphery, the average current account of the Periphery group began to deteriorate precipitously, while the Core accrued increasing surpluses.

---

[120] The current account is the sum of a country's balance of trade plus net income and direct payments. A positive current account balance indicates that the country is a net seller to the world, while a negative balance indicates it is a net purchaser.

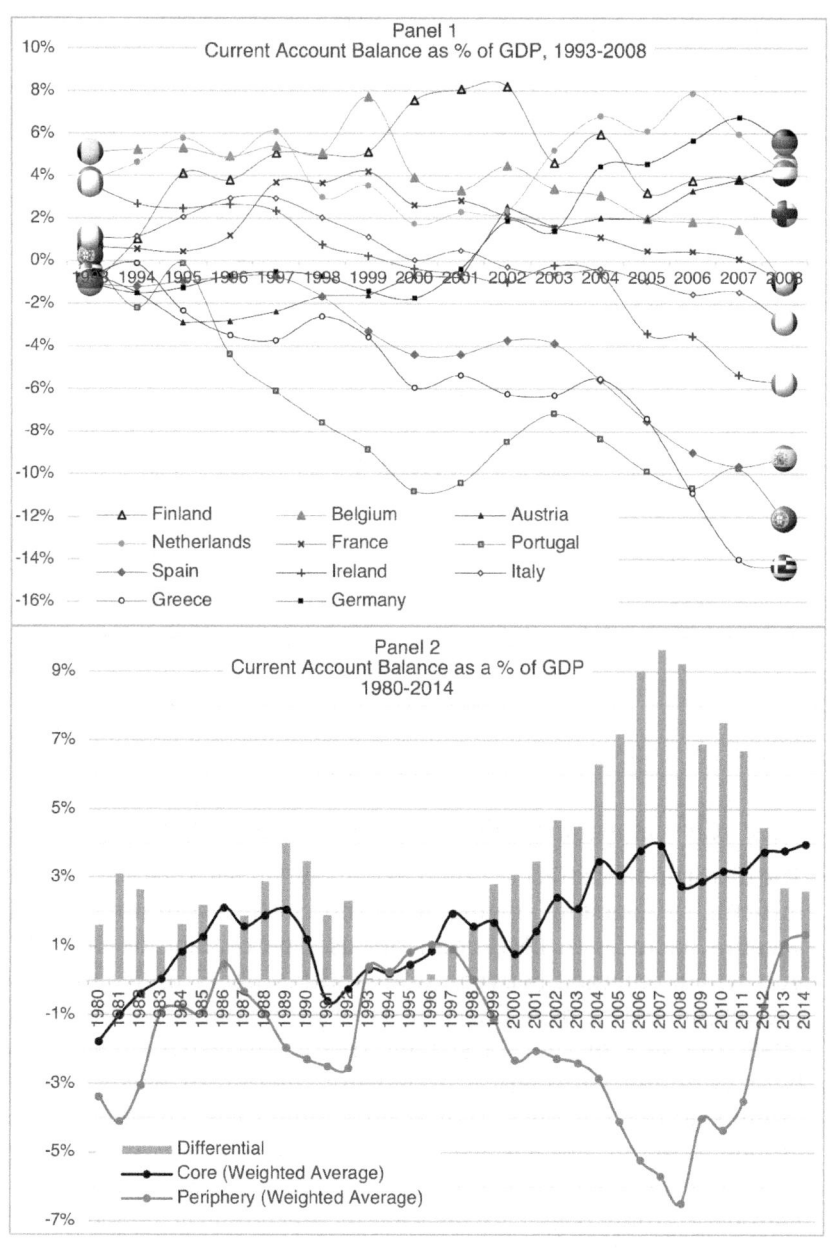

Figure 3.10 Current account balance as percentage of GDP: Periphery countries versus Core countries[121]

---

[121] IMF, 'Current Account Balance, % GDP'. Core weighted average in Panel 2 excludes Luxembourg due to data unavailability.

The root of this imbalance is a breakdown in the role of capital in the financial system under low real interest rates and outsized capital flows.[122] From a theoretical perspective, the role of the finance system may be decomposed into five fundamental functions: Effective payments, mobilization of funds, pooling of risk, appraisal of creditworthiness and monitoring the use of funds.[123] Of these, the latter two functions are determinative of growth and competitiveness. This is so because creditors will demand a higher premium from businesses with a higher probability of failure, restricting credit to productive investments. What matters for growth is not just large amounts of credit, but the effectiveness and quality of that credit.[124]

Where credit is universally cheap and abundant, however, it does not play its normal 'watchdog' role in the economy.[125] There is a de-linking between the cost and quantity of available finance and conditions of domestic production at national level.[126] Non-productive borrowers in the Periphery may access international credit through domestic banks at the same real cost (or lower) as highly productive firms in the Core – with no hope of contributing to the national increase in output needed to pay it back.[127] The OECD notes: 'there is a powerful feedback mechanism between domestic weaknesses in credit quality and the overall availability of credit'.[128]

Empirical work by Mendoza and Terrones studying seventy credit booms in sixty-one countries finds that credit booms are common

---

[122] Fagan and Gaspar, 'Adjusting to the Euro', 5; Thomas Mayer, 'Euroland's Hidden Balance-of-Payments Crisis' (2011) Deutsche Bank Research EU Monitor No 88, 2; Enrique Mendoza and Marco Terrones, 'An Anatomy of Credit Booms and their Demise' (2012) 15 Economía Chilena 4, 4; Carmen Reinhart and Vincent Reinhart, 'Capital Flow Bonanzas: An Encompassing View of the Past and Present' (2008) NBER Working Papers, 9; Guillermo Calvo, 'Capital Flows and Capital-Market Crises: The Simple Economics of Sudden Stops' (1998) 1 J Appl Econ 35; Lane and McQuade, 'Credit Growth'.

[123] Patrick Honohan, 'To What Extent Has Finance Been a Driver of Ireland's Economic Success?' (2006) ESRI Quarterly Economic Commentary 59, 61; Ross Levine, 'Finance and Growth: Theory and Evidence' in Philippe Aghion and Steven Durlauf (eds), Handbook of Economic Growth (Elsevier Science, 2005) 870–881.

[124] Jeffrey Wurgler, 'Financial Markets and the Allocation of Capital' (2000) 58 J Financ Econ 187.

[125] Honohan, 'To What Extent?', 60.

[126] Barnes, 'Unsustainable Imbalances', 10; Jürgen von Hagen and Boris Hofman, 'Macroeconomic Implications of Low Inflation in the Euro Area' (2004) 15 N Amer J Econ Financ 5; Boris Hofman and Hermann Remsperger, 'Inflation Differentials among the Euro Area Countries: Potential Causes and Consequences' (2005) 16 J Asian Econ 403.

[127] Lane and Pels, 'Imbalances', 4.

[128] OECD, Euro Area 2012, 31.

under managed exchange rates and have a systemic relationship with boom-bust cycles in asset prices, real inflation, balance-of-payment imbalances and banking crises.[129] Fagan et al. model a drop in interest rates on a small periphery country and confirm that the result is a private-sector consumption boom, real appreciation, upward pressure on wages and external trade imbalances.[130] In the EMU, numerous studies confirm that interest rate convergence and capital flows caused current account deteriorations and unprecedented build-ups in household debt.[131]

It should be emphasized that the external debts mapped in this section are simply not a public-sector debt phenomenon.[132] The rapid credit expansion and external indebtedness of the Periphery economies can only be, as Gavilán et al. conclude, 'rationalised as the natural reaction of the economy to the observed developments in interest rates'.[133] Fagan and Gaspar summarize the commonalities of the Periphery experience so adroitly that it bears repeating here:

> The process of interest rate convergence was accompanied by a boom in final expenditures of households [. . .] in the converging countries. This was accompanied by a sharp rise in the household debt ratio. [. . .] In contrast, *fiscal balances were remarkably similar across the two groups of countries.* [. . .] The boom in domestic expenditure fuelled by credit growth triggered a deterioration in the current account balance and a build-up of foreign debt. In addition, the converging countries experienced a sizeable real appreciation vis-a-vis the core group.[134]

3.2.3   Reallocation to Non-Tradable Consumption and Competitive Divergence

Although unprecedented in scale, the essential tenets of this process are well known. Credit expansion has a deleterious effect on competitiveness

[129] Mendoza and Terrones, 'Credit Booms'.

[130] Gabriel Fagan, Vitor Gaspar and Alfredo Pereira, 'Macroeconomic Adjustment to Structural Change' in Gyorgy Szapary and Jürgen Von Hagen (eds), *Monetary Strategies for Joining the Euro* (Edward Elgar Publishing Ltd, 2004).

[131] Wendy Carlin, 'Heterogeneity in the Euro Area and Why It matters for the Future of the Currency Union' in Beblavy, Cobham and Ódor (eds), *Euro Area and Financial Crisis*; Giavazzi and Spaventa, 'Current account', 203–217; Stark, 'Lessons', 549; Philip Lane and Gian Maria Milesi-Ferretti, 'Cross-Country Incidence of the Global Financial Crisis' (2011) 39 IMF Econ Rev 77; and sources above, n 122.

[132] Lane, 'Sovereign Debt Crisis', 54: 'The credit boom in this period was not primarily due to government borrowing.'

[133] Angel Gavilán et al., 'The Crisis in Spain: Origins and Developments' in Beblavy, Cobham and Ódor (eds), *Euro Area and Financial Crisis*, 91.

[134] Fagan and Gaspar, 'Adjusting to the Euro', 14 (emphasis added).

as demand in the non-tradable sector draws away capital from efficient investments in the tradable sector.[135] The result is not only external indebtedness, but real appreciation and long-term competitive divergence. Conceptually, each country's economy can be divided into a tradable sector, which sells outputs abroad and is subject to international productivity competition; and a non-tradable sector, which does not sell on the international market and is less exposed to international productivity competition. The tradable sector produces goods which are sold on the international market and increases the balance-of-payments of the country. The non-tradable sector absorbs resources but does not contribute to the net income of the country. The housing sector is a ready example of the latter: Housing investment is particularly reactive to low real interest rates,[136] yet when two Irish residents build and swap houses, the money exchanged does not add to the country's balance-of-payments with the world. Instead, there is an indirect real appreciation from the transaction, as the increase in economic activity hires away capital from the tradable sector. If the tradable sector wants it back, it will have to pay more. This causes real appreciation.

This effect is widely visible in the periphery countries. The OECD finds that 'export-oriented activities became squeezed by over-heating domestic demand', as credit inflows went 'to fund consumption or loss-making property investments'.[137] The overall share of industry to gross value added declined sharply in Periphery countries, while construction and services in the non-tradable sector expanded.[138]

Figure 3.11 shows the real effective exchange rates (REER) of the Periphery and Core groups from 1993 (Maastricht), and the percentage increase/decrease for all countries to 2007 (the last year before the crisis). It shows an average real appreciation of 10% in the Periphery group and an average real devaluation of 1.3% in the Core group. Between 1993 and 2007, Periphery products had become, on average, 11% more expensive than the Core.

---

[135] Olivier Blanchard, 'Current Account Deficits in Rich Countries' (2007) 54 IMF Staff Papers 191; Ricardo Reis, 'The Portuguese Slump and Crash and the Euro Crisis' (2013) 46 Brookings Papers on Economic Activity 143, 162; Balázs Égert and Rafal Kierzenkowski, 'Exports and Property Prices in France: Are they Connected?' (2014) 37 World Econ 387; Enrique Mendoza, 'Real Exchange Rate Volatitlity and the Price of Nontradable Goods in Economies Prone to Sudden Stups' (2006) 6 Economía 103; Lane, 'Capital Flows', 2–3 and sources cited above nn 122, 129–131.

[136] European Commission, 'The EU Economy: 2006 Review' (2006) European Economy No 6, 163.

[137] OECD, Euro Area 2012, 35, 74.

[138] OECD, Euro Area 2012, 76; Philip Lane, 'The Real Effects of European Monetary Union' (2006) 20 J Econ Persp 47.

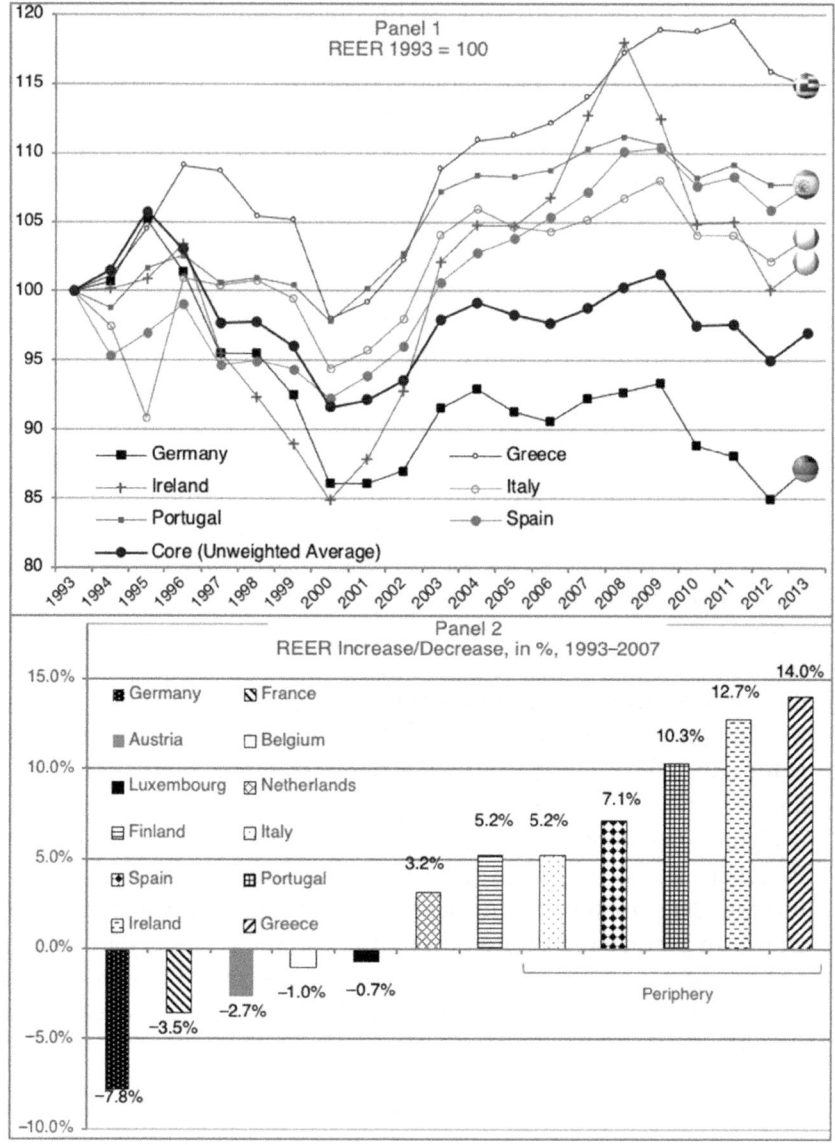

Figure 3.11 Real effective exchange rates[139]

[139] REER is the nominal effective exchange rate (NEER) index, adjusted for relative movements in national price or cost indicators of the home county, selected countries and the euro area. A NEER index is the ratio (here expressed on the base 1993 = 100) of an index of a currency's period-average exchange rate to a weighted geometric average of selected competitor currencies. World Bank, 'REER (PX.REX.REER)'.

3.2.4   Analysis: The Failure of the Multilateral Surveillance Procedure

By the end of the euro's first decade, the damage done to the current account positions of the Periphery was unprecedented in over thirty years of economic data (See Figure 3.10 in Section 3.2.2), and far exceeded the post-World War II norm for OECD countries.[140] A range of empirical work finds that Periphery external deficits were not linked to increases in potential output capable of financing them.[141] On a staggering scale, capital flows were financing investments that would never generate the increases in national wealth needed to pay them back.

The question then necessarily arises: Where was the European Union? Under Articles 121 and 126 TFEU, the Commission's latitude to monitor economic policy is extremely broad, 'potentially encompassing any national economic policy and thus reaching every aspect of economic activity in the Member States'.[142] Under Article 121(4) TFEU, if national economic policies were based on a misjudging of economic fundamentals, or risked 'jeopardizing the property functioning of economic and monetary union', EU institutions were expected to identify them and raise the alarm.[143] And yet, as Adamski concludes:

It is hardly disputable that the pre-crisis macroeconomic coordination of structural reform policies [...] failed to raise the alarm on deteriorating competitiveness of peripheral countries and growing bubbles on assets markets. It failed even more badly at reducing them.[144]

EU surveillance assessments prior to the crash make sobering reading. Mere months before Ireland's fatal €375bn bank guarantee, the Commission's EMU@10 report hailed the EMU as 'a major success', misattributing Periphery current account deficits to an 'accelerated catching-up process' and remarking the strong performance of Spain, Ireland and Greece.[145] Yet a year later, it recognized that any gains in economic

---

[140] OECD, *Euro Area 2012*, 35.
[141] Florence Jaumotte and Piayporn Sodsriwiboon, 'Current Account Imbalances in the Southern Euro Area' (2010) IMF Working Paper No 139; Giavazzi and Spaventa, 'Current account', 201; Gavilán et al., 'Origins', 91; Lane, 'Capital Flows', 9.
[142] Adamski, '(Misguided) Constitution', 51.
[143] Art. 6(2), 10(1) Reg 1466/97.
[144] Dariusz Adamski, 'National Power Games and Structural Failures in the European Macroeconomic Governance' (2012) 49 CMLR 1319, 1351.
[145] European Commission, *EMU@10: Successes and Challenges after Ten Years of Economic and Monetary Union* (European Economy No 2, 2008).

growth had been 'wiped out' by macroeconomic imbalances that reached 'an all-time high' at about the time the EMU@10 report was written.[146] *The Economist* fairly points out that the Commission's forecasts for 2008 (when the crisis was already front-page news) had the EMU growing at 2% in 2008 and 1.8% in 2009 (the final numbers were −0.3% in 2008 and −2.8% in 2009).[147]

A central question for the literature is explaining how current account deficits in the Periphery grew so far beyond the capacity of national economies to finance them, evidently without detection.[148] This section points to two causes. The first was the failure of interest rates to rise *on their own* to the violation of the solvency condition in the absence of the liquidity constraint. The second was the failure of EU surveillance to detect this due to information asymmetries familiar to fiscal federalism theory.

Ordinarily, the Commission's stated assumption that current account deficits are part of an 'accelerated catching-up process' is unproblematic: Convergence theory predicts that a 'catching up' country will experience a higher current account deficit before future export surpluses.[149] In a country with limited liquidity and no bailout expectation, investors can be assumed left to their devices because two forces will prevent such deficits from progressing from the 'natural side effect of a healthy process of convergence' to 'symptoms of future sovereign insolvency'.[150] These are:

The inter-temporal budget constraint (or the solvency condition) requires that, first, credit is put to productive purposes which will generate future surpluses and investment gains to pay it off; and, second, that credit expansion slows and ceases as the economy approaches the limit of its potential output. As shown in Sections 3.2.1–3.2.3, this condition was violated under the single interest rate: Credit was not put to productive purposes and interest rates did not rise as the Periphery approached, and then exceeded, potential output.

[146] European Commission, 'Reinforcing Economic Policy Coordination' (Communication) COM(2010) 250 final, 22–23.

[147] Buttonwood, 'The Perils of Planning on the Basis of Economic Forecasts' *The Economist* (26 Novermber 2015).

[148] Mayer, 'Hidden Balance-of-Payments Crisis', 2.

[149] See sources cited above, n 97.

[150] Giavazzi and Spaventa, 'Current Account', 201–203.

The liquidity constraint is the effect of dwindling stocks of money on interest rates. When growth is funded domestically, potential output has a clear limit: the stock of national savings to finance it.[151] There is a natural 'crowding out' of consumptive borrowing as dwindling pools of money appreciate in value, and only efficient firms are able to access increasingly expensive capital.[152]

Put simply, these constraints mean investors will cease pouring money into a sector which will no longer generate the returns needed to pay it back. In EMU, this did not happen: credit remained perfectly elastic in response to consumptive demand because there was no 'crowding out' from higher-risk premiums – despite above-average inflation and deteriorating output potential.[153] Giavazzi and Spaventa explain:

Models establishing the optimality of current account deficits in a catching-up process implicitly assume that the inter-temporal budget constraint is satisfied, so that the accumulation of foreign liabilities is matched by future surpluses [...] the growth pattern of the countries under consideration was unsustainable because it violated the solvency constraint: the counterpart of the capital inflows was a boom of non-tradable residential construction or a growth of consumption. [A] common monetary policy targeting the average inflation rate of the area did nothing (nor could it do much) to prevent the extraordinary growth of credit that fuelled the growing imbalances.[154]

That is straightforward enough. But if interest rates would not rise *on their own* under the single interest rate, why did the MSP fail to detect that such capital flows were *not* going to productive investment, but instead to consumption and asset bubbles?

Fiscal federalism theory provides an answer to this. There is, at institutional level, a significant information asymmetry problem.[155] EU surveillance shines its light down on top-level general government

[151] Giavazzi and Spaventa, 'Current Account', 201.
[152] Gibson, 'Interest Rates', 434–345: 'this liquidity effect is so widely recognised [...] that it might be called the reigning view on the relation between money and interest rates'.
[153] EEAG Report 2011, 77–78; Barnes, 'Unsustainable Imbalances', 5–12.
[154] Giavazzi and Spaventa, 'Current Account' 201–203.
[155] Oates, 'Towards a Second-Generation', 35; Mariano Tommasi and Federico Weinschelbaum, 'Centralization vs Decentralization: A Principal-Agent Analysis' (2007) 9 J Public Econ Theory 369; Massimo Bordignon, Paulo Manasse and Guido Tabellini, 'Optimal Regional Redistribution Under Asymmetric Information' (2001) 91 Am Econ Rev 709; Oates, 'Towards a Second-Generation', 353.

balances and capital flows, but is twice removed from groundswell economic movements underpinning those balances.[156] Oates explains:

Thus, there exists an asymmetry of information: local governments know the preferences of their own residences and other local circumstances, but the central government does not.[157]

If interest rates do not rise in response to country risk, all of the 'symptoms of future insolvency' spilling out into the Member States are local phenomena.[158] They are not found in the general government balance. They are found in above-equilibrium house prices in Madrid; a hotel construction boom in Dublin; rising car imports in Greece; and myriad other idiosyncratic booms across thousands of European townships. They are found on the books of countless domestic agents exceeding their own individual budget constraints.[159] These are hard for supranational institutions to identify (and nearly impossible for them to respond to). From their view, it simply looks like beneficial capital flows are flowing into credit-worthy Periphery banks. Only 5% of loans to the non-banking sector were issued directly from foreign banks, and it is worth noting that the lenders with the most toxic exposures to periphery bonds were Spanish *Cajas* and German *Landesbanken* – regional banks that would not have been under EU supervision even under EU Banking Union.[160] For this reason, the EU proved no better, and in many cases much worse, than national authorities at detecting symptoms of insolvency. Other international surveillance regimes, such as IMF surveillance, suffered the same handicap.[161]

Local authorities, on the other hand, are well placed to perceive and respond to local information from markets and electorates (which levy

---

[156] Pisani-Ferry, *Aftermath*, 144 refers to 'streetlamp syndrome'.

[157] Oates, 'Towards a Second-Generation', 35.

[158] Giavazzi and Spaventa, 'Current Account', 215–216 note: 'there were no foreign investors investing specifically in assets earmarked for construction activity: foreign investors would lend to [. . .] domestic banking institutions which would then finance the construction industry'.

[159] Vítor Constâncio, 'European Monetary Integration and the Portuguese Case' in Carsten Detken, Vitor Gaspar and Gilles Noblet (eds), *The New EU Member States: Convergence and Stability* (Third ECB Central Banking Conference, ECB 2005), 211–212.

[160] Barnes et al., 'Minimising Risks', 12; Thorsten Beck, 'Why the Rush? Short-Term Crisis Resolution and Long-Term Bank Stability' in Thorsten Beck (ed.), *Banking Union for Europe: Risks and Challenges* (CEPR 2012).

[161] Manuela Moschella, 'Monitoring Macroeconomic Imbalances: Is EU Surveillance More Effective than IMF Surveillance?' (2014) 52 JCMS 1273, 1277, 1279; IMF Independent Evaluation Office, *IMF Performance in the Run-Up to the Financial and Economic Crisis: IMF Surveillance in 2004–2007* (IMF, 2011), 42.

their costs on national institutions directly). But as long as credit-supply conditions are unresponsive to regional risk, there is little they can do about them.

The collapse of the Irish banking sector is elucidative. Three reports commissioned in the wake of the crisis point to two causes, one on the domestic (demand) side and the other on the international (supply) side.[162]

On the supply side, overleveraging was the result of unresponsive interest rates and credit flows which exceeded the entire GDP of the state. On the demand side, the crisis was caused by exposure to, and the collapse of, the domestic property bubble. Yet on that side, domestic banking and housing weaknesses were well-prodded by Irish economists and regulators.[163] By 2003, academic consensus in Ireland was that housing prices had overshot equilibrium and would fall, triggering recessionary pressures.[164] Financial Stability Reports between 2004 and 2006 considered a range of potential overvaluations, from 55% to 73%.[165] Stress tests in 2004 and 2006 accounted for up to a 20% fall in housing prices.[166] Significant domestic shocks were highly expected.

But from the international (supply) side perspective, there was little to fear so long as Irish banks sat perched atop an international credit pipeline gushing twice the volume of the national economy. The IMF's 2006 Financial System Stability Assessment concluded that the Irish financial system 'seems well placed to absorb the impact of a downturn in either house prices or growth more generally' and 'domestic lending institutions have adequate capital buffers to cover a range of large but plausible hypothetical shocks that reflect the

---

[162] Patrick Honohan, The Irish Banking Crisis: Regulatory and Financial Stability Policy 2003–2008 (Central Bank of Ireland, 2010); Klaus Regling and Max Watson, A Preliminary Report on the Sources of Ireland's Banking Crisis (Government of Ireland Publications Office, 2010); and The Nyberg Report.

[163] For example, Alan Barrett et al., Medium-Term Review 2005–2012 (ESRI, 2005) 90–93; Morgan Kelly, 'On the Likely Extent of Falls in Irish House Prices' (2007) ESRI Quarterly Economic Commentary 42; The Nyberg Report, iv: 'The financial regulator was clearly aware of many of these problems.'

[164] Honohan, Irish Banking Crisis 89.

[165] Honohan, Irish Banking Crisis 93.

[166] Central Bank and Financial Services Authority of Ireland, Financial Stability Review 2004 (FSA Ireland, 2004); Central Bank and Financial Services Authority of Ireland, Financial Stability Review 2006 (FSA Ireland, 2006); Honohan, Irish Banking Crisis 87; Honohan, 'Resolving Ireland's Banking Crisis', 220.

above risks'.[167] Similarly, 'EU Council Opinions were favourable [and] did not focus very strongly on vulnerabilities arising from monetary conditions'.[168] The OECD praised Irish regulators.[169]

The *causa sine qua non* of the failure of multilateral surveillance is, once again, the disconnection of credit prices from macroeconomic fundamentals prevailing at national level. With interest rates unresponsive to regional risk, supranational institutions are simply ill-placed to perceive local signals from markets and electorates about the character of local interest rate adjustment, and are unable to respond to them. Local authorities are well placed for this, but as long as credit-supply conditions are unresponsive to regional risk, there is little they can do about their cause.[170]

Studies investigating alternative explanations for the crisis, such as national economic policies,[171] or even financial exposure to the United States,[172] do not provide alternate explanations to the chain of causality between interest rates, capital flows and net external indebtedness charted in this chapter.[173] Garicano et al. conclude:

Although there are alternative explanations for the euro crisis, the view that the credit bubble itself is the source of the disturbance is hard to counter. [...] Our reading of the evidence is thus that the causality mainly runs from the credit bubble to the real changes and not in the opposite direction.[174]

---

[167] IMF, *Ireland: Financial System Stability Assessment Update* (IMF Country Report No 06/292, 2006), 5. Other IMF reports were equally sanguine: IMF, *Staff Report for the 2005 Art. IV Consultation: Ireland* (IMF, 2005), 11; IMF, *Staff Report for the 2006 Article IV Consultation: Ireland* (IMF, 2006), 10.

[168] *The Regling & Watson Report*, 20.

[169] OECD, *Economic Survey: Ireland* (OECD, 2008) 8, 41, 51.

[170] Barnes, 'Unsustainable Imbalances', 31.

[171] Vitor Gaspar and Miguel St Aubyn, 'Adjusting to the Euro – the Contrast between Portugal and Spain' (10 Years of the Euro Conference, University of Minho, Braga, Portugal, May 2009).

[172] Andrew Rose and Mark Spiegel, 'Cross-Country Causes and Consequences of the 2008 Crisis: Early Warning' (2011) 24 Jpn World Econ 1; Andrew K Rose and Mark M Spiegel, 'Cross-Country Causes and Consequences of the 2008 Crisis: International Linkages and American Exposure' (2010) 15 Pacific Econ Rev 340; Hamid Faruqee and Jaewoo Lee, 'Global Dispersion of Current Accounts: Is the Universe Expanding' (2009) 56 IMF Staff Papers 574.

[173] Fagan and Gaspar, 'Adjusting to the Euro', 28; Barnes, 'Unsustainable Imbalances', 10; Barnes et al., 'Minimising Risks', 12.

[174] Jesús Fernández-Villaverde, Luis Garicano and Tano Santos, 'Political Credit Cycles: The Case of the Eurozone' (2013) 47 J Econ Persp 145, 146.

3.3   The Sovereign Debt Crisis and the Failure of the EDP

The final failure of the Maastricht architecture is the failure of the excessive deficit procedure to prevent the sovereign debt crisis and, more fundamentally, to enforce budgetary discipline according to its own terms.[175] This section identifies a number of reasons for this, but primary among them is that sovereign debt is not a common causal denominator of the Euro Crisis at all – real interest rates, private-sector credit, and macroeconomic imbalances are. As Skouras concludes:

Consequently, it is difficult to accept that the euro zone's problem is excessive sovereign debt. This official diagnosis misses the root of the crisis.[176]

3.3.1   Not a Sovereign Debt Crisis

Figure 3.12 compares the aggregate trajectories of gross government debt with domestic credit to the private sector, both measured in percentage of GDP. The result is startling. Contrary to the official wisdom, the gross debt accumulations leading to the crisis accrued all but entirely in the private sector. While Periphery government debt-to-GDP ratios fell by an average of 20% between Maastricht and the crisis, Periphery private-sector debt increased by an approximate average of *150%* over the same period. It is this pattern which binds the crisis-hit Periphery countries and distinguishes them from the Core. As the IMF concludes: 'The roots of the financial crash stretch back to the preceding seven years of low interest rates [...] *Fiscal policy did not play a major role in the run up to the crisis.*'[177]

Figures 3.13–3.18 examine this claim in further detail by decomposing public- and private-sector debt accumulation by country. Even in Greece (Figure 3.15), the *causa sine qua non* of the crisis must be traced to the private sector: In that country, government debt increased 11% over fifteen years (1993–2008), while private-sector

---

[175] Commission Blueprint, 2. Demosthenes Ioannou and Livio Stracca, 'Have the Euro Area and EU Governance Worked? Just the Facts' (2014) 34 Eur J Polit Econ 1.
[176] Skouras, 'Lessons', 55.
[177] IMF, *Initial Lessons of the Crisis* (IMF, 2009), 7 (emphasis added).

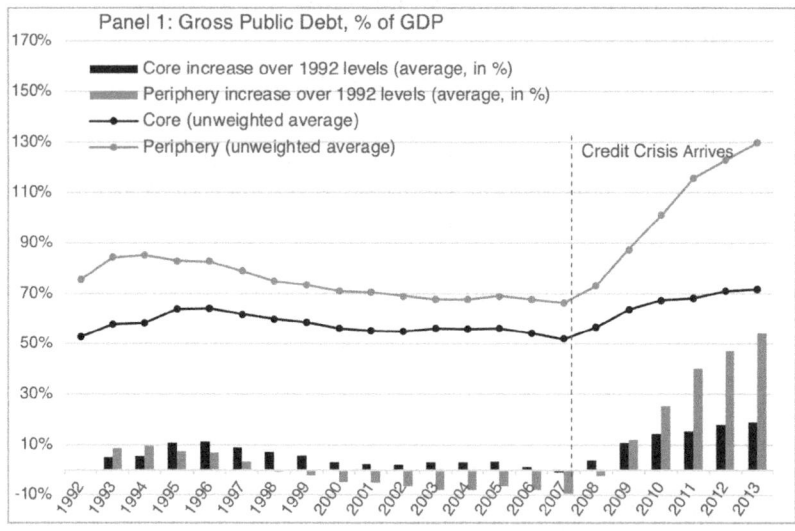

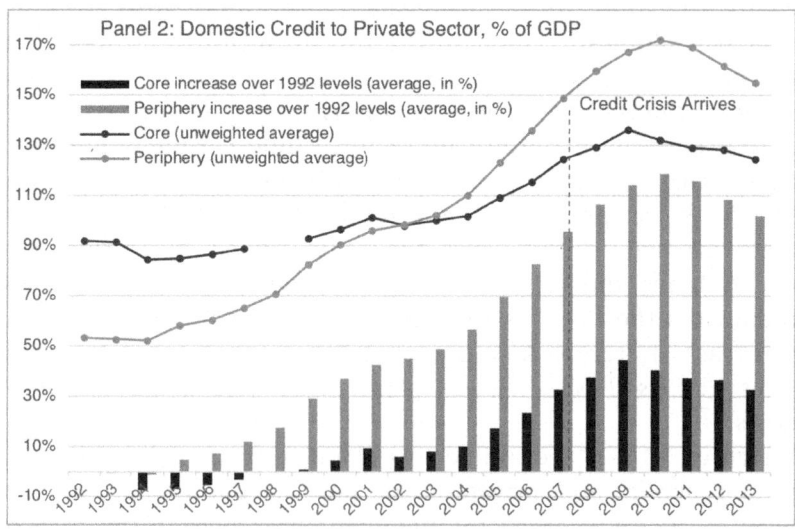

Figure 3.12 Credit growth by sector: government versus private sector[178]

[178] 'Credit Crisis Arrives' denotes August 9, 2007, when BNP Paribas froze redemption funds for three investment funds, signalling the arrival of the global financial crisis in Europe. Panel 1: Eurostat, 'Consolidated gross debt (gov_10dd_3dpt1)'. Panel 2: World Bank, 'Domestic Credit to Private Sector (% of GDP) (FS.AST.PRVT.GD.ZS)'. Core average and per cent increase for 1998 excluded due to data unavailability. Core average for 1993 and 1999 excludes Luxembourg due to data unavailability.

debt increased by a whopping 249%.[179] In Ireland (Figure 3.14) the gross government debt/GDP ratio fell a remarkable 52.87% between 1993 and 2008 (from 94.1% to 44.3% of GDP), while private-sector domestic credit expanded over 400%. All of the Periphery countries exhibit the same pattern. Private debt – not public debt – is the cause of the sovereign debt crisis.[180] Hübner concludes:

Let us not get it wrong. The sovereign debt crisis did not start with Greece and its roots are not public debt, at least not directly.[181]

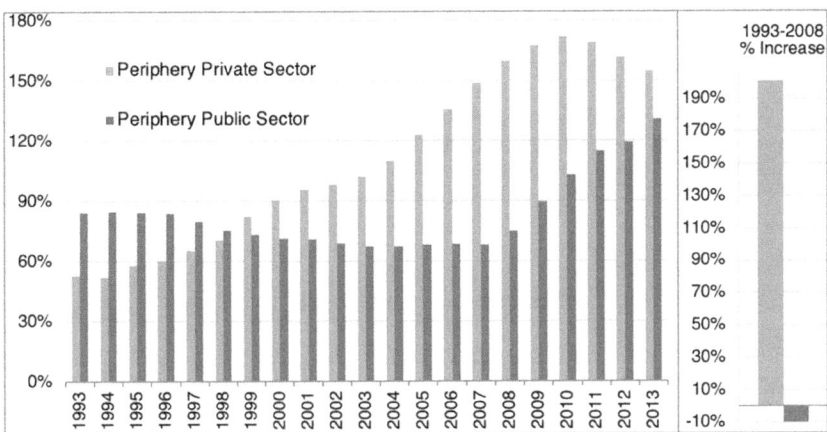

Figure 3.13 Gross government debt versus private-sector domestic credit (percentage of GDP): Periphery countries[182]

[179] Georgios P Kouretas, 'The Greek Debt Crisis: Origins and Implications' (2010) 57 Panoeconomicus, 391, 293.

[180] IMF, 2013 Article IV Consultation (Euro Area), 58; OECD, Euro Area 2012 37–38; Lane, 'Sovereign Debt Crisis', 54 excerpted above, n 132; Fagan and Gaspar, 'Adjusting to the Euro', 14 excerpted in Section 3.2.2 at n 134; Barnes, 'Unsustainable Imbalances', 31.

[181] Kurt Hübner, 'Eurozone: Creeping Decay, Sudden Death or Magical Solution' in Fin Laurson (ed.), The EU and the Eurozone Crisis (Ashgate, 2013), 26.

[182] Aggregates calculated as unweighted averages. 1993–2008 per cent increase is average per cent increase over 1993 levels. Eurostat, 'Consolidated Gross Debt (gov_10dd_3dpt1)'; World Bank, 'Domestic Credit to Private Sector (% of GDP) (FS.AST. PRVT.GD.ZS)'.

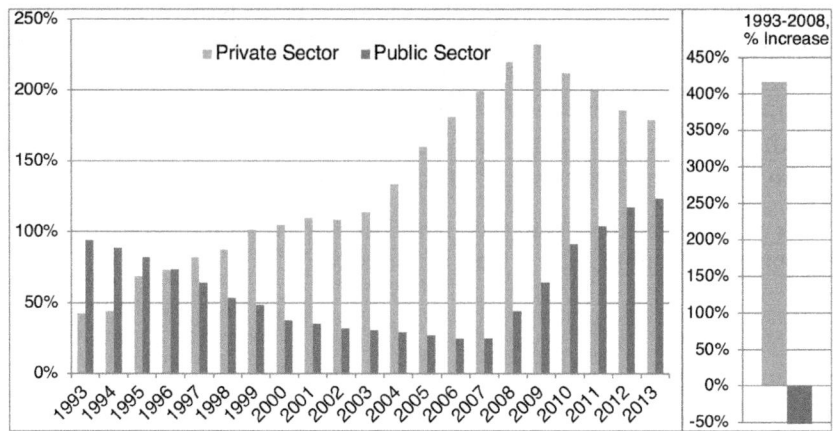

Figure 3.14 Gross government debt versus private-sector domestic credit (percentage of GDP): Ireland[183]

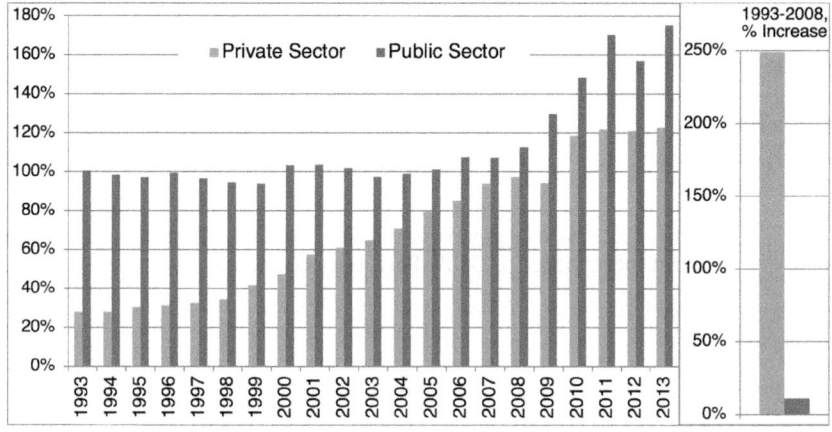

Figure 3.15 Gross government debt versus private-sector domestic credit (percentage of GDP): Greece

[183] Figures 3.14–3.18: Comparison of gross public debt with domestic credit to private sector. Government data from 1995: Eurostat, 'Consolidated Gross Debt (gov_10dd_3dpt1)'. Government data to 1994 from IMF, 'General Government Gross Debt (% of GDP)'. Private sector: World Bank, 'Domestic Credit to Private Sector (% of GDP) (FS.AST.PRVT.GD.ZS)'.

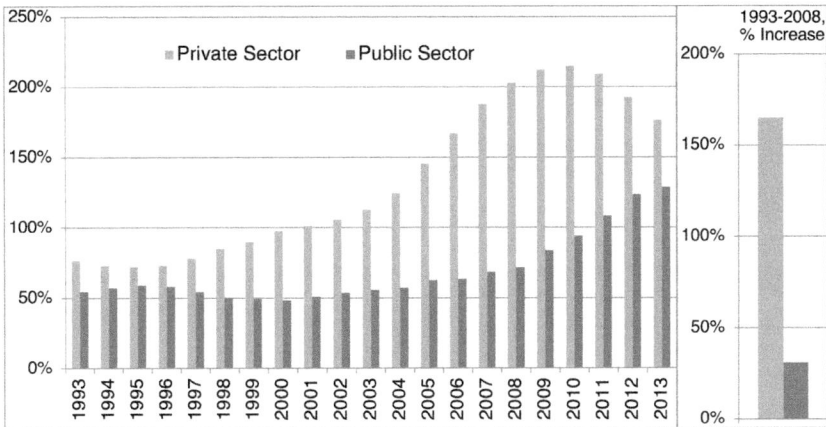

Figure 3.16 Gross government debt versus private-sector domestic credit (percentage of GDP): Portugal

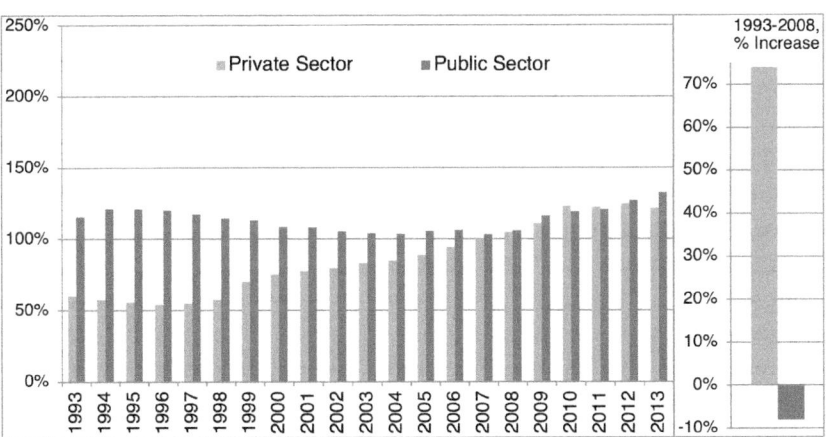

Figure 3.17 Gross government debt versus private-sector domestic credit (percentage of GDP): Italy

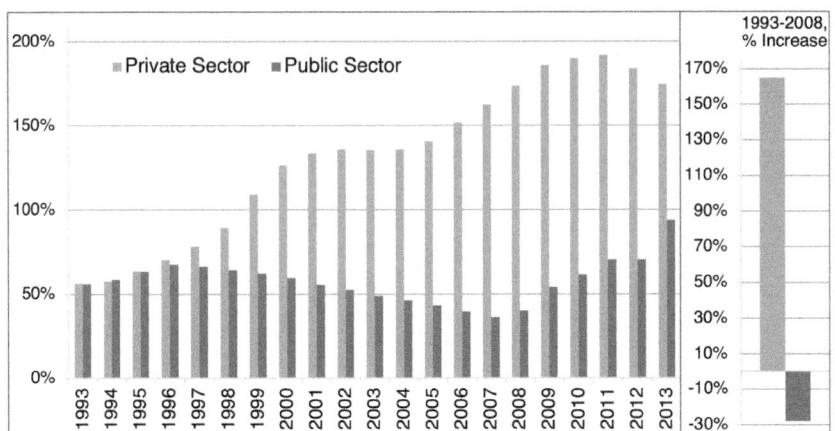

Figure 3.18 Gross government debt versus private-sector domestic credit (percentage of GDP): Spain

3.3.2   The European Sovereign Debt Crisis

The 'sovereign debt crisis', properly so named, refers to but the final link in the chain of causality: The rise in sovereign bond spreads beginning in August 2007 (see Figure 3.19). This phase of the crisis unfolded in two stages.

The first 'financial' stage began with the arrival of the United States' subprime crisis on European shores in August 2007, when BNP Paribas froze redemptions on three funds, citing an inability to value certain structured products.[184] As banks found themselves unable determine which among them was credit-worthy and which contained a vault of poisoned assets, counterparty risk increased dramatically, and interest rates rose.[185] The balance-sheet and bank-lending channels were thrown into reverse: Inter-bank funding markets seized, causing a liquidity crisis, and banks began to deleverage.[186] Property assets could not be used as collateral, highly leveraged Periphery banks could no longer take short-term loans at negative or negligible rates, and the credit-fuelled imbalances built up under the euro began to implode.[187]

---

[184] Boyd, 'BNP Paribas Freezes Funds'.

[185] Viral V Acharya and Philip Aschnable, 'Do Global Banks Spread Global Imbalances? The Case of Asset-Backed Commercial Paper during the Financial Crisis of 2007–09' (2010) 58 IMF Econ Rev 37; Pisani-Ferry, *Aftermath* 7.

[186] Barnes et al., 'Minimising Risks', 15; Caruana and Avdjiev, 'Sovereign creditworthiness', 78.

[187] For example, house prices fell by 1/3 in Ireland, 1/4 in Spain, and 1/5 in Greece by 2012: OECD, *Euro Area 2012*, 32.

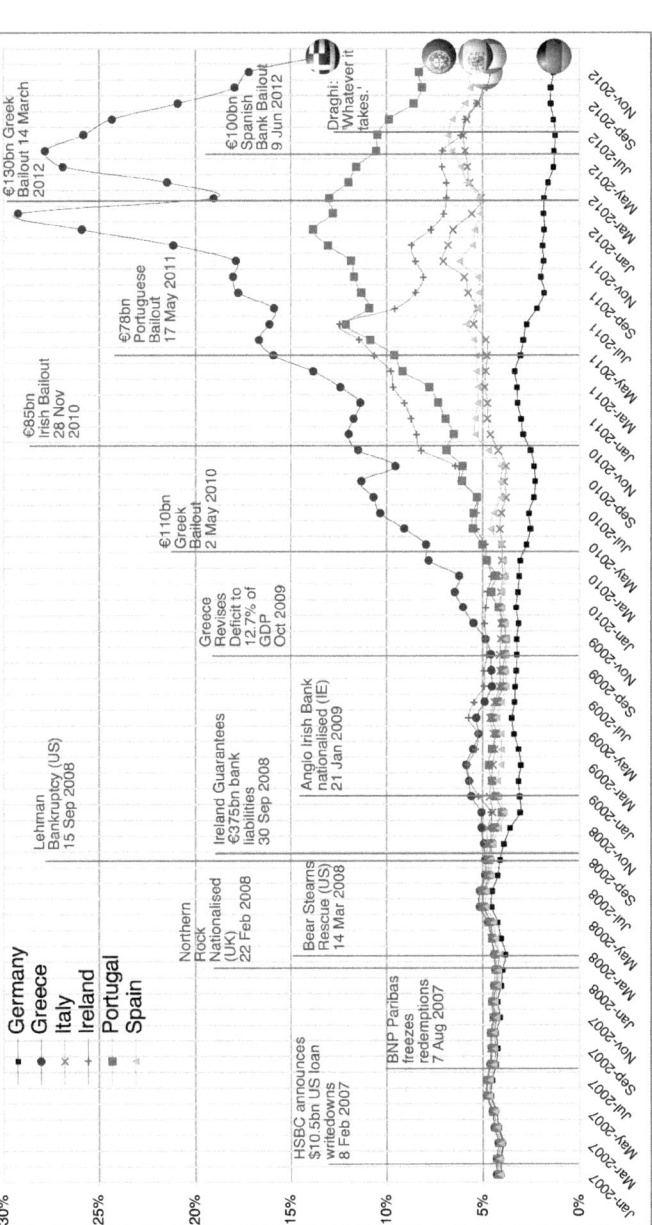

Figure 3.19 The sovereign debt crisis: interest yields on long-term government bonds[188]

[188] Eurostat, 'EMU convergence criterion series – monthly data (online data code irt_lt_mcby_m)' (*Eurostat*, http://epp.eurostat.ec.europa.eu accessed 26 November 2014). 'Whatever it takes' marker refers to ECB President Mario Draghi's July 26, 2012 announcement that 'the ECB is ready to to whatever it takes to save the euro'. ECB, 'Speech by Mario Draghi, President of the ECB at the Global Investment Conference (London, 26 July 2012) www.ecb.europa.eu/press/key/date/2012/html/sp120726.en.html accessed 22 June 2020.

While Member States had managed to comply nominally with the SGP leading to accession, the structural deterioration which built up *within* the SGP meant that fiscal balances would begin to fail at the first downturn in revenues.[189] The EDP failed to account for revenues from asset bubbles, which made them structurally unsound in the event of a correction in external funding.[190] In the event, the retrenchment of external funding was immense: Core countries withdrew investment from Periphery countries in a magnitude of 71.2% of GDP in Ireland, 20% of GDP in Greece, 18.1% of GDP in Spain, 17.4% of GDP in Portugal and 15.3% of GDP in Italy.[191] The consequent collapse of revenues boosted by unsustainable booms saw the average government balance of Periphery countries sink from close to balance (−1.78%) in 2006 to −13.1% by 2010.[192]

The second, 'sovereign debt' phase of the crisis emerged in 2008 as private-sector write-downs migrated to the public sector.[193] Cracks began to show between government bond yields with the nationalization of Northern Rock (UK) in February 2008, and the rescue of Bear Stearns (USA) in March 2008.[194] The 'sovereign debt crisis' only truly emerged, however, following the announcement of the €375bn bank guarantee by the Irish government (a commitment amounting to well over twice GNP) in September 2008, followed by the nationalization of Anglo Irish Bank in January 2009 (on a scale equivalent to 20% of Irish GDP).[195]

These guarantees signalled the risks for governments with large private-sector external debts, and the separation between the 'financial' crisis and government finances ended.[196] By March 2009, Periphery spreads over German bonds had widened to 274bps for Ireland, 285bps for Greece, 144bps for Italy, 166bps for Portugal and 101bps for Spain. As sovereign debt began to deteriorate, the balance-sheet

---

[189] Morris et al., 'Reform and Implementation', 16.

[190] Commission, 'Reinforcing Economic Policy Coordination' COM(2010) 250 final, 3.

[191] IMF, 'Euro Area: Selected Issues' (IMF, 2013), 4. See Gian Maria Milesi-Ferretti and Cedric Tille, 'The Great Retrenchment: International Capital Flows During the Global Financial Crisis' (2011) 26 Econ Policy 285.

[192] Eurostat, 'Deficit/Surplus (gov_10dd_edpt1)'.

[193] See sources cited above, Section 3.3.1, n 180.

[194] Ashoka Mody and Damiano Sandri, 'The Eurozone Crisis: How Banks and Sovereigns Came to Be Joined at the Hip' (2012) 27 Econ Policy 199, 203; Vincent Reinhart, 'A Year of Living Dangerously: The Management of the Financial Crisis in 2008' (2011) 25 J Econ Persp 71.

[195] Nyberg, *The Nyberg Report* 77; Mody and Sandri, 'Joined at the Hip', 206.

[196] Mody and Sandri, 'Joined at the Hip', 204; Lane, 'Sovereign Debt Crisis', 55; Skouras, 'Lessons', 53.

channel returned shocks back downwards to banks: Sovereign debt write-downs led to write-downs on bank balance sheets, which increased doubts about the sovereign's ability to support them, leading to further sovereign write-downs, and so on.[197]

In the midst of this spiral, Greece announced that its debt data had been inaccurately reported for years, and issued a revised deficit forecast of 12.7% of GDP in October 2009 – double the existing estimate of 6%.[198] It is this revelation to which the mischaracterization of the 'sovereign debt crisis' is owed.[199] Pisani-Ferry laments that, had Ireland sought a bailout first, 'the focus of the discussion on European crisis would have been completely different' – focused on cheap credit and macroeconomic imbalances, not cultural failings. The Irish, he adds, 'are not known for spending too much time on the beaches'.[200]

Following the announcement, foreign claims on the public sectors of Greece, Ireland, Italy, Portugal and Spain dropped from €586bn in the third quarter of 2009 to €335bn mid-way through 2011 – a fall of approximately 42%.[201] Greek bonds began to peel away from Irish bonds immediately, causing it to seek €110bn in assistance by May 2010.[202] Portuguese and Irish bond yields rose together in 2010, resulting in Ireland seeking €85bn in assistance in November, and Portugal following suit for €78bn in May 2011. Italian and Spanish spreads rose over 400 bps over the level of Germany in 2012, resulting in Spain seeking €100bn in assistance to bail out its banks.

This final result – the 'sovereign debt crisis' properly so named – is the *raison d'etre* of the EDP. Yet the EDP is not merely ineffective at intervening in this cascade – it is incapable of doing so.[203] For example, Ireland

---

[197] Paolo Angelini, Giuseppe Grande and Fabrio Panetta, 'The Negative Feedback Loop between Banks and Sovereigns' (2014) Banca D'Italia Occasional Papers No 213; Reis, 'Slump and Crash', 177; Niccolò Battistini, Marco Pagano and Saverio Simionelli, 'Systemic Risk and Home Bias in the Euro Area' (2013) European Economy Economic Papers No 494; Viral Acharya, Itamar Dreschler and Philipp Schnable, 'A Pyrrhic Victory? Bank Bailouts and Sovereign Credit Risk' (2014) 69 J Finance 2689.

[198] Lane, 'Sovereign Debt Crisis', 56. The 12.7% figure was subsequently revised upwards to 15.4% of GDP. Gibson et al., 'Greek Financial Crisis', 504.

[199] Lane, 'Sovereign Debt Crisis', 56.

[200] Pisani-Ferry, *Aftermath*, 52.

[201] Caruana and Avdjiev, 'Sovereign Creditworthiness', 81.

[202] Greek bonds ultimately rose to over 29% until it received a second bailout of €130bn in February 2012.

[203] Clemens Feust and Andreas Peichl, 'European Fiscal Union: What is it? Does it Work? And Are There Really "No Alternatives"?' (2012) 13 CESifo Forum 3, 3; Giavazzi and Spaventa, 'Current Account', 218 and sources cited below, nn 206–207.

and Spain were praised for their budget surpluses in 2007, only to have that praise rendered irrelevant by the collapse of private-sector credit imbalances: By 2011, Ireland's debt had risen from 25% to 108% of GDP and Spain's from 40% to 70% of GDP.[204] Across the EMU as a whole, the collapse of private-sector imbalances caused government balances to deteriorate from +0.6% of GDP in 2007 to −7% in 2010 – 'wiping out the results of twenty years of consolidation'.[205] In the face of this result, the EDP is worse than useless – it is procyclical. The EDP deactivates when countries are 'temporarily boosted by tax-rich activity' from 'unsustainable booms',[206] and is then unable to penalize crisis-hit countries in recessions once the booms have collapsed (both because sanctions become destabalizing and because that is when counter-cyclical spending is called for).[207] The EDP was never capable of countering the groundswell credit incentives which led to the Euro Crisis.

3.3.3   The Futility of Centralized Fiscal Governance: A Counterfactual

The statement of this chapter is that the sovereign debt crisis is the culmination of an economic breakdown that began with a mispricing of credit – not fiscal profligacy. The necessary implication is that centralized fiscal governance, failed or otherwise, is irrelevant to the economic cascade traced in this chapter (if not an aggravating factor). This is verifiable with a brief counterfactual – that is, could any alternative fiscal policies have been adopted to cause or prevent the cataclysmic accumulation of external debt in the Periphery?

The answer, according to several critiques, is no. First and most obviously, the chain of causality identified in this chapter is not capable of running in reverse (from sovereign debt to macroeconomic imbalances, etc.). Ordinarily, governments affect the composition of external debt through several instruments: Capital controls (restricting capital inflows or outflows), trade policy (targeting sector-specific inflows/outflows), monetary policy (interest rates and base money), and fiscal policy

---

[204] Jean Pisani-Ferry, 'The Eurozone and the Streetlamp Syndrome' (*Bruegel*, http://bruegel.org accessed 28 September 2016.

[205] Commission, 'Reinforcing Economic Policy Coordination' COM (2010) 250 final, 3.

[206] Commission, 'Reinforcing Economic Policy Coordination' COM (2010) 250 final, 3.

[207] Graham Bishop, 'The Future of the Stability and Growth Pact' (2003) 6 Int Financ 297, 300–301; Patrick Leblond, 'The Political Stability and Growth Pact is Dead: Long Live the Economic Stability and Growth Pact' (2006) 44 JCMS 969, 982; Adams et al., 'European Budgetary Constraints', 3; Crawford, *One Money?*, 290; Jean-Claude Trichet, 'International Policy Coordination in the Euro Area: Toward an Economic and Fiscal Federation by Exception' (2013) 35 J Policy Model 473, 479.

(affecting the rate of domestic absorption). Under EMU, the first two are banned and the third is the exclusive competence of the Union, fixed at euro aggregates. That leaves fiscal policy.[208] But fiscal policy cannot cause (nor is it correlated with) the train of low real interest rates, unprecedented credit expansion, capital flows and private-sector indebtedness mapped in this chapter. Real interest rates are, in fact, 'a monetary phenomenon' – not a political or fiscal one.[209] As Patnaik observes:

> The proposition that the size of the fiscal deficit affects the level of [real] interest rates is theoretically and completely erroneous, which in turn makes the budgetary strategy fundamentally flawed.[210]

The best fiscal policy can do is attempt to dampen absorption, but even then it is not clear that fiscal policy is effective at affecting absorption in the private sector at all – and certainly not on the scale required to combat broken credit incentives.[211] Constraining the current account is 'well beyond direct policy influence' in an open-market currency union.[212] For example, Abbas et al. find that a 1% of GDP increase in the fiscal balance will increase the current account by a mere 0.2%–0.3% of GDP.[213] When one recalls that capital flows from France and Germany alone were 120% of Irish GDP, the futility of trying to replace failed credit incentives with fiscal policy govern-ance becomes obvious. The scale of financial commitment required to offset the 'monetary phenomenon' of low real interest rates

---

[208] De Grauwe, *Economics of Monetary Union* (2020), 8–23, 111–115 and 221. On the role of fiscal policy in a currency union: Jordi Gali and Tommaso Monacelli, 'Optimal Monetary And Fiscal Policy in a Currency Union' (2008) 76 J Int Econ 116; Michael Kumhof and Douglas Laxton, 'Fiscal Deficit and Current Account Deficits' (2009) IMF Working Paper No 237; Laura Bardone and Vito Ernesto Reitano, 'Italy in the Euro Area: The Adjustment Challenge' in Marco Buti (ed.), *Italy in EMU: The Challenges of Adjustment and Growth* (Palgrave Macmillan, 2013), 68 and sources cited above, Chapter 2, Section 2.2.2, n 62.

[209] Rapach and Wohar, 'Monetary Phenomenon?'. See also: Frederic Miskin, 'Understanding Real Interest Rates' (1988) 70 Am J Agr Econ 1064, 1071.

[210] Prabhat Patnaik, 'On Fiscal Deficits and Real Interest Rates' (2001) 36 Econ Polit Weekly 1160.

[211] Philip Lane, 'External Imbalances and Fiscal Policy' (2010) IIIS Discussion Paper No 314, 1; George Alogoskoufis, 'Greece's Sovereign Debt Crisis: Retrospect and Prospect' (2012) Hellenic Observatory Papers on Greece and Southeast Europe, GreeSE Paper No 54, 4; Vanda Almeida et al., 'Fiscal Policy in a Small Euro Area Economy' (2012) Banco de Portugal Working Papers No 16.

[212] Dabrowski, 'Fiscal and Macroeconomic Governance', 16. See also Blanchard, 'Current Account Deficits in Rich Countries'.

[213] Ali AM Abbas et al., 'Fiscal Policy and the Current Account' (2010) 59 IMF Econ Rev 603.

would undermine the fiscal stability of entire countries.[214] For this reason, a 2002 OECD Economics Department Working Paper argued that fiscal policy should *not* be used to counter overheating demand due to too-loose monetary conditions, since the scale of intervention needed to dampen it would undermine budgetary stability (and that is if it is not futile altogether, which it seems it may be).[215]

Detragiache and Hamann's study of exchange rate stabilization operations in Greece, Ireland, Portugal and Italy found no clear relationship in any of those countries between fiscal policy and disinflation.[216] Gaspar and St Aubyn find that starkly different fiscal policies in Spain and Portugal between 1995 and 2005 (Spain being prudent and Portugal expansionary) made little difference to their external debts.[217] The adjustment pattern is dominated by the private-sector reaction to the fall in interest rates irrespective of the differences in fiscal policies deployed against it. Lane makes a similar finding comparing the fiscal policies of Ireland and Spain against Greece and Portugal: 'the only strong correlation is between aggregate net flows and the net flows of non-financial corporations'.[218] Other studies reach similar conclusions.[219] As Gavilán et al. conclude: 'fiscal tightening would have helped very little in attenuating the build-up of the economy's external imbalance over this period'.[220] Adamski observes:

No EU institutional measures could prevent macroeconomic imbalances from becoming unsustainable [...] Diminishing real interest rates induced both the societies and the governments to drink from the poisoned chalice of overspending.[221]

[214] As Lane, 'External Imbalances', 18, observes, whatever stabilization policy is used, the long-term fiscal position must remain sustainable if it is to be useful.

[215] Claude Giorno, Peter Hoeller and Christine De La Maisonneuve, 'Overheating in Small Euro Area Economies: Should Fiscal Policy React?' (2002) 2 OECD Economics Department Working Papers 323.

[216] Enica Detragiache and Alfonso J Hamann, 'Exchange Rate-Base Stabilization in Western Europe: Greece, Ireland, Italy and Portugal' (1997) IMF Working Paper 75, 25.

[217] Gaspar and St Aubyn, 'Portugal and Spain'.

[218] Lane, 'Capital Flows', 11.

[219] Lane and McQuade, 'Credit Growth', 3; Barnes, 'Unsustainable Imbalances', 31.

[220] Quite the opposite, attempts to diminish current account deficits by increasing the primary surplus may have the opposite effect due to various 'crowding in' effects (the space left by government will be filled by private capital, worsening the current account deficit). Gavilán et al., 'Origins', 91–92; António Afonso, 'Expansionary Fiscal Consolidations in Europe: New Evidence' (2010) 17 Applied Economics Letters 105; Dabrowski, 'Fiscal and Macroeconomic Governance', 18.

[221] Adamski, 'Power Games', 1324–1326.

3.3.4   Analysis: The Failure and Abrogation of the Excessive Deficit Procedure

The EDP's inability to instil fiscal discipline is not just economic; it is also institutional. The EDP is fundamentally non-credible on its own terms. By 2011, the SGP had been exceeded ninety-seven times, and no sanctions for violation had ever been imposed.[222] Eyraud and Wu note that 'about half of the countries have missed the 60 percent debt ceiling more than half the time', and public debt for the euro area as a whole has exceeded the 60% debt limit every year since 1999.[223] Yet the procedures of the EDP are *mandatory* – if countries were openly flouting the rules, the Council was expected to enforce them.[224] The EEAG finds that, irrespective of the 'widespread failure' of economic surveillance, the EDP has in any event 'been ignored in virtually all its dimensions'.[225]

There are two reasons for this. The first is constitutional, and well-predicted by fiscal federalism theory: cooperative outcomes in economic policy simply 'cannot be enforced by conventional legal techniques'.[226] Under a single currency, the only tool for dealing with mounting current account deficits is structural reform. This entails significant costs to be borne unequally among citizens. The Commission, for example, states that 'the consolidation of public finances requires setting priorities and making hard choices', and EU involvement in this process is 'crucial'.[227] But, to put it mildly, these 'hard choices' are not for the Union to make.[228] They are not even for national executives to make. Decisions on public revenue and public expenditure are, in the words of the BVerfG, 'a fundamental part of the ability of a constitutional state to democratically shape itself' and 'the core of parliamentary rights in democracy'.[229] The EDP simply cannot compel Member States to defy markets and electorates when those forces state that they should do otherwise.[230] As shown in Chapter 2, the SGP as originally designed was dependent on the 'feeding through

---

[222] EEAG Report 2011, 94. See also: Groeteke and Mause, 'Debt Brakes', 287.
[223] Luc Eyraud and Tau Wu, 'Playing by the Rules: Reforming Fiscal Governance in Europe' (2015) IMF Working Paper 67, 12; EEAG Report 2011, 79.
[224] Arts. 3(4), 7 of Regulation 1467/97. Lastra, *Legal Foundations*, 254.
[225] EEAG Report 2011, 79.
[226] Joerges, 'Economic Constitution', 15.
[227] Commission, 'Reinforcing Economic Policy Coordination' COM (2010) 250 final, 2.
[228] Fabian Amtenbrink and Jakob De Haan, 'Reforming the Stability and Growth Pact' (2006) 31 EL Rev 402, 404.
[229] *Euro Rescue Package (Germany)* [122].
[230] Adamski, '(Misguided) Constitution', 58.

of reputation costs to public opinion or financial markets' to function.[231] It was never designed (nor could it be designed) to stymie or replace those forces if they pulled in the opposite direction.

The second reason for its failure is institutional, and arises from the first: the SGP itself is simply not credible. For example, in 2002 the Council eschewed Commission recommendations to issue warnings to Germany and Portugal, declining to even put the recommendation to a vote.[232] In 2004, Greece was placed under budgetary surveillance by the Commission and the Council, but sanctions were never applied, despite the IMF's finding that 'data shortcomings are a recurring problem in Greece'.[233] Instead, surveillance was lifted in 2007 – a little over a year before Greece issued its revised deficit forecast of −12.7% of GDP.[234]

The EDP was most definitively eviscerated in 2003, when excessive deficit procedures were initiated against France and Germany for flaunting the debt rules,[235] and, instead of declaring 'no effective action' and issuing notice (the final step before sanctions) as required by the rules, the Council issued 'Conclusions' professing to put the procedures in abeyance.[236]

In the aftermath of the Franco–German rebellion, the SGP was amended in 2005 to make it more reflective of 'macro-fiscal inter-linkages' under the pretence that this would make it more credible. Under the MSP, the deficit requirement of 'close to balance or in surplus' (−0.5% of GDP) was replaced with differentiated MTOs of up to −1% of GDP, discounts were provided for anticipated structural reforms, and the obligation to achieve 'sustained convergence' was

---

[231] Commission, 'Strengthening Economic Governance and Clarifying the Implementation of the Stability and Growth Pact' COM (2004) 581 final, 8.

[232] European Council, Conclusions of 12 February (2002) EUCO 6108/02, 9, 22.

[233] IMF, *Staff Report for the 2009 Art. IV Consultation (Greece)* (IMF, 2009), 20–21.

[234] 'Report on Greek Government Deficit and Debt Statistics' COM (2010) 1 final.

[235] The Commission found that France 'did not take measures' required to correct its excessive deficit, and that the targets had been similarly 'abandoned' by Germany: Commission Recommendation for a Council Decision giving notice to Germany, in accordance with Art. 104(9) of the EC Treaty, SEC (2003) 1317 final, 2; Commission Recommendation for a Council Decision giving notice to France, in accordance with Art. 104(9) of the EC Treaty, SEC (2003) 1121 final.

[236] ECOFIN Council Conclusions of 25 November 2003 14492/1/03 REV 1 (en) (Presse 320) 15–19. When challenged, the ECJ confirmed that the EDP could be put in abeyance any time the Commission failed to achieve the sufficient political majority for sanctions (though the 'Conclusions' themselves were annulled on the basis that they were not contemplated by the EDP procedure). *Case C-27/04 Commission v. Council*, [34], [81]–[86].

replaced by an obligation to achieve the MTO over the cycle.[237] Under the EDP, the deadlines for taking effective action and imposing sanctions were both doubled, and a new one-year extension for 'unexpected adverse economic events' was added where the Council was previously supposed to issue notice.[238] If breached, the −2% of GDP trigger for the 'exceptional and temporary' escape clause was replaced with a 'negative annual GDP volume' and/or an 'accumulated loss of output during a protracted period of very low annual GDP volume growth relative to its potential' (effectively widening the exception to any downturn), and a litany of 'other relevant factors' were added before an excessive deficit could be found.[239]

Instead of increased attention to macro-fiscal linkages, the SGP was suddenly just compatible with a wider range of outcomes. For a country with a 70% debt-to-GDP ratio, the EDP was compatible with any result from a return to balance to a deterioration of 10 percentage points within a decade.[240] Scenarios for Greek debt ranged comfortably between 70% and 130% of GDP by 2015.[241]

This did not just undermine the credibility of the SGP, it undermined the entire system of rules in Articles 121–126 TFEU – including the 'no bailout' clause.[242] The Franco–German rebellion concerned the application of Article 126(8)–(9) TFEU – not just the secondary-law SGP.[243] Primary EU law called for the enforcement of the EU's rules, and this was not done.[244] As Rodden concludes:

> The European [EDP] proved to be unenforceable [...] Those half-hearted efforts at hierarchical regulation inadvertently undermined market discipline by sending significant signals about the central government's lack of credibility.

---

[237] Arts. 1(1), 2a Council Regulation (EC) No 1055/2005 of 27 June 2005 amending Regulation No 1466/97 on the strengthening of the surveillance of budgetary positions and the surveillance and coordination of economic policies [2005] OJ L 174/1.

[238] Arts. 1(2), 1(3) Reg 1056/2005, amending Art. 3, 5, Reg 1467/97.

[239] Art. 1(1), Reg 1056/2005, amending Art. 2 Reg 1467/07. See: Lastra, *Legal Foundations*, 262.

[240] Morris et al., 'Reform and Implementation', 24–25.

[241] Morris et al., 'Reform and Implementation', 39.

[242] Adamski, 'Power Games', 1337: 'Hollow Enforcement Is Always Conducive to Moral Hazard.'

[243] Daniel Gros, Thomas Mayer and Angel Ubide, *The Nine Lives of the Stability Pact: A Special Report of the CEPS Macroeconomic Policy Group* (CEPS, 2004), 4.

[244] Helge Berger, Jakob De Hann and David-Jan Jansen, 'Why has the Stability and Growth Pact Failed?' (2004) 7 Int Financ 235, 236; Lastra, *Legal Foundations*, 269–272.

[. . .] Weak or half-hearted regulation may have been worse than no regulation at all.[245]

If the EDP had worked, the entire 'sovereign debt' narrative of the crisis might have been avoided. Yet the EDP still failed to apply on its own terms even after the amendments. In first year of the new rules, a mere four of twelve EMU Member States complied with their MTOs.[246] In 2005, Germany violated its EDP recommendations and, instead of sanctions, the Council granted it a two-year extension *despite* the reformed EDP only introducing extensions by up to one year.[247] In 2005, the *Financial Times* observed:

[I]t is becoming increasingly clear that the markets will have to provide the Eurozone with the financial discipline that governments seem unable to muster. The Eurozone's original straitjacket, the growth and stability pact, has been made more flexible, but five of the 12 member governments are still in breach of it.[248]

3.4   Conclusions: Economic Criteria for EU Federalism

The *causa sine qua non* of the crisis is a severe mispricing of private and public debt caused by a failure of Articles 121–126 TFEU to induce markets to differentiate between sovereign borrowers under a (now-realized) bailout expectation. The model did not fail because investors failed to appropriately price sovereign default risk, and it did not fail because of sovereign debt. The model failed because markets (correctly) assessed that the 'no bailout' rule was non-credible, and (correctly) guessed that the EU would sooner re-interpret the Treaties than allow a Member State to default. The failure of the Maastricht model is a failure of EU institutions and EU law.

The operational hypothesis of this chapter, that exposure to hard budget constraints and market discipline are indispensable requirements for fiscal discipline in a decentralized EMU, appears robust at each stage of the analysis. The chain of causality traced in this chapter is not capable of running in reverse (from fiscal policy to net external indebtedness or credit expansion), and there are no common public debt factors which separate 'Core' from 'Periphery' groups. Whatever

---

[245] Rodden, 'Can Market Discipline Survive?', 45.

[246] Morris et al., 'Reform and Implementation', 27.

[247] Morris et al., 'Reform and Implementation', 36. See further: Feldstein, 'Euro and the Stability Pact', 424.

[248] Editorial, 'ECB Shows Its Hand'.

other economic characteristics divide the Member States, the single price of credit remains the 'common factor behind the evolution of their situations'.[249]

[3.1] The chain of causality in this chapter begins with the elimination of individuated interest rate spreads along the maturity spectrum of sovereign bonds due to a widespread bailout expectation. As the *Bundesbank* president concludes, 'this expectation put downward pressure on risk premiums on government bonds, thus distorting the pricing system; and we all know what happened next'.[250] [3.1.2] Nominal interest rate convergence resulted in a 'severe mispricing of risk of both private and public assets' according to keystone indicators of macroeconomic risk;[251] [3.1.3] Below Taylor-rule interest rates precipitated the damaging feedback cycle predicted by the 'Walters Critique'; and [3.1.4] Private-sector domestic credit expanded to 232% of GDP in Ireland, 212% of GDP in Spain, 187% in Portugal, 94.28% in Greece and 66% of GDP in Italy by 2009. [3.1.5] Low or negative real interest rates under the single nominal rate – not sovereign debt – is the denominator that binds Periphery countries to the chain of causality in this chapter and distinguishes them from the Core.

[3.2.1] Massive amounts of capital (particularly gross debt) entered Periphery economies with no liquidity- or exchange-risk premium, exceeding the capacity of their host states to finance them. [3.2.2] This fuelled current account imbalances unprecedented in over thirty years of economic data. [3.2.3] The Multilateral Surveillance Procedure failed to apprehend unprecedented macroeconomic imbalances due to a systemic breakdown in the cost-levying function of credit (at national level) and severe information asymmetries (at EU level).

[3.3] The failure of the Excessive Deficit Procedure is both institutional and fundamental. Institutional, because the EU's fiscal rules suffer from endemic credibility failure. Fundamental, because the EDP is economically unavailing and irrelevant, if not an aggravating factor, to the cascade of economic indicators in this chapter. [3.3.1] Excessive deficits are not the cause of the crisis – real interest rates and private-sector credit are. [3.3.2] The 'sovereign debt crisis', properly

---

[249] Pisani-Ferry, *Aftermath*, 51.
[250] Weidmann, 'Crisis Management'.
[251] Commission Blueprint, 3.

so-called, is but the final symptom of deeply rooted imbalances caused by the disconnection of credit from underlying economic conditions. [3.3.3] Causality is incapable of running in reverse: Real interest rates are, in fact, a monetary phenomenon – not a fiscal one, and no optimal fiscal policy is shown to be capable of causing – or preventing – the crisis.

The lesson extracted from this analysis is that hard budget constraints and market discipline are indispensable to European fiscal federalism.[252] This is not (only) because the EU's fiscal governance institutions are not credible and do not work. It is because there is no institutional counter capable of overriding the inexorable pull of millions of private individuals responding, in their economic and political lives, to the dysfunctional cost incentives of cheap credit under a sovereign bailout expectation.

[252] Sinn, *Euro Trap*, 6; Stark, 'Lessons', 544–545.

4 Constitutional Criteria for EU Fiscal Federalism

Chapters 1–3 yield two constitutional criteria for European fiscal federalism which will be applied and tested throughout Part II of this book.

First, any model of European fiscal federalism must preserve the fiscal sovereignty of the twenty-seven (formerly twenty-eight) constitutional democracies which form the basis of its legal order. In so far as the EU is founded upon the principles of conferral, it can have no powers other than what the Member States have given it and, *nemo plus iuris,* what the Member States have given it is limited by their own constitutional identities. The three tests to be applied in that respect are:

No unlawful *restrictions* on budgetary sovereignty: A restriction on budgetary sovereignty must not 'fetter the budget legislature to such an extent that the principle of democracy is violated', that is, 'with the effect that it or a future Parliament can no longer exercise the right to decide the budget on its own';[1]

No unlawful *conferral* of budgetary sovereignty: A delegation of budgetary sovereignty must not compromise the principle that 'the [national] Parliament remains the place in which autonomous decisions on revenue and expenditure are made';[2] and

No structural *impairments* of fiscal sovereignty: finite financial dispositions must not be of structural significance to the parliament's right to decide on the budget and shape the economic and social life of the state.[3]

---

[1] *Euro Rescue Package (Germany)* [104] and sources cited in Chapter 1, Section 1.3.1.1, n 482.
[2] *Euro Rescue Package (Germany)* [124] and sources cited in Chapter 1, Section 1.3.1.1, n 483.
[3] *ESM II (Germany)* [173] and sources cited in Chapter 1, Section 1.3.1.1, n 484.

Second, hard budget constraints and market discipline in sovereign bond markets are indispensable requirements for the guiding principles of price stability and fiscal discipline binding on the mandate for EMU in Article 119(3) TFEU. As shown in Chapters 2 and 3 of this book, these conditions are economic antecedents of financial stability in a decentralized currency union with a federal structure. However, these rules also entrench a decentralized model of 'classical' or 'market-preserving' fiscal federalism that preserves the autonomous budgetary competences of national parliaments. The hypothesis to be applied in Part II is that alternate systems of fiscal federalism not constructed upon these principles must not be compatible with the constitutional authorization for EMU,[4] and therefore must not be compatible with deeper constitutional boundaries of the EU legal order as a whole. In particular, the BVerfG has held that the 'no bailout rule' and 'no monetary financing rule' safeguard the *Bundestag*'s 'national budgetary responsibility', and Germany's constitutional identity would be violated if the *Stabilitätsgemeinschaft* became a 'liability community' through the 'direct or indirect communitarisation of state debts'.[5]

---

[4] See, for example, *Brunner (Germany)* [80]–[89]: the *Stabilitätsgemeinshaft* in Articles 119–127 TFEU is 'the basis and subject-matter of the German Act of Accession'. See also Chapter 1, Section 1.3.2, nn 547–552.

[5] *ESM I (Germany)* [203] and cases cited in Methods and Introduction, n 61.

Part II

5 The Emergent Centralized Architecture of European Fiscal Federalism

Part II of this book pursues the second undertaking of this study: to identify which institutional configurations of fiscal federalism theory remain empirically and theoretically implementable within the constitutional boundaries of the EU legal order. It will test the veracity of the constitutional criteria extracted in Part I; examine the emerging model of EU 'fiscal union' against the constitutional boundaries of the EU legal order as a whole; and conduct a data-backed analysis of the structure of public finance incentives in EMU from the perspective of fiscal federalism theory. The analysis seeks to identify which models of fiscal federalism are compatible with the European legal order and, of those remaining, which models result in a stable economic equilibrium based on real economic data.

This chapter embarks on this process with the task of taxonomy, classifying the emergent post-crisis European model from the perspective of fiscal federalism theory in order to determine what it demands from the EU legal order to 'work'. In terms of the throughline, it begins where Part I left off: The abrogation of the Maastricht architecture and the pursuit of a new model in the wake of the sovereign debt crisis.

Section 5.1 begins by providing a brief overview of the amendments to the fiscal architecture effected since the crisis. Section 5.2 then classifies the new model from the perspective of fiscal federalism theory. Section 5.3 considers the demands placed on the European legal order by this model and provides directions for the remainder of Part II of this study. This chapter finds that successive amendments to the EU public finance architecture have supplanted the decentralized model of fiscal federalism inscribed in the EU Treaties with a highly centralized model of proto-fiscal union comprised of four pillars:

Conditional financial assistance, which principal architecture is now comprised mainly of the European Stability Mechanism (ESM) and Article 136(3) TFEU;

Centralized macroeconomic governance, which architecture is comprised principally of a new Macroeconomic Imbalance Procedure (MIP) and Excessive Imbalance Procedure (EIP);

Centralized fiscal governance, which architecture is comprised principally of the Multilateral Surveillance Procedure (MSP), the Excessive Deficit Procedure (EDP) and the intergovernmental Treaty on Stability, Coordination and Governance (TSCG); and

Centralized governance of Member State budgetary frameworks, which architecture is comprised of the European Semester and a web of secondary EU law that inserts binding interlinkages into Member State budgetary frameworks.

5.1   Overview of Reforms

The reformation of the Treaty model began on 2 May 2010 with the announcement of a €110bn package of bilateral loans to Greece.[1] This was followed the same year by the creation of the European Financial Stabilisation Mechanism (EFSM), a €60bn bailout mechanism founded under EU law,[2] and the European Financial Stability Facility (EFSF), a special-purpose vehicle established by the EMU Member States with a €440bn lending capacity.[3] In 2012, these mechanisms were eclipsed by the ESM, a €705bn intergovernmental organization subscribed by the nineteen EMU Member States with a €500bn lending capacity.[4] In 2017 the Commission proposed to bring the ESM into the EU legal order as a permanent 'European Monetary Fund' (EMF) to provide the embryo of an EU fiscal Union capable of providing

---

[1] Eurogroup, 'Statement by the Eurogroup' (2 May 2010).
[2] Reg 407/2010 establishing a European financial stabilisation mechanism [2010] OJ L 118/1.
[3] EFSF Framework Agreement (2014) www.efsf.europa.eu/attachments/20111019_efsf_framework_agreement_en.pdf accessed 31 December 2014; EFSF Consolidated Articles of Association (23 April 2014) www.efsf.europa.eu/attachments/EFSFStatusCoordonnes%2023AVRL2014.pdf accessed 31 December 2014.
[4] Treaty Establishing the European Stability Mechanism [2012] OJ L 91/1.

a macroeconomic stabilization function (among other things).[5] These fiscal developments have been accompanied by a series of 'unconventional' monetary policy instruments, most recently the Outright Monetary Transactions Programme (OMT) and the Public Sector Purchase Programme (PSPP), which have had a decisive effect on reducing government bond spreads.[6]

In order to stabilize the new model and safeguard the price stability monetary union, the counterpart to the communitarization of risk has been an unprecedented extension of EU governance into national budgetary processes and economic competences. Reforms began in 2011 with a package of legislation known as the 'six pack', consisting of three regulations expanding and reinforcing the SGP;[7] two regulations introducing the MIP and extending EU governance into the realm of (previously excluded) macroeconomic policy;[8] and Directive 2011/85/ EU, which sets out binding requirements for national budgetary frameworks.[9] In 2013 this was followed by the 'two pack', consisting of Regulation 472/2013, which introduced a governance regime for financial assistance programmes,[10] and Regulation 473/2013, introducing new requirements for national budgetary procedures for EMU countries.[11]

---

[5] Commission Proposal for an EMF (2017). For a critical analysis see Hannes Hofmeister, 'From ESM to EMF and Back' (2019) 29 Swiss Rev Int'l & Eur L 367.

[6] See Chapter 6, Section 6.1.6 and sources cited.

[7] Council Regulation (EU) No 1175/2011 of 16 November 2011 amending Council Regulation (EC) No 1466/97 on the strengthening of the surveillance of budgetary positions and the surveillance and coordination of economic policies [2011] OJ L 306/12; Council Regulation (EU) No 1177/2011 of 8 November 2011 amending Regulation (EC) No 1467/97 on speeding up and clarifying the implementation of the excessive deficit procedure [2011] OJ L 306/33; Council Regulation (EU) No 1173/2011 of 16 November 2011 on the effective enforcement of budgetary surveillance in the euro area [2011] OJ L 306/1.

[8] Council Regulation (EU) No 1176/2011 of 16 November 2011 on the prevention and correction of economic imbalances [2011] OJ L 306/25; Council Regulation (EU) No 1174/ 2011 of 16 November 2011 on the prevention and correction of economic imbalances [2011] OJ L 306/25.

[9] Council Directive 2011/85/EU of 8 November 2011 on requirements for budgetary frameworks of the Member States [2011] OJ L 306/41.

[10] Council Regulation (EU) No 472/2013 of 21 May 2014 on the strengthening of economic and budgetary surveillance of Member States in the euro area experiencing or threatened with serious difficulties with respect to their financial stability [2013] OJ L 140/1.

[11] Council Regulation (EU) No 473/2013 of 21 May 2013 on common provisions for monitoring and assessing draft budgetary pans and ensuring the correction of excessive deficit of the Member States in the euro area [2013] OJ L 140/11.

In March 2012, this framework was accompanied by the TSCG, an intergovernmental treaty formed under public international law (outside the EU Treaties) that is nonetheless interlaced with secondary EU law.[12] The centrepiece of the TSCG is the 'Fiscal Compact', a justiciable obligation on Member States to institute a 'balanced budget rule' in national law of constitutional or permanent character, or otherwise guaranteed to be respected throughout the budgetary process.[13] In 2017 the Commission proposed to bring the Fiscal Compact under (binding and supreme) secondary EU law with the dubious justification that 'Its objective [i.e., enacting balanced budgets] cannot be sufficiently achieved by the Member States and can be better achieved at Union level.'[14]

Until 2012, revisions to the overall model of fiscal federalism appeared merely incidental to *ad hoc* and piecemeal responses to the crisis, with apparently only belated consideration of whether these elements would amount to a coherent economic model, and whether that model might adhere to the Treaties.[15] Bilateral loans to Greece, for example, took place outside the Treaties, with conditionality inscribed in secondary EU law,[16] and no justification of legality.[17] Recourse to Article 122(2) TFEU (the only exception to the 'no bailout' rule in EMU) could not be had, since the loans came from the Member States. In other cases, crisis measures outpaced committees assigned to give them sober legal aforethought. The question of a crisis resolution framework under EFSM/EFSF financial assistance, for example, was assigned to a task force in March 2010,[18] only to have both the EFSF and EFSM come into existence before the task force could submit its report in October 2010 (it did not conclude that financial assistance was

---

[12] Treaty on Stability, Coordination and Governance in the Economic and Monetary Union (TSCG), Brussels, 2 March 2012, ITS (2013) 13.

[13] Art. 3, TSCG. The Fiscal Compact is Title III TSCG. It binds the nineteen Member States in EMU, plus Bulgaria, Denmark and Romania.

[14] Commission, Proposal for a Council Directive strengthening fiscal responsibility and the medium-term budgetary orientation in the Member States' COM(2017) 824 final, 6.

[15] Merino, 'Financial Assistance', 1614.

[16] Council Decision 2010/320/EU of 10 May 2010 addressed to Greece with a view to reinforcing and deepening fiscal surveillance and giving notice to Greece to take measures for the deficit reduction judged necessary to remedy the situation of excessive deficit [2010] OJ L 145/6.

[17] The only justification was that it was 'to be considered ultimate ratio, meaning in particular that market financing is insufficient.' *Statement by the Heads of State or Government of the Euro Area* (Brussels 25 March 2010).

[18] European Council, Conclusions of 25–26 March (2010) EUCO 7/10.

reconcilable with the existing Treaties).[19] By that time, a combined €198bn in bailouts had been issued under three separate legal instruments. The EFSM was later to be tacitly recognized by both the European Council and the ECJ as wanting a proper legal basis,[20] and in December 2010 'a limited treaty change' was agreed to replace the EFSF/EFSM with the ESM – only to have the ESM enter into force *before* the amendment to Article 136 TFEU thought necessary to provide it sufficient legal cover.[21]

The architecture of EU fiscal federalism is now a bewildering and inchoate constellation of over twenty separate legal instruments in various legal forms, both within and without the framework of the Treaties, which both cross-amend and interlace with each other.[22]

It should be emphasized that the architecture set out here and picked apart for the duration of this study is as-yet inchoate. In June 2012, the 'Four Presidents' Report' envisioned 'a fully-fledged fiscal union' entailing, *inter alia*, a power to rewrite Member State budgets, mutualized debt, and the 'joint exercise of sovereignty'.[23] This was followed by the Commission's 'Blueprint for a deep and genuine economic and monetary union' which called for a 'full banking union', a 'full fiscal union', a 'full economic union' and a 'full political union'. The completed union would:

[I]nvolve a political union with adequate pooling of sovereignty with a central budget as its own fiscal capacity and *a means of imposing budgetary and economic decisions on its members* ... [24]

In 2015 the *Five Presidents' Report* enunciated a multi-stage plan to use EU mechanisms 'forcefully' and centralize Member State fiscal policy

---

[19] Council of the EU, *Strengthening Economic Governance in the EU: Report of the Task Force to the European council* (15301/10 Brussels, 21 October, 2010), para 57. The mechanisms became operational in May 2010. See further: Section 6.1.

[20] See Chapter 6, at nn 40–41.

[21] European Council, Conclusions of 28–29 October 2010 (Brussels, 20 November 2010) EUCO 25/1/10 Rev 1, para 2.

[22] For excellent overviews and analyses: Damian Chalmers, 'The European Redistributive State and a European Law of Struggle' (2012) 18 ELJ 667; Alexandre De Streel, 'The Evolution of the EU Economic Governance since the Treaty of Maastricht: An Unfinished Task' (2013) 20 MJ 336; Kenneth Armstrong, 'The New Governance of EU Fiscal Discipline' (2013) 38 EL Rev 601; Chiti and Pedro, 'Constitutional Implications'; Tuori and Tuori, *Eurozone Crisis*, 85–117; Craig, 'Economic Governance', 19; Fabbrini, *Economic Governance*, 2–10; Adamski, *Redefining Economic Integration*, 36–70.

[23] Van Rompuy, *Towards a Genuine EMU* 3, 6.

[24] Commission Blueprint 30 (emphasis added).

under 'binding [. . .] EU legislation, as sovereignty over policies of common concern would be shared and strong decision-making at euro area level would be established'.[25]

The legal landscape remains unchanged at the time of writing, though Commission meeting minutes shows that a 'new phase' has begun.[26] This 'next phase' 'would be more intrusive', 'coordinating or even harmonising taxes', with EU institutions 'able to insist on certain spending priorities'.[27] Work to make *ex ante* coordination of economic policies binding under EU law has begun,[28] and the use of 'solidarity mechanisms' (i.e. financial conditionality) as the basis of binding debt contracts is now commonplace.[29] In late 2015, Commission minutes confirmed that Stage 2 of the plan to bring binding debt contracts within the EU legal order was underway,[30] while some in the Council Legal Service have energetically called for the removal of the 'no bailout' rule on the basis that 'The rationale of the prohibition, founded on the logic that Member States remain sovereign for their budgets, would not exist any more should [. . .] Member States no longer be sovereign for their budgetary decisions.'[31]

It is clear, however, that the present framework has met the limits of the Treaties.[32] The proposals for a centralized power of EU institutions to rewrite national budgets are deeper extensions of the four-pillar

---

[25] Juncker et al., *Five Presidents' Report*, 9.

[26] Minutes of the 2111th meeting of the Commission held in Strasbourg (Winston Churchill) on Tuesday 13 January 2015 PV(2015) 2111 final; Minutes of the 2117th meeting of the Commission held in Brussels (Berlaymont) on Wednesday February 2015 PV(2015) 2117 final; Minutes of the 2143rd meeting of the Commission held in Brussels (Berlaymont) on 21 October 2015 PV(2015) 2143 final; Minutes of the 2155th meeting of the Commission held in Brussels (Berlaymont) on Friday 5 February 2016 PV(2016) 2155 final; Minutes of the 2158th meeting of the Commission held in Brussels (Berlaymont) on 24 October 2016 PV(2016) 2158 final.

[27] Quentin Peel, 'Germany and Europe: A Very Federal Formula' *Financial Times* (London 9 February 2012) www.ft.com/intl/cms/s/0/31519b4a-5307-11e1-950d-00144feabdc0.html #axzz3VZyP8kdL accessed 27 March 2015.

[28] Euro Area Summit Statement of 24 October 2014, accessible at: www.consilium.europa .eu/en/press/press-releases/2014/10/eurosummit-brusel-24-ï%C3%ADjna-2014/ accessed 24 November 2015.

[29] See: Section 7.5. See further: European Commission, 'Minutes of the 2158th meeting', 21; Minutes of the 2145th meeting of the Commission held in Brussels (Berlaymont) on 11 November 2015 PV(2015) 2145 final, 19–20.

[30] European Commission, 'Minutes of the 2143rd Meeting', 19–20.

[31] Merino, 'Financial Assistance', 1632.

[32] Commission Blueprint, 26, 'the innovations brought [. . .] are reaching the limit of what is possible under the current Treaties [. . .] once adopted, the EU will largely have exhausted the limits of its legislative competence'.

model identified by this chapter, but they have no legal basis in the Treaty.

Nevertheless, the foundation stones have been sunk, and the layout is clearly classifiable from the perspective of fiscal federalism theory. The new model conforms to the pattern of a highly centralized *proto*-fiscal union comprised of four pillars:

The first is conditional financial assistance under the EFSM (Article 122(2) TFEU), and the EFSF and ESM (Article 136(3) TFEU), supplemented by various 'unconventional' policy instruments deployed by the ECB, in particular the OMT and PSPP. This legal architecture is deconstructed in Chapter 6 and Chapter 7 (see Section 7.5).

The second is centralized economic governance under the MIP and EIP, which expand sanction-backed EU governance to virtually all areas of fiscal, economic and social policy. This architecture is deconstructed in Chapter 7 (see Section 7.4).

The third is centralized fiscal governance under Articles 121 and 126 TFEU. Under this pillar, new sanctions have been inserted into both limbs of the SGP and coupled with the introduction of RQMV, rendering the application of sanctions virtually automatic. This, combined with the operationalization of the concept of a 'significant observed deviation from the MTO',[33] has expanded the sanction-backed 'hard law' disciplines of EU governance from the 3% and 60% debt limits, to the whole panoply of economic, social and welfare decisions which constitute that balance. This has been accompanied by a significant deepening of vertical legal restraints. Included in this category is the TSCG which, though founded under public international law, is nonetheless interlaced with EU law.[34] This architecture is deconstructed in Chapter 7 (see Section 7.3.2).

The fourth is centralized governance of budgetary frameworks. All of the above procedures are now fully integrated into an annual coordination cycle under the 'European Semester', which integrates EU economic governance procedures into Member State budgetary frameworks. This architecture is deconstructed in Chapter 7 (see Section 7.2).

---

[33] See Chapter 7, Section 7.3.1.
[34] See Chapter 7, Section 7.3.2.

All of these machineries, their legal bases and their operations are examined in-depth in the remaining three chapters of this book. For present purposes, it is sufficient to remark here that the border between EU law and national fiscal competence is now criss-crossed with legal sutures that bind national budgetary outcomes to EU processes, rules and recommendations. Among other things, secondary EU law now sets out binding requirements for, *inter alia*, Member State budgetary frameworks,[35] budgetary targets and objectives,[36] draft budgetary plans,[37] medium-term fiscal plans and SCPs,[38] constitutional correction mechanisms,[39] MTO adjustment paths,[40] budgetary forecasts,[41] budgetary planning,[42] statistical and macofiscal assessments[43] and national fiscal rules.[44] From the perspective of fiscal federalism theory, this is an institutional configuration that is far more apt to unitary states than any of the federations touched upon this book. As Wyplosz (in a comparison of eighteen countries, both unitary and federal) concludes, the EU's new fiscal governance regime 'is both more encompassing and more intrusive than what is found in federal *and* unitary states'.[45]

5.2   Classification of the New Model

From the perspective of fiscal federalism theory, the economic and legal taxonomy of a given federal model depends on its placement on a continuum between 'centralized' or 'surveillance' models of fiscal union, and 'classical' decentralized fiscal federalism (known as 'ideal-type' federalism, 'market-preserving federalism', or 'self-preserving federalism' in the public economics literature).[46] Within these federal states, institutional arrangements for fiscal discipline fall along a spectrum from pure market discipline to centrally imposed fiscal

---

[35] Arts. 2(d), 3 Directive 2011/85/EU; Art. 3(1) Reg 473/2011.
[36] Art. 2(c),(e) Directive 2011/85/EU.
[37] Art. 6(1) Reg 473/2011.
[38] Art. 4(1) Reg 473/2011.
[39] Arts. 5(2)(a), 9 Reg 473/2013.
[40] Arts. 4, 5 Reg 1466/97; Art. 4(1) Reg 473/2013.
[41] Art. 4 Directive 2011/85/EU.
[42] Arts. 4, 6(2) Directive 2011/85/EU; Art. 5 Reg 473/2013.
[43] Art. 15(2) Reg 479/2009.
[44] Arts. 5, 6(2) Directive 2011/85/EU; 5 Reg 473/2013.
[45] Wyplosz, 'Centralization-Decentralization', 17 (emphasis added).
[46] See sources cited in Methods and Introduction, at nn 68–69 and the analysis in Chapter 8.

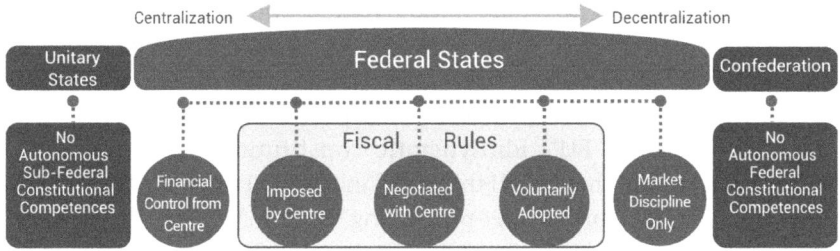

Figure 5.1 Institutional constraints on sub-federal budgetary policy[49]

rules and legal governance.[47] A rich literature has developed to determine the optimum selection of institutional characteristics in a given constitutional and economic federal system.[48]

Occupying one end of the federalism spectrum, highly centralized federations such as Germany impose a high degree of fiscal control over their constituent states through centralized decision-making, financial transfers and fiscal rules.[50] Occupying the other end of the spectrum lie highly decentralized 'classical' or 'ideal-type' federations such as the United States,[51] Switzerland[52] and Canada,[53] which exercise no federal oversight of state-level finances, and in which state treasuries are not under the umbrella of a 'fiscal union' of the sort proposed in 2012 by the Commission.[54] Beyond either extreme of this spectrum lie non-federal systems of government: A 'confederation' is one in which the central authority has no sovereignty independent of the cumulative choices of

---

[47] This book relies on the taxonomy proposed by Ter-Minassian and Craig, 'Subnational Borrowing', and often used by the IMF to assess borrowing constraints. See IMF, *Macro Policy Lessons for a Sound Design of Fiscal Decentralization* (IMF Fiscal Affairs Department, 2009), 40; Singh and Plekhanov, 'Subnational Government Borrowing'; Eyraud and Gomez Sirera, 'Constraints', 93–97.

[48] See Chapter 8.

[49] See, further, the typology in Eyraud and Gomez Sirera, 'Constraints', 94. Here, 'Financial Control from Centre' refers to legal instruments which allow the federal government to intercede in certain spending or revenue competences of sub-federal governments. This may include systems of co-government which prevent sub-federal governments from acting unilaterally; a high degree of federal control over sub-federal revenues; or policy conditions tied to federal grants, transfers or loans that impact policies outside federal competence.

[50] Bishop et al., *Market Discipline*, 2.

[51] See Chapter 8, Section 8.2.3.

[52] See Chapter 8, Section 8.2.2.

[53] See Chapter 8, Section 8.2.4.

[54] Commission Blueprint; Van Rompuy, *Towards a Genuine EMU*.

its individual members; and a unitary state is one in which the central government is supreme: tax and revenue powers may be devolved by statute, but the central government may abrogate the acts of devolved governments or unilaterally curtail their powers.[55]

Setting aside the EU's idiosyncratic constitutionalism debate, the 'Maastricht model' that is still inscribed in the EU Treaties falls squarely upon the 'classical' or 'market-preserving' end of the federal spectrum. The EU's 'federal' budget may be relatively small in comparison to most federations (which does not necessarily reflect the outsized scope of its legal competences)[56] but the model generally adheres to the 'classical' or 'ideal-type' federalism: The Union and the Member States each have their own autonomous expenditure and revenue competences, and both are (in principle) supreme within their spheres.

The reforms identified in this chapter constitute a fundamental departure from that model. The layout outlined in this chapter is that of a highly centralized *proto*-fiscal union that relies on centrally imposed fiscal rules and the co-option of national fiscal competences to ensure fiscal discipline.

In that regard, some terminological idiosyncrasies of EU politics must be remarked at the outset. In the fiscal federalism literature, the difference between a federal state and a unitary one is the existence of two independent, self-governing and 'co-equally supreme' governments, each exercising autonomous federal and sub-federal fiscal capacities side by side.[57] Certain tax and spending competences are exercised independently by the federal government, certain others are exercised independently by the states, and neither can exert control over or curtail the competences of the other. In the fiscal federalism literature, a fiscal 'union' may refer to the independent tax and expenditure capacities of the *federal government*, but it does *not* necessarily imply the mutualization of sub-federal tax and spending competences.

In EU politics, however, 'federal', 'federalism' and 'fiscal union' are often used to denote the centralization of Member State competences in

---

[55] Wheare, *Federal Government*, 31–32.

[56] Federal expenditures typically range from between 10% and 30% of GDP in comparative federations, compared to around 1% of EU GDP. However, in Canada, the United States, Switzerland and Germany, both federal and state governments maintain a large civil service, while the EU operates by 'co-opting' Member State executives, so the federal spending comparison is not a straightforward proxy for centralization. Iain Begg, 'Fiscal Federalism, Subsidiarity and the EU Budget Review' (2009) SIEPS Report No 1, 28.

[57] Kenneth Wheare, *Federal Government* (Oxford University Press, 1987), 10–15. See further Wallace Oates, *Fiscal Federalism* (Harcourt Brace Jovanovich, 1972).

the Union.[58] 'Fiscal union', as it is used by EU institutions in the Commission Blueprint and the *Five Presidents' Report*, does not refer (as the literature on federalism does), to the existence of independent *federal* tax and spending competences (which model the EU already has). It refers to the vertical centralization of *Member State* tax and spending competences in the Union – or, as the Commission so puts it, 'a means to imposing budgetary and economic decisions on its members'.[59] Indeed, if the reforms charted in this chapter are evidence of 'federalisation', the model enunciated here is closer to a unitary state than any model of federalism considered in Chapter 8 of this book. As Fabbrini observes:

Indeed, in the United States, *because of the federal system of government,* it would arguably be impossible for the federal government to mandate to the states the incorporation of specific budgetary rules in the state constitutions and to require state legislatures and governors to submit draft budgets for prior approval in Washington DC.[60]

5.3   Demands on the European Legal Order and Operational Hypotheses

The demands placed on the European legal order by these reforms are significant. The emergent federal architecture supplants a legal pillar of decentralized fiscal sovereignty (an entrenched 'no bailout' law) for a legal feature of unitary states – financial assistance and centralized governance of sub-federal economic competences. The constitutional boundaries underlying this architecture, however, have not changed. Nor have the Treaty provisions which protect them. As stated by the *Bundesbank*, 'the no bail-out principle, member states' national responsibility for their own fiscal policy as well as investors' individual responsibility for their investment decisions remain constitutional components of monetary union'.[61]

---

[58] Charles Kennedy, 'European 'Federalism' Isn't What You've Been Told It Is' *The Guardian* (2 July 2014) www.theguardian.com/commentisfree/2014/jul/02/european-federalism-eu-debate-superstate accessed 30 October 2016. See, for example, The Spinelli Group, 'Manifesto' (*Spinelli Group*, 2016) www.spinelligroup.eu accessed 12 December 2016, 3–4.
[59] Commission Blueprint, 31.
[60] Fabbrini, 'Paradox', 34.
[61] Deutsche Bundesbank, 'Monthly Report: August 2011', 63.

The first hypothesis of this book is that hard budget constraints and market discipline are indispensable requirements for the principles of price stability and fiscal discipline (Article 119(3) TFEU) in an EMU bound by the fiscal sovereignty of its Member States. If that is so, systems of fiscal federalism which substitute hard budget constraints for financial transfers and centralized legal governance must not be compatible with the guiding principles of price stability and fiscal discipline, and must not be compatible with the boundaries of the legal architecture in Chapter 1 'Economic Policy' of Title VIII, Part III TFEU.

The second hypothesis of this book is that any model of European fiscal federalism must preserve the fiscal sovereignty of the twenty-seven (formerly twenty-eight) constitutional democracies which form the basis of its legal order. If that is correct, legal architectures of fiscal federalism which depend on centralized legal governance and financial transfers may not be compatible with the constitutional boundaries of the EU legal order as a whole, and therefore illusory or unenforceable as stable structures of federalism. Yet in order to stabilize the new model and safeguard the price stability monetary union, EU economic governance has been broadened to virtually all areas of fiscal, economic and social policy, and imbued with strictures of increasingly precise and binding force. EU-legislated norms increasingly prescribe – in great detail and on pain of punitive sanctions or direct legal enforcement – substantive policy choices which are ordinarily the legislative competences of Europe's constitutional democracies. If the model is to 'work', it is now dependent upon the credibility and enforceability of these constituent legal mechanisms.

Applying these observations to the EU's emerging fiscal architecture, this chapter poses three operational hypotheses which will structure the remaining chapters of Part II:

[Chapter 6] First, instruments of financial assistance and centralized legal governance, being such a departure from the criteria of hard budget constraints and market discipline inscribed in the Treaty at Maastricht, must not conform to the legal architecture in Articles 121–126 TFEU of Chapter 1 'Economic Policy' of Title VIII, Part III TFEU for the guiding principles of price stability and fiscal discipline as a matter of EU law.

[Chapter 7] Second, financial assistance and centralized legal governance, being such a departure from the principle of fiscal sovereignty, may not conform to the constitutional boundaries underlying the EU legal order as a whole. If that is so, the good functioning of the new model may now be dependent on the operation of legal machineries which are beyond the limits of the EU legal order, and vulnerable to repudiation under Member State 'constitutional identity' jurisprudence. In pursuit of that hypothesis, Chapter 7 conducts a piece-by-piece deconstruction of the economic governance framework to identify instruments which, explicitly or implicitly, trespass on constitutional boundaries of fiscal sovereignty set out in the rulings of national constitutional courts.

[Chapter 8] Third, according to the Treaty drafters (and this book), hard budget constraints and market discipline are indispensable institutional criteria for fiscal discipline in a decentralized federation bound by the fiscal sovereignty of its Member States. If that is so, financial assistance and centralized legal governance must not conform to the criteria for price stability and fiscal discipline as a matter of theoretical and empirical fiscal federalism. To test this hypothesis, Chapter 8 evaluates EMU against the fiscal federalism literature and existing comparative models to evaluate which systems will 'work' in the EU for the achievement of these principles.

By proceeding through these three analyses, Part II will attempt to identify which architectures of fiscal federalism are compatible with the constitutional boundaries of the EU legal order and, within those remaining, what criteria EU fiscal federalism must meet in order to remain permanent and stable as a matter of law and economics.

6 The Constitutional Boundaries of Economic and Monetary Union under EU Law

The first operational hypothesis to be examined in Part II is that financial assistance and centralized legal governance, being such a departure from hard budget constraints and market discipline, must not conform to the legal architecture inscribed in Articles 121–126 TFEU for the purpose of fiscal discipline as a matter of EU law.

In *Pringle* v. *Ireland* the ECJ ruled that conditional financial assistance is both contemplated by the existing Treaties and capable of fulfilling the teleology of the 'logic of the markets' in ensuring fiscal discipline.[1] In that case, the Court interpreted Articles 122–125 TFEU against the teleology of price stability and fiscal discipline, and sanctioned the economic abrogation of the 'no bailout' rule through the establishment of the ESM and Article 136(3) TFEU – instead entrusting budgetary discipline to centralized legal governance under Articles 121 and 126 TFEU. The Court interpreted Article 125 TFEU as follows:

> It is apparent from the preparatory work relating to the Treaty of Maastricht that the [. . .] prohibition laid down in art.125 TFEU ensures that the Member States *remain subject to the logic of the market* when they enter into debt, since that *ought to prompt them to maintain budgetary discipline.* [. . .] Given that that is the objective pursued by art.125 TFEU, it must be held that that provision *prohibits the Union and the Member States from granting financial assistance as a result of which the incentive of the recipient Member State to conduct a sound budgetary policy is diminished.*[2]

The Court then ruled that financial assistance will be compatible with Article 125 where three conditions are met: (1) Member States must remain responsible for their commitments to their creditors and

---

[1] *Pringle* v. *Ireland* [135]–[145].
[2] *Pringle* v. *Ireland* [136]–[137] (emphasis added).

subject to the 'logic of the markets' when they enter into debt;[3] (2) financial assistance must be subject to strict conditionality to preserve the incentive for fiscal discipline;[4] and (3) financial assistance must be *ultima ratio* indispensable for the financial stability of the euro area as a whole.[5]

This *ratio decidendi* is the gateway through which EU fiscal federalism passed from a decentralized 'ideal-type', founded on hard budget constraints, to a 'centralized' model of financial assistance and legal governance. This is so because, of the three conditions named by the Court, only strict conditionality is of disciplinary force, and, as will be seen, this is exclusively defined and enforced through the EU's fiscal governance procedures under Article 121 and 126 TFEU. According to the Court in *Pringle* v. *Ireland*, ESM conditionality only ensures that 'the recipient Member States *comply with measures adopted by the Union* [...] to ensure that the Member States pursue a sound budgetary policy'.[6] This abrogates a legal instrument of decentralized federalism (an entrenched 'no bailout' law) and sinks a legal pillar of fiscal union (centralized fiscal governance) in its place.

This surgery was effected according to a single overarching *ratio decidendi*: financial assistance is compliant with the Treaty because EU economic governance is sufficient to preserve the incentive for fiscal discipline (and so safeguard price stability).[7] Were it not so, the conditions set out by the ECJ in *Pringle* v. *Ireland* would not be met, and financial assistance would be unlawful under the EU Treaties.[8]

This chapter examines and applies that *ratio decidendi* as a matter *de jure*. It concludes, unavoidably, that conditional financial assistance under Article 136(3) TFEU and the ESM is not reconcilable with the legal architecture in the Treaties. This emerges from an analysis of the allocation of competences (within which it does not sit) and an analysis of the substantive provisions of Articles 121–126 TFEU (to which it does not adhere). When the sovereign debt crisis arrived, there was no legal competence and no institutions allowing the Member States or the

---

[3] *Pringle* v. *Ireland* [137]–[139].
[4] *Pringle* v. *Ireland* [135]–[137], [143].
[5] *Pringle* v. *Ireland*, [136], [142]–[145].
[6] *Pringle* v. *Ireland* [143] (emphasis added).
[7] *Pringle* v. *Ireland* [135]–[137]. Sebastian Grund and Mikael Stenström, 'A Sovereign Debt Restructuring Framework for the Euro Area' (2019) 42 Fordham Int'l LJ 795, 818: 'The maxim of primary EU Law is thus to preserve the incentives for member states to pursue sound budgetary policies.'
[8] *Pringle* v. *Ireland* [136]–[137].

Union to share the burdens of the crisis, and Articles 122–125 TFEU expressly precluded the possibility of bringing one into existence.[9] By restoring an interpretation of the 'no bailout' rule that was rejected under Articles 104–104a of the Commission's draft Treaty at Maastricht, the ECJ would seem to have reached back through history, brushed aside the stated will of the Treaty drafters, plucked the (rejected) Commission draft Treaty from the floor of Maastricht, and enacted it into primary law.

Yet, proceeding on the basis that *Pringle* v. *Ireland* is an authoritative interpretation of Article 125 TFEU from the internal perspective of EU law, it remains that the legal instruments of conditional financial assistance can only be lawful in so far as the conditions set out by the ECJ in *Pringle* v. *Ireland* are indeed met.[10] But they are not: (1) The instruments in Articles 14 and 16–18 TESM declare on their face that Member States shall *not* be subject to the 'logic of the markets' when they enter into debt,[11] and Articles 8(4) and 25(2)–(3) TESM *do* create a guarantee that discharges the liability of the debtor;[12] (2) financial assistance under Articles 14 and 18 TESM is *not* subject to strict conditionality;[13] and (3) the instruments under Articles 14 and 18 TESM are issued exclusively where it is *not* 'indispensable for the stability of the euro area as a whole'.[14] Taking *Pringle* v. *Ireland* as a correct interpretation of Article 125 TFEU, it is clear that the legal architecture now established under Article 136(3) TFEU is incompatible with the Treaties.

Notwithstanding that the ECJ has already made its ruling in *Pringle* v. *Ireland*, this analysis remains vital because, as shown in Chapter 1, the text of the Treaty is but the litmus paper for determining whether EU law coheres with deeper constitutional boundaries underlying the EU legal order itself. It is uncontroversial that both fiscal rules and market discipline are used in federations for fiscal discipline. However, suitability for budgetary discipline cannot be assumed – rarely will these antipodal mechanisms work in the same way in

---

[9] Chiti and Pedro, 'Constitutional Implications', 698; Stark, 'Lessons', 543; Peroni, 'Crisis of the Euro', 189.

[10] *Pringle* v. *Ireland* [136]–[137]: The activation of financial assistance 'is not compatible with art.125 TFEU *unless*' those conditions are met (emphasis added). See similarly *Gauweiler III (Germany)* [192] 'Against this backdrop, one must assume that the Court of Justice considers the conditions it specified [...] to be legally binding.'

[11] See Section 6.3.2, nn 246–249.

[12] See Section 6.3.2.

[13] See Section 6.3.3 nn 267–275.

[14] See below, Section 6.3.4.

different contexts.[15] Furthermore, they yield federal systems of starkly opposite character, requiring entirely different constitutional foundations. Centralized debt constraints imply an abdication of fiscal sovereignty and a mutualization of risk; bailout prohibitions entrench fiscal sovereignty and market discipline. Discomfiture with the allocation of competences in Articles 2(3), 3(1)(c) and 5(1) TFEU, or the architecture in Articles 121–126 TFEU, therefore provides the first testable indication that an amendment to the federal structure may be incompatible with deeper constitutional fault lines underlying the European legal order as a whole.[16] This chapter proceeds as follows.

Section 6.1 briefly outlines the legal architecture of conditional financial assistance. Since the creation of the EFSM and EFSF, there have been four conditional finance instruments: One under EU law (the EFSM), one under private law (the EFSF), one under public international law (the ESM), and one by the ECB (the OMT). All of these instruments have now been superseded or subsumed within the legal framework of Article 136(3) TFEU and the TESM. Section 6.1 summarizes the salient features of these instruments and the analytical framework developed by the ECJ for their legality.

Section 6.2 concludes that the new legal architecture of conditional financial assistance is fundamentally incompatible with the allocation of competences under the Treaties. There is but one avenue for financial assistance in the 'Economic Policy' Chapter of the TFEU – Article 122(2) – and this is preclusive of any other mechanisms as a matter of law, whether Member State or EU competence. The Treaty drafters were acutely aware that they precluded all other avenues for financial assistance under the Treaty, and made this explicit throughout the preparatory work.[17] Applying the analytical framework of the ECJ, the EFSM, EFSF, ESM and OMT simply cannot be reconciled within the division of competences for economic and monetary policy in Articles 2(3), 3(1)(c) and 5(1) TFEU.

Section 6.3 concludes that conditional financial assistance is incompatible with Articles 122–125 TFEU and comprehensively in breach of

---

[15] Massimo Bordignon, 'Fiscal Decentralization: How to Harden the Budget Constraint' in Servaas Deroose et al. (eds), *Fiscal Policy Surveillance in Europe* (Palgrave Macmillan, 2006), 109; Richard Bird and François Vaillancourt, *Fiscal Decentralization in Developing Countries* (Cambridge University Press, 1998), 34: 'one cannot take an institution from a specific setting, plant it in the alien soil of another environment, and expect to obtain the same results'.

[16] *Lisbon (Germany)*, [210]; *Weiss Decision (Germany)* [158].

[17] See Chapter 2, Section 2.3.1.

the three conditions set down in *Pringle* v. *Ireland* for its legality. The application of *Pringle* v. *Ireland* to the Treaty framework repeatedly 'fails on its own terms'.[18]

Section 6.4 concludes by describing how national constitutional courts have duly crimped these mechanisms to the shape of Member State constitutional identities, and marks the implication for EU fiscal federalism: there simply isn't a constitutional basis for a credible financial assistance backstop in the EU.

6.1   The Legal Architecture of Conditional Financial Assistance

6.1.1   *The Bilateral Greek Loan Facility*

Conditional financial assistance emerged with the announcement of a €110bn package of bilateral loans to Greece on 1 May 2010,[19] with EMU Member States providing €80bn and the IMF providing €30bn.[20] Policy conditionality was set out in an Intercreditor Agreement, incorporated into a Council Decision, and integrated into the normal SGP procedure.[21] The first disbursement of €20bn took place at a floating rate of three-month EURIBOR + 300bps for the first three years, and three-month EURIBOR + 400bps thereafter.[22]

6.1.2   *The European Financial Stabilisation Mechanism*

On 11 May 2010, the Council adopted Regulation 407/2010 establishing the EFSM under Article 122(2) TFEU, a bailout mechanism with the ability to raise €60bn against the EU budget for a loan volume of €40bn.[23] EFSM funding of €22.5bn was first issued to Ireland in December 2010 at cost + 292.5bps with a maximum maturity of 7.5 years.[24] In May 2011, €26bn was issued to Portugal at cost + 215bps with

---

[18]   Gunnar Beck, 'The Court of Justice, Legal Reasoning, and the *Pringle* Case – Law as the Continuation of Politics by Other Means' (2014) 39 EL Rev 234, 244. See also Adams et al., 'European Budgetary Constraints', 9.

[19]   Eurogroup, 'Statement by the Eurogroup' (2 May 2010).

[20]   European Commission, 'The Economic Adjustment Programme for Greece' (2010) European Economy Occasional Papers No 61, 8, 26.

[21]   See Sch 1–2 of the Euro Area Loan Facility Act 2010, No 7 of 2010 (Ireland); Council Decision 2010/320/EU.

[22]   European Commission, 'Adjustment Programme for Greece', 1, 26.

[23]   Reg 407/2010.

[24]   Arts. 1(5)–(6), Council Implementing Decision 2011/77/EU of 7 December 2010 on granting Union financial assistance to Ireland [2011] OJ L 30/34.

a maximum average maturity of 7.5 years.[25] These costs were successively watered-down over the course of nearly two-dozen amendments, such that by October 2011 the price of EFSM loans was reduced to cost, and average maximum maturities were extended – first to 12.5 years (in October 2011),[26] and then to 19.5 years (in June 2013).[27]

6.1.3   The European Financial Stability Facility

The EFSF was founded alongside the EFSM, outside of EU law, in the form of a Luxembourg *société anonym*.[28] Endowed with an effective loan volume of €440bn, the EFSF was financed by debt instruments against an 'irrevocable and unconditional guarantee' issued by EMU Member States according to an adjusted ECB capital key.[29] The EFSF issued €17.55bn as part of the €85bn package for Ireland in November 2010,[30] €26bn as part of a €78bn package for Portugal in May 2011[31] and was the method of disbursement for the €110bn Greek bailout in July 2011.[32]

The cost of EFSF assistance (cost + 200bps for three years and 300bps thereafter, with a maximum maturity of 7.5 years)[33] was considerably less punitive from the outset and also subsequently watered down. In July 2011, the cost was reduced to 3.5% (close to cost) and maximum maturities were extended to 30 years with a grace period of 10 years.[34]

---

[25] Art. 1 Council Implementing Decision 2011/334/EU of 30 May 2011 on granting Union financial assistance to Portugal [2011] OJ L 159/88.

[26] Council Implementing Decision 2011/682/EU of 11 October 2011 amending Implementing Decision 2011/77/EU [2011] OJ L 269/31; Council Implementing Decision 2011/683/EU of 11 October 2011 amending Implementing Decision 2011/344/EU [2011] OJ L 269/32.

[27] Council Implementing Decision 2013/313/EU of 21 June 2013 amending Implementing Decision 2011/77/EU [2013] OJ L 173/40; Council Implementing Decision 2013/323/EU of 21 June 2013 amending Implementing Decision 2011/344/EU [2013] OJ L 175/47.

[28] Its constitutive legal instruments consist of an executive agreement, the private SPV under the EFSF Articles of Association, and the EFSF Framework Agreement, cited in Chapter 5, n 3.

[29] See Arts. 2(3)–(6), 6 of the EFSF Framework Agreement; EFSF Articles of Association paras 3–4.

[30] 'Master Financial Assistance Facility Agreement' 22 December 2010) www.efsf.europa .eu/attachments/Master%20FFA%20Ireland.pdf accessed 25 February 2015.

[31] Council Implementing Decision 2011/344/EU.

[32] ECOFIN, 'Financial Assistance to Greece' (*ECOFIN*, 20 October 2014) ec.europa.eu/econ omy_finance/assistance_eu_ms/greek_loan_facility/index_en.htm accessed 2 January 2015.

[33] Art. 2(8)–(9) EFSF Framework Agreement.

[34] European Council, *Statement by the Heads of State or Government of the Euro Area and EU Institutions* (Brussels, 21 July 2011).

By August 2014 the final weighted average maturity was 20.8 years for Ireland and Portugal, and 32.38 years for Greece.[35]

6.1.4   Article 136(3) TFEU

The European bailouts posed acute legal problems under the Treaties. First, as the German Chancellor insisted two months before the first bailout: 'We have a treaty under which there is no possibility of paying bailouts to states in difficulty.'[36] Second, there was no legal basis for EU financial assistance in the Treaties outside Article 122(2) TFEU, which only applies when a Member State is threatened by severe difficulties 'caused by *natural disasters* or exceptional circumstances *beyond its control*'.[37] Yet it was widely doubted that this criteria was met.[38] For example, the EFSM was last used in July 2015 to provide a €7.16bn bridge loan to Greece, which only became necessary in the first place because Greece was ineligible to access the €7.2bn remaining in its bailout programme because it had repudiated its terms in 2014 and continued to accumulate a gross debt of nearly 180% of GDP.[39]

The lack of an adequate legal basis was tacitly acknowledged by the European Council in December 2010,[40] and confirmed by the ECJ in *Pringle,* which concluded: 'Article 122(2) TFEU does not constitute an appropriate legal basis for any financial assistance from the Union to Member States who are experiencing, or are threatened by, severe financing problems.'[41]

Faced with such exposure, certain quarters on the European Council became anxious 'to have a clear Treaty basis for action in order to

---

[35] EFSF, 'Lending Operations' (*EFSF,* 14 August 2015) www.efsf.europa.eu/about/oper ations/index.htm accessed 25 February 2015.

[36] Andreas Illmer, 'Angela Merkel Rules Out German Bailout for Greece' *Deutsche Welle* (Berlin 1 March 2010) www.dw.com/en/angela-merkel-rules-out-german-bailout-for-greece/a-5299788 accessed 1 September 2013.

[37] Art. 122(2) TFEU.

[38] Palmstorfer, 'To Bail Out', 780; Jonathan Tomkin, 'Contradiction, Circumvention and Conceptual Gymnastics: The Impact of the Adoption of the ESM Treaty on the State of European Democracy' (2013) 14 German LJ 169, 171; Sideek M Seyad, 'A Legal Analysis of the European Financial Stabilisation Mechanism' (2011) 26 JIBLR 421, 423.

[39] Council of the EU, 'EFSM: Council Approves €7bn Bridge Loan to Greece' (*Council of the EU,* 17 July 2015) www.consilium.europa.eu/en/press/press-releases/2015/07/17-efsm-bridge-loan-greece/ accessed 18 July 2015.

[40] Council Decision 2011/199/EU of 25 March 2011 amending Article 136 of the TFEU with regard to a stability mechanism for Member States whose currency is the euro [2011] OJ L 91/1, r 4; European Council, Conclusions of 16–17 December 2010 (2010) EUCO 30/1/10 r 1.

[41] *Pringle* v. *Ireland* [116].

forestall any adverse judgment of the German Constitutional Court'.[42] Yet, as the *Economist* reported, the European Council also could not 'risk crossing the Irish constitutional court's threshold, set in the 1987 Crotty judgment, for submitting treaty changes to a referendum'.[43] The a-legal expansion of conditional financial assistance was already being impinged by the constitutional boundaries discussed in Part I of this book.

For this reason, in December 2010 – less than a year since the Lisbon Treaty had entered into force – the European Council agreed 'a limited treaty change required to that effect, not modifying article 125 TFEU ("no bail-out" clause)'.[44] To that end, the European Council adopted Decision 2011/199/EU inserting a new Article 136(3) into the TFEU.[45] Article 136(3) TFEU states:

> The Member States whose currency is the euro may establish a stability mechanism to be activated if indispensable to safeguard the stability of the euro area as a whole. The granting of any required financial assistance under the mechanism will be made subject to strict conditionality.

Decision 2011/199/EU was adopted under the 'simplified procedure' of Article 48(6) TEU, which allows the European Council to amend the provisions of Part III of the TFEU by unanimity, subject to two conditions: (1) the procedure may only be used to amend the provisions of Part III of the TFEU; and (2) the procedure may not be used to increase the competences conferred on the Union.

The legality of Decision 2011/199/EU therefore rests on two claims. The first claim is that establishing the ESM under Article 136(3) does not extend or intrude on the Union competences for economic 'coordination' (Articles 2(3) and 5(1) TFEU), giving financial assistance (Article 122(2) TFEU) or monetary policy (Articles 3(1)(c) and 127 TFEU). This is because these are competences of the Union under Articles 2(3), 3(1)(c) and 5(1) TFEU – provisions in Part I of the TFEU which Article 48(6) TEU cannot amend. For this reason, the Commission,[46] the European

---

[42] House of Lords European Union Committee, *Amending Article 136 TFEU* (10th Report of Session 2010–2011), 6.
[43] Charlemagne, 'A Grim Take of Judges and Politicians' *The Economist* (4 November 2010) www.economist.com/node/17414379 accessed 25 February 2015.
[44] European Council Conclusions of 28–29 October 2010, para 2.
[45] Council Decision 2011/199/EU.
[46] European Commission, 'Opinion on the draft European Council Decision Amending Article 136 TFEU with regard to a stability mechanism for Member States whose currency is the euro' COM(2011) 70 final.

Parliament,[47] and the ECB[48] all asserted that Article 136(3) TFEU does nothing to permit or involve any EU or Member State institution in activities within the competence of another.

The second claim is that Article 136(3) TFEU does not create a derogation from Article 125 TFEU, but merely has 'declaratory value' of an extant (and unwritten) *lex specialis* to the 'no bailout' rule.[49] This is so because Article 125 TFEU was not amended – the 'no bailout' rule is still binding just as it was drafted at Maastricht.[50] Moreover, as the ESM came into effect *before* Article 136(3) TFEU, the legal premise of the ESM is that the amendment does not much matter – the bailout mechanism was anyways permitted under the 'no bailout' rule.[51]

These claims are examined below, but for present purposes it is sufficient to note that the legal justification for the Treaty amendment is that the Treaty amendment is entirely redundant.

6.1.5   The European Stability Mechanism

It is on this basis that the Treaty Establishing the European Stability Mechanism (TESM) entered into force on 27 September 2012, nearly eight months before Decision 2011/199/EU.[52] The ESM is an intergovernmental organization endowed with a total subscribed capital of €705bn and a total lending capacity of €500bn.[53] It is governed principally by a Board of Governors (BoG) consisting of the EMU Finance Ministers.[54] There are three aspects of the ESM relevant to the constitutional boundaries in this book: Its funding model, the role of EU institutions and its financial instruments.

---

[47] European Parliament resolution of 23 March 2011 on the draft European Council Decision amending Art. 136 TFEU with regard to a stability mechanism for Member States whose currency is the euro (C7-0014/2011–2010/0821 (NLE)).

[48] ECB, Opinion of the European Central Bank of 17 March 2011 on a draft European Council Decision amending Art. 136 TFEU with regard to a stability mechanism for Member States whose currency is the euro (CON/2011/24), para 5.

[49] Merino, 'Financial Assistance', 1629.

[50] Christian Calleiss, 'From Fiscal Compact to Fiscal Union? New Rules for the Eurozone' (2012) 14 CYELS 101, 112.

[51] *Pringle* v. *Ireland* [183]–[185].

[52] Decision 2011/199/EU came into effect 1 May 2013.

[53] Annex II TESM.

[54] Decisions capable of increasing financial liability are taken by unanimity on the BoG, the exception being an 'emergency' support procedure taken by a super-QMV of 85% (intended to give Germany a blocking minority): Arts. 4–5 TESM.

First, the ESM is endowed with its own authorized capital stock in the amount of €705bn.[55] Contributions are assessed according to a modified ECB subscription key, and Article 8(4) commits its signatories 'irrevocably and unconditionally' to provide their contribution to the authorized stock and to meet all capital calls on a timely basis.[56] Capital calls are governed by Article 9 TESM, and may be made to cover losses (Article 9(2)) or avoid default on payment obligations (Article 9(3)).[57] Importantly, Article 8(5) TESM states that the liability of each ESM member 'shall be limited, in all circumstances, to its portion of the authorised capital stock' and that 'No ESM Member shall be liable, by reason of its ownership, for obligations of the ESM.'[58] However, Article 25(2) TESM states that if one or more members fail to meet a capital call, a revised call will be made for which the remaining members will be jointly and automatically liable for the unpaid portion under Article 8(4) TESM.[59] Member States are therefore jointly and severally liable for ESM capital up to the amount of their authorized capital stock. This is discussed in Section 6.3.2, but it suffices to note that it is perfectly and legally possible that a single stalwart contributor may become automatically liable for all of its recalcitrant fellows' obligations to the ESM.

The second matter of concern is the significant entwinement between the TESM and EU law. The Commission is tasked with assessing requests for ESM stability support (in hand with the ECB),[60] negotiating ESM economic conditionality (in hand with the ECB),[61] ensuring that the ESM macroeconomic programme is enacted into EU law by the Council,[62] and overseeing compliance with the ESM programme under the EU's economic governance procedures.[63] Once agreed, the macroeconomic adjustment programme is simultaneously approved by the Eurogroup and inscribed in a *binding* Council Decision,[64] and approved by the BoG of the ESM (which are the same individuals), and signed by the Commission on their behalf.[65] Importantly, under Regulation 473/2013:

---

[55] Art. 8(1) TESM.
[56] Arts. 8(4), 11 TESM.
[57] Arts. 9(2)-(3) TESM.
[58] Art. 8(5), 11(1) TESM.
[59] Arts. 25(2), 8(4) TESM.
[60] Art. 6 Reg 472/2013; Arts. 4(4), 13(1) TESM.
[61] Art. 7(1) Reg 472/2013; Art. 13(3) TESM.
[62] Art. 7(1)-(2) Reg 472/2013.
[63] Art. 7 Reg 472/2013; Art. 13(3) TESM.
[64] Art. 7(2) Reg 472/2013.
[65] Art. 13(3)-(5) TESM.

The Commission shall ensure that the [MoU] signed by the Commission on behalf of the ESM or the EFSF is fully consistent with the macroeconomic adjustment programme approved by the Council.[66]

The third matter of concern is the terms of the ESM's financial instruments. The TESM contemplates five support facilities, as follows:

Loans may be provided where a Member State has lost market access because lenders will only provide financing 'at excessive prices that would adversely impact the sustainability of public finances'.[67]

Precautionary Financial Assistance[68] may be granted in the form of a precautionary credit line (PCCL) for countries where 'the economic and financial situation is still fundamentally sound' under a list of specific criteria,[69] or an enhanced conditions credit line (ECCL) if they do not meet the PCCL criteria but the general financial situation nonetheless 'remains sound'.[70]

Bank Recapitalisation Assistance is to be granted if a crisis situation in the financial sector would 'pose a serious risk to the Euro Area as a whole or the ESM Member'.[71]

The Primary Market Support Facility (PMSF) contemplates primary bond market interventions to allow Member States 'to maintain or restore their market access' if there are risks to financial stability on the basis of an ECB analysis.[72]

The Secondary Market Support Facility (SMSF) allows for secondary bond purchases with the same objective where the recipient's economic and financial situation is still essentially 'sound'.[73]

As the ESM does not derive its legal basis from the Treaties, the premise is that all of these instruments are within the competence of the Member States and their use is compliant with the 'no bailout' rule.

---

[66] Art. 7(2) Reg 472/2013. See also Art. 13(3) TESM.

[67] Art. 16 TESM; Art. 1, ESM Guideline on Loans (ESM, 2014).

[68] Art. 14 TESM.

[69] Art. 2(4) *ESM Guideline on Precautionary Financial Assistance* (ESM, 2012).

[70] Art. 2(4) ESM.

[71] Art. 15 TESM; Art. 2(1), ESM Guideline on Financial Assistance for the Direct Recapitalisation of Institutions (ESM, 8 December 2014).

[72] Arts. 17(1) TESM. Art. 1, *ESM Guideline on the Primary Market Support Facility* (ESM, 2012).

[73] Art. 18 TESM, Arts. 1–2, *ESM Guideline on the Secondary Market Support Facility* (ESM, 2014).

6.1.6   Unconventional Monetary Policy Instruments

Monetary instruments and institutions are, in principle, outside the strict scope of this book because they are not institutions of fiscal federalism unless the central bank takes on a role as initial provider of capital or some other characteristic of fiscal federalism. ECB monetary policy instruments can therefore remain outside the scope of this book in so far as they do not breach the prohibition on monetary financing in Article 123 TFEU – a conclusion no court has yet reached.[74] However, as will be shown, the ECB's OMT and PSPP instruments are part of the same 'analytical framework' developed by the ECJ to delineate the boundaries of economic and monetary policy, and the validity of the ESM must therefore be established against the analytical framework of these instruments.[75]

The OMT was announced in August 2012 and has never been implemented (notwithstanding its decisive impact on bond markets).[76] The OMT programme consisted of *ex ante* unlimited secondary market purchases of Member State bonds experiencing high default risk premia, subject to compliance with ESM conditionality.[77] In *Gauweiler* v. *Bundestag*, the ECJ upheld the legality of this instrument against an alleged breach of Articles 123 and 127 TFEU on the basis that secondary bond market interventions for the stated purpose of reducing unsustainable risk premia fell within the ECB's competence for monetary policy.[78]

As will be shown, however, the ESM and OMT are *prima facie* possessed of the same instrument (secondary market bond purchases), pursuant to the same immediate objective (lowering interest rates through purchases on secondary markets), and are tied to the same economic conditionality (the OMT is predicated on ESM conditionality). The only substantive difference between them would seem to be their effects on

---

[74] For criticism: Groeteke and Mause, 'Debt Brakes'; Thomas Beukers, 'The New ECB and Its Relationship with the Eurozone Member States' (2013) 50 CMLR 1579; Sinn, *Euro Trap*, 5.

[75] Case C-492/17 *Weiss* EU:C:2018:815 (Opinion of AG Wathelet) [95], [97].

[76] ECB, 'Press Release: Technical features of Outright Monetary Transactions'(Frankfurt 6 September 2012). www.ecb.int/press/pr/date/2012/html/pr120906_1.en.html accessed 5 March 2015. See 'OMT Draghi Whatever It Takes' marker in Figure 3.19, Chapter 3, Section 3.3.2.

[77] The OMT was the latest in a long line of 'unconventional' monetary policy instruments. See Arie Krampf, 'From the Maastricht Treaty to Post-crisis EMU: The ECB and Germany as Drivers of Change' (2014) 22 Journal of Contemporary European Studies 303.

[78] *Gauweiler (CJEU)* [76].

price stability: The (economic policy) ESM affects inflation, while the (monetary policy) OMT is sterilized, and does not. The ESM and OMT are therefore mirror images of each other, tracing overlapping issues of competence, and this has direct relevance with regards to the issue of competence for financial assistance.

The final instrument, the PSPP, provides for the purchase of euro-denominated public-sector bonds on secondary markets.[79] The PSPP contains notable design differences which distinguish it from the OMT. First, the PSPP is one of four sub-programmes of the Expanded Asset Purchase Programme (APP), a larger quantitative easing programme which is activated and ceases based on the ECB's 2% inflation criteria – not risk premiums in a given Member State.[80] Second, PSPP purchases are made in all Member States in accordance with the ESCB's capital key. Unlike the OMT, they are not made 'selectively', targeting only those Member States whose interest rates are rising under market discipline.[81] Third, PSPP purchases cannot exceed 33% of bonds from a single issue, or 33% of the outstanding bonds of a single issuer, so investors cannot always count on selling their holding to the ESCB.[82] Fourth, PSPP bonds must be rated Credit Quality Step 3 or higher.[83] This is unlike the OMT, which boosted Member States with low credit but left stable countries out of it.

The one significant issue not shared with the OMT, however, is that the PSPP has resulted in the purchase of over €2 trillion in public-sector bonds since its enactment, with demonstrable effects on financing conditions.[84] On this basis, in *Weiss* v. *Bundestag* the BVerfG ruled the PSPP *ultra vires* due to the apparently disproportionate effects on economic policy *stricto sensu*.[85] The *Weiss* v. *Bundstag* litigation therefore comprises part of the same 'analytical framework' for identifying the constitutional boundaries of economic and monetary policy.

---

[79] Art. 3(1) Decision (EU) 2015/774 of the ECB of 4 March 2015 on a secondary markets public-sector asset purchase programme (ECB/2015/10) [2015] OJ L 121/20. Decision 2015/774 was severally amended and supplemented before being replaced by Decision (EU) 2020/188 of the ECB of 3 February 2020 on a secondary markets public-sector asset purchase programme (ECB/2020/9) [2010] OJ L 39/12.

[80] Recital (3) Decision 2015/774; *Weiss (CJEU)*, [34], [54], [57], [84]–[88], [133]–[134].

[81] Art. 6(2) Decision 2015/774; *Weiss (CJEU)*, [96], [120], [140]

[82] Art. 5(1)–(2) Decision 2015/774; *Weiss (CJEU)*, [89], [124]–[125], [141].

[83] Art. 3 Decision 2015/774; *Weiss (CJEU)* [142].

[84] *Weiss Decision (Germany)*, [169], [224], [227].

[85] *Weiss Decision (Germany)*, [123]–[133].

6.1.7   The Interpretations of the ECJ under Title VIII of Part III TFEU

The analytical framework for assessing competence for these instruments lies in a trilogy of rulings by the ECJ on the legality of the ESM, OMT and PSPP under Articles 2(3), 3(1)(c) 5(1) and 121–127 TFEU.

The leading case, *Pringle* v. *Ireland*, arose on a preliminary reference from the Supreme Court of Ireland pursuant to a constitutional challenge by Irish *Teachta Dála* (TD) Thomas Pringle.[86] It had two limbs.

First, on competence grounds, it was argued, *inter alia*, that Decision 2011/199/EU and the TESM unlawfully infringed on the EU's monetary and economic competences and therefore breached EU law and the Irish Constitution.[87] This is so because financial assistance and economic coordination are competences of the Union, on one side of the competence fence (Articles 122(2) and 121/126 TFEU), and so is monetary stability, on the other side (Article 3(1)(c) TFEU). If the ESM were to do either of these things, it would infringe the allocation of competences and violate the terms of Article 48(6) TEU by which Article 136 TFEU was amended. And yet, by definition, the ESM must fall on at least one side of that fence (and would appear to straddle both sides).

Second, on substantive grounds, it was argued that Decision 2011/199/EU amending Article 136(3) TFEU and the TESM entailed 'a direct and substantive breach' on the 'no bailout' principle.[88] Pringle argued:

> The TESM subverts and reverses the 'no bail-out' principle. It provides for a permanent 'bail-out' scheme that would allow for massive – and [...] unlimited – borrowing. [...] This is a most profound change from a 'no bail-out' EMU to a 'bail-out' EMU.[89]

The second major case, *Gauweiler* v. *Bundestag*, concerned a German challenge to the OMT initiated by 11,000 applicants alleging a breach of Articles 123 and 127 TFEU.[90] In June 2015 the ECJ applied an objectives-based test to rule that the OMT's objective of 'bringing about a fall in – or even the elimination of – excessive risk *premia*' fell within the ECB's competence for price stability because it was done with the objective of 'safeguarding an appropriate monetary policy transmission

---

[86] *Pringle* v. *Ireland (Ireland)*.
[87] Thomas Pringle, 'Written Observations in Case C-370/12 *Pringle* v. *Ireland*' (*Extompore*, 27 November 2012) www.extempore.ie/2012/10/17/thomas-pringles-written-submissions-to-the-court-of-justice/c-370–12-observations-of-t-pringle-as-filed-2/ accessed 3 May 2017, 8.
[88] Pringle, 'Written Observations', 28–34 [3.49].
[89] Pringle, 'Written Observations', 8.
[90] *Gauweiler Reference (Germany)*.

and the singleness of the monetary policy' – which in turn provides for price stability.[91] The case returned to the BVerfG in June 2016, where the German court ruled the OMT *did* exceed the competences of the ECB, but that the breach would not be 'manifest' so far as it complied with six conditions on its operation.[92]

In the third major case, *Weiss* v. *Bundestag*, the ECJ again applied its objectives-based test to uphold the PSPP against alleged breaches of Articles 123 and 127 TFEU, ruling that its objective was price stability (not monetary financing) and that it was suitable and appropriate to achieving 2% inflation.[93] The CJEU reasoned that the Treaty drafters did not intend to make an absolute separation between economic and monetary policy.[94]

Upon returning to the BVerfG in *Weiss Decision (Germany)*, the German court rejected the ECJ's objectives-based test on the basis that the ECJ 'abandoned the distinction between economic and monetary policy'[95] and 'manifestly exceeded the judicial mandate conferred upon the CJEU in Art. 19(1) TEU' such that the ECJ's interpretation itself constituted 'an *ultra vires* act that is not binding upon the [BVerfG]'.[96] The BVerfG pointed to economic effects which were larger, or 'at least comparable in weight' to the PSPP's monetary objectives, and held that the PSPP was also *ultra vires* for failing to establish proportionality *stricto sensu*.[97] The BVerfG rejected the contention that the Treaties did not make an absolute separation between economic and monetary policies. According to the BVerfG: 'this reasoning is flawed not least given that the European Union only has an exclusive competence for monetary policy'.[98]

6.2 Conformity with the Allocation of Competences

This section examines the establishment of conditional financial assistance under Article 136(3) TFEU and the ESM within this analytical framework. It concludes that there is no legal basis for conditional

---

[91] *Gauweiler (CJEU)* [76], [46]–[49].
[92] See the six conditions set down in *Gauweiler Decision (Germany)* [174], [205]–[207] listed below, in Section 6.2.1, n 136.
[93] *Weiss (CJEU)*, [74]–[81].
[94] *Weiss (CJEU)*, [61]–[62].
[95] *Weiss Decision (Germany)*, [162].
[96] *Weiss Decision (Germany)*, [154].
[97] *Weiss Decision (Germany)*, [134]–[137], [170]–[174] [177]–[178].
[98] *Weiss Decision (Germany)*, [142].

financial assistance in the Treaties outside Article 122(2) TFEU, and no way to reconcile the ESM under Article 136(3) TFEU with the boundaries of competence according to the analytical framework set out by the ECJ. The starting point for the analysis is Articles 2(1) and 2(2) TFEU. Under those articles, Member States may not adopt legally binding acts in areas of exclusive union competence, and may act in shared competences only 'to the extent that the Union has not exercised its competence'. Monetary policy (Article 3(1)(c) TFEU), financial assistance (Article 122(2) TFEU), and economic coordination (Articles 2(3), 5(1) TFEU) are all competences possessed and occupied by Union institutions under the Treaties.

To take account of the overlapping issues of competence between the ESM, EFSM, EFSF and OMT, this analysis merges these instruments into a single analytical framework devolved into four cumulative assessments.

[6.2.1] First, it considers whether the objective of the ESM under Article 136(3) TFEU, namely, 'to meet the financing requirements of ESM Members [...] if indispensable to safeguard the financial stability of the euro area',[99] is reconcilable with the division between economic and monetary policy given the obvious parallels with the OMT's objective of 'bringing about a fall in – or even the elimination of – excessive risk *premia*' to safeguard 'an appropriate monetary policy transmission and the singleness of monetary policy'.[100]

[6.2.2] Second, it considers whether Member State financial assistance through the ESM under Article 136(3) TFEU is reconcilable with the EU's competence for financial assistance occupied by the EFSM under Article 122(2) TFEU.

[6.2.3] Third, it considers whether ESM conditionality trespasses upon the Union's economic 'coordination' competence or falls within Member State economic competence proper. If the former, this would mean the TESM is *ultra vires* Member State competence, and Decision 2011/199/EU exceeds Article 48(6) TEU by amending the Union's competence in Articles 2(3) and 5(1) TFEU.

[6.2.4] Finally, it considers whether the involvement of EU institutions in the ESM involves them in Member State economic policy. If so, then Decision 2011/199/EU would exceed Article 48(6) TEU by

---

[99] *Pringle v. Ireland*, [96].
[100] *Gauweiler (CJEU)* [76], [47].

extending the competences of the Union, and the TESM would violate the requirement in Article 13(2) TEU that EU institutions act only 'within the limits of the powers conferred [in] the Treaties'.

The apparent difficulties in meeting these criteria should be noted at the outset. Taken cumulatively, a positive finding of legality requires the ESM to reconcile several apparently disjunctive criteria:

[6.2.1] On one hand, secondary-market bond purchases for the stability of the monetary union by the ESM must fall decisively within economic policy; on the other hand, secondary bond purchases for the stability of the monetary union by the ECB must fall decisively within monetary policy;

[6.2.2] On one hand, the EFSF/ESM must not intrude upon the competences of the EFSM for financial assistance; on the other hand, the ESM must be allowed to directly subsume the tasks and financial assistance programmes of the EFSM;

[6.2.3] One one hand, the ESM must fall decisively outside the scope of EU law; on the other hand, the EU institutions and EU acts governing every step of its operations must not be doing anything outside the scope of EU law; and

[6.2.4] On one hand, the EU can have no power to dictate economic policy and Member States can have no power to coordinate it; on the other hand, ESM conditionality is negotiated on behalf of the Member States by EU institutions and is only lawful if it is fully consistent with measures enacted under EU law.

If the ESM is genuinely reconcilable with the fault lines running through the Treaties, it must be clear that it is not based upon an 'accumulation of contradictions with and circumventions of the Union legal order'.[101]

6.2.1   Incompatibility with the Boundaries of Economic and Monetary Policy Competence

Articles 136(3) TFEU and 3 TESM state that the competence of the ESM is to 'safeguard the stability of the *euro area* as a whole'.[102] This sounds suspiciously like monetary policy – the exclusive competence of the Union. Indeed, outside Article 136(3) TFEU, the Treaties employ the

---

[101] Tomkin, 'Conceptual Gymnastics', 187.
[102] Art. 136(3) TFEU; Art. 3 TESM.

term 'stability' exclusively in the context of the 'price stability'.[103] In that respect, the complainant in *Pringle* argued that '*the fundamental and defining purpose of the ESM is rooted* in Union monetary policy', and the ESM would have a 'direct impact' on inflation and price stability in the euro area.[104]

In *Pringle* v. *Ireland*, the ECJ concluded that the ESM fell wholly within the province of Member State economic policy. This conclusion was reached on an objectives-based test that discounts indirect (but often concrete) effects of an instrument.[105] The objective of the ESM, namely, 'to meet the financing requirements of ESM Members [. . .] if indispensable to safeguard the financial stability of the euro area',[106] was held to be 'clearly distinct' from the aims of monetary policy because indirect effects on inflation were to be excluded from the analysis:

> Even if the activities of the ESM might influence the rate of inflation, such an influence would constitute only the indirect consequence of the economic policy measures adopted.[107]

In *Gauweiler (Reference) (Germany)*, the BVerfG applied the ECJ's *Pringle* judgment verbatim to the OMT.[108] The BVerfG observed that, like the ESM, the *immediate* objective of the OMT was to 'neutralise spreads on government bonds of selected Member States of the euro currency area which have emerged in the markets and which adversely affect the refinancing of these Member States'.[109] Although this might subsequently or *indirectly* influence the rate of inflation – per *Pringle* – 'such an influence would constitute only the indirect consequence of the economic policy measures adopted'.[110] The BVerfG alleged a 'manifest breach' under its *ultra vires* jurisdiction.[111]

In *Gauweiler* v. *Bundestag (CJEU)*, the ECJ upheld the OMT. According to the ECJ, the OMT's purpose of 'bringing about a fall in – or even the elimination of – excessive risk *premia*' was done with the objective of safeguarding 'an appropriate monetary policy transmission and the

---

[103] Arts. 3(3)(1) TEU; 119(2)–(3), 127(1), and 282(2)TFEU; Art. 2(1) Statute of the ECB.
[104] Pringle, 'Written Observations', paras 3.22, 3.25 (emphasis in original).
[105] *Pringle* v. *Ireland*, [53]–[55].
[106] *Pringle* v. *Ireland*, [96].
[107] *Pringle* v. *Ireland* [56], [97].
[108] *Gauweiler Reference (Germany)* at [55], [70].
[109] *Gauweiler Reference (Germany)* at [55], [70].
[110] *Pringle* v. *Ireland* [56], [96]–[97].
[111] *Gauweiler Reference (Germany)* at [39]–[40].

singleness of the monetary policy'.[112] This was then assimilated within the ECB's competence for price stability as follows:

> First, the objective of safeguarding the singleness of monetary policy *contributes* to achieving the objectives of that policy [price stability] in as much as, under Article 119(2) TFEU, monetary policy must be 'single'.
>
> Secondly, the objective of safeguarding an appropriate transmission of monetary policy is likely both to preserve the singleness of monetary and *to contribute* to its primary objective which is to maintain price stability.[113]

'Contribute' is italicised here to emphasize that these objectives are brought under price stability by their secondary effects – their achievement 'contributes' to price stability. Price stability, in fact, only arises as a tertiary (thrice removed) *possible* and *partial* indirect consequence from the initial objective of lowering risk premia.

To compare, in *Pringle* v. *Ireland* the ECJ held that [1] secondary bond market operations[114] [2] have the purpose of 'meet[ing] the financing requirements of ESM Members',[115] in order [3] 'to safeguard the financial stability of the euro area'.[116] Thereafter [4] 'effects on the inflation level' could be discounted as 'only the indirect consequence of the economic policy measures adopted'.[117]

In *Gauweiler* v. *Bundestag*, the ECJ held that [1] secondary bond market operations [2] have the purpose of 'the reduction of the financing costs of the State concerned',[118] in order to [3] repair the 'transmission of monetary policy decisions to the economy and the singleness of monetary policy'.[119] Thereafter, [4] 'the objective of safeguarding an appropriate transmission of monetary policy is *likely* both to preserve the singleness of monetary policy and to *contribute* to its primary objective, which is to maintain price stability'.[120] Price stability itself does not even arise in this chain of causality at all – it is only [5] a possible consequence to be taken

---

[112] *Gauweiler (CJEU)* [76], [47].

[113] *Gauweiler (CJEU)* [48]–[50] (emphasis added).

[114] *Pringle* v. *Ireland*, [141].

[115] *Pringle* v. *Ireland* [96]–[97].

[116] *Pringle* v. *Ireland* [96]–[97].

[117] *Pringle* v. *Ireland* [96]–[97].

[118] *Gauweiler (CJEU)* [76].

[119] *Gauweiler (CJEU)* [58].

[120] *Gauweiler (CJEU)* [49], [58] (see also [80]) (emphasis added).

up in future.[121] This is *Pringle*, turned inside out. Financial assistance comes long before price stability in the chain of causality.[122]

Yet, discounting 'indirect effects' under the objectives-based test is not even the only problem with these cases.[123] Even if one accepts the objectives-based test in principle, it cannot be avoided: the OMT and ESM rely upon the *exact same* instrument (targeted secondary bond purchases triggered by financial instability);[124] with the *exact same* purpose ('the reduction of the financing costs of the State concerned');[125] subject to the *exact same* financial conditionality (OMT purchases are contingent on ESM conditionality),[126] pursuant to the *exact same* objective:

'to support the good functioning of the government debt markets of ESM Members in exceptional circumstances where the lack of market liquidity threatens financial stability' (as the ESM words it);[127] or

'to ensure depth and liquidity in those market segments which are dysfunctional' (as the ECB words it).[128]

The ECJ's response to that charge is that the OMT is triggered by the need to 'safeguard monetary policy transmission and the singleness of monetary policy', and so retains its own criteria as to whether bond purchases are warranted 'from a monetary policy objective'.[129] But this makes little sense. The OMT is triggered when the singleness and transmission of monetary policy is threatened by rising default risk, and default risk only arises due to the *prospect of default*. Since any Member State default would end the 'singleness of monetary policy' and the 'stability of the euro area' in equal measure, this amounts to a permanent guarantee that the ECB

---

[121] *Gauweiler (AG Cruz-Villalón)* [136].
[122] See Petch, 'Outright Monetary Transactions', 18 applying the test of criminal intent.
[123] Paul Craig, 'Pringle: Legal Reasoning, Text, Purpose and Teleology' (2013) 20 MJ 3 5; Beck, 'Continuation of Politics', 241–242; Thomas Beukers and Bruno De Witte, 'The Court of Justice Approves the Creation of the European Stability Mechanism Outside the EU legal Order: *Pringle*' (2013) 50 CMLR 805, 831.
[124] Cf: Art. 18 ESCB and Art. 18 TESM. See Jürgen Bast, 'Don't Act beyond Your Powers: The Perils and Pitfalls of the German Constitutional Court's Ultra Vires Review' (2014) 15 German LJ 167, 176.
[125] *Gauweiler (CJEU)* [240]. Cf Art. 1, ESM Guideline on the SMSF and ECB, 'Monthly Bulletin September 2012' (2012) ECB Monthly Bulletin 7, 7–8.
[126] *Gauweiler (AG Cruz-Villalón)* [145].
[127] Art. 1, ESM Guideline on the SMSF.
[128] Trichet, 'ECB's Response'; ECB, 'OMT Press Release'. See further sources cited above, n 123.
[129] *Gauweiler (CJEU)* [62]. See also: *ECB Monthly Bulletin October 2012*, 8.

will use its monetary policy instruments to guarantee against default.[130] ECB President Draghi somewhat gives this away, revealing that the OMT had no specific 'trigger' beyond a general 'sense of worsening of the crisis' and 'the sudden increase in the shorter part of the yield curve for several countries [and] other symptoms of market fragmentation'.[131]

Yet the ECB has no competence to prevent the worsening of financial crises and stop sovereign bond market spreads from fragmenting.[132] For this reason, in *Gauweiler (Germany)*, the BVerfG rejected this justification out of court, stating:

As for the European Central Bank claiming to safeguard the current composition of the euro currency area [...] this is obviously not a task of monetary policy but one of economic policy, which remains a responsibility of the Member States.[133]

It is defensible to conclude that the ESM is an act of economic policy on the objectives-based test in isolation, but the Union cannot have it both ways. Whatever test is used, it is impossible to conclude that both instruments are separately, implicitly and simultaneously countenanced by the allocation of competences in the Treaty. If that is so, the ECJ's interpretation of at least one of these instruments must exceed those bounds, and its applicability must fall subject to the *ultra vires* and constitutional identity rulings of national courts.

Proof for this proposition is set out in the final ruling of the BVerfG in *Gauweiler Decision (Germany)*, in which the BVerfG inveighed against the ruling of the ECJ;[134] concluded that it failed to 'completely remove the character of the OMT programme insofar as it encroaches upon economic policy';[135] and accepted that the OMT was not a 'manifest' breach of competence only in so far as that (technically supreme) act of EU law

---

[130] William Buiter and Clemens Grafe, 'Reforming EMU's Fiscal Policy Rules: Some Suggestions for Enhancing Fiscal Sustainability and Macroeconomic Stability in an Enlarged European Union' in Mario Buti (ed.), *Monetary and Fiscal Policies in EMU: Interactions and Coordination* (Cambridge University Press, 2003), 25.

[131] Mario Draghi and Vítor Constâncio, 'Introductory Statements to the Press Conference (with Q&A)' (Frankfurt am Main, 2 August 2012).

[132] Indeed, this was the ECB's argument in *Euro Rescue Package (Germany)* [90]. See further Editorial, 'Financing via the Money Press'.

[133] *Gauweiler Decision (Germany)* [72].

[134] *Gauweiler Decision (Germany)* [182]–[189].

[135] *Gauweiler Decision (Germany)* [196].

complied with six conditions on its operation.[136] The BVerfG then placed the *Bundesbank* and *Bundestag* in the position of monitoring compliance with those conditions.[137] According to the BVerfG, the German *Bundesbank* 'may only participate in the programme's implementation *if and to the extent that*' those substantive conditions are met.[138]

6.2.2   Incompatibility with the Boundaries of Union Financial Assistance

The ECJ's conclusion that ESM financial assistance is not monetary policy merely leads to a subsequent problem. Financial assistance is an EU competence under Article 122(2) TFEU, and it is a mechanism enacted under that article – the EFSM – which the ESM was designed to replace. As the complainant in *Pringle* argued:

> In so doing, it is clearly envisaged that the ESM should exercise *a competence which has been both conferred on and exercised by the Union*.[139]

In *Pringle* v. *Ireland*, the ECJ avoided this conclusion by holding that Union financial assistance (Article 122(2) TFEU) and Member State financial assistance (Article 136(3) TFEU) occupy two distinct fields of competence: The EFSM occupies the field of *ad hoc* financial assistance to a Member State which is in difficulties caused by exceptional occurrences beyond its control, and the ESM occupies the field of permanent financial assistance to safeguard the financial stability of the euro area as a whole.[140] But on any ostensible application of the criteria by which the ECJ divides these fields, both mechanisms must occupy the same field.

First, the ESM under Article 136(3) TFEU is held not to overlap with the EFSM because Articles 2(3) and 5(1) TFEU restrict EU economic

---

[136] *Gauweiler Decision (Germany)* [174], [205]–[207], [220]. The six conditions are: (1) Purchases must not be announced in advance, (2) the volume of purchases must be limited from the outset, (3) a minimum period must be observed between the issuance of government bonds and their purchase by the ESCB that is defined from the outset and prevents the issuing conditions from being distorted, (4) the ESCB must only purchase government bonds of Member States that have bond market access, (5) purchased bonds must only be held to maturity in exceptional cases, and (6) purchases are restricted or ceased, and purchased bonds are remarketed, should continuing intervention become unnecessary.

[137] Gauweiler Decision (Germany) [174], [205]–[207], [220].

[138] *Gauweiler Decision (Germany)* [220] (emphasis added).

[139] Pringle, 'Written Observations', 25 (emphasis in original).

[140] *Pringle* v. *Ireland* [65]–[68], [105], [120]; Case C-370/12 *Pringle* v. *Ireland* EU:C:2012:675 (View of AG Kokott) [125].

competence 'to the adoption of coordinating measures'. [141] For this reason, according to the Court, Article 122(2) TFEU does not confer any specific power on the EU to establish a stability mechanism such as the ESM, which provides financial assistance for the stability of the euro area as a whole.[142] In short, the EFSM is a mere coordination measure; the ESM is not. But this is a curious finding to make, given that it is Article 136(3) TFEU which requires coordination through economic conditionality, and it is the ESM which coordinates financial assistance by the Member States. Article 122(2) says nothing about strict conditionality and the EFSM uses the EU's own resources, so it does not entail any 'coordination' whatsoever.[143] The Court applies this criterion backwards: The ESM coordinates, the EFSM does not.

Second, the ECJ divides the ESM and EFSM by their objectives and criteria: The EFSM is activated in the event of difficulties caused by exceptional occurrences beyond Member State control, while the ESM is activated in the event of instability to the euro area as a whole.[144] But this cannot be tenable for the simple reason that both the ESM and EFSM perform the *exact same* function for the *exact same* states in the *exact same* circumstances.[145] The ECJ itself acknowledges this, admitting, 'the ESM will [. . .] *assume the tasks hitherto allocated temporarily to the EFSM*' namely – 'providing, *where needed, financial assistance* to euro area Member States'.[146] And even if such programmes were not directly passed between them, their objectives and criteria for activation are anyways identical: Both Article 122(2) and 136(3) TFEU apply – and have applied – to safeguard the financial stability of the euro area.[147] The ECJ attempts to avoid this by describing the purpose of Article 136(3) as the

---

[141] *Pringle v. Ireland* [64]–[65], [104]–[105].

[142] *Pringle v. Ireland* [64]–[65], [104]–[105].

[143] The Commission had previously stated that pooling Member State bailout funds fell within its duty to 'coordinate': European Commission, 'Adjustment Programme for Greece', 26.

[144] *Pringle v. Ireland*, [104]–[105].

[145] Roderic O'Gorman, 'Thomas Pringle v. Government of Ireland, Ireland and the Attorney General' (2013) 50 Ir Jur 221.

[146] *Pringle v. Ireland*, [99], [103] (emphasis added).

[147] The explicit purpose of the EFSM regulation was to 'ensure fiscal sustainability *in the euro area*' by stopping interest rate contagion through the euro area. Cf: Council of the EU, 'Press Release 9596/10'; R (1), (4) and Art. 1 Reg 407/2010. See further Stanislas Adam and Javier Mena Parras, 'The European Stability Mechanism through the Legal Meanderings of the Union's Constitutionalism: Comment on Pringle' (2013) 38 EL Rev 848, 859.

'management of financial crises which, notwithstanding such preventative action as might have been taken, might nonetheless arise'.[148] Yet it is difficult to imagine how this does not precisely describe the situation Article 122(2) is meant to govern: A crisis which arises despite any preventative action that might have been taken is, by definition, 'an exceptional occurrence beyond the control of a Member State' within the wording of Article 122(2).

Third, the two mechanisms cannot be rendered distinct on the basis that the EFSM is '*ad hoc*' and the ESM is 'permanent.'[149] The issuance of *financial assistance* – the object of both Articles 122(2) and 136(3) – is coterminous on any reading. Both articles activate financial assistance in a period of financial instability, and both contemplate its termination as soon as that instability ceases to persist.[150]

The entire edifice is arbitrary. Both mechanisms could, with less mendacity, be seen to occupy the field of 'financial assistance to a Member State'. The ECJ itself perhaps lets this slip, noting that nothing in Article 122 TFEU 'indicates that the Union has exclusive competence *to grant financial assistance to a Member State*'.[151] Shared or not, if that is the competence at issue, then it is a Union competence pre-emptive of a Member State mechanism under Article 2 (1)–(2) TFEU.

As one final proof, it should be noted that the EFSF acted in conjunction with the EFSM as part of the same financial assistance operations, and the EFSF, as a Member State mechanism, has the same legal position as the ESM (and also passes its financial programmes to the ESM).[152] In that circumstance, there can be little doubt that Member State and EU financial assistance do the same thing. It is not possible to reconcile the EFSM, EFSF and ESM to their respective boundaries of competence on the criteria set down by the ECJ.

6.2.3   Incompatibility with the Boundaries of Competence for Economic Coordination

The third problem with permitting conditional financial assistance under Article 136(3) TFEU is that Articles 2(3) and 5(1) TFEU confer

---

[148] *Pringle* v. *Ireland*, [58].
[149] *Pringle* v. *Ireland*, [65], [104]–[105].
[150] Recitals (1), (4); Art. 2 Reg 407/2010. Cf: Art. 3 TESM. See Adam and Parras, 'Legal Meanderings', 858; Borger, 'Predicament in *Pringle*', 128.
[151] *Pringle* v. *Ireland*, [120] (emphasis added).
[152] Arts. 39–40 TESM.

competence for economic coordination on the Union. Yet this is something which the ESM, by pooling Member State funds and imposing a macroeconomic adjustment programme, also appears to do. If Articles 2(3) or 5(1) describe an exclusive or shared Union competence, then the ESM will unlawfully encroach on that competence pursuant to Articles 2(1)–(2) TFEU.

Article 2(5) TFEU could have provided a third possibility. That article states that in certain areas and under certain conditions, the Union can 'support, coordinate or supplement' the actions of the Member States 'without thereby superseding their competence in these areas'. Some authors argue (convincingly) that the competence for economic coordination 'is a special one' that falls within this category, neither pre-empting nor precluding Member State coordination.[153]

But this is not the route the ECJ took. The ECJ did not uphold ESM conditionality by recognizing that Member States *also* retain their own competence for economic coordination.[154] It ruled that ESM conditionality does not trespass on EU 'coordination' because ESM conditionality is not coordination at all. It merely ensures consistency with 'the measures taken by the Union in the area of co-ordination' under EU law.[155] This is significant because, by holding that the ESM must be separate from the 'coordination' competence of the Union, the Court proceeds on the basis that economic coordination must be an EU competence capable of pre-empting Member State economic coordination.

But the Court's conclusion, that the ESM does not 'coordinate' because it is instead concerned exclusively with the 'management of financial crises which nonetheless arise' (as the Court held that it was),[156] is rather difficult to reconcile with the wording of the TESM. The stated purpose of the PCCL under Article 14 TESM is that of 'reinforcing the credibility of [. . .] economic performance'.[157] This applies, no less, to Member States which have 'a track record of access to international capital markets on reasonable terms' and 'whose economic conditions are still sound'.[158] Similarly, the PCCL/ECCL and SMSF

---

[153] Koen Lenaerts and Piet Van Nuffel, *European Union Law* (3rd ed., Sweet & Maxwell, 2011), 128–129; Steve Peers, 'The Stability Treaty: Permanent Austerity or Gesture Politics' (2012) 8 ECL Review 404, 410; Calleiss, 'New Rules', 105; Palmstorfer, 'To Bail Out'; Servais and Ruggeri, 'EU Constitution', 50; Lastra, *Legal Foundations*, 249.

[154] *Pringle* v. *Ireland*, [108], [64], [174].

[155] *Pringle* v. *Ireland*, [110]–[113].

[156] *Pringle* v. *Ireland*, [58].

[157] Arts. 1, 2(2), ESM Guideline on the PCCL and ECCL.

[158] Arts. 1, 2(2), ESM Guideline on the PCCL and ECCL.

provide financing to countries 'whose economic conditions are *still sound*', in order to '*reinforce* credibility' . . . '*before* they face major difficulties raising funds in the capital markets'.[159]

The ESM declares, on its face, that these are coordination measures, not indispensable finance measures.

The reply to that charge is that ESM conditionality is still not coordination because, as Merino so puts it, the objective of conditionality 'is to avoid building a rival universe of economic coordination outside of the EU Treaties to the detriment of the competence of economic coordination under the EU Treaties'.[160] For this reason, the ECJ holds that so long as ESM conditionality merely apes EU macroeconomic adjustment programmes, it would 'not constitute an instrument for the coordination of the economic policies of the Member States'.[161]

But this causes more problems than it solves. Since conditionality is only legal when it ensures 'full consistency' with EU policy coordination, this proves only that Member State policy conditionality is, *prima facie*, unlawful. The ESM can point to the EU's rules, but it can have none of its own. Coordination beyond the measures set out under EU law would encroach on the Union competence. This traps the ESM in another legal paradox: As will be shown in Section 6.3.3, the ECJ later rules (in the same judgment no less) that strict conditionality is necessary for the ESM to be lawful under the 'no bailout' rule.[162] But if strict conditionality may have no force beyond EU law, this reduces that requirement to compliance with substantive EU policy prescriptions in the realm of economic policy (which, it must be recalled, the Union has no competence in).[163]

6.2.4 Incompatibility with the Boundaries of Competence for Economic Policy

The ECJ's conclusion that the ESM is (Member State) economic policy proper, not (EU) economic coordination, poses yet another problem. If the ESM is Member State competence, then it must be economic policy proper – and not mere coordination. And yet, as noted in Section 6.1.5

---

[159] Art. 1, ESM Guideline on the PCCL and ECCL; Art. 1, ESM Guideline on the SMSF (emphasis added).
[160] Merino, 'Financial Assistance', 1635.
[161] *Pringle* v. *Ireland*, [110]–[112].
[162] *Pringle* v. *Ireland*, [69], [136]–[137].
[163] *Pringle* v. *Ireland*, [69], [72], [111], [121], [143], [151]. See Beukers and De Witte, '*Pringle*', 840.

above, each stage of the ESM's instruments are governed by EU law and administered by EU institutions.[164] If that is so, this must necessarily involve EU institutions in activities beyond the competences of the Union contrary to Article 13(2) TEU.

It is important to note that it was accepted during the preparatory work of Decision 2011/199/EU that the amendment of Article 136(3) TFEU under the simplified procedure would be unlawful if it incorporated the involvement of EU institutions, as it would require the conferral of new competences on the Union and therefore could not be effected by Article 48 TEU.[165] It is for this reason that Decision 2011/199/EU contains no mention of EU institutions – it is a 'deliberate move to avoid a question of competence'.[166] Instead, the role of EU institutions was set out in a 'Term Sheet' – a commitment which would have been unlawful if it had been included in Decision 2011/199/EU itself.[167] Yet this, too, should be unlawful: The ECJ has held since *Defrenne* that the Member States cannot modify the Treaty through an informal agreement.[168]

In *Pringle* v. *Ireland*, the ECJ turned a blind eye to this informal agreement and limited its scrutiny to the text of the TESM itself.[169] Having done so, the ECJ held that the EU involvement of the Commission and ECB in the ESM is lawful because:

> [T]he duties conferred on the Commission and ECB within the ESM Treaty, important as they are, *do not entail any power to make decisions of their own.* Further, the activities pursued by those two institutions within the ESM Treaty *solely commit the ESM.*[170]

This, too, is rather difficult to reconcile with the terms of either the TESM or Regulation 472/2013.[171] First, under Article 7 of Regulation 472/2013, ESM macroeconomic programmes are duplicated in EU Council decisions, and these decisions are binding in their entirety on the parties to

---

[164] See Section 6.1.5, nn 60–66.

[165] Beukers and De Witte, '*Pringle*', 812. See European Parliament Resolution of 23 March 2011 on Article 136 TFEU.

[166] O'Gorman, '*Pringle* v. *Ireland*', 228.

[167] Beukers and De Witte, '*Pringle*', 812.

[168] *Defrenne* [58].

[169] *Pringle* v. *Ireland* [75]. For criticism: Craig, '*Pringle*', 6; O'Gorman, '*Pringle* v. *Ireland*', 228.

[170] *Pringle* v. *Ireland* [160]–[164] (emphasis added).

[171] Angelos Dimopoulos, 'The Use of International Law as a Tool for Enhancing Governance in the Eurozone and its Impact on EU Institutional Integrity' in Adams, Fabbrini and Larouche (eds), *Constitutionalization of European Budgetary Constraints* (Hart, 2014), 51; Craig, 'Economic Governance', 27–18; O'Gorman, '*Pringle* v. *Ireland*'', 229.

whom they are addressed under Article 288 TFEU. Second, the Commission and ECB have a virtually autonomous right to negotiate, supervise, and sanction macroeconomic programmes that include dictates on healthcare spending, pensions and wage negotiations, and which will bind Member States under secondary EU law.[172] Third, according to *Pringle* v. *Ireland*, the legality of the ESM framework depends on the conclusion that 'the [MoUs] concluded by the ESM [...] must be fully consistent with EU law',[173] and, under Regulation 472/2013:

The Commission shall ensure that the [MoU] signed by the Commission on behalf of the ESM or the EFSF is fully consistent with the macroeconomic adjustment programme approved by the Council.

How is it that the terms of these macroeconomic programmes are not acts of EU institutions, but the Member States are legally prohibited – by an act of EU law – from enacting something other than policies selected by the Commission and ECB and enacted into binding EU law by the Council?

As will be shown in Chapter 7 (Section 7.5) all of this has forced the ECJ into an untenable position. The Commission and ECB have a power, under binding secondary EU law, to select specific economic policy objectives when drafting macroeconomic programmes, and these decisions are: acts of EU institutions capable of grounding an action for non-contractual liability under Article 340 TFEU;[174] enacted in EU Council Decisions under Regulation 472/2013, which are binding under Article 288 TFEU;[175] acts which constitute '*binding legal commitments* with the Commission [and] ECB';[176] acts which condition the purchase of secondary bonds under the OMT;[177] reviewable acts of EU institutions according to established case law;[178] and acts that impose 'binding'[179] and 'mandatory'[180] obligations to implement specific measures in economic policy.[181]

---

172   Art. 6 Reg 472/2013; Art. 13 TESM.
173   *Pringle* v. *Ireland*, [174].
174   *Ledra* v. *Commission*, [55]-[59], [67].
175   Art. 7 Reg 472/2013; *Florescu*, [31]-[36], [41] (see also [49]-[55]); Joined Cases C-105–109/15 P *Mallis* v. *Commission and ECB* EU:C:2016:294 (Opinion of AG Wathelet), [85]-[94].
176   *Dowling* v. *Minister of Finance* [2013] IESC 27, [41.2](4); Case C-41/15 *Dowling et al.* v. *Minister for Finance* EU:C:2016:473 (Opinion of AG Wahl), [25]. See: Section 7.5.4.
177   *Gauweiler (AG Cruz-Villalón)* [145].
178   Case C-409/13 *Council* v. *Commission* EU:C:2015:217, [70]-[74]; Case C-613/14 *James Elliott Construction Limited* v. *Irish Asphalt Limited* EU:C:2016:821.
179   See sources cited above, n 176.
180   *Florescu*, [41] (see also [35]-[36] [49]-[55]); *Juízes Portugueses*, [46] (see also [49]).
181   Case C-64/16 *Associaçao Sindical dos Juízes Portugueses* v. *Tribunal de Contas* EU:C:2017:395 (Opinion of AG ØE), [52].

However, if the CJEU acknowledges these as acts of EU institutions, then it will be difficult not to acknowledge that they are also *ultra vires*. So it does not. The issue is examined in greater detail where it arises with regards to fiscal sovereignty in Chapter 7.[182] For present purposes it is sufficient to remark that, EU law or not, economic conditionality drafted by EU institutions and governed or enforced by EU law is not contemplated by the Treaty.

6.3 Conformity with the Substantive Law of the Treaty

In addition to the allocation of competences, in order for the ESM to be lawful, financial assistance must be permissible under the 'no bailout' rule inscribed in the Treaty since Maastricht. As Article 125 TFEU is not amended, financial assistance under Article 136(3) TFEU is still a violation of EU law unless it can be shown that it is *already* permitted under the 'no bailout' rule. As the ECJ held in *Pringle*, the amendment of Article 136 TFEU has no legal effects on its own – 'the right of a Member State to conclude and ratify the TESM is not subject to the entry into force of Decision 2011/99.'[183]

Article 125(1) TFEU consists of two sentences, the first addressed to the Union and the second addressed to the Member States. In identical terms, those sentences state that:

> [The Union/A Member State] *shall not be liable for or assume the commitments of* central governments, regional, local or other public authorities, other bodies governed by public law, or public undertakings of any Member State, without prejudice to mutual financial guarantees for the joint execution of a specific project. [Emphasis added]

There are two competing interpretations of this provision among legal scholars, and *Pringle* v. *Ireland* has done little to quell the dispute. The broad (purposive) interpretation is of a 'no bailout' rule *stricto sensu*. This view enjoys resilient support among legal commentators and has a strong textual basis in the Treaty.[184] Ruffert and others point out

---

[182] See below, Chapter 7, Section 7.5.

[183] *Pringle* v. *Ireland* [185].

[184] Lars Feld and Thushyanthan Baskaran, 'Federalism, Budget Deficits and Public Debt: On the Reform of Germany's Fiscal Constitution' (2010) 6 Rev Law Econ 365, 379; Matthias Ruffert, 'The European Debt Crisis and European Union Law' (2011) 48 CMLR 1777, 1786; Palmstorfer, 'To Bail Out'; Adamski, 'Power Games'; Craig, 'Pringle'; Borger, 'Predicament in *Pringle*', 130; Beck, 'Continuation of Politics', 244; Tuori and

that the language of Article 125(1) is 'rather explicit'.[185] It states that the Member States and the Union *'shall not'* engage in such activities – language which implies a 'hard obligation and thus a prohibition'.[186] Article 125(2) TFEU itself refers to the 'prohibitions' set out in Articles 123, 124 and 125(1) TFEU, and Declaration No. 6 on Article 100 EC refers to Article 125 as the *'no* bail-out *rule'*.[187] The ECJ itself slips into this language in *Pringle*, where it refers to the 'no bailout clause' – literally, a provision that allows for *no* bailouts.[188] As shown in Chapter 2, this interpretation finds explicit support in the *travaux préparatoires*: The purpose of Article 125 is 'to dispel any investor's doubt, or *hope,* about the risk they run in financing governments',[189] and so 'ensure that the financial markets exercise a degree of discipline'.[190]

The narrow interpretation, by contrast, is derived from a literal reading of the text of Article 125 TFEU. On this view, the wording 'shall not be liable for or assume the commitments of' prohibits only direct relationships of *guarantee* that result in the direct assumption of liability to a Member State's creditors.[191] As the Commission argues, 'Lending to a euro-area Member State – as opposed to assuming its debt – is not in contradiction with Article 125 TFEU.'[192] A proponent of this interpretation, Merino explains it this way:

> Any direct relationship of guarantee with a Member State's creditors would breach the no-bailout clause. However, this prohibition does not appear to extend to types of financial assistance, such as loans or credits [...] where the beneficiary of the assistance is held to pay them back.[193]

It is important to emphasize this difference in scope: Under the narrow interpretation, the concern of Article 125 TFEU is not the financing of another Member State's liabilities, only *how* they are

---

Tuori, *Eurozone Crisis,* 119–120; Michelle Everson, 'An Exercise in Legal Honesty: Rewriting the Court of Justice and the Bundesverfassungsgericht' (2015) 21 ELJ 474.
[185] Ruffert, 'Debt Crisis', 1785. See also: Lastra, *Legal Foundations,* 253; Antonio Estella, *Legal Foundations of EU Economic Governance* (Cambridge University Press, 2018), 19.
[186] Palmstorfer, 'To Bail Out', 775.
[187] Declaration No 6 (emphasis added). See also Palmstorfer, 'To Bail Out', 775.
[188] *Pringle v. Ireland* [129], [132].
[189] Commission, 'A Stability Pact', 15–16 (emphasis added).
[190] Monetary Committee, EMU beyond Stage I (1990), 2.
[191] Phoebus Athanassiou, 'Of Past Measures and Future Plans for Europe's Exit from the Sovereign Debt Crisis: What Is Legally Possible (and What Is Not)' (2011) 36 EL Rev 558; Paul De Grauwe, 'The Greek Crisis and the Future of the Eurozone' (2010) 2 Intereconomics 89, 91.
[192] Commission, 'Reinforcing Economic Policy Coordination' COM(2010) 250 final, 10.
[193] Merino, 'Financial Assistance', 1627.

financed. The Union/Member States could, theoretically, finance a Member State's liabilities in perpetuity, as long as no direct guarantee exists between the lending Member State and the debtor's creditors.

In *Pringle* v. *Ireland*, the ECJ adopted the narrow interpretation.[194] It did so in three stages. First, on a textual analysis of Article 125 TFEU, the Court ruled that the wording 'shall not be liable for' or 'assume the commitments of' did not prohibit all types of financial assistance in any form.[195] Second, the Court verified its textual analysis with a comparison of the wording of Articles 122(2) and 123 TFEU: since those provisions did not also prohibit *all* forms of financial assistance whatsoever in the same terms, this proved that Article 125 TFEU did not preclude *all* financial assistance whatsoever.[196] Third, the Court identified three teleological purposes underpinning Article 125 TFEU: Market discipline, budgetary discipline, and the financial stability of the EMU as a whole.[197] From this, the Court ruled that financial assistance is permitted under Article 125 where three conditions are met:

> First, because Member States must remain subject to the 'logic of the markets when entering into debt', a Member State receiving financial assistance must remain 'responsible for its commitments to its creditors' (even if it may use its bailout funds to repay them).[198]
>
> Second, financial assistance will be lawful '*provided* that the conditions attached to such assistance are such as to prompt that Member State to *implement* a sound budgetary policy'.[199]
>
> Third, financial assistance may only be granted *ultima ratio* – 'when such support is indispensable to safeguard the financial stability of the euro area as a whole and of its Member States'.[200]

On these conditions, the ECJ held that the ESM and Article 136(3) complied with the teleology of Article 125 TFEU, and were therefore lawful.[201]

---

[194] *Pringle* v. *Ireland*, [130].
[195] *Pringle* v. *Ireland*, [130].
[196] *Pringle* v. *Ireland* [131]–[132].
[197] *Pringle* v. *Ireland* [136], excerpted above, n 2.
[198] *Pringle* v. *Ireland* [137]–[139].
[199] *Pringle* v. *Ireland* [137] (emphasis added).
[200] *Pringle* v. *Ireland* [142]–[145].
[201] *Pringle* v. *Ireland* [137].

This section argues, first, that this interpretation of Article 125 TFEU is fundamentally incompatible with the Treaties and the teleologies to which it is meant to subscribe. However, proceeding on the basis that it is authoritative from the internal perspective of EU law, it remains that the legal instruments of conditional financial assistance can only be lawful in so far as the conditions set out by the ECJ in *Pringle* v. *Ireland* are indeed met. According to the Court, the activation of financial assistance 'is not compatible with art.125 TFEU *unless*' they are met.[202] But they are not. The ESM's instruments do not comply with any of the formal conditions laid down by the ECJ.

6.3.1 Conditional Financial Assistance Is Incompatible with the Treaties

At the outset, it must be explained why there is ample reason to doubt the veracity of *Pringle* v. *Ireland* as a correct statement of Article 125 TFEU and the boundaries of the EMU architecture, even as a matter of pure EU law.

First, under ordinary rules of statutory interpretation, the textual interpretation of a provision must not be inconsistent with, or circumvent the plain meaning of, the text of the law.[203] In that regard, Article 125(1) TFEU is nothing if not 'clear and precise'.[204] The words 'shall not', 'prohibition', and '*no* bail-out rule' do not avail of any unwritten exceptions.[205] There is certainly no textual basis for exceptions in the event of instability in the euro area and strict conditionality.[206]

Second, the ECJ rules that financial assistance is lawful because the ESM 'does not act as a *guarantor* of the debts of the recipient Member State' and does not '*guarantee* the debt' of defaulting members because 'the defaulting ESM Member State remains bound to pay its part of the capital'.[207] But if becoming a 'guarantor' under a 'guarantee' is what is prohibited, the ECJ's interpretation does not even do this. As Tomkin points out, a *guarantee* in law 'does not necessarily or even ordinarily affect the primary liability of a debtor'.[208] Andrews and Millet, *Law of*

[202] *Pringle* v. *Ireland* [136]–[137].
[203] Oliver Jones, *Bennion on Statutory Interpretation* (Sixth ed., Lexis Nexis, 2013), 421–424.
[204] Lastra, *Legal Foundations*, 253.
[205] Palmstorfer, 'To Bail Out', 775; Ruffert, 'Debt Crisis', 1785–1786.
[206] Beukers and De Witte, '*Pringle*', 838; Borger, 'Predicament in *Pringle*', 134–135; Everson, 'Legal Honesty', 479 and Palmstorfer, 'To Bail Out', 775; Ruffert, 'Debt Crisis', 1785–1786.
[207] *Pringle* v. *Ireland*, [138]–[139], [144]–[145].
[208] Tomkin, 'Conceptual Gymnastics', 181.

Guarantees, note that, 'The essential distinguishing feature of a contract of guarantee is that the liability of the guarantor is always ancillary, or secondary, to that of the principal, who *remains primarily liable to the creditor*.'[209] The literal interpretation again 'fails on its own terms'.[210]

Third, if 'bailouts' are what is being prohibited, the narrow interpretation does nothing of the sort.[211] It must be recalled that the preparatory work was quite clear on the purpose of the 'no bailout' rule: It was to 'be clear that neither the Community nor the Member States stand behind a Member State's debts',[212] and 'to dispel any investor's doubt, or *hope*, about the risk they run in financing governments'.[213] There can be little doubt that the narrow interpretation does not accomplish either of these things.[214]

Fourth, as shown in Chapter 2, Article 125 TFEU is but the 'final piece' of an integrative structure that prohibits all access to non-market public finance under Articles 122–125 TFEU.[215] This interlocking framework would not have this effect if public finance could be provided through any one of the three barred doorways (Articles 123, 124 or 125 TFEU) outside of Article 122(2) TFEU. The corralling of any finance-seekers into the 'out of control emergency' test of Article 122(2) TFEU is rendered completely ineffective if just one of its constituent barriers is compromised. Allowing financial assistance, where previously there was none, undeniably negates a system constructed to dispel any investor's 'hope' of that possibility.

In that respect, the ECJ's cross-textual comparison of Articles 122, 123 and 125 TFEU in *Pringle* fell far short of what might properly be termed a systemic analysis.[216] The Court undertook a purely textual comparison of these provisions – it did not recognize the legal framework as having any effect greater than its disaggregated parts.[217] But on a systemic reading, if there were meant to be some silent, unspecified avenue for

---

[209] Geraldine Andrews and Richard Millet, *Law of Guarantees* (6th ed., Sweet & Maxwell, 2011), 1–001–005 (see also 1–013).

[210] Beck, 'Continuation of Politics', 244.

[211] Palmstorfer, 'To Bail Out', 775.

[212] Monetary Committee, EMU beyond Stage I (1990), 2.

[213] Commission, 'A Stability Pact', 15–16 (emphasis added).

[214] Beck, 'Continuation of Politics', 243.

[215] Borger, 'Predicament in *Pringle*', 119. See also Louis, 'Guest Editorial', 977 and Chapter 2, Section 2.3.1 of this book.

[216] For criticism: Bardutzky and Fahey, 'Judicial Review of the Legal Instruments of the Eurozone', 356; Borger, 'Predicament in *Pringle*', 134.

[217] *Pringle* v. *Ireland* [131]–[132]. Cf: *Gauweiler (AG Cruz-Villalón)* [131].

financial assistance in EMU, it would seem necessary to replicate the provisions of Article 143 TFEU for the euro area. As Palmstorfer points out, Article 143 belongs to the oldest parts of the Treaty.[218] Yet the Treaty drafters didn't use that provision for the EMU or create a new one in its likeness. They rescinded it.[219] Under the text of the Treaty, EMU countries cannot access financial assistance on the same basis that non-EMU countries can under Article 143 TFEU.[220] All that exists in the way of a financial assistance umbrella in EMU is Article 122(2) TFEU, which is limited to *Union* financial assistance for severe difficulties caused by natural disasters or exceptional occurrences beyond a Member State's control.[221]

The Court's take-away from this is that the very existence of Article 122(2) proves that Article 125 is not absolute. That much is self-evident – the latter cannot render the former redundant. The obvious way to reconcile these provisions would therefore be to conclude that, *lex specialis derogat legi generali*, Article 122(2) is an exception to Article 125.[222]

But that would mean that Article 125 *is* a general prohibition on all forms of financial assistance, which would preclude the ESM because it is provided outside Article 122(2) TFEU, and so this conclusion is denied by the ECJ.[223] Instead, the Court posits that Article 122(2) proves there are routes for financial assistance which fall *outside* the scope of Article 125 – of which Article 122(2) is merely one.[224] However, the reasoning that financial assistance is already permitted *outside* of Article 125, rather than through exceptions to that rule, is logically impossible: if that were the case, it would be impossible for Article 125 to impose its three substantive conditions on loans, as the Court subsequently finds that it does.[225] This may be explained simply: *expressio unius*, a prohibition whose scope is limited to *guarantees* could not *also* place such restrictions as 'indispensability' and 'strict conditionality' on *loans* if they were outside its scope.

The Court's interpretation of Article 122(2) as a route around, not through, Article 125, also renders Article 122(2) itself redundant.[226]

[218] Palmstorfer, 'To Bail Out', 779.
[219] See Chapter 2, Section 2.3.1.4.
[220] Athanassiou, 'What Is Legally Possible', 569.
[221] See above, Chapter 2, Section 2.3.1.4.
[222] Borger, 'Predicament in *Pringle*' 134; Merino, 'Financial Assistance', 1633; Athanassiou, 'What Is Legally Possible', 561.
[223] Borger, 'Predicament in *Pringle*', 134,
[224] *Pringle* v. *Ireland* [130]–[131].
[225] See above, Section 6.3, nn 198–201 for the conditions.
[226] Palmstorfer, 'To Bail Out', 778.

Article 125(1) contains two identical sentences, one addressed to the Union and one addressed to the Member States. Since both sentences are identical, they must have identical meaning. The only exception to either sentence in the Treaties is Article 122(2) TFEU, which allows only for *Union* financial assistance in circumscribed circumstances. There is no exception for the Member States. But since the sentences are identical, if there is an (unwritten) Article 136(3)-sized hole in the sentence applying to Member States, there must also be an (unwritten) Article 136(3)-sized hole in the sentence applying to the Union. This renders Article 122(2) TFEU redundant because, under Article 122(2), 'The occurrence has to be exceptional and not manageable under any other Treaty provisions.'[227] If there were always a silent (and much broader) exception to the 'no bailout' rule in the Treaty, Article 122(2) has no function.[228] This interpretation violates the rule against surplusage.

AG Kokott offers that perhaps Article 122(2) is a competence provision – a power which the Member States do not need.[229] But this, too, violates the rule against surplusage. If Article 122(2) were a standalone *competence* for Union financial assistance rather than a *lex specialis*, this would render the first sentence of Article 125(1) redundant. This is so because the EU can only ever act within its competences. Why ban *Union* bailouts under Article 125 if they can never be given outside of the conditions of Article 122(2) in the first place?[230] That cannot be correct either.

The better view is that both articles do what they say they do: Article 125(1) applies the same prohibition to both the Member States and the Union, and Article 122(2) creates a *lex specialis* for the Union.[231] If it were otherwise, financial assistance would simply not need to comply with either provision.

Finally, from a teleological viewpoint, the interpretation of the 'no bailout' rule adopted in *Pringle* v. *Ireland* is uncannily reminiscent of Articles 4–4a of the 1990 Commission draft treaty that was roundly rejected at Maastricht for the purpose of budgetary discipline.[232]

---

[227] Louis, 'Guest Editorial', 981.
[228] Beck, 'Continuation of Politics', 240.
[229] *Pringle* v. *Ireland (View of AG Kokott)* [125].
[230] Palmstorfer, 'To Bail Out', 778; Borger, 'Predicament in *Pringle*', 129.
[231] Merino, 'Financial Assistance', 1633; Borger, 'Predicament in *Pringle*' 134; Boris Ryvkin, 'Saving the Euro: Tensions with the European Treaty Law in the European Union's Efforts to Protect the Common Currency' (2012) 45 Cornell Int'l LJ 227, 238; Everson, 'Legal Honesty', 479.
[232] See Chapter 2, Section 2.3.1.4.

Like the first condition set out in paragraphs 137–139 of *Pringle* v. *Ireland*,[233] Article 104a of the Commission draft treaty was based on the narrow interpretation of the 'no bailout' principle, prohibiting only 'the granting [. . .] of an unconditional guarantee in respect of the public debt of a Member State'.[234] Second, like the condition set down at paragraphs 136–137 of *Pringle* v. *Ireland*,[235] the Commission draft treaty permitted financial assistance in the form of loans or budgetary interventions when it was subject to conditionality.[236] Third, like the *ultima ratio* condition in paras 96 and 142 of *Pringle*,[237] the Commission draft treaty stated that financial assistance could only be given where 'a Member State is in difficulties or is seriously threatened with difficulties'.[238] *Pringle* v. *Ireland* appears to have enacted into primary EU law the very interpretation which was rejected and precluded by the Treaty drafters at the creation of the EMU for fiscal discipline.

In any event, putting all that aside, it remains that the ESM violates all three conditions set down in *Pringle* v. *Ireland* for compatibility with Article 125 TFEU.

6.3.2   The ESM Does Not Meet the First Condition Set Down by the ECJ

The first condition set down by the ECJ in *Pringle* v. *Ireland* is that Member States remain subject to the 'logic of the markets when they enter into debt' and responsible for their commitments to their creditors for their existing debts.[239] Neither condition is met by the ESM.

At the outset, the Court offers no account of how the rule that a Member State 'remains responsible for its commitments to its creditors' preserves the 'logic of the markets' at all, especially if all involved know the Member State's debts are backstopped by the ESM.[240] Only AG Kokott offers some explanation, opining that although creditors will, 'as a rule', benefit from a bailout, there remains uncertainty as to whether the assistance will actually lead

---

[233] *Pringle* v. *Ireland* [137]–[139]: financial assistance is lawful where 'the ESM will not act as guarantor of the debts of the recipient Member State'.

[234] Art. 104a of the Draft Treaty in Commission, *Contributions by the Commission*, 43.

[235] *Pringle* v. *Ireland* [136]–[137]: Article 125 does not prohibit forms of financial assistance that are not guarantees where they are subject to financial conditionality.

[236] Art. 104 of the Draft Treaty, excerpted in Chapter 2, Section 2.3.1.4, n 138.

[237] *Pringle* v. *Ireland* [96], [142]: financial assistance may be given where Member States 'are experiencing or are threatened by severe financing problems' or if 'indispensable for the financial stability of the euro area as a whole'.

[238] Art. 104 of the Draft Treaty, excerpted above, Chapter 2, Section 2.3.1.4, n 138.

[239] *Pringle* v. *Ireland* [135], [137]–[139].

[240] Borger, 'Predicament in *Pringle*', 136.

to 'complete or even partial satisfaction of the Member State's creditors'.[241] Setting aside the problem that this is inconsistent on its face (if creditors will 'as a rule' benefit from support to a debtor, then it is inevitably accompanied by a partial satisfaction of those creditors), this description of 'market logic' would surely earn a flunking grade on a sixth-form exam.[242] Most obviously, since a creditor can *never* truly know if a debtor will use new resources to pay off a debt, if transfers did not improve the creditworthiness of a borrower, no other sources of finance (such as taxes, transfers, etc.) would either. But of course they do.[243] As will be shown in Chapter 8, several German *Länder* provide notable examples of being free from the 'logic of the markets' due to what creditors believe is 'a rather straightforward guarantee of subnational debt'.[244] Yet Germany's 'straightforward guarantee' – written in constitutional law – would not be caught by the *Pringle* test: German transfers are provided to *Länder* governments, not their creditors.

Second, it must be recalled that, according to the 1989 Monetary Committee, the purpose of the 'no bailout' rule is to 'ensure that the financial markets [. . .] discipline unsound budgetary policies by imposing differential terms on its paper and *ultimately by refusing to lend*'.[245]

Yet thwarting this objective is written explicitly into the ESM's financial instruments. ESM loans are provided 'where a Member State has lost access to market financing' because lenders will only provide financing 'at excessive prices that would adversely impact the sustainability of public finances.'[246] The objectives of the PMSF/SMSF are 'to allow the ESM Members to maintain or restore their market access',[247] and to provide financing where 'the lack of market liquidity threatens financial stability'.[248] Most acutely, the PCCL/ECCL 'secure the possibility to access ESM assistance *before* they [Member States] face major difficulties raising funds in the capital markets', thereby helping ESM members to

---

[241] *Pringle* v. *Ireland (View of AG Kokott)*, [148], [151]–[152].

[242] See Beck, 'Continuation of Politics', 239 for criticism.

[243] Thomas Courchene, 'Subnational Budgetary and Stabilization Policies in Canada and Australia' in James M Poterba and Jürgen Von Hagen (eds), *Fiscal Institutions and Fiscal Performance* (University of Chicago Press, 1999), 344.

[244] Jonathan Rodden, 'Achieving Fiscal Discipline in Federations: Germany and the EMU' in Deroose et al. (eds), *Fiscal Policy Surveillance*, 151. See Chapter 8, Section 8.2.1.3.

[245] Monetary Committee, EMU Beyond Stage I (1990) (emphasis added).

[246] Art. 16 TESM; Art. 1, ESM Guideline on Loans.

[247] Arts. 17(1) TESM. Art. 1, *ESM Guideline on the PMSF*.

[248] Art. 1, *ESM Guideline on the SMSF*.

'maintain continuous access to market financing' by 'ensuring an adequate safety-net'.[249] In that case, Member States are insulated from market discipline *before* it can even be brought to bear. The ESM's instruments provide financing *exclusively* in situations which the 'logic of the markets' would prohibit.[250]

As though to make an embarrassment of *Pringle* v. *Ireland*, the ESM's website proudly states that 'conditions on the loans from the EFSF and ESM are much more favourable than those in the market'.[251] Indeed. Interest rates on EFSM/EFSF/ESM programmes have been fixed at 'well below market level' and, as the *Bundesbank* finds, 'future incentives for sound public finances were [in fact] weakened'.[252] The first bailout (to Greece) was set at a floating rate of three-month EURIBOR + 300bps for the first three years, and three-month EURIBOR + 400bps thereafter.[253] The second bailout (to Ireland) was set at cost + 292.5bps, with a maximum maturity of 7.5 years.[254] The third bailout (to Portugal) was set at cost + 215bps with a maximum average maturity of 7.5 years.[255] By October 2011, the price of EFSM loans was reduced to cost, while the average maximum maturity was extended – first to 12.5 years (in October 2011), then to 19.5 years (in June 2013).[256] By 2012 and 2013, ESM bailouts to Spain and Cyprus were going for between EURIBOR −0.06% and EURIBOR −0.21%.[257] In July 2015, when Greece was found ineligible to access €7.2bn in its bailout programme, the EFSM gave it a €7.16bn bridge loan at cost + 10bps.[258] Yet it still required debt relief to remain solvent, so its programme has now been

---

[249] Art. 1, *ESM Guideline on the PCCL and ECCL*.

[250] Craig, 'Pringle', 8.

[251] ESM, 'Financial Assistance: Greece' (*ESM*, 2020) www.esm.europa.eu/assistance/greece accessed 29 October 2020.

[252] Deutsche Bundesbank, 'Monthly Report: August 2011', 63.

[253] European Commission, 'Adjustment Programme for Greece', 26.

[254] Arts. 1(5)–(6), Council Implementing Decision 2011/77/EU; IMF, Ireland: Letter of Intent, Memorandum of Economic and Financial Policies, and Technical Memorandum of Understanding (3 December 2010) www.imf.org/external/np/loi/201 0/irl/120310.pdf accessed 2 January 2014.

[255] Art. 1(5) Council Implementing Decision 2011/334/EU.

[256] See sources cited above, Section 6.1.2, nn 26–27.

[257] European Stability Mechanism 'Issue of EURO 12,000,000,000 Floating Rate Notes due December 2015 under the Debt Issuance Programme' (ESM, Final Terms dated 7 December 2012) available at: www.esm.europa.eu/assistance/spain/index.htm accessed 5 November 2015.

[258] See sources cited above, Section 6.1.4, n 39.

amortized to 2060 and EMU countries have now agreed to begin paying Greece to implement reforms it already agreed.[259]

This is not market pricing. Member States received a discount *below the base rate*, 'contradicting both IMF standards and practice'.[260] In an environment of negative interest rates, this is free money – at a cost to the lender. The *Bundesbank* complains:

This weakens the foundations of monetary union, which is based on the principles of national fiscal responsibility and the disciplining effect of capital markets [. . .] assuming the rules continue to be breached, protection from the capital market is ultimately granted at extremely beneficial conditions that were even much more favourable than those for some countries providing assistance.[261]

Finally, the last redoubt of the narrow interpretation is that Article 125 TFEU is, in all circumstances, an absolute prohibition on guarantees where the debtor's liability to the creditor is discharged by the guarantor.[262] Yet this condition, too, is not met by the ESM. As noted in Section 6.1.5 of this chapter, Article 25(2) TESM states that if one or more members fails to meet a capital call, a revised capital call will be made for which the remaining members will be jointly and automatically liable for the unpaid portion.[263] The others are committed, 'irrevocably and unconditionally' to fulfil that obligation.[264] Once that is done, Article 25(3) TESM states that if the defaulting Member State 'settles its debt' to the ESM, the capital 'shall be returned to the other ESM Members' – not the ESM.[265] This is precisely the narrow form of guarantee the ECJ says is prohibited under Article 125 TFEU. If a Member State does not repay the ESM, it never has to – its liability to the ESM is discharged. It may ultimately repay its fellows pursuant to Article 25(3) or it may not, but any money the ESM receives will be given back to its guarantors because they have already paid off its debt. In the narrow sense of the literal interpretation of Article 125 TFEU, they

[259] ESM, 'ESM Programme for Greece: Repayment Schedule' (*ESM*, 2014) www
.esm.europa.eu/assistance/greece accessed 29 October 2020. Francesco Guarascio and Renee Maltezou, 'Greece Gets Debt Relief from Euro Zone' *Reuters* (21 June 2018) www
.reuters.com/article/us-eurozone-greece/greece-gets-debt-relief-from-euro-zone-idUSKBN1JH3FM accessed 22 June 2018.

[260] Zeitler, 'Experience and Adjustments', 248.

[261] Deutsche Bundesbank, 'Monthly Report: August 2011', 64.

[262] *Pringle* v. *Ireland* [137], [144]–[146].

[263] Arts. 8(4), 25(2) TESM.

[264] Arts. 8(4), 9(3) TESM.

[265] Art. 35(3) TESM.

'assume the commitments of' the other Member State to the ESM and 'become liable for' their obligations to the ESM. This does not comply with the narrowest redoubt of *Pringle* v. *Ireland* for legality under Article 125 TFEU.

6.3.3 *The ESM Does Not Meet the Second Condition Set Down by the ECJ*

The second condition set down by the Court is that, in order to fulfil the teleology of budgetary discipline, financial assistance is only lawful '*provided* that the conditions attached to such assistance are *such as to prompt* that Member State to *implement* a sound budgetary policy'.[266]

Once again, the ESM makes something of an embarrassment of this condition. Under PCCL/ECCL guidelines, the only conditions to be met are the normal criteria which apply under the Stability and Growth Pact and, even then, a Member State which is subject to an Excessive Deficit or Excessive Imbalance Procedure 'may still access a PCCL',[267] and an ECCL 'shall be open to ESM Members that do not comply with some of the eligibility criteria'.[268] The SMSF is even worse – it remains 'open to an ESM Member outside of a macro-economic adjustment programme'.[269] It applies *without any financial conditionality at all*.

In short, financial assistance may be issued with no more, and certainly no stricter, measures than apply to Member States which receive no financial assistance whatsoever.[270]

Even where conditions are applied, it can hardly be said that such conditions are sufficient to prompt Member States to '*implement* a sound budgetary policy'.[271] All the fears of the Treaty drafters have come to pass:[272] Conditionality is watered-down by politics and secret deals, including interventions by the Commission;[273] Commission minutes

---

[266] *Pringle* v. *Ireland* [136]–[137].
[267] Art. 2(2)(a)–(c) ESM Guideline on the PCCL and ECCL.
[268] Art. 2(4) ESM Guideline on the PCCL and ECCL.
[269] Art. 2(2) ESM Guideline on the SMSF.
[270] See also Art. 7(12) Reg 472/2013: the EU's obligation to impose conditionality does not apply to 'any new ESM financial instrument for which the ESM rules do not provide for a macroeconomic adjustment programme'.
[271] *Pringle* v. *Ireland* [136]–[137].
[272] See discussion in Chapter 2, Section 2.3.1.4.
[273] Francesco Guarascio, 'EU gives Budget Leeway to France "Because It Is France" – Juncker' *Reuters* (Brussels 31 May 2016) www.reuters.com/article/eu-deficit-france-idUSL8N18S3PL accessed 31 May 2016; Dariusz Adamski, *Redefining European Economic Integration* (Cambridge University Press, 2018), 62–63.

enunciate a 'political approach' to applying EU fiscal rules;[274] and the cost of financial assistance has fallen from EURIBOR + 400bps and a maturity of 7.5 years to EURIBOR −21bps, with amortizations kicked to 2058. Where a country fails to meet terms, it will not be cut off – it will receive a bridge loan at cost + 10bps and debt relief. Leaked IMF minutes lament that, due to Commission interference, EU bailout conditions are not credible – disbursements will be made even if conditions are not met – and that this has, *in fact*, reduced the impetus to follow sound budgetary policy.[275]

6.3.4   The ESM Does Not Meet the Third Condition Set Down by the ECJ

The final condition set out in *Pringle* v. *Ireland* is an *ultima ratio* one: 'the activation of financial assistance by means of [. . .] the ESM is not compatible with Article 125 TFEU unless it is indispensable for the financial stability of the euro area as a whole'.[276]

There is no textual basis in the Treaty for this condition. Instead, this *ultima ratio* condition implies that, where financial assistance is indispensable for the stability of the euro area, an act which would normally breach the teleology of fiscal discipline suddenly does not. Athanassiou, a proponent of this interpretation, explains that because market discipline would result in the default of an over-indebted Member State in a crisis (rather than sustainability) the logic of the 'no bailout' rule is 'suspended' during a threat to sovereign solvency, and bailouts which would ordinarily be prohibited are suddenly allowed.[277]

But this makes little sense. If Article 125 TFEU only applies up until the moment that some final, marginal decision pushes a country's liabilities over the edge of sustainability, the failure to conduct prudent policy would lead, in every case, to the mutualization for the liabilities accrued. It is *only* in such circumstances that the 'no-bailout' rule has

---

[274] European Commission, 'Minutes of the 2111th Meeting', 18.

[275] See: Meeting minutes between the head of the IMF's European Department (Poul Poulsen) and the IMF's Mission to Greece (Delia Velkouleskou), excerpted as follows: 'THOMSON: They [Greece] are not on track to meet the criteria. That is the whole point. They essentially need to agree to make our targets the baseline [. . .] but if they don't, they will still disburse. Right? VELKOULESKOU: Yeah, that's right. [. . .] I think actually politically for them [the Greeks] it is possible to give on both of these things [conditionality]. But they don't have any incentive [to agree conditionality] and they know that the Commission is willing to compromise, so that is the problem.' Delia Velkouleskou, Poul Thomsen and Iva Petrova, 'Transcript of 9 March 2016 IMF Teleconference on Greece' (Wikileaks Release: 2 April 2016).

[276] *Pringle* v. *Ireland* [136]. See: Art. 12(1) TESM.

[277] Athanassiou, 'What Is Legally Possible', 561–562.

a function, since it is *only* the possibility of default which causes interest rates to rise.[278]

But the veracity of this condition does not much matter because, once again, the ESM does not meet it. The PCCL/ECCL facilities, for example, will '*support sound policies* and *prevent* crisis situations' by allowing ESM members 'access to ESM assistance *before* they face major difficulties raising funds in the capital markets' and to 'maintain *continuous access to market financing* by reinforcing the credibility of their macroeconomic performance'.[279] The PCCL, ECCL and SMSF facilities can only be activated 'where the economic and financial situation is still fundamentally sound' and where there is an *absence* of bank solvency problems that would 'pose systemic threats to the stability of the euro area banking system'.[280]

In short, these instruments may *only* be issued in circumstances in which they are *not* indispensable to safeguard the stability of the Euro Area as a whole.

6.4   Conclusion: Conditional Financial Assistance Is Not Compatible with the Treaties

As a matter of EU law, *Pringle* v. *Ireland* supplants a legal pillar of decentralized fiscal federalism (an entrenched 'no bailout' law) with a legal pillar of unitary states: centralized fiscal transfers and governance of sub-federal economic and fiscal competences. The conclusion of this chapter is that conditional financial assistance is simply not reconcilable with the legal architecture for fiscal discipline inscribed in the Treaties.

[6.2] The new legal architecture of conditional financial assistance is fundamentally incompatible with the allocation of competences under the Treaties. There is but one avenue for financial assistance in the 'Economic Policy' Chapter of the TFEU – Article 122(2) – and this is preclusive of any other mechanisms as a matter of law, whether Member State or EU competence. There is no way to reconcile the EFSM, EFSF, ESM and OMT with the division of competences for

---

[278] Beck, 'Continuation of Politics', 240; Palmstorfer, 'To Bail Out', 777.
[279] Art. 1 *ESM Guideline on the PCCL and ECCL* (emphasis added).
[280] Art. 2, ESM Guideline on the SMSF; Art. 2(2) *ESM Guideline on the PCCL and ECCL* (emphasis added).

economic and monetary policy according to the analytical framework set out by the ECJ.

[6.3] The legal architecture of conditional financial assistance is incompatible with Articles 122–125 TFEU. [6.3.1] The interpretation of Article 125 TFEU in *Pringle* v. *Ireland* hearkens to a 'conditional bailouts' rule that was rejected by the Treaty drafters at Maastricht, and the ESM does not comply with any of the conditions set down by the ECJ: [6.3.2] Member States are *not* subject to the 'logic of the markets' when they enter into debt and the TESM *does* contain a guarantee that discharges the liability of the debtor; [6.3.3] financial assistance is *not* subject to strict conditionality such as to preserve budgetary discipline; and [6.3.4] it is given where it is *not* indispensable for the stability of the euro area as a whole.

The inability to genuinely reconcile the ESM's legal framework with the Treaties provides the first testable indication that conditional financial assistance has exceeded the architecture of fiscal federalism inscribed in the Treaty, and is now dependent on the continuous acquiescence of Member State *ultra vires* and constitutional identity jurisdictions. Proof for this proposition is found in *Gauweiler (Germany)* and *Weiss (Germany)*, in which the BVerfG ruled that the ECJ's analytical framework failed to resolve the 'overlap' between the ESM, OMT and PSPP, and concluded that the latter two instruments do, in fact, exceed the boundaries of Member State economic policy, placing conditions on the operation of the OMT,[281] and ruling the PSPP *ultra vires* altogether.[282] Further proof is found in the string of 2011 ESM rulings in which the German, Irish, Austrian, Finnish, Polish and Estonian constitutional courts and committees duly subjected the ESM to their own constitutional tests for fiscal sovereignty, capping financial dispositions to the extent of national parliamentary authorization – despite the fact that the ECJ did not read any such limits into the TESM in *Pringle* v. *Ireland*.[283] Despite permissive interpretations by the ECJ from the internal perspective of EU law, conditional financial assistance has clearly come up against the constitutional boundaries identified in Part I of this book.

This is significant, for several reasons. First and most obviously, the tests for fiscal sovereignty defined in Part I entail that national

---

[281] *Gauweiler Decision (Germany)* [174], [200], [205]–[207] and [196]: 'The restrictive parameters developed by the Court of Justice do not completely remove the character of the OMT programme insofar as it encroaches upon economic policy.'

[282] *Weiss Decision (Germany).*

[283] For these cases see Chapter 1, Section 1.3.1, nn 473–480. Cf: *Pringle* v. *Ireland* [144]–[146].

parliaments must retain final legal authority over financial contributions to other Member States – and this includes the capacity to withdraw from the TESM or, if necessary, to withhold capital calls.[284] This
means that markets cannot price risk on the assumption that the EU's
keystone fiscal backstop will be able to extract the necessary capital
calls from its members in a crisis. The fact that the ESM is already
'massively over-collateralized' and yet has not won an overall AAA
rating constitutes evidence of this.[285]

Second, the lending capacity of the ESM cannot be assumed to have
any increased capacity beyond its €500bn lending capacity because no
parliament has authorized an increase to the €700bn in authorized
capital. This means that markets will always be able to price the limits
of the EU's fiscal backstop, putting the ESM itself at risk of downgrades
in anything greater than a middling financial crisis.[286] As modelling by
Bauer and Herz concludes, 'the ESM is likely to act as a crisis accelerant
rather than a stabilizer in the most likely case of requests for medium-
sized financial supports from distressed ESM members at a time when
other ESM countries might be unwilling or unable to provide new
capital'.[287] Incidences such as Moody's 2012 downgrade of the ESM
due to 'the high correlation in credit risk which Moody's believes is
present among the [ESM]'s largest financial supporters' (i.e. France)
offer further evidence of this.[288]

Third, the Commission's 2017 proposal to bring the ESM into the EU
legal order as an EMF through an amendment under Article 352 TFEU
would have also faltered on these boundaries. This is so, first, because
Article 352 TFEU cannot serve as a basis for the widening of EU
powers,[289] and the EMF would require an extension of EU competence
into economic policy, *contra* the ruling in *Pringle* v. *Ireland* that the ESM is

---

[284] See the three tests and sources cited in Chapter 1, Section 1.3.1.1, at nn 482–484.
[285] Bauer and Herz, 'Reforming the ESM', 637, 643: 'as indicated by the current sub-AAA
rating and time-varying ESM rating, markets obviously do not entirely trust ESM
member states to honour in full their obligation to provide callable capital'.
[286] Bauer and Herz, 'Reforming the ESM', 646.
[287] Bauer and Herz, 'Reforming the ESM', 636. See also EEAG Report 2011, 33.
[288] Moody's, 'Rating Action Moody's Downgrades ESM' (*Moody's*, 30 November 2012) www
.moodys.com/research/Moodys-downgrades-ESM-to-Aa1-from-Aaa-and-EFSF-
to-PR_261114 accessed 15 September 2016.
[289] Opinion 2/94 *Accession of the Community to the ECHR* [1996] ECR I-1781; EU:C:1996:143
[30]; *EU Accession to the ECHR*, [38]. See Hannes Hofmeister, 'European Monetary Fund –
The Commission's Proposal to Establish a European Monetary Fund: A Critical
Analysis' (2018) 5 ALJ 139, 153–154.

Member State competence.[290] Second, the EMF proposal would require the assumption of parliamentary competences over the amount and use of financial resources, imbuing ESM financial obligations with the supremacy of EU law under the ultimate judicial control of the ECJ – and this is contrary to Member State fiscal sovereignty and constitutional identity jurisprudence.[291] In December 2018, the Euro Summit decided not to integrate the ESM into the EU legal order.[292]

All of this is to say that there simply isn't a constitutional basis for a credible financial assistance backstop in the EU. Models which depend on this will not be suitable for EU fiscal federalism as a matter of economics or of law. More concerningly, the inability to reconcile these instruments with the allocation of competences and substantive legal architecture in the Treaties provides the first testable indication that the new model now being pursued is likely to be incompatible with deeper constitutional fault lines running beneath the boundaries of the Treaty. This leads to the two remaining hypotheses tested in the final chapters of this book:

[Chapter 7] Instruments of conditional financial assistance and centralized legal governance, being incompatible with the boundaries of the Treaty architecture in the realm of fiscal competence, must not conform to the deeper constitutional boundaries of fiscal sovereignty underlying the EU legal order as a whole; and

[Chapter 8] Financial assistance and centralized legal governance, being incompatible with the Treaty architecture for hard budget constraints and market discipline in Articles 121–127 TFEU, must not conform to the institutional requirements for price stability, budgetary discipline and sustainable balance of payments as a matter of fiscal federalism theory.

---

[290] *Pringle* v. *Ireland* [64]–[68], [105], [120]

[291] It has not helped that the Commission has watered-down the voting requirements in the ESM and given EU institutions a say in negotiating conditionality and approving financial assistance: Hofmeister, 'European Monetary Fund', 146–148, 154–155.

[292] Euro Summit meeting 14 December 2018 – statement (EURO 503/18). See further: Hofmeister, 'ESM to EMF'.

7   The Constitutional Boundaries of Member State Fiscal Sovereignty

The preceding analysis found that the legal architecture of conditional financial assistance does not conform to the allocation of competences in Articles 2(3), 3(1)(c) and 5(1) TFEU, and does not conform to the substantive provisions for fiscal discipline and price stability under Articles 119–127 TFEU. The purpose of this chapter is to examine the new legal architecture of EU economic governance against deeper constitutional boundaries underlying the EU legal order as a whole.

This is necessary because the design of fiscal federalism inscribed in the Treaties since Maastricht established an incentive framework for – yet remained hived-off from – the economic and social competences of Europe's constitutional democracies. As shown in Chapter 2, Articles 121–126 TFEU were drafted to internalize the costs of economic policy choices under hard budget constraints and market discipline, and so obviate the need to govern them. The abrogation of the 'no bailout' clause has ruptured this barrier. As Chalmers observes, 'Provision has now been made for unlimited fiscal transfers between the euro-area states.'[1] To stem the dysfunctional cost incentives identified in Chapter 3 and make this model 'work', EU legislation has stretched athwart the gap between legal orders and made amendments directly to national budgetary laws. It is now centralized legal governance, not decentralized market discipline, which is tasked with ensuring budgetary discipline and economic stability in the EU.[2]

Yet the hypothesis of this book is that systems of fiscal federalism which substitute decentralized market discipline for centralized legal

---

[1] Chalmers, 'Law of Struggle', 667.
[2] Kelemen and Teo, 'Focal Points', 365; Fabbrini, 'Paradox', 22.

governance and fiscal transfers are not compatible with deeper constitutional boundaries of fiscal sovereignty underlying the EU legal order. If that is correct, the instruments established by the EU for this task are likely to exceed the EU Treaties and intrude on constitutional boundaries set out in Member State *Kompetenz-Kompetenz* and constitutional identity jurisprudence. Such instruments may be unenforceable against EU Member States as written under EU law, and therefore illusory or ineffective as stable structures of European fiscal federalism. In pursuance of that hypothesis, this chapter conducts a piece-by-piece deconstruction of the economic governance framework to identify EU legal instruments that trespass on a previously set or acknowledged boundary by the CJEU or a constitutional court, and are therefore placed in legal territory subject to *ultra vires* or constitutional identity jurisdictions – and vulnerable to repudiation by Europe's constitutional courts.

The conclusion of this chapter is that the new model of EU fiscal federalism is comprehensively dependent, for its stable functioning, on instruments which are manifestly beyond the boundaries of the EU legal order and perhaps may exist only in so far as they are not actually enforced as the binding and supreme EU law they appear to be. Fully seven out of the eight legal mechanisms examined in this chapter contain at least one instrument which exceeds the EU legal order and professes to bind national constitutional organs in the exercise of their exclusive economic competences, contrary to Member State *Kompetenz-Kompetenz* and fiscal sovereignty jurisprudence.

At the outset, it should be noted that this analysis is not concerned with instruments that raise the costs of poor economic choices through fines or financial sanctions, but which are not legally binding as a matter of *law*. Binding legal force will be defined here as legal obligations which acquire the force of the supremacy of EU law, are capable of giving rise to infringement proceedings under Articles 258–260 TFEU, and so are capable of supplanting Member State economic policy by legal decree (not merely financial penalty).[3] The criteria for identifying such an act is simple: the failure to take the legislated-for economic policy decision will, in principle, lead to a breach of (directly applicable and supreme) EU law.

---

[3] This is narrower than hard law in the positivist sense: Case C-16/16 P *Belgium v. Commission (Gaming Recommendation)* EU:C:2017:959 (Opinion of AG Bobek), [74].

The acts which concern this chapter occur along two dimensions: The horizontal allocation of competences and the vertical penetration of EU law into parliamentary domains of fiscal policy.

First, when measured along the horizontal dimension, EU economic governance no longer bears any resemblance to the legislative competences of the Union. Under the MSP/EDP, budgetary surveillance has expanded from the simple tabulation of the 3% and 60% debt limits to line-by-line analyses of the whole panoply of economic, social and welfare decisions which constitute that balance. Further, the introduction of the MIP/EIP has brought virtually all aspects of economic and social policy within reach of 'hard law' disciplines of EU sanctioning procedures, such that the lines are increasingly blurred between the task of tabulating budgetary sums and fine-tuning the national economy.[4] Once these procedures are activated, Member States will receive highly specific, sanction-backed policy recommendations in areas for which there is little doubt the Union has no competence to legislate. Sanction-backed economic recommendations do not distinguish between policy fields in which the EU has some competence, such as energy policy, and those which would clearly be *ultra vires* at EU level (such as direct taxation).[5] They do not differentiate between those policies which fall under EU legislation (such as fisheries) and those which do not (such as education).[6] They do not even differentiate between those with cross-border effects (such as foreign investment), and those that exclusively concern the internal organization of the social state (such as the relocation of social housing).[7] Nor do they contain any assessments of subsidiarity. As Bekker warns, the wrapping-together of policy fields that fall Treaty-wise within different competences and modes of action suggests the EU could be penetrating domains of Member State fiscal sovereignty via the back door of economic coordination.[8]

---

[4] All CSRs include the following caveat: 'In order to take account of their interlinkages, the two programmes [economic and fiscal programmes] have been assessed at the same time.'

[5] See, for example, Council Recommendation of 14 July 2015 on the 2015 National reform Programme of Italy and delivering a Council opinion on the 2015 Stability programme of Italy [2015] OJ C 272/16.

[6] See, for example, Council Recommendation of 8 July 2014 on the National Reform Programme of 2014 of Italy and delivering a Council opinion on the Stability Programme of Italy, 2014 [2014] OJ C 247/11.

[7] Council Recommendation of 14 July 2015 on the 2015 National Reform Programme of the United Kingdom and delivering a Council opinion on the 2015 Stability Programme of the United Kingdom [2015] OJ C 272/06.

[8] Sonja Bekker, 'EU Coordination of Welfare States after the Crisis: Further Interconnecting Soft and Hard law' (2014) 19 Int Rev Public Adm 296, 297.

Second, when measured by their vertical legal effects, many of these instruments appear to conflict with tests laid out for democratic legitimation under Member State constitutional identity jurisprudence. In *ESM (Germany)*, for example, the BVerfG stated that an intrusion into 'fundamental fiscal decisions on public revenue and public expenditure [and] decisions on the shaping of the social state' would violate the constitutional identity of Germany.[9] In that case it ruled that the TSCG did not do this because it 'does not grant the European Commission authority to impose specific substantive requirements for the structuring of budgets'.[10] Other constitutional courts have ruled on similar lines.[11] Yet granting authority to impose specific substantive requirements for the structuring of budgets is the stated objective of several EU law instruments enacted since that decision.[12] Norms produced under the EU's 'coordination' competence no longer resemble the 'soft law' coordination framework of the OMC. Instead, the new framework 'in many ways entails a return to "command and control" regulation' that stretches beyond democratic accountability under either the community or intergovernmental method.[13] Scholars sifting through the framework repeatedly find structures which appear 'remarkably a-legal',[14] suffer from 'legitimacy gaps',[15] or fall into 'grey zones' between national and EU law.[16] As Menéndez remarks, 'all these changes imply a clear break from the Maastricht "model" [...] it is hard to keep on affirming that Member States retain the power to conduct their fiscal policy autonomously'.[17]

If that is so, it poses a basic challenge to the boundaries of conferral and fiscal sovereignty upon which the legitimation of EU law depends.[18]

---

[9] *ESM II (Germany)*, [164].

[10] *ESM II (Germany)*, [244].

[11] *TSCG (France)* [26]–[27]; *TSCG (Austria)* [5.3]–[5.5.1], [6.4]; *TCSG (Belgium)*, [B.8.4].

[12] See, for example, rr (2), (12) and Art. 1(c) of Reg 473/2013; r (19) of Directive 2011/85/EU (excerpted below, Section 7.2.1, at n 54); European Commission, Economic Governance Review' COM(2014) 905 final, 4. See further below, Sections 7.2.2 and 7.3.2.

[13] Pernice, 'Domestic Courts', 313; Chalmers, 'Law of Struggle', 683; Chiti and Pedro, 'Constitutional Implications', 684–685; Hinarejos, *Constitutional Perspective*, 88.

[14] Chalmers, 'Law of Struggle', 682.

[15] Alexandre De Streel, 'EU Fiscal Governance and the Effectiveness of Its Reform' in Adams, Fabbrini and Larouche (eds), *Constitutionalization of European Budgetary Constraints* (Hart, 2014), 101.

[16] Mark Dawson, 'The Legal and Political Accountability Structure of 'Post-Crisis' EU Economic Governance' (2015) 53 JCMS 976, 984.

[17] Menéndez, 'Constitutional Mutation', 129.

[18] Peter Lindseth, 'Power and Legitimacy in the Eurozone: Can Integration and Democracy be Reconciled?' in Adams, Fabbrini and Larouche (eds), *Constitutionalization of European Budgetary Constraints*, 390.

European constitutions do not authorize the 'a-legal' exercise of power, and there are no 'gaps' between constitutional orders. Each boundary of EU competence is, in principle, a border with national constitutional law. In economic policy, this means fiscal sovereignty – the core of constitutional identity.

This chapter proceeds as follows: Section 7.1 begins with a brief overview of the European governance procedures as they operate at EU level. Section 7.2 then examines EU legislation governing Member State budgetary frameworks. Section 7.3 examines binding interlinkages with EU fiscal governance regimes, and Section 7.4 follows by examining binding interlinkages with EU macroeconomic governance regimes. Section 7.5 concludes by examining the EU legal architecture governing conditional financial assistance.

7.1   Overview of Economic and Fiscal Governance Procedures at EU Level

The economic governance architecture consists of five integrated procedures: The European Semester; the Multilateral Surveillance Procedure (MSP); the Excessive Deficit Procedure (EDP); the Macroeconomic Imbalance Procedure and Excessive Imbalance Procedure (MIP/EIP); and financial conditionality under the EFSM/EFSF/ESM. Throughout these procedures, EU institutions generate policy outputs (in the form of MoUs, recommendations, decisions or opinions) that are established, incorporated or enforced through a constellation of secondary EU legislation under the 'six pack', 'two pack' and 'Stability and Growth Pact'. The design of these mechanisms at EU level can seem, at times, almost intentionally abstruse, but for now it simplifies matters to state that each of these procedures are designed to enshrine and enforce a core obligation at EU level.

[7.2] The first procedure is the European Semester, an annual surveillance and coordination cycle that fully integrates the MSP/EDP/MIP/EIP and Member State budgetary frameworks into a single integrated timeline for the evaluation and approval of budgetary plans.[19] Member States must submit annual Stability and Convergence Programmes (SCPs) setting out medium-term fiscal plans and National Reform Programmes (NRPs)

---

[19] Art. 2-a Reg 1466/97; Art. 4 Reg 473/2013.

concerning structural reforms by 20 April each year;[20] submit their draft budgetary plans for approval by 15 October;[21] and, if approved, adopt the budget by 31 December each year.[22] If the Commission finds that the budget is in 'particularly serious non-compliance' with the recommendations of the Commission and Council, it will give an opinion to that effect and request that the budget be redrafted.[23] The central obligation under the European Semester is for Member States to 'take due account of the guidance addressed to them in the development of their economic, employment and budgetary policies *before* taking key decisions on their national budgets for the succeeding years'.[24] Previously, the only duties to 'take due account' under the SGP applied to the Union's discretion.[25]

[7.3] The second procedure is the Multilateral Surveillance Procedure (MSP). The central obligation under the MSP is to comply with the country-specific Medium-Term Objective (MTO).[26] The MTO is a three-year target for the structural deficit set within a prescribed range of -1% of GDP and balance or surplus,[27] with a per annum reduction of 0.5% of GDP in the cyclically adjusted structural deficit as a benchmark, net of one-off and temporary measures.[28] In order to support the MTO, Member States must also now comply with an expenditure benchmark linked to

---

[20] SCPs, NRPs and medium-term fiscal plans may all be the same document: Arts. 2-a(2)(d), 3(3) and 7(3) Reg 1466/97; Art. 4(1) Reg 473/2013.

[21] Art. 6(1) Reg 473/2013. See also Arts. 3(2), 3(3) Reg 479/2009.

[22] Art. 7 Reg 473/2013.

[23] Art. 7(2) Reg 473/2014.

[24] Art. 2-a(3) Reg 1466/97.

[25] See Council Regulation (EC) No 1056/05 on speeding up and clarifying the implementation of the excessive deficit procedure [2005] OJ L 174/5, r (6). An EU law obligation to 'take due account' is capable of binding decision-makers, such that legislation which precludes due account of those factors may be set aside for inconsistency: Case C-427/12 *Commission v. European Parliament* EU:C:2014:170 [46]–[52]; Case C-481/14 *Hansson v. Jungpflanzen Grünewald GmbH* EU:C:2016:419 [37]–[40]; *Belgium v. Commisssion (Gaming Recommendation)* (AG Bobek), [99]–[100].

[26] Art. 2a Reg 1466/97.

[27] The TSCG further constricts this to an MTO of better than -0.5% of GDP for its signatories, unless the debt-to-GDP ratio is significantly below the 60% threshold and risks to long-term sustainability are low: Arts. 3(1b), (1d) TSCG.

[28] If the Member State is within three years of an EDP, the adjustment path will be the cyclically adjusted minimum linear structural adjustment (MLSA) necessary to ensure compliance by the end of the three-year transition period. See: Art. 5 1466/97; Art. 3 1467/97; Specifications of the Council of 5 July 2016 on the implementation of the Stability and Growth Pact and Guidelines on the format and content of Stability and Convergence Programmes, accessible at: https://ec.europa.eu/economy_finance/eco nomic_governance/sgp/pdf/coc/code_of_conduct_en.pdf accessed December 8 2019, 9.

potential GDP growth.[29] A 'significant observed deviation' from the MTO (generally defined as a deviation of >0.5% of GDP)[30] triggers new sanctioning mechanisms under the MSP, which may result in more specific recommendations, enhanced surveillance, a declaration of 'no effective action', and sanctions.[31] This is linked to further legal effects under rules legislated into national budgetary frameworks by Directive 2011/85/EU, Regulation 473/2013, and the TSCG, each examined in Section 7.3.

[7.3] The third procedure is the Excessive Deficit Procedure (EDP), or the 'corrective' arm of the SGP. Under the EDP, Member States must comply with two variables. First, they must comply with the 3% of GDP deficit limit in Article 126(2)(a) TFEU, unless either: (i) the ratio has declined substantially and continuously and reached a level that comes close to 3%; or (ii) the excess over 3% is 'exceptional and temporary' and the ratio remains 'close' to 3%.[32] Second, they must comply with the 60% of GDP debt limit unless the ratio is 'sufficiently diminishing' and approaching 60% at a 'satisfactory pace'.[33]

[7.4] The fourth is the MIP/EIP. The core duty under the MIP/EIP is to correct 'macroeconomic imbalances' and 'excessive imbalances'. Macroeconomic imbalances are 'any trend giving rise to macroeconomic developments which are adversely affecting, or have the potential adversely to affect, the proper functioning of the economy of a Member State or of the [EMU] or of the Union as a whole'.[34] Excessive imbalances are 'severe imbalances, including imbalances that jeopardize or risks jeopardising the proper functioning of the economic and monetary union'.[35]

[7.5] The fifth is the legal architecture governing macroeconomic adjustment programmes for EFSM, EFSF or ESM financial assistance. All EFSM/EFSF/ESM conditionality has now been institutionalized in the EU legal order under Regulation 472/2013. The core duty which applies under Regulation 472/2013 is to implement macroeconomic adjustment programmes that in turn must be 'fully consistent with' the

---

[29] Arts. 5(1)(a)–(b), 9(1)(a)–(b) Reg 1466/97.
[30] Arts. 6(2), 10(2) Reg 1466/97.
[31] Arts. 2-a(3), 2-ab(2), 6(2), 9(2), 10(2), 11 Reg 1466/97; Arts. 4(1), 5 Reg 1173/2011.
[32] Art. 1, Protocol (no 12) on the excessive deficit procedure; Art. 2(2) Reg 1467/97. See also: Arts. 3(1)(c),(d) TSCG.
[33] A 'satisfactory pace' is the differential between actual debt and the 60% reference value at a rate of 1/20th per annum. 'Sufficiently diminishing' means an annual improvement in the cyclically-adjusted budget balance of 0.5% of GDP. Art. 2(1a) Reg 1467/97; Council, Specifications on the SGP, 9.
[34] Art. 2(1) Reg 1176/2011.
[35] Art. 2 Reg 1176/2001.

outputs of EU institutions issued in the above procedures.[36] Financial conditionality is enacted into EU Council decisions or Council implementing decisions and then fed into the procedures of the MSP/EDP/MIP/EIP.[37]

Compliance with each of these core duties is enforced at EU level through the successive, ratcheting procedures of the European Semester, MSP, EDP and MIP/EIP. Each stage of these procedures is accompanied by the issuance of detailed, sanction-backed economic policy recommendations adopted by the Commission or Council under Articles 121(2), 121(4), 126(3) and 126(5)–(9) TFEU.[38]

As the EU has no competence in economic policy, all of these procedures' rules are legislated, interpreted, monitored and enforced under the Union's 'coordination competence' in Articles 2(3) and 5(1) TFEU, upon the legal bases of Articles 121(6) TFEU and 126(14) TFEU.

Article 126(14) TFEU provides a legal basis for the adoption of rules and definitions for the application of the Protocol on the EDP – a sanctioning procedure at EU level.

Article 121(6) TFEU empowers the Council to adopt regulations setting out detailed rules for two stages of the MSP – Commission monitoring under Article 121(3) TFEU and Council recommendations under Article 121(4) TFEU.

The limits of this competence must be emphasized at the outset: The EU has no competence to set national economic and fiscal policy objectives, amend national budgetary processes, or determine the composition of revenues and expenditures.[39] Neither the Treaty debt targets nor the policies recommended to meet them are legally binding. Excessive deficits and debts above 3% or 60% of GDP are *not* prohibited under EU law – Article 126(10) TFEU is clear that infringement proceedings cannot be initiated for breach of the debt limits[40] – and the obligations to adhere to the MTO or correct 'imbalances' are found nowhere in the Treaties.

Under this division of competences, surveillance and sanctions under EU law are justified because they set a political incentive framework for, yet are hived off from, the economic and social competences of Europe's

---

[36] Art. 7(2) Reg 472/2013.
[37] Art. 7 Reg 472/2013; Art. 3 Reg 407/2010; Art. 13(3)–(5) TESM.
[38] See Section 7.3.4 on the operation of sanctions at EU level.
[39] See sources cited above, in Methods and Introduction, n 24.
[40] Art. 126(10) TFEU states: 'The rights to bring actions provided for in Articles 258 and 259 may not be exercised within the framework of paragraphs 1 to 9 of this Article.' See further Chapter 2, Sections 2.3.2–2.3.3 and Hahn, 'Constant Legal Duty', 85.

constitutional democracies.[41] That a national debt should become more costly at 60% of GDP is a political agreement inscribed in the Treaty as a clarion for markets and electorates; whether this should give way to healthcare or schooling (or be heeded at all) is for the national parliament to decide. There is, in principle, no violation of the European legal order in so far as EU economic policy prescriptions do not take on legal effects, and a failure to implement them cannot lead to infringement proceedings. As Dawson explains:

> So long as [country-specific recommendations] are simply 'recommendations,' their legal effects, and therefore their capacity to override limits prescribed in EU/national constitutional orders, is limited. [...] The 'soft' coordination of national policies at the European level is justified so long as it operates parallel to, rather than supplants, the ordinary legislative process.[42]

However, the below analysis will show that, far from mere fines and coordination at EU level, the machineries picked apart in this chapter are underpinned by a webwork of binding interlinkages which have stretched athwart the gap between legal orders and made amendments directly to national budgetary frameworks so as to bind them to EU governance systems. Under the constellation of EU legislation examined in this chapter, economic recommendations are no longer merely advisory, and the EU's economic 'coordination' procedures no longer operate parallel to the ordinary legislative process. The border between EU and national competence is now criss-crossed with legal sutures that bind national budgetary outcomes to EU processes, rules, recommendations and policy outputs.

7.2   Binding Vertical Interlinkages with the European Semester

The first interlinkages dissected here are two complex legal machineries capable of imbuing the European Semester and its outputs with binding force in Member State budgetary frameworks.

[7.2.1] First, a constellation of provisions under Directive 2011/85/EU,[43] Regulation 473/2013,[44] and Regulation 479/2009[45] (as amended

---

[41] Francesco Costamanga, 'The Impact of Stronger Economic Policy Co-ordination on the European Social Dimension: Issues of Legitimacy' in Adams, Fabbrini and Larouche (eds), *Constitutionalization of European Budgetary Constraints*, 360.

[42] Dawson, 'Accountability Structure', 986.

[43] Arts. 1–14 Directive 2011/85/EU; Arts. 2a-7 Reg 1466/97.

[44] Arts. 3–4, 6 Reg 473/2013.

[45] Arts. 9–15 Reg 479/2009.

in 2015)[46] aim to ensure that the Commission's technical definitions, forecasted outcomes and calculated MTO are automatically reproduced in national law and internalized into the budgetary process. As will be shown, these constrain the choices of national budgetary decision-makers both *ex ante*, at the stage of policy formulation, and *ex post*, at the stage of budgetary legislation.

[7.2.2] The second machinery studied here is what is referred-to as the 'budgetary veto'. This has two components. First, in near-identical terms, Articles 3, 4 and 6 of Regulation 473/2013 state that Member State budgetary procedures, medium-term budgetary plans and draft budgetary plans 'shall be consistent with', *inter alia*, all recommendations and opinions issued under Regulation 1466/97 (the MSP), Regulation 1467/97 (the EDP), Regulation 1176/2011 (the MIP/EIP) and Regulation 473/2013. Second, under Article 7(2) of Regulation 473/2013, if the Commission identifies 'particularly serious non-compliance' with those obligations, it will deliver an 'Opinion' requesting that the budget be re-drafted. As Regulation 473/2013 cannot be interpreted in such a way that a national budget can be both 'consistent with' EU recommendations (for the purposes of Articles 3, 4 and 6) and in 'serious non-compliance with' those same EU recommendations (for the purposes of Article 7(2)), a failure to take the legislated-for decision will, as will be shown, result in a technical breach of directly applicable secondary EU law.

7.2.1   EU Legislation Binds Budgetary Frameworks to EU Macrofiscal Assessments

The first architecture is a webwork of EU legislation that automatically circumscribes budgetary objectives and policy choices in the context of the European Semester.

The backbone of this webwork is Directive 2011/85/EU. Applicable to all Member States, Directive 2011/85/EU lays down detailed rules governing national medium-term budgetary frameworks;[47] statistical and accounting rules;[48] rules and procedures governing economic forecasts;[49]

---

[46] Council Reg (EU) 2015/759 of 29 April 2015 amending Reg (EC) No 223/2009 on European Statistics [2015] OJ L 123/90.

[47] Medium-term budgetary frameworks are 'the set of arrangements, procedures, rules and institutions that underlie the conduct of budgetary policies of general government'. Art. 2 Directive 2011/85/EU.

[48] Art. 3 Directive 2011/85/EU.

[49] Art. 4 Directive 2011/85/EU.

numerical fiscal rules;[50] the budgetary enactment process;[51] the setting of policy priorities and MTOs;[52] and the establishment of independent fiscal councils.[53] It intends, in no uncertain terms, to bind Member States to EU-legislated frameworks, rules, assessments and macrofiscal outcomes. Recital 19 states:

Medium-term budgetary frameworks are strictly instrumental in ensuring that budgetary frameworks of the Member States are *consistent with the legislation of the Union*.[54]

Traditionally, EU legislation requiring Member States to produce or harmonize technical outputs are justified because either: (a) the data is necessary for the exercise of one of the *competences of the Union*;[55] or (b) the data merely informs national policymakers under *non-binding coordination mechanisms* at EU level.[56] The machinery of technical legislation picked apart in this section is different. Directive 2011/85/EU and its accompanying instruments have implanted binding interlinkages with EU procedures into national law in a manner that can automatically define policy choices.

At the centre of this framework is the MTO. As will be shown, the MTO takes on both constitutional and 'hard law' effects in national law under a webwork of EU law instruments and the TSCG.[57] Yet the MTO is a numerical value calculated according to a mathematical formula at EU level. This means the objective of the budget is the numerical sum of the numbers put into it – not the outcome of political choice by elected officials. As the EU Statistical Programme states:

---

[50] Arts. 5–6 Directive 2011/85/EU.
[51] Arts. 9–14 Directive 2011/85/EU.
[52] Arts. 9–10 Directive 2011/85/EU.
[53] Arts. 12–14 Directive 2011/84/EU.
[54] Recital 19, Directive 2011/85/EU (emphasis added).
[55] For example, Art. 388 TFEU permits 'adoption of measures for the production of statistics where necessary for the *performance of the activities of the Union*.' See also Council Regulation (EU) No 549/2013 of 21 May 2013 on the European system of national and regional accounts in the European Union [2013] OJ L 174/1, r 1.
[56] For example, Article 126(14) TFEU permits measures for a political coordination mechanism at *EU level*. See also Council Regulation (EC) No 479/2009 of 25 May 2009 on the application of the Protocol on the excessive deficit procedure [2009] OJ L 145/1.
[57] See below, Sections 7.2.2, 7.3.2, 7.3.3.

[T]he nature of statistics has changed. They are no longer merely one source of information for policy-making purposes, but are now at the very heart of the decision-making process.[58]

No issues of fiscal sovereignty arise in so far as elected budgetary executives and legislatures remain legally free, as a matter of EU law, to prefer their own macrofiscal assessments or disregard the EU's altogether when selecting the primary budgetary objective or formulating policy. Without exception, Europe's constitutional democracies guarantee the right to elect a legislature with the freedom to choose its own budgetary objectives or pursue purely social factors instead of an EU-calculated MTO or EU economic forecasts.[59]

The question therefore arises: Are Member States legally free, as a matter of EU law, to arrive at their own macrofiscal assessments or to disregard the MTO altogether for other political objectives? This section argues that they are not. The machinery described here has three components.

7.2.1.1   Component 1: Budgetary Legislators are Bound to EU Technical Frameworks

The first component is Article 4(1) of Directive 2011/85/EU. Article 4(1) states that Member State budgetary planning 'shall be based on the most likely macrofiscal scenario or on a more prudent scenario'.[60] This mirrors an obligation under Regulation 1466/97 which formerly only applied to SCPs for budgetary coordination *at EU level*, and so now extends that obligation into *Member State* budgetary procedures *at Member State level*.[61] Article 4(1) further states that those forecasts must be compared with 'the values contained in the Commission's forecasts' under a comply or explain principle.[62] The obligation to base the budget on the most likely macrofiscal scenario, however, is not qualified by a comply or explain rule.

Article 4(1) is sufficiently clear and precise to constitute a binding legal obligation. As the Commission states, 'the precise requirement of Regulation 1466/97 is that they must be based on the most likely

---

[58]   Council Reg (EU) No 99/2013 on the European statistical programme 2013–17 [2013] OJ L 39/12, r 14.

[59]   As stated in *TCSG (Belgium)*, [B.8.4], 'It is up to the democratically elected legislature not only to approve the budget annually, but to set medium-term budgetary objectives.'

[60]   Art. 4(1) Directive 2011/85/EU.

[61]   Cf: Arts. 3(2a), 7(2a), Reg 1466/97.

[62]   Art. 4(1) Directive 2011/85/EU.

macro-fiscal scenario or on a more prudent scenario'.[63] As forecasts must be compared with that of the Commission, to the extent the most likely national forecast aligns with that of the Commission, the Member State will be bound to it. They are prohibited by Article 4(1) from choosing the second-most prudent scenario.

7.2.1.2 Component 2: Member State Fiscal Institutions are Bound to EU Technical Assessments

Article 4(1) alone does not preclude a Member State from coming up with its own 'most likely scenario', but here Articles 6(1)(b) of Directive 2011/85/EU and 4(4) of Regulation 473/2013 add a second component to this machine. Article 4(4) of Regulation 473/2013 states that national medium-term fiscal plans and draft budgets must be based on macro-fiscal assessments produced or endorsed by independent bodies,[64] and Article 6 of Directive 2011/85/EU states that Member State fiscal rules must determine compliance based on independent analysis carried out by independent bodies.[65] EU legislation then establishes the requirements, mandates and functional operations of those bodies.[66]

Once again, this may pose no constitutional difficulties for this book so long as these independent bodies are not imposed by EU law, where their macrofiscal assessments are their own, and/or where they do not have automatic legal effects binding on Member State budgetary authorities. However, this is not the case.

First, these 'independent bodies' are legally, functionally and financially connected to EU institutions. They derive their existence and mandates from secondary EU legislation;[67] they fall under the purview of a 'European Fiscal Board' (EFB) established by the Commission to 'coordinate national fiscal councils';[68] they are governed by an EU-legislated 'National Statistical Institute' (NSI) which must have 'sole responsibility for deciding on processes, statistical methods, standards

---

[63] Commission, 'Vade mecum on the SGP' (2013) European Economy Occasional Papers No 151, 25.

[64] Art. 4(4) Reg 473/2013 states that medium-term fiscal plans and draft budgets must be based on independent macroeconomic forecasts (see also Art. 5), and Art. 2(1)(b) defines 'independent macroeconomic forecasts' as 'forecasts *produced or endorsed* by independent bodies.'

[65] Art. 6(1)(b) Directive 2011/85/EU.

[66] See below nn 67–78.

[67] Reg 473/2013 r 18; Arts. 4 6(1)(b) Directive 2011/85/EU; Art. 5 Reg 223/2009.

[68] European Commission Decision (EU) 2015/1937 of 21 October 2015 establishing an independent advisory European Fiscal Board [2015] OJ L 282/37.

and procedures' in the Member States;[69] they are required to engage in a 'permanent technical dialogue' with the Commission to 'ensure consistency' in their 'independent macroeconomic forecasts';[70] they are subject to direct technical assistance, targeted financial grants, and 'any other interventions needed' by the Commission;[71] they must calculate public accounts using an inventory of methods, procedures and sources adopted by the Commission;[72] the Commission is empowered to take binding decisions regarding the interpretation of those methods, procedures and sources;[73] statistical institutions are subject to direct supervision by the Commission to ensure quality and compliance;[74] the Commission is empowered to conduct on-site 'dialogue' visits, 'methodological' visits, and 'conduct all investigations necessary' to review data, monitor processes, verify accounts and investigate non-compliance;[75] and the Commission may unilaterally re-write data where there are unresolved methodological disagreements between the NSI and the Commission.[76]

It is no small irony that EU legislation has created 'independent' fiscal institutions which are bound to the Commission by all the criteria which render them independent from Member State legislators. Indeed, the EFB itself does not meet the standards for independence from the Commission that the ECB considers to be necessary at Member State level.[77] As stated by the EFB: 'there is insufficient separation between the independent economic analysis by expert staff in the Commission and the political deliberations'.[78]

Furthermore, the technical outputs produced by this legal framework have demonstrable legal effects. Since medium-term fiscal plans and national draft budgets must be based on the macrofiscal scenario produced under Article 4(1) of Directive 2011/85/EU, and this assessment must be produced or endorsed by the EU-governed 'independent' bodies, national legislators are no longer free to make their own assessment

---

[69] Art. 5(1) Reg 223/2009, as amended by Art. 1(2) Reg 2015/759.
[70] Art. 4(5) of Directive 2011/85 EU establishes the duty, and Art. 2(1) of Reg 473/2013 transfers it to the independent bodies.
[71] Recital (21), Arts. 8, 10 Reg 99/2013.
[72] Art. 9(2) Reg 479/2009.
[73] Art. 10(1) Reg 479/2009.
[74] Art. 8(1) Reg 479/2009.
[75] Art. 11a–11b Reg 479/2009; Art. 8(3) Directive 1173/2011.
[76] Art. 15(2) (see also Arts. 8(1) 11(3)(b)(s)) Reg 479/2009.
[77] ECB, 'Fiscal Councils in EU Countries' (2014) ECB Monthly Bulletin June 1996, 98. Cf: ECB, 'The Creation of a European Fiscal Board' (2015) 7 ECB Economic Bulletin 48, 30.
[78] European Fiscal Board, *Annual Report 2019* (European Fiscal Board, 2019), 75.

of which scenario to follow at all. In Italy's 2018's budgetary process, for example, the EU Commission rejected Italy's draft budget on the basis that, *inter alia*, 'Italy does not comply with the requirement established by Article 4(4) of Regulation (EU) No 473/2013, as the macroeconomic forecasts underlying [the] draft budgetary plan have not been endorsed by an independent body'.[79]

That is well known at EU level, but the lesser-known 2015 dialogue between Ireland's Central Statistics Office (CSO) and the Commission under Regulation 479/2009 is perhaps more instructive of the effects at national level.

In 2015, the CSO concluded that Ireland's water utility, Irish Water, should not be classified under the government sector according to the European System of Accounts (ESA) rules.[80] The Commission disagreed.[81] This led to a terse exchange in which the CSO found that the Commission's assessment suffered from factual inaccuracies, was 'difficult to understand', and was inappropriately subjective.[82] It concluded: 'Having reviewed the structures of Irish Water we cannot accept [the Commission's] conclusion.'[83] However, Article 10 of Regulation 479/2009 empowers the Commission to take decisions regarding the application of the ESA, and the ESA Regulation is binding on Member States. The CSO was therefore required to reproduce the technical assessment of the Commission (with which it thoroughly disagreed).[84] This resulted in over €600 million being added to the government deficit.[85]

---

[79] Commission Opinion of 23.10.2018 on the Draft Budgetary Plan of Italy COM(2018) 7510 final, para 8.

[80] Central Statistics Office, 'Sector Classification of Irish Water in the Irish National Accounts' (CSO, 25 March 2015) www.cso.ie/en/surveysandmethodology/nationalac counts/classificationdecisions/classificationofirishwater accessed 18 April 2015.

[81] Letter from Eduardo Barredo Capelot, European Commission, to Jennifer Banim, CSO, The classification of Irish Water, Ares(2015)1436637 (2015 April 1).

[82] Letter from Jennifer Banim, CSO, to Eduardo Capelot, European Commission (17 April 2015), 5.

[83] Letter from Jennifer Banim to Eduardo Capelot (17 April 2015); Central Statistics Office, 'Information Notice: Classification of Irish Water' (CSO, 30 July 2015) www.cso.ie/en/ nationalaccounts/classificationdecisions/classificationofirishwater accessed 18 April 2015.

[84] Department of Finance, *Ireland's Stability Programme April 2015* (Republic of Ireland, 2015), 15, lamented that the classification of Irish Water was taken by the Commission through a 'closed process'.

[85] Cliff Taylor, 'CSO Provisionally Puts Irish Water on State Books' *The Irish Times* (3 April 2015) www.irishtimes.com/news/politics/cso-provisionally-puts-irish-water-on-state-books-1.2164485 accessed 18 April 2016.

That this results in an extra €600 million for the purpose of calculating compliance with the SGP *at EU level* is uncontroversial. What brings this into the realm of controversy is that it does not just result in €600 million for the SGP at *EU level*, but under *Member State* budgetary laws implanted there by EU legislation. It must be recalled that Ireland's budgetary decision-makers are legally bound, by Directive 2011/85/EU and Article 4(4) of Regulation 473/2013, to base their budgetary frameworks and draft budgetary plans on economic forecasts '*produced or endorsed by independent bodies*', and independent bodes are legally bound to the Commission's classification of Irish Water under Regulation 479/2009.[86] The Irish independent fiscal body is therefore required to reproduce the Commission's assessment of the appropriate MTO adjustment path, and the Irish budgetary executive is required to enact a budget which reproduces the MTO adjustment path of the independent body. This drags a budgetary obligation which is not binding under the Treaty into the realm of binding law.

7.2.1.3   Component 3: Member State Fiscal Rules are Bound to EU Technical Assessments

It may be contested that all of this is *ex ante*: it binds the process leading up to the decision to choose the parameters and objectives of the budget, but not the actual decision. This is because although Article 10 of Directive 2011/85/EU states that Member States' 'annual budget *legislation*' must be consistent with the medium-term budgetary framework, it also states that 'any departure from those provisions shall be duly explained'.[87] The obligation applying to Member States' actual budget legislation is only comply or explain.

But it is here that a third component closes the circle. That is the role of the independent bodies in fiscal rules inserted into national law by Directive 2011/85/EU and Regulation 473/2011. The operation of those fiscal rules is examined in detail below (see Sections 7.3.2 and 7.3.3), but for present purposes it is sufficient to state that Member States are *required by EU law* to establish fiscal rules in *national law* which enforce the MTO *established under EU law*, under supervision of 'independent' fiscal bodies mandated and implanted there *by EU law* using statistical outputs *determined by EU law*.

---

[86] Art. 10(1) Reg 479/2009.
[87] Art. 10 Directive 2011/85/EU.

First, under Articles 6(1)(b) of Directive 2011/85/EU and 5(1) of Regulation 473/2011, it is the 'independent' fiscal bodies which are responsible for monitoring compliance with the MTO and numerical fiscal rules imposed by Article 5 of Directive 2011/85/EU (see Section 7.3.3 for discussion of these rules).[88]

Second, under Article 5(1)(a) of Regulation 473/2013, it is the independent fiscal bodies which are responsible for triggering the constitutional correction mechanism of the TSCG, which incorporates, into the national budgetary process, the MTO 'as established in Article 2a Regulation 1466/97' – i.e. the EU-calculated MTO (see Section 7.3.1 on the MTO).[89] Under Article 5(2)(a) Regulation 473/2013, the independent fiscal body is required to make that assessment *on the basis of an assessment made by the Commission* under Regulation 1466/97 (see Section 7.3.2).[90]

Under these procedures, the Commission can be assured that, if an elected budgetary executive somehow arrives at their own medium-term macrofiscal objective contrary to the rules described above, the Commission's chosen MTO should be enforced against that executive by the EU-legislated fiscal councils, using EU-legislated fiscal rules, on the basis of EU-legislated numerical triggers.

Furthermore, as Directive 2011/85/EU and Regulation 473/2013 are enacted using Articles 121(6) and 126(14) TFEU, non-implementation or non-compliance with this framework is not excluded from infringement proceedings. Article 126(10) TFEU only excludes paragraphs (1)–(9) of Article 126 from infringement proceedings.[91] This leads to a curious result: While the 3% and 60% limits in the Treaty are not legally binding and cannot be subject to infringement proceedings, there is nothing to exclude a Member State being brought before the ECJ for failure to base and enforce its *internal budgetary enactment process* on the 'most likely' fiscal scenario produced by the Commission or EU-legislated

---

[88] Art. 5(1) Reg 473/2013 is excerpted below, Section 7.3.3.2 at n 200. Art. 6(1)(b) Directive 2011/85/EU states: 'country-specific numerical fiscal rules shall contain specifications as to [. . .] (b) the effective and timely monitoring of compliance with the rules, based on reliable and independent analysis carried out by independent bodies . . .'

[89] Art. 5(1)(a) Reg 473/2013 is excerpted below, Section 7.3.3.2 at n 200.

[90] Art. 5(2)(a) of Reg 473/2013 states that the 'independent bodies' shall assess the need to activate the correction mechanism under the Fiscal Compact 'in accordance with Art. 6(2) [Reg 1466/97]' – a provision which refers to the assessment of a 'significant observed deviation' by the Commission. Art. 6(2) is excerpted below, Section 7.3.2.3 at n 165.

[91] See above, Section 7.1, n 40.

fiscal councils and enforced under the budgetary framework imposed by Directive 2011/85/EU and Regulation 473/2013.

7.2.1.4   Independent Macrofiscal Assessments are Acts of EU Law

If elected budgetary officials are bound by EU law to base their budgetary objectives on macrofiscal assessments which are also acts of EU law, this would raise the prospect of an *ultra vires* breach going to the heart of fiscal sovereignty. The question therefore arises: Are the macrofiscal assessments produced by EU-legislated fiscal councils acts of the institutions, bodies, offices or agencies of the Union as described in Article 267 TFEU?

According to the reasoning of the ECJ in *James Elliott Construction* v. *Irish Asphalt*, the answer is yes.[92] *Irish Asphalt* concerned the so-called 'New Approach' of technical harmonization under Directive 89/106.[93] Under that regime, the Commission asks 'independent private-law standards bodies' (ISBs) to draw up technical standards for industrial products. If the ISB chooses to accept the mandate, it may then draw up the relevant standard, and the Commission may publish a reference to the standard in the Official Journal. Products meeting those standards enjoy a presumption of conformity with the Directive.[94]

In *Irish Asphalt*, the ECJ held that such technical outputs were acts of EU law. This was so according to a three-stage test. First, the ECJ concluded that ISB standards 'while indeed adopted by bodies which cannot be described as "institutions, bodies, offices or agencies of the union" *are by their nature measures implementing or applying an act of EU law*', and '*provisions forming part of the European legal system*'.[95] Second, the Court found that the ISB technical standards were not truly independent, but '*strictly governed by the essential requirements defined by that directive, initiated, mandated and monitored by the Commission*'.[96] Third, the work of the ISBs was mandated by EU law;[97] 'initiated, managed and monitored by the

---

[92]   Case C-613/14 *James Elliott Construction Limited* v. *Irish Asphalt Limited* EU:C:2016:821. For comment: Kai P Purnhagen, 'Voluntary "New Approach" Technical Standards are Subject to Judicial Scrutiny by the CJEU! The Remarkable CJEU Judgment "Elliott" on Private Standards' (2017) 8 Eur J Risk Regul 586.

[93]   Council Directive 89/106/EEC of 21 December 1988 on the approximation of laws, regulations and administrative provisions of the Member States relating to construction products [1989] OJ L 40/12.

[94]   Arts. 4(1), 4(2)(a) Directive 89/106/EEC.

[95]   *Irish Asphalt* [34] (emphasis added). See also: Case C-613/14 *James Elliott Construction Limited* v. *Irish Asphalt Limited* EU:C:2016:63 (Opinion of AG Campos Sánchez-Bordona), [44]–[45].

[96]   *Irish Asphalt* [43] (emphases added). See also: *Irish Asphalt (AG Sánchez-Bordona)*, [41], [55].

[97]   *Irish Asphalt*, [44].

Commission';[98] 'subject to detailed monitoring by the Commission';[99] and acquired legal effects as a consequence of their incorporation into acts of EU law.[100]

Applying any and all of these tests, it is impossible to avoid the conclusion, *a fortiori*, that the technical outputs of the 'independent' fiscal bodies that bind budgetary legislators in this chapter are also acts of EU law.

First, the 'New Approach' ISBs are independent private bodies which can autonomously accept/refuse mandates issued by the Commission. This is unlike the 'independent' fiscal bodies discussed in this section, which derive their existence and mandates from EU law, and which are not autonomous (they cannot choose to accept or refuse to produce certain statistics, for example). Second, the 'New Approach' directive is not mandatory: ISBs can develop their own standards or refuse the Commission's specifications, and economic operators can choose to follow them or not. This is unlike the fiscal bodies in this chapter, which have no choice as to whether or not to follow the requirements of the Commission when producing macrofiscal and accounts assessments. Third, ISB standards do not take on legal effects unless the Commission selects them, and operators are not bound to those standards which are approved. This is unlike the macrofiscal assessments produced by ISBs, which *are* binding on budgetary executives *ex ante*, and do trigger EU-legislated fiscal rules *ex post*.

In sum, the 'independent' fiscal bodies discussed in this chapter are bound in every corner by EU law and EU institutions. The implications of this are discussed below in conjunction with the discussion of the budgetary veto, which follows.

7.2.2   EU Legislation Binds Substantive Budgetary Policy: The Budgetary Veto

The EU's macrofiscal governance framework is accompanied by a second, even more remarkable, legal machinery that has become known as the Commission's 'budgetary veto'. This has three components.

7.2.2.1   Component 1: Inconsistent Draft Budgetary Plans

The first component is Article 6(1) of Regulation 473/2013. It states:

---

[98] *Irish Asphalt*, [43].
[99] *Irish Asphalt*, [45].
[100] *Irish Asphalt*, [43] See also: *Irish Asphalt (AG Sánchez-Bordona)* [56]–[58].

Member States shall submit annually to the Commission and to the Eurogroup a draft budgetary plan for the forthcoming year by 15 October. That draft budgetary plan *shall be consistent with* the recommendations issued in the context of the SGP and, where applicable, with recommendations issued in the context of the annual cycle of surveillance, including the macroeconomic imbalances procedure as established by Regulation (EU) No 1176/2011, and with opinions on the economic partnership programmes referred to in Article 9.[101]

This obligation, to 'be consistent with', encompasses all recommendations and opinions issued under Regulation 1466/97 (the MSP), Regulation 1467/97 (the EDP), Regulation 1176/2011 (the MIP/EIP), Regulation 473/2013 and any other outputs issued in the context of the European Semester.[102]

The imperative 'shall be consistent with' has been interpreted as sufficiently precise to constitute a binding obligation under EU law. For example, the Commission has been under a legal obligation to ensure that financial conditionality is 'consistent with' EU law since *Pringle* v. *Ireland*,[103] and in *Ledra* v. *Commission* this was interpreted as requiring something less than 'obedience and full conformity' between two texts, but something more than 'compatibility and non-contradiction between them'.[104] In that case, the ECJ held that this wording constituted a binding obligation on a decision-maker to 'refrain from signing a memorandum of understanding whose consistency with EU law it doubts'.[105]

The relative imprecision of the obligation of 'consistency' in Regulation 473/2013 therefore does not matter to the conclusion that there is a binding secondary EU law threshold beyond which Member State legislation will no longer comply with substantive policy outputs of EU institutions and, therefore, Regulation 473/2013. Moreover, as will become apparent momentarily, the threshold will not always be ambiguous.

7.2.2.2   Component 2: Particularly Serious Non-Compliance

The second component in this machinery is Article 7(2) of Regulation 473/2013. Under Article 7(2), if the Commission identifies 'particularly

---

[101] Art. 6(1) Reg 473/2013 (emphasis added).
[102] For the contents of such plans, see: Art. 6(3)(a)-(h) Reg 473/2013.
[103] *Pringle* v. *Ireland* [163]-[164].
[104] Joined Cases C-8-10/15 *Ledra et al.* v. *Commission and ECB* EU:C:2016:290 (Opinion of AG Wahl) [72].
[105] *Ledra* v. *Commission*, [58]-[60], [67].

serious non-compliance' with the obligation under Article 6(1), the Commission (not the Council) will deliver an opinion to that effect and 'request' that the budget be re-drafted.[106] This process will repeat until the budget is found compliant. Recital 20 provides guidance on the definition of 'particularly serious non-compliance':

> This will be the case, in particular, where the implementation of the draft budgetary plan would *put at risk the financial stability of the Member State concerned* or risk jeopardising the proper functioning of the [EMU] or where the implementation of the draft budgetary plan would entail an *obvious significant violation of the recommendations adopted by the Council* under the SGP.[107]

Two features of this definition are italicised. First, there is no cross-border element. Member States will be in particularly serious non-compliance where they put at risk the financial stability of their own country and no others. Second, the concept of 'particularly serious non-compliance' includes a violation 'of the recommendations adopted by the Council' – it has nothing to do with the debt limits in the Treaty. It is perfectly likely that a Member State may be in 'non-compliance' for ignoring the Union's preferred allocation of social, education, health or employment spending.

The Commission's Opinion in Article 7(2), when read in isolation, is obviously non-binding. The Opinion is not a binding instrument under Article 288 TFEU, there is no legal basis for a budgetary veto under Article 121 TFEU, and the 'request' that the budget be re-drafted is in the language of a non-binding invitation.[108] Taking Article 7(2) in isolation, if a Member State elects to thumb its nose at the Opinion and enact its original budget, it may do so as a matter of law.

However, the obligation in Article 6(1) *is* worded as a binding legal obligation.[109] Read together, it would be surprising indeed if Regulation 473/2013 could be interpreted in such a way that a national budget can be both 'consistent with' EU recommendations for the purposes of Article 6(1), and in 'particularly serious non-compliance' with those same EU recommendations for the purposes of Article 7(2). There is, therefore, a threshold for 'consistency' under Regulation 473/2013, and that threshold is a matter for the Commission to decide.

---

[106] Art. 7(2) Reg 473/2013.
[107] Recital 20 Reg 473/2013 (emphasis added).
[108] Case C-16/16 P *Belgium* v. *Commission (Gaming Recommendation)* EU:C:2018:79, [31]. Cf: *Belgium* v. *Commisssion (Gaming Recommendation) (AG Bobek)*, [105]: a recommendation worded as an 'invitation' may nonetheless be binding.
[109] *Ledra* v. *Commission*, [58]–[60], [67]; *Ledra* v. *Commission (AG Wahl)*, [72].

Because of this interaction, it is difficult to read the two provisions in any way other than the following: If the Commission finds a draft budget in 'serious non-compliance' under Article 7(2), the Member State is in breach of Article 6(1) of Regulation 473/2013, and will be so until the Commission approves the budget.

7.2.2.3 Component 3: Particularly Serious Non-Compliant Budgetary Procedures

The obvious defence to that reading is that Article 6(1) only binds *draft* budgetary plans – a set of documents placed on a table at EU level. It does not bind the budgetary executive or legislature in so far as the real budget may legislate for a different outcome altogether.

But here Articles 3 and 4(1) of Regulation 473/2013 introduce a final component to this machinery. Those articles do not bind a set of documents at EU level. They state, in near-identical terms to Article 6(1) (recited above, Section 7.2.2.1), that the entirety of the *'Member States budgetary procedure'*,[110] and the 'medium-term fiscal plans produced in accordance with their *medium-term budgetary framework'*,[111] shall be consistent with recommendations issued in the annual cycle of surveillance.

As defined in Article 2(1)(e) of Directive 2011/85/EU, the 'medium-term budgetary framework' encapsulates the budgetary framework in its entirety, including the setting of policy priorities, the MTO, and the enforcement of numerical fiscal rules required under Directive 2011/85/EU and Regulation 473/2013.[112]

This closes the circle. A Member State that is able to persist in legislating a budget in 'particularly serious non-compliance' with EU economic policy prescriptions can hardly be said to have implemented a budgetary framework which 'is consistent with' the obligation imposed by Article 3 of Regulation 473/2013. Once again, they may be subject to infringement proceedings for breach or failure to implement secondary EU law.

In actual practice, of course, launching infringement proceedings against an elected government for failing to internalize EU edicts within Member State economic competence would be nothing short of political suicide for the Commission. Instead, the Commission has used

---

[110] Art. 3 Reg 473/2013.
[111] Art. 4(1) Reg 473/2013.
[112] Art. 2(1)(e) Directive 2011/85/EU; Art. 2(1)(c) Reg 473/2013.

concessions won in negotiations over the budgetary veto as reason not to initiate the EU's SGP financial sanctioning procedures in the first place. Far from effecting an enforceable obligation against Member States, this has simply moved the non-credibility of the EU's own sanctioning procedures to the front of the process. But perhaps this is the point: there is no constitutional basis for governing Member State budgetary policies, so binding instruments of EU law capable of that effect may only exist in so far as they are not actually enforced. Nonetheless, the button on this legal machinery remains in place, should it ever be pressed.

Italy's 2018/2019 budgetary process is instructive. In 2018 Italy submitted a draft budgetary plan with a planned structural deterioration of −0.8% of GDP − a deviation of 1.4% of GDP from the MTO adjustment path.[113] This is significant, since a deviation of 0.5% is a 'significant deviation' for the purposes of the EDP.[114] This forced the Commission to wield its budgetary veto for the first time, finding (twice) that Italy's draft budget was in 'particularly serious non-compliance' with the recommendations of the Council.[115] Ultimately, however, any sort of legal consequence was averted when the Commission accepted a reduction in the structural deterioration to −0.2% of GDP in order to avoid opening an EDP at all, putting an end to the matter.[116]

And yet, as the EFB has pointed out, Italy's revised budget still entailed a structural deviation from the adjustment path of 0.8% of GDP, which 'still amounts to a significant deviation from the required adjustment path towards the MTO'.[117] This means that Italy's fiscal plans (Article 4), draft budget (Article 6) and domestic *budgetary procedure itself* (Article 3) were in breach of Regulation 473/2013 − directly applicable secondary EU law. There is nothing here to preclude infringement proceedings for breach of Regulation 473/2013 and non-implementation of Directive 2011/85/EU.

7.2.2.4 The Legal Basis of the Budgetary Veto

Recommendations or opinions adopted in the context of the European Semester do not derive from a legal basis to adopt binding legislation.

---

[113] Commission Opinion of 23 October 2018 on the Draft Budgetary Plan of Italy, para 11.
[114] Art. 6(3) Reg 1466/97.
[115] Commission Opinion of 23 October 2018 on the Draft Budgetary Plan of Italy; Commission Opinion of 21 November 2018 on the revised Draft Budgetary plan of Italy COM(2018) 8028 final.
[116] Commission Letter to Italy (19 December 2018) Ares(2018) 7351969.
[117] Commission Opinion of 21 November 2018 on the revised Draft Budgetary plan of Italy, 36.

Absent some incorporation into binding EU law, even a clear, unconditional and unequivocal recommendation will not be capable of binding force under Article 288(5) TFEU.[118] The purpose of recommendations under Articles 121(2),(4) or 126(3),(5),(7) or (9) TFEU is to give substance to the procedures *at EU level* for sanctioning the 3% and 60% debt limits – which are themselves not legally binding.[119] From the harmless safety of this 'coordination' competence, the EU may issue recommendations and opinions that run the full gamut of economic policy from taxation to 'improving work-life balance'.[120] AG Bobek explains:

The Member States are fully entitled to entirely disregard the content of a recommendation without there being any possibility of direct or indirect sanctions. [...] There can be neither any positive, nor negative obligations flowing from a recommendation. *A recommendation also cannot be used to define a standard or an indeterminate legal notion that will then, after having been given content by that recommendation, be enforced against as Member State or an individual.*[121]

But, as a result of Regulation 473/2013, the recommendations in this section no longer meet this definition. It is well settled that a non-binding recommendation *can* be imbued with legal force through incorporation into binding EU law and thereby cease to be a 'true' recommendation.[122] In *Germany et al.* v. *Commission*, for example, the ECJ held that the EU's 'coordination' competence in social policy would not encroach on Member States' exclusive social policy powers only *in so far as* they are not covered by other provisions of EU law.[123] Similarly, in *Grimaldi*, the ECJ held:

[I]t must be stressed that [recommendations] in question cannot be regarded as having no legal effect [...] in particular where they cast light on the interpretation of national measures adopted in order to implement them or where they are designed to supplement binding Community provisions.[124]

Herein the problem lies. In principle, a failure to adopt the 'recommended' outcome will lead to a breach of Articles 3, 4(1) and 6(1) of

---

[118] Case C-322/88 *Grimaldi* v. *Fonds des Maladies Professionnelles* [1989] ECR 4407; EU: C:1989:646 [13]–[14]; Case C-526/14 *Kotnik et al.* EU:C:2016:102 [38]–[39]; *Belgium* v. *Commission (Gaming Recommendation)*, [26].

[119] See above, Section 7.1, n 40.

[120] European Commission, Annual Growth Survey 2016 COM(2015) 690 final, 11.

[121] *Belgium* v. *Commisssion (Gaming Recommendation) (AG Bobek)*, [168] (emphasis added).

[122] *Grimaldi* [16]; *Belgium* v. *Commisssion (Gaming Recommendation) (AG Bobek)*, [147].

[123] Joined Cases 281, 283–285, 287/85 *Germany et al.* v. *Commission* [1987] ECR 2303; EU: C:1987:351, [14], [27]–[36].

[124] *Grimaldi* [18]–[19].

Regulation 473/2013, which is binding in its entirety and directly applicable in EMU Member States. Non-binding recommendations for policies outside EU competence are therefore drawn into an EU statutory framework and taken as the point of enforcement under binding and supreme secondary EU law.

7.2.3   Conclusion: Two Infringements of Member State Fiscal Sovereignty

Under Articles 3, 4(1), 4(4), 5(1)–(2), 6(1) and 7(2) of Regulation 473/2013, and Articles 4–6 and 10 of Directive 2011/85/EU, an elected budgetary executive who sits down to map out the appropriate macrofiscal objective for her country will find herself hemmed in by an inescapable pathway bound by secondary EU law.

[7.2.1] *Ex ante*, elected budgetary legislators are legally bound, as a matter of EU law, to base the budget upon the most likely macrofiscal assessment of the Commission or the EU-governed 'independent' fiscal body as to the appropriate MTO, and this binds the parameters of the budget through the entire budgetary procedure. *Ex post*, under Article 5 of Directive 2011/85/EU, Article 3 of Regulation 473/2013 and Article 3 TSCG, Member States are then required to legislate fiscal rules to enforce compliance with the MTO. Under Articles 6(1)(b) of Directive 2011/85/EU and 5(2)(a) of Regulation 473/2013, these are to be monitored and triggered by the EU-governed fiscal bodies. For EMU countries, this is to be done on the basis of the Commission's assessment of a 'significant observed deviation' under Article 6(2) of Regulation 1466/97 (see Section 7.3.2). According to recent ECJ case law, the macrofiscal outputs which so bind elected budgetary executives in this section are acts of EU law.[125]

[7.2.2] Second, the Commission is then given a trigger for a budgetary veto that binds budgetary policies directly, such that failure to internalize or secure the prescribed EU policy outcome in a Member State's own budgetary framework will lead to a breach of Articles 3, 4(1) and/or 6(1) of Regulation 473/2013 – even if this only concerns specific substantive economic policy choices, and even where there are no spillovers to the Union.

This is extremely problematic for the constitutional boundaries of EU fiscal federalism. The legal bases for Regulation 473/2013 and Directive 2011/85/EU are Articles 121(6) TFEU and 126(14) TFEU. Article 126(14) provides a legal basis for rules and definitions for the application of the

---

[125] *Irish Asphalt*, [34], [43]–[45].

Protocol on the EDP – a sanctioning procedure *at EU level*. Similarly, Article 121(6) empowers the Council to adopt regulations setting out detailed rules for two stages of the MSP: Commission monitoring under Article 121(3) and Council recommendations under Article 121(4) – both procedures *at EU level*. Neither article provides a legal basis to bind Member States to macrofiscal assessments of EU institutions or prescribe budgetary outcomes in national law.

And yet, as has just been shown, these mechanisms do, in fact, profess to bind the entire budgetary enactment process. Ireland's Medium-Term Budgetary Framework under Regulation 473/2013, for example, states that the EU's fiscal rules 'must be complied with in every one of the processes and outputs of our fiscal planning process, and in the implementation of the annual budget'.[126] It further states:

> It is important to note that these are fiscal rules with which Ireland must comply, whether they arise as a result of *EU legislation which has been given effect through Irish legislation* or *EU legislation with direct effect*.[127]

There is no legal basis for EU legislation with such effects.

In that regard, as shown in Chapter 1, the litmus test for evaluating whether a fetter on budgetary autonomy amounts to a deprivation of the right to vote is whether control over that policy is relinquished, such that the fetter is irreversible by an equivalent act of the parliament in the future.[128] In *Euro Rescue Package (Germany)* and *ESM (Germany)*, the leading cases on this test, the BVerfG held:

> A necessary condition for the safeguarding of political latitude in the sense of the core of identity of the constitution (art.20(1) and (2), art.79(3) BL), is that the budget legislature makes its decisions on revenue and expenditure free of other-directedness on the part of the bodies and of other Member States of the European Union and remains permanently 'the master of its decisions'.[129]

It is clear that the framework just described could not meet this test. This framework intercedes to grip each stage of the decision-making process for the drafting of a budget; it is not voluntary (because it is enacted under binding EU law); the budgetary legislator is not accountable to the voter in the development of its macrofiscal policies (because

---

[126] Department of Finance, *Medium-Term Budgetary Framework* (Republic of Ireland, 2014), 9.

[127] Department of Finance, *Medium-Term Budgetary Framework* (Republic of Ireland, 2014), 26 [emphasis added]. See, similarly *Juízes Portugueses (AG ØE)*, at footnote 43.

[128] *Euro Rescue Package (Germany)* [124], [127]; *ESM II (Germany)* [168]–[170].

[129] *ESM I (Germany)* [197]. See also: *ESM II (Germany)* [164]; *Euro Rescue Package (Germany)* [127].

it must choose the MTO adjustment path yielded by the EU law framework); and, as binding secondary EU law, it cannot be reversed by a unilateral action of the Member State parliament in the future. The only possible conclusion to be drawn is that these instruments are manifestly beyond the boundaries of the EU legal order and may perhaps exist only in so far as they are not actually enforced like the binding EU law instruments they appear to be. This is not only constitutionally illegitimate but, as will be shown in Chapter 8, these instruments are utterly ineffective and furthermore injurious to good principles of fiscal federalism.

7.3   Binding Vertical Interlinkages with EU Fiscal Governance

The second architecture of concern to this chapter is a webwork of EU fiscal governance legislation that imbues the 3% and 60% debt values, plus a third variable – the MTO, found nowhere in the Treaty – with legal effects in national law.

The main substantive norm leveraged in this section is the MTO. At EU level, the MTO is enforced under a reinforced 'hard law' MSP, complete with its own sanctioning mechanism under a reverse-QMV voting procedure. At Member State level, the MTO will bind Member State budgetary processes under Directive 2011/85/EU and Regulation 473/2013,[130] and it will take on legal effects under fiscal rules imposed by the TSCG,[131] Directive 2011/85/EU;[132] and Regulation 473/2013.[133] As Chalmers observes, it is the MTO 'which moves States into a regime where their budgetary planning is co-governed by the EU institutions'.[134]

[7.3.1] The analysis therefore begins by examining the question of where the MTO comes from: That is, whether Member States are legally free to legislate their own MTOs. It finds that it is the *Commission* and the *Council* under Articles 5(1) and 9(1) of Regulation 1466/97 – not the Member State – which define the appropriate MTO and adjustment path towards it for the purposes of enforcement under Directive 2011/

---

[130] See Section 7.2, in particular Section 7.2.1. Arts. 4–6, 9–14 Directive 2011/85/EU; Arts. 3, 4(1), 6(1), 5(2)(a) Reg 473/2013.
[131] Art. 3(1)(b) TSCG; Art. 5(1),(2) Reg 473/2013. See Section 7.3.2.
[132] Arts. 5–6 Directive 2011/85/EU. See Section 7.3.3.
[133] Arts. 3, 4(1), 6(1) Reg 473/2013. See Section 7.2.2.
[134] Chalmers, 'Law of Struggle', 679. See also Eyraud and Wu, 'Playing by the Rules', 17

85/EU, Regulation 473/2013, and the TSCG. The MTO is legislated by the Union.

[7.3.2] Second, the TSCG requires EMU countries to enforce the MTO 'through provisions of binding force and permanent character, preferably constitutional' to ensure that the MTO is binding on the legislative process.[135] This is not an instrument of EU law. However, Article 5 of Regulation 473/2013 states that compliance with the correction mechanism must be placed in the hands of an 'independent' fiscal council, implanted there by EU law, and determined on the basis of the Commission's declaration of a 'significant observed deviation' under Article 6(2) of Regulation 1467/97 of the SGP.[136] This *is* an instrument of EU law. This spans the boundary between legal orders and co-opts the Fiscal Compact, inserting the Commission's determination under Article 6(2) of Regulation 1466/97 into national constitutional correction mechanisms.

[7.3.3] Third, Directive 2011/85/EU – binding and supreme secondary EU law – requires Member States to have in place fiscal rules which enforce compliance with, *inter alia*, the MTO and the 3% and 60% debt limits.

[7.3.4] Fourth, the MTO is enforced by new sanctions and reverse QMV (RQMV) voting under both limbs of Articles 121 and 126 TFEU. The effect of the new framework is that, while the Union has no competence in economic policy, the Commission is, 'as a rule', presumed to be able to enumerate a detailed list of economic policy measures and then issue fines that are adopted automatically unless the Council votes to stop it under a RQMV burden.[137] Compounding matters, RQMV for all new sanctions is defined in accordance with Article 238(3)(b) TFEU, requiring 72% of the Member States comprising 65% of the population.[138] This means the Commission can pass sanctions against a mid-sized EMU state (e.g., Portugal or Greece) against a numerical super-majority of seventeen countries,[139] or an overwhelming population majority of up to 97.80%,[140] so long as two countries representing 35+1% of the population, or six countries with any population, abstain.

---

[135] Art. 3(1)–(2) TSCG.
[136] Art. 5(1)–(2) Reg 473/2013. Arts. 6(2) and 10(2) Reg 1466/97 provide for the significant observed deviation.
[137] Articles 2-a(3), 2-ab(2), 6(2) Reg 1466/97, Art. 2a Reg 1497/96, and Regs 1173–1174/2011.
[138] Art. 12(2) Reg 1173/2011; 5(2) Reg 1174/2011; Art. 7 TSCG.
[139] See below, Section 7.3.4.1, n 227 for this voting scenario.
[140] See below, Section 7.3.4.1, n 228 for this voting scenario.

This section concludes that the mechanisms analysed in Section 7.3.2 and 7.3.3, in conjunction with the MTO under Section 7.3.1, entail several *ultra vires* norms which intrude on Member State fiscal sovereignty according to constitutional identity rulings in four countries and a related opinion of the Council Legal Service. The RQMV sanctioning framework in Section 7.3.4, however, does not amount to a violation of the boundaries in this book because it does not co-opt or restrict parliamentary fiscal powers as a matter of law.

7.3.1   Significant Observed Deviation from the MTO as Trigger for Enforcement

Since the MTO is alleged to take on such legal force, it is vital to begin with a discussion of where it comes from.

To begin with, the legal basis for the MTO is an instrument of EU law: Article 2a of Regulation 1466/97 states that 'Each member State shall have a differentiated MTO [. . .] within a defined range between −1.0% of GDP and balance or surplus.'[141] Two features of this article are of note.

First, not any budgetary objective will do. A Member State could only set 'the alleviation of poverty' as its primary budgetary objective in so far as this is does not result in an MTO outside the defined range of −1% of GDP.

Second, nowhere in Regulation 1466/97 does it state where the MTO comes from. Article 2a states that each country 'shall have' an MTO, but does not state who is responsible for the definitive calculation. It is a curious case of what Dawson calls 'rolling' legal enforcement, where each Member State 'shall have' a thing to implement, but legal accountability for that thing is not attributable to either Member State or EU institutions.[142]

The first possibility is that the MTO is attributable to the Member States. There are two pieces of evidence for this: the methodology for the MTO is set out in a non-binding code of conduct;[143] and the first chronological appearance of the MTO in the European Semester states that countries 'shall present' their MTO as part of their SCPs submitted in April each year.[144]

A closer look reveals otherwise, however. First, as shown in Section 7.2.1, under Article 4 of Directive 2011/85/EU and Articles 4(4)

---

[141] Art. 2a Reg 1466/97.
[142] Dawson, 'Accountability Structure', 984.
[143] Council, Specifications on the SGP.
[144] Arts. 3(2) and 7(2) of Reg 1466/97 and 4 of Reg 473/2013.

and 2(1)(a)-(b) of Regulation 473/2014, budgetary executives are *required by EU law* to establish their MTO on the most likely scenario, compared against the Commission's forecasts, and calculated or endorsed by 'independent' fiscal institutions that are comprehensively governed by the Commission under EU law.[145]

Second, as shown in Section 7.2.2, Member State budgetary frameworks, budgetary plans and medium-term fiscal plans must be 'consistent with', *inter alia,* any and all recommendations issued under Regulations 1466/97, 1467/97, 1176/2011 and 473/2013.[146] This includes, obviously, the MTO.[147] This creates a sort of circular legal duty: Member States may 'present' their own MTOs, but only if these MTOs are 'consistent' with those of the Commission and Council. Otherwise, they will be in non-compliance with Regulation 473/2013 in the manner described in Section 7.2.2 above.

Third, once the MTO is 'presented', it is for the Council and Commission, under Articles 5(1) and 9(1) of Regulation 1466/97, to assess whether the economic assumptions underpinning the MTO are plausible, appropriate and sufficient to achieve the MTO over the cycle.[148] It is the statistical value determined at *this* stage and in *those articles* which takes on legal force under the terms of the TSCG,[149] Directive 2011/85/EU[150] and Regulation 473/2013.[151] Article 5(2)(a) of Regulation 473/2013, for example, defines significant observed deviation from the MTO 'in accordance with Article 6(2) of Regulation 1466/97', which empowers the Commission to make that determination against the MTO in Article 5(1) of Regulation 1466/97.

Finally, in order to operationalize the MTO and imbue it with coercive force, the 'six-pack' introduced the concept of a 'significant observed deviation' from the MTO or the adjustment path towards it.[152] In general terms, a 'significant observed deviation' will occur where the

---

[145] See Sections 7.2.1.1–7.2.1.2.

[146] Arts. 3, 4(1), 6(1) Reg 473/2013.

[147] Commission, 'Vade mecum', 23: 'compliance [is assessed against the] previous year's country-specific recommendation [. . .] in terms of the [MTO].'

[148] Arts. 5(1)–(2), 9(1)–(2) Reg 1466/07. On the calculation of the appropriate MTO, see: Commission, 'Vade mecum', 23–24, 26–27; European Commission, 'Making the Best Use of the Flexibility within the Existing Rules of the Stability and Growth Pact' COM (2015) 12 final, 6, Annex 2.

[149] Art. 3(1)(b) TSCG; Art. 5(2)(a) reg 473/2013 discussed below, Section 7.3.2.3.

[150] Arts. 4–5, 9–14 Directive 2011/85/EU, in particular 5(b), discussed below, Sections 7.3.3.1–7.3.3.2.

[151] Arts. 3, 4(1), 6(1) Reg 473/2013, discussed above, Section 7.2.2.

[152] Arts. 6(2), 10(2) Reg 1466/96.

Commission finds a deviation from the MTO adjustment path of >0.5% of GDP.[153] In the event of such a deviation, the Commission will now issue an autonomous warning to the Member State under Article 6(2) or 10(2) of Regulation 1466/96 (previously this was issued by the Council).[154]

At EU level, the Commission warning triggers the new sanctioning mechanisms of the MSP, which may result in more specific recommendations, enhanced surveillance, a declaration of 'no effective action' and sanctions.[155]

At Member State level, however, the Commission warning is linked to legal effects under rules legislated into national budgetary frameworks by Articles 5-6 of Directive 2011/85/EU, Article 5(1)-(2) of Regulation 473/2013, and Article 3(1) of the TSCG. The EU MTO is the one taken as the point of enforcement for all of these systems, upon the trigger of the Commission warning. The remainder of this Section 7.3 follows the MTO through each of these systems.

7.3.2 EU Legislation Vertically Integrates the Commission Warning into the TSCG

Articles 5(1)-(2) of Regulation 473/2013 insert the Commission warning under Article 6(2) of Regulation 1466/97 into the Fiscal Compact of the TSCG to procure enforcement of the EU-legislated MTO. This mechanism has three components.

7.3.2.1   Component 1: The TSCG 'Balanced Budget' Rule

Article 3 TSCG requires the Contracting Parties to introduce a 'balanced budget' rule into national law through provisions 'of binding force and permanent character, preferably constitutional, or otherwise guaranteed to be fully respected and adhered to throughout the national budgetary process'.[156] Under Article 3(1)(b) and 4 TSCG, compliance with this rule will be achieved where the annual structural balance is 'within its country-specific MTO *as defined in the Stability and Growth Pact*', or within the MTO adjustment path, also evaluated '*in line with the revised Stability and Growth Pact*'.[157] Deviations may only be excepted in

---

[153] Arts. 6(2)–(3) and 10(2)–(3) of Reg 1466/97. See also Council, Specifications on the SGP, 7; Commission, 'Vade mecum', 38.

[154] Arts. 6(2), 10(2) Reg 1466/96.

[155] Arts. 2-a(3), 2-ab(2), 6(2), 9(2), 11 Reg 1466/97. See below, Section 7.3.4 on sanctions at EU level.

[156] Art. 3(1)–(2) TSCG.

[157] Art. 3(1)(b) TSCG (emphasis added).

exceptional circumstances defined in identical terms to those of the SGP,[158] and Article 4 TSCG imports the adjustment pace for excessive debts 'as provided for in Article 2(1a) of Regulation [1467/97]' (i.e. the SGP).[159]

The most significant feature of the 'balanced budget rule' is therefore that it is not a balanced budget rule at all. As Van Mallegheim points out, it 'is really a rule to keep the structural budgetary position at its country-specific medium-term [and] therefore originates in the existing framework of the fiscal supervision of EU Member States'.[160] In that respect, the TSCG also implements Article 5 of Directive 2011/85/EU, which requires Member States to enact numerical rules which ensure respect for the MTO established under the SGP (see Section 7.3.3).

7.3.2.2 Component 2: Significant Observed Deviation and the Fiscal Compact

To enforce this rule, Article 3(1)(e) TSCG requires contracting parties to establish an automatic 'constitutional correction mechanism', which 'shall be triggered automatically' in the event of 'significant observed deviations from the [MTO] or the adjustment path towards it'.[161]

It should be noted that, under Regulation 1466/97, it is the Commission alone which is empowered to identify a 'significant observed deviation' and issue an autonomous warning to that effect under Article 121(4) TFEU.[162] However, there is nothing in the TSCG itself to link Article 3(1)(e) TSCG to the Commission's assessment under Regulation 1466/97.[163] The concepts are obviously intended to align, but as a matter of law the Member States have not, by signing the TSCG, chosen to bind their constitutional laws to the Commission warning in the EU's MSP procedure.

---

[158] Arts. 3(1)(c), 3(3) TSCG.
[159] That is, a reduction 1/20th per year as a benchmark: Art. 4 TSCG.
[160] Pieter-Augustijn Van Malleghem, '(Un)Balanced Budget Rules in Europe and America' in Adams, Fabbrini and Larouche (eds), *Constitutionalization of European Budgetary Constraints*, 163.
[161] Art. 3(1)(e) TSCG.
[162] Arts. 6(2), 10(2) Reg 1466/96.
[163] Commission, 'Common Principles on National Fiscal Correction Mechanisms' COM (2012) 342 final, 342: 'trigger points may rely on either EU-level criteria, country-specific criteria, or both'.

7.3.2.3   Component 3: Secondary EU Law Binds the Constitutional Correction Mechanism

It is here where Regulation 473/2013 – binding secondary EU law – intercedes to co-opt the constitutional correction mechanism. First, Article 5(1) of Regulation 473/2013 requires Member States to empower the 'independent' fiscal bodies discussed in Section 7.2.1 with triggering fiscal rules for the enforcement of the MTO 'as established in Article 2a of Regulation (EC) No 1466/97'.[164] Second, Article 5(2)(a) of Regulation 473/2013 then states that the independent fiscal bodies are required to make that assessment on the basis of the assessment made by the Commission under Article 6(2) of Regulation 1466/97:

> Those bodies shall, where appropriate, provide public assessments with respect to national fiscal rules, inter alia relating to: (a) the occurrence of circumstances leading to the activation of the *correction mechanism for cases of significant observed deviation* from the [MTO] or the adjustment path towards it *in accordance with Article 6(2) of [Regulation 1466/97]*.[165]

Here, Article 5(2)(a) of Regulation 473/2013 stretches athwart the gap between legal orders and inserts the 'significant observed deviation' – defined, identified and activated by the Commission under Article 6(2) of Regulation 1466/97 – into the TSCG. By completing this link, Regulation 473/2013 wires national constitutional correction mechanisms to the MSP, placing the trigger in the autonomous hands of the Commission under Article 6(2) of Regulation 1466/97. Ireland's Medium-Term Budgetary Framework, for example, states that the requirement for a correction plan under its automatic correction mechanism is triggered automatically, 'if the European Commission addresses a warning under Article 6(2) of Regulation 1466/97'.[166] Many Member States have interpreted it along similar lines. Eleven Member States have given their EU-legislated independent fiscal councils a role in triggering national correction mechanisms.[167] Twelve Member States have placed their fiscal councils in charge of *ex post* fiscal rule assessment.[168]

---

[164] Art. 5(1) Reg 473/2013 excerpted below, in Section 7.3.3.2 at n 200.
[165] Art. 5(2)(a) of Reg 473/2013 (emphasis added).
[166] Department of Finance, *Medium-Term Budgetary Framework* (Ireland, 2014), 36.
[167] Michal Horvath, 'EU Independent Fiscal Institutions: An Assessment of Potential Effectiveness' (2018) 56 JCMS 504, 509.
[168] Horvath, 'EU Independent Fiscal Institutions', 509.

Thus, in a rather neat coup, the medium-term objective chosen by EU institutions is now enforced by national constitutional courts on the Commission's say-so. What makes this legally problematic, however, is that it is Article 5(2)(a) Regulation 473/2013, directly applicable and supreme EU law – not an intergovernmental treaty – which crosses the competence fence and inserts this link. As Fabbrini concludes:

The Fiscal Compact is bringing about centralization in the governance of the Euro-zone that is significantly greater than that existing in the United States. [...] This is ironic considering that EU member states have systematically discarded a federalist arrangement for the governance of the Euro-zone as being incompatible with state sovereignty.[169]

7.3.2.4   Assessment: An Exceedance of the EU Legal Order and Infringement of Fiscal Sovereignty

This is problematic for the subject matter of this book. The EU law alternative to this mechanism – that is, a regulation based on Article 126 or 136 TFEU imposing a constitutional correction mechanism – would certainly be *ultra vires* and a violation of constitutional identity. This is why the TSCG was signed outside the European legal order in the first place. The objective of the TSCG, 'domestic legal and constitutional change',[170] through 'provisions [which] cannot be simply altered by the ordinary budgetary law',[171] could not be effected by EU legislation.[172] However, the TSCG remains heavily intertwined with EU law, and at least two vital pieces of this machine – the establishment of independent fiscal councils and the triggering of the TSCG – are set out in a Directive and Regulation, which *are* binding under EU law.[173]

In that regard, as shown in Chapter 1, the litmus test for an unconstitutional restriction on budgetary sovereignty is whether it could be reversed by an equivalent unilateral action of the elected parliament in the future.[174] The standard applied, according to the leading cases of

[169] Fabbrini, 'Paradox', 35.
[170] Armstrong, 'New Governance', 604.
[171] Commission, 'Common Principles', 3.
[172] Editorial, 'Reinforced Economic Union', 1–3, 10–11; Leonard Besselink and Jan-Herman Reestman, 'Editorial: The Fiscal Compact and the European Constitutions: "Europe Speaking German"' (2012) 8 ECL Review 1, 5–6; Calleiss, 'New Rules', 105; Armstrong, 'New governance', 604.
[173] *TSCG (Austria)*, [B.2]. See Giovanni Boggero and Pasquale Annicchino, 'Who Will Ever Kick Us Out? Italy, the Balanced Budget Rule and the Implementation of the Fiscal Compact' (2014) 20 Eur Pub L 247, 251.
[174] See: Section 1.3.1, in particular Section 1.3.1.2.

the BVerfG, is that 'the democratic process remains open and that legal re-evaluations may occur on the basis of other majority decisions'.[175] The TSCG, as an intergovernmental treaty, passes this test, because the legislature remains free to enter into (and withdraw from) treaties containing commitments regarding future spending behaviour.[176] Other courts have ruled on similar lines.[177] Articles 5(1)(a)–(2)(a) of Regulation 473/2013, however, do not pass this test. As directly applicable and supreme EU law, they are not reversible by an equivalent unilateral action of the national parliament. The only possible conclusion is that Articles 5(1)(a) and 5(2)(a) of Regulation 473/2013 are an infringement of fiscal sovereignty.

The first proof for this proposition is the BVerfG's decision in *ESM II (Germany)*. In that case, the BVerfG held that the TSCG correction mechanism was a lawful restriction on the budgetary autonomy of the *Bundestag* because the TSCG, as an intergovernmental treaty, could be reversed by an equivalent action of the parliament in the future.[178] An EU law measure would not. The BVerfG held:

The [TSCG] *grants the bodies of the European Union no powers which affect the overall budgetary responsibility of the German Bundestag* and *does not force [Germany] to make a permanent commitment regarding its economic policy that it can no longer reverse.* It is true that [. . .] the Contracting Parties rely on principles which are to be proposed by the European Commission and which concern in particular the nature, size and time-frame of the corrective action to be taken (including under exceptional circumstances), and the role and independence of the institutions responsible at the national level for monitoring compliance with the deficit and indebtedness criteria. This, however, *does not grant the European Commission authority to impose specific substantive requirements for the structuring of the budgets.*[179]

This is no longer the case. Regulation 473/2013 was enacted after the *ESM (Germany)* litigation was brought, however Regulation 473/2014 *does* grant the Commission the power to trigger the constitutional mechanism that affects the budgetary responsibility of the *Bundestag*; Regulation 473/2013 *is* directly applicable and supreme EU law which *does* force Germany to make a permanent commitment that is *not* reversible by an equivalent majority of the *Bundestag* in the future (because it is secondary EU law); and Regulation 473/2013 *does* grant

---

[175] *ESM II (Germany)* [173].
[176] *ESM II (Germany)* [172]–[173].
[177] *TCSG (Belgium)*, [B.8.4]; *TSCG (France)* [26]–[27]; *TSCG (Austria)* [5.3]–[5.5.1], [6.4].
[178] *ESM II (Germany)*, [164], [168], [162]–[173], [242]–[245].
[179] *ESM II (Germany)*, [242]–[245] (emphasis added).

the Commission the authority to impose specific substantive requirements for the structuring of state budgets.[180] According to this decision,
the addition of Regulation 473/2013 to the TSCG framework no longer
meets the constitutional identity test in Germany.

The second proof for this proposition is the ruling in *TSCG (France)*. In
that case, the *Conseil Constitutionnel* held that the TSCG did not 'infringe
the essential conditions for the exercise of national sovereignty'
because it did not define the procedures according to which the mechanism must be triggered and left Member States free to define these
procedures in accordance with their own constitutional law. It stated:

> Considering that the 'correction mechanism' which the States undertake to put
> in place must be 'triggered automatically' 'in the event of significant observed
> deviations from the medium-term objective or the adjustment path towards it'
> [. . .] *these provisions do not define either the procedures according to which this mechanism
> must be triggered or the measures which must be implemented as a result; that they
> therefore leave the States free to determine these procedures and measures in accordance
> with their constitutional law.*[181]

Once again, this is no longer the case. Regulation 473/2013 was not in
issue in *TSCG (France)*, but that instrument now *defines the procedures
according to which this mechanism must be triggered* and, since the trigger
is in directly applicable and binding EU law, no longer leaves the states
free to determine these procedures in accordance with their constitutional law.

The third is *TSCG (Austria)*, wherein the VfGH ruled that the tasks
conferred on the Commission in the TSCG could be lawfully conferred
by the 'ordinary legislator' without a 'total revision' by the constitutional legislator because it granted no power in budgetary policy to the
Union beyond that already granted under the Austrian Accession Act.[182]
It was a purely intergovernmental treaty – not EU law – which conferred
tasks on the Commission and thus fell within 'part of [the ordinary
legislator's] policy-making role within the democratic parliamentary
system foreseen by the Federal Constitutional Act'.[183] It held:

> The [TSCG] *is a treaty under international law outside the scope of Union Law* [. . .]
> neither is the transfer of competences to the European Union bodies of such
> nature which would exceed the scope of what is admissible under constitutional

---

[180] On this latter issue, see above, Section 7.2.2.
[181] *TSCG (France)* [26]–[27] (emphasis added).
[182] *TSCG (Austria)* [5.3]–[5.5.1], [6.4].
[183] *TSCG (Austria)* [6.3].

law, nor are the constitutional law provisions which govern the federal budget thereby violated.[184]

Once again, Regulation 473/2013 is not an international treaty and therefore not within the ordinary legislator's policymaking role within the Federal Constitutional Act on that basis. It is EU law – not the TSCG – conferring a role on the Commission. This also seems to conflict with a rule in another case, *ESM (Austria)*, where the VfGH considered, *obiter dictum*, that a conferral of budgetary policy on the Union would affect the fundamental principles of the constitution, rendering it unconstitutional without a total revision of the Constitution.[185] In that particular case the TESM did not do so, because it did not hand the EU a power to dictate economic policy and so it was not a treaty by which the contractual bases of the EU were modified.[186] But Regulation 473/2013 does seem to do so, because it inserts EU law and EU institutions into constitutional fiscal rules in Member State law.

In a fourth case, *TSCG (Belgium)*, the *Cour constitutionnelle* held that the TSCG did not infringe Belgian constitutional identity because the TSCG was still an international treaty, and thus the commitment to the MTO was still an act of the budgetary competences of the legislator. It held:

> It is up to the democratically elected legislator not only to approve the budget annually, but to set medium-term budgetary objectives. It can contract these commitments in concert, especially in a treaty.[187]

Regulation 473/2013 was also not considered in this decision, but it is *not* an exercise of the democratically elected legislator with competence to approve the budget annually. As shown above in Section 7.3.1, the legislator does not set the MTO, and Regulation 473/2013 is not an international law treaty by which the legislator's commitment to contract its competence in concert remains its own – it is imposed by EU law.

A final indication that this instrument exceeds the boundaries of the EU legal order can be seen in the Council Legal Service's opinion on another part of the TSCG – Article 8(1). Article 8(1) TSCG states if the Commission finds that a party has failed to comply with the obligation

---

[184] *TSCG (Austria)*, [5.5.1] (emphasis added).
[185] *ESM (Austria)*, discussed above, Chapter 1, Section 1.2.2.1 at n 351, and Section at 1.3.1, n 475. See further Claudia Mayer, 'ESM Treaty in Accordance with the Austrian Constitution' (2013) 7 ICL Journal 385, 399.
[186] Mayer, 'ESM Treaty in Accordance with the Austrian Constitution', 399.
[187] *TCSG (Belgium)*, [B.8.4].

to enact the constitutional correction mechanism, the matter 'will be brought to the Court of Justice by one or more Contracting Parties'.[188] This presents an analogous problem to that of Regulation 473/2013. As Craig explains:

This cannot conceal the substantive reality, which is that Art. 8 TSCG is seeking to do by the back door what it cannot do by the front. Article 8 TSCG gives the Commission the 'trigger' as to whether a legal action should be brought.[189]

The Council Legal Service was of the opinion that Article 8 did not make the Commission the initiator of the action, because 'an act of a Member State taken in a situation of "tied competence" remains an act of this Member State'.[190] This is convincing. But this only heightens the case against Article 5(2)(a) of Regulation 473/2013 because it is *not* the intergovernmental TSCG which requires Member States to give effect to the Commission warning under Article 6(2) of Regulation 1466/97 – it is a provision of EU law which does so. A *fortiori* the Legal Service's view on Article 8 TSCG, it is not a case of 'tied competence', because the fetter tying the Member State to EU law is an instrument of EU law.

The only possible conclusion is that Article 5(2)(a) of Regulation 473/2013 is in violation of the principle of conferral and a manifest trespass on Member State fiscal sovereignty. To defuse this latent conflict, Articles 5(1)(a) and 5(2)(a) of Regulation 473/2013 must be amended so as to withdraw the imposition of the Commission trigger from the TSCG framework. Given that Member States are anyways likely to define their mechanisms on the basis of Article 6(2) of Regulation 1466/97 of their own accord, this is an utterly unnecessary and needlessly risky over-extension of EU law. As Menéndez wryly observes:

A ruling of the ECJ fining say the French state for a wrong transposition of [the TSCG] after the transposition was enshrined into the French Constitution and approved in a referendum would perhaps be the last judgement ever rendered by the ECJ.[191]

---

[188] Art. 8(1) TSCG.

[189] Paul Craig, 'The Stability, Coordination and Governance Treaty: Principle, Politics and Pragmatism' (2012) 37 EL Rev 231, 246.

[190] Council of the European Union 5788/12 (Brussels, January 26, 2012), 5. See: Craig, 'Stability, Coordination and Governance Treaty', 246.

[191] Menéndez, 'Constitutional Mutation', 133.

7.3.3 Directive 2011/85/EU Binds Member States to EU-Legislated Fiscal Rules

The third instrument that binds Member State budgetary policy is Directive 2011/85/EU. The stated purpose of the Directive is to 'lay down detailed rules concerning the characteristics of the budgetary frameworks of the Member States [...] necessary to *ensure Member States' compliance* with obligations under the TFEU'.[192] It should be noted that 'compliance' connotes a far stricter obligation than the requirement of 'consistency' found to constitute a binding obligation in Section 7.2.2, above. In *Ledra* v. *Commission and ECB*, AG Wahl explained:

> [T]he two terms of 'compliance' and 'consistency' should not be confused. Indeed, from a legal standpoint, they refer to two rather different concepts: the former requires obedience and full conformity between two texts, whereas the latter is satisfied by the mere compatibility and non-contradiction between them.[193]

Thus, Directive 2011/85/EU seeks, in no uncertain terms, to amend national fiscal frameworks so as to bind them to EU fiscal rules. The machinery deconstructed here has three components.

7.3.3.1 Component 1: EU Law Imposes Fiscal Rules which Enforce EU Reference Values

First, Article 5 of Directive 2011/85/EU states that Member States must have numerical rules in force to enforce the 3% deficit limit, the 60% debt limit and the MTO. It states:

> Each Member States shall have in place numerical fiscal rules which are specific to it and which effectively promote compliance with its obligations deriving from the TFEU in the area of budgetary policy [...] Such rules shall promote in particular:
> (a) compliance with the reference values on deficit and debt set in accordance with the TFEU;
> (b) the adoption of a multiannual fiscal planning horizon, including adherence to the Member State's medium-term budgetary objective.[194]

---

[192] Art. 1 Directive 2011/85/EU.
[193] *Ledra* v. *Commission (AG Wahl)*, [73].
[194] Art. 5 Directive 2011/85/EU. Art. 6(2) further harmonizes escape clauses.

The duty to 'effectively promote compliance' is a novel imperative that is typically interpreted as a duty to establish some financial penalty or disincentive which comes to bear on rule-breakers.[195] This is unlikely to be sufficiently clear and precise to constitute a binding legal obligation to enforce the 3% deficit, 60% debt and MTO.[196] However, Directive 2011/85/EU must be read in combination with Article 2a of Regulation 1466/97, which provides:

The respect of the [MTO] shall be included in the national medium-term budgetary frameworks in accordance with Chapter IV [Article 5] of [Directive 2011/85/EU].

This effectively amends the language of 'promote compliance' to 'shall respect' where it concerns the MTO. This language *is* capable of constituting a binding legal obligation under EU law,[197] and therefore *is* capable of making enforcement of the MTO a legal obligation under binding EU law – an intent perhaps made explicit by Article 7 of Directive 2011/85/EU, which states that 'annual budget *legislation* [. . .] shall reflect country-specific numerical rules in force'.[198]

7.3.3.2 Component 2: EU Law Binds the Enforcement Mechanism

Articles 6(1)(b) of the Directive and 5(1) of Regulation 473/2013 then require Member States to place compliance with these rules in the hands of the independent bodies examined in Section 7.2.1.2 above. Article 6(1)(b) states that compliance with the rules must be based on the analysis of the independent bodies,[199] and Article 5(1) of Regulation 473/2013 imbues those independent bodies with the mandate to enforce the MTO using numerical rules under the Directive. Article 5(1) states:

Member States shall have in place independent bodies for monitoring compliance with:
(a) numerical fiscal rules incorporating in the national budgetary processes their [MTO] as *established in Article 2a [Reg] 1466/97*;

---

[195] Case C-384/02 *Grøngaard and Bang* [2005] ECR I-09939; EU:C:2005:708 (Opinion of AG Maduro), [24].
[196] Case C-301/10 *Commission v. UK (Urban waste water)* EU:C:2012:36, [64].
[197] Case C-179/14 *Commission v. Hungary* EU:C:2016:108, [102]. See also Case C-342/14 *X-Steuerberatungsgesellschaft* v. *Finanzamt Hannover-Nord* EU:C:2015:827, [25]-[47]; Case C-298/14 *Brouillard* v. *Belgium* EU:C:2015:652, [47].
[198] Art. 7 Directive 2011/85/EU (see also Art. 10).
[199] Excerpted above, Section 7.2.1.3, n 88.

(b) numerical fiscal rules *as referred to in Article 5 of Directive 2011/85/EU.*[200]

The interaction of these articles is rather remarkable. Instruments of EU law cannot lawfully compel Member States to implement economic edicts for which the Union has no competence. EU legislation cannot, as national legislation might, bind the budgetary powers of the elected executive or legislature to a certain numerical target;[201] set procedural rules which govern the entirety of the legislative process;[202] set rules governing the setting of policy priorities and budgetary objectives;[203] regulate the constitutional relationships between levels of government in a Member State;[204] or govern the economic policy priorities of Member States.[205]

And yet, Directive 2011/85/EU, on its face, professes to do all these things. It does not do so directly, however – such legislation would be overtly *ultra vires.* Instead, the Directive and the Regulation seek to establish or amend national laws which *do* accomplish all these things. They implant fiscal rules in Member State law, then create fiscal institutions independent of national legislators, and then legislate a legal mandate for those fiscal institutions to enforce those fiscal rules.

7.3.3.3   Assessment: An Exceedance of Competence

This cannot be other than an excess of competence. The legal basis for Directive 2011/85/EU is Article 126(14) TFEU. This provides a basis for laying down detailed rules and definitions for how the excessive deficit procedure is to be applied *at EU level.* Curiously, however, this is how Directive 2011/85/EU describes its objectives:

Since the objective of this Directive, namely *uniform compliance with budgetary discipline* as required by the TFEU, cannot be sufficiently achieved by the Member States and can therefore be better achieved at the level of the Union, the Union may adopt measures, in accordance with the principles of subsidiarity as set out in Article 5 of the TEU.[206]

There are two glaring problems with this.

---

[200]   Art. 5(1) Reg 473/2013 (emphasis added).
[201]   Art. 2(c) Directive 2011/85/EU.
[202]   Art. 2(d) Directive 2011/85/EU.
[203]   Art. 2(e) Directive 2011/85/EU.
[204]   Art. 2(g) Directive 2011/85/EU.
[205]   Art. 2(3) Directive 2011/85/EU.
[206]   Rec 28, Directive 2011/85/EU (emphasis added).

First, the EU has no competence to achieve 'uniform compliance' with budgetary discipline, or ensure budgetary discipline at all. Budgetary discipline is not even a legal duty on the Member States: Article 126(10) TFEU is quite clear: The 3% and 60% reference values are not binding as a matter of law.[207] The EU's 'coordination' competence under Articles 2(3) and 5(1) TFEU is not a legal basis to amend *national budgetary laws* so that the debt/deficit values – plus a third variable, the MTO, found nowhere in the Treaty – takes effect in national law.

Second, even if there was such an EU competence to ensure budgetary discipline (which there is not) the notion that the EU can better manage national budgets in accordance with subsidiarity is so self-evidently flawed that it questions the entire basis for a democratic state. This is likely why the objective is described in terms of 'uniform' compliance – some reason must be given for why Europe's constitutional democracies cannot govern their own finances. But 'uniform compliance with budgetary discipline' appears nowhere in the Treaty. It is made up.

The result is a rather convoluted circumvention of the barriers of competence in an area of Member State fiscal sovereignty. Secondary EU law places Member States under a legal duty, to place themselves under a legal duty, to comply with the EU's fiscal rules – which themselves are not legal duties. A Member State whose budgetary framework allows financial legislation to breach the EU's numerical rules without enforcement will be in breach of EU law – even though the numerical rules themselves are not binding EU law. There is nothing in Directive 2011/85/EU or Regulation 483/2013 to enable one to avoid this conclusion.[208] Under Article 288(3) TFEU, a directive is binding. Member States must 'adopt all the measures necessary to ensure that the provisions of [a Directive] [are] fully effective and so guarantee achievement of the prescribed result'.[209]

The unavoidable conclusion is that Directive 2011/85/EU is *ultra vires* its legal basis and incompatible with the case law on Member State fiscal sovereignty cited above. Infringement proceedings against a Member State for, say, failing to implement Directive 2011/85/EU because it failed to enforce its country-specific MTO against the legislature would

---

[207] See above, Section 7.1 n 40.

[208] *SNHCA (Slovenia)* [49]: 'Such entails that [Slovenia] must not [. . .] adopt measures which would jeopardize the attainment of the aim of Directive 2011/85/EU, i.e. uniform respect for budgetary discipline.'

[209] Case C-277/13 *Commission* v. *Portugal* EU:C:2014:2208, [43]–[44]. See also: Joined Cases C-,179,188–190/94 *Dillenkofer et al.* [1996] ECR I-4867, [48].

perhaps yield yet another instrument that 'can perhaps only exist so long as it is not made use of'.[210]

7.3.4   The Effect of New Sanctions and Reverse-Burden Voting Rules

The final issue raised by the fiscal governance framework is the introduction of new sanctions and RQMV throughout both limbs of each of the MSP/EDP and MIP/EIP procedures enacted under Articles 121 and 126 TFEU.

If one were to look at the EU Treaties, under the twenty-one paragraphs of Articles 121 and 126 TFEU, there is only one fiscal obligation and one legal sanction: Member States must comply with the 60% and 3% of GDP debt and deficit limits or, under Article 126(11) TFEU, they may be fined up to 0.5% of GDP by their fellows voting in the Council by ordinary QMV.

No longer.

First, new sanctions have been interspersed throughout the MSP/EDP/ MIP/EIP procedures *before* a Member State is fined at the end of the EDP in Article 126(11). A Member State may now be fined a deposit of 0.2% of GDP following a declaration of 'no effective action' for deviation from the MTO under the MSP (Article 121(4) TFEU);[211] sanctions of 0.1% of GDP following a finding of an excessive imbalance under the MIP/EIP (Article 126(5) TFEU);[212] sanctions of 0.1% of GDP following 'non-compliance' with the recommendations of the Council under the MIP/ EIP (Article 126(8) TFEU);[213] a deposit of 0.2% of GDP following a declaration of 'particularly serious non-compliance' with the recommendations of the Council after launching the EDP (Article 126(5) TFEU);[214] a deposit of 0.2% of GDP following a decision of 'no effective action' under the EDP (Article 126(8) TFEU);[215] and, finally, fines of up to 0.5% of GDP for breach of the 3% and 60% debt limits (Article 126(11) TFEU).

Lattermost instance excepting, all of these new fines are for something *other* than the debt limits in the Treaty. They penalize failures to respect the MTO or specific Council recommendations.

---

[210]   Menéndez, 'Constitutional Mutation', 133.
[211]   Arts. 6(2), 10(2) Reg 1466/97. See also Arts. 4 and 5 of Reg 1173/2011.
[212]   Art. 3 Reg 1174/2011.
[213]   Art. 10(4) Reg 1176/2011; Art. Reg 1174/2011.
[214]   Article 5(1),(2)–(4) Reg 1173/2011.
[215]   Arts. 4(1), 5 Reg 1173/2011.

Secondly, under Regulations 1173/2011 and 1174/2011, all of these 'new' fines are adopted automatically unless rejected by 'reinforced' RQMV defined in accordance with Article 238(3)(b) TFEU, which requires 72% of the Member States comprising at least 65% of the population to reject the proposal.[216] However, as Regulations 1173/ 2011 and 1174/2011 cannot amend the Treaty, there are three stages of the sanctioning procedures (Article 121(4), Article 126(8) and Article 126(11) TFEU) which the Treaties say are still to be taken by ordinary QMV under Article 126(12) TFEU:

(i) The adoption of recommendations on the existence of an excessive deficit (Article 126(6) TFEU),[217] excessive imbalance (Article 121(4) TFEU),[218] or significant deviation from the MTO (Article 121(4) TFEU);[219]

(ii) The decision establishing 'no effective action' under the EDP (Article 126(8) TFEU);[220] and

(iii) The decision levying the sanctions of up to 0.5% of GDP under Article 126(11) TFEU.

Thus, while the new 2011 sanctions are virtually automatic, if one looks to these QMV 'gateways' in the Treaty, no sanctions should be possible without the active support of 55% of the Member States with 65% of the population.

But this is where Article 7 TSCG intervenes to flip the remaining voting rules in the Treaty for EMU countries. That article requires signatories to 'commit to supporting the proposals or recommendations' submitted by the Commission in the context of the EDP 'unless a qualified majority of them are opposed'.[221] This effectively switches all of the remaining gateways under the EDP for EMU countries: RQMV now applies to the decision on the existence of an excessive deficit (Article 126(6) TFEU), the decision on 'no effective action' (Article 126(8) TFEU), the decision to give notice (Article 126(9) TFEU) and all of the decisions to sanction (Article 126(11) TFEU).

---

[216] MSP: Arts. 4, 5 Reg 1173/2011. EDP: Arts. 4(1), 5, 6(2), 8(2) Reg 1173/2011. MIP/EIP: Art. 5 Reg 1175/2011 and Art. 3 Reg 1174/2011. Under Arts. 12(2) of Reg 1173/2011 and 5(2) of Reg 1174/2011, QMV is defined in accordance with Article 238(3)(b) TFEU.

[217] Art. 3(1)–(3) Reg 1467/97.

[218] Art. 7(1)–(2) Reg 1176/2011.

[219] Art. 6(2), 10(2) Reg 1466/97.

[220] Art. 4(1) Reg 1467/97.

[221] Art. 7 TSCG.

The effect of the new framework is that, while the Commission has no competence in economic policy, it is, 'as a rule',[222] presumed to be able to enumerate detailed economic policy measures and sanction Member States who do not comply over a large numerical and demographic majority in the Council.[223] The issue for this section is whether this constitutes a violation or restriction of budgetary sovereignty under the tests set out in Section 1.3.1 of this book.

7.3.4.1 Reinforced RQMV and the Community Method

The effect of introducing 'reinforced' RQMV into this paradigm has been carefully and illuminatingly documented by Van Aken and Artige.[224] First and most obviously, 'reinforced' RQMV means that the support needed for the Commission to pass its policies or sanctions against an EMU country is lowered considerably – from eleven countries (55.55%) *and* 66% of the population, to either two countries with 35.1% of the population, or six countries with any population.[225] The second effect is that abstentions effectively count as 'yes' votes.[226] This means the Commission could, for example, sanction Greece or Portugal against a numerical super-majority opposition of sixteen states to two,[227] or a population majority of 97.80%,[228] with *zero* positive votes of support. The thresholds between these extremes change markedly depending on the Member State at issue, but in all cases the Commission can sanction a country against an overwhelming numerical and demographic opposition of Europe's states and citizens. This

---

[222] See legislation cited above, n 137.

[223] For analysis see Chalmers, 'Law of Struggle', 688; De Streel, 'EU Fiscal Governance', 92–94.

[224] Wim Van Aken and Lionel Artige, 'A Comparative Analysis of Reverse Majority Voting' in De Witte, Héritier and Trechel (eds), *The Euro Crisis and the State of European Democracu* (European University Institute, 2013), 129.

[225] Art. 12(2) Reg 1173/2011; 5(2) Reg 1174/2011; Art. 7 TSCG.

[226] Van Aken and Artige, 'Reverse Majority Voting', 141

[227] Author's calculations based on composition and population of EMU countries at 13 September 2020. This scenario imagines a recommendation to sanction Greece, with Austria, Belgium, Cyprus, Estonia, Finland, France, Ireland, Italy, Latvia, Lithuania, Luxembourg, Malta, Netherlands, Portugal, Slovakia, Slovenia and Spain (sixteen countries with 60.87% of the population) voting against sanctions, and Germany and Spain (two countries with 39.13% of the population) in favour or abstaining. Greece does not vote.

[228] This scenario imagines a recommendation to sanction Greece, with Austria, Belgium, Finland, France, Germany Ireland, Italy, Lithuania, the Netherlands, Portugal, Slovakia and Spain (twelve states with 97.8% of the population) voting against sanctions, and Cyprus, Estonia, Latvia, Luxembourg, Malta, and Slovenia (six countries with 2.2% of the population) in favour or abstaining. Greece does not vote.

does not seem to adhere to the most basic principles of democratic accountability, let alone the Community method. As the BVerfG states:

> All systems of representative democracy have this in common: a will of the majority that has come about freely and taking due account of equality is formed, either in the constituency or in the assembly which has come into being proportionally, by the act of voting.[229]

Under the 'community method', democratic legitimation for EU acts is provided by the citizens directly, through the European Parliament; and indirectly, through the Council. However, the European Parliament has no legislative role in the MSP/EDP/MIP/EIP and exerts no decision-making influence on recommendations or sanctions.[230] This leaves the Council to legitimate these decisions. In a fact sheet on its website, the Commission insists that the Council is where responsibility for sanction-backed economic recommendations lies.[231] But this is disingenuous. How can the Council be responsible for an act of the Commission which occurs without any positive action from the Council, and which a sizeable majority on the Council are powerless to stop? This would appear to be irreconcilable with the formula for representative democracy under the 'community' method.

7.3.4.2   Reverse QMV and Member State Fiscal Sovereignty

However, this section concludes this is not likely to infringe on Member State fiscal sovereignty, for two reasons. First, as shown in Section 1.3.1.2, the test for an unlawful restriction of fiscal sovereignty is that the restriction is not reversible by an equivalent act of the parliament in the future. In that regard, Regulation 1173/2011 does not interfere with QMV control over the activation of EU sanctions because, as noted above, each stage is preceded by a QMV 'gateway' under the (unamended) Article 126 TFEU. The real culprit that flips the gateways here is Article 7 TSCG – an intergovernmental treaty.

   This has led some scholars to argue that Article 7 TSCG constitutes a circumvention or amendment of Article 126 TFEU in violation of the

---

[229] *Lisbon (Germany)* [191].
[230] Menéndez, 'Constitutional Mutation', 134; Chalmers, 'Law of Struggle', 692.
[231] European Commission, 'Fact Sheet Q&A: Country-specific recommendations 2015' (*European Commission Press Release Database*, 13 May 2014) http://europa.eu/rapid/press-release_MEMO-15-4968_en.htm accessed 27 February 2016.

amendment procedures in Article 48 TEU.[232] These arguments have merit. However, it remains that, as an intergovernmental treaty, the TSCG is unilaterally reversible by an equivalent act of the national parliament, and so does not infringe the test for an unlawful restriction on fiscal sovereignty under the case law set out in Section 1.3.1 of this book.[233]

Second, since it is a public international law agreement by Member States to modify the conditions on which they will pay a fine, the test which might otherwise apply to a fetter within control of parliament is a structural impairment of fiscal autonomy (see Section 1.3.1.4). Under that test, a finite impairment of fiscal autonomy from an agreement to pay money will not infringe the requirements of the democratic state so long as 'the democratic process remains open and that legal re-evaluations may occur on the basis of other majority decisions and that an irreversible legal prejudice to future generations is avoided'.[234] In *ESM (Germany)* budget commitments of €190,024,800,000 (approximately 50% of all central government expenditure) did not constitute an infringement of fiscal sovereignty because it did not impair the parliament's ability to shape the economic and social life of the state.[235] By that standard, fines of up to 0.5% of GDP simply fall within the margin of appreciation afforded to the legislator by even the most assertive constitutional court (so long as a subsequent parliament can end its commitment to that sanctioning mechanism in the future).

7.3.5 Conclusion: Three Infringements of Member State Fiscal Sovereignty

This section finds that three out of the four fiscal governance mechanisms examined in this Section 7.3 infringe a constitutional boundary identified in this book.

[7.3.1] First, it is the MTO produced by the *Commission* and the *Council* under Articles 5(1) and 9(1) Regulation 1466/97 – not the assessment of the Member State – which is enforced for the purposes of Directive 2011/85/EU; Regulation 473/2013; and Article 3(1)(b) TSCG (as co-opted by Article 5(2)(a) of Regulation 473/2013).

---

[232] Craig, 'Stability, Coordination and Governance Treaty', 238; Alan Dashwood, 'The United Kingdom in a Re-formed Union' (2013) 38 EL Rev 737, 744.

[233] *ESM II (Germany)* [172]–[173]; *TSCG (France)* [26]–[27]; *TSCG (Austria)* [5.3]–[5.5.1], [6.4];*TCSG (Belgium)*, [B.8.4].

[234] *ESM II (Germany)* [173]–[174]; *Euro Rescue Package (Germany)* [131]; and cases cited above, Chapter 1, Section 1.3.1.1, n 484.

[235] *ESM I (Germany)* [240]; *ESM II (Germany)* [185].

[7.3.2] Second, Article 5(2)(a) of Regulation 473/2013 spans the boundary between legal orders and co-opts the Fiscal Compact, inserting the Commission's warning under Article 6(2) Regulation 1466/97 into an intergovernmental treaty that binds Member State constitutional law. This conflicts with the constitutional identity rulings of four Member State constitutional courts and the Council Legal Service's opinion on 'tied competence'.

[7.3.3] Third, by professing a legal competence to ensure 'uniform compliance with budgetary discipline', Directive 2011/85/EU is *ultra vires* its legal basis and penetrates the boundaries of Member State fiscal sovereignty. There is no EU competence to amend *national budgetary laws* so that the 3% or 60% debt values – plus a third variable, the MTO, found nowhere in the EU Treaties – take effect in national law.

[7.3.4] The 'reinforced' RQMV procedures appear be incompatible with the 'community' method; however, the tests for an unlawful restriction or structural impairment of fiscal sovereignty are not met.

7.4 Binding Vertical Interlinkages with EU Macroeconomic Governance

This fourth section of this chapter is concerned with binding EU legislation enforcing macroeconomic recommendations issued in the context of the EU's MIP/EIP procedure.

The procedure begins with the adoption of the Alert Mechanism Report (AMR), which evaluates Member States against a macroeconomic 'scoreboard' consisting of fourteen headline variables and twenty-eight auxiliary indicators designed to indicate macroeconomic imbalances.[236] Seven indicators relate to internal imbalances, seven relate to external imbalances, and the scoreboard has expanded over time.[237] A finding of an imbalance or excessive imbalance on one of those headline variables will activate the MIP/EIP, after which Member States will receive highly specific, sanction-backed recommendations in 'areas specifically excluded from EU interference by the Treaty'.[238] Once activated, the Member State must submit a far-reaching 'Corrective Action Plan' (CAP), potentially encompassing any aspect of economic, social and welfare policy, based on Commission and Council

---

[236] The AMR is established by Arts. 3, 4 Reg 1176/2011, under Art. 121(2) TFEU.

[237] See Alert Mechanism Report 2019 Statistical Annex COM(2018) 758 final, 15–24.

[238] Dawson and de Witte, 'Constitutional Balance', 840.

recommendations.[239] Once again, the Member State may be found in 'non-compliance' and sanctioned where the Member State's CAP is rejected or where the 'Member State concerned has not taken the corrective action recommended by the Council'.[240]

This section examines three aspects of this procedure which extend EU policy norms beyond the legislative competences of the Union and appear to imbue them with legal force under EU law.

7.4.1 Component 1: The Scope of the Macroeconomic Scoreboard

The first aspect of concern is the remarkable discretion afforded to the Commission under Regulation 1176/2011 to choose the economic variables that are included in the macroeconomic scoreboard, and therefore the competences for which Member States may be brought under the system of co-government.[241] Under Article 4(7) of Regulation 1176/2011, the task of drafting and deciding what goes into the scoreboard belongs entirely to the Commission. Under that article:

The Commission shall assess the appropriateness of the scoreboard, including the composition of the indicators, the thresholds set and the methodology used, and it shall adjust or modify them where necessary. The Commission shall make changes in the underlying methodology and composition of the scoreboard and the associated thresholds public.

The only substantive parameters imposed on the Commission's discretion are set out in Article 4(3) of Regulation 1176/2011, which states that the 'scoreboard shall, inter alia, encompass indicators which are useful in the early identification of (a) internal imbalances [and] (b) external imbalances', and then gives a short list of variables that should be included for each, such as public and private indebtedness and the current account.[242] Outside of this open list of variables (and a duty to 'consult' the ESRB on any financial indicators chosen)[243] there is no institutional oversight or substantive limit on the Commission's discretion whatsoever.

Accountability issues arose immediately. The European Parliament's review of the first Commission scoreboard, for example, complained that the Commission had just cited the 'available economic literature'

---

[239] Art. 8 Reg 1176/2011.
[240] See Art. 10(4) Reg 1176/2011 and Art. 3(1) Reg 1174/2011.
[241] For excellent analyses on this point, see Chalmers, 'Law of Struggle', 682–684; Dawson, 'Accountability Structure', 987; Menéndez, 'Constitutional Mutation', 128.
[242] Art. 4(7) Reg 1176/2011.
[243] Art. 4(5) Reg 1176/2011.

in support of its chosen variables without 'providing a single specific reference'.[244]

Since this inauspicious start, the scoreboard has expanded to a list of indicators that bears no resemblance to the legislative competences of the Union. The first macroeconomic scoreboard in February 2012 consisted of ten headline indicators and eighteen auxiliary indicators appropriately confined to those variables specified in Article 4(3) of Regulation 1176/2011.[245] In November 2012, an eleventh indicator relating to financial sector liabilities was added, at which time the Commission assured that it 'does not foresee the addition of new indicators to the scoreboard'.[246] Then, less than a year later, the Commission introduced eight social indicators to the auxiliary list, despite noting that 'employment and social policies fall very largely under the national competence of the Member States'.[247] Then in September 2015 the Commission moved three of these social indicators (the activity rate, long-term unemployment and youth unemployment) to the headline scoreboard.[248] It appeared to acknowledge that it had broken from the legislative basis for the MIP, stating:

The inclusion of these variables into the scoreboard shall not have legal implications nor change the focus of the MIP, which remains aimed at preventing the emergence of harmful macroeconomic imbalances and ensuring their correction. To this purpose, no additional employment and social indicators should a priori be added to the scoreboard in the future.[249]

Yet the very next month, in October 2015, Commission minutes described a new 'highly political' strategy to add more social indicators to the MIP,[250] such as 'access to healthcare and the level of social protection', and proposed that 'reference criteria be set to measure those factors'.[251] The stated objective for this was not the stability of

---

[244] European Parliament Resolution of 15 December 2011 on the Scoreboard for the surveillance of macroeconomic imbalances: envisaged initial design' P7_TA(2011) 0424, para 11.

[245] European Commission, Alert Mechanism Report 2013 COM(2012) 68 final, 3.

[246] European Commission, Alert Mechanism Report 2014 COM(2013) 790 final, 22.

[247] European Commission, 'Strengthening the Social Dimension of the Economic and Monetary Union' COM(2013) 690 final, 4.

[248] European Commission, 'Adding Employment Indicators to the Scoreboard of the Macroeconomic Imbalance Procedure' SWD Ref. Ares (2015) 5426195.

[249] Commission, Employment indicators, 1.

[250] European Commission, 'Minutes of the 2143rd meeting', 22.

[251] European Commission, 'Minutes of the 2145th meeting', 36.

EMU, but 'to rally the support of the people of Europe for the project of deepening EMU'.[252]

It is hard to imagine this meeting any test of controlled delegation.[253] To rally political support for deepening EMU is far outside the stated purposes of the EU's coordination competence. Quite contrary to the Commission's statement that expanding the scoreboard has no legal implications, the scoreboard determines the scope of the MIP/EIP, and therefore the fields of policy in which Member States will be governed by EU institutions. As Chalmers observes, 'the thresholds for determining when States enter and exit this sphere of co-government are very unstable: something which offends the very idea of limited government'.[254]

7.4.2 Component 2: 'Imbalances' and 'Excessive Imbalances'

The second matter of concern is the Commission's discretion to determine whether a Member State is suffering from an 'Imbalance' or 'Excessive Imbalance', and thus activate the trigger which determines when a Member State needs to be governed by EU institutions.

Under Article 2 of Regulation 1176/2011, 'Imbalances' are defined as 'any trend giving rise to macroeconomic developments which are adversely affecting, or have the potential adversely to affect, the proper functioning of the economy *of a Member State* or of the [EMU] or of the Union as a whole'. 'Excessive Imbalances' are 'severe imbalances, *including* imbalances that jeopardise or risk jeopardising the proper functioning of the economic and monetary union'.[255]

The definitions of 'Imbalances' and 'Excessive Imbalances' are therefore not restricted to the scope of the EU's legislative competences; they are not limited to cross-border situations; and they are not limited to the stability of the monetary union. Under Regulation 1176/2011, 'imbalances' include economic trends that affect the 'functioning of the economy of a Member State' individually, and 'excessive imbalances' are not confined to imbalances that 'risk jeopardising the proper functioning of the [EMU]'. The governance regime extends to virtually *any* macroeconomic development within a Member State, even purely internal ones.

---

[252] European Commission, 'Minutes of the 2143rd meeting', 22.
[253] Case 9/56 *Meroni* v. *Haute autorité* EU:C:1958:7, 152; Case 10/56 *Meroni* v. *Haute autorité* EU:C:1958:8, 173.
[254] Chalmers, 'Law of Struggle', 682–684.
[255] Art. 2 Reg 1176/2011 (emphasis added).

Then, once a variable on the scoreboard 'flashes', Regulation 1176/ 2011 gives the Commission a virtually open-ended mandate to investigate and adjudge the significance of any suspected imbalances through an In-Depth Review (IDR).[256] Article 5(2) even goes so far as to permit the use of 'qualitative information' in the analysis,[257] and Article 3(2) adds that 'conclusions shall not be drawn from a mechanical reading of the scoreboard indicators,' further muddying what an 'imbalance' even is. Perhaps unsurprisingly, a recent study of Commission recommendations found that 'the EU makes significant political choices about which imbalances are judged to be excessive and which are judged not excessive'.[258]

As commentators such as Dawson and Chalmers have illuminatingly pointed out, the indeterminacy of these norms makes it nigh impossible to hold the Commission's application of the rules to any sort of legal or democratic accountability.[259] AMRs are transmitted to the European Parliament, the Council and the EESC, but they have no amending role in the assessments.[260] Similarly, the only provision for the European Parliament is the Economic Dialogues, which do not begin until later stages of the MIP, and do not impact the reviews.[261] National parliaments are excluded entirely. Member States are represented at this stage only in the Council and the Eurogroup, which may adopt conclusions or 'discuss' AMRs, but have no ability to alter the content.[262]

Judicial review for excess of discretion would be just as elusive. Establishing an unlawful act of a EU institution in the performance of its tasks requires establishing that the institution 'manifestly and gravely disregarded the limits on its discretion'.[263] This standard is difficult to overcome at the best of times. It would be nigh impossible where the Commission can make changes to the 'methodology and composition of the scoreboard and the associated thresholds'

---

[256] Art. 5 Reg 1176/2011
[257] Art. 5(2) Reg 1176/2011.
[258] Konstantinos Efstathou and Guntram Wolff, 'Is the European Semester Effective and Useful?' (2018) Bruegel Policy Contribution Issue No 9, 1.
[259] Dawson, 'Accountability Structure', 987; Chalmers, 'Law of Struggle', 682–684.
[260] Art. 3(4) Reg 1176/2011. Chalmers, 'Law of Struggle', 692.
[261] Art. 14(1) Reg 1176/2011; Art. 6 Reg 1174/2011; Arts. 3(9), 7(1),(4),(10), 18 Reg 472/2013; Art. 15 Reg 473/2013.
[262] Article 3(4) Reg 1173/2011; Art. 4(4) Reg 1175/2011.
[263] Case C-352/98 *Bergaderm and Groupil* v. *Commission* [2000] ECR I-5291; EU: C:2000:3611, [43].

autonomously,[264] and furthermore asserts that 'there is no automatic or mechanical interpretation' of the scoreboard, 'but rather a qualitative assessment'.[265]

7.4.3 Component 3: Economic Recommendations Are Incorporated into Binding EU Law

The final matter of concern is the interaction with Regulation 473/2013. As explained in Section 7.2.2, Regulation 473/2013 states that EMU Member States' budgetary procedures, medium-term fiscal plans and draft budgets themselves 'shall be consistent with', *inter alia*: 'recommendations issued in the context of the annual cycle of surveillance, including the macroeconomic imbalances procedure as established by Regulation (EU) No 1176/2011'.[266]

In this context, this unpacks as follows: Once the MIP/EIP has been activated, the Council may adopt a Commission recommendation for preventative or corrective action under Article 121(2) or 121(4) TFEU.[267] If the IDR results in a finding of 'excessive imbalances', EMU Member States must submit a Corrective Action Plan (CAP) that must be based on, and consistent with, EU recommendations.[268]

These EU recommendations include detailed, sanction-backed policy recommendations in areas for which there is little doubt the Union has no competence to legislate. Country-specific recommendations specify policies for, *inter alia*, elder care,[269] court docket backlogs,[270] youth vocational training and school evaluations,[271] childcare,[272] city

[264] Art. 4(7) Reg 1176/2011.
[265] European Commission, *First Alert Mechanism Report on macroeconomic imbalances in Member States* (MEMO/12/104, 2012).
[266] Arts. 3(3), 4(1), 6(1) Reg 473/2013.
[267] Arts. 6(1) (MIP), 7(1)–(2) (EIP) Reg 1176/2011.
[268] Art. 8(1) Reg 1176/201; Art. 9(1)–(2) Reg 473/2013. Cf: Koen Lenaerts, 'EMU and the EU's Constitutional Framework' (2014) 39 EL Rev 753, 766–767.
[269] Council Recommendation of 10 July 2012 on the National Reform Programme 2012 of Italy and delivering a Council opinion on the Stability Programme of Italy, 2012–2015 [2012] OJ C 219/14, para 4.
[270] Council Recommendation of 9 July 2013 on the National Reform Programme 2013 of Italy and delivering a Council opinion on the Stability Programme of Italy, 2012–2017 [2013] OJ C 217/11, para (12).
[271] Council Recommendation of 8 July 2014 on the NRP of Italy, para 6.
[272] Council Recommendation of 8 July 2014 on the National Reform Programme 2014 of Ireland and delivering a Council opinion on the Stability Programme of Ireland 2014 [2014] OJ C 247/07, para 14.

planning policy,[273] and 'work-life balance'.[274] Nor do Commission minutes show much internal concern for the limits of competence. In the same breath, Commission minutes propose 'targeted measures to boost employment among vulnerable groups', measures to 'plug the gaps in social safety nets' and measures targeting 'health care or in favour of children, in terms of early schooling and assistance'.[275] By 2016, Commission minutes expressed 'satisfaction that, for example, questions such as the pay gap between men and women', 'the efficiency of the judiciary', and 'the quality of health care systems and access to good quality care' had been deployed in the context of the European Semester.[276]

None of these policies are within the competences of the Union. Most are not even relevant to economic imbalances. As Efstathiou and Wolff marvel, 'to our surprise a sizable share of recommendations, such as on childcare, are also labelled as relevant for resolving macroeconomic imbalances'.[277]

Yet these recommendations then become the object of enforcement under Regulation 473/2013 because, under Articles 10(4) of Regulation 1176/2011 and 3(1) of Regulation 1174/2011, the Council will issue a decision establishing 'non-compliance' and trigger fines if, in the Commission's view, the Member State 'has not taken the corrective action *recommended by the Council*'.[278]

This imbues the recommendations under the MIP/EIP with binding force in the same manner as the 'budgetary veto' discussed above in Section 7.2.2, by stretching a binding EU law obligation over (formerly) non-binding recommendations in fields of economic policy. A Member State whose economic policies are in 'non-compliance' under Article 10(4) of Regulation 1176/2011 can hardly be said to conform to the binding obligation to have a budgetary framework 'consistent with' those same obligations for the purposes of Articles 3, 4(1) and 6(1) of Regulation 473/2013. The effect of this obligation was discussed in Section 7.2.2; however, it suffices to recall here that 'consistency' requires nothing less than 'compatibility and non-contradiction'

---

[273] Council Recommendation of 14 July 2015 on the NRP of the UK, rec 2.
[274] See, for example, Council Recommendation on NRP and Stability Programme Italy 2015, (19) and para 5.
[275] Commission, 'Minutes of the 2126th Meeting'.
[276] European Commission, 'Minutes of the 2158th Meeting', 21.
[277] Efstathou and Wolff, 'Effective and Useful?', 1.
[278] Art. 10(4) Reg 1176/2011 (emphasis added). This triggers fines under Article 3 Reg 1174/2011.

between economic policies,[279] and refraining from approving an economic programme whose consistency one doubts.[280] In this way, 'non-binding' economic recommendations under the MIP/EIP are drawn into the binding requirements of Regulation 473/2013 and used as the 'triggering rule' for directly effective and supreme EU law.[281] As stated by AG Bobek in his recent opinion on recommendations, if a recommendation were a 'true' recommendation, it could not 'create a legislative "shortcut" or a "pre-emption" by excluding certain actors from the later legislative process'.[282] But this is what this procedure does.

7.4.4   Conclusion: An Ultra Vires Intrusion on Fiscal Sovereignty

The primary legal basis for the instruments which comprise the MIP/EIP – Regulations 1174/2011, 1176/2011 and 473/2013 – is Article 121(6) TFEU. The limitations of this article were discussed above (see Sections 7.1 and 7.2.2.4), but suffice it to recall here that Article 121(6) TFEU does not provide a legal basis to bind Member States to substantive economic policies prescribed by EU institutions.[283]

Indeed, neither Regulations 1174/2011 nor 1176/2011 do this. True, they require Member States to submit a CAP that is consistent with EU recommendations in a range of policy areas that are outwith the legislative competences of the Union. True, also, Member States are bound to take recommendations into account.[284] True, again, this is a legal device clearly drafted with 'the ambition to induce compliance on the part of its addressees' with real positivist legal force analogous to that identified by AG Bobek's recent opinion on recommendations in *Gaming Recommmendation*.[285] As AG Bobek has opined, requiring Member States to 'designate, to monitor, to notify, to evaluate, to collect data and to report back to the Commission by specific dates on all those (entirely

---

[279] *Ledra* v. *Commission (AG Wahl)*, [72].

[280] *Ledra* v. *Commission*, [58]–[60], [67].

[281] See also Melanos Markakis and Paul Dermine, 'Bailouts, the Legal Status of Memoranda of Understanding, and the Scope of Application of the EU Charter: *Florescu*' (2018) 55 CMLR 643, 666; René Repasi, 'Judicial Protection against Austerity Measures in the Euro Area: *Ledra* and *Mallis*' (2017) 54 CMLR 1123, 1141.

[282] *Belgium* v. *Commisssion (Gaming Recommendation) (AG Bobek)*, [169].

[283] See discussion in Section 7.1 and Section 7.2.2.4.

[284] *Grimaldi*, [18]; *Belgium* v. *Commisssion (Gaming Recommendation) (AG Bobek)*, [99]–[100]. On the duty to 'take due account' see above, Section 7.1, n 25.

[285] *Belgium* v. *Commisssion (Gaming Recommendation) (AG Bobek)*, [93]–[95].

voluntary) activities [in a field outside EU competence] reaches the quality of an advanced Jedi mind trick.'[286]

No doubt. But it remains that the CAP is merely a document submitted at EU level. The secondary EU law obligation of consistency imposed on the CAP does not bind actual economic policies as a matter of law. If a Member State wishes to submit a compliant CAP to comply with the Regulations, and then disregard it in the policies it chooses to implement, there is little in Regulations 1174/2011 or 1176/2011 that could ground infringement proceedings for doing so.

Regulation 473/2013 is a different matter. As explained in Section 7.2.2, this *does* create a mechanism capable of binding Member States as a matter of law, because 'non-compliance' with the recommended outcome in the context of the MIP/EIP will lead to a breach of Articles 3, 4(1) and 6(1) of Regulation 473/2013 which, under Article 288 TFEU, is binding in its entirety and directly applicable in all Member States. An obligation to implement a recommendation *can* be imbued with legal force through incorporation into binding EU law,[287] or as stated by AG Bobek, through the creation of 'a separate and distinct sanction for failing to do so'.[288]

As this framework compels the exercise of substantive economic policies within the competence of national parliaments, the fiscal sovereignty test which would apply in this context is that discussed in Section 1.3.1.3 on unlawful conferrals of fiscal sovereignty.[289] As the BVerfG so put it in *Lisbon (Germany)*:

> [A] transfer of the right of the *Bundestag* to adopt the budget and control its implementation by the government [would] violate the principle of democracy and the right to elect the German *Bundestag* in its essential content if the determination of the type and amount of the levies imposed on the citizen were supranationalised to a considerable extent. [. . .] In this area, the responsibility concerning social policy in particular is subject to the democratic decision-making process, which citizens want to influence through free and equal elections. Budget sovereignty is where political decisions are planned to combine economic burdens with benefits granted by the state.[290]

---

[286] *Belgium* v. *Commisssion (Gaming Recommendation) (AG Bobek)*, [132].

[287] *Germany et ors* v. *Commission*, [14], [27]–[36]; *Grimaldi* [18]–[19]; *Belgium* v. *Commisssion (Gaming Recommendation) (AG Bobek)*, [91]–[93], [100].

[288] *Belgium* v. *Commission (Gaming Recommendation) (AG Bobek)*, [105] (see also [120]).

[289] See cases cited above, Chapter 1, Section 1.3.1.1, n 483 and Section 1.3.1.3.

[290] *Lisbon (Germany)* [228]–[232].

In *ESM (Germany)*, the BVerfG stated that an intrusion into 'fundamental fiscal decisions on public revenue and public expenditure [and] decisions on the shaping of the social state' would violate the constitutional identity of Germany.[291] In that case, it held that the TSCG did not do so because it 'does not grant the European Commission authority to impose specific substantive requirements for the structuring of budgets'.[292]

Regulation 473/2013, however, *does* grant EU institutions authority to impose specific substantive requirements for the structuring of budgets, because it uses economic policy norms issued in the context of the MIP/EIP as the point of enforcement under directly applicable and supreme EU law.

Once again, the only possible conclusion to be drawn is that requiring Member States to internalize economic policy prescriptions under binding secondary EU law is manifestly beyond the boundaries of the EU legal order, and such instruments may perhaps exist only in so far as they are not actually enforced. If macroeconomic governance is to be restored to the confines of its legal basis, the machinery of the 'budgetary veto' in Regulation 473/2013 must be dismantled so that non-compliance with MIP/EIP recommendations no longer triggers a breach of binding and supreme legal obligations under Regulation 473/2013.

7.5 Binding Interlinkages with EFSM, EFSF and ESM Financial Conditionality

The final (and perhaps most important) legal architecture of concern to this chapter is that surrounding the macroeconomic adjustment programmes attached to EFSM, EFSF and ESM financial assistance. All EFSM/EFSF/ESM financial assistance conditionality has now been institutionalized in the EU legal order under Regulation 472/2013, in conjunction with Regulation 407/2010 and the TESM. Under those instruments, the Commission is tasked with assessing requests for stability support (in hand with the ECB),[293] negotiating and drafting economic conditionality (in hand with the ECB),[294] and ensuring that

---

[291] *ESM II (Germany)* [164], [244]. See also: *ESM II (Germany)* [164]; *Euro Rescue Package (Germany)* [127].
[292] *ESM II (Germany)* [164], [244].
[293] Art. 6 Reg 472/2013; Arts. 4(4), 13(1) TESM; Art. 3 Reg 407/2010 (EFSM).
[294] Art. 7(1) Reg 472/2013; Art. 13(3) TESM; Art. 3 Reg 407/2010 (EFSM).

conditionality is 'fully consistent with the macroeconomic adjustment programme' enacted into EU law by the Council.[295] EFSM conditionality is set out in an MoU signed by the Commission on behalf of the EFSM under Regulation 407/2010,[296] while ESM conditionality is set out in an MoU signed by the Commission on behalf of the ESM under Regulation 472/2013 and the TESM.[297] Once agreed, the macroeconomic adjustment programme is simultaneously enacted in Council decisions or Council implementing decisions, and these decisions are binding under Article 288 TFEU.[298] The macroeconomic adjustment programme is then fed into the procedures of the MSP/EDP/MIP/EIP, where its content supersedes all other surveillance and reporting requirements.[299]

As this book is concerned with the boundaries of the EU legal order, this section is mainly concerned with acts of EU law imbued with the supremacy of EU law and, by that effect, capable of requiring Member States to set aside conflicting social, economic and fiscal policy choices within their own constitutional competences. As Markakis and Dermine so put it:

Litigants need to strike at the core: they need to strike at the source of these measures [. . .] [w]hen you believe that a measure is illegal, you need to be able to uproot its normative source.[300]

Under EU law, there are three procedures by which an act of EU law may be challenged on grounds that it is illegal or *ultra vires*: An action for annulment (Article 263 TFEU); a preliminary reference (Article 267 TFEU); or a claim for damages (Article 340 TFEU). At the outset, Article 340 TFEU is no help because an award of damages does not annul the *ultra vires* measure, and a claim for non-contractual liability will not lie against a tortious EU act where the illegality is one of competence.[301] This leaves Articles 263 and 267 TFEU. Under those articles, judicial review is possible once a measure has legal effects, whether at EU or national level.[302] This encompasses legislative acts, implementing acts

---

[295] Art. 7(2)–(3) Reg 472/2013; Art. 3(8) Reg 407/2010 (EFSM).
[296] Art. 3(5) Reg 407/2010.
[297] Art. 7(2) Reg 472/2013; Art. 13(4) TESM.
[298] Art. 7(2) Reg 472/2013; Art. 3(2),(7) Reg 407/2010.
[299] Arts. 10–13 Reg 472/2013.
[300] Markakis and Dermine, 'Bailouts', 649.
[301] Case 5/71 *Schöppenstedt* v. *Council* [1971] ECR 975; EU:C:1971:116, [11]; Joined Cases C-120–121/06 P *FIAMM* v. *Council and Commission* [2008] ECR I-06513; EU:C:2008:476, [176]–[184].
[302] Case 60/81 *IBM* v. *Commission* [1981] ECR 2639; EU:C:1981:264 [9]; Joined Cases C-68/94 and C-30/95 *France et al.* v. *Commission* [1998] ECR I-1375; EU:C:1998:148 [62].

and delegated acts, including EU regulations, directives, decisions and any other *sui generis* acts which produce binding legal effects, whatever their form.[303] A ruling that an EU act is valid and enforceable under those articles therefore affirms that the act is a binding and supreme act of EU law.

To date, however, the CJEU has repeatedly declined direct actions and preliminary references challenging the validity of macroeconomic adjustment programmes on the basis that the impugned instruments are not binding acts of the Union or, if they are, that the EU act is not challengeable because the national implementation of that act is not attributable to the EU law.[304] On this basis, the CJEU has rejected dozens of challenges to conditions imposed by economic policy instruments including, *inter alia*:

- Mous negotiated and signed by the Commission on behalf of the ESM;[305]
- Mous negotiated and signed by the Commission on behalf of the EU's EFSM;[306]
- Council Decisions and Council Implementing Decisions;[307]
- Statements of the Eurogroup setting out financial assistance conditionality;[308]
- Statements of the ECB;[309] and

Preliminary references may be admissible regarding acts without legal effects: *Irish Asphalt*, [34].

[303] Joined Cases 8–11/66 *Cimenteries CBR et al.* v. *Commission* [1967] ECR 75; EU:C:1967:7, [91]; Case 22/70 *Commission* v. *Council (ERTA)* [1971] ECR 26; EU:C:1971:32, [42]; *IBM* v. *Commission*, [9]; Case C-303/90 *France* v. *Commission* [1991] ECR I-5315; Case C-325/91 *France* v. *Commission* [1993] ECR I-3283; Case C-39/93 *Syndicat Français de l'Express International (SFEI)* v. *Commission* [1994] ECR I-2681; Case C-57/95 *France* v. *Commission* [1997] ECR I-1627, [23]; Case C-521/06 P *Athinaïki Techniki* v. *Commission* [2008] ECR I-5829; EU:C:2008:422, [42]-[44]; Case C-31/13 P *Hungary* v. *Commission* EU:C:2014:70, [54]-[55]; Joined Cases C-463/10, 475/10 P *Deutsche Post and Germany* v. *Commission* EU:C:2011:656, [36]-[38].

[304] The jurisdiction of the court is confined to provisions of EU law: Case C-185/08 *Latchways and Eurosafe* v. *Kedge Safety Systems BV* [2010] ECR I-10025; EU:C:2010:619; Case C-361/07 *Polier* v. *Najar* [2008] ECR I-6; EU:C:2008:16, [9].

[305] *Ledra* v. *Commission*, [52]-[55].

[306] Case C-128/12 *Sindicato dos Bancários do Norte et al.* v. *BPN* EU:C:2013:149, [12]; Case C-264/12 *Sindicato Nacional dos Profissionais de Seguros e Afins* v. *Fidelitate Mudial* EU:C:2014:2036, [19]; Case C-665/13 *Sindicato Nacional dos Profissionais de Seguros e Afins* v. *Via Directa* EU:C:2014:2327, [14].

[307] Case T-541/10 *ADEDY, Papaspyros and Iliopoulos* v. *Council* EU:T:2012:626, [71]-[76]; Case T-215/11 *ADEDY et al.* v. *Council* EU:T:2012:626, [64].

[308] Joined Cases 105-109/15 P *Mallis* v. *Commission*.

[309] Case C-64/14 P *Von Storch et al.* v. *ECB* EU:C:2016:846, [36]-[38].

- MoUs negotiated and signed by the Commission for BoP assistance.[310]

The (increasingly tenuous) position of the CJEU is therefore that the implementation of EFSM/EFSF/ESM macroeconomic programmes in the Member States has nothing to do with EU law. As will be shown, this has become a vexing and expensive problem for private litigants. As a symptom of the boundaries of this book, however, it is expository. As will be shown, the acts at issue include binding secondary EU law instruments under Article 288 TFEU;[311] they include 'the adoption of directives or decisions' under EU regulations and EU Treaty provisions;[312] they include EU acts capable of grounding actions for damages;[313] they include acts of EU institutions within the meaning of Article 267(b) TFEU;[314] they include EU acts according to established ECJ case law;[315] and they impose 'binding'[316] and 'mandatory'[317] obligations to implement 'specific measures' in economic policy,[318] which implementation 'constitutes an implementation of EU law'.[319] But, if a challenge is ever raised on *ultra vires* or illegality grounds, it will be met with the response that they are not EU law or, if they are, that they are not challengeable because it was not the implementation of EU law which affected the position of the litigants.

The problem, it seems, is that the EU has no competence to regulate the policies which these instruments do, clearly, regulate, so the ECJ cannot acknowledge that they are binding acts of EU law without implicitly recognizing that they are also *ultra vires*. So it does not. This is not only constitutionally illegitimate, but it renders them illusory or unenforceable against Member States as effective legal implements of EU fiscal federalism: Member State courts can (and do) strike them

---

[310] Case C-434/11 *Corpul National al Politistilor* v. *MAI* EU:C:2011:830, [16]; Case C-462/11 *Cozman* v. *Teatrul Municipal Târgoviste* EU:C:2011:831, [13]-[15]; Case C-134/12 *MAI et al.* v. *Corpul National al Politistilor* EU:C:2012:288, [12]-[14]; Case C-369/12 *Corpul National al Politisilor* v. *MAI* EU:C:2012:725, [15].

[311] Art. 7 Reg 472/2013; Art. 3 Reg 407/2010. See, for example, cases cited above, n 307.

[312] *Florescu*, [31]-[36], [41] (see also [47]-[48]); *Mallis* v. *Commission (AG Wathelet)* [85]-[94].

[313] *Ledra* v. *Commission*, [55]-[59], [67].

[314] *Florescu*, [35]-[36]; Case C-258/14 *Florescu et al.* v. *Romania* EU:C:2016:995 (Opinion of AG Bot) [49]-[55]; *Juízes Portugueses*, [46], [49].

[315] Case C-409/13 *Council* v. *Commission* [70]-[74]; Case C-613/14 *Irish Asphalt*, [35].

[316] *Dowling* v. *Minister of Finance* [2013] IEHC 27 [41.2](4); Case C-41/15 *Dowling (AG Wahl)* (Opinion of AG Wahl) [25].

[317] *Florescu*, [41] (see also [35]-[36], [49]-[55]); *Juízes Portugueses*, [46] (see also [49]).

[318] *Juízes Portugueses (AG ØE)*, [52].

[319] *Juízes Portugueses (AG ØE)*, [53].

down without facing a claim of EU supremacy. The Portuguese *Tribunal Constitucional*, for example, has ably struck down numerous economic measures contained in Council Decisions and other instruments which it considered to be binding EU law.[320] Other courts have also done so.[321] There is perhaps no clearer demonstration that the new cornerstone of EU fiscal federalism is outside the boundaries of the EU legal order than that it is repeatedly disowned by the ECJ and subsequently struck down by Member State constitutional courts.

7.5.1   Denial of Actions against Financial Conditionality Instruments

The original sin underlying all this case law is the first *ultra vires* challenge to conditional financial assistance in *Pringle* v. *Ireland*. As discussed in Section 6.2.4, the ECJ fended-off an *ultra vires* challenge to EU institutions acting in the ESM by ruling that the role of EU institutions did not unlawfully trespass on economic policy because their tasks 'do not entail any power to make decisions of their own' and 'solely commit the ESM'.[322] The first decision on conditional financial assistance was therefore that the EU institutions are not acting *ultra vires* because (or in so far as) they only act as functionaries of the Member States and have no power to make or impose economic policy commitments in their own right. From this flawed starting point, the CJEU has been forced to tie itself into knots to avoid remarking a breach of this boundary of competence.

In 2011–2012 the CJEU dismissed a series of Romanian preliminary references challenging economic restructuring measures imposed under an MoU signed by the *Commission* on behalf of the *Union* under Article 143 TFEU – primary EU law. The CJEU held that the reference

---

[320] *State Budget 2012 (Portugal)*, [3] 'These memoranda are binding on the Portuguese State, insofar as they are based on legal instruments of [. . .] European Union law.' See also *State Budget 2011 (Portugal)* (Case 72/11) Judgment 396/2011, [5]; *State Budget 2013 (Portugal)* (Cases 2/2013, 5/2013, 8/2013, 11/20133) Judgment 187/2013, [29]; *Pensions Convergence (Portugal)* (Case 1260/13) Judgment 862/2013; *State Budget 2014 (Portugal)* (Case 14/14) Judgment 413/2014; *Pay Cuts 2014–2018 (Portugal)*, [8], [16] and [12] (referring to 'undoubtedly binding rules of the European Union'); *Special Sustainability Contribution (Portugal)*; *Public Workers Requlification (Portugal)* (Case 754/13) Judgment 474/2013; *Labour Code (Portugal)* (Case 531/12) Judgment 602/2013. See further: *Fidelitate Mundial* [15]; *Via Directa*, [10].

[321] See, for example, *Athens Water Supply and Sewerage Company S.A. (Greece)* Decision 2906/2014; ECLI:EL:COS:2014:0523A190612E4344 (Συμβούλιο της Επικρατείας); *Koutselini-Ioannidou (Cyprus)* (reduction of pensions unconstitutional independently of any obligations under EU law).

[322] *Pringle* v. *Ireland* [160]–[164], above, Chapter 6, Section 6.2.4, n 170.

contained nothing sufficient to establish that the restructuring measures were 'intended to implement EU law'.[323]

In 2012, the CJEU dismissed a string of Portuguese preliminary references concerning EU Charter challenges to restructuring measures
taken under an MoU signed by *the Commission* on behalf of the EFSM
for *Union financial assistance* provided under an *EU regulation*. In each case,
the CJEU declined the reference on the basis that it 'did not contain any
specific evidence to support the view that that law was intended to
implement EU law'.[324] This was so even though the measures were
soon to be, or had already been, enacted in a Council Decision,[325] and
the Portuguese court twice reasserted its reference because it considered the measures EU acts within the scope of the Charter.[326]

In the 2016 *Mallis* group of cases, the CJEU dismissed five direct
actions brought by depositors in Cypriot banks against ESM conditionality set out in a Eurogroup Statement.[327] The applicants argued that the
terms which caused the bailing-in of their deposits at two Cypriot banks
were assessed, negotiated, drafted and agreed by the Commission and
ECB, and were, in reality, *ultra vires* acts of those EU institutions. But the
CJEU held that the bailout terms were not acts of EU institutions,
because, per *Pringle* v. *Ireland*, 'the duties conferred on the Commission
and the ECB within the ESM Treaty do not entail any power to make
decisions on their own and [. . .] commit the ESM alone'.[328] This was so
despite the fact that: 'the Commission [. . .] was responsible for negotiating the [MoU] with the Republic of Cyprus';[329] that it 'includes formula-
tions that might seem categorical';[330] and that those obligations were to
be incorporated into binding secondary EU legislation.[331]

---

[323] See cases cited above, n 310.

[324] See cases cited above, n 306.

[325] While in the first Portuguese case (C-128/12), the Council Decision was enacted after
the offending measures at national level, in the latter two cases (C-264/12 and C-665–
13), the Council Decision was enacted first in time (see cases cited above, Section 7.5,
n 306).

[326] *Fidelitate Mundial* [15]; *Via Directa*, [10].

[327] Joined Cases 105–109/15 P *Mallis* v. *Commission*.

[328] Case T-327/13 *Mallis* v. *Commission and ECB* EU:T:2014:9 09, [45]; Joined Cases 105–109/15
P *Mallis* v. *Commission*, [55]–[57].

[329] Case T-327/13 *Mallis* v. *Commission* [61].

[330] Case T-327/13 *Mallis* v. *Commission* [61]. Approved in Joined Cases 105–109/15 P
Mallis v. *Commission* [57].

[331] Council Implementing Decision 2013/463/EU of 13 September 2013 on approving the
macroeconomic adjustment programme for Cyprus and repealing Decision 2013/236/
EU [2013] OJ L 250/50.

In the 2016 *Ledra* group of cases, the CJEU dismissed five actions for annulment brought against the same depositor bail-in terms in the MoU signed by the Commission on behalf of the ESM.[332] Once again, the claimants argued that the Commission and ECB 'are the true authors of the bail-in implemented in Cyprus' and therefore the bail-ins were *ultra vires* acts of those institutions.[333] This time, the ECJ recognized that the duty of the Commission under EU law to ensure that the MoU was 'consistent with EU law' necessarily entailed act(s) of that institution capable of grounding a claim in damages.[334] However, the impugned measures were not acts of EU law challengeable for invalidity under Article 263 TFEU because, per *Pringle*, 'the duties conferred on the Commission and the ECB within the TESM do not entail any power to make decisions on their own and [. . .] solely commit the ESM'.[335]

This has led to some frankly objectionable results.[336]

First and most obviously, the conditionality programmes negotiated and drafted by the Commission do not solely commit the ESM. Under Article 7 of Regulation 472/2013, the conditions negotiated and signed by the Commission are incorporated into EU Council Decisions, and these decisions are binding in their entirety on the parties to whom they are addressed under Article 288 TFEU. As Dermine observes: 'Such Council Decisions are fully-fledged EU acts, perfectly reviewable under Article 263.'[337]

Second, contrary to what is stated by the Court, the Commission does not only act under duties conferred by the ESM outside EU law.[338] Regulation 472/2013 – binding secondary EU law – governs every subsequent and ongoing financial assistance procedure by the ESM.[339] It is that *EU regulation* which grants the Commission and ECB a virtually autonomous right to dictate and supervise macroeconomic

---

[332] *Ledra* v. *Commission*.
[333] *Ledra* v. *Commission* [49].
[334] *Ledra* v. *Commission* [55]-[59], [67].
[335] *Ledra* v. *Commission* [50].
[336] See Dimopoulos, 'Institutional Integrity', 50–51; Craig, 'Economic Governance', 27–18; O'Gorman, '*Pringle* v. *Ireland*', 229; Anastasia Poulou, 'The Liability of the EU in the ESM Framework' (2017) 24 MJ 127; Paul Dermine, 'The End of Impunity? The Legal Duties of 'Borrowed' EU Institutions under the European Stability Mechanism Framework' (2017) 13 Eur Const Law Rev 369, 379–381; Markakis and Dermine, 'Bailouts', 662; Repasi, '*Ledra* and *Mallis*'.
[337] Dermine, 'End of Impunity?', 379–380. See also: Markakis and Dermine, 'Bailouts', 654–655; Repasi, '*Ledra* and *Mallis*', 1147.
[338] Cf: Markakis and Dermine, 'Bailouts', 649.
[339] Arts. 6–7, 9–14 Reg 472/2013. See further: Poulou, 'Liability of the EU', 134.

programmes that, at present, include dictates on healthcare spending, pensions and wage negotiations, and which bind Member States under secondary EU law.

Third, according to *Pringle* v. *Ireland* and *Ledra* v. *Commission*, the legality of the ESM framework depends on the conclusion that 'the [MoUs] concluded by the ESM [. . .] must be fully consistent with EU law',[340] and the Commission has a duty under EU law to ensure 'that the [MoUs] concluded by the ESM are consistent with EU law'.[341] Importantly, under Article 7 of Regulation 472/2013:

> The Commission shall ensure that the [MoU] signed by the Commission on behalf of the [ESM] is *fully consistent with the macroeconomic adjustment programme approved by the Council.* [Emphasis added]

How is it that the terms of these macroeconomic programmes are not acts of EU institutions, but, under Article 7 of Regulation 472/2013, the Member States are legally prohibited – by an act of EU law – from enacting anything other than policies fully consistent with policies selected by the Commission and enacted into binding EU law by the Council? The fact that the Commission has a power and duty under EU law to include or refuse to include terms means that it is not, obviously, doing nothing.

Furthermore, as Repasi points out, Regulation 472/2013 does not link the disbursement of financial assistance to compliance with the macroeconomic adjustment programme approved by the Council (nor could it, because the EFSF/ESM are not EU institutions).[342] The Council Decisions imposing conditionality would remain in force if EFSF/ESM conditionality were scrapped (and vice versa). This means that the Council Decisions under Regulation 472/2013 are *standalone legal obligations* to implement the economic adjustment programme. This shows that the Council, too, is not doing nothing.

One must take a moment to imagine this procedure from the view of the aggrieved litigant: When a Member State requests financial assistance from the ESM, the Commission and ECB assess, negotiate, agree and monitor the macroeconomic adjustment programme simultaneously on behalf of the Union under EU law (Article 7 Regulation 472/ 2013), and on behalf of the ESM (Article 13 TESM). The conditions are then simultaneously passed to a meeting of the Eurogroup (in which the

---

[340] *Pringle* v. *Ireland*, [174]; *Ledra* v. *Commission*, [57]–[58].
[341] *Pringle* v. *Ireland*, [164]; *Ledra* v. *Commission*, [57]–[58].
[342] Repasi, '*Ledra* and *Mallis*', 1148.

ECB and Commission participate),[343] and a meeting of the ESM BoG (chaired by the President of the Eurogroup and in which the Commission and ECB participate).[344] Once approved, ESM conditionality is simultaneously signed by the Commission (on behalf of the ESM),[345] and enacted into a *binding Council Decision* by the Union in its Eurogroup configuration.[346] It is important to note, as AG Wathelet points out, that the Eurogroup, the ESM BoG and the EMU Council are 'composed of exactly the same members'.[347] Indeed, this entire procedure could be accomplished without anyone leaving or entering the room.

So who is responsible for the terms of the macroeconomic adjustment programme? Under Regulation 472/2013, the Commission is under a legal duty to ensure that 'the [MoU] signed by the Commission on behalf of the ESM or the EFSF is fully consistent with the macroeconomic adjustment programme approved by the Council'.[348] But the Commission is not legally responsible for its contents, because that would be *ultra vires*, per *Pringle*.[349] The Eurogroup is not an institution capable of creating binding EU legal acts, and is therefore not legally responsible for its contents either, per *Mallis*.[350] The Council Decision is also not challengeable, however, because its application is interposed with national implementing law, per the Greek,[351] Romanian[352] and Portuguese[353] cases on EFSM and BoP conditionality. The only entity accountable for the depositor bail-in is the ESM. But this, alas, is not an institution of the Union and cannot be challenged before the ECJ.

Thus, the same twenty-one people (the EMU finance ministers plus the Commission and ECB), sitting in three identical configurations, are completely immune from judicial review at EU level because the only configuration which is not acting *ultra vires* is that of the ESM – which, as explained above in Sections 6.2.3–6.2.4 per *Pringle*, is only lawful if it replicates EU financial conditionality to the letter anyways.[354] For the

---

[343] Art. 1, Protocol of the Eurogroup.
[344] Art. 5(3) TESM.
[345] Art. 13(4) TESM.
[346] Art. 7(2), 7(3) Reg 472/2013.
[347] Joined Cases 105–109/15 P *Mallis v. Commission (AG Wathelet)*, [71].
[348] Art. 7(2) Reg 472/2013. *Pringle v. Ireland*, [164]; *Ledra v. Commission*, [57]-[59].
[349] *Pringle v. Ireland*, [160]-[164]. See Section 6.2.4.
[350] Joined Cases 105–109/15 P *Mallis v. Commission*, [55]-[57].
[351] Cited above, Section 7.5, n 307.
[352] Cited above, Section 7.5, n 310 and *Florescu*, [40], [42].
[353] Cited above, Section 7.5, n 306.
[354] See above, Chapter 6, Sections 6.2.3–6.2.4; *Pringle v. Ireland*, [111].

aggrieved lay litigant, this Kafkaesque affair must look more like a Monty Python sketch than the ultimate safeguard for stability in an improved model of EU fiscal federalism.

7.5.2   Denial of Direct Actions against EU Macroeconomic Adjustment Programmes

In a second category of cases, litigants have filed direct actions against acts that are *undeniably* binding acts of EU law, in particular EU Council Decisions.[355] In those cases the ECJ has denied the connection between the EU act and the implementing measure by applying its case law on direct concern and holding, in essence, that it is probably not the binding EU law instrument that is faithfully being implemented by the Member State, but another, non-EU norm.[356] This is so even where the measure is a binding EU law instrument that would appear to be clear, precise and leave no discretion to the addressee.[357]

The *ADEDY* v. *Council* cases are instructive.[358] In those cases, the litigants challenged Council Decisions enacted under Article 126 TFEU pursuant to Greece's bailout programme. Those decisions contained a list of highly specific imperatives, including the following:

> Greece shall adopt the following measures by the end of September 2010: [. . .] (b) a unified statutory retirement age of 65 years . . .[359]

Since it is difficult to imagine an imperative as clear and automatic as 'set the retirement year at 65 by 30 September 2010', the applicants contested:

> [T]he measures which may be decided upon by the Council under the [EDP] and included in its decisions cannot be prescribed specifically, explicitly and without room for deviation, since that competence is not conferred upon the Council by the Treaties.[360]

---

[355] Case T-541/10 *ADEDY*; Case T-215/11 *ADEDY*.

[356] In direct actions, a measure will not be of direct concern unless it directly affects the legal situation of the individual, or is clear, precise and unconditional and leaves no discretion to the addressees entrusted with the task of implementing it: Joined Cases 41–44/70 *International Fruit Co* v. *Commission* [1971] ECR 411; EU:C:1971:53; Case 123/77 *UNICME et al.* v. *Council* [1978] ECR 845; Case 11/82 *Piraïki Patraïki et al.* v. *Commission* [1985] ECR 207; EU:C:1985:18.

[357] For criticism, see Markakis and Dermine, 'Bailouts', 650.

[358] Case T-541/10 *ADEDY*; Case T-215/11 *ADEDY*.

[359] Council Decision 2010/486/EU of 14 September 2010 [2010] OJ L 241/12 and Council Decision 2010/320/EU, in particular at Arts. 2(1)(f) and 2(2)(b).

[360] Case T-215/11 *ADEDY*, [2010] OJ C 186/54.

Yet the Court concluded that these provisions were not acts of EU institutions capable of direct concern. In Case T-541/10 the Court held (perhaps preposterously) that the requirement to set the retirement age at 65 'left a very wide discretion to the Greek authorities to define the content of the law which was to implement it'.[361]

These cases are remarkable, however, in that they do not avoid the conclusion that the EU decision is a legal act of economic policy. In fact, they appear to confirm as much. In Case T-541/10, for example, the Court accepted that the Decision 'sets a clear objective which must be achieved by the reduction of the bonuses paid to civil servants, that is to say the saving of a certain sum per year'.[362] The Court appears to confirm the main point of this chapter – that the EU does legislate economic policy; it just cannot acknowledge its hand at the controls if it is caught doing so.

7.5.3 Denial of Preliminary References against EU Macroeconomic Adjustment Programmes

Perhaps unsurprisingly, national courts believing themselves to be applying binding EU law have taken an increasingly dim view of this disownership of EU macoroeconomic adjustment programmes. In a third class of cases, a series of pointed preliminary references have pressed the CJEU to acknowledge acts which are *undeniably* EU law.[363] These acts include EU Council Decisions,[364] Council Implementing Decisions[365] and MoUs signed by *the Commission* on behalf of *the Union* under *EU regulations*.[366]

In these cases, the ECJ has adopted either of two approaches. The first approach has been to avoid the issue entirely and decide the reference on an issue that does not require the Court to state whether the economic edict is EU law or not.[367] The second is to find that while, yes, the Council Decision or MoU is an act of EU law, it did not specify the precise

---

[361] Case T-541/10 *ADEDY*, [71]–[76]. See also: Case T-215/11 *ADEDY*, [64].

[362] Case T-541/10 *ADEDY*, [70].

[363] Case C-64/16 *Juízes Portugueses* [2016] OJ C 156/32; Case C-214/14 *Florescu et al.* v. *Romania* [2014] OJ C 292/14 [4]; Case C-41/15 *Dowling et al.* v. *Minister for Finance* [2015] OJ C 138/31; Case C-526/14 *Kotnik et al.* v. *Državni zbor Republike Slovenije* [2015] OJ C 81/04, 1(a).

[364] *Juízes Portugueses (AG ØE)*, [4] and footnote 40; *Juízes Portugueses*, [14]; *Florescu*, [56].

[365] *Dowling* v. *Minister for Finance*, [11]–[13].

[366] *Florescu*, [7]–[9], [35]–[36]; *Juízes Portugueses (AG ØE)*, [45], [52]–[53].

[367] See, for example, *Juízes Portugueses*, *Dowling* v. *Minister of Finance*, and references below, at nn 383–384 and 390.

measure the Member State adopted in order to achieve the objective set by the Union, so the measure in issue not an act of EU law.[368]

Sometimes this has looked mendacious.[369] Sometimes it has not,[370] but even where it could be asserted without mendacity, it is still problematic.

The first such case is *Florescu v. Romania*. *Florescu* is a case concerning BoP assistance outside EMU, but is nonetheless elucidative because it deploys the same acts which are deployed alongside EFSM/ESM financial assistance. In that case, the ECJ acknowledged that an MoU signed by the Commission for Union financial assistance under Article 143 TFEU was an 'act of an EU institution within the meaning of Article 267(b) TFEU'.[371] It also accepted that this act 'contain[ed] a number of economic policy requirements'[372] which were set down by the Council through 'the adoption of directives or decisions',[373] and were 'mandatory'.[374] And yet, the ECJ held that, although a 'mandatory' act of EU institutions, the act was to 'be interpreted as meaning that it does not require the adoption of national legislation such as that at issue in the main proceedings'.[375]

But this is still problematic.[376] The ECJ found that a mandatory act of EU law set 'predefined economic objectives'.[377] If EU acts are setting economic policy objectives, then this is still plainly *ultra vires* under the ECJ's objectives-based analytical framework for identifying economic policy competence described in Chapter 6.[378] Taking the measures in *Florescu* as an example, EU acts imposing 'the objective of reducing public sector wage costs' and 'the key parameters of the pension system' are just as far outside EU competence as any more specific measure used to implement them would be.[379] As AG Bot concluded, it is therefore 'irrelevant, in that regard, that the [MoU] leaves a discretion to

---

[368] *Florescu* [40] and cases above, nn 306–310.
[369] Case T-541/10 *Case T-541/10 ADEDY* [71]-[76]; *Case T-215/11 ADEDY* [64]; *Dowling v. Minister for Finance*, [51]-[52].
[370] *Florescu (AG Bot)*, [58]-[60]; *Florescu* [40], [42].
[371] *Florescu*, [35]-[36].
[372] *Florescu*, [38].
[373] *Florescu*, [31]-[33].
[374] *Florescu*, [41].
[375] *Florescu*, [40], [42].
[376] See also Markakis and Dermine, 'Bailouts', 659–661.
[377] *Florescu*, [34]; *Florescu (AG Bot)*, [58].
[378] See above Sections 6.1.7 and 6.2.1.
[379] *Florescu*, [56], [46]-[47]; *Florescu (AG Bot)*, [68]-[69].

Romania to decide on the measures best able to ensure compliance with those commitments'.[380]

Juízes Portugueses is a second example. In that case, a Council Implementing Decision required Portugal to 'adopt [...] measures of a specific nature' set out in a EFSM MoU, namely, 'a single wage scale during 2014 [to ensure] the consistency of remuneration policy across all careers in the public sector'.[381] AG AØ concluded that this was undeniably an EU act, and therefore national discretion over the measures to implement it could not 'call that analysis in question'.[382] In the subsequent ECJ judgment, the Court did not address the binding EU law nature of the Decision,[383] but it noted in passing that the measures at issue 'were adopted because of *mandatory requirements* linked to eliminating the Portuguese State's excessive budget deficit and in the context of an *EU programme* of financial assistance to Portugal'.[384] But if that is so, once again, imposing requirements such as a single wage scale across all careers in the public sector,[385] 'reduc[ing] the public sector wage bill', or reforming 'the key parameters of the pension system',[386] are all just as far beyond EU competence as any lesser, more specific measures implemented to carry them out would be.

Dowling v. *Minister of Finance* provides another doozy.[387] That case concerned a challenge to conditionality imposed on Ireland in an EFSM MoU signed by the Commission and specified in a Council Implementing Decision pursuant to Regulation 407/2010 under Article 122(2) TFEU. One of those conditions was to ensure the recapitalization of certain banks by the end of July 2011. To implement this condition, the Minister adopted a Direction Order recapitalizing Irish Life and Permanent plc (Irish Life) by direct capital injection of €2.7bn in July 2011, acquiring 99.2% of its shares. Irish Life shareholders applied to set aside the recapitalization, arguing that it was contrary to Second

---

[380] *Florescu (AG Bot)*, [70].

[381] *Juízes Portugueses (AG ØE)*, [52].

[382] *Juízes Portugueses (AG ØE)*, [52].

[383] The ECJ brought the issue within the scope of the EU Charter by focusing on the fact that it involves courts of the Member States within the meaning of Article 19(1) TEU. See: Monica Claes and Matteo Bonelli, 'Judicial Serendipity: How Portuguese Judges Came to the Rescue of the Polish Judiciary' (2018) 14 Eur Const Law Rev 622.

[384] *Juízes Portugueses*, [46] (emphasis added) (see also [49]).

[385] *Juízes Portugueses (AG ØE)*, [52].

[386] *Florescu*, [46]–[47].

[387] *Dowling* v. *Minister for Finance*, [46]–[47].

Council Directive 77/91/EEC (the Second Directive), which protects shareholders against such scenarios.[388]

The Irish court's *Dowling* reference foreclosed the usual escape routes taken to avoid acknowledging EU acts in economic policy. The ECJ could not deny that the act was EU law, because the Council Implementing Decision and MoU were clearly EU acts, adopted under an EU regulation, on behalf of the EU. Nor would it be able to deny that the Minister's Direction Order was implementing those acts, because if the Direction Order was a purely national act then it could not prevail over the Second Directive (binding and supreme EU law) in a conflict with it. Nor would it be able to find that the recapitalization was an act of Member State discretion, because the Irish Court predicated its reference on a finding of fact: that the Irish state had no discretion to implement it another way.[389]

Instead, the ECJ held that the Second Directive did not cover the situation either way. Because the Second Directive only covered normal circumstances and the crisis was exceptional, it concluded:

> [T]he Second Directive [did not] preclude an exceptional measure, taken by the national authorities [...] with the objective of preventing a systemic risk and ensuring the financial stability of the European Union [...] *the nature of the national authority which issued that order being of no relevance in that regard.*[390]

But one might be forgiven for wondering if couching this ruling in words like 'measure taken by the national authorities' is meant to obscure the inference that the EU is imposing economic policy on a Member State. Because the inference seems otherwise hard to avoid. First, the objective of the measure identified by the ECJ is that of 'ensuring the financial stability of the European Union' – and this is the objective of EU financial assistance under Article 122(2) TFEU.[391] Second, the ECJ accepted that 'the recapitalisation of national banks [...] was also laid down by [...] Implementing Decision 2011/177 [in accordance with] Regulation No 407/2010 – itself adopted on the basis of Article 122(2) TFEU'.[392] In other words, the recapitalization was imposed by EU law. Third, the ECJ accepted that Ireland had no

---

[388] [1977] OJ L 26/1.
[389] *Dowling* v. *Minister for Finance*, [47]–[48].
[390] *Dowling* v. *Minister for Finance*, [51]–[52] (emphasis added).
[391] See: Recital 5 and Art. 1 Reg 407/2010 establishing 'a Union stabilisation mechanism to preserve the financial stability of the European Union'.
[392] *Dowling* v. *Minister for Finance*, [46].

discretion in recapitalizing as it did, so it was not a measure adopted within the Member State's discretion.[393]

7.5.4   An Unsustainable Choice between the Ultra Vires and the Unenforceable

There are two glaring problems with this case law. First and most obviously, the ECJ still has not answered the problem that EFSM and ESM macroeconomic programmes are reproduced or incorporated into EU Council decisions, and these decisions are binding in their entirety under Article 288 TFEU. Even if the ESM MoU imposes the same or equivalent conditionality, Council Decisions are legally binding and supreme EU law – the MoU is not. It seems odd to conclude that Member States are complying solely with the MoU and not the same terms set out in binding Council Decisions. This problem was admitted by AG Wathelet in *Mallis*, who noted:

> Up to now, however, any measures contained in an MoU adopted under the ESM have also been contained, in varying degrees of detail, in a Council Decision adopted under the FEU Treaty by the Council, a procedure perhaps dictated by the fear *that the MoU is not legally binding*. The Council decisions [. . .] support the view that national measures adopted [. . .] constitute an implementation of EU law.[394]

No answer has been forthcoming on how to reconcile this with the EU legal order, except to say that the Member States probably don't have that binding EU law in mind when they faithfully execute it to the letter. And yet, as the ECJ acknowledged in *Florescu*, *both* 'the objectives set out in [the Council Decision] *as well as* those set out in the [MoU] are sufficiently detailed and precise to permit the inference that [the national measure] is to implement *both* the memorandum and that decision, and thus EU law'.[395]

Second, the MoU cases ignore the reality that the Commission and Council *do* take decisions which can only be attributed to their own acts according to existing case law.[396] However, if the CJEU acknowledges these acts as acts of EU institutions, then it will be difficult not to acknowledge that they are also *ultra vires*. *Mallis* and *Ledra* are elucidative of the dilemma. In *Mallis*, the ECJ held that a measure would be imputed

---

[393] Dowling v. Minister for Finance, [47]–[48].
[394] Joined Cases 105–109/15 P Mallis v. Commission (AG Wathelet) [85]–[94] (emphasis added).
[395] Florescu, [48] (emphasis added).
[396] See cases cited above, Section 6.2.4, nn 174–181 and Section 7.5, nn 312–319.

to an EU institution where it was an 'expression of a decision-making power' of that institution.[397] Yet in *Ledra* the ECJ found that the Commission's duty to ensure that the MOU is 'fully consistent with EU law' was a stronger duty than the mere 'best efforts' obligation AG Wahl had considered it to be – it was a 'true performance obligation',[398] capable of grounding an action for non-contractual liability against *the Commission* (note: not the ESM).[399] So, not only does the Commission draft the thing, but it has a power to stop the ESM from doing something which the Commission does not want it to do. Its decision-making power is *decisive.* Yet in both cases, challenges to this same act on *ultra vires* grounds were dismissed because the legality of the ESM framework depends on the conclusion that the Commission and ECB do not have 'any power to make decisions on their own and [...] solely commit the ESM'.[400] But these are disjunctive propositions. The Union cannot have it both ways. As Polou points out:

> Had the EU institutions no actual power to make decisions in the framework of the ESM, the [ECJ] could not have interpreted the monitoring of the compliance of the MoU with EU law as one of their duties.[401]

Such cases have evidently tied the European Courts into an untenable position. The Opinion of AG Wahl in *Dowling* evinces this quandary perfectly. On the one hand, AG Wahl accepted that:

> To be sure [...] Ireland was giving effect to the condition for financial assistance to recapitalise its banks, as laid down in Article 3(5)(a) and (7)(g) of the Implementing Decision ...[402]

On the other hand, since this would render the measure *ultra vires*, AG Wahl demurred:

> That said, I must admit to being more hesitant with regard to the argument that EU law obliged Ireland to recapitalise as it did [...] In that connection, as the Commission rightly pointed out at the hearing, the Implementing Decision is ultimately rooted in Article 122(2) TFEU, a provision which refers to providing 'financial assistance' under 'conditions', rather than conferring

---

[397] Joined Cases 105–109/15 P *Mallis* v. *Commission*, [57].
[398] Dermine, 'End of Impunity?', 375. See: *Ledra* v. *Commission*, [55]–[59].
[399] *Ledra* v. *Commission* [55] [58]–[60], [67].
[400] *Pringle* v. *Ireland* [160]–[164]; *Ledra* v. *Commission*, [55]; Case T-327/13 *Mallis* v. *Commission* [41]–[50]; Joined Cases 105–109/15 P *Mallis* v. *Commission* [55]–[57].
[401] Poulou, 'Liability of the EU', 135.
[402] *Dowling (AG Wahl)* (Opinion of AG Wahl) [55]–[57], [91].

upon the European Union the power to set binding economic policy objectives.[403]

These instruments thus typify the essential thrust of this chapter: The new model of European fiscal federalism is comprehensively dependent, for its functioning, on instruments of EU law which are manifestly beyond the boundaries of the EU legal order and may perhaps exist only in so far as they are not actually enforced as the binding secondary EU law they appear to be.

By breaching its 'no financial assistance' rules and involving itself in macroeconomic stability programmes, the EU has found itself entwined in fields of law very far beyond the scope of its legal competences. This is no basis for the stability of EU fiscal federalism. It is not only constitutionally illegitimate and ripe for repudiation but, as will be shown in Chapter 8, it is inimical to principles of good fiscal federalism.

7.6   Conclusion: A Model of Legal Governance the EU Legal Order Cannot Support

The conclusion of this chapter is that the fiscal governance architecture upon which the European *proto*-fiscal union depends is manifestly incompatible with the European legal order. At EU level, the new model depends, for its effective operation, on continuous Member State acquiescence to intensified governance regimes which bear no relation to the legislative competences of the Union;[404] which extend the unilateral discretion of the Commission;[405] and which fail to adhere to the 'community method' or 'intergovernmental method' at EU level.[406]

At Member State level, it is dependent on a complex and beguiling 'quasi-legislative' legal framework that stretches athwart the gap between legal orders to inject binding EU economic policies directly into Member State law. The term 'quasi-legislative' is used here because, while economic policy recommendations *themselves* are not formally binding, EU legislation has implanted vehicles in Member State legal orders to meet these prescriptions at the border and shuttle them into national law. The result of these interlinkages is a sort of

---

[403] *Dowling (AG Wahl)* (Opinion of AG Wahl) [55]–[57].
[404] See: Section 7.4.1.
[405] See: Sections 7.4.2 and 7.5.
[406] See: Section 7.3.4.

conjunctive direct effect: The EU has no conferred constitutional authority to dictate economic policy by legal decree, but the result is the same – the EU writes the policy prescription, and national courts must enforce it under binding secondary EU law. This is a feature of unitary states that the European constitutional order simply cannot support.

[7.2] First, a complex constellation of provisions under Articles 3, 4(1), 4(4), 5(1)–(2), 6(1) and 7(2) of Regulation 473/2013, and Articles 4–6 and 10(4) of Directive 2011/85/EU, have made substantial amendments to national fiscal frameworks such that a failure to internalize EU macro-fiscal assessments and numerical targets will lead to a breach of EU legislation both directly and indirectly as result of budgetary laws implanted there by EU legislation. [7.2.1] A budgetary framework which allows the government to depart from the macrofiscal assess-ments of the Commission or the EU-governed fiscal body will be in breach of EU law for failing to adhere to the required scenario produced by the Commission or EU-legislated fiscal body;[407] for failing to adopt a budget endorsed by the EU-legislated fiscal body;[408] and for failing to internalize EU numerical targets under national fiscal laws implanted there by EU legislation.[409] [7.2.2] Then, under Article 7(2) of Regulation 473/2013, the Commission may declare the draft budget in 'particularly serious non-compliance' with the obligations in Articles 3, 4(1) and 6(1) of Regulation 473/2013, even if this only concerns specific substantive economic policy choices, and even where there are no spillovers to the Union. These machineries grip each link in the 'chain of legitimation' that appears *ultra vires* their legal basis and contrary to Member State constitutional identity jurisprudence.

[7.3] Second, the MTO assessed by the Commission and the Council under Article 5(1) of Regulation 1466/97 defines the appropriate MTO adjustment path for the purposes of Directive 2011/85/EU, Regulation 473/2013, and the TSCG.[410] [7.3.2] Article 5(2)(a) of Regulation 473/2013 then stretches athwart the gap between legal orders and inserts the Commission warning in Article 6(2) of Regulation 1466/97 into the constitutional correction mechanism of the TSCG. [7.3.3] Directive 2011/85/EU places Member States under a legal duty, to place

---

[407] Articles 4(1) and 10 of Directive 2011/85/EU.

[408] Articles 4(4), 5 of Reg 473/2013, in conjunction with Directive 4(1) and 10 of Directive 2011/85/EU.

[409] Articles 5 of Reg 473/2013 and 5 of Directive 2011/85/EU. See Section 7.2.1.

[410] See Section 7.3.1, nn 149–151.

themselves under a legal duty, to comply with the EU's fiscal rules – which themselves are not legal duties. These binding interlinkages with the EU fiscal governance regime exceed their legal bases and bind Member State budgetary legislators in a manner contrary to the explicit rulings of Member State constitutional courts in *ESM (Germany)*, *TSCG (France)*, *TSCG (Belgium)* and *TSCG (Austria)*.[411]

[7.4] The expansive scope of the MIP/EIP, combined with Article 10(4) of Regulation 1176/2011, extends the legal machinery of the 'budgetary veto' in Section 7.2.2 of this chapter to essentially *any* economic situation in a Member State – even if there are no spillovers to the Union and no overlap with any of the Union's competence. This arrangement is incompatible with the test for unlawful dispositions of fiscal sovereignty under the 'constitutional identity' jurisprudence set out in Section 1.3.1 of this book.

[7.5] The new legal architecture of conditional financial assistance is comprehensively dependent, for its functioning, on instruments which are manifestly beyond the boundaries of the EU legal order and may perhaps exist only in so far as they are not enforced. MoUs negotiated and signed by the Commission for EU financial assistance under 122(2) TFEU,[412] EU Council Decisions and Council Implementing Decisions,[413] statements of the Eurogroup,[414] and MoUs negotiated and signed by the Commission for the ESM,[415] cannot be enforced as directly applicable and supreme EU law because they legislate policy outcomes that are manifestly beyond the boundaries of the EU legal order and are vulnerable to repudiation by national constitutional courts. Accordingly, the (increasingly tenuous) position of the CJEU is that these are not acts of EU law at all. This renders them ineffective as instruments of fiscal federalism. Member State courts can (and do) strike them down without facing a claim of EU supremacy.[416]

This abstruse governance network is no basis on which to place the stability of a brave new model of EU fiscal federalism. The injection of binding strictures into Member State fiscal policy is not only constitutionally illegitimate but, as will be shown in Chapter 8, it is utterly ineffective and furthermore injurious to

---

[411] See cases cited above, Section 7.3.2.4, nn 178–187.
[412] See cases cited above, Section 7.5, n 306.
[413] See cases cited above, Section 7.5, n 307 and Section 7.5.3, nn 364–365.
[414] Joined Cases 105–109/15 P *Mallis v. Commission*.
[415] See cases cited above, Section 7.5, n 305.
[416] See cases cited above, Section 7.5, n 320.

good principles of fiscal federalism. There is simply no constitutional basis for centralized fiscal governance in the EU. Models of fiscal federalism which depend on this are fundamentally incompatible with the boundaries of Member State fiscal sovereignty, and legal instruments which implement them are likely to prove unavailing and unenforceable against Member States as stable structures of federalism.

8 Principles of Fiscal Federalism for the European Union

The preceding analyses have found that financial assistance and centralized fiscal governance do not conform to the allocation of competences in the Treaty; do not conform to the legal architecture for the guiding principles of price stability and fiscal discipline; and do not conform to the constitutional boundaries of Member State fiscal sovereignty underlying the limits of the EU legal order as a whole.

This chapter evaluates established principles of fiscal federalism theory and empirical outcomes from the EU and four comparative federations in order to determine which systems of fiscal federalism can indeed 'work' to ensure fiscal discipline (and, hence, price stability) in a large, decentralized economic and monetary union bound by the fiscal sovereignty of its constituent constitutional democracies.

The constitutional constraints on the selection of fiscal federalism models for the EU are, by now, clear. The model chosen must, first, preserve the fiscal sovereignty of its Member States; and, second, it must be empirically and theoretically suitable for ensuring the guiding principles of fiscal discipline and price stability.

The first half of this chapter, Section 8.1, reviews the literature on fiscal federalism in order to extract the legal determinants of fiscal discipline in a fiscal federation. This is necessary because the essential premise of the nascent EU *proto*-fiscal union is that centralized legal governance can enforce fiscal discipline in a federation with an established bailout precedent and institutionalized financial assistance. This is the essential premise of the *ratio decidendi* in *Pringle* v. *Ireland*,[1] and recent proposals by the

---

[1] *Pringle* v. *Ireland* [136]–[137].

Commission and the Presidents of the EU institutions endorse this premise.[2] Following the abrogation of the 'no bailout' rule the new model depends on law, rather than economics, to 'limit the moral hazard of member states running up unsustainable debts and turning again and again to the E.U. for bailouts'.[3] Section 8.1 seeks to determine whether, and if so under what circumstances, this premise may hold.

The literature examining that question is extensive. The various strands of fiscal federalism theory have sought to identify the institutional precepts for fiscal stability, as well as the various 'pathologies of federalism' which undermine it.[4] The bailout hazard or 'soft budget constraints',[5] the 'flypaper effect' of fiscal transfers,[6] electoral 'wars of attrition' over structural reforms,[7] and the (in)effectiveness of fiscal rules in large diverse federations,[8] are all pathologies whose underlying incentive structures are well understood. The literature also yields some rather certain lessons on how to avoid them. As Blume and Voigt observe:

Summarising the available empirical evidence, it seems fair to say that we know quite a bit about the effects of substantive rules within (federal) states [...] [t]he literature on the fiscal effects of fiscal institutions is well established, as is the underlying theory.[9]

Section 8.1 extracts five lessons for European fiscal federalism:

[8.1.1] First, legal fiscal rules are *never* credible in a large, decentralized federation in the absence of market discipline. Fiscal rules do not have a direct or endogenous relationship with empirical outcomes;

---

[2] See the institutional proposals cited in Methods and Introduction, n 81.

[3] Kelemen and Teo, 'Focal Points', 365.

[4] For surveys and important characteristics of self-preserving federalism: Weingast, 'Market-Preserving Federalism'; McKinnon, 'Market-Preserving Fiscal Federalism'; Ter-Minassian and Craig, 'Subnational Borrowing'; Weingast, 'Second Generation Fiscal Federalism', 281–283; Wibbels, 'Bailouts, Budget Constraints, Leviathans'; Erik Wibbels, *Federalism and the Market* (Cambridge University Press, 2005), 17–53; Oates, 'Towards a Second-Generation', 363; Jenna Bednar, *The Robust Federation: Principles of Design* (Cambridge University Press, 2009); Bordo et al., 'Lessons from History'; Prakash Chandra Jha, 'Theory of Fiscal Federalism: An Analysis' (2015) 17 J Soc Econ Dev 241.

[5] See below, Section 8.1 at nn 22–24 and Section 8.1.2.

[6] See below, Section 8.1.3, in particular n 104.

[7] Alberto Alesina and Allan Drazen, 'Why are Stabilizations Delayed' (1991) 81 Am Econ Rev 1170.

[8] Eyraud and Gomez Sirera, 'Constraints', 108; Ter-Minassian, 'Fiscal Rules', 8; Foremny, 'Sub-National Deficits', 89; Rodden and Eskeland, 'Lessons and Conclusions', 455, 459.

[9] Blume and Voigt, 'Budget Institutions', 238.

elected policymakers are not deterred by fiscal rules; and even where debt brakes are effective, the cost-levying function of legal sanctions can almost never outweigh the cost/benefit incentives of subsidized credit and voter preferences if market discipline is put out of work.

[8.1.2] Second, legal fiscal rules do not work effectively under soft budget constraints. Bailout expectations indicate that fiscal rules themselves are not credible, and soft budget constraints actively undermine the cost-levying function of fiscal rules (i.e. the discount on debt from a bailout expectation is nearly always more than any regulatory fine that could be levied).

[8.1.3] Third, the condition of fiscal symmetry, wherein expenditure competences are matched by command over equivalent own revenues, is an indispensable condition for fiscal discipline. Fiscal transfers (especially bailouts) distort marginal incentives, refract institutional accountability and cause soft budget constraints. Fiscal rules are not capable of correcting such incentives once they are in motion.

[8.1.4] Fourth, decentralized expenditure and revenue autonomy is necessary for credible fiscal rules. Governments that cannot increase revenues to pay down debts or increase expenditures to deal with downturns will breach fiscal rules or seek fiscal transfers to fill the gap. The EU's expansive fiscal governance framework and proposals for tax base harmonization undermine the conditions of fiscal autonomy.

[8.1.5] Finally, fiscal rules are neither necessary nor necessarily desirable in a decentralized federation. The institutional preconditions for effective fiscal rules are not very distinct from the preconditions for 'ideal type' or 'self-preserving' fiscal federalism to exist in the first place,[10] and improperly designed fiscal rules may introduce their own pathologies into an otherwise stable federal system. The EU lacks the institutional preconditions essential for the operation of effective fiscal rules, and the EU's fiscal rules themselves do not comport with the minimum criteria of clarity, transparency and strength necessary to make them work.

In simple terms, the literature suggests that centralized fiscal rules are *not* capable of replacing market discipline in a decentralized federation

---

[10] See above, n 4.

with an institutionalized bailout expectation.[11] History cautions that centralized debt brakes *never* work in a decentralized fiscal federation without market discipline, and the IMF warns that fiscal rules adopted 'without the prerequisites adequately in place are unlikely to be sustained and may end up undermining policy credibility'.[12] As Foremny's study of fifteen countries from 1995 to 2008 concludes: 'only deficits in unitary countries can be avoided by tying the government's hands with fiscal rules, while they are ineffective in federations'.[13] Numerous studies reach similar findings: fiscal rules 'are neither necessary nor sufficient to ensure fiscal discipline at the subnational level' and 'fiscal rules cannot substitute for a properly designed system of intergovernmental relations'.[14]

Section 8.2 applies the five determinants of fiscal discipline extracted in Section 8.1 to a comparative analysis of the EMU and four advanced federations: the Federal Republic of Germany, the Swiss Confederation, the United States of America and Canada. These federations are chosen for this analysis because they are the four oldest federations in the world, and the most appropriate to the European Union according to both a 'most-similar cases' and a 'prototypical cases' methodology.[15] The analysis seeks to test the extracted determinants in operation and evaluate which models will 'work' in the EU. It finds that the five principles extracted from Section 8.1 are robust theoretical and empirical determinants of fiscal discipline. The emergent European 'fiscal union' is inconsistent with basic principles of fiscal federalism theory, and lacks the institutional preconditions necessary for its fiscal rules to 'work'. Accordingly, the new European model has not reduced sovereign debt, it has not improved implementation rates of EU policy recommendations, and it has not applied on its own terms. The new EU model of fiscal federalism simply does not work.

The analysis concludes with five institutional preconditions necessary for fiscal discipline in the European EMU: [8.1.1] Market discipline; [8.1.2] hard budget constraints; [8.1.3] fiscal symmetry; [8.1.4] Member State expenditure and revenue autonomy; and [8.1.5] simpler, less

---

[11] See discussion below, Sections 8.1.1–8.1.2 and sources cited in Methods and Introduction, n 79.

[12] IMF, *Anchoring Expectations*, 15.

[13] Foremny, 'Sub-National Deficits', 86.

[14] Ter-Minassian, 'Fiscal Rules', 2, 8. See, further, the sources cited in Methods and Introduction, n 79, and below, Section 8.1, nn 34–46.

[15] On case selection in this context see below, Section 8.2, n 192.

flexible, more decentralized fiscal rules (if any fiscal rules at all). The overarching lesson for the EU is clear: hard budget constraints and market discipline are indispensable for the fundamental guiding principles of fiscal discipline and price stability in an EMU bound by the fiscal sovereignty of its Member States.

8.1 Principles of Fiscal Federalism for the European Union

Fiscal federalism theory may be divided into two generations. First Generation Fiscal Federalism (FGFF) theory is concerned with how to efficiently allocate tax and spending functions to different levels of government.[16] FGFF is based around Oates' 'Decentralisation Theorem' which posits that, unless there are offsetting spillovers or economies of scale, decentralization is typically more welfare-enhancing than a centralized allocation of outputs.[17] This is based on two findings. First, in a variant of the principal-agent problem, the central government is subject to information asymmetries.[18] Second, central governments are prevented from tailoring the composition of local public outputs, while local governments, financed by local resources, more closely represent local needs and resources.[19] Over-centralization results in a uniform, 'one size fits none' level of public output.[20] As de Tocqueville once posited it:

> In great centralized nations the legislator is obliged to give a character of uniformity to the laws, which [. . .] cannot adapt itself to the exigencies and the customs of the population, which is a great cause of trouble and misery.[21]

Second Generation Fiscal Federalism (SGFF) theory is concerned with structural pathologies that improperly designed institutions can wreak

---

[16] See Oates, *Fiscal Federalism*; Wallace Oates, 'An Essay on Fiscal Federalism' (1999) 37 J Econ Lit 49; Jha, 'Theory of Fiscal Federalism', 242–244.
[17] Oates, *Fiscal Federalism*, 35, 54
[18] Oates, 'Towards a Second-Generation', 353.
[19] Ben Lockwood, 'Distributive Politics and the Costs of Centralization' (2002) 69 Rev Econ Stud 313; Timothy Besley and Stephen Coate, 'Centralized versus Decentralized Provision of Local Public Goods: A Political Economy Approach' (2003) 87 J Public Econ 2611.
[20] Oates, 'Evolution of Fiscal Federalism', 314–319.
[21] Alexis De Tocqueville, *Democracy in America*, vol. I (Vintage Books, Random House 1945, first published in 1838).

on the public sector and even the economy as a whole.[22] Central to SGFF is the theory of soft budget constraints. The theory originated in the work of Kornai on government support in socialist economies, and describes the situation in which an enterprise expects to be bailed-out in the event of failure.[23] The essential tenet is that a government cannot credibly abstain from supporting a loss-making enterprise once it has provided initial capital and, where that is so, the enterprise will face perverse incentives to underperform. The theory has since been expanded and applied to fiscal federalism.[24] Where a sub-federal government can expect a bailout from central authorities, it does not face a fixed envelope of resources and so does not bear the full marginal cost of an increase in debt.[25] Interest premia do not rise in proportion to own liabilities and revenues, and the government is incentivized to contract for debt beyond the length of its own resources. Feld and Schaltegger summarize:

These incentives particularly hold in federal systems [. . .] if excessively indebted regions can expect a bailout. Whenever sub-central governments perceive that the federal government provides them with funds to cope with their financial or economic stress, any effort to consolidate their budgets becomes incredible or may simply not gather the necessary popular support in a region.[26]

Federations evince a broad range of strategies for dealing with these problems. Institutional arrangements for fiscal discipline range from direct controls on spending, borrowing and taxation (as in a unitary state), to pure market discipline.[27]

The EU relies primarily on fiscal rules. A fiscal rule is an instrument which imposes a constraint on fiscal policy expressed in a summary

---

[22] Qian and Weingast, 'Preserving Market Incentives', 85; Oates, 'Towards a Second-Generation', 356–364; Weingast, 'Second Generation Fiscal Federalism', 82–283; Jha, 'Theory of Fiscal Federalism', 244–245 and sources cited above, n 4, and in Methods and Introduction, n 69.

[23] János Kornai, '"Hard" and "Soft" Budget Constraint' (1980) 35 Acta Oeconomica 231; János Kornai, 'The Soft Budget Constraint' (1986) 39 Kyklos 3; János Kornai, Paul Maskin and Gerard Roland, 'Understanding the Soft Budget Constraint' (2003) 41 J Econ Lit 1095.

[24] Yingyi Qian and Gérard Roland, 'Federalism and the Soft Budget Constraint' (1998) 88 Am Econ Rev 1143; Timothy Goodspeed, 'Bailouts in a Federation' (2002) 9 Int Tax Pub Finan 409, 410–418; Jonathan Rodden, Hamilton's Paradox: The Promise and Perils of Fiscal Federalism (Cambridge University Press, 2006), 50–71; Rodden, 'Achieving Fiscal Discipline', 138–144; Timothy Goodspeed, 'Soft Budget Constraints in Decentralized Government' (2017) 221 Hacienda Pública Esp 112.

[25] Rodden, Hamilton's Paradox, 80–94.

[26] Feld and Schaltegger, 'Decentralized Governments', 116.

[27] See Chapter 5, Section 5.2, nn 47–49 and Figure 5.1.

indicator of fiscal performance, such as the government deficit, borrowing, debt, expenditure, or other economic indicators.[28]

In support of this approach, there is a ponderous international literature which finds that fiscal rules *can* lead to improved fiscal outcomes in federal states.[29] Depending on their design and institutional setting, fiscal rules have been associated with lower overall gross debt,[30] lower expenditures,[31] smaller deficits[32] and lower risk premia.[33]

However, this same literature which finds that fiscal rules *can* improve outcomes also stresses that fiscal rules do not necessarily do so at all.[34] In a sample of forty-nine countries, von Hagen and Eichengreen find that fiscal rules are associated with *increased* debt, because they accompany more injurious incentives, like bailout expectations and fiscal transfers.[35] Fornasari et al.'s thirty-one country panel study found no consistent effects on subnational deficits from fiscal rules.[36] Reuter's study of eleven EU Member States from 1994 to 2012 yields similar

[28] George Kopits and Steve Symansky, 'Fiscal Rules' (1998) IMF Occasional Paper No 162.

[29] For surveys: James M Poterba, 'Balanced Budget Rules and Fiscal Policy: Evidence from the States' (1995) 48 Natl Tax J 329; Heiko Burret and Lars Feld, 'Political Institutions and Fiscal Policies' (2014) 12 DICE Report 3; Dominik Maltritz and Sebastian Wüste, 'Determinants of Budget Deficits in Europe' (2014) 48 Econ Model 222, 230–233.

[30] D Roderick Kiewiet and Kristin Szakaty, 'Constitutional Limitations on Borrowing: An Analysis of State Bonded Indebtedness' (1996) 12 JLEO 62; Stephen Tapp, 'The Use and Effectiveness of Fiscal Rules in Canadian Provinces' (2013) 39 Can Public Admin 45, 46.

[31] Mark Crain and James Millar, 'Budget Process and Spending Growth' (1990) 31 WMLR 1021.

[32] Henning Bohn and Robert Inman, 'Balanced-Budget Rules and Public Deficits: Evidence from the U.S. States' (1996) 45 Carnegie-Rochester Conference Series on Public Policy 13; Alberto Alesina and Roberto Perotti, 'Budget Deficits and Budget Institutions' in Poterba and Von Hagen (eds), *Fiscal Institutions*, 13; Jaoquim Ayuso-i-Casals et al., 'Beyond the SGP – Features and Effects of EU National-level Fiscal Rules' in Servaas Deroose, Elena Flores and Laurent Moulin (eds), *Policy Instruments for Sound Fiscal Policies: Fiscal Rules and Institutions* (Palgrave Macmillan, 2009), 651.

[33] Feld et al., 'Sovereign Bond Market Reactions to No-Bailout Clauses and Fiscal Rules – The Swiss Experience' (2017) 70 J Int Money Financ 319 and sources cited below, Section 8.1.1, n 67.

[34] Jürgen von Hagen, 'A Note on the Empirical Effectiveness of Formal Fiscal Restraints' 44 J Public Econ 199, 209; Suzanne Kennedy and Janine Robbins, 'The Role of Fiscal Rules in Determining Fiscal Performance' (2001) Government of Canada, Department of Finance Working Paper, 4; Bordignon, 'Fiscal Decentralization', 109; Ayuso-i-Casals et al., 'Beyond the SGP', 651; IMF, *Anchoring Expectations*, 15; Rommerskirchèn, 'Financial Market Behaviour', 836 and sources cited in Methods and Introduction, n 79.

[35] Jürgen Von Hagen and Barry Eichengreen, 'Federalism, Fiscal Restraints and European Monetary Union' (1995) 48 Am Econ Rev 134.

[36] Francesca Fornasari, Stephen B Webb and Heng-fu Zou, 'The Macroeconomic Impact of Decentralized Spending and Deficits: International Evidence' (2000) 1 Ann Econ Fin 403.

results,[37] and Imbeau finds higher debt variations in states with fiscal rules than states with none.[38] Martinez-Vasquez and Vulovic's fifty-seven country panel study concludes: 'none of the broad types [of regulations for subnational government borrowing] seem to have a significant direct effect on the narrow definition of fiscal sustainability at the subnational level'.[39]

It seems that fiscal rules are not determinative of empirical outcomes while other factors, such as bailout expectations and fiscal transfers, are.[40] This idea, that fiscal rules do not always 'work', should sound familiar in the EU, where twenty-five countries had their own fiscal rules prior to the arrival of the crisis, and yet the SGP has been violated over 141 times by all but two countries (Luxembourg and Estonia).[41]

Fiscal rules can even be harmful. The OECD warns that 'inappropriate fiscal rules can be destabilising' in an otherwise well-functioning federation.[42] This is so because, as the Lamfalussy paper and the British delegation warned at Maastricht, they signal the vulnerability of the central government to the fortunes of its states and invite larger, more injurious pathologies of soft budget constraints.[43] As the OECD explains: 'the implicit guarantee that requiring permission to borrow creates can weaken the effectiveness of financial market discipline'.[44] As the analysis below shall bear out, swapping decentralization for centralized fiscal governance is an inauspicious choice for a diverse federation. Rommerskirchen's review of the literature concludes:

---

[37] Heinrich Reuter, 'National Numerical Fiscal Rules: Not Complied with, but Still Effective?' (2015) 39 Europe J Polit Economy 67 (fiscal rules are complied-with only half of the time in EU countries).

[38] Louis Imbeau, 'Deficits and Surpluses in Federated States: A Review of the Public Choice Empirical Literature' (Annual Conference of the Canadian Political Science Association, Winnipeg, 3 June 2004), 19.

[39] Jorge Martinez-Vazquez and Violeta Vulovic, 'How Well Do Subnational Borrowing Regulations Work?' in Naouki Yochino and Peter Morgan (eds), *Central and Local Government Relations in Asia: Achieving Fiscal Sustainability*(Edward Elgar, 2017), 161, 212–213.

[40] Singh and Plekhanov, 'Subnational Government Borrowing', 24–35, and sources cited in Methods and Introduction, n 79.

[41] See Methods and Introduction, nn 87–88, and Chapter 3, Section 3.3.4, nn 222–223. Only Greece, Cyprus and Malta had no numerical fiscal rules at all in the 1990–2005 period. See: European Commission, 'Fiscal Rules Database' (*DG ECFIN*, 2014) http:// ec.europa.eu/economy_finance/db_indicators/fiscal_governance/fiscal_rules/index_en .htm accessed 24 December 2015.

[42] OECD, *Economic Surveys: Canada 2010*, 93. See also IMF, *Anchoring Expectations*, 15.

[43] See above, Chapter 2, Section 2.2.4, at nn 93–96 and Section 2.3.3, nn 171–172.

[44] OECD, *Economic Surveys: Canada 2010*, 93.

These [investigations] do not present sufficiently strong evidence in order to give empirical support for the promotion of new fiscal rules across Europe [...] fiscal rules may well be influenced by pressures from the sovereign bond market, rather than the other way around.[45]

The literature converges on five determinants of fiscal discipline in a federal system: [8.1.1] Market discipline, [8.1.2] hard budget constraints under a 'no bailout' rule, [8.1.3] fiscal symmetry, [8.1.4] expenditure and revenue autonomy, and [8.1.5] appropriately designed fiscal rules (if fiscal rules are introduced at all).[46]

8.1.1 Market Discipline

The first determinant is market discipline. Market discipline is the ultimate enforcer of hard budget constraints.[47] Financial markets are, after all, the supply side of government borrowing. Under conditions of market discipline, a government which borrows against a fixed envelope of resources will face an increased marginal cost on each spending decision down the path to insolvency until, eventually, it becomes 'cheaper to make expenditure cuts and/or raise money through taxes at home than to continue to borrow, and [borrowers] change their behaviour'.[48] Markets are also particularly suited to this task: First because they are democratic (unlike EU conditionality, markets do not impose specific policies on electorates); and second because they are credible – loss-bearing investors tend to be unsentimental about political justifications used to poke holes in EU rules, like cyclical downturns or earthquake relief.

Yet market discipline has been set out of work by the EU's institutionalized bailout expectation. Assuming the EU's new model functions as intended, its efficacy is now dependent on fines (under the SGP), economic conditionality (under the EFSM/EFSF/ESM), or on judicial enforcement (under the TSCG). In short, it is dependent on legal enforcement. This is the *modus operandi of* EU governance and the normal role of legal

---

[45] Rommerskirchèn, 'Financial Market Behaviour', 839–840.

[46] See, Groeteke and Mause, 'Debt Brakes', 281–282; Eyraud and Gomez Sirera, 'Constraints', 105–112; Ter-Minassian, 'Fiscal Rules'; Rodden, *Hamilton's Paradox*, 50–71 and sources cited above, n 4.

[47] Lane, 'Market Discipline', 55–58; Robert Inman, 'Transfers and Bailouts: Enforcing Local Discipline with Lessons from US Federalism' in Rodden, Eskeland and Litvack (eds), *Challenge of Hard Budget Constraints*, 62–66; Fabrizio Balassone, Daniele Franco and Raffaela Giordano, 'Market-Induced Fiscal Discipline', *Public Debt* (Banca d'Italia, 2004), 410.

[48] Hallerberg, 'Fiscal Federalism Reforms', 130.

enforcement: to alter behaviour by setting legal rules and threatening enforcement by a central authority.[49] The question for EU federalism is whether this can *replace* market discipline in hardening the inter-temporal budget constraint.

The efficacy of fiscal rules *vis-à-vis* market discipline is often difficult to extricate. Not only are both used for the same task, but their preconditions overlap. For example, both market discipline and fiscal rules are empirically effective where there are no transfer dependencies, no bailout expectations, and a high degree of expenditure and revenue autonomy.[50] Conversely, neither appears particularly effective without those conditions – and bailout expectations are fatal to both.[51] It is an unfortunate lesson of the literature that the very conditions which make for effective fiscal rules are the same conditions which make them unnecessary. This long left it unclear whether law can *replace* market discipline on its own strength. However, a growing literature parsing the simultaneity bias of fiscal rules finds that it cannot.

First, the causal mechanism of law – legal rules and coercive enforcement by a central authority – does not have an endogenous relationship with fiscal outcomes.[52] The very same empirical literature which shows that fiscal rules 'work' also shows that 'there is essentially no evidence that these laws are directly enforced'.[53] For example, fiscal rules in the United States are somehow empirically effective, but in the 160-year history of fiscal rules across forty-nine American states, only once has a judicial sanction ever been levied (and not until 2004).[54] Similarly, in the EU, the SGP has been violated over 141 times by all but two countries (Luxembourg and Finland), yet no sanction has ever been imposed.[55] The IMF remarks the same phenomenon globally: Even where there is 'a deliberate intent to breach the numerical limits'

[49] Kelemen and Teo, 'Focal Points', 356.
[50] Ter-Minassian, 'Fiscal Rules'; Douglas Sutherland, Robert Price and Isabelle Joumard, 'Fiscal Rules for Sub-Central Governments: Design and Impact' (2005) OECD Economics Department Working Papers No 52, 28–37; Eyraud and Gomez Sirera, 'Constraints', 108.
[51] Ter-Minassian, 'Fiscal Rules', 8; Sutherland et al., 'Design and Impact', 25; Eyraud and Gomez Sirera, 'Constraints', 90, 112.
[52] Kelemen and Teo, 'Focal Points', 366.
[53] James Alt and Robert Lowry, 'A Visible Hand?' (2001) 13 Econ Politics 49, 51.
[54] Kelemen and Teo, 'Focal Points', 356; Richard Briffault, 'Courts, Constitutions and Public Finance' in Elizabeth Garret, Elizabeth Graddy and Howell Jackson (eds), *Fiscal Challenges: An Interdisciplinary Approach to Budget Policy* (Cambridge University Press, 2008), 418, 429.
[55] See Methods and Introduction, nn 87–88 and Chapter 3, Section 3.3.4, nn 222–223.

sanctions are 'generally difficult to implement' and, typically, 'never intended to be used'.[56] Clearly, the effect of fiscal rules does not lie in their application, because they 'are rarely, if ever, enforced'.[57]

The intuitive reply is that they must work by deterrence – the harsher the judicial penalty, the better the effect on creditworthiness. But this is not so.[58] Kelemen and Teo find that clear and transparent fiscal rules with no consequences whatsoever appear more effective than unclear rules with strict legal enforcement (if fear of enforcement were what mattered, the opposite should be true).[59] Other studies yield similar results: Clear budgetary frameworks work better – and provide a better impact on creditworthiness – than severe fiscal rules, even when they are not backed by a credible threat of legal enforcement.[60]

Indeed, Delledonne points out that political office-holders seem 'neither strongly nor properly influenced by financial constitutional provisions'.[61] They hardly need to fear being dragged before the courts for legislating a corpulent budget. Even budgetary-conscious, constitutionally armed courts will apply a 'light touch' review to budgets, 'as matters of public policy best left to legislatures'.[62] The notion that courts will enforce fiscal rules 'is clearly denied by the US experience', where courts have proven 'remarkably shy' in wielding them.[63] Indeed, they have been just as likely to undermine them, preferring to uphold financing for, say, public education or pension commitments.[64] The same phenomenon is visible in the EU.[65]

---

[56] IMF, *Anchoring Expectations*, 33.
[57] Alt and Lowry, 'Visible Hand?', 52.
[58] Kelemen and Teo, 'Focal Points', 356–358.
[59] Kelemen and Teo, 'Focal Points', 362–365.
[60] Tapp, 'Fiscal Rules in Canadian Provinces', 47; Xavier Debrun and Manmohan S Kumar, 'The Discipline-Enhancing Role of Fiscal Institutions: Theory and Empirical Evidence' (2007) IMF Working Papers No 171; Alberto Alesina, 'Fiscal Adjustments: Lessons from Recent History' (ECOFIN meeting in Madrid, April 15 2010), 11–13; Fabio Canova and Evi Pappa, 'The Elusive Cost and the Immaterial Gains of Fiscal Constraints' (2006) 90 JPE 1291, 1312; and sources cited below, nn 73–77.
[61] Giacomo Delledonne, 'A Legalization of Financial Constitutions in the EU? Reflections on the German, Spanish, Italian and French Experiences' in Adams, Fabbrini and Larouche (eds), *Constitutionalization of European Budgetary Constraints* (Hart, 2014), 196.
[62] Kelemen and Teo, 'Focal Points', 358, 366.
[63] Delledonne, 'Legalization of Financial Constitutions', 196.
[64] Richard Briffault, 'The Disfavored Constitution: State Fiscal Limits and State Constitutional Law' (2003) 34 Rutgers LJ 956, 907; Fabbrini, *Economic Governance*, 103–105.
[65] Delledonne, 'Legalization of Financial Constitutions', 19; Rudolf Streinz, 'The Limits of Legal Regulation' in Ringe and Huber (eds), *Bail-outs, the Euro and Regulation*, 242.

Finally, even if the costs of fiscal rules *were* levied, such costs suffer from a serious incentive handicap. As explained in the following section, if market discipline has been put out of work, the pull of voter preferences and the discount on debt under a bailout expectation will usually outweigh any regulatory fine that might be imposed.

In sum, legal fiscal rules are too indirect, too unlikely to bite, and too ineffective to explain their own relationship with fiscal outcomes. There is no endogenous causal mechanism between fiscal rules and outcomes; governments are not deterred by fiscal rules; and the cost-levying function of sanctions can never outweigh the cost/benefit incentives of markets and voter preferences. And yet, as the IMF points out, fiscal rules will not be effective 'unless the cost of breaking the rule is higher than the benefit of doing so'.[66] So what is it, then, that makes the cost of breaking a rule higher than the benefit, if there is virtually no risk that legal sanctions will be imposed?

Market discipline. While there is no direct application of force between fiscal rules and empirical outcomes, there is a direct relationship between fiscal rules and bond spreads, on the one hand, and bond spreads with government behaviour, on the other.[67] Market discipline is 'felt before and would be far more painful than any penalty that might eventually be meted out by a court',[68] and markets reward strong fiscal rules and penalize governments that break them – even if the fiscal rule is never brought to bear.[69] Alt and Lowry, for example, find that American states with no carry-over balanced-budget rules (BBRs) pay about 7.3bps less than states with no laws, but are then punished disproportionality for running consecutive

---

[66] IMF, *Anchoring Expectations*, 33.

[67] Alt and Lowry, 'Visible Hand?'; Kelemen and Teo, 'Focal Points'; James M Poterba and Kim Rueben, 'State Fiscal Institutions and the US Municipal Bond Market' in Poterba and Von Hagen (eds), *Fiscal Institutions*, 204; James M Poterba and Kim S Rueben, 'Fiscal News, State Budget Rules, and Tax-Exempt Bond Yields' (2001) 50 J Urban Econ 537; Balassone et al., 'Market-Induced Discipline'; Craig Johnson and Kenneth Kriz, 'Fiscal Institutions, Credit Ratings and Borrowing Costs' (2005) 25 Public Budg Finance 84; Silvia Ardagna, Francesco Caselli and Timothy Lane, 'Fiscal Discipline and the Cost of Public Debt Service: Some Estimates for OECD Countries' (2007) 7 BEJM 1; Laubach, 'New Evidence'; Anna Iara and Guntram Wolff, 'Rules and Risks in the Euro Area' (2014) 34 Eur J Polit Econ 222.

[68] Kelemen and Teo, 'Focal Points', 358.

[69] Alt and Lowry, 'Visible Hand?', 67. See also Poterba and Rueben, 'State Fiscal Institutions', 204.

deficits.[70] Reuter's study of eleven EU countries from 1994 to 2012 finds that governments take little action to avoid breaching a fiscal rule but, once breached, will attempt to return to it once it is surpassed – even though no legal sanctions are brought to bear. Thus, 'actual legal compliance with such rules may not necessarily be important for their economic effects'.[71] This allows researchers a chance to break the simultaneity bias: Markets penalize governments for breaching fiscal rules even when their own legal sanctions do not, and markets escalate costs exponentially the more a deficit is repeated beyond the rule when legal sanctions do not.[72] Markets enforce fiscal rules, not courts.

Kelemen and Teo demonstrate that to the extent fiscal rules work, they do so by acting as a focal point that facilitates decentralized punishment of sovereigns by bond markets – and this 'provides a more plausible explanation of the causal mechanism through which balanced budget rules work' than enforcement of the rules themselves.[73] The United States General Accounting Office, for example, finds that market discipline is the most important causal explanation for compliance with fiscal laws in American states.[74] Canova and Pappa find that neither strict nor weak BBRs have an effect on excessive deficit or debt levels, but those accompanied by 'clearly stated and easily verifiable' triggers for enforcement, do.[75] Other studies reach similar conclusions: Fiscal rules 'work better where they provide a clear focal point for investors, not where they are designed to be stringently enforced by judicial authorities'.[76] As Briffault concludes: 'The real discipline for the state comes from capital markets.'[77]

---

[70] Alt and Lowry, 'Visible Hand?', 67.

[71] Reuter, 'National Numerical Fiscal Rules', 77.

[72] Kelemen and Teo, 'Focal Points', 363–365; Alt and Lowry, 'Visible Hand?', 52; Sutherland et al., 'Design and Impact', 36–37; Tamim Bayoumi, Morris Goldstein and Geoffrey Woglom, 'Do Credit Markets Discipline Sovereign Borrowers? Evidence from US States' (1995) 27 J Money Credit Bank 1046; and sources cited above, n 67.

[73] Kelemen and Teo, 'Focal Points', 381 (also 356–357, 366).

[74] US General Accounting Office, *Balanced Budget Requirements: State Experiences and Implications for the Federal Government* (GAO/AFMD-93-58BR, 1993), 4.

[75] Canova and Pappa, 'Elusive Costs', 1312.

[76] Kelemen and Teo, 'Focal Points', 356. See also Alesina, 'Fiscal Adjustments', 11–12; Blume and Voigt, 'Budget Institutions', 236, 238–239, 245–246; Balassone et al., 'Market-Induced Discipline', 418; Alt and Lowry, 'Visible Hand?', 54; Van Malleghem, '(Un)Balanced', 165–168; Reuter, 'National Numerical Fiscal Rules', 68; IMF, *Anchoring Expectations*, 33, and sources cited above, n 60.

[77] Richard Briffault, *Balancing Acts: The Reality Behind State Balanced Budget Requirements* (Twentieth Century Fund Press, 1996), 61.

8.1.2   Hard Budget Constraints and a Credible 'No Bailout' Rule

The essential cause of the soft budget constraint is the inability of the central authority to credibly commit to refuse a bailout.[78] This is typically described in a sequential game theoretic known as the 'bailout game'.[79] In the bailout game, the central authority commits itself to a 'no bailout' policy so that it is not exposed to sub-federal liabilities,[80] and markets and sub-federal treasuries then assess whether the 'no bailout' commitment is credible.[81]

Where markets perceive that the liabilities of the debtor will be financed by a guarantor, the creditworthiness of the debtor is assessed by the capacity of the guarantor to bail it out, rather than its own finances, and the borrower does not bear the full marginal costs of an increase in debt.[82] The debtor is not only able to borrow beyond the length of its own revenues, but it has an incentive to do so because a portion of the costs are 'shifted' to the centre.[83] This only heightens the scale of eventual calamity: While bailouts lower interest rates for an individual borrower, they do not dispel the underlying risk – they merely share it out.[84] Kirsch and Rühmkorft, for example, find that financial assistance does not prevent defaults from unsustainable debt at all – financial assistance 'raises average debt levels causing an overall increase in the probability of default'.[85]

The first and most important condition for fiscal discipline is therefore a credible commitment to a 'no bailout' rule – fiscal rules or not.[86] Fiscal rules will not ensure fiscal discipline without it.[87] Oates explains:

---

[78] Qian and Roland, 'Soft Budget Constraint', 1143 and sources cited above, Section 8.1, n 24.

[79] Rodden, *Hamilton's Paradox*, 50–71.

[80] The 'centre' or 'central authority' may be the central government, the central bank, a confederacy of governments, or an international institution such as the ESM. Balassone et al., 'Market-Induced Discipline', 394; Groeteke and Mause, 'Debt Brakes' 294–295.

[81] Rodden, *Hamilton's Paradox*, 48–118 and sources cited above, Section 8.1, n 24.

[82] Rodden and Eskeland, 'Introduction', 4.

[83] Oates, 'Towards a Second-Generation', 365.

[84] Stuart Landon and Constance Smith, 'Government Debt Spillovers and Creditworthiness in a Federation' (2000) 33 Can J Econ 634; Feld et al., 'No-Bailout Clauses and Fiscal Rules; Eva Jenkner and Zhongjin Lu, 'Sub-National Credit Risk and Sovereign Bailouts-Who Pays the Premium?' (2014) IMF Working Paper No 20; Faini, 'Fiscal Policy and Interest Rates'.

[85] Florian Kirsch and Ronald Rühmkorf, 'Sovereign Borrowing, Financial Assistance, and Debt Repudiation' (2017) 64 Econ Theory 777, 777.

[86] Bordo et al., 'Lessons from History', 482.

[87] Ter-Minassian, 'Fiscal Rules', 8; Groeteke and Mause, 'Debt Brakes', 297–298; Eyraud and Gomez Sirera, 'Constraints', 112: 'Constraints are not binding if subnational

[I]t is important to understand that in such a framework [where bailouts exist], perverse fiscal behaviour is essentially built into the system. This is not simply a case where fiscal advisors can rely on directing public authorities to behave in responsible ways [. . .] The system itself induces fiscally irresponsible behaviour: It is *endogenous* to the system. The solution to the problem thus involves a fundamental reform of political and fiscal institutions to alter the whole structure of incentives.[88]

So why is it, exactly, that fiscal rules cannot work alongside bailouts? First, a bailout expectation does more than insulate governments from market discipline – it actively undermines the cost-levying function of fiscal rules.[89] Unless non-compliance with a fiscal rule is costly enough to outweigh the benefits of a marginal increase in debt, it is 'rather unlikely that such jurisdictions would voluntarily reduce borrowing/ expenditures and increase taxes/fees'.[90] If bailouts are afoot, this is rarely the case. The discount on interest rates will subsidize the cost incurred by breaking the rule (and may reduce that cost to zero).[91] Empirical work by Feld et al., for example, finds that introducing a fiscal rule reduces interest premia by 10bps, versus 25bps for a no-bailout commitment.[92] Thus, 'the introduction of a reasonably strong fiscal rule [. . .] apparently falls short of the quantitative effect of the credible no-bailout regime.'[93] It seems countries with soft budget con-straints have higher debts, higher expenditures, require more fiscal transfers and spend their funds less efficiently – even if strong fiscal governance systems are in place.[94]

Second, a bailout precedent signals that the centre is exposed to the fortunes of its ward, and so is unlikely to enforce a 'no bailout' commitment *or* financial penalties that might nudge it closer to

governments know that they can appeal to the center for additional resources. A strong central government commitment is key to ensuring that institutional arrangements such as fiscal rules are enforced [and] also necessary to preserve the effectiveness of market mechanisms.'

[88] Oates, 'Towards a Second-Generation', 361.
[89] Hallerberg, 'Fiscal Federalism Reforms', 131; Landon and Smith, 'Ceditworthiness in a Federation', 635–638; Feld et al., 'Bond Market Reactions'.
[90] Groeteke and Mause, 'Debt Brakes', 291.
[91] Rodden, 'Achieving Fiscal Discipline', 144 and sources cited above, n 89.
[92] Feld et al., 'No-Bailout Clauses and Fiscal Rules'.
[93] Lars Feld et al., 'No-Bailout Clauses and Fiscal Rules', 328.
[94] Alexander Fink and Thomas Stratmann, 'Institutionalized Bailouts and Fiscal Policy: Consequences of Soft Budget Constraints' (2011) 64 KYKLOS 366; Braun and Trein, 'Federal dynamics', 808; Von Hagen and Eichengreen, 'Fiscal Restraints'; Imbeau, 'Deficits and Surpluses', 19; Martinez-Vazquez and Vulovic, 'Do Subnational Borrowing Regulations Work?', 208.

default.[95] In countries with a bailout precedent, sub-federal governments are more likely to receive a bailout than be fined for breaching fiscal rules.[96] The EU provides its own evidence for this: Over the
hundred-odd breaches of the SGP since its inception, the EU has
dispensed over €500.07bn in bailouts, and levied €0.00 in fines.[97]

8.1.3   Vertical Fiscal Symmetry

The third determinant of fiscal discipline in a federal system is fiscal
symmetry.[98] This is the condition wherein the expenditure responsibilities of each level of government are matched with independent command over an equivalent revenue capacity.[99] Fiscal symmetry ensures
that the supply of public goods is tailored to local citizens' willingness
to pay, and each bears the costs of its own mismanagement.[100] Each
government 'stands on its own bottom'.[101] Oates explains:

> There is fairly general agreement that for a sound fiscal system, the various
> levels of government need their own sources of tax revenues [. . .] having to rely
> on own revenues (rather than transfers) provides incentives for a more careful
> balancing of the two sides of the ledger. A condition of vertical fiscal imbalance
> (or 'transfer dependency') is said to exist where own-revenue systems are weak
> and lower level governments rely heavily on transfers from above.[102]

Fiscal asymmetries break the link between costs and benefits, incentiv-
izing governments to rely on fiscal transfers rather than their own
revenue base.[103] This is bad. According to the vast empirical phenomenon known as the 'flypaper effect', transfers simply do not have the

---

[95] Rodden, 'Achieving Fiscal Discipline', 159; Jonathan Rodden, 'Can Market Discipline
     Survive in the US Federation?' in Paul E Peterson and Daniel Nadler (eds), *The Global Debt
     Crisis: Haunting US and European Federalism* (Brookings Institution, Press 2014), 43–45.

[96] Sutherland et al., 'Design and Impact', 25; Rodden, 'Achieving Fiscal Discipline', 138;
     Eyraud and Gomez Sirera, 'Constraints', 100–101, at footnote 17.

[97] For the calculation of this €500.07bn figure, see above, Methods and Introduction, n 89.

[98] IMF, *Macro Policy Lessons*, 14.

[99] Mancur Olson, 'The Principle of "Fiscal Equivalence"' (1969) 59 Am Econ Rev 479, 483;
     Oates, *Fiscal Federalism*, 33–35; Feld and Schaltegger, 'Decentralized Governments', 116;
     Weingast, 'Second Generation Fiscal Federalism', 283–284.

[100] Charles Blankart and Achim Klaiber, 'Subnational Government Organisation and
      Public Debt Crises' (2006) 26 IEA 48, 49.

[101] Richard Bird and Andrey Tarasov, 'Closing the Gap: Fiscal Imbalances and
      Intergovernmental Transfers in Developed Federations' (2004) 22 Environment and
      Planning C: Government and Policy 77, 78.

[102] Wallace Oates, 'On the Theory and Practice of Fiscal Decentralization' (2006) IFIR
      Working Paper No 5, 23.

[103] Jonathan Rodden, 'Reviving Leviathan: Fiscal Federalism and the Growth of
      Government' (2003) 57 IO 695, 697.

same effect on public finances as own revenues.[104] The effect of a fiscal transfer is an unmatched increase in expenditure that exceeds the increase which would occur were the revenues generated locally. In other words, fiscal transfers increase net spending – own revenues do not. This effect is, as Rodden's forty-four country panel study of 1978–1997 data concludes, 'one of the most enduring empirical results in public economics'.[105]

Furthermore, fiscal asymmetries imply that more expenditure is funded from a common pool and, as central governments become entwined in paying for sub-federal local goods, they become politically accountable for those goods and vulnerable to soft budget constraints.[106] As Foremny so puts it, 'the higher the dependency on central government grants and transfers, the higher the expectation of a bailout'.[107]

The incentive-sapping effects of fiscal transfers are multifarious. Fiscal transfers impede fiscal consolidations,[108] increase government debt,[109] disincentivize efficient investment[110] and perpetuate, rather than close, gaps between regions.[111] As Oates observes:

[I]ntergovernmental grants often do not function as the normative theory would have them do, even in the context of a system of relatively hard budget constraints.[112]

---

[104] James Hines and Richard Thaler, 'The Flypaper Effect' (1995) 9 J Econ Persp 217; Stephen Bailey and Stephen Connolly, 'The Flypaper Effect: Identifying Areas for Further Research' (1998) 95 Public Choice 335; Shama Gamkhar and Anwar Shah, 'The Impact of Intergovernmental Fiscal Transfers' in Robin W Boadway and Anwar Shah (eds), *Intergovernmental Fiscal Transfers: Principles and Practice* (The World Bank, 2007).

[105] Rodden, 'Reviving Leviathan', 705.

[106] David Wildasin, 'Externalities and Bailouts' (1997) World Bank Policy Research Working Papers No 1843; Oates, 'Fiscal Decentralization', 19; IMF, *Macro Policy Lessons*, 18; Rodden, 'Achieving Fiscal Discipline', 143.

[107] Foremny, 'Sub-National Deficits', 88.

[108] Feld and Baskaran, 'Federalism', 383; Rodden, 'Achieving Fiscal Discipline', 144, 155

[109] Jonathan Rodden, 'The Dilemma of Fiscal Federalism: Grants and Fiscal Performance around the World' (2002) 46 Am J Polit Sci 670, 670; Luc Eyraud and Lusine Lusinyan, 'Vertical Fiscal Imbalances and Fiscal Performance in Advanced Economies' (2013) 60 J Monetary Econ 571.

[110] Rodden and Eskeland, 'Lessons and Conclusions', 452; John Joseph Wallis and Barry R Wieingast, 'Dysfunctional or Optimal Institutions?' in Garrett, Graddy and H Jackson (eds), *Fiscal Challenges*, 362–363.

[111] Thomas Courchene, 'A Market Perspective on Regional Disparities' (1981) 7 Can Public Policy 506, 509; McKinnon, 'Market-Preserving Fiscal Federalism', 83–85; Fabio Padovano, *The Politics and Economics of Regional Transfers: Decentralization, Interregional Redistribution and Income Convergence* (Edward Elgar, 2007), 4–14.

[112] Oates, 'Fiscal Decentralization', 25.

In most cases, fiscal rules cannot out-muscle such incentives. Martinez-Vazquez and Vulovic's analysis of fifty-seven countries from 1990 to 2008 finds that none of the broad types of subnational borrowing regulations have a significant influence on fiscal sustainability where there is high dependence on intergovernmental transfers.[113] Studying a panel of thirteen federations, Eyraud and Gomez Sirera, and Cotarelli and Guerguil, find that well-designed fiscal constraints 'cannot compensate for flaws in the decentralization framework – such as [...] mismatches between revenue and expenditure responsibilities'.[114] Other large-panel empirical studies yield similar conclusions.[115]

There is a role for fiscal transfers in FGFF theory, but they must be designed so that they do not interfere with fiscal symmetry in the first place. The literature points to three basic conditions to be met if transfers are not to do so, but the overarching prescription is clear: 'local authorities need to rely on their own revenues for financing *at the margin* so that decisions to expand public programs are made in full light of the additional costs'.[116] The three conditions are as follows. First, transfers should be limited to two purposes, *ex ante* capacity equalization (equalization transfers), or spillover internalization (efficiency transfers) – they should not finance the general budget (where they become available for financing marginal expenditure).[117] Second, they should not provide *ex post* bailouts, to finance inefficient liabilities already incurred.[118] Third, they must be clear, predictable and customized to their purpose.[119] This typically requires some form of institutional authority to guard against the predation of sub-federal competences through the 'golden leash' – the use of federal spending

---

[113] Martinez-Vazquez and Vulovic, 'Do Subnational Borrowing Regulations Work?' 161, 207–208, 213.

[114] Carlo Cottarelli and Martine Guerguil, *Designing a European Fiscal Union* (Routledge, 2015), 7; Eyraud and Gomez Sirera, 'Constraints', 108.

[115] Von Hagen and Eichengreen, 'Fiscal Restraints', 137; Singh and Plekhanov, 'Subnational Government Borrowing'; Santiago Lago-Peñas, Jorge Martinez-Vazquez and Agnese Sacchi, 'Fiscal Stability during the Great Recession: Putting Decentralization Design to the Test' (2020) 54 Reg Stud 919.

[116] Oates, 'Evolution of Fiscal Federalism', 324–326 (emphasis in original).

[117] Bird and Vaillancourt, 'Fiscal Decentralization', 13, 32, 37; Oates, 'Towards a Second-Generation', 352, 363; Oates, 'Evolution of Fiscal Federalism', 317, 323–327.

[118] Rodden and Eskeland, 'Lessons and Conclusions', 441–442.

[119] Oates, 'Evolution of Fiscal Federalism', 326; Isabelle Joumard and Per Mathis Kongsrud, 'Fiscal Relations across Government Levels' (2003) OECD Economics Department Working Papers No 375, 36–41.

powers to impose conditions in policy fields outside federal competence, resulting in a malign feedback cycle of fiscal asymmetry.[120] It should be noted that the EU bailout programmes conform to the most distortive fiscal transfer possible. Take Greece's 2010 bailout programme.[121] It is an *ex post* bailout (softening the inter-temporal budget constraint), to the general government budget (where it has in fact been used to finance marginal expenditure),[122] and it is attached to a 'golden leash' of conditions stretching from the retirement age to direct taxation, refracting political responsibility in all those areas in which it applies.[123]

8.1.4   Revenue and Expenditure Autonomy

The fourth determinant of fiscal discipline in a federation is expenditure and revenue autonomy.

The case for *revenue* autonomy is obvious. Where a sub-federal government is unable to respond on its own to an anticipated deficit by expanding its tax base, it will have no choice but to break its fiscal rule or pressure other governments or the central bank for financial assistance.[124] As Gunlicks puts it, 'If the federal government has control over revenues, it is going to be difficult to sustain a meaningful federal system.'[125] Once again, this condition seems more determinative of fiscal outcomes than fiscal rules: Foremny's analysis of EU-15 fiscal rules from 1995 to 2008 finds that increasing tax autonomy increases fiscal responsibility, lowers bailout expectations, and constrains spending in federations.[126] Fiscal rules, by contrast, are not effective in federal states,[127] and fiscal rules that constrain revenue autonomy are known to reduce creditworthiness.[128]

---

[120] Braun, 'German Fiscal Federalism', 237–239, 260; McKinnon, 'Market-Preserving Fiscal Federalism', 86.

[121] Council Decision 2010/320/EU; Council Decision 2010/486/EU.

[122] Mehreen Khan, 'Brussels Voices Concerns over Greek Spending Plans' (*Financial Times*, 20 December 2016) www-ft-com.elib.tcd.ie/content/04e10bc8-f6c5-355d-b22b-bec086f7ed0a accessed 27 December 2016.

[123] Notably, two leaders of bailout recipient countries have referred to their bailout agreements as a 'coup'. Suzanne Lynch, 'Europe Is Looking at Ireland and Does Not Like What It Sees' *Irish Times* (2 March 2016).

[124] Groeteke and Mause, 'Debt Brakes', 290; Von Hagen and Eichengreen, 'Fiscal Restraints', 137; Weingast, 'Second Generation Fiscal Federalism', 283; Rodden, *Hamilton's Paradox*, 10.

[125] Arthur Gunlicks, *The Länder and German Federalism* (Manchester University Press, 2003), 164.

[126] Foremny, 'Sub-National Deficits'.

[127] Foremny, 'Sub-National Deficits', 86.

[128] See below, Section 8.1.5.1, n 140.

The case for *expenditure* autonomy is also more intuitive than it might sound. As Alesina points out, if an electorate exhorts non-compliance with a fiscal rule, 'there is virtually no rule which can induce an unwilling government to do so'.[129] Increasing accountability through decentralization is the better way to improve outcomes, because it aligns responsibility for expenditures with the electorates which must pay for them. Rodden and Wibbels, for example, find that higher expenditure decentralization is associated with smaller deficits.[130] Bartolini et al.'s study of nineteen OECD countries finds that a 1% increase in decentralized spending improves the consolidated budget balance by over 4 percentage points, and has beneficial effects on fiscal stability in a crisis.[131] Lago-Peñas et al. reach similar findings.[132]

8.1.5   The Design of Effective Fiscal Rules

Fiscal rules are neither necessary nor necessarily desirable in a decentralized federation. That is not to say that fiscal rules cannot be beneficial, but inappropriate fiscal rules can introduce their own design flaws into the system.[133] Fiscal rules must therefore be designed correctly.

There are a number of ways to index the strength of a fiscal rule, but three main methodologies dominate: The Advisory Commission on Inter-governmental Relations (ACIR) index,[134] the Inter-American Development Bank (IADB) index of borrowing autonomy[135] and the EU Commission's Fiscal Rules Strength Index (FRSI).[136] The literature

---

[129] Alesina, 'Fiscal Adjustments', 15.
[130] Jonathan Rodden and Erik Wibbels, 'Beyond the Fiction of Federalism: Macroeconomic Management in Multitiered Systems' (2002) 4 World Politics 494, 520.
[131] David Bartolini et al., 'Fiscal Decentralization in Times of Financial Crises' (2018) 64 CESifo Econ Stud 456.
[132] Lago-Peñas et al., 'Fiscal Stability', 927. Cf: Timothy Goodspeed, 'Decentralization and Intra-Country Transfers in the Great Recession: The Case of the European Union' (2020) 54 Reg Stud 931, 939.
[133] OECD, *Economic Surveys: Canada 2010*, 93.
[134] The ACIR index depends on two scores: (1) The strictness of the balanced-budget objective (i.e., whether *ex ante/ex post*, annual or multi-annual, and whether automatic); and (2) whether the rule has a binding legal basis (such as constitutional law).
[135] The IADB ranks the debt rules primarily based on the flexibility of the limit – that is, whether debt is subject to a numerical constraint or authorization to exceed it is required; and the extent to which ownership of financial institutions may increase borrowing autonomy or support contingent liabilities. See Sutherland et al., 'Design and Impact'.
[136] The FSRI is based on the methodology of Servaas Deroose, Laurent Moulin and Peter Wierts, 'National Expenditure Rules and Expenditure Outcomes: Evidence for EU Member States' (2006) 1 *Wirtschaftspolitische Blätter* 27.

has produced a miscellany of similar indices.[137] The criteria vary under these methodologies, but the main factors weighed in the balance are: (1) the type of fiscal rule; (2) strength of the rule (e.g. constitutional rules outperform statutory ones); (3) enforcement mechanism (e.g. independent/ automatic *ex post* enforcement outperforms *ex ante* political commitments); and (4) clarity and transparency.

8.1.5.1   Sub-Criterion 1: Type of Rule

The first criterion is the type of rule. There are four main types, depending on the aggregate they constrain: (1) Debt rules typically set a numerical limit for debt or deficits; (2) balanced-budget rules (BBRs) require the budget to reach equilibrium on an annual or cyclical basis; (3) expenditure limits constrain expenditure to specific aggregates or purposes; and (4) revenue rules set ceilings or floors on taxes.[138]

Of these, two are particularly doubt-worthy: spending limits do not seem particularly effective,[139] and revenue restrictions are correlated with *negative* creditworthiness.[140]

BBRs and debt limits are the most effective, and this is what is notionally used in the EU under Directive 2011/85/EU and the TSCG.[141] However, it should be noted that these are only effective if the budget rules rely on *ex post* enforcement – *ex ante* rules (rules based on budgetary plans that do not have consequences for deviations after it is enacted), and rules which allow budgetary carry-overs or adjust with the economic cycle, do not have the same effects.[142] Considering that such criteria matter so much to their effectiveness, Directive 2011/85/

---

[137] See, for example, Robert Inman, 'Do Balanced Budget Rules Work? US Experience and Possible Lessons for the EMU' in Horst Siebert (ed.), *Quo Vadis Europe?* (Mohr Siebeck, 1997), 4; James Poterba, 'Do Budget Rules Work?' in Alan J Auerbach (ed.), *Fiscal Policy: Lessons from Economic Research* (MIT Press, 1997) 53; Jürgen Von Hagen, 'Fiscal Rules and Fiscal Performance in the EU and Japan' (2005) CEPR Discussion Paper No 5330; Tapp, 'Fiscal Rules in Canadian Provinces', 46.

[138] For a review: Andrea Schaechter et al., 'Fiscal Rules in Response to the Crisis – Towards the "Next-Generation" Rules. A New Dataset' (2012) IMF Working Paper No 187; IMF, *Fiscal Policy: How to Select Fiscal Rules* (IMF Fiscal Affairs, 2018).

[139] Shanna Rose, 'Institutions and Fiscal Sustainability' (2010) 63 Nat Tax J 807, 823–824; Tapp, 'Fiscal Rules in Canadian Provinces', 45; Eyraud and Wu, 'Playing by the Rules', 20.

[140] Xavier Debrun et al., 'Tied to the Mast? National Fiscal Rules in the European Union' (2008) 54 Econ Policy 299, 343; Poterba and Rueben, 'State Fiscal Institutions', 197.

[141] For analysis, see Chapter 7, Sections 7.3.2 and 7.3.3.

[142] Rose, 'Fiscal Sustainability', 821; Bohn and Inman, 'Balanced-Budget Rules', 48–49; Briffault, *Balancing Acts*, 19.

EU and the TSCG actually prescribe quite little.[143] As noted in Section 7.3.2.1, while notionally called 'balanced budget rules', these laws do not say whether they are *ex post* or *ex ante* rules and they do not, in fact, require governments to adhere to a numerical balance, but rather to achieve a cyclical MTO – 'a benchmark which is easily and frequently modified'.[144]

8.1.5.2   Sub-Criterion 2: Strength

Once the correct rule is chosen, 'strength' is governed by a balance of strictness and flexibility.[145] A rule which is too strict and brittle, or too flexible and weak, will be non-credible.

Strictness is necessary because a government is unlikely to choose unpopular cuts or tax hikes to comply with a rule unless circumventing it is infeasible.[146] Stricter rules – those that are based on *ex post* numerical constraints, independently enforced, inscribed in constitutional law, and broad enough to capture off-balance-sheet circumvention – are correlated with better outcomes.[147] Notable design flaws include too-flexible exceptions, inadequate oversight, or targets and escape clauses that are within the control of government to define or amend.[148]

On the other hand, a rule which is so strict that it precludes responses to legitimate economic imperatives will not be durable, and may simply increase creative accounting and decrease budget transparency along the way.[149] Legislators are ultimately accountable to electorates, and will only respect a fiscal rule if the utility of doing so exceeds the utility of evading, breaking or simply scrapping it.[150] Manasse's model of this trade-off, for example, finds that the penalty for breaching a fiscal rule must be 'unreasonably high' to offset the reward of stabilization for an

---

[143] Van Malleghem, '(Un)Balanced', 164–166.

[144] Boggero and Annicchino, 'Kick Us Out?', 257.

[145] Kennedy and Robbins, 'Fiscal Performance', 3; Buiter and Grafe, 'Reforming EMU's Fiscal Rules', 58.

[146] Groeteke and Mause, 'Debt Brakes', 291.

[147] See sources cited above, Section 8.1, nn 29–33.

[148] Debrun et al., 'Tied to the Mast?', 301–302.

[149] Sutherland et al., 'Design and Impact', 26–27; IMF, *Anchoring Expectations*, 15; von Hagen, 'Empirical Effectiveness', 205; James Alt, David Dreyer Lassen and Wehrner Joachim, 'It Isn't Just about Greece: Domestic Politics, Transparency and Fiscal Gimmickry in Europe' (2014) 44 Br J Polit Sci 707, 707–716.

[150] IMF, *Anchoring Expectations*, 33; Paolo Manasse, 'Deficit Limits and Fiscal Rules for Dummies' (2007) IMF Staff Papers No 455, 458; Simpson and Wesley, 'Effectively Hollow?', 308.

elected policymaker.[151] An unbending fiscal rule will thus prove brittle in a downturn.

The 1999–2005 SGP is a perfect specimen of a debt brake at once both too strict and too brittle: The law could not be complied-with in a downturn, so it was defused by political capture.[152] The 2005–2011 SGP, by contrast, is a specimen of a rule which is too flexible and weak.[153]

The post-2011 fiscal rules vary under these criteria, but, in general, appear to fare little better. Under the amended SGP, sanctions only bite once the target level is breached *and* this is not excused by the economic cycle *and* the efforts to return to the MTO are insufficient.[154] In 2015, the Commission released its 'flexibility communication' outlining no less than seven accounting exceptions under its 'margin of interpretation'.[155] In particular, its interpretation of 'appropriate annual improvement of the cyclically-adjusted budget balance' means the 0.5% benchmark will only ever apply to a country with a negative output gap of better than −1.5% of GDP.[156] Then, if the target is not met, neither the TSCG nor the SGP will bite where there is 'an unusual event outside the control of the Contracting Party' or a 'period of severe economic downturn' – all of which are also applied flexibly.[157] As Ódor and Kiss lament,

Paradoxically, the system relies on so many rules that in many cases the final verdict is in fact a discretionary decision by the European Commission/ Council.[158]

The MIP/EIP fares even worse: the IMF finds that the Commission has exercised 'excessive discretion in enforcement' and 'held back in applying the enforcement tools at its disposal – even though several countries have been diagnosed with excessive imbalances'.[159]

---

[151] Manasse, 'Deficit Limits', 466.
[152] See Chapter 3, Section 3.3.4, at nn 235–236. See further Joerges, 'Economic Constitution', 11; Dermot Hodson and Imelda Maher, 'Soft Law and Sanctions: Economic Policy Co-ordination and Reform of the Stability and Growth Pact' (2004) 11 J Eur Public Policy 798.
[153] See Chapter 3, Section 3.3.4, at nn 237–241.
[154] Eyraud and Gomez Sirera, 'Constraints', 103 suggest this scaled approach reflects a lack of credible enforcement tools.
[155] Commission, 'Flexibility within the SGP'.
[156] Commission, 'Flexibility within the SGP', 20
[157] Commission, 'Flexibility within the SGP', 17.
[158] L'udovít Ódor and Gábor Kiss, 'Lost in Complexity' in Ódor (ed.), *Rethinking Fiscal Policy*, 191
[159] IMF, *Euro Area Policies: Selected Issues* (IMF Country Report No 15/205, 2015).

Nor does the TSCG help matters. The amended German, Spanish and Italian fiscal rules, for instance, all contain emergency exceptions determined by absolute majority.[160] This makes the exceptions even easier to trigger than fiscal rules in the United States or Switzerland, where exceptions are typically determined by supermajority (and those are still unlikely to be enforced).[161] Energetic use of this flexibility is widely in evidence.[162]

8.1.5.3   Sub-Criterion 3: Sanctions

As noted above in Section 8.1.1, there is good reason to doubt the utility of sanctions. Nonetheless, if a fiscal rule is to 'work', whatever sanction it wields must actually be applied. Most obviously, this requires that the rule not be under the thumb of the executive. This is apparent from the Franco-German SGP rebellion of 2004,[163] the constant cycle of re-drafting fiscal rules in the United States and Canada,[164] and indeed globally – the IMF finds that a quarter of all debt brakes worldwide were suspended or scrapped in the first year of the 2008 crisis alone.[165] One solution to this is to establish independent monitoring.

Short of making sanctions fully automatic, however, they are difficult to make credible even under 'independent' monitoring. Debrun et al. find that independent fiscal watchdogs 'cannot credibly exert a direct constraint on day-to-day policy choices' and are 'only weakly correlated with subsequent policy changes'.[166] In countries with bailout precedents, sub-federal governments are more likely to receive a bailout than be sanctioned for breaching fiscal rules, regardless of how they are monitored.[167] In the EU, the Commission plays the role of independent watchdog, but its minutes are replete with examples of political capture.[168] As the Commission's 2020 Economic Governance Review

---

[160] Delledonne, 'Legalization of Financial Constitutions', 194; Groeteke and Mause, 'Debt Brakes', 286; Boggero and Annicchino, 'Kick Us Out?', 247.

[161] See below, Sections 8.2.2 and 8.2.3.

[162] Daniel Gros and Cinzia Alcidi, 'The Case of the Disappearing Fiscal Compact' (CEPS Commentary, 5 November 2015).

[163] See Chapter 3, Section 3.3.4.

[164] Tapp, 'Fiscal Rules in Canadian Provinces'; Kiewiet and Szakaty, 'Constitutional Limitations on Borrowing', 76.

[165] IMF, *Anchoring Expectations*, 3.

[166] Xavier Debrun, Marc Gérard and Jason Harris, 'Fiscal Watchdogs and Sound Fiscal Policy' in Vitor Gaspar, Sanjeev Gupta and Carlos Mulas-Granados (eds), *Fiscal Politics* (IMF, 2017), 327.

[167] See sources cited above, n 96.

[168] See, for example, European Commission, 'Minutes of the 2155th Meeting', 15; European Commission, 'Minutes of the 2117th Meeting', 25.

admits, despite widespread failures to comply with the 3% and 60% debt limits, 'Enforcing the debt reduction benchmark [...] has proven politically and economically difficult.'[169]

Conditional financial assistance under the EFSM/EFSF/ESM is (theoretically) intended to bolster enforcement, because a recalcitrant government will supposedly lose the benefit of its next bailout instalment. But this doesn't work either, because the Commission, the governments in the Council and the ECB have simply moved into the position of Kornai's initial provider of capital. For example, the EFSF/ESM alone now hold more than half of Greece's entire government debt.[170] This explains why, for example, Greece was not cut off when it was found ineligible to access €7.2bn in its bailout programme in July 2015 – it received a €7.16bn bridge loan at cost + 10bps. As Groeteke and Mause lament: 'there will still be no politically independent enforcer of the Stability and Growth Pact'.[171]

8.1.5.4   Sub-Criterion 4: Clarity and Transparency

As explained above, clarity and transparency are what will govern the effectiveness of a fiscal rule, not necessarily the legal weight of the axe which hangs above it.[172] As Van Mallegheim concludes:

Enshrining a [fiscal rule] into a document of constitutional or equivalent rank seems more of a symbolic gesture to appease markets than an effective means of preventing excessive deficits.[173]

Fiscal rules must be designed with this reality in mind: The gavel cannot supplant the bank and the ballot box, and complex rules merely confound their true enforcers. Tapp's study of fiscal rules in Canadian provinces from 1981 to 2007 is typical:

The key characteristic of effective rules appears to be the specificity of the rule's requirements, such as having clear numerical objectives.[174]

In that regard, the EU's new fiscal rules also fail at this vitally important hurdle. First, the proliferation of targets under the new system has

---

[169] Commission, Economic Governance Review (2020), 7.
[170] ESM, 'Financial Assistance: Greece' (ESM, 2020) www.esm.europa.eu/assistance/greece accessed 29 October 2020; Guarascio and Maltezou, 'Greece Gets Debt Relief'.
[171] Groeteke and Mause, 'Debt Brakes', 287.
[172] See sources cited above, Section 8.1.1, nn 52–77, in particular Kelemen and Teo, 'Focal Points', 356, 366.
[173] Van Malleghem, '(Un)Balanced', 165.
[174] Tapp, 'Fiscal Rules in Canadian Provinces', 47.

rendered it essentially unintelligible.[175] As the Commission's Economic Governance Review concludes, the new governance framework is characterized by 'different indicators', each with their 'own eligibility criteria' and 'various escape clauses', which has 'increased its complexity and reduced its transparency'.[176] Perhaps ridiculously, 'Those multiple rules do not always yield the same conclusion in terms of compliance.'[177]

Second, the 'triggers' which set off the SGP and TSCG – the concepts of a structurally balanced, 'cyclically-adjusted balance net of one-off and temporary measures'; the MTO adjustment path; and 'country-specific sustainability risks' – are famously nebulous concepts for measuring compliance.[178] The Commission notes that the system 'relies heavily on variables that are not directly observable and are frequently revised, such as the output gap and the structural balance'.[179] Estimates of the structural deficit widely vary by institution (the Commission, IMF and OECD all 'produce significantly different estimates' for potential GDP even though all use standard methodologies),[180] and the average error in estimating GDP growth *after the year has actually ended* is 0.5% of potential GDP per year.[181] This is a huge margin of error, considering that 0.5% is precisely the floor of the Fiscal Compact. Menendez complains: '"structural deficit" is an indeterminate concept [. . .] it may well turn out to be a fully discretionary constitutional term'.[182]

This same dilemma plagues the MIP/EIP which, by all accounts, appears unenforceable.[183] The triggers for the MIP/EIP – the concepts of 'imbalance' and 'excessive imbalance' – have no firm quantitative basis at all, leaving 'great room for arbitrary judgement'.[184] The EFB

[175] IMF, *Staff Report for the 2014 Article IV Consultation (Euro Area Policies)* (IMF, 2014); Eyraud and Wu, 'Playing by the Rules', 16–17.
[176] Commission, Economic Governance Review (2020), 10.
[177] Commission, Economic Governance Review (2020), 10.
[178] Van Malleghem, '(Un)Balanced', 168; Menéndez, 'Constitutional Mutation', 137.
[179] Commission, Economic Governance Review (2020), 10.
[180] IMF, 'Ireland: Selected Issues' (2015) IMF Country Report No 15/78, 8.
[181] Buttonwood, 'Perils of Economic Forecasts'; IMF, *2014 Article IV Consultation (Euro Area)*, 12; Eyraud and Wu, 'Playing by the Rules', 19. *Ex ante* predictions fare much worse: Jeffrey Frankel and Jesse Schreger, 'Over-Optimistic Official Forecasts and Fiscal Rules in the Eurozone' (2013) 149 Rev World Econ 247, 248; Roel Beetsma, Massimo Giuliodori and Peter Wierts, 'Planning to Cheat: EU Fiscal Policy in Real Time' (2009) 24 Econ Policy 753, 682.
[182] Menéndez, 'Constitutional Mutation', 137.
[183] See Section 8.2.5.4. See also Commission, Economic Governance Review (2020), 12–14.
[184] Dabrowski, 'Fiscal and Macroeconomic Governance', 15. See further Section 7.4.2

observes that despite seventy-six findings of 'imbalances', and twenty-eight 'excessive imbalances', the EIP has never been activated: 'Given the lack of explanation by the Commission [...] the process seems political rather than technical.'[185] The MIP/EIP is not more effective than OECD or IMF surveillance (with no enforcement whatsoever),[186] and the Commission finds that compliance has declined over time, likely due to 'reduced financial market pressure'.[187] Efstathiu and Wolff confirm this.[188]

Nor does the TSCG assist much. The MTO and the adjustment path on which it is based are moving targets; the deficit is structural, which makes the assessment subject to 'abstraction of the economic cycle of booms and busts'; and the objective of 'balanced budget' is, in reality, −1%, −0.5% or the MTO, depending on the circumstance.[189] Kelemen concludes:

> Because the [TSCG] focuses on strengthening the legal enforceability of balanced budget rules but leaves the rules themselves extremely vague, it is unlikely to prove effective.[190]

8.1.6   Determinants of Fiscal Discipline from the Literature on Fiscal Federalism

This analysis extracts five determinants of fiscal discipline in a decentralized system of fiscal federalism:

[8.1.1] The first is market discipline. Market discipline is the ultimate enforcer of hard budget constraints. Legal fiscal rules, by contrast, are not effective in a decentralized federation in the absence of market discipline.

[8.1.2] The second is hard budget constraints under a credible 'no bailout' commitment. Neither market discipline nor fiscal rules work effectively under soft budget constraints, and the empirical impact of a 'no bailout' rule significantly outweighs the impact of fiscal rules.

[8.1.3] The third is fiscal symmetry. Fiscal symmetry is an indispensable condition for fiscal discipline in a federal system. Fiscal rules are

---

[185] EFB, *Assessment of EU Fiscal Rules* (European Fiscal Board, 2019), 54.
[186] See below, Section 8.2.5.4 in particular sources cited in n 529.
[187] Commission, Economic Governance Review (2020), 12–14.
[188] Konstantinos Efstathiou and Guntram Wolff, 'What Drives National Implementation of EU Policy Recommendations?' (2019) Bruegel Working Paper No 4 1, 6.
[189] Van Malleghem, '(Un)Balanced', 162.
[190] Kelemen and Teo, 'Focal Points', 361. See also Kelemen, 'Law, Fiscal Federalism, Austerity', 396.

not capable of counteracting the distortive incentives of fiscal asymmetries and transfer dependency once they are in motion.

[8.1.4] The fourth is expenditure and revenue autonomy. Decentralization of expenditure and revenue autonomy increases fiscal sustainability, lowers bailout expectations, reduces spending and improves responsiveness to economic crises.

[8.1.5] The fifth is appropriately designed fiscal rules. The EU lacks the essential preconditions necessary for the operation of effective fiscal rules, and the EU's fiscal rules do not meet the endogenous design criteria necessary for their effectiveness.

8.2 Comparative Systems of Fiscal Federalism for the European Union

In order to test these legal determinants in operation, the remainder of this chapter conducts a comparative analysis of the world's oldest fiscal federations: the United States of America (established 1789), the Swiss Confederation (1848), Canada (1867) and the Federal Republic of Germany (reconstituted in 1949 following the German *Reich*, established 1871). These four comparators are the longest-running laboratories in which theories of fiscal federalism are developed and tested.[191] Together, they combine for nearly two-and-a-half centuries of empirical data across over 106 sub-federal government units.

The federations selected for this analysis have been chosen according to a most similar cases methodology and a prototypical cases methodology.[192] On all relevant variables for this study, these four federations chosen are widely recognized as the most relevant comparators for the EMU: They are consistently ranked among the most decentralized OECD federations in terms of sub-national revenues, expenditure and public employment; they are characterized by well-developed financial markets and a high degree of cultural and socio-economic heterogeneity;

---

[191] Comparative analysis in this field is a necessity exhorted by European constitutional scholars and economists alike: Adams et al., 'European Budgetary Constraints', 7; Fabbrini, *Economic Governance*, 12; Eyraud and Gomez Sirera, 'Constraints', 101 and sources cited below, n 195.

[192] A 'most similar cases' methodology implies that these federations provide useful control factors for the main variables not central to this study, but differ in the terms of the object of this study. A 'prototypical cases' methodology implies that their different institutional patterns are prototypical of the competing models of European fiscal federalism examined in this book. Ron Hirschl, 'The Question of Case Selection in Comparative Constitutional Law' (2005) 53 AJCL 125.

and all are currency unions running a price-stability monetary policy.[193] They differ, however, in terms of the object of this study: Each occupies a different place on the institutional spectrum of fiscal restraints, bailout mechanisms and fiscal transfers. Switzerland, the United States and Canada are prototypical decentralized federations that provide useful proxies for the 'classical' or 'market-preserving' model of fiscal federalism. Germany, by contrast, is a highly centralized 'surveillance' federation characterized by bailout expectations, weak market discipline and centralized legal constraints, that provide a useful proxy for the (bailouts + fiscal rules) model christened in *Pringle* v. *Ireland* as the basis for fiscal discipline in EMU.[194] As regards the design of their transfer systems, all four are spaced roughly equally along the federal spectrum.

Importantly, all four of these comparators encountered the soft budget constraint problem now faced by the EU in their history. How each federation dealt with this problem is credited with the stability (or not) of sub-federal finances. The lessons for EMU are obvious, and the comparisons widely noted.[195]

8.2.1   The Federal Republic of Germany

The Federal Republic of Germany is something of a 'disguised unitary state', plagued by transfer dependency, over-centralization and soft budget constraints.[196] The 'agony of central power', or the 'German problem' of fiscal federalism, has plagued German federalism through three separate constitutions.[197] Ritschl summarizes:

---

[193] Canada, the United States, Switzerland and Germany are the four most decentralized countries in public revenues as % of GDP; four of the five most decentralized in public expenditures as % of GDP; and four of the six most decentralized in public staff expenditure: OECD, *Regions and Cities at a Glance* (OECD 2018), 115, 117, 133.

[194] *Pringle* v. *Ireland* [136]–[137]. See Jörg Broschek, 'Pathways of Federal Reform: Australia, Canada, Germany and Switzerland' (2014) 45 Public Choice 51, 56–57.

[195] Henning and Kessler, 'Fiscal Federalism'; Mélitz, 'How to Save the Euro?', 342; Fabbrini, *Economic Governance*, 12–13, 49–52; Rodden, 'Can Market Discipline Survive?', 44–48; Dabrowski, 'Fiscal and Macroeconomic Governance', 9; Vitor Gaspar, 'The Making of a Continental Financial System: Lessons for Europe from Early American History' in Gaspar et al. (eds), *Fiscal Politics*, 436–437.

[196] Charlie Jeffery, 'Cycles of Conflict: Fiscal Equalization in Germany' (2003) 13 Reg Fed Stud 22, 23.

[197] Carsten Hefeker, 'The Agony of Central Power: Federalism in the German Reich' (2001) 5 Eur Rev Econ Hist 119; Jörg Broschek, 'Historical Institutionalism and the Varieties of Federalism in Germany and Canada' (2011) 42 Publius: The Journal of Federalism 662, 676; Henrik Enderlein and Camillo Von Müller, 'German Federalism at the Crossroads' in Peterson and Nadler (eds), *The Global Debt Crisis*, 134; Gunlicks, *German Federalism*, 164–203.

Germany's debt position [. . .] is not so much the result of prudence but rather of past misdemeanour and debt forgiveness. Certainly, it is not a measure of the comparative success of German fiscal policy or even the superiority of its social institutions [. . .] there is not a single episode in German debt history since the 1830s in which the ratio of debt to income was reduced by methods other than default.[198]

The German *Reich* established in 1871 was plagued by common-pool incentives and laboured under mounting debt ratios that increased from 30% of GDP (1872) to 60% (1914), reaching 131% by 1918.[199] In 1920, the Weimar Constitution instated a system of joint taxes collected by the centre and then transferred to the *Länder*, giving the *Bund* 'a virtual monopoly of direct and indirect taxation'.[200] Predictably, Weimar Germany was once again plagued by common-pool incentives (including an expensive equalization system).[201] After WWI, Germany defaulted on its international creditors in 1931 and was released from reparations in 1932.[202] Then in 1934, under Nazi Germany, the *Länder* parliaments 'ceased to exist as meaningful federal units' and became administrative units governed wholly by the centre.[203]

After WWII, claims on Germany by Marshall aid recipients were blocked by American occupation policy until 1953 (and later waived).[204] Once again starting with a clean ledger, this time the Allies insisted on a new tax system in which the *Bund* and *Länder* would each have authority 'over only those taxes it needed to meet its responsibilities'.[205] The Allies also rejected a fiscal equalization system, so that the *Länder* would not fall under the 'golden leash' and become agents of the *Bund*.[206] However, two vestiges of the German tendency for

[198] Albrecht Ritschl, 'Sustainability of High Public Debt: What the Historical Record Shows' (1996) CEPR Discussion Paper No. 1357, 20.

[199] Heiko Burret, Lars Feld and Ekkehard Köhler, 'Sustainability of Public Debt in Germany – Historical Considerations and Time Series Evidence' (2013) 233 Jahrb Natl Okon Stat 291, 296–30; Ritschl, 'Sustainability', 14; Broschek, 'Historical Institutionalism', 670; Hefeker, 'Federalism in the German Reich', 129.

[200] Gerald Feldman, *The Great Disorder* (Oxford University Press, 1993), 160–161; Gunlicks, *German Federalism*, 165.

[201] Dan Stegarescu, *Decentralised Government in an Integrating World*, vol. 34 (Physica-Verlag, 2006), 120–121.

[202] Ritschl, 'Sustainability', 13–20; Burret et al., 'Public Debt in Germany', 296.

[203] Gunlicks, *German Federalism*, 165. See also: Maiken Umbach, *German Federalism: Past, Present, Future* (Palgrave Macmllan, 2002), 123.

[204] Ritschl, 'Sustainability', 19; JL Simpson, 'The Agreement on German External Debts' (1957) 6 ICLQ 472.

[205] Gunlicks, *German Federalism*, 167.

[206] Gunlicks, *German Federalism*, 167.

centralization remained in the 1949 Constitution: First, the *Bund* retained a residual right to tap into *Länder* direct taxes, making them 'in effect joint taxes'.[207] Second, an ambiguous provision stating that the *Bund* 'may make grants' was used to resurrect a fiscal equalization system.[208] Almost immediately, the decentralized model began to draw back into a centralized system. Reforms in 1955 and 1969 replaced the separate taxation powers with joint taxation and extensive fiscal transfers, binding the *Länder* 'into arrangements of joint decision-making, leaving no room for unilateral exit options'.[209] Nineteen constitutional reforms between 1949 and 2006 re-centralized competences in the *Bund*.[210]

Today, German fiscal federalism is characterized by four main features:

Shared Revenues: Joint taxes under Article 106(3) BL constitute approximately 75% of total revenues, and up to 88% of *Länder* revenues.[211] Article 106(3) BL divides income tax (42.5%/42.5%) and corporation tax (50%/50%) evenly between *Länder* and *Bund*, while VAT is divided 53%/45% in favour of the *Bund*.[212] As all three taxes are determined by federal law, the alteration of this tax base is not within the control of individual *Länder*.

Horizontal Fiscal Equalization: Article 107 BL provides for a fiscal equalization system that equalizes allocated expenditures (fiscal need) with actual revenues (fiscal capacity).[213] Need is based on an average figure for all *Länder*, then adjusted by population size and density. Capacity is determined by the total tax revenues of the *Länder*, adjusted per capita. Wealthier *Länder* are then taxed in progressive bands between 15% and 80% of the amount that their per capita revenue capacity exceeds the average, while poor *Länder*

---

[207] Gunlicks, *German Federalism*, 168. Stegarescu, *Decentralised Government*, 122.
[208] Gunlicks, *German Federalism*, 168.
[209] Broschek, 'Historical Institutionalism', 677. See also: Gunlicks, *German Federalism*, 168–173.
[210] Jan Schnellenbach, 'German Federalism at the Crossroads: Renegotiating the Allocation of Competencies in a New Financial Environment' in Richard Eccleston and Rick Krever (eds), *The Future of Federalism* (Edward Elgar, 2017), 152.
[211] Gunlicks, *German Federalism*, 176–181; Groeteke and Mause, 'Debt Brakes', 290.
[212] Schnellenbach, 'German Federalism', 156.
[213] Annalisa Fedelino and Sven Jari Stehn, 'Fiscal Incentive Effects of the German Equalization System' (2009) IMF Working Paper 124, 7; Gunlicks, *German Federalism*, 178–179; Bundesministerium der Finanzen, *The Federal Financial Equalisation System in Germany* (Bunesministerium der Finanzen, 2016), 2–6.

are entitled to receive subsidies up to 92% of the per capita average, and 37.5% above that.

Supplementary Grants: After equalization, the federal government provides supplementary grants to *Länder* whose capacity per inhabitant is less than 99.5% of the average, up to approximately 77.5% of the shortfall.[214] The combination of fiscal transfers and supplementary grants assures equalization to about 98%–99.5% of the German average.[215]

Centralized Debt Brakes: Since 1969, Germany has had in place a constitutional debt brake in the form of a balanced-budget 'golden rule' (no borrowing to fund expenditure). This proved manifestly ineffective, and was replaced in 2009 by a balanced-budget debt brake (*Schuldenbremse*) (Article 109(3) BL), which applies to *Länder* budgets from 2020.

8.2.1.1 Vertical Fiscal Asymmetry and Transfer Dependency

Germany is characterized by severe fiscal asymmetry. On the expenditure side, approximately 20%–25% of *Länder* expenditures are determined by federal laws.[216] On the revenue side, however, roughly 75% of *Länder* revenue is provided by joint taxes.[217] Because the *Länder* cannot control this tax base it is, in effect, a massive fiscal transfer from a federal tax.[218] The tax base directly controlled by the *Länder* amounts to less than 5% of total tax revenues,[219] and, since much of that is determined in the *Bündesrat*, only about 2% of *Länder* resources could be considered 'own revenue' within their discretion.[220]

Perhaps unsurprisingly, Rodden finds that German *Länder* are far and away the most transfer-dependent states when compared with other centralized federations such as Australia and Spain, which are in turn more transfer-dependent then even the most dependent American states and Canadian provinces.[221] Cottaralli and Guerguil rank them similarly.[222]

---

[214] Bundesministerium der Finanzen, *Financial Equalisation System*, 4–6.
[215] Unicredit, *Handbook of German States* (Unicredit, 2012), 13–15; Rodden, 'Achieving Fiscal Discipline', 151.
[216] Enderlein and Von Müller, 'German Federalism', 140.
[217] Groeteke and Mause, 'Debt Brakes', 290–291.
[218] Bird and Tarasov, 'Closing the Gap', 81.
[219] Enderlein and Von Müller, 'German Federalism', 139.
[220] Fedelino and Stehn, 'Fiscal Incentive', 6.
[221] Rodden, 'Achieving Fiscal Discipline', 147–150.
[222] Cottarelli and Guerguil, *Designing European Fiscal Union*, 3.

Consistent with the literature, these transfers are incredibly distortive. Rodden finds 'no indication of adjustment among recipient states at all' to revenue downturns and 'no indication that the recipient states restrain themselves when revenue growth is unexpectedly strong'.[223] Seitz et al. and Federlino and Stehn find that net-recipient *Länder* increase unsustainable budget policies in reliance on fiscal transfers.[224] Jochimsen (among others) points to the mismatch between available revenues and expenditure as a structural problem in which 'every actor has an incentive to let someone else pay their bill while, perversely, incentives for their own activities and effort vanish'.[225]

8.2.1.2 Limited Expenditure and Revenue Autonomy

Since *Länder* are unable to unilaterally raise revenues in order to balance the budget, this leaves expenditure cuts. Yet *Länder* have little incentive to match expenditures to revenues, because whatever adjustments they make are neutralized by a fiscal transfer scheme that guarantees 99.5% of the overall average per capita tax revenue.[226] Jochimsen finds that a marginal increase of €1.00 in tax revenue relative to expenditures will be offset by a reduction in transfer payments by €0.90.[227] So, simply foregoing the tax rise or expenditure cuts might 'buy the government more votes than spending the remaining €0.10 on public goods'.[228] By the same token, raising an additional marginal euro in tax for a rich *Länder* will increase its payment into the transfer system by 15%–80% of the marginal unit raised.[229] This 'kills incentives to run a proper economic policy'.[230]

---

[223] Rodden, 'Achieving Fiscal Discipline', 155.

[224] Helmut Seitz, 'Subnational Government Bailouts in Germany' (1999) Zentrum für Europäische Integrationsforschung Working Paper No 20, 10; Fedelino and Stehn, 'Fiscal Incentive', 3.

[225] Beate Jochimsen, 'Fiscal Federalism in Germany: Problems, Proposals and Chances for Fundamental Reforms' (2008) 17 German Politics 541, 552. See also Braun, 'German Fiscal Federalism'; Jeffery, 'Fiscal Equalization'.

[226] Christian Baretti, Bernd Huber and Karl Lichtblau, 'A Tax on Tax Revenue' (2002) 9 Int Tax Pub Finan 631; Jonathan Rodden, 'Soft Budget Constraints and German Federalism' in Rodden, Eskeland and Litvack (eds), *Challenge of Hard Budget Constraints*, 172; Rodden, 'Achieving Fiscal Discipline', 151; Feld and Baskaran, 'Federalism', 375.

[227] Jochimsen, 'Fiscal Federalism in Germany', 545. See also: Fedelino and Stehn, 'Fiscal Incentive', 13.

[228] Jochimsen, 'Fiscal Federalism in Germany', 545.

[229] Bird and Tarasov, 'Closing the Gap', 96; Gunlicks, *German Federalism*, 179.

[230] Helmut Seitz, 'Fiscal Policy, Deficits and Politics of Subnational Governments: The Case of German Laender' (2000) 102 Public Choice 183, 189.

As predicted by the literature, Germany's constitutional debt brake cannot out-muscle such incentives.[231] Foremny finds that increasing tax autonomy to something equivalent to that of Spanish states would reduce deficits by 7.5%, *ceteris paribus*, where fiscal rules have proven incapable of doing the same.[232] Feld and Baskaran warn that Germany's new debt brake 'needs to be complemented by tax autonomy for the German *Lander*' in order to be effective.[233] Others reach similar conclusions.[234]

8.2.1.3 Soft Budget Constraints and Market Discipline

Market discipline is 'virtually set out of work by the construction of the German fiscal federalism system'.[235] Bailouts were constitutionalized in German federalism in 1992, when the BVerfG ordered the *Bund* to provide financial support to two *Länder*, Bremen and Saarland, in 'extreme budgetary distress'.[236] An OECD Economics Department paper notes:

Constitutional [rules] can weaken incentives for sub-central governments to behave prudently. The most egregious example of this is the constitutional ruling in Germany that requires the federal government to provide financial support to the heavily indebted Laender [sic] of Saarland and Bremen. The consequences of this ruling make it nearly impossible for the central government to resist bailouts in the future.[237]

As it presently stands, German *Länder* simply 'cannot go bankrupt' – they will be bailed-out by the federal government.[238] Accordingly, markets ceased to apply differentiated default risk to *Länder* following the Saarland/Bremen ruling.[239] Fitch merged all *Länder* ratings into the rating of the *Bund*, citing the Saarland/Bremen ruling for the proposition that no German state would be allowed to default so long as the *Bund* is

---

[231] See Sections 8.1.3–8.1.4 and sources cited.
[232] Foremny, 'Sub-National Deficits', 102. See also: Fedelino and Stehn, 'Fiscal Incentive'.
[233] Feld and Baskaran, 'Federalism', 365.
[234] Jochimsen, 'Fiscal Federalism in Germany', 552; Groeteke and Mause, 'Debt Brakes', 291.
[235] Seitz, 'Government Bailouts', 11.
[236] *Finanzausgleich II (Germany)* (2BvF 1, 2/88, 1/89 & 190): BVerfGE 86, 148.
[237] Sutherland et al., 'Design and Impact', 36.
[238] Jochimsen, 'Fiscal Federalism in Germany', 550; Kirsten Heppke-Falk and Guntram Wolff, 'Moral Hazard and Bail-Out in Fiscal Federations: Evidence for the German Länder' (2008) 61 KYKLOS 425, 440; Enderlein and Von Müller, 'German Federalism', 153.
[239] Rodden, 'Achieving Fiscal Discipline', 149–155; Enderlein and Von Müller, 'German Federalism', 140.

solvent.[240] S&P and Moody's still rate *Länder* separately; however, all sixteen *Länder* enjoy an Aa1 rating or above, despite wildly different base-risk calculations.[241] Institutional investors have followed suit. UniCredit, for example, states:

The fact that the four German states have very high debt levels is old hat [...] a German state cannot fail to fulfil its financial obligations unless the Bund and the other states are no longer able to provide financial assistance.[242]

Rodden finds that, with average debt-to-own revenue ratios of nearly 2,000%, German *Länder* 'would not be creditworthy if their debt burdens were assessed relative to their own meagre taxes'.[243] Numerous studies show that *Länder* bond yields are completely disconnected from important indicators of risk – despite several *Länder* being severely in excess of the solvency condition when measured by their own finances.[244]

8.2.1.4 Fiscal Rules and Fiscal Outcomes

Germany has had a balanced-budget 'golden investment rule' enshrined in its constitution since 1969.[245] And yet, it has proved useless in the face of soft budget constraints. Between 1991 and 2005 the debt limits were exceeded sixty-eight times by the *Länder* and seven times by the *Bund*.[246] Where the fiscal rule was not violated, it was circumvented.[247] Kirchhoff points out that an exception to the rule in the event of a 'disturbance of the overall equilibrium' has been activated every year since 1970.[248] Legal enforcement and independent oversight

---

[240] Seitz, 'Government Bailouts', 21; Unicredit, *Handbook of German States*, 16.
[241] For an overview of S&P and Moody's ratings, see: Unicredit, *Handbook of German States*, 3–9; Groeteke and Mause, 'Debt Brakes', 292.
[242] Unicredit, *Handbook of German States*, 6, 19.
[243] Rodden, 'Achieving Fiscal Discipline', 150.
[244] Alexander Schultz and Guntram Wolff, 'The German Sub-national Government Bond Market' (2009) 229 J Econ Stat 61; Thushyanthan Baskaran, 'Soft Budget Constraints and Strategic Interactions in Subnational Borrowing: Evidence from the German States, 1975–2005' (2011) 71 J Urban Econ 114, 124; Fedelino and Stehn, 'Fiscal Incentive', 10; Heppke-Falk and Wolff, 'Moral Hazard', 434; Jochimsen, 'Fiscal Federalism in Germany', 546; Groeteke and Mause, 'Debt Brakes', 291–295; Enderlein and Von Müller, 'German Federalism', 135.
[245] Arts. 110, 115 BL.
[246] Groeteke and Mause, 'Debt Brakes', 285.
[247] Kennedy and Robbins, 'Fiscal Performance', 8; Groeteke and Mause, 'Debt Brakes', 285; Delledonne, 'Legalization of Financial Constitutions', 186.
[248] Kirchhof, 'Debt Brake', 56.

also proved futile.[249] Indeed, the BVerfG's Saarland/Bremen ruling granted bailouts while recognizing that both *Länder* had violated the Basic Law for *fifteen consecutive years*.[250] Jochimsen observes:

> Lander politicians face strong incentives to finance public expenditures via debts because they know that, in the end, there will be a bailout. Existing rules to prevent over-indebtedness of the Bund or the Lander have proved to be nothing but a paper tiger.[251]

In 2009, Germany replaced its 'golden rule' with a balanced-budget 'debt brake' (*Schuldenbremse*). A structurally balanced deficit of 0.35% of GDP must be achieved 'without revenue from credits' by the *Bund* from the end of 2015, and from 2020 for the *Länder*.[252] Yet economists already point to many endogenous flaws shared with its predecessor: The *Schuldenbremse* concerns the *ex ante* structural balance, and therefore accounts for cyclical oscillation using the same models that have made the EU's fiscal rules malleable targets,[253] numerous 'gladly used' creative accounting avenues remain open,[254] and an escape clause for economic deviations from 'normal conditions' apes the 'disturbance of the overall equilibrium' clause activated every year for the past forty years.[255] Groeteke and Mause conclude:

> Overall, the analysis of a number of crucial design issues suggest that the 2009 German debt brake is actually not a credible commitment to slow down or stop the 'drive' further into public debt [. . .] These issues will appear in all European countries which copy the German debt brake as agreed in the 2012 EU 'Fiscal Compact'.[256]

The German 'surveillance' model, of centralized legal debt brakes + bailout expectations, does not work. By 2000, the gap in competitiveness and wealth between 'rich' and 'poor' *Länder* had become 'far greater than anything known before unification'.[257] The 1969 debt

---

[249] Jochimsen, 'Fiscal Federalism in Germany', 547–548.

[250] Seitz, 'Government Bailouts', 16; Rodden, 'Achieving Fiscal Discipline', 154.

[251] Jochimsen, 'Fiscal Federalism in Germany', 542. See also Groeteke and Mause, 'Debt Brakes', 295.

[252] Arts. 109, 115 BL.

[253] Groeteke and Mause, 'Debt Brakes', 284.

[254] Groeteke and Mause, 'Debt Brakes', 285.

[255] Kirchhof, 'Debt Brake', 56, 60; Feld and Baskaran, 'Federalism', 385–386.

[256] Groeteke and Mause, 'Debt Brakes', 289–290.

[257] Hans Machenstein and Charlie Jeffery, 'Financial Equalization in the 1990's: On the Road Back to Karlsruhe?' in Charlie Jeffery (ed.), *Recasting German Federalism: The Legacies of Unification* (Pinter, 1999), 169.

rule has presided over 'a systemic upward-ratcheting of subnational debt',[258] and the *Länder* are plagued by 'a long-term structural debt problem'.[259] Germany's aggregate gross debt-to-GDP ratio increased by nearly 300% from 1970 (18.6%) to 2009 (73% of GDP).[260] Prior to the 2008 financial crisis, twelve of sixteen *Länder* had deficits breaching the constitutional rule, and three were in a state of emergency.[261] Burret et al. find that most *Länder* have unsustainable finances.[262] 'Given the magnitude of this debt', Kirchhoff concludes, 'it is surprising that public finances in Germany are regarded as sound'.[263]

8.2.2   The Swiss Confederation

The Swiss Confederation is a highly decentralized heterogeneous federation that evinces all the characteristics of the classical 'ideal type' of market-preserving federalism: [8.2.2.2] Cantonal expenditure and revenue capacities are symmetrical; [8.2.2.1] Swiss Cantons have total autonomy over their own tax base and rates, with constitutional protection against predation by the Federal Council; [8.2.2.4] Cantonal finances are subject to no federal oversight or borrowing restrictions; and [8.2.2.3] Cantons are subject to market discipline under a credible 'no bailout' rule. Accordingly, when the crisis arrived in 2008, twenty-four of twenty-six Swiss Canton were in surplus (two had deficits of <1% of GDP),[264] and no Swiss Canton has ever defaulted or been bailed-out by the Confederation.

8.2.2.1   Expenditure and Revenue Autonomy

The Federal Council imposes no rules and exercises no oversight of Cantonal expenditure and revenue competences. Article 3 of the Swiss Constitution ascribes all residual competences to the Cantons, and Federal legislation impacts on few Cantonal spending responsibilities.[265]

---

[258] Baskaran, 'Soft Budget Constraints', 124.
[259] Feld and Baskaran, 'Federalism', 370.
[260] Feld and Baskaran, 'Federalism', 370; Baskaran, 'Soft Budget Constraints', 117.
[261] Braun, 'German Fiscal Federalism', 244–245.
[262] Heiko Burret, Lars Feld and Ekkehard Köhler, '(Un)Sustainability of Public Finances in German Laender: A Panel Time Series Approach' (2016) 53 Econ Model 254.
[263] Kirchhof, 'Debt Brake', 54.
[264] IMF, 'Net Lending/Borrowing (% GDP)'.
[265] Kurt Stalder and Sigrid Röhrs, *Answers to OECD Questionnaire: Fiscal Rules for Cantons and Communes* (Insitut für Finanzwissenschaft und Finanzrecht, 2005), 3; Gebhard Kirchgässner, 'Swiss Confederation' in Anwar Shah (ed.), *The Practice of Fiscal Federalism: Comparative Perspectives* (McGill-Queen's University Press, 2007), 318; Adian Vatter, *Swiss Federalism: The Transformation of a Federal Model* (Routledge, 2018), 24–27, 57–63.

On the revenue side, Article 128 of the Swiss Constitution allocates corporate and personal tax to the Cantons, and these taxes account for 95% of their total tax revenue.[266] Moreover, all taxes not specifically assigned belong to the Cantons under the Constitution, so there is little room for federal encroachment.[267] Cantons set their own bases and rates, and unfettered tax competition is seen as an important driver of the competitiveness of the country.[268]

8.2.2.2   Vertical Fiscal Symmetry

Swiss Cantonal expenditures (~41.6% of general government expenditures) and revenues (~40.8% of general government revenues) are symmetrical and larger than federal responsibilities (at ~31.4% of expenditures).[269] A fiscal equalization system which existed since 1959 failed to achieve its objectives and was reformed in 2004.[270] Areas of joint responsibility are small and progressively decreasing (falling from fifty overlapping responsibilities to thirty-three from 2004).[271] The 2004 reform of Swiss federalism increased fiscal symmetry in two ways. First, seventeen areas of joint expenditure responsibility were disentangled, most of which (ten) have been returned to the Cantons.[272] Second, conditional grants which led to 'creeping centralization' over preceding decades were eliminated and replaced with a new *ex ante* resource equalization system.[273]

The new equalization system aims to equalize Cantonal resources to 85% of the average *potential* revenues of the Cantons, according to a basket of the main tax bases belonging to the Cantons. Expenditures and actual revenues are no longer part of the equalization formula.[274]

---

[266] Feld and Baskaran, 'Federalism', 381.

[267] Johanna Schnabel, 'Switzerland' in Dietmar Braun, Christian Ruiz-Palmero and Johanna Schnabel (eds), *Consolidation Policies in Federal States* (Routledge, 2016), 79–80; Vatter, *Swiss Federalism*, 186–203.

[268] Stalder and Röhrs, *OECD Questionnaire*, 14.

[269] Schnabel, 'Switzerland', 79–80 (2016 figures).

[270] Vatter, *Swiss Federalism*, 186–195; Schnabel, 'Switzerland', 80.

[271] IMF, 'Switzerland: 2012 Article IV Consultation' (2012) IMF Country Report No 12/106, 34; Vatter, *Swiss Federalism*, 189–194.

[272] Braun, 'German Fiscal Federalism', 257; Vatter, *Swiss Federalism*, 186–195.

[273] Stalder and Röhrs, *OECD Questionnaire*, 15; Feld and Baskaran, 'Federalism', 381; Vatter, *Swiss Federalism*, 186–203.

[274] Two parts of the existing transfer system remain. First, there is a temporary cohesion fund, which compensates Cantons that lose funds as a result of the changes to the amounts they received prior to the amendment (this amount is being reduced by 5% per annum from 2015 and should be eliminated within eighteen years). Second, the reforms have not done away with cost-equalization transfers designed to reduce financial inequalities arising from external factors (such as topography) or special

This moves away from the German system, based on expenditures, and closer to the Canadian system – based on the *potential* tax base. In so doing, it preserves incentives to raise a marginal unit of capital, since Cantonal obligations or entitlements will not rise or fall with actual tax receipts.[275] Transfers are largely horizontal, with 'donor' Cantons contributing up to 70% of the amount,[276] and the federal government supplying the difference if Cantons are still not at the guaranteed minimum of 85% after horizontal transfers.[277] However, as the amount is capped to 85% of average potential, the scheme still redistributes far fewer marginal resources than the German system (amounting only to about 4% of Cantonal revenues).[278]

Baun and Train find that Switzerland responded to the crisis better – and with less destabalization to the federal framework – than more centralized federal states, even though the Cantons and Federation pursued 'anti-crisis policies in a rather independent manner, without formally coordinating the measures'.[279] Others make similar observations supporting the versatility of Swiss decentralization in responding to crises.[280]

8.2.2.3 Hard Budget Constraints and Market Discipline

Swiss Cantons operate under hard budget constraints.[281] This was tested at Cantonal level in the mid-1990s, when a succession of Cantons came under market pressure for the implicit liabilities of cantonal banks and were not given bailouts; and again in *Leukerbad (Switzerland)*, wherein the Supreme Court upheld Valais' right to reject

---

financial burdens from which other jurisdictions profit (such as hospitals), which the Federation still pays into. See further, sources cited above, n 273.

[275] Vatter, *Swiss Federalism*, 192–193.

[276] Braun, 'German Fiscal Federalism', 254; Dietmar Braun and Philipp Trein, 'How Do Fiscally Decentralized Federations Fare in Times of Crisis? Insights from Switzerland' (2016) 26 Reg Fed Stud 199, 212; Sean Mueller and Soeren Keil, 'The Territoriality of Fiscal Solidarity: Comparing Swiss Equalisation with European Union Structural Funding' (2013) 5 Perspect Fed 123, 134.

[277] In practice this has been significant: in 2018 the Federal Government made 59.5% of equalization payments, and 65.6% of all payments: Vatter, *Swiss Federalism*, 192.

[278] Nils Soguel, 'The Future of Swiss Federalism: The Challenge of Fiscal Stabilization Policy in the Absence of Coordination' in Eccleston and Krever (eds), *Future of Federalism*, 176.

[279] Braun and Trein, 'Insights from Switzerland', 203.

[280] Soguel, 'Future of Swiss Federalism', 182–189; Feld and Schaltegger, 'Decentralized Governments'; Schnabel, 'Switzerland', 90–91.

[281] IMF, '2012 Article IV Consultation (Switzerland)', 35; Rodden, 'Achieving Fiscal Discipline', 156.

a bailout demand from Leukerbad (seen by some as a precedent for Federal/Cantonal bailout games).[282] As a result, the IMF notes that lenders and rating agencies assess each Canton separately, and bond markets exert strong pressure on Cantonal and municipal finances.[283]

8.2.2.4   Fiscal Rules and Fiscal Outcomes

No centrally imposed fiscal rules apply to Swiss Cantons. As Braun observes:

> The federal government has no regulatory powers with regard to the borrowing of the states. The system depends on market discipline.[284]

Competition for investment has, however, produced a heterogeneous array of fiscal rules within the cantons themselves. The heterogeneity of these rules precludes full examination here, but most (Aargau, Bern, Friboug, Glarus, Lucerne, Neuchâtal, Nidwalden, Obwalden, Schaffausen, St Gallen and Valais) have deficit limits which constrain the current budget and the investment budget.[285] Some (Appenzell Ausserhoden, Basel County, Geneva, Grisons, Solothurn, Vaud and Zürich) have deficit rules that leave the investment budget unconstrained. A minority (Basel City, Schwyz, Thurgau, Ticino, Uri and Zug) rely on procedural or material rules that do not impose a numerical deficit limit or non-discretionary sanctions.[286] Only Appenzell Innerhoden – which 'has basically never run deficits' – has no fiscal rule in place at all.[287] These rules vary widely in strictness, cyclicality and enforcement, which can range from automatic deficit-linked tax increases (Basel County, Fribourg, Neuchâtel, Nidwalden, Schwyz, Vaud and Zurich), to automatic deficit carry-overs (Nidwalden) or expenditure cuts (Aargau).[288]

---

[282] *Munizipalgemeinde Leukerbad* Decisions 2C4/2000, 2C5/1999, 2C4/1999 and 2C1/2001 of 3 July 2003 (Federal Supreme Court of Switzerland). Braun, 'German Fiscal Federalism', 247; Stalder and Röhrs, *OECD Questionnaire*, 18. Feld and Baskaran, 'Federalism', 379; Feld et al., 'Bond Market Reactions'.

[283] IMF, '2012 Article IV Consultation (Switzerland)', 34–35.

[284] Braun, 'German Fiscal Federalism', 257.

[285] Heiko Burret and Lars Feld, '(Un)intended Effects of Fiscal Rules' (2018) 52 Eur J Polit Econ 166, 186.

[286] Burret and Feld, '(Un)intended Effects of Fiscal Rules', 170, 186.

[287] Schnabel, 'Switzerland', 92.

[288] Stalder and Röhrs, *OECD Questionnaire*, 3; Feld and Baskaran, 'Federalism', 378–379; Burret and Feld, '(Un)intended', 170, 186; Feld et al., 'Bond Market Reactions' 325.

Swiss fiscal rules correlate with better fiscal outcomes.[289] Cantons with strict fiscal rules are more effective at smoothing spending over the economic cycle than those without,[290] Swiss rules are generally effective at constraining their targeted variables,[291] and stronger rules are rewarded with lower bond yields.[292]

Is this to say that fiscal rules are responsible for the stability of Swiss Federalism? It does not seem so. Scholars parsing the simultaneity bias of Swiss fiscal outcomes find that they also correspond to market discipline and voter preferences, even if institutions are held constant.[293] Stalder and Röhrs' report to the OECD is typical: 'Fiscal rules had no influence on the spending patterns of the cantons and communes.'[294] Schnabel observes that 'market discipline has been the main driving force behind the adoption of fiscal rules' in Switzerland,[295] and Feld et al. find that the quantitative impact of the credible 'no bailout' regime in Switzerland far outweighs the impact of fiscal rules on bond yields.[296] The IMF concludes, for this section:

The Swiss system of fiscal federalism is working well. To summarise, a rationalised system of intergovernmental fiscal relations (including clear task assignments, rationalised equalization flows, a no-bail-out presumption, and a considerable degree of tax autonomy) has delivered a general culture of fiscal discipline and laid the basis for a credible commitment to and consistent compliance with fiscal rules.[297]

---

[289] Burret and Feld, 'Political Institutions'; Burret and Feld, '(Un)intended', 168 and sources cited.

[290] Stalder and Röhrs, *OECD Questionnaire*.

[291] Burret and Feld, '(Un)intended'.

[292] Feld et al., 'Bond Market Reactions', 328.

[293] Bernard Dafflon and Francesc Pujol, 'Fiscal Preferences and Fiscal Performance: Swiss Cantonal Evidence' (2000) 2 Int Public Manag Rev 54; Francesc Pujol and Luc Weber, 'Are Preferences for Fiscal Discipline Endogenous?' (2003) 114 Public Choice 421; Lars Feld and John Matsusaka, 'Budget Referendums and Government Spending: Evidence from Swiss Cantons' (2003) 87 JPL 2703; Dominique Küttel and Peter Kugler, 'Explaining Yield Spreads of Swiss Canton Bonds: An Empirical Investigation' (2008) 16 FMPM 208; Küttel and Kugler, 'Yield Spreads of Swiss Cantons'; Braun, 'German Fiscal Federalism', 247–248. Cf: Friedrich Heinemann, Steffen Osterloh and Alexander Kalb, 'Sovereign Risk Premia: The Link between Fiscal Rules and Stability Culture' (2014) 41 J Int Money Financ 110, 124.

[294] Stalder and Röhrs, *OECD Questionnaire*, 11.

[295] Schnabel, 'Switzerland', 80.

[296] Feld et al., 'Bond Market Reactions', 328 (introducing a fiscal rule reduces interest premia by 10bps, versus 25bps for a 'no bailout' commitment).

[297] IMF, '2012 Article IV Consultation (Switzerland)', 36.

8.2.3 The United States of America

The United States of America is another highly decentralized federation that evinces the primary characteristics of an 'ideal type' market-preserving federalism: [8.2.3.1] There is clear vertical fiscal symmetry between state and federal governments; [8.2.3.2] there are no federal constraints on state budgets; and [8.2.3.3] bond markets exert strong pressure on state finances.

Yet American federalism is particularly relevant to the EU, for three reasons: First, there is no federal equalization system in the United States. This makes it unique among the federations in this chapter. Second, like the EU, the United States federal budget has historically been small (amounting to just 2%–3% of GDP until the 1930s, compared to around 1% in the EU).[298] Third, the United States began its life under an implicit bailout expectation, but managed to switch its federal 'type' partway through its history. The first period of American fiscal federalism, from 1790 to 1842, began with the assumption of state war debts, was characterized by soft budget constraints and ended with a wave of state defaults. The second period began in 1842, when the Federal Congress took costly action to restore hard budget constraints, refusing to bail out state infrastructure debts. This caused nine state defaults and impaired market access for a further four.[299] Yet today, this episode is widely credited with nearly two centuries of state financial stability.[300]

8.2.3.1 Vertical Fiscal Symmetry

The relatively small size of the United States federal budget to the 1930s encouraged the footprint of the federal budget to develop within independent federal public goods, with no role for fiscal equalization or bailouts. Today, there is high degree of fiscal symmetry and no federal equalization programme in the United States.[301] Sub-federal government revenue amounts to approximately 59.6% of total general government revenue, and 46.2% of spending.[302] There are no federal tax coordination

---

[298] Dabrowski, 'Fiscal and Macroeconomic Governance', 9.

[299] See below, Section 8.2.3.3, at nn 323–326.

[300] Thomas Sargent, 'Nobel Lecture: United States Then, Europe Now' (2012) 120 J Polit Econ 1; Van Malleghem, '(Un)Balanced', 153–155; Rodden, 'Can Market Discipline Survive?', 46–48.

[301] Daniel Béland and André Lecours, 'Fiscal Federalism and American Exceptionalism: Why Is There No Federal Equalization System in the United States?' (2014) 34 J Public Policy 303.

[302] Cottarelli and Guerguil, Designing European Fiscal Union, 3.

or harmonization systems restricting state tax autonomy (though some states voluntarily ape the federal tax code).[303] The federal spending power does play a natural countercyclical role, but federal countercyclical redistribution arises *de facto*, within federal responsibilities themselves (federal programmes such as Medicaid and education account for personal incomes and so are inherently redistributive).[304] Estimates of regional stabilization range from 'virtually non-existent' at 0.8% of state domestic product,[305] to as much as 15% of state domestic product or 16%–28% of personal income.[306] Because redistributive formulae are confined within federal spending competences, however, 'they do not relieve state and local governments of debt obligations'.[307]

The United States' response to the 2008 financial crisis is elucidative. The federal government played a stabilization role by enacting a total direct injection of 1.4% of GDP in 2009 under the $787bn *American Recovery and Reinvestment Act* (ARRA),[308] effecting fiscal stimulus by increasing federal spending programmes (45% of the programme, or $357bn), cutting federal taxes (37%, or $288bn), and through transfers to states (18% or $144bn) – over 90% of which was for Medicaid ($86.9bn) and education ($53.6bn). The sheer scale of the programme gave rise to some concerns over fiscal asymmetry,[309] but it is worth noting that the state stabilization portion of the programme did not allow states to 'retain any portion of the [fund] for State purposes' – all funds were required to be used for specific public services and could not be added to the general budget or used to pay debts.[310] The ARRA has since been phased out without lasting detriment to fiscal symmetry.[311]

---

[303] Schnabel, 'United States', 97.
[304] Schnabel, 'United States', 98. Cf: Rodden, 'Can Market Discipline Survive?', 52–53; Béland and Lecours, 'American Exceptionalism', 306 (arguing that cost-matching grants heighten inequalities).
[305] Jürgen Von Hagen, 'Fiscal Arrangements in a Monetary Union: Some Evidence from the US' in Donald Fair, Christian De Boissieu and Julian Alworth (eds), *Fiscal Policy, Taxation and the Financial System in an Increasingly Integrated Europe* (Kluwer, 1992), 356.
[306] Jacques Mélitz and Frédéric Zumer, 'Regional Redistribution and Stabilization by the Center in Canada, France, the UK and the US: A Reassesment and New Tests' (2002) 86 J Public Econ 263, 264, 279, 284; Kevin H. O'Rourke and Alan M. Taylor, 'Cross of Euros' (2013) 27 Journal of Economic Perspectives 167.
[307] Henning and Kessler, 'Fiscal Federalism', 29.
[308] American Recovery and Reinvestment Act of 2009 (ARRA), Pub L 111–115; 122 Stat 115.
[309] Schnabel, 'United States', 106; OECD, *Economic Surveys: United States 2010* (OECD, 2012), 85; Rodden, 'Can Market Discipline Survive?', 52–53.
[310] *Guidance on the State Fiscal Stabilization Fund Program* (US Department of Education, 2009), 32–33.
[311] Schnabel, 'United States', 106.

8.2.3.2   Revenue and Expenditure Autonomy

The federal government exercises no oversight or authority over State fiscal competences. American states have complete revenue and expenditure autonomy, and unfettered tax and policy competition is considered a beneficial driver of competitiveness in the United States.[312]

In principle, the United States Constitution would seem ripe for federal 'golden leash' predations of state competences. Federal and state tax factors and expenditure competences overlap extensively, and the federal competence for 'general welfare' under Section 8 of the United States Constitution has been interpreted to permit spending in areas outwith the federal legislative power.[313] However, this has not been accompanied by competence takeovers due to a strong institutional authority in the form of the United States Supreme Court, which conceives of American states as equal sovereign polities.[314] As enunciated by Justice Kennedy in *US Term Limits* v. *Thornton*:

Federalism was our nation's own discovery. The Framers split the atom of sovereignty. It was the genius of their idea that our citizens would have two political capacities, one state and one federal, each protected from incursion by the other.[315]

The Supreme Court has guarded against fiscal competence takeovers by pruning conditionality attached to federal spending back to the scope of federal legislative competences.[316] The Federal Government and American states may make co-investments for the achievement of specific objectives, but the Federal Government cannot impose or attach

---

[312] Cottarelli and Guerguil, *Designing European Fiscal Union*, 3; Schnabel, 'United States', 97; Rodden, *Hamilton's Paradox*, 141–145.

[313] *United States* v. *Butler*, 297 US 1, 65–66 (1936) (US Supreme Court).

[314] *Hans* v. *Louisiana*, 34 US 1 (1890); *Shelby County, Alabama* v. *Holder Jr (Attorney General) et al*, 570 US 529 (2013). See further: Inman, 'Transfers and Bailouts', 76; Paul E Peterson and Daniel J Nadler, 'Competitive Federalism under Pressure' in Peterson and Nadler (eds), *The Global Debt Crisis*, 20–21; Schnabel, 'United States', 97; Fabbrini, *Economic Governance*, 52.

[315] *US Term Limits Inc* v. *Thornton*, 514 US 779 (1995) (US Supreme Court).

[316] *New York* v. *United States* 505 US 144 (1992), 176–177 (unconstitutional to require states to 'take title' to waste as a condition of a federal-state negotiated agreement, as it required states to legislate according to the federal scheme); *National Federation of Independent Business* v. *Sebelius* 567 US (2012) (unconstitutional to attach conditions to Medicare grant for which non-compliance leads to loss of all Medicaid funding); *Printz* v. *United Sates* 521 US 898: (unconstitutional to co-opt state police to execute federal mandate).

conditions which require states to implement policies in areas of state competence. Federal legislation governing state budgetary policies – such as the EU instruments examined in Chapter 7 – would be unconstitutional in the United States.[317]

8.2.3.3   Hard Budget Constraints and Market Discipline

The Federal Congress established in 1788 was saddled with $52m in Continental Congress debts from the War of Independence, in addition to $25m held by the American states – a volume amounting to 40% of GDP.[318] With no equivalent means of taxation to extinguish its debt, in 1790 the Federal Congress assumed state debts in exchange for the states' abdication of the state tax base on imports.[319]

This allowed the Federal Congress to back its own debt issues, but it had an unintended secondary effect: From 1790 to 1842, United States federalism was characterized by implicit bailout expectations, soft budget constraints, and state debt unsustainability. As Henning and Kessler summarize, throughout this period, 'the possibility of a federal bailout of states was a reasonable expectation; moral hazard was substantially present'.[320]

As is now familiar to the literature, this precipitated a wave of unsustainable borrowing. Between 1820 and 1843, state debts increased from $4m (1820) to $231.6m (1843) – an increase of 5,700%.[321] Adams (1890) observes:

There is no question but that the assistance of the general government, coming at the time when it did, is largely responsible for the carelessness with which local obligations were incurred.[322]

By 1842, several states faced insolvency and, citing the precedent of 1790, proposed that $200,000,000 of federal stock should be exchanged for state securities to pay off state debts.[323] Yet, this time, the bailout was denied. The immediate consequences were costly: Nine states

---

[317] For this point: Fabbrini, *Economic Governance*, 26.
[318] John C Miller, *The Federalists: 1789–1801* (Harper & Row, 1960), 37–38; Sargent, 'Nobel Lecture', 12.
[319] Sargent, 'Nobel Lecture', 12–14.
[320] Henning and Kessler, 'Fiscal Federalism', 10.
[321] Henry Adams, *Public Debt* (D. Appleton and Company, 1890), 318; John Joseph Wallis, 'Constitutions, Corporations and Corruption: American States and Constitutional Change, 1842 to 1852' (2005) 65 J Econ Hist 211, 216.
[322] Adams, *Public Debt*, 327.
[323] Adams, *Public Debt*, 332.

defaulted on their debts.[324] Of these, five (Arkansas, Florida, Louisiana, Michigan, Mississippi) repudiated all or some of their debts, and four were forced to renegotiate with creditors (Illinois, Indiana, Maryland, Pennsylvania).[325] A further four (Alabama, New York, Ohio, Tennessee) narrowly escaped default.[326]

Yet this 1842 episode may 'be properly regarded as marking an epoch in the constitutional development of the States'.[327] By the end of the decade, over half of the American states had enacted budget laws in order to get back in good with markets, and most undertook difficult reforms, innovating their tax bases and setting off the inter-state tax competition which still characterizes United States federalism.[328] Nearly two centuries later, markets still monitor state finances closely and price default risk in a manner that impels states to act consistently with their solvency.[329] Between 2001 and 2007, the average spread between American states was wider than the bond spreads between EU states – despite much narrower debt dispersion.[330] Spillovers are also few: a deterioration in one state's credit outlook does not cause a deterioration in others,[331] and Ang and Longstaff find 'much less systemic risk among U.S. sovereigns than among Eurozone sovereigns'.[332] In other words, the United States struggled out of precisely the bailout trap into which the EU has now fallen.[333]

---

[324] Arthur Grinath III and John Joseph Wallis, 'Debt, Default and Revenue Structure: The American State Debt Crisis in the Early 1840s' (1997) NBER Historical Paper No 97; Arthur Grinath III, Richard E Sylla and John Joseph Wallis, 'Sovereign Debt and Repudiation: The Emerging-Market Debt Crisis in the US States' (2004) NBER Working Paper No 10753; William B English, 'Understanding the Costs of Sovereign Default: American State Debts in the 1840's' (1996) 86 Am Econ Rev 259, 261–267.

[325] BU Ratchford, *American State Debts* (Duke University Press, 1941), 114.

[326] Wallis, 'Constitutional Change', 216.

[327] Adams, *Public Debt*, 335.

[328] Kelemen, 'Law, Fiscal Federalism, Austerity', 384.

[329] Bayoumi et al., 'Credit Markets'; Morris Goldstein and Geoffrey Woglom, 'Market-Based Fiscal Discipline in Monetary Unions: Evidence from the US Municipal Bond Market' in Matthew Canzoneri, Vittorio Grilli and Paul Masson (eds), *Market-Based Fiscal Discipline in Monetary Unions: Evidence from the US Municipal Bond Market* (Cambridge University Press, 1992); Inman, 'Transfers and Bailouts', 63–64; Rodden, 'Can Market Discipline Survive?', 47–48.

[330] Henning and Kessler, 'Fiscal Federalism', 26.

[331] Henning and Kessler, 'Fiscal Federalism', 26–27.

[332] Andrew Ang and Francis Longstaff, 'Systemic Sovereign Credit Risk: Lessons from the U.S. and Europe' (2011) 60 J Money Econ 493, 494.

[333] Sargent, 'Nobel Lecture', 26.

8.2.3.4   Fiscal Rules and Fiscal Outcomes

There is no federal oversight of American state debts. Self-imposed fiscal rules emerged at state level under a period of intense market discipline following the 1842 episode, but 'these legal restrictions are, themselves, largely an endogenous response to the external discipline of the credit markets'.[334]

At the time of writing, 49 states had some form of BBR in place.[335] The heterogeneity of these laws precludes full description here, but, in brief, 44 states require the governor to submit a balanced budget, 41 states require the legislature to enact a balanced budget, and 29 states are not able to carry a deficit into future years.[336] In 35 states, at least some element of the fiscal rule is enacted into constitutional law, while 10 states are purely legislative.[337] Forty states also attempt to limit gross debt, and 28 fetter expenditures or revenues to an eclectic mix of variables from oil revenues (Alaska) to sales tax (North Dakota).[338] As a rule, enforcement mechanisms are weak or non-existent.[339]

A ponderous body of research finds that American states comply with fiscal rules because of market discipline, not legal enforcement.[340] A United States General Accounting Office survey of 49 states, for example, found that the primary impetus for fiscal adjustment is market discipline.[341] By contrast, 'Factors such as enforcement provisions, sanctions and court decisions were cited by only a few officials as being significant motivators.'[342] Rodden concludes, for this section:

This [1842] episode marked the beginning of a long period of successful market discipline among the US states [...] Unlike other political unions described

---

[334] McKinnon, 'Market-Preserving Fiscal Federalism', 75. See also Wallis, 'Constitutional Change', 212; Henning and Kessler, 'Fiscal Federalism', 17.

[335] The exception is Vermont. National Association of State Budget Officers, *Budget Processes in the States 2015* (NASBO, 2015); Martinez-Vazquez and Vulovic, 'Do Subnational Borrowing Regulations Work?' 161, 174.

[336] National Association of State Budget Officers, *Budget Processes*.

[337] National Association of State Budget Officers, *Budget Processes*, 52.

[338] National Association of State Budget Officers, *Budget Processes*, 55; Kennedy and Robbins, 'Fiscal Performance', 12.

[339] See James M Poterba, 'Budget Institutions and Fiscal Policy in US States' (1996) 86 Am Econ Rev 395, 395; National Association of State Budget Officers, *Budget Processes* and sources cited above, Section 8.1.1, nn 54, 57.

[340] Kelemen and Teo, 'Focal Points', 381; Briffault, *Balancing Acts*, 61; Eyraud and Gomez Sirera, 'Constraints', 111–112; and sources cited above, Section 8.1.1, nn 52–64, 67–70, 72–77 and Section 8.2.3.3, n 329.

[341] US General Accounting Office, *Balanced Budget Requirements*.

[342] US General Accounting Office, *Balanced Budget Requirements*.

above, the US federal government has not endeavoured to limit the deficits or debts of the US States. Yet without any hierarchical oversight or regulation, throughout the twentieth century the deficits and debt burdens of the US states have been quite low in comparison with entities in most other federations.[343]

8.2.4 Canada

Like the EU, Canada is another large, decentralized monetary union whose provinces differ in terms of economic endowments, population, size, geography and language.[344] Worse, Canada's economy is inextricably entwined with the United States – the origin of the 2008 crisis.

And yet, the global financial crisis had relatively light effects on Canada. It had no tottering debts and no imbalances to burst. In 2007–2008 the provinces posted a combined $11.2bn surplus – the seventh in nine years (the federal government achieved its eleventh-straight surplus, amounting to $9.6bn).[345] Since Canada established its 'no bailout' commitment in 1936, in the past eighty years no province has ever defaulted.

Canadian federalism has evolved from a centralized constitution into the most decentralized federation exhibited in this chapter: [8.2.4.1] There is no federal oversight over the budgetary polices of the provinces; [8.2.4.2] Canada is characterized by a high degree of vertical fiscal symmetry; and [8.2.4.3–8.2.4.4] market discipline – not fiscal rules – plays a strong role in disciplining fiscal policy. In short, Canada is the antithesis of Europe's nascent fiscal union.[346] Bird and Tassonyi summarize:

Canada is one of the most decentralized countries in the world. Canadian provinces [...] face essentially no constitutional restraints on tax rates, bases or collection systems and no requirement to harmonize either with each other or with the federal government. [...] Moreover, if provinces wish to borrow, they may borrow as and from whom they wish, with no central review or control. There are no federal controls at all over provincial borrowing, internal or external.[347]

[343] Rodden, 'Can Market Discipline Survive?', 47.
[344] Canadian federal territories are excluded from this analysis, as they are federal jurisdictions.
[345] OECD, *Revenue Statistics 2014 – Canada* (OECD, 2014); Statistics Canada, 'Revenue and Expenditures' (*Statistics Canada*, 6 January 2016) www.statcan.gc.ca/tables-tableaux/sum-som/l01/cst01/govt02b-eng.htm accessed 10 September 2016.
[346] Amy Nuget, James Pearce and Richard Simeon, 'The Resilience of Canadian Federalism' in Peterson and Nadler (eds), *The Global Debt Crisis*, 214, 219.
[347] Richard Bird and Almos Tassonyi, 'Constraints on Provincial and Municipal Borrowing in Canada: Markets, Rules and Norms' (2001) 44 Can Public Admin 84, 85–86.

8.2.4.1   Revenue and Expenditure Autonomy

Canada did not begin life as a decentralized federation. The *British North America Act* 1867 (BNA Act) establishing the Dominion of Canada resolved all residual powers to the Dominion parliament, and gave it a power to disallow provincial statutes in certain competences.[348] The Dominion also had near-total control over revenues: Section 91(3) of the BNA Act empowered the Dominion to raise money 'by any mode or system of taxation' and ascribed tariffs – around 80% of revenues at that time – to the Dominion.[349]

From this inauspiciously centralized foundation, the jurisprudence of the Privy Council from 1880 to the 1930s nonetheless 'elevated the provinces to coordinate status with the Dominion'.[350] The Privy Council expanded provincial powers in competence disputes by looking to provincial competences to act first, such as civil and property rights (which it interpreted broadly), and only secondarily looking to federal heads of power such as the residuary and federal trade and commerce powers (which it interpreted narrowly).[351] For example, provincial competence over 'direct' taxes was interpreted to include sales taxes,[352] and the federal 'paramountcy' doctrine was restricted to circumstances where one law necessarily violated the other.[353] In *AG Canada* v. *AG Ontario*, the Privy Council famously described Canadian provinces as 'watertight compartments' and ruled that the federal residuary power was not a residuary power at all, but a delimited federal competency like any other.[354] The centralizing powers of pre-emption

---

[348]   Sections 90–91 British North America Act 1867 (UK) 30 & 31 Vict, c 3 [1985] RSC App II, No 5 (BNA Act).

[349]   BNA Act 1867, ss. 91. See Peter Hogg, *Constitutional Law of Canada* (Carswell, 2013), 5-15 – 5-16, 6-1.

[350]   Hogg, *Constitutional Law of Canada*, 5-18. See also : Eugénie Broullet and Bruce Ryder, 'Key Doctrines in Canadian Legal Federalism' in Peter Oliver, Patrick Macklem and Nathalie Des Rosiers (eds), *The Oxford Handbook of the Canadian Constitution* (Oxford University Press, 2017).

[351]   Hogg, *Constitutional Law of Canada*, 5-18 – 5-20; Francis Reginald Scott, 'Centralization and Decentralization in Canadian Federalism' (1951) 29 Can Bar Rev 1095; Louise-Philippe Pigeon, 'The Meaning of Provincial Autonomy' (1951) 29 Can Bar Rev 1126.

[352]   *Liquidators of Maritime Bank* v. *Receiver General of New Brunswick* [1892] AC 437 (Privy Council).

[353]   *Hodge* v. *The Queen* [1883] UKPC 59, 1–12; (1883) 9 App Cas 11; *Attorney General of Ontario* v. *Attorney General of the Dominion of Canada*, [1894] UKPC 13; [1894] AC 189; *The Grand Trunk Railway Company of Canada* v. *Attorney General of the Dominion of Canada* [1906] UKPC 72; [1907] AC 65, [4]; *Smith* v. *The Queen*, [1960] SCR 776, [5]; *Multiple Access* v. *McCutcheon*, [1982] 2 SCR 161, [39]–[49].

[354]   *Attorney General of Canada* v. *Attorney General of Ontario (Labour Conventions)* [1937] AC 326, 354; [1937] 1 DLR 673, 12.

fell into disuse by the 1930s and are now 'constitutional dead letters, whose use by Ottawa against either Quebec or western Canada would provoke political crisis'.[355] In *Hodge* v. *the Queen*, the Privy Council stated that provincial powers were as sovereign and plenary as those of the Imperial Parliament itself:

> Provincial Legislatures [...] are in no sense delegates of or acting under any mandate from the Imperial Parliament. [...] Within [its] limits of subjects and area the Local Legislature is supreme, and has the same authority as the Imperial Parliament, or the Parliament of the Dominion.[356]

Today, provincial governments spend more than the federal government and have a larger revenue base. On the revenue side, Provinces claim over 66% of personal and corporate direct taxation, about 50% of sales tax revenues and 100% of resource revenues.[357] The total federal share of revenues is less than half – around 45%.[358] Provinces are not obligated to keep the federal tax base, levy their own taxes or match the federal tax rate. Since 1962, the federal government has offered 'collection' agreements, offering to collect taxes without charge for any province which apes the federal tax base.[359] However, provinces may choose to administer their own tax base, for which the federal government provides an 'abatement', resiling its tax rate on shared tax factors to make room for the provincial taxing powers.[360] According to a long-settled convention described thusly by the Government of Canada:

> [T]he decision of a provincial Legislature to exercise its constitutional right not to participate in any programme, even given a national consensus, should not result in a fiscal penalty being imposed on the people of the province.[361]

On the expenditure side, there is no form of institutionalized coordination in the Canadian federation. Economic coordination is often described as 'federal-provincial diplomacy',[362] or intergovernmental

---

[355] Nuget et al., 'Canadian Federalism' 206. See also Hogg, *Constitutional Law of Canada*, 5–19.

[356] *Hodge* v. *The Queen (Canada)*. See also *Liquidators of Maritime Bank (Canada)*.

[357] Courchene, 'Stabilization Policies', 308; OECD, *Revenue Statistics 2014 – Canada*.

[358] Sources Courchene, 'Stabilization Policies', 308; OECD, Revenue Statistics 2014 – Canada.

[359] Hogg, *Constitutional Law of Canada*, 6–5; Francis Reginald Scott, 'The Constitutional Background of the Taxation Agreements' (1955) 2 McGill LJ 1 783–784.

[360] Hogg, *Constitutional Law of Canada*, 6–6.

[361] Government of Canada, *Federal-Provincial Grants and the Spending Power of Parliament* (Queen's Printer, 1969), 36.

[362] Richard Simeon, *Federal-Provincial Diplomacy: The Making of Recent Policy in Canada* (University of Toronto Press, 2006).

'confederalism', in which economic objectives are negotiated as between co-equally supreme sovereigns.[363]

Canada's federal spending power plays a countercyclical role (estimates of regional stabilization tend to range around 10%–14% of personal income or 15%–20% of GDP),[364] but even at the height of the 2009 federal stimulus (at 4% of GDP), federal spending accounted for 43% of public expenditures, compared to 57% by the provinces.[365] Like in the United States and Switzerland, federal countercyclical spending occurs through automatic stabilizers that arise consequentially from the federal budget, using federal revenues, within federal competences.[366] For example, the federal stimulus package in the global financial crisis came mainly through cost-matching investments and direct spending in infrastructure, amounting to about $8bn in federal funds, $6bn in provincial funds and approximately 7,000 infrastructure projects (municipal projects were usually funded at 33% each).[367] Much like Switzerland and the United States, the provinces and federal government ran their own stimulus programmes parallel to each other in a decentralized manner without long-term economic or political instability to the constitutional framework.[368] As Brown observes:

The Canadian system has remained decentralised during the initial crisis response and the subsequent consolidation, especially with respect to fiscal policy.[369]

8.2.4.2   Vertical Fiscal Symmetry

The share of provincial revenues (56%) and federal revenues (44%) almost perfectly matches provincial expenditures (57%) and federal (43%) expenditures.[370] Like the United States, Canadian provinces have

---

[363] David Cameron and Richard Simeon, 'Intergovernmental Relations in Canada' (2002) 32 Publius 49, 50, 55–56; Nuget et al., 'Canadian Federalism', 206–207; Jennifer Smith, *Federalism* (UBC Press, 2014), 101.

[364] Mélitz and Zumer, 'Regional Redistribution', 284; Tigran Poghosyan, Abdelhak Senhadji and Carlo Cottarelli, 'The Role of Fiscal Transfers in Smoothing Regional Shocks: Evidence from Existing Federations' (2016) IMF Working Paper No 141.

[365] OECD, *Economic Surveys: Canada 2012* (OECD, 2012), 21.

[366] Poghosyan et al., 'Existing Federations'.

[367] Nuget et al., 'Canadian Federalism', 217; OECD, *Economic Surveys: Canada 2012*, 21–22.

[368] OECD, *Economic Surveys: Canada 2012*, 21–22; OECD, *Economic Surveys: Canada 2010*, 73.

[369] Douglas Brown, 'The Financial Crisis and the Future of Federalism in Canada' in Eccleston and Krever (eds), *Future of Federalism*, 73.

[370] Statistics Canada, 'Revenue and Expenditures'. Geneviève Tellier and Louis Imbeau, 'Budget Deficits and Surpluses in the Canadian Provinces: A Pooled Analysis' (European Public Choice Society Annual Conference, Berlin, April 2004), 5.

complete fiscal autonomy, despite extensively overlapping tax factors and expenditure competences, and despite a federal 'spending power' that allows Canada to spend on public goods in areas that mainly fall under provincial jurisdiction.[371] Cottarelli and Guerguil rank Canadian provinces as the second-least transfer-dependent in the world (slightly behind Swiss Cantons) – German *Länder* are 228% more transfer-dependent.[372]

This is remarkable, considering Canada has four federal-provincial transfer programmes on the books: the Canada Health Transfer (CHT), the Canada Social Transfer (CST), the Fiscal Stabilization Program (FSP) and the Federal Equalization Program.[373]

The CST is an unconditional per capita block transfer for tertiary education and other social programmes,[374] and the CHT is a per capita cash and tax-point healthcare transfer.[375] Both are funded by the federal government under a federal mandate and substantively unconditional. With the exception of vague, largely undefined, CHT standards (i.e. accessibility, comprehensiveness, portability, public administration and universality),[376] conditional transfers have completely disappeared from Canadian federalism – seen as 'just another opportunity for federal meddling in provincial affairs' by provincial electorates.[377] These programmes have not led to soft budget constraints, and markets and electorates continue to differentiate between provincial/federal financial obligations.[378]

The FSP is an *ex post* revenue-stabilization programme that bears several injurious hallmarks warned-against by SGFF theory.[379] Yet it has nonetheless 'atrophied to near insignificance' as a feature of Canadian federalism.[380] In principle, the FSP allows the Federal Government to

---

[371] Andrew Petter, 'Federalism and the Myth of the Federal Spending Power' (1989) 60 Can Bar Rev 34; Colleen Flood, William Lahey and Bryan Thomas, 'Federalism and Health Care in Canada: A Troubled Romance?' in Oliver et al. (eds), *Handbook of the Canadian Constitution*; Hoi Kong, 'The Spending Power in Canada' in Oliver et al. (eds.), *Handbook of the Canadian Constitution*.

[372] Cottarelli and Guerguil, *Designing European Fiscal Union*, 3.

[373] *Federal-Provincial Fiscal Arrangements Act*, R.S.C. 1985 c. F-8.

[374] *Fiscal Arrangements Act (Canada)*, s. 24.3.

[375] *Fiscal Arrangements Act (Canada)*, s. 24.

[376] *Fiscal Arrangements Act (Canada)*, s. 24(a). See Courchene, 'Stabilization Policies', 312; Bird and Tassonyi, 'Different Approaches', 44; OECD, *Economic Surveys: Canada 2012*, 25–27.

[377] Nuget et al., 'Canadian Federalism', 209.

[378] OECD, *Economic Surveys: Canada 2012*, 25–26; Bird and Tassonyi, 'Different Approaches', 44, 87–88.

[379] *Fiscal Arrangements Act (Canada)*, s. 5.

[380] Trevor Tombe, 'An (Overdue) Review of Canada's Fiscal Stabilization Program' (2020) IRRP Insight No 31, 4.

increase transfers to provinces following a sudden and significant year-over-year drop in non-resource revenues exceeding 5%. However, several constraints have prevented this from morphing into an *ex post* transfer programme: First, provinces are only eligible if the drop in revenues exceeds 5% of revenues in a year, and declines in resource revenues are counted only if the decline in resource revenues exceeds 50%.[381] This means the programme is hard for provincial governments to spoof, because rather catastrophic economic circumstances are needed to trigger it. Second, as stated by the Government of Canada, the programme only compensates for 'revenue declines due to economic downturns not for declines due to provincial decisions to reduce taxes; policy changes made by the province in the rate or in the structure of provincial taxes are factored out when measuring revenue declines'.[382] Third, the FSP distributes a maximum of $60 per person – a limit set in 1986 that has not increased with inflation (effectively reducing it in half). The FSP therefore poses little risk of soft budget constraints for the simple reason that it is measly. For example, in 2015/2016 Alberta received an FSP transfer of $249m in response to a revenue loss of between ~$7.2bn and $8.8bn. As Eisen and Hill observe: 'the program did almost nothing to help Alberta cope with its revenue loss'.[383]

The most significant transfer programme for this book is the Federal Equalization Program, an *ex ante* tax equalization programme.[384] The system calculates entitlements by selecting a basket of provincial tax-base factors and calculating an average tax rate for those factors according to what is known as the 'ten-province standard'.[385] The total of these calculations yields the province's 'fiscal capacity', which is then divided by its population

[381] Government of Canada, 'Backgrounder: The Fiscal Stabilization Program' (*Government of Canada*, 23 February 2016) www.canada.ca/en/department-finance/news/2016/02/ba ckgrounder-the-fiscal-stabilization-program.html accessed 6 December 2019.

[382] Government of Canada, 'The Fiscal Stabilization Program'.

[383] Ben Eisen and Tegan Hill, 'Canada's Stabilization Program Overdue for a Rethink' (*Fraser Institute*, 19 June 2020) www.fraserinstitute.org/blogs/canadas-stabilization-program-overdue-for-a-rethink accessed 6 August 2020; Bev Dahlby, 'Reforming the Federal Fiscal Stabilization Program' (2019) 12:18 University of Calgary SPP Briefing Paper 1.

[384] *Fiscal Arrangements Act (Canada)*, s. 3.

[385] *Fiscal Arrangements Act (Canada)*, s. 3.2–3.5. See Édison Roy-César, *Canada's Equalization Formula* (Library of Parliament Publication No 2008–20-E, 2008).

to provide a per capita figure.[386] If a province has potential per-capita revenues below this level, it will be entitled to a transfer to the amount of the average. Transfers are from the federal treasury and they are unconditional.

Two characteristics mark this out from comparable systems in Germany and Switzerland. First, unlike Germany, it is not based on *actual* revenues, or the expenditure needs of any particular province.[387] If a province earns more *actual* per capita revenues through tax-base innovation than the formula computes, it will get to keep both its transfer and its revenues. By the same token, a province which spends too much or raises too little cannot expect an increase in transfers to balance the budget.[388] The marginal incentive is maintained.[389]

Second, unlike the German and Swiss systems, 'have' provinces do not make transfers to 'have not' provinces. For 'have' provinces, the equalization programme is not a transfer system at all. All equalization payments come from federal revenues and are paid out by the Consolidated Revenue Fund of Canada – 'strictly a federal program'.[390] Rich provinces will not be taxed for good performance, because they do not pay for the transfer at all.

8.2.4.3 Hard Budget Constraints and Market Discipline

The Canadian federation in the 1930s faced choices that were similar to those faced in the United States in 1842, Germany in 1992 and the EU today. Most importantly, Canada learned the same lesson that the United States learned in 1840 and the EU has yet to learn: As Maxwell and MacG so put it in 1936, fiscal federalism requires provinces to be 'allowed to go broke at their own sweet will'.[391]

The Canadian Dominion formed in 1867 had a high degree of fiscal asymmetry. Like today's EU Member States, Canadian provinces were

---

[386] *Fiscal Arrangements Act (Canada)*, s. 3.4.

[387] OECD, *Economic Surveys: Canada 2012*, 26.

[388] Courchene, 'Stabilization Policies', 316–318. Nor is it justiciable, as in Germany: Hogg, *Constitutional Law of Canada*, 6–10.

[389] Bird and Vaillancourt, 'Fiscal Decentralization', 32, 34; Bird and Tassonyi, 'Provincial and Municipal Borrowing', 90 at fn 26.

[390] Joe Ruggeri, *Equalization Reform in Canada: Principles and Compromises* (Fiscal Federalism and the Future of Canada, the Institute of Intergovernmental Relations, Queen's University Kingston, September 28–29, 2006), 8.

[391] JA Maxwell and DA MacG, 'The Adjustment of Federal-Provincial Financial Relations' (1936) 2 Can J Econ Polit Sci 374, 383, 379.

responsible for all major social, redistributive and countercyclical spending functions: unemployment insurance, pensions, 'relief' (welfare) payments, health and education.[392] Unlike today's EU countries, however, they also had a constrained tax base.[393] When the Great Depression hit, provincial debt skyrocketed as a result of spending on federal 'relief' obligations, and provincial revenues could not be adequately stretched to cover them.[394] Provincial bonded debt and treasury bills increased by 48% between 1929 and 1933 (from $848,501,200 to $1,255,713,300), of which 95% was directly attributable to federal 'relief' obligations.[395]

The Dominion responded to the crisis by, *inter alia*, issuing $116,527,200 in loans to BC, Alberta, Saskatchewan and Manitoba. Most of this was never repaid – one-third of Saskatchewan's debt was written off, while most of the rest was extended to a thirty-year maturity before disappearing from public accounts after 1977.[396]

Like the 1790 assumption of American state war debts, this bailout resulted in soft budget constraints and led to Canada's first – and only – provincial default.[397] Under this bailout precedent, in 1935 the young Province of Alberta embarked on a (now-familiar) train of 'loose financial management, wildly-optimistic capital expansion projects and poor judgment', which shortly bankrupted the province and pushed it to seek another bailout in March 1936.[398] This time, the bailout was denied. Alberta defaulted on $3.2m in maturing debt on 1 April 1936 and stayed in default until 1945, by which time it had defaulted on $33.4m in principal and $28.6m in interest.[399] Writing at the 1936 Round Table on Public Finance, Maxwell and MacG encapsulate the lessons learned by Canada thusly:

---

[392] Bird and Tassonyi, 'Provincial and Municipal Borrowing', 90; Maxwell and MacG, 'Federal-Provincial Financial Relations'.
[393] Income and commodity taxation were pre-empted by the Dominion, and the provincial tax base (mainly on gasoline, motor vehicles, corporations, inheritances and amusements) was relatively inflexible. Maxwell and MacG, 'Federal-Provincial Financial Relations', 381.
[394] Maxwell and MacG, 'Federal-Provincial Financial Relations', 377–378, 381.
[395] Maxwell and MacG, 'Federal-Provincial Financial Relations', 379.
[396] Bird and Tassonyi, 'Different Approaches'; Mac Joffe, *Provincial Solvency and Federal Obligations* (Macdonald-Laurier Institute, 2012), 39–40.
[397] Robert Ascah, *Politics and Public Debt: The Dominion, the Banks and Alberta's Social Credit* (University of Alberta Press, 1999), 53.
[398] Ascah, *Politics and Public Debt*, 56 (see generally 53–80); Joffe, *Provincial Solvency*, 37.
[399] Joffe, *Provincial Solvency*, 37.

The suggestion [has been made] that while the provincial revenues cannot be greatly expanded through the efforts of the provincial governments themselves, they can be expanded by increasing the unconditional subsidies paid by the Dominion. An advocate of this plan must neglect or brush aside all Canadian experience with these subsidies because they have from the outset been an apple of discord in Dominion-provincial relations, they have led to provincial extravagance, and they have intensified [. . .] political friction between the Dominion and the provinces due to real or imagined infringement of provincial autonomy.[400]

For those apt to listen, Maxwell and MacG may just as well be speaking to a conference on EU fiscal federalism today.

Today, there is no bailout expectation in Canadian federalism. Instead, Canadian federalism presents 'an extreme test of the viability of market-constrained decentralization'.[401] Constitutional amendments in 1941 and 1951 disentangled the fiscal asymmetries and 'relief' obligations which caused the 1935 crisis.[402] Although the 1930s episode has led some to argue that Canada is still a limited 'bailout' federation,[403] three empirical findings contradict this. First, credit rating agencies apply different ratings to each province, and do not identify a bailout expectation for Canadian provinces as they do for German or EMU states.[404] Second, market discipline has proven both effective and instrumental in disciplining provincial debt levels throughout the 1980s,[405] 1990s[406] and 2000s.[407] Despite several recessions over these decades and no centralized fiscal constraints, these periods are widely regarded as some of 'the most successful examples of fiscal

---

[400] Maxwell and MacG, 'Federal-Provincial Financial Relations', 379–382.

[401] Bird and Tassonyi, 'Provincial and Municipal Borrowing', 87.

[402] This confirms the lesson that unfunded federal mandates lead to soft budget constraints. See Bird and Tassonyi, 'Different Approaches'; Maxwell and MacG, 'Federal-Provincial Financial Relations', 379; Singh and Plekhanov, 'Subnational Government Borrowing', 4–5.

[403] Nuget et al., 'Canadian Federalism', 214 argue that bond yields for small, equalization-receiving provinces do not reflect market risks.

[404] Provinces are subject to harder budget constraints than the federal government: Rodden, *Hamilton's Paradox*, 143. On EMU and German credit ratings, see above, Chapter 3, Section 3.1.2 and Chapter 8, Section 8.2.1.3.

[405] Ronald Kneebone, 'Deficits and Debt in Canada: Some Lessons from Recent History' (1994) 20 Can Pub Pol'y 152.

[406] Courchene, 'Stabilization Policies', 331

[407] OECD, *Economic Surveys: Canada 2010* 69–71; Virginie Traclet, 'Monetary and Fiscal Policies in Canada: Some Interesting Principles for EMU?' (2004) Bank of Canada Working Paper No 28 ; Bordo et al., 'Lessons from History', 464.

consolidation in recent history'.[408] Third, empirical evidence shows that provinces respond to ratings changes and are better at managing deficits – 'largely because markets make them do so' – than they are at managing surpluses (to which no market constraints apply).[409] Bird and Tassonyi conclude:

[I]t appears to be widely accepted by provincial governments, and their constituents, that they are responsible for their own actions and that there will be no federal bailout [...] as has been clear since the beginning of public-sector borrowing in Canada, credit markets clearly exert effective discipline on pubic-sector borrowers.[410]

8.2.4.4   Fiscal Rules and Fiscal Outcomes

Courchene summarizes federal coordination of provincial finances as follows:

In a word, there is no coordination! Moreover, any monitoring of provincial finances is done by the capital markets (bond-rating agencies), not by Ottawa. [...] Phrased differently, the provinces can tax and spend as they wish and they can borrow as long as they can find markets for their bonds.[411]

Six (formerly eight) Canadian provinces have, however, enacted some form of fiscal rule of their own accord.[412] Provincial fiscal rules are ceaselessly being re-drafted, but the genus of the current rules owes to a period of raised market pressure in the 1990s.[413] At the time of writing, Ontario,[414] Alberta[415] and British Columbia[416] require the budget to be balanced *ex ante*. Saskatchewan,[417] Manitoba[418] and Quebec[419] require the budget to be balanced *ex post*. Nova Scotia and New Brunswick used to have BBRs, but scrapped them in 2009 and 2015,

---

[408] OECD, *Economic Surveys: Canada 2010*, 69.
[409] Bird and Tassonyi, 'Provincial and Municipal Borrowing', 102.
[410] Bird and Tassonyi, 'Provincial and Municipal Borrowing', 91, 101.
[411] Courchene, 'Stabilization Policies', 324–325.
[412] Stephen Tapp, *Canadian Experiences with Fiscal Consolidations and Fiscal rules* (Office of the Parliamentary Budget Officer, 2010); Tapp, 'Fiscal Rules in Canadian Provinces', 63.
[413] Tellier and Imbeau, 'Budget Deficits', 4; Liu (2011), 40, 52.
[414] *Fiscal Sustainability, Transparency and Accountability Act*, S.O. 2019, c. 7.
[415] *Fiscal Planning and Transparency Act*, S.A. 2015, c. F-14.7.
[416] *Budget Transparency and Accountability Act*, S.B.C. 2000, c 23; *Balanced Budget and Ministerial Accountability Act*, S.B.C. 2001, c 28.
[417] *The Growth and Financial Security Act*, S.S. 2008, c. G-81.
[418] *The Fiscal Responsibility and Taxpayer Protection Act*, C.C.S.M. 2018 c. F84.
[419] *Balanced Budget Act*, C.Q.L.R. 2001 c. E-12.00001.

respectively.[420] Newfoundland and Labrador, and Prince Edward Island, have never adopted BBRs. As a rule, enforcement mechanisms 'are not well defined for any of the provinces and territories', and all are plagued by loose escape clauses 'that would allow governments to bypass the constraints'.[421] The OECD notes that 'no external/independent bodies exist' to monitor the rules, and there is little or no possibility that any of the rules could be enforced in the courts.[422]

Canadian fiscal rules are, however, correlated with improved fiscal outcomes. Tapp's 2013 study of Canadian fiscal rules from 1981 to 2007 finds that the average improvement in the budget was around 0.8% of GDP for provinces which enacted BBRs, and the debt-to-GDP ratio was 1% of GDP better for provinces with debt rules.[423] Stronger fiscal rules also out-performed weaker ones.[424]

Is the lesson to be gleaned that Canadian fiscal stability is a result of legal fiscal rules? Hardly. Canadian fiscal rules are more likely to be scrapped than applied.[425] Tapp finds that 40% of Canadian fiscal rules were repealed, amended or allowed to lapse between 1981 and 2007, and the remaining rules crumbled in 2008, as soon as 'the benefits of doing so were judged to exceed the political costs'.[426] As Bird and Tassonyi conclude: 'The more important lesson appears to lie in the flexibility of the Canadian political system and its ability and willingness to respond to market signals.'[427]

Studies parsing provincial fiscal rules and budget outcomes attribute the Canadian fiscal record to market discipline. Simpson and Wesley's 2012 study is typical: 'Our analysis shows that BBLs had no discernible effect in restraining expenditure growth relative to revenue growth in most provinces.'[428] MacKinnon finds that announcements and actions by rating agencies triggered fiscal consolidation efforts in

---

[420] *Finance Act*, S.N.S. 2010, c. 2, s. 59(2); *Fiscal Transparency and Accountability Act*, S.N.B. 2014, c. 63.

[421] Jonathan Millar, 'The Effects of Budget Rules on Fiscal Performance and Macroeconomic Stabilization' (1997) Bank of Canada Working Paper No 15, 7. See also OECD, *Economic Surveys: Canada 2010*, 87.

[422] OECD, *Economic Surveys: Canada 2010*, 72.

[423] Tapp, 'Fiscal Rules in Canadian Provinces', 62.

[424] Tapp, 'Fiscal Rules in Canadian Provinces', 53.

[425] OECD, *Economic Surveys: Canada 2010*, 89–90.

[426] Tapp, 'Fiscal Rules in Canadian Provinces', 50.

[427] Bird and Tassonyi, 'Provincial and Municipal Borrowing', 91.

[428] Simpson and Wesley, 'Effectively Hollow?', 291.

Saskatchewan, for example (not fiscal rules).[429] Tapp finds that fiscal rules were adopted as part of consolidation plans, during fiscal consolidations, or to 'lock-in' completed adjustments.[430] Moreover, 'improvements also occurred in provinces that did not adopt fiscal rules'.[431] Millar makes similar findings.[432] As Schnable concludes, 'a look at consolidation episodes confirms the functioning of market discipline'.[433] Bird and Tassonyi conclude, for this section:

> Democracy *plus* markets [...] thus works to overcome a number of institutional features that on their face might seem conducive to flagrant fiscal misbehaviour by provincial governments. In Canada [...] budget rules [...] can be effective only through the working of the same forces – and if those forces work, it is not clear that much is gained by legislating such rules.[434]

8.2.5   The European Economic and Monetary Union

The model of fiscal union taking root in EMU supplants a legal fulcrum of decentralized federalism (an entrenched 'no bailout' law) with a legal characteristic of unitary states: financial transfers and centralized governance of Member State fiscal policy. The *ratio* governing the legality of this shift, per *Pringle* v. *Ireland*, is that centralized governance can ensure fiscal discipline in a federated monetary union with an established bailout precedent and institutionalized financial assistance.[435] This is the essential economic premise upon which the emerging European fiscal union is based, and recent proposals by the Five Presidents and the European Commission espouse this premise.[436] The stated policy wisdom behind the emergent fiscal union implies that the unique 'design flaw' at the heart of EMU was the centralization of monetary policy (a good thing) while leaving fiscal policy at national level (a bad thing).[437] EU policy documents often recite the refrain that the EU

---

[429] Janice MacKinnon, *Minding the Public Purse: The Fiscal Crisis, Political Trade-Offs and Canada's Future* (McGill Queen's University Press, 2003), 118–119.

[430] Tapp, 'Fiscal Rules in Canadian Provinces', 50.

[431] Tapp, 'Fiscal Rules in Canadian Provinces', 50, 52.

[432] Millar, 'Budget Rules', 7–8.

[433] Schnabel, 'Canada', 68–69.

[434] Bird and Tassonyi, 'Different Approaches', 101 (emphasis in original).

[435] See *Pringle* v. *Ireland* [136]–[137] and discussion above, Chapter 6, at nn 1–8.

[436] See proposals cited in Methods and Introduction, n 81.

[437] European Commission, 'Economic Governance Review' COM(2020) 55 final, 2; Commission Reflection Paper (2017), 7, 15–17, 25; Trichet, 'Federation by Exception', 474–476; European Commission, 'Building a Strengthened Fiscal

is somehow 'unique' in combining a centralization of monetary policy with 'decentralised fiscal and economic policies under the responsibility of Member States'.[438] Establishing a fiscal union and centralizing fiscal governance, so the argument goes, will rectify this error.[439]

Theory and evidence from the EMU's four comparators refute this hypothesis. Contrary to the 'sui generis' myth of European exceptionalism, the EMU is far from 'unique' in combining monetary centralization with a loose coordination of fiscal policy. Even if that were not so, the prevailing political prescriptions seem conspicuously deaf to the fact that the Euro Crisis was simply not caused by fiscal profligacy or lack of a federal macrofiscal spending capacity.[440]

8.2.5.1   Soft Budget Constraints and Bailout Expectations

First and foremost, theory, history and evidence show clearly that legal sanctions cannot replace market discipline as a disciplining force in a decentralized federation.[441] Legal sanctions can never outweigh the dysfunctional incentives of markets and voter preferences under soft budget constraints; bailout expectations indicate that fiscal rules themselves are non-credible; and soft budget constraints actively undermine the cost-levying function of fiscal rules.[442] In the EU, this would seem correct as an empirical matter: Rule-breakers are demonstrably more likely to receive a bailout (which count stands at €500.07bn dispersed over eight separate bailout agreements for five EMU Member States) than to face sanctions under EU law (which count stands at €0.00 fines levied).[443]

The sanctification of permanent financial assistance in *Pringle* v. *Ireland* has sterilized Article 125 TFEU as a matter of economics,[444]

Framework in the European Union' (2013) European Economy Occasional Papers No 150, 5

[438] Commission, Economic Governance Review (2020), 2.

[439] Commission Blueprint, 31–33, 38–49; Commission Reflection Paper (2017), 7, 15–17; David Ziblatt, 'Between Centralization and Federalism in the European Union' in Peterson and Nadler (eds), *The Global Debt Crisis*, 113.

[440] Rommerskirchèn, 'Financial Market Behaviour', 836; De Grauwe and Ji, 'How Much Fiscal Discipline?', 349, excerpted above, Chapter 3, at n 11.

[441] See, *inter alia*, sources cited above, Methods and Introduction, n 79, and Sections 8.1.1–8.1.2.

[442] See Sections 8.1.1–8.1.2.

[443] For the calculation of this figure, see Methods and Introduction, n 89.

[444] Wyplosz, 'Centralization-Decentralization', 19; Bordo et al., 'Lessons from History', 481–482.

and of law,[445] so 'removing a cornerstone of Europe's model of fiscal federalism'.[446] In accordance with the predictions of this study, markets have been under-pricing economic risks in the periphery since the European bailouts.[447] Italy's gross debt (134.8% of GDP in 2019) is now larger than Greece's at the height of the crisis (126.7% of GDP in 2009),[448] but the yield on its ten-year bonds (1.19% in 2019) is less than AAA-rated American Treasuries (2.14%).[449] So are Portugal's (0.76%) and Spain's (0.66%).[450] Portugal, whose bonds were junk-rated until September 2017 and lower-medium grade thereafter,[451] has been paying the same or less for its long-term debt than AAA-rated Australian debt since 2014.[452] Ireland, the fourth most indebted country in Europe in the crisis, borrowed for 2.37% less than a year after exiting its bailout programme in 2013.[453] Finally, Greece – a country the IMF said would be insolvent unless given debt relief – borrowed at 4.95% in one of its first bond issues (contrast this with AAA-rated New Zealand bonds, which were priced at 4.2%).[454] Even during the peak of the crisis, when the ECB claimed bond yield spreads were unjustified, countries in the euro *still* faced *less* pressure than countries with equivalent debt characteristics outside it.[455]

8.2.5.2   Expenditure and Revenue Autonomy

Second, the model christened by *Pringle* v. *Ireland* and charted in the Commission Blueprint and the *Five Presidents' Report* creates 'fiscal union' by vertically co-opting Member State revenues and expenditure competences. It does not create 'fiscal union' by establishing its own.

[445] Van Malleghem, '(Un)Balanced', 157.
[446] Sonja Puntscher Riekmann and Doris Wydra, '"Obligations of Good Faith": On the Difficulties of Building US-Style EU Federalism' (2015) 21 Contemporary Politics 201, 213. See, similarly, sources cited in Methods and Introduction, n 3.
[447] ECB, *Financial Stability Review 2013* (May, 2013), 11, 35.
[448] Eurostat, 'Consolidated Gross Debt (gov_10dd_3dpt1)'.
[449] OECD, 'Long-Term Interest Rates'.
[450] 2019 rates. OECD, 'Long-Term Interest Rates'.
[451] Trading Economics, 'Portugal – Credit Rating' (*Trading Economics*, 24 April 2020) tra dingeconomics.com/portugal/rating accessed 12 November 2020.
[452] Average of 2.50% for Portugal, and 2.59% for Australia between 2014 and 2019. OECD, 'Long-Term Interest Rates'; Legrain, 'Ignoring Eurozone Risks'.
[453] OECD, 'Long-Term Interest Rates'. See also: Legrain, 'Ignoring Eurozone Risks'.
[454] Editorial, 'IMF-EU Feud over Greece's Debt'; Legrain, 'Ignoring Eurozone Risks'; Eurostat, 'Maastricht Criterion Interest Rates (irt_lt_mcby_a)'; OECD, 'Long-Term Interest Rates'.
[455] Hallerberg, 'Fiscal Federalism Reforms', 135; Barry Eichengreen, *The Crisis and the Euro* (*Mimeo*, University of California Berkeley, 2009).

This is a well-known recipe for dysfunction. Second only to the 'no bailout' rule, no other clearer lesson can be gleaned than that expenditure and revenue autonomy is absolutely necessary for fiscal discipline.[456] It is worrying, then, that all of the EU's current and proposed reforms regarding binding macroeconomic governance,[457] binding EU-set deficit targets,[458] binding interlinkages with Member State budgetary processes[459] and tax harmonization,[460] seek to centralize power in the EU and impair the autonomy of national governments.

The Commission Blueprint, for example, allows EU institutions to veto and take control of policies in national policy areas – such as by adjusting tax rates or freezing categories of fiscal spending – if the government does not implement EU recommendations.[461] There is no justification under either FGFF or SGFF for this. What is described in these proposals is closer to a unitary state than anything presented in the literature on federalism.[462] As Wyplosz concludes:

[A]t no point [do] the five presidents provide any justification for this centralization step. Observing that structural reforms are needed to promote prosperity, is a far cry from justifying further centralization.[463]

The centralization of budgetary constraints does nothing to address the causes of the sovereign debt crisis and instead 'strip[s] away the shock absorbers most economies rely on' to ensure macroeconomic stabilization.[464] On the expenditure side, Henning and Kessler caution that 'creating stringent state-level debt brakes in Europe without a capacity for countercyclical stabilisation would be a serious

---

[456] See Section 8.1.4.
[457] See Chapter 7, Section 7.4.
[458] See Chapter 7, Section 7.3.3.
[459] See Chapter 7, Section 7.2.
[460] See European Commission, 'Common Consolidated Corporate Tax Base (CCCTB)' (*Commission*, 1 October 2016) https://ec.europa.eu/taxation_customs/business/com pany-tax/common-consolidated-corporate-tax-base-ccctb_en accessed 22 December 2019. For comment: Clemens Fuest, 'The European Commission's Proposal for a Common Consolidated Corporate Tax Base' (2008) 24 Oxford Rev Econ Pol 720; Brady Gordon, 'Tax Competition and Harmonisation under EU Law: Economic Realities and Legal Rules' (2014) 39 EL Rev 790.
[461] Commission Blueprint, 31, 38–49; Trichet, 'Federation by Exception', 479.
[462] Wyplosz, 'Centralization-Decentralization', 17. For similar assessments, see Methods and Introduction, n 72.
[463] Wyplosz, 'Centralization-Decentralization', 23.
[464] The Economist, 'Not a Government Debt Crisis'. See Bayoumi and Eichengreen, 'Restraining Yourself'.

mistake'.[465] Others raise the same alarm.[466] For the EU, crimping Member State macroeconomic stabilization capacities may ultimately mean a choice between breaking the fiscal rule or breaking the 'no bailout' rule. Either way, there will be a trauma to the constitutional framework: The debt rules will be broken and the Member State will provide the stimulus, or the 'no transfer union' rule will be broken and the EU/ECB must provide the stimulus. Indeed, this is precisely what has occurred.[467] Commission meeting minutes, for example, note with satisfaction that, 'As regards the OECD's calls for expansionist fiscal policies [...] this was precisely the direction being taken by the [ECB] in its monetary policy.'[468] This objectionable state of affairs lies at the crux of the BVerfG's *ultra vires* ruling on the PSPP.[469] Thus, restricting expenditure and revenue autonomy only causes the spillover problems they are meant to solve.[470] Von Hagen and Eichengreen explain:

[T]he pressure for the central government to provide tax smoothing and automatic-stabilization services through a system of fiscal federalism will be greater where restrictions on borrowing by subcentral governments prevent the latter from providing these services themselves. [...] Thus, restraints on the budgetary freedom of subcentral governments will encourage the transfer of fiscal authority to the centre and will increase the demand for central government borrowing, ultimately weakening financial stability.[471]

The days of Member State revenue autonomy may also soon be numbered. Gordon, for example, argues that the EU's recidivistic Common Consolidated Corporate Tax Base (CCCTB) proposal 'immobilises the tax base', and 'decreases GDP, raises tax rates, decreases investment [and] decreases revenue', counter to the objectives of the internal market and EU tax policy.[472]

To the extent that EU reforms centralize control over Member State expenditure and revenue competences, the EU is violating the oldest rules and rationales of fiscal federalism. Fabbrini's criticism is apt: In repeatedly discounting the United States' federal model as being 'too

---

[465] Henning and Kessler, 'Fiscal Federalism', 30.
[466] Menéndez, 'Constitutional Mutation', 138 and sources cited below, n 470.
[467] Steinberg and Vermeiren, 'Germanized Euro Area?'.
[468] European Commission, 'Minutes of the 2158th Meeting', 22.
[469] *Weiss Decision (Germany)*, [134]-[137], [170]-[174] [177]-[178].
[470] Lago-Peñas et al., 'Fiscal Stability', 920; Bartolini et al., 'Fiscal Decentralization', 456–467.
[471] Von Hagen and Eichengreen, 'Fiscal Restraints', 136–137.
[472] Gordon, 'Tax Competition and Harmonisation', 806, 807 (and sources cited).

centralized and centripetal for the EU', the Union has instead 'ended up establishing a regime that is much less respectful of state sovereignty than the US federal system'.[473]

8.2.5.3   Vertical Fiscal Asymmetry

Third, the structural symmetries required for fiscal discipline are well-understood, and should not be ignored.[474] Conditional transfers and centrally imposed fiscal rules undermine fiscal symmetry and signal the vulnerability of the centre to the fortunes of its states. Rodden and Eskeland warn:

> [C]entral control, especially when it comes to borrowing and investment, is not likely to provide a satisfactory long-term answer to the problem of subnational fiscal discipline, especially in large, diverse federations.[475]

As described in Chapter 2, the EU has had all the elements of a symmetrical 'ideal-type' model since Maastricht: Instead of establishing an *ex post* 'bailout' capacity to finance governments coping with economic shocks, the EU was given its own budget and runs its own programmes independently, 99% of which comes from 'own resources' and 75% of which are customs duties and sugar levies – which the Member States do not share.[476] The Union's budget is simply too small to provide the side-by-side provision of public goods seen in Canada or the United States, but this is probably right: All of the EU's economic stabilizers are at Member State level, as are all of the revenues needed to finance them, and this in turn is aligned at the same level as electoral accountability.[477]Attempting to introduce centralized transfers and legal governance into this system lacks any theoretical justification from the perspective of fiscal federalism theory.[478] Indeed, the first major study commissioned by the European Commission applying fiscal federalism theory to spending competences in the EU found that macroeconomic stabilization functions should *not* be assigned to EU level.[479] The

---

[473] Fabbrini, 'Paradox', 2.

[474] Wyplosz, 'Centralization-Decentralization', 7 excerpted above, Methods and Introduction, at nn 19, 67, 97.

[475] Rodden and Eskeland, 'Lessons and Conclusions', 455, 459. See also Foremny, 'Sub-National Deficits', 86.

[476] Commission, 'New Budgetary Instruments', 2–4; Mario Monti et al., *Future Financing of the EU* (Commission, 2016).

[477] Giandomenico Majone, 'From Regulatory State to a Democratic Default' (2014) 52 JCMS 1216, 1218.

[478] Wyplosz, 'Centralization-Decentralization', 18.

[479] ECORYS, CPB and IFO, *A Study on EU Spending* (European Commission, 2008), 33.

Commission admits as much: 'Given their central role in the economy, national budgets will continue to be the main fiscal policy instrument for Member States to adjust to changing economic circumstances.'[480]

The nascent fiscal union plotted by the *Five Presidents' Report*, the Commission 'Blueprint' and subsequent proposals – which include conditional fiscal transfers and a 'fiscal stabilization function'[481] – shows an explicit disregard for the essential principles of fiscal autonomy and symmetry.[482]

So what accounts for it? Besides the permeating 'ever closer union' teleology, the main touted economic justification is the need to provide a stabilization capacity in the event of asymmetric shocks.[483] The crisis, so the argument goes, proved that shock absorbers at national level were simply too small for the weight of the imbalances created under the euro.[484] A larger fiscal capacity would have been better able to do the job.

One must not be misled, however. In no federation has a federal budget ever been created chiefly for macroeconomic stabilization purposes,[485] and it would not do anything to intervene in the chain of causality tracked through the Euro Crisis in Chapter 3. It is true that both OCA theory and FGFF theory call for a countercyclical macroeconomic stabilization function, but neither require fiscal stabilizers to be placed at federal (or supranational) level.[486] The earliest works tending to assign macreconomic stabilization to federal level have been challenged by 'a long list of studies' showing that decentralization probably has better – but certainly no worse –

[480] Commission, 'New Budgetary Instruments', 13.
[481] Juncker et al., *Five Presidents' Report*; Commission Blueprint; Commission, 'New Budgetary Instruments', 13–16; Commission Proposal for an EMF (2017).
[482] Wyplosz, 'Centralization-Decentralization', 23.
[483] See above, n 481. See also: Trichet, 'Federation by Exception', 478; Dabrowski, 'Fiscal and Macroeconomic Governance', 8, 11.
[484] Most of the deterioration of public finances during the 2008 crisis was due to automatic stabilizers – not discretionary increases in stimulus spending: Eyraud and Wu, 'Playing by the Rules', 9.
[485] Agnès Bénassy-Quéré et al., 'Reconciling Risk Sharing with Market Discipline: A Constructive Approach to Euro Area Reform' (2018) CEPR Policy Insight No 91, 2; Dabrowski, 'Fiscal and Macroeconomic Governance', 12.
[486] For this point: Dabrowski, 'Fiscal and Macroeconomic Governance', 8, 11–12. Under OCA theory, see Chapter 2, Section 2.2.2, nn 59–66. Under FGFF theory, see Oates, 'Essay on Fiscal Federalism', 1121.

effects on stability.[487] What *is* required is that, wherever macroeconomic stabilization expenditures are placed, there is symmetry between expenditure and revenue competences.[488] This principle is placed in jeopardy by the current direction of institutional reform in the EU.

In order to assign the EU a stabilization role without recourse to common-pool funding, the fiscal capacity assigned to it would need to amount to between 2% and 10% of Union GDP, encompassing 'far-going tax schemes, social transfers, and other expenditure responsibilities'.[489] As Dabrowski warns, this may not only be 'politically unrealistic', but it 'may also be economically dysfunctional [...] it can contradict the basic principles of fiscal federalism'.[490] This is because, under fiscal federalism theory, 'there is little scope for the centralization of any of [education, health, social security, housing, public order and safety, economic affairs and services] functions to the EU level, for instance'.[491]

In view of these obvious obstacles to a truly independent federal spending capacity, the Union is in pursuit of what Hinarejos calls the 'centralization' or 'surveillance' model.[492] Under this model, Member States retain all taxing powers (but the EU will govern their tax bases!),[493] and the EU enforces fiscal discipline through centralized supervision or direct control of state budgets. Since EU taxing power remains limited, fiscal stabilization spending is funded through common-pool fiscal transfers (like the EFSM) or debt mutualization (like the ESM).[494] Proponents of European fiscal union protest that other currency unions have this.[495]

Once again, one should not be misled. Calls for a US-style 'transfer union' and 'mutual risk sharing' are fundamentally mischaracterized. The United States is not a 'transfer union', and there is no

---

[487] Lago-Peñas et al., 'Fiscal Stability', 920 (and sources cited); Bartolini et al., 'Fiscal Decentralization'.

[488] See Oates, 'Evolution of Fiscal Federalism', 319 and Section 8.1.3 above, nn 98–115.

[489] Dabrowski, 'Fiscal and Macroeconomic Governance', 11. The MacDougall report called for a budget of 5%–7% of GDP. Wolff, 'A Budget for Europe's Monetary Union' argues for a budget of 2% for a countercyclical role.

[490] Dabrowski, 'Fiscal and Macroeconomic Governance', 12.

[491] Wyplosz, 'Centralization-Decentralization', 9.

[492] Hinarejos, *Constitutional Perspective*, 182–183.

[493] See Commission, 'CCCTB'. For criticism: Gordon, 'Tax Competition and Harmonisation'.

[494] See, for example, Trichet, 'Federation by Exception', 478.

[495] See Riekmann and Wydra, 'US-Style Federalism', 203; Benjamin J Cohen, 'Why Can't Europe Save Itself? A Note on a Structural Failure' (2015) 21 Contemporary Politics 220, 221.

mutual risk sharing between American states, Canadian provinces or Swiss cantons in that sense at all. In federal monetary unions where a central capacity plays a macroeconomic stabilization role, this is done through automatic stabilizers arising consequently from federal taxes and federal spending within federal competences.[496] It is *not* done by establishing common-pool revenue incentives, co-opting state competences, and then providing *ex post* bailouts through intergovernmental transfers. Cottarelli and Guerguil's study of thirteen federations finds that changes in federal transfers in response to cyclical shocks are 'neither large nor common' – fiscal stabilization occurs 'as a by-product of the centralization of revenues and spending', not transfers to state budgets.[497] Spending mechanisms offset approximately only 15%–20% of common shocks (and less for asymmetric shocks)[498] – a number 'roughly in line with the share of federal taxes' in GDP.[499] Furthermore, federal governments 'always finance themselves through their own taxes', and the lion's share of stabilization is left to sub-federal levels even in the most mature federations.[500] Poghosyan et al. conclude that simply transferring Member State revenue and expenditure competences to the centre will not improve stabilization, *ceteris paribus*:

To the extent that these central revenue and spending functions are transferred from local governments, the overall countercyclical response of transfers (central plus local) will not change, and *ceteris paribus* the ability of states to cushion the impact of shocks will not improve greatly following centralization.[501]

Anyways, one may question if it is really needed at all. Poghosyan et. al find that transfers to state budgets play only a 'limited role' in

---

[496] Poghosyan et al., 'Existing Federations', 2; Torsten Persson and Guido Tabellini, 'Federal Fiscal Constitutions: Risk Sharing and Moral Hazard' (1996) 64 Econometrica 632, 624.

[497] Cottarelli and Guerguil, *Designing European Fiscal Union*, 6. Tigran Poghosyan, Abdelhak Senhadji and Carlo Cottarelli, 'The Role of Fiscal Transfers in Smoothing Regional Shocks' in Carlo Cottarelli and Martine Guerguil (eds.), *Designing a European Fiscal Union* (Routledge, 2015) 78, 81.

[498] From 4% in Canada to 11% in the United States: Poghosyan et al., 'Smoothing Regional Shocks (2015)', 81.

[499] Cottarelli and Guerguil, *Designing European Fiscal Union*, 5.

[500] Cottarelli and Guerguil, *Designing European Fiscal Union*, 4.

[501] Poghosyan et al., 'Smoothing Regional Shocks (2015)', 81.

cushioning the impact of regional shocks in fiscal federations,[502] and Dabrowski points out the history of EMU is devoid of any real examples of asymmetric shocks used to justify fiscal union.[503] The only real asymmetric shock identified in Chapter 3 was internal imbalances caused by interest-rate convergence and markets pricing-in the mutulization of risk.[504] A central fiscal capacity would do nothing to offset this problem, and much to compound it. *Bundesbank* President Weidmann explains:

> In order to strengthen the principle of liability at the level of sovereign states [...] liability and control must be in equilibrium. In the Maastricht framework, both liability and control were, essentially, located at national level. During the crisis, however, we moved away from this: control remained national, whereas liability has been increasingly transferred to the European level. While national governments take independent decisions on debt, the community is liable for the consequences. This set-up is a breeding ground for renewed unsound developments.[505]

For this reason, as Dabrowski concludes, 'such proposals will lead to building a dysfunctional fiscal union which encourages moral hazard behaviour by both national authorities and financial markets'.[506] Others raise the same alarm.[507] Van Malleghem concludes:

> Paradoxically, the policy response to the crisis might be even more threatening to the survival of the eurozone and, indeed, the EU as a whole.[508]

8.2.5.4   Fiscal Rules and Fiscal Outcomes

Finally, as an empirical matter, it is clear that the EU's expansive fiscal governance regime is no more credible than its predecessors.[509] Eyraud et al. find that the extensive reforms of Stability and Growth Pact over 2005–2013 'have not had any evident

---

[502] Poghosyan et al., 'Smoothing Regional Shocks (2015)', 60; Cottarelli and Guerguil, *Designing European Fiscal Union*, 5.

[503] Dabrowski, 'Fiscal and Macroeconomic Governance', 8.

[504] See above, Chapter 3, Section 3.1.4, at n 73; Charles Wyplosz, 'The Common Currency: More Complicated than It Seems' in Harald Badinger and Volker Nitsch (eds.), *Routledge Handbook of the Economics of European Integration* (Routledge, 2015), 108.

[505] Weidmann, 'Crisis Management'.

[506] Dabrowski, 'Fiscal or Bailout Union', 46.

[507] Zeitler, 'Experience and Adjustments', 246; Sinn, *Euro Trap*, 6.

[508] Van Malleghem, '(Un)Balanced', 151.

[509] IMF, *2014 Article IV Consultation (Euro Area)*, 12; Eyraud and Wu, 'Playing by the Rules', 10–22, 26–28; Smits, 'Crisis Response', 1162; Commission, Economic Governance Review (2020), 7–10; Groeteke and Mause, 'Debt Brakes', 297–299.

impact on compliance'.[510] The Commission's 2019 Economic Governance review concludes:

Some Member States' debt ratios have in fact continued to rise or, at best, have stabilised. Some highly indebted Member States still have deficits that do not provide a sufficient safety margin towards the 3%-of-GDP reference value, despite favourable economic conditions. They also remain far from their medium-term budgetary objectives. Those observations [...] suggest that the enforcement of the fiscal rules did not make a material difference in the cases where the enforcement of fiscal discipline was most necessary.[511]

It other words, it does not work. It is no small wonder, then, that the Commission continues to promote more of the same.[512] Allowing Member States a margin of error of 0.5% of GDP, this author counts 141 breaches of the 3% deficit limit by twenty-four countries between 1999 and 2018 (only Estonia, Luxembourg, Finland and Sweden maintained deficits better than −3.5% of GDP),[513] and eighteen countries with multi-year periods in breach of the 60% debt limit (fourteen were in breach at the end of 2018).[514] The general government debt of both the EMU and the EU as a whole has exceeded 60% of GDP every year since 1999.[515] No sanctions have ever been imposed.

The Maastricht criteria do not appear to be constraining. If anything, Blume and Voight find that the Maastricht limits are associated with higher total expenditure.[516] In 2018, aggregate general public debt as a percentage of GDP in both EMU (85.8%) and the EU as a whole (80.3%) was the same as it was in 2010 (the year before the 'six pack' was enacted) at 85.8% and 79.6%, respectively.[517] The EFB finds that, despite extensive amendments to the governance framework, 'noncompliance has been the rule rather than the exception [...] EU rules have failed to impose

---

[510] Luc Eyraud, Vitor Gaspar and Tigran Poghosyan, 'Fiscal Politics in the Euro Area' in Gaspar et al. (eds.), *Fiscal Politics*, 429.
[511] Commission, Economic Governance Review (2020), 7.
[512] Commission, Economic Governance Review (2020), 8. For criticism: Pernice, 'Domestic Courts', 297, 302.
[513] Eurostat, 'Deficit/Surplus (gov_10dd_edpt1)'.
[514] Only the Czech Republic, Estonia, Latvia, Lithuania, Luxembourg, Poland, Romania, Slovenia, Sweden (since 2000) and Denmark (since 2000) have complied with the 60% debt limits since 1999. Eurostat, 'Consolidated Gross Debt (gov_10dd_3dpt1)'.
[515] Eurostat, 'Consolidated Gross Debt (gov_10dd_3dpt1)'.
[516] Blume and Voigt, 'Budget Institutions', 237.
[517] Eurostat, 'Consolidated Gross Debt (gov_10dd_3dpt1)'. From 2014–2018 there has been gradual reduction from 93% to 85.8% in EMU and from 87% to 80.4% in the EU as a whole. See EFB, *Assessment*, 28.

sufficient fiscal discipline in high debt countries to generate a convergence of public debt to safer levels'.[518]

The political cavortings splayed across the pages of the *Financial Times* each year as the Commission pretends it will enforce the SGP (or that enforcement would matter even if it did) have become farcical. Portugal and Spain are fined €0.00;[519] Italy's budget is found in 'particularly serious non-compliance' by the Commission, which then drops the entire procedure a few weeks later;[520] and France has been subject to some stage of the excessive deficit procedure in fourteen of the eighteen years since it first received an 'early warning' in 2002, with no sanctions ever being applied.[521] It is clear that EU fiscal governance does not work and markets do not care about it;[522] the charade should be dropped. It only puts the weaknesses of EU fiscal governance on display and encourages moral hazard.

Attempts to enforce a countercylclical policy under the MSP, Fiscal Compact and Directive 2011/85/EU do not work either. The Commission laments that, despite the extensive deepening of the countercylcical MTO framework, 'nevertheless, Member States' fiscal policies have remained largely pro-cycliclical'.[523] The EFB finds that 'the majority of Member States are estimated to be currently below their MTOs and a significant gap with the MTO remains [...] some Member States (Belgium, France, Italy, Poland, Portugal, Slovenia and Slovakia) have never achieved their MTO'.[524]

---

[518] EFB, *Assessment*, 30–31.

[519] Mehreen Khan, 'Brussels Avoids Hitting Spain and Portugal with Budget Fine' (*Financial Times*, 2016) www.ft.com/content/0c1c6dab-5f50-326a-ad92-47ec440d6923 accessed 2 December 2019.

[520] Mehreen Khan, 'Dutch Question Brussels' Explanation on Italian Budget' *Financial Times* (London 7 March 2019) www.ft.com/content/a389f924-40c5-11e9-9bee-efab61506f44 accessed 12 September 2020.

[521] Its latest EDP was abrogated in 2018 despite exceeding both the 3% and 60% debt limits, and in 2019 its 'planned deficit for 2020 provide[d] *prima facie* evidence of the existence of an excessive deficit'. Commission, 'Report from the Commission: France' COM (2020) 538 final 1, 1.

[522] Tony Barber, 'The Markets, Not Brussels, Will Determine Italy's Fate' *Finanial Times* (London 21 November 2018) www.ft.com/content/d2009da0-ed7b-11e8-89c8-d36339d835c0 accessed 12 September 2020 and sources cited above, Chapter 3, Section 3.3.2, n 207.

[523] Commission, Economic Governance Review (2020), 8 and (at 47): excluding countries whose gap with the MTO is <0.5% of GDP, 'the descending trend of adjustment remains'.

[524] EFB, *Assessment*, 46.

The MIP/EIP has fared little better. The MIP has been triggered several times since its enactment, with 104 findings of 'imbalances' and 28 'excessive imbalances'.[525] Only one Member State (Slovenia) has ever reduced its 'excessive imbalances' to 'no imbalances', and the number of excessive imbalances has been increasing.[526] Yet no EIP has ever been launched. Implementation of recommendations is poor. The rate of full/substantial implementation was just 6% in 2012, and had declined to 0% in 2019.[527] As a report commissioned by the European Parliament concludes, 'The key conclusion [...] is that the European Semester is not effective.'[528]

Remarkably, implementation rates under EU governance (including bailout programmes) are not better than the implementation rates of the OECD's unilateral recommendations (which have no coordination or enforcement mechanisms whatsoever), and the rate of implementation has not increased relative to the pre-crisis (pre-amendment) period.[529]

Beefed-up enforcement mechanisms do not help either: Despite much stronger legal enforcement tools in fiscal policy, the response rate for fiscal recommendations is only somewhat higher (44% on average in 2012–2014) than macroeconomic recommendations (32% in 2012–2014), a difference 'which is not particularly high and suggests that the European Semester is not particularly effective in enforcing the EU's fiscal rules'.[530] The EFB finds no 'clear difference in compliance between the two arms of the SGP', and 'compliance rates among countries under the corrective arm of the SGP *drop* by 10 percentage points when countries under macroeconomic adjustment [bailout] programmes are excluded'.[531] The ECB concludes that 'The EU's economic governance framework [...] has so far not induced sufficient

---

[525] Smits, 'Crisis Response', 1155; EFB, *Assessment*, 54.

[526] EFB, *Assessment*, 53–54.

[527] European Parliament Economic Governance Support Unit, *Implementation of the Macroeconomic Imbalance Procedure: State of Play August 2020* (European Parliament PE 497/739, 2020). See also IMF, *Euro Area Policies: Selected Issues*; Efstathiou and Wolff, 'National Implementation'.

[528] Zsolt Darvas and Álvaro Leandro, *Economic Policy Coordination in the Euro Area under the European Semester* (European Parliament PE 542680, 2015), 5–6.

[529] Darvas and Leandro, *Economic Policy Coordination*, 11 (overlap between recommendations is not sufficient to explain the lack of difference). See also Moschella, 'EU Surveillance More Effective than IMF?', 1283.

[530] Darvas and Leandro, *Economic Policy Coordination*, 14.

[531] EFB, *Assessment*, 31 (emphasis added).

implementation of national structural reforms.'[532] The IMF concurs.[533] Efstatiou and Wolff conclude:

There is no evidence that these stricter processes matter for implementation rates, whereas *macroecnomic fundamentals and market pressure* are important determinants of implementation progress.[534]

Viewed in the light of fiscal federalism theory, none of this should be surprising. As concluded in Chapter 3, the cold reality is that it is futile to centrally govern outcomes which are, in reality, determined by myriad private individuals responding, in their economic and political lives, to the dysfunctional cost incentives of a sovereign bailout expectation built into the basic price of credit.

8.3   Conclusion: Principles of Fiscal Federalism for the EU

The stated premise underpinning the EU's new model is that centralized financing of Member State debt is compatible with fiscal discipline so long as it is accompanied by centralized governance of economic policies.[535] This chapter finds that this is, quite simply and profoundly, wrong. History cautions that centralized debt brakes *never* work in a decentralized fiscal federation without market discipline,[536] and economists already find the new fiscal arrangements in the EU less credible than their predecessors.[537]

[8.1] There are four institutional determinants of fiscal discipline in a large decentralized fiscal federation: [8.1.1] Market discipline; [8.1.2] hard budget constraints; [8.1.3] fiscal symmetry; and [8.1.4] expenditure/revenue autonomy. [8.1.5] A fifth determinant, fiscal rules, are neither necessary nor necessarily desirable in a federation, but can only ever be an adjunct to a well-functioning system of fiscal federalism – they cannot replace it (and may even ruin it). The literature 'offers several warnings about the effective capacity of fiscal rules to constrain the

---

[532] ECB, 'The Creation of Competitiveness Boards in the Context of Striving towards a Genuine Economic Union' (2015) 7 ECB Economic Bulletin 28.

[533] IMF, *Euro Area Policies: Selected Issues*, 87.

[534] Konstantinos Efstathiou and Guntram Wolff, 'EU Policy Recommendations: A Stronger Legal Framework Is Not Enough to Foster National Compliance' (*Vox EU*, CEPR, 17 July 2019) https://voxeu.org/article/stronger-eu-legal-framework-not-enough-foster-national-compliance accessed 20 July 2020 (emphasis added).

[535] *Pringle* v. *Ireland* [136]–[137].

[536] See Sections 8.1.1–8.1.2 and sources cited in Methods and Introduction, n 79.

[537] See Section 8.2.5.4 and sources cited.

action of the political branches in the budgetary domain',[538] and such instruments 'only create more opportunities for the types of behaviour they seek to prevent'.[539] Dabrowski concludes:

Summing up, the EU and EMU have moved definitively from a 'no bail out' principle to conditional bail out policy with a parallel attempt to strengthen formal fiscal rules of disputable efficiency. It is worrisome that the dominant tone of the debate on the Eurozone's fiscal union seems to go even further in this direction.[540]

[8.2] The five determinants extracted in Section 8.1 appear to be robust determinants of fiscal discipline. In Canada, the United States and Switzerland, state-level governments (1) are exposed to market discipline under credible 'no bailout' commitments; (2) have complete expenditure and revenue autonomy; (3) evince a high degree of fiscal symmetry; and (4) there are no mechanisms for federal oversight of state-level budgetary policies. Despite this, when the crisis arrived in 2008, none of the fifty American states had an average deficit of more than 1% of GDP, none of the ten Canadian provinces had an average deficit of more than 2% of GDP (most had a deficit of <1%), and 24 of 26 Swiss Canton were in surplus (two had deficits of <1% of GDP).[541] All State/Provincial/ Cantonal sectors have staid records of fiscal stability throughout the twentieth century, dating to the Great Depression or beyond.[542]

[8.2.1] The 'centralization' or 'surveillance' model of German fiscal federalism does not work. Under the 'agony of central power', the German Federal Republic is plagued by transfer-dependency and soft budget constraints that insulate *Länder* from market discipline. Despite having the strongest grade of fiscal rule inscribed in constitutional law, German fiscal federalism is an empirical failure. There is 'not a single episode in German debt history since the 1830s in which the ratio of debt to income was reduced by methods other than default'.[543] Most *Länder* had unsustainable finances most of the time over the period of 1950–2011.[544] Prior to the arrival of the 2008 financial crisis, twelve of sixteen *Länder* had deficits

---

[538] Adams et al., 'European Budgetary Constraints', 8.
[539] Von Hagen and Eichengreen, 'Fiscal Restraints', 137.
[540] Dabrowski, 'Fiscal or Bailout Union', 41.
[541] IMF, 'Net Lending/Borrowing (% GDP)'; Simon Hurst and Thomas Rühl, 'Swiss Cantons in the Red' (*CreditSuisse*, 5 May 2015) www.credit-suisse.com/us/en/articles/articles/ne ws-and-expertise/2015/05/en/half-of-swiss-cantons-in-th-red.html accessed 14 November 2016.
[542] Rodden, *Hamilton's Paradox*, 141–142.
[543] Ritschl, 'Sustainability', 20.
[544] Burret et al., '(Un)Sustainability'.

breaching the constitutional rule, and three were in a state of emergency.[545]

[8.2.5] In the EU, centralized fiscal governance has, *in fact*, proven institutionally non-credible and empirically ineffective. The new model has not reduced sovereign debt; it has not improved implementation rates of EU policy recommendations (even over OECD and IMF systems with no enforcement whatsoever); and it has not applied on its own terms. Over the course of 141 breaches of the 3% deficit limit by twenty-four countries between 1999 and 2018, and 132 findings of imbalances/excessive imbalances, the EU's centralized governance model has imposed €0.00 in sanctions, and dispensed €500.07bn in bailouts.[546] Wyplosz concludes:

> The original sin of European monetary union is undoubtedly the reliance on the Stability and Growth Pact to establish fiscal discipline. The cardinal sin was the *de facto* dismissal of the no-bailout clause when it became binding for the first time. Paradoxically, the potentially effective instrument, the no-bailout clause, was abandoned while the flawed instrument, the pact, was not just retained but further 'strengthened.' From the point of view of fiscal discipline institutional arrangements, the eurozone is much weaker now than it was before the crisis.[547]

The hypothesis of this book, that market discipline and hard budget constraints are indispensable for sound public finances and a sustainable balance of payments in an EMU bound by the fiscal sovereignty of its Member States, appears robust at each stage of investigation. The literature on fiscal federalism is quite unequivocal: there is no institutional counter to myriad private individuals responding, in their economic and political lives, to dysfunctional cost incentives. To that end, this chapter concludes with five principles of fiscal federalism which the European EMU must meet if it is to remain stable as a matter of law and economics: [8.1.1] Market discipline; [8.1.2] hard budget constraints; [8.1.3] fiscal symmetry; [8.1.4] decentralized fiscal autonomy; and [8.1.5] simple, less malleable, and more credible fiscal rules (if any fiscal rules at all).

---

[545] Braun, 'German Fiscal Federalism', 244–245.

[546] This €500.07bn figure encompasses all EU bailouts from May 2010 and 31 December 2016 and excludes an additional combined €43.35bn out of an agreed €60.75 in BoP assistance to Romania, Latvia and Hungary. See Methods and Introduction, n 89.

[547] Wyplosz, 'Fiscal Discipline in a Monetary Union without Fiscal Union', in Ódor Lu (ed), *Rethinking Fiscal Policy after the Crisis* (Cambridge University Press, 2017), 185.

Conclusion

In order to remain stable and permanent as a matter of law and economics, European fiscal federalism must do two things: It must, first, be compatible with the constitutional boundaries of the European legal order; and, second, it must 'work' – that is, it must not be economically unstable. The conclusion of this book is as follows.

First, Member State fiscal sovereignty is a permanent constitutional constraint upon the application of fiscal federalism theory in the EU. In so far as the limits of EU competence are governed by the principle of conferral, the EU can have no powers other than what the Member States have given it, and what the Member States have given it is limited by their own constitutional identities.[1] Not only has economic and fiscal policy not been conferred on the Union under Articles 2(3) and 5(1) TFEU, it cannot ever be so conferred without abrogating, *inter alia*, basic principles of the democratic state (Article 20 BL) shielded by the 'eternity clause' (Article 79(3)) of the German Basic Law. Numerous other Member State courts have drawn similar boundaries around their own constitutional formulas for parliamentary fiscal sovereignty. Chapter 1 extracted three constitutional tests that constrain the application of fiscal federalism theory in the European legal order: [1.3.1.2] no unlawful *restrictions* on fiscal sovereignty;[2] [1.3.1.3] no

---

[1] See Chapter 1, Section 1.2.2 and cases cited. For further judicial statements to that effect, see cases cited in Methods and Introduction, n 25.

[2] A restriction on budgetary sovereignty must not 'fetter the budget legislature to such an extent that the principle of democracy is violated', that is, 'with the effect that it or a future Parliament can no longer exercise the right to decide the budget on its own'. *Euro Rescue Package (Germany)* [104] and sources cited in Chapter 1, Section 1.3.1.1, n 482.

unlawful *conferral* or *delegation* of fiscal sovereignty;[3] and [1.3.1.4] no structural *impairments* of fiscal sovereignty through finite financial dispositions of structural significance to the budget.[4]

Second, hard budget constraints and market discipline are indispensable for the guiding principles of price stability and fiscal discipline in a decentralized federation bound by the fiscal sovereignty of its Member States. Systems of fiscal federalism theory which substitute hard budget constraints for centralized legal governance are not compatible with the guiding principles of price stability and fiscal discipline, and are not compatible with the constitutional boundaries of the EU legal order as a whole. In particular, the BVerfG has held that the 'no bailout rule' and 'no monetary financing rule' safeguard the *Bundestag's* 'national budgetary responsibility', and that Germany's constitutional identity would be violated if the *Stabilitätsgemeinschaft* should become a 'liability community' through the 'direct or indirect communitarization of state debts'.[5] Chapter 8 extracted five principles of fiscal federalism for European Economic and Monetary Union: [8.1.1] market discipline; [8.1.2] hard budget constraints under a credible 'no bailout' rule; [8.1.3] fiscal symmetry; [8.1.4] Member State expenditure and revenue autonomy; and [8.1.5] simple, less malleable, less centralized fiscal rules (if any fiscal rules at all). The nascent EU *proto*-fiscal union meets none of these conditions and, accordingly, does not work.

In sum, the model chosen for European fiscal federalism must preserve the fiscal sovereignty of its constitutional democracies and it must have market discipline under hard budget constraints. As for the selection of an appropriate model for EU fiscal federalism, this book proposes that the three constitutional tests identified in Chapter 1[6] and the five principles identified in Chapter 8[7] provide an intersecting set of criteria for assessing which models of fiscal federalism are compatible

---

[3] Delegation or conferral of budgetary decision-making must not compromise the principle that 'the [national] Parliament remains the place in which autonomous decisions on revenue and expenditure are made'. *Euro Rescue Package (Germany)* [124] and sources cited in Chapter 1, Section 1.3.1.1, n 483.

[4] Finite financial dispositions must not be of structural significance to the parliament's right to decide on the budget such that it causes an irreversible prejudice to future majority decisions and cannot be reversed by an equivalent action by the parliament in the future: *ESM II (Germany)* [173] and sources cited in Chapter 1, Section 1.3.1.1, n 484.

[5] *ESM I (Germany)* [203] and cases cited in Methods and Introduction, n 61.

[6] Listed in Chapter 1, Section 1.3.1.1, at nn 482–484 and Section 1.4, at nn 574–576.

[7] See Sections 8.1.1–8.1.5.

and implementable within the boundaries of the EU legal order as a matter of law and economics.

In that respect, this book suggests that the EU has embarked upon a model of 'fiscal union' that is fundamentally incompatible with the European legal order, and furthermore adherent to a formula for disequilibrium that is well-established in theory and well-evidenced in history. The model advanced does not work and cannot be implemented; its implementation requires the abrogation of conferral and fiscal sovereignty, upon which the constitutionality of Member State participation in the Union depends. If Europe is not to continue further down this lonely, troubled path, the misguided myth of '*sui generis*' European exceptionalism must not become an excuse to ignore every fundamental lesson of fiscal federalism and OCA theory. History is littered with federal architectures pulled apart by the creeping pathologies of SGFF theory spreading across the constitutional framework with each marginal contract for debt.[8] As Sinn forbodes:

> Kornai predicted in 1980 that soft budget constraints would lead to the demise of the communist economic system. The Eurozone currently runs the risk of sharing this fate.[9]

Over two centuries of history and data from 106 sub-central governmental units in Germany, Canada, Switzerland and the United States admonish that the flaw at the heart of EMU is not the budgetary freedom of national electorates, nor their economic diversity, nor the small size of the EU budget. The fatal flaw at the heart of the euro is the pooling of risk and the centralization of fiscal governance. Under this system, interest rates do not rise in response to risk,[10] governments do not act,[11] and electorates do not feel the costs of their own debts.[12] When the

---

[8] See sources cited above, Methods and Introduction, n 98, and Sections 8.2.1, 8.2.3 and 8.2.4, pointing to the United States to 1842, Canada to 1936, and Germany from 1830–1918, 1920–1939, and 1955 to its 2020 debt brake.

[9] Sinn, *Euro Trap*, 6.

[10] See Section 3.1. See also, for example, Editorial, 'Standard & Poor's Raises Greece Rating by Two Notches' *The Irish Times* (22 July 2015) www.irishtimes.com/business/economy/standard-poor-s-raises-greece-rating-by-two-notches-1.2292676 accessed 9 May 2016.

[11] See Section 3.3. See also, for example, Fiona Reddan, '"Urgent" Action Needed to Boost Ireland's Competitiveness' *The Irish Times* (31 July 2015). www.irishtimes.com/business/economy/urgent-action-needed-to-boost-ireland-s-competitiveness-1.2302541 accessed 9 May 2016.

[12] See Section 3.2. See also, for example, Arthur Beesley, 'Irish Access to Low Debt Costs Reflects Market Confidence' *The Irish Times* (24 July 2015) www.irishtimes.com/business/economy/irish-access-to-low-debt-costs-reflects-market-confidence-1.2295223 accessed 9 May 2016.

credit market adjusts, the terms of reform are selected and enforced by the Union through its new governance architecture outside the constitutional apparatus for legitimation of fiscal policy – not the voters who must bear them. Systems of law which develop to enforce such conditions must then inevitably conflict with Member State 'constitutional identity' jurisprudence. This is manifestly incompatible with the integrity of the EU legal order. As Wyplosz concludes:

> Fiscal discipline is thoroughly needed, but centralization is not necessary. [...] The main objective must be to decentralize both the design of fiscal rules and their implementation, while restoring the no-bailout clause. Ignoring this clause has opened the way to further centralization, which is a major source of conflict and an approach that will ultimately fail.[13]

The conclusions presented here are extracted from this study as follows.

Chapter 1 identified two permanent constitutional boundaries that constrain European fiscal federalism *de lege lata* and *de lege ferenda*:

> First, any model of European fiscal federalism must preserve the fiscal sovereignty of its twenty-seven constituent constitutional democracies. National parliamentary control over fundamental decisions on public finance and expenditure is 'a fundamental part of the ability of a constitutional state to democratically shape itself', 'the core of parliamentary rights in democracy', and 'an essential manifestation of constitutional democracy'.[14] Under Member State *Kompetenz-Kompetenz* and constitutional identity jurisprudence, a trespass on parliamentary fiscal competences may require the Member States to repudiate the advance (refusing to ratify or apply the EU law) or withdraw from the Union altogether.[15]

> The second constitutional boundary is comprised of the fundamental guiding principles of price stability and 'fiscal discipline' (i.e. sound public finances and a sustainable balance of payments) set forth in Article 119(3) TFEU. According to the BVerfG, these principles of the *Stabilitätsgemeinshaft* are 'the basis and subject-matter of the German Act of Accession'.[16] This encompasses price stability (Article 127 TFEU), the prohibition on monetary financing (Article 123 TFEU), the 'no bailout' clause (Article 125 TFEU), and the stability criteria of the 'Stability and Growth Pact' (Articles 121,126

---

[13] Wyplosz, 'Centralization-Decentralization', 26.
[14] *Euro Rescue Package (Germany)* [107], [127].
[15] See cases cited in Methods and Introduction, n 37.
[16] *Brunner (Germany)* [89] and cases cited above, Chapter 1, Section 1.3.2, nn 547–552.

TFEU).[17] These provisions are not themselves limits of constitutional identity, however they do shield basic principles of the democratic state (Article 20 BL) and human dignity (Article 1 BL), which *are* part of the constitutional identity shielded by the German 'eternity clause' (Article 79(3) BL) and are *not* amendable, *lex lata* or *de lege ferenda*.

In Chapter 2 the principles of fiscal sovereignty, price stability and fiscal discipline were found to penetrate three levels of investigation: The *travaux préparatoires* and the mandate for EMU (Article 119 TFEU); the allocation of competences in economic policy (Articles 2(3) and 5(1) TFEU); and the technical architecture governing public finance itself (Articles 121–126 TFEU). By those provisions, EU fiscal federalism was shown to rest on two principles: (1) Fiscal sovereignty – the EU has no competence in fiscal policy and Member States are responsible for their own budgetary policies; and (2) market discipline – Member States are exposed to hard budget constraints and market discipline for the achievement of fiscal discipline. As the Bundesbank explains:

The founding principle of the euro area was to leave the responsibility for fiscal policy in the hands of each individual member state [...] As an incentive to establish sound budgetary policy, it was codified in the Maastricht Treaty that neither the Community nor the member states may be liable for or assume the debt of another member state. The consequences of unsound fiscal policy, for example in the form of rising financing costs due to risk premiums on interest rates, were meant to be concentrated on the member state in question and not shared between other countries in the currency union as would be the case with joint liability or a transfer union.[18]

Chapter 3 showed that the *causa sine qua non* of the Euro Crisis is a severe mispricing of private and public debt caused by a failure of Articles 121–126 TFEU to induce markets to differentiate between sovereign borrowers under a (now-realized) bailout expectation. The model did not fail because investors failed to appropriately price risk; it did not fail because of the accumulation of sovereign debt; and it did not fail due to the inability of the central (EU) authority to control the finances of its Member States. The model failed because markets (correctly) guessed that the 'no bailout' rule was non-credible, and (correctly) guessed that

---

[17] *Brunner (Germany)* [89], [204]–[205]; *Euro Rescue Package (Germany)* [181]–[182]; *ESM I (Germany)* [203]–[204]; *Gauweiler Reference (Germany)* [32].

[18] Deutsche Bundesbank, 'Monthly Report: August 2011', 62.

the EU would sooner re-interpret the Treaties than allow a Member State to default. As Rodden observes of the lessons of fiscal federalism:

The European Monetary Union has fallen prey to exactly the same problem, and it seems to be failing in an even more spectacular fashion [...] the European Union confirmed suspicions that it cannot tolerate outright default by a member states. [...] It is not surprising that these crises are interpreted as failures of market discipline. Unsustainable borrowing took place in part because market actors (correctly) interpreted the higher-level government's no-bailout commitments as not credible. It is just as appropriate, however, to interpret them as failures of hierarchy. [H]alf-hearted efforts at hierarchical regulation inadvertently undermined market discipline by sending significant signals about the central government's lack of credibility. Moreover, the very act of attempting to regulate the borrowing of member states signals a certain level of responsibility.[19]

Chapter 4 set out the two criteria for EU fiscal federalism which emerged from Chapters 1–3: First, any model of EU fiscal federalism must preserve the fiscal sovereignty of the twenty-seven constituent constitutional democracies at the basis of its legal order. Second, hard budget constraints and market discipline are indispensable for price stability and fiscal discipline in an EMU bound by Member State fiscal sovereignty.

Part II tested and applied these criteria against the emergent European *proto*-fiscal union, and examined which models of fiscal federalism are compatible with the boundaries of EU law.

Chapter 5 found that, by supplanting a legal cornerstone of decentralized federalism (an entrenched 'no bailout' law) with financial assistance and centralized fiscal governance, the EU has sunk the foundation of an institutional configuration that is far more apt to unitary states than a decentralized federal monetary union.

Chapter 6 examined whether the instruments of conditional financial assistance enacted since the crisis are reconcilable with the legal architecture inscribed in the Treaties as a matter of EU law. Following the analytical framework developed by the ECJ in *Pringle*, *Gauweiler* and *Weiss*, it found that they are not. This provided the first testable indication that the demands of the emerging new model are incompatible with the boundaries of the EU legal order. There simply isn't a constitutional basis for a credible financial assistance backstop in the EU.

Chapter 7 examined whether the fiscal governance architecture enacted since the crisis is reconcilable with the constitutional

---

[19] Rodden, 'Can Market Discipline Survive?', 45.

boundaries of Member State fiscal sovereignty underlying the EU legal order as a whole. It found that the new architecture is dependent, for its stable functioning, on instruments which are beyond the boundaries of the EU legal order and which profess to bind national legislators in economic/fiscal policy, contrary to Member State constitutional identity jurisprudence. This is not only legally unsound, but economically ineffective and injurious to good principles of fiscal federalism.

Chapter 8 applied the lessons of fiscal federalism theory to extract principles for EMU and evaluate which models of fiscal federalism will 'work' given the constitutional boundaries of the EU legal order. It concluded that the incumbent political prescriptions for a centralized EU fiscal union are incompatible with the fundamental guiding principles of EMU under Article 119(3) TFEU. Centralized fiscal rules *never* work in a decentralized federation without market discipline, and contemporary economists already find the new governance framework less credible than its predecessor. The EU's new 'centralized' model has not reduced sovereign debt; it has not improved implementation rates of EU policy recommendations; and it has not even been enforced under its own terms. Instead, the EU's *proto*-fiscal union has institutionalized the dysfunctional cost incentives behind the Euro Crisis. The analysis identified five determinants of fiscal discipline in a decentralized federal system: market discipline; hard budget constraints under a credible 'no bailout' rule; fiscal symmetry; expenditure and revenue autonomy; and less malleable, more credible, and less centralized fiscal rules (if any fiscal rules at all).

In sum, there are two permanent constitutional requirements with which any model of European fiscal federalism must comply if it is to remain stable and permanent in law and economics: The European Union must, first, preserve national constitutional formulas for the exercise of fiscal sovereignty; and, second, it must expose Member State finances to individuated market discipline under hard budget constraints.

Proposed Directions for Future Research and Reform

The conclusion of this book points to two prescriptions for future study and reform.

The first is that hard budget constraints and market discipline must be restored at all costs. This is not (only) because government debt remains unsustainably high (it is), but because yields on government debt set the basic cost of credit across the entire economy. There simply is no institutional counter to the inexorable pull of millions of private individuals responding, in their economic and political lives, to the dysfunctional incentives of cheap credit. If the EMU is not to follow historical precedents into the dustbin of broken federal arrangements, it must be able to withstand the default of its individual members.[1] In that regard, the European Union must learn the same lesson that the United States learned in 1840 and Canada learned in 1936: As Maxwell and MacG put it in the formative years of Canadian federalism, federalism requires states to be 'allowed to go broke at their own sweet will'.[2] The *Bundesbank* pleads:

> It is imperative that the no bail-out rule that is still enshrined in the treaties and the associated disciplining function of the capital markets be strengthened, and not fatally wounded.[3]

This requires a significant departure from the incumbent objective of EU policy, which, as Buchheit and Gulati describe it, 'to date has had a single objective – to convince the markets that all Eurozone sovereign debt enjoys an implicit official sector backstop [. . .] and to reward it by

---

[1] Deutsche Bundesbank, *Approaches to Resolving Sovereign Debt Crises in the Euro Area* (Monthly Report: July, 2016), 41.

[2] Maxwell and MacG, 'Federal-Provincial Financial Relations', 379.

[3] Deutsche Bundesbank, 'Monthly Report: August 2011', 11.

accepting coupons below what they would have demanded for the stand-alone credit risk of a Eurozone sovereign borrower'.[4] In that respect, the introduction of collective action clauses (CACs) into all EMU Member State debt contracts from 1 January 2013 under Article 12 TESM (Euro CACs) was a welcome first step in restoring incentives in a European model of 'classical' federalism.[5] A new draft TESM agreed by the Eurogroup (endorsed but not yet ratified at the time of writing) will bolster this by introducing a 'single limb' procedure to make it easier for a qualified majority of creditors to approve a restructuring across all government bond series, thereby precluding holdout creditors from acquiring a blocking minority on an individual series.[6] Further proposals for a European Sovereign Debt Restructuring Framework (ESDRF) may also help restore the economic and political credibility of restructuring in those instances where such contractual mechanisms fail.[7] Promising proposals for inclusion in an ESDRF include automatic maturity extensions if a country obtains financial assistance;[8] splitting government bonds into multiple tranches of differing priority;[9] mandatory restructuring with financial

---

[4] Lee Buchheit and Mitu Gulati, 'Sovereign Debt Restructuring in Europe' (2018) 9 Global Policy 65, 66.

[5] From 2013 all EMU countries are required to imbue their debt contracts with CAC's that allow a majority of holders of an individual bond series to agree to modify repayment terms, which then become binding on all other creditors (the majority differs depending on the adjustment and voting procedure). Under Art. 12 TESM, a country that appears to be insolvent must negotiate a comprehensive restructuring plan with its creditors. See further: Deutsche Bundesbank, *Resolving Sovereign Debt Crises*, 48–49; ECB, 'The European Stability Mechanism' (2011) ECB Monthly Bulletin (July) 71, 78–82; Michael Bradley and Mitu Gulati, 'Collective Action Clauses for the Eurozone' (2013) 18 Rev Fin 2045.

[6] Art. 12(4), DRAFT revised text of the Treaty Establishing the European Stability Mechanism as agreed by the Eurogroup on 14 July 2019, accessible at www .esm.europa.eu/about-esm/esm-reform accessed 22 December 2020. See further: IMF, *Strengthening the Contractual Framework to Address Collective Action Problems in Sovereign Debt Restructuring* (IMF, 2014); Giuseppe Bianco, 'Collective Action Clauses in the Eurozone: One Step Forward, Two Steps Back' (2014) 16 Eur J L Reform 713, 727; Deutsche Bundesbank, *Resolving Sovereign Debt Crises*, 49; Grund and Stenström, 'Sovereign Debt Restructuring', 828.

[7] See the learned consideration of proposals in Grund and Stenström, 'Sovereign Debt Restructuring', 814–816.

[8] IMF, *Executive Board Approves Exceptional Access lending Framework Reforms* (IMF Press Release, 28 January 2016); Deutsche Bundesbank, *Resolving Sovereign Debt Crises*, 47; Beatrice Weder di Mauro and Jeromin Zettelmeyer, *The New Global Financial Safety Net*, vol. 4 (Centre for International Governance Innovation, 2017).

[9] Deutsche Bundesbank, *Resolving Sovereign Debt Crises*, 51.

assistance;[10] procedures that progressively reduce CAC voting thresholds over a period of time;[11] emergency procedures to override existing contractual limits (subject to review by an adjudicative body);[12] preventing creditors from recovering more than the market value of their bonds at the time a restructuring offer is accepted;[13] and automatically reprofiling sovereign debt or immunizing state assets from creditor attachment if a bailout is obtained.[14]

Nevertheless, it must be cautioned that creditor restructuring is unlikely under conditions of soft budget constraints.[15] Creditors are unlikely to accept a large haircut if they believe that, by holding out long enough, their debtor will receive financial assistance.[16] This is particularly problematic where the EU and its Member States have moved into the position of Kornai's provider of capital (recall that the EFSF/ESM alone hold over half of Greece's entire debt).[17] As the experience of Germany informs, as long as the 'federal' economic constitution is read by markets as permitting the bailout of sub-units, 'threats by the federation to allow states to enter into a default or debt restructuring with private creditors have extremely limited scope'.[18] Buchheit and Gulati explain:

> Investors in Euro-area sovereign bonds need to be disabused of the belief that taxpayers will bail them out at par in the event of another crisis; the result they have come to expect after the last crisis. To the extent that they continue to nuture that belief, they will neither analyze nor price their sovereign lending correctly. [...] Strengthening collective action clauses – the solution proposed by

---

[10] Bénassy-Quéré et al., 'Risk Sharing with Market Discipline', 13; Grund and Stenström, 'Sovereign Debt Restructuring', 825–828.

[11] Deutsche Bundesbank, *Resolving Sovereign Debt Crises*, 59–60.

[12] Grund and Stenström, 'Sovereign Debt Restructuring', 823.

[13] Grund and Stenström, 'Sovereign Debt Restructuring', 843.

[14] Committee on International Economic Policy and Reform, *Revisiting Sovereign Bankruptcy* (Brookings, 2013), 40; Lee Buchheit, Mitu Gulati and Ignacio Tirado, 'Reprofiling Sovereign Debt' (2015) 30 JIBLR 19; Grund and Stenström, 'Sovereign Debt Restructuring', 843–844.

[15] Deutsche Bundesbank, *Resolving Sovereign Debt Crises*, 45–46.

[16] In the 2012 Greece restructuring, for example, holdouts famously blocked the restructuring of €6 billion in foreign-law bonds (which Greece paid in full after obtaining its bailout). See Sebastian Grund, 'Restructuring Government Debt under Local Law: The Greek Case and Implications for Investor Protection in Europe' (2017) 12 CMLJ 253, 254; Grund and Stenström, 'Sovereign Debt Restructuring', 804.

[17] ESM, 'Financial Assistance: Greece' (*ESM*, 2020) www.esm.europa.eu/assistance/greece accessed 29 October 2020; Guarascio and Maltezou, 'Greece Gets Debt Relief'.

[18] Enderlein and Von Müller, 'German Federalism', 153.

some commentators – will be pointless unless backed by a willingness to use the clauses in a crisis to facilitate a debt workout.[19]

There is no sugar-coating the pill that must be swallowed: the EMU must return to a 'no bailout' regime.

This is why *credible* legal enforcement of the Treaties is needed. The interests of EU institutions and Member States are always likely to pull in favour of a bailout – this is why the 'no bailout' rule wasn't left to a political mechanism in the first place. From the view of fiscal federalism theory, calls from some in the Council Legal Service for the removal of Article 125 TFEU in order to eliminate the last irritants of fiscal sovereignty are fundamentally misconceived.[20] Fiscal federalism, being concerned with the optimum decentralization of democratic and economic goods, is one area inherently at tension with 'ever closer union' – which, taken to its logical conclusion, implies the centralization of all decision-making power in one building. As Dabrowski complains: When weighed against the data on fiscal federalism, 'the claim for closer political and fiscal union sounded more like a creed rather than something based on well-founded academic arguments'.[21]

If there is to be a Treaty amendment, this must only be to bolster the 'no bailout' rule in the Treaty and redress the interpretation of the ECJ that Article 125 TFEU is a mere prohibition on specific forms of guarantee. It must be recalled that the problem with Article 125 TFEU is not that Member State executives re-wrote the Treaty to allow bailouts – they didn't.[22] The problem with Article 125 TFEU is that the ECJ reinterpreted it contrary to the apparent intention of the Treaty drafters at Maastricht. This must be addressed.

If an amendment to Article 125 TFEU seems a bridge too far, one (lesser) alternative is to further constrict the conditions by which Member States can give financial assistance under Article 136(3) TFEU itself, using the same Article 48(6) TEU by which it was enacted. But it is not clear that the EU has all that much to fear from restoring the 'no bailout' clause at all. Indeed, the private restructuring of Greek debt was

[19] Buchheit and Gulati, 'Sovereign Debt Restructuring', 65.
[20] Merino, 'Financial Assistance' excerpted above, Chapter 5, Section 5.1, at n 31.
[21] Dabrowski, 'Fiscal and Macroeconomic Governance', 5.
[22] As noted in Section 6.1.4, they couldn't re-write the Treaty because, *inter alia*, an amendment which altered the essential scope of the Union or permitted large-scale fiscal transfers would come up against boundaries set by, *inter alia*, the German and Irish constitutional identity jurisprudence.

the largest creditor restructuring *in history*,[23] yet it did not lead to the much-feared contagion and destruction of EMU.[24] The path the EMU has chosen seems a much surer (if longer) road to perdition.

The second proposed direction offered by this book is a framework for establishing a central budgetary capacity of sufficient heft to perform an adequate countercyclical role (the primary justification for fiscal union), but one that does not conflict with the constitutional boundaries of the EU legal order. In that respect, the conclusion of this book is that any model of European fiscal federalism must (1) preserve the fiscal sovereignty of its constitutional democracies, and (2) have market discipline under hard budget constraints. This book does *not* state that a central fiscal capacity – a 'fiscal union' – of sufficient heft to perform a countercyclical role is incompatible with the European legal order. It simply states that the particular 'fiscal union' christened in *Pringle* v. *Ireland* and the *Five Presidents Report* is incompatible with the European legal order.[25] This is because it requires the abrogation of the principle of conferral and Member State fiscal sovereignty, upon which the constitutionality of Member State participation in the Union depends.[26]

However, it must also be recalled that, as noted in Section 5.2 above, the model of 'fiscal union' bandied about by Union institutions is something of a perversion of the term. 'Fiscal union', according to the Commission Blueprint and the *Five Presidents' Report*, does not refer, as the literature does, to the existence of independent *federal* tax and spending competences (which model the EU already has). It refers to the co-option of *Member State* tax and spending competences by the Union – or, as the Commission so puts it, to 'a means to imposing budgetary and economic decisions on its members'.[27]

This is wrong. But the tests for Member State fiscal sovereignty identified in this book do not preclude an *independent* federal tax base. They simply mean that Member State fiscal policy must be exercised in accordance with the constitution's unamendable structures; or, if it cannot be so exercised, then the impingement on fiscal sovereignty

---

[23] Grund and Stenström, 'Sovereign Debt Restructuring', 378.

[24] Buchheit and Gulati, 'Sovereign Debt Restructuring', 66.

[25] Wolfgang Münchau, 'Better No Fiscal Union than a Flawed One' *Financial Times* (18 October 2015).

[26] See further sources cited above, Chapter 1, n 21.

[27] Commission Blueprint, 31.

must not be so severe that it violates the constitutional democracy in its essential content. The three tests are:

[1.3.1.2] A restriction on budgetary sovereignty must not 'fetter the budget legislature to such an extent [...] that it or a future parliament can no longer exercise the right to decide the budget on its own';[28]

[1.3.1.3] A disposition of budgetary sovereignty must not compromise the principle that 'the [national] parliament remains the place in which autonomous decisions on revenue and expenditure are made';[29] and

[1.3.1.4] Fiscal policy decisions must not be of structural significance to the parliament's right to decide on the budget, such that 'the democratic process remains open and that legal re-evaluations may occur on the basis of other majority decisions and that an irreversible legal prejudice to future generations is avoided'.[30]

With certainty, this prohibits the co-option of *Member State* expenditure competences, and the mutualization of *Member State* revenue competences to finance them. It does not, however, prohibit separate expenditure and revenue competences of the Union, provided they 'do not grant the European Commission authority to impose specific substantive requirements for the structuring of budgets', and do not deprive European constitutional democracies of the 'substance of the power to rule'.[31]

In that regard, the 'classical' model of fiscal federalism inscribed in the Treaty at Maastricht, and visible in Canada, the United States and Switzerland, does not appear to trespass on any of the tests set out in this book. Federal and state governments may spend in the same territory, on the same people, and even on the same goods, but they cannot bind each other. This includes an independent fiscal union with sufficient heft to play an adequate countercyclical role alongside independent state treasuries. Whether this should be built in Europe for political reasons is its own debate,[32] but if that is what is desired, the three constitutional tests identified in Chapter 1[33] and the five principles

---

[28] *Euro Rescue Package (Germany)* [104] and sources cited in Section 1.3.1.1, n 482.

[29] *Euro Rescue Package (Germany)* [124] and sources cited in Section 1.3.1.1, n 483.

[30] *ESM II (Germany)* [173] and sources cited in Section 1.3.1.1, n 484.

[31] *ESM II (Germany)* [244].

[32] Studies applying fiscal federalism theory to the EU typically find that macroeconomic stabilization functions should *not* be assigned to EU level: See Chapter 8, Section 8.2.5.3 and sources cited.

[33] Section 1.3.1.

identified in Chapter 8[34] provide a reference point for how to achieve it within the boundaries of the EU legal order.

Take Canada. The Federal Government and the Provinces both have extensive and overlapping tax and expenditure competences. Each citizen is subject to two separate and equal governments. A student of law in British Columbia (BC) will, for example, receive two expenditure packages of student funding: one from the federal government and one from her province. If the province goes broke, she may still rely on the federal, and vice versa; but at no point will one of her governments transfer her taxes to the treasury of the other because it could not keep its commitments to its creditors. Canada and BC may make mutual investments, such as in healthcare or highways, but these are assessed on their merits and neither can legislate objectives for the competences of the other. Indeed, she controls them separately: She may vote to have one increase their spending and the other reduce it. But she cannot have one government impose rules on the other.

If BC should decide to compete with its low-tax neighbour Alberta by expanding its tax base and lowering its tax rate, it may do so without restriction by federal legislation. Both the federal and provincial governments have overlapping tax powers on income, but the federal government provides 'abatements', resiling its base on shared factors to make room for the provincial taxing powers.[35] There are no recidivistic 'CCCTB' proposals coming down from dubious legal bases at federal level to co-opt or stamp out tax competition in the provinces.

Applying the tests applied in this book, does this 'fiscal union' intrude on fundamental decisions on public revenue, expenditure and the shaping of the social state,[36] such that the BC legislature no longer 'remains the place in which autonomous decisions on revenue and expenditure are made'?[37] Clearly it does not. Does the 'overall responsibility, with sufficient political discretion regarding revenue and expenditure, still rest with the [Provincial Legislature]'?[38] Clearly it does. If the BC constitution were the German constitution, it seems the entire 'chain of

---

[34] Sections 8.1.1–8.1.5.

[35] The provinces are not required to raise rates to the amount of the abatement, and the federal government will not increase its rate if the province does not use the unoccupied tax factor. Hogg, *Constitutional Law of Canada* 6.5.

[36] *Euro Rescue Package (Germany)* [107], [122], [228]; *ESM I (Germany)* [195]; *ESM II (Germany)* [161]–[165]; *Parliamentary Information (ESM & EPP) (Germany)* [114]; *Lisbon (Germany)* [228], [232].

[37] *ESM I (Germany)* [195]; *ESM II (Germany)* [161]–[165].

[38] *Lisbon (Germany)* [228]–[232].

legitimation' between, the voter (Article 38(2) BL), exercising the right to vote on an autonomous parliament, free of other-directedness (Article 38(1) BL), possessed of the substance of the power to rule (Articles 20(2) BL) would remain intact (Article 79(3) BL).

As regards the scale of spending capacity needed to assign the EU its sought countercyclical stabilization role, Section 8.2.5.3 suggested the EU would need to be able to provide a total direct injection (outlays plus revenue measures) of between 2% and 10% of Union GDP. The 2009 United States fiscal stimulus, for example, amounted to a total direct injection (outlays plus revenue measures) of $200bn, or 1.4% of GDP in 2009.[39] In Canada, the height of the 2009 federal stimulus reached nearly 4% of GDP.[40] The Member States would have to share some additional tax factors to give the EU a nest-egg of this size. But in theory this, too, would seem marginally within the tests for permissible impairments of fiscal autonomy under German law – particularly if the national parliament retains the right to re-occupy shared tax factors in the future (through a Canadian-style abatement or otherwise).[41]

Is such an arrangement politically possible? It is not for this book to say. The doctrine of supremacy will prove an intractable obstacle, so long as giving the EU any direct tax powers will inevitably result in challenging the autonomy of the Member States' own.[42] After all, direct tax harmonization is already the stated agenda of EU institutions with no legal competence in direct taxation at all. But perhaps if there were not so many 'back doors' attempting to enter upon the exclusive expenditure/revenue competencies of the EU's twenty-seven (formerly twenty-eight) constitutional democracies, the peoples of Europe might be less hesitant to entrust the Union with its own.[43]

---

[39] OECD, *Economic Surveys: United States 2010*, 85.

[40] OECD, *Economic Surveys: Canada 2012*, 21.

[41] See above, Sections 1.3.1.4–1.3.1.5, in particular Section 1.3.1.5.

[42] As Fabbrini, *Economic Governance*, 199 notes, 'in all the areas in which the EU *has* competence (including competences it shares with the member states), the EU member States are no longer free to step outside the framework of EU law and regulate a given field'.

[43] See, for example, Irish Taoiseach Enda Kenny referring to the CCCTB as 'tax harmonisation by back door'. Arthur Beesley, 'Common EU Corporate Tax Rate Back to Haunt Kenny' *The Irish Times* www.irishtimes.com/news/common-eu-corporate-tax-rate-back-to-haunt-kenny-1.447314 accessed 25 January 2015; and Lynch, 'Europe Is Looking at Ireland'.

Bibliography

Guidance on the State Fiscal Stabilization Fund Program (US Department of Education 2009)

'Master Financial Assistance Facility Agreement' (22 December 2010) www
.efsf.europa.eu/attachments/Master FFA Ireland.pdf accessed
25 February 2015

'Report of the Study Group 'Economic and Monetary Union 1980' (1975) II/675/3/
74 – E fin

Selected Case-Law of the Constitutional Court of the Republic of Latvia: 1996–2017
(Constitutional Court of the Republic of Latvia 2018)

'V-136(3) TFEU / VIII-TESM: Constitutional Change through Euro Crisis Law:
A Multi-level Legal Analysis' (European University Institute, 2015) http://euro
crisislaw.eui.eu/ accessed 9 April 2016

Aalto P, 'Accession of Finland to the European Union: First Remarks' (1995) 20 EL
Rev 618

Abbas AA, Bougha-Hagbe J, Fatás AJ, Mauro P and Velloso RC, 'Fiscal Policy and
the Current Account' (2010) 59 IMF Econ Rev 603

Acharya V, Dreschler I and Schnable P, 'A Pyrrhic Victory? Bank Bailouts and
Sovereign Credit Risk' (2014) 69 J Finance 2689

Acharya VV and Aschnable P, 'Do Global Banks Spread Global Imbalances? The
Case of Asset-Backed Commercial Paper during the Financial Crisis of 2007–
09' (2010) 58 IMF Econ Rev 37

Adam S and Parras JM, 'The European Stability Mechanism through the Legal
Meanderings of the Union's Constitutionalism: Comment on Pringle' (2013)
38 EL Rev 848

Adams H, *Public Debt* (D. Appleton 1890)

Adams M, Fabbrini F and Larouche P, 'The Constitutionalization of European
Budgetary Constraints: Effectiveness and Legitimacy in Comparative
Perspective' in Adams M, Fabbrini F and Larouche P (eds), *The
Constitutionalization of European Budgetary Constraints* (Hart 2014)

Adams M, Fabbrini F and Larouche P (eds), *The Constitutionalization of European
Budgetary Constraints* (Hart 2014)

Adamski D, 'Europe's (Misguided) Constitution of Economic Prosperity' (2013) 50 CMLR 47

Adamski D, 'National Power Games and Structural Failures in the European Macroeconomic Governance' (2012) 49 CMLR 1319

Adamski D, *Redefining European Economic Integration* (Cambridge University Press 2018)

Afonso A, 'Expansionary Fiscal Consolidations in Europe: New Evidence' (2010) 17 Applied Economics Letters 105

Afonso A and Strauch R, 'Fiscal Policy Events and Interest Rate Swap Spreads: Evidence from the EU' (2007) 17 Int Fin Markets, Inst and Money 261

Ahrend R, 'Monetary Ease: A Factor behind Financial Crisis? Some Evidence from OECD Countries' (2010) 4 Economics 1

Aizenman J, 'US Banking over Two Centuries: Lessons for the Eurozone Crisis' in Beck T (ed), *Banking Union for Europe* (CEPS 2012)

Albert R, 'Constitutional Handcuffs' (2010) 42 Ariz St L J 663

Albert R, 'The Expressive Function of Constitutional Amendment Rules' (2013) 59 McGill LJ 225

Albi A, 'Could the Post-Communist Constitutional Courts Teach the EU a Lesson in the Rule of Law?' (2010) 47 CMLR 791

Albi A, 'Europe Agreements in the Light of Sovereignty and Legitimacy: The Case of Estonia' in Kellermann AE, De Zwaan J and Cruczi J (eds), *EU Enlargement* (TMC Asser Press 2001) 195

Albi A, 'Supremacy of EC Law in the New Member States: Bringing Parliaments into the Equation of "Co-operative Constitutionalism"' (2007) 3 EuConst 35

Albi A and Bardutzky S (eds), *National Constitutions in European and Global Governance* (Springer 2019)

Alesina A, *Fiscal Adjustments: Lessons from Recent History* (ECOFIN meeting in Madrid, 15 April 2010)

Alesina A and Drazen A, 'Why are Stabilizations Delayed' (1991) 81 Am Econ Rev 1170

Alesina A and Perotti R, 'Budget Deficits and Budget Institutions' in Poterba JM and Von Hagen J (eds), *Fiscal Institutions and Fiscal Performance* (University of Chicago Press 1999)

Alesina A, Hausmann R, Hommes R and Stein E, 'Budget Institutions and Fiscal Performance in Latin America' (1999) 59 J Dev Econ 253

Alesina A, De Broack M, Prati A, Tabellini G, Obstfeld M and Rebelo S, 'Default Risk on Government Debt in OECD Countries' (1992) 7 Econ Policy 427

Allard C, Bluedorn J, Bornhorst F and Furceri D, 'Lessons from the Crisis: Minimal Elements for a Fiscal Union in the Euro Area' in Cottarelli C and Guerguil M (eds), *Designing a European Fiscal Union* (Taylor & Francis 2014)

Allard C, Koeva Brooks P, Bluedorn JC, Bornhorst F, Christopherson K, Ohnsorge F and Poghosyan T, 'Toward a Fiscal Union for the Euro Area' (IMF Staff Discussion Note, 2013)

Almeida V, Casto G, Mourinho Félix R and Maria JR, 'Fiscal Policy in a Small Euro Area Economy' (2012) Banco de Portugal Working Papers No 16

Alogoskoufis G, 'Greece's Sovereign Debt Crisis: Retrospect and Prospect' (2012) Hellenic Observatory Papers on Greece and Southeast Europe, GreeSE Paper No 54

Alt J and Lowry RC, 'A Visible Hand? Bond Markets, Political Parties, Balanced Budget Laws, and State Government Debt' (2001) 13 Econ Politics 49

Alt J, Lassen DD and Joachim W, 'It Isn't Just about Greece: Domestic Politics, Transparency and Fiscal Gimmickry in Europe' (2014) 44 Br J Polit Sci 707

Amtenbrink F and De Haan J, 'Economic Governance in the European Union: Fiscal Policy Discipline versus Flexibility' (2003) 40 CMLR 1075

Amtenbrink F and De Haan J, 'Reforming the Stability and Growth Pact' (2006) 31 EL Rev 402

Andrews G and Millet R, Law of Guarantees (6th ed., Sweet & Maxwell 2011)

Ang A and Longstaff F, 'Systemic Sovereign Credit Risk: Lessons from the U.S. and Europe' (2011) 60 J Money Econ 493

Angelini P, Grande G and Panetta F, 'The Negative Feedback Loop between Banks and Sovereigns' (2014) Banca D'Italia Occasional Papers No 213

Ardagna S, Caselli F and Lane T, 'Fiscal Discipline and the Cost of Public Debt Service: Some Estimates for OECD Contries' (2007) 7 BEJM 1

Armstrong K, 'The New Governance of EU Fiscal Discipline' (2013) 38 EL Rev 601

Ascah R, Politics and Public Debt: The Dominion, the Banks and Alberta's Social Credit (University of Alberta Press 1999)

Athanassiou P, 'Of Past Measures and Future Plans for Europe's Exit from the Sovereign Debt Crisis: What Is Legally Possible (and What Is Not)' (2011) 36 EL Rev 558

Avbelj M and Komárek J (eds), Constitutional Pluralism in the European Union and Beyond (Hart Publishing 2012)

Ayuso-i-Casals J, Hernández DG, Moulin L and Turrini A, 'Beyond the SGP – Features and Effects of EU National-level Fiscal Rules' in Deroose S, Flores E and Moulin L (eds), Policy Instruments for Sound Fiscal Policies: Fiscal Rules and Institutions (Palgrave Macmillan 2009)

Baele L, Ferrando A, Hördahl P, Krylova E and Monnet C, 'Measuring Financial Integration in the Euro Area' (2004) 20 Oxford Rev Econ Policy 509

Bailey SJ and Connolly S, 'The Flypaper Effect: Identifying Areas for Further Research' (1998) 95 Public Choice 335

Bakshi G and Chen Z, 'Inflation, Asset Prices, and the Term Structure of Interest Rates in Monetary Economies' (1996) 9 Rev Financ Stud 241

Bakshi G and Chen Z, 'Inflation, Asset Prices, and the Term Structure of Interest Rates in Monetary Economies' (1996) 9 Rev Financ Stud 241

Balassone F, Franco D and Giordano R, 'Market-Induced Fiscal Discipline: Is there a Fall-Back Solution for Rule Failure?', Public Debt (Banca d'Italia 2004)

Baldwin R and Giavazzi F, The Eurozone Crisis: A Consensus View of the Causes and a Few Possible Solutions (CEPR Press 2015)

Bank for International Settlements, 'Consolidated Banking Statistics: Foreign Claims by Nationality of Reporting Banks, Immediate Borrower Basis ' (BIS, 2014) www.bis.org/statistics/consstats.htm accessed 27 November 2014

Baquero Cruz J, 'The Legacy of the Maastricht-Urteil and the Pluralist Movement' (2008) 14 ELJ 389

Baratta R, 'Legal Issues of the "Fiscal Compact"' in De Witte B and others (eds), *The Euro Crisis and the State of European Democracy* (European University Institute 2013) 31

Barber T, 'The Eurozone's Fiscally Lax Nations Are at It Again' *Financial Times* (3 November 2014)

Barber T, 'The Markets, Not Brussels, Will Determine Italy's Fate' *Finanial Times* (London 21 November 2018) www.ft.com/content/d2009da0-ed7b-11e8-89c8-d36339d835c0 accessed 12 September 2020

Bardone L and Reitano VE, 'Italy in the Euro Area: The Adjustment Challenge' in Buti M (ed), *Italy in EMU: The Challenges of Adjustment and Growth* (Palgrave Macmillan 2013)

Bardutzky S and Fahey E, 'Who Got to Adjudicate the EU's Financial Crisis and Why? Judicial Review of the Legal Instruments of the Eurozone' in Adams M, Fabbrini F and Larouche P (eds), *The Constitutionalization of European Budgetary Constraints* (Hart Publishing 2014)

Bardutzky S, 'The Future Mandate of the Constitution of Slovenia: A Potent Tradition Under Strain' in Albi A and Bardutzky S (eds), *National Constitutions in Europe and Global Governance* (Springer 2019)

Baretti C, Huber B and Lichtblau K, 'A Tax on Tax Revenue: The Incentive Effects of Equalizing Transfers: Evidence from Germany' (2002) 9 Int Tax Pub Finan 631

Barnes S, 'Resolving and Avoiding Unsustainable Imbalances in the Euro Area' (2010) OECD Economics Department Working Papers No 827

Barnes S, Lane PR and Radziwill A, 'Minimising Risks from Imbalances in European Banking' (2010) OECD Economics Department Working Papers No 828

Baroncelli S, 'The Independence of the ECB after the Economic Crisis' in Adams M and others (eds), *The Constitutionalization of European Budgetary Constraints* (Hart Publishing 2014) 125

Barrett A, Fitz Gerald J, Bergin A, Kearney I, Duffey D, Garrett S and McCarthy Y, *Medium-Term Review 2005–2012* (ESRI, 2005)

Barro R and Sala-i-Martin X, *Economic Growth* (2nd ed., MIT Press 2003)

Bartolini D, Sacchi A, Salotti S and Santolini R, 'Fiscal Decentralization in Times of Financial Crises' (2018) 64 CESifo Econ Stud 456

Baskaran T, 'Soft Budget Constraints and Strategic Interactions in Subnational Borrowing: Evidence from the German States, 1975–2005' (2011) 71 J Urban Econ 114

Bast J, 'Don't Act Beyond Your Powers: The Perils and Pitfalls of the German Constitutional Court's Ultra Vires Review' (2014) 15 German LJ 167

Battistini N, Pagano M and Simionelli S, 'Systemic Risk and Home Bias in the Euro Area' (2013) European Economy Economic Papers No 494

Bauer C and Herz B, 'Reforming the European Stability Mechanism' (2020) 58 JCMS 636

Bayoumi T and Eichengreen B, 'Restraining Yourself: The Implications of Fiscal Rules for Economic Stabilization' (1995) 4 IMF Staff Papers 32

Bayoumi T, Goldstein M and Woglom G, 'Do Credit Markets Discipline Sovereign Borrowers? Evidence from US States' (1995) 27 J Money Credit Bank 1046

BBC, 'Row Over "Stupid" EU Budget Rules' *BBC* (17 October 2002) http://news .bbc.co.uk/2/hi/business/2336823.stm accessed 14 December 2014

Beck G, 'The Court of Justice, Legal Reasoning, and the Pringle Case – Law as the Continuation of Politics by Other Means' (2014) 39 EL Rev 234

Beck H and Prinz A, 'The Trilemma of a Monetary Union: Another Impossible Trinity' (2012) 47 Intereconomics 39

Beck T, 'Why the Rush? Short-Term Crisis Resolution and Long-Term Bank Stability' in Beck T (ed), *Banking Union for Europe: Risks and Challenges* (CEPR 2012)

Beck T, Levine R and Loayza N, 'Finance and the Sources of Growth' (2000) 58 J Financ Econ 261

Bednar J, *The Robust Federation: Principles of Design* (Cambridge University Press 2009)

Beesley A, 'Common EU Corporate Tax Rate Back to Haunt Kenny' *The Irish Times* www.irishtimes.com/news/common-eu-corporate-tax-rate-back-to-haunt-kenny-1.447314 accessed 25 January 2015

Beesley A, 'Irish Access to Low Debt Costs Reflects Market Confidence' *The Irish Times* (24 July 2015) www.irishtimes.com/business/economy/irish-access-to-low-debt-costs-reflects-market-confidence-1.2295223 accessed 9 May 2016

Beetsma R, Giuliodori M and Wierts P, 'Planning to Cheat: EU Fiscal Policy in Real Time' (2009) 24 Econ Policy 753

Begg I, 'Fiscal Federalism, Subsidiarity and the EU Budget Review' (2009) SIEPS Report No 1

Bekker S, 'EU Coordination of Welfare States after the Crisis: Further Interconnecting Soft and Hard law' (2014) 19 Int Rev Public Adm 296

Béland D and Lecours A, 'Fiscal Federalism and American Exceptionalism: Why Is There No Federal Equalisation System in the United States?' (2014) 34 J Public Policy 303

Belov M, 'Constitutional Courts as Ultimate Players in Multilevel Constituent Power Games: The Bulgarian Case' in Belov M (ed), *Courts, Politics and Constitutional Law* (Routledge 2020)

Belov M and Tanchev E, 'The Bulgarian Constitutional Order, Supranational Constitutionalism and European Governance' in Albi A and Bardutzky S (eds), *National Constitutions in European and Global Governance* (Springer 2019)

Bénassy-Quéré A, Brunnermeier M, Enderlein H, Farhi E, Fratzscher M, Fuest C, Gourinchas P-O, Martin P, Pisani-Ferry J, Rey H, Schnabel I, Véron N, Weder di Mauro B and Zettelmeyer J, 'Reconciling Risk Sharing with Market Discipline: A Constructive Approach to Euro Area Reform' (2018) CEPR Policy Insight No 91

Berger H, De Hann J and Jansen D-J, 'Why Has the Stability and Growth Pact Failed?' (2004) 7 Int Financ 235

Bermann GA, 'Taking Subsidiarity Seriously: Federalism in the European Community and the United States' (1994) 2 Columbia L Rev 331

Bernanke B and Gertler M, 'Inside the Black Box: The Credit Channel of Monetary Policy Transmission' (1995) 9 J Econ Persp 27

Bernanke B, Gertler M and Gilchrist S, 'The Financial Accelerator in a Quantitative Business Cycle Framework' in Taylor J and Woodford M (eds), *Handbook of Macroeconomics*, vol 1 C (North-Holland 1999)

Bernanke B, Gertler M and Gilchrist S, 'The Financial Accelerator in a Quantitative Business Cycle Framework' in John Taylor and Michael Woodford (eds), *Handbook of Macroeconomics*, vol 1 C (North-Holland 1999) 1531

Bernanke B, Gertler M and Gilchrist S, 'The Financial Accelerator and the Flight to Quality' (1996) 87 Rev Econ Stat 1

Bernitz U, 'Sweden and the European Union: On Sweden's Implementation and Application of European Law' (2001) 38 CMLR 903

Bernoth K, Von Hagen J and Schuknecht L, 'Sovereign Risk Premiums in the European Government Bond Market' (2012) 31 J Int Money Financ 975

Besley T and Coate S, 'Centralized versus Decentralized Provision of Local Public Goods: A Political Economy Approach' (2003) 87 J Public Econ 2611

Besselink L and Claes M, 'The Netherlands: The Pragmatics of a Flexible, Europeanised Constitution' in Albi A and Bardutzky S (eds), *National Constitutions in European and Global Governance* (Springer 2019)

Besselink L and Reestman J-H, 'Editorial: The Fiscal Compact and the European Constitutions: "Europe Speaking German"' (2012) 8 ECL Review 1

Besselink L, 'Curing a "Childhood Sickness"? On Direct Effect, Internal Effect, Primacy and Derogation from Civil Rights' (1996) 3 MJ 165

Besselink L, 'National and Constitutional Identity Before and After Lisbon' (2010) 6 Utrecht L Rev 36

Besselink LF, 'The Parameters of Constitutional Conflict after Melloni' (2014) 39 EL Rev 531

Beukers T and De Witte B, 'The Court of Justice Approves the Creation of the European Stability Mechanism outside the EU legal Order: *Pringle*' (2013) 50 CMLR 805

Beukers T, 'The New ECB and Its Relationship with the Eurozone Member States' (2013) 50 CMLR 1579

Bianco G, 'Collective Action Clauses in the Eurozone: One Step Forward, Two Steps Back' (2014) 16 Eur J L Reform 713

Bini Smaghi L, 'Challenges for the Euro Area and the World Economy' (The Group of Thirty 63rd Plenary Session, Rabat, 28 May 2010)

Bini Smaghi L, Padoa-Schioppa T and Papadia F, 'The Transition to EMU in the Maastricht Treaty' (1994) Essys in International Finance No 194

Bird R and Tarasov A, 'Closing the Gap: Fiscal Imbalances and Intergovernmental Transfers in Developed Federations' (2004) 22 Environment and Planning C: Government and Policy 77

Bird R and Tassonyi A, 'Constraining Subnational Fiscal Behaviour in Canada – Different Approaches, Similar Results?' in Rodden J, Eskeland GS and Litvack J (eds), *Fiscal Decentralisation and the Challenge of Hard Budget Constraints* (MIT Press 2003)

Bird R and Tassonyi A, 'Constraints on Provincial and Municipal Borrowing in Canada: Markets, Rules and Norms' (2001) 44 Can Public Admin 84

Bird R and Vaillancourt F, 'Fiscal Decentralization in Developing Countries: An Overview' in Bird R and Vaillancourt F (eds), *Fiscal Decentralization in Developing Countries* (Cambridge University Press 1998)

Bishop G, 'The Financial Market Alternative' in Cowie H (ed), *Towards Fiscal Federalism: Federal Trust Conference Report* (Federal Trust for Education and Research 1992)

Bishop G, 'The Future of the Stability and Growth Pact' (2003) 6 Int Financ 297

Bishop G, Damrau D and Miller M, *Market Discipline CAN Work in the EC Monetary Union* (Salomon Brothers 1989)

Blanchard O and Giavazzi F, 'Current Account Deficits in the Euro Area: the End of the Feldstein-Horioka Puzzle?' (2002) 2 Brookings Papers on Economic Activity 147

Blanchard O, 'Current Account Deficits in Rich Countries' (2007) 54 IMF Staff Papers 191

Blankart C and Klaiber A, 'Subnational Government Organisation and Public Debt Crises' (2006) 26 IEA 48

Bloomberg Editorial Board, 'Hey, Germany: You Got a Bailout Too' *Bloomberg* (New York 23 May 2012) www.bloombergview.com/articles/2012-05-23/merkel-should-know-her-country-has-been-bailed-out-too accessed 6 December 2014

Blume L and Voigt S, 'The Economic Effects of Constitutional Budget Institutions' (2013) 29 Eur J Polit Econ 236

Boadway RW, 'Public Economics and the Theory of Public Policy' (1997) 30 Can J Econ 753

Bogdandy Av and Bast J, 'The European Union's Vertical Order of Competences: The Current Law and Proposals for its Reform' (2002) 39 CMLR 227

Boggero G and Annicchino P, 'Who Will Ever Kick Us Out? Italy, the Balanced Budget Rule and the Implementation of the Fiscal Compact' (2014) 20 Eur Pub L 247

Bohn H and Inman R, 'Balanced-Budget Rules and Public Deficits: Evidence from the U.S. states' (1996) 45 Carnegie-Rochester Conference Series on Public Policy 13

Boivin J, 'The "Great" Recession in Canada: Perception vs Reality' *Bank of Canada* (Montreal 28 March 2011) www.bankofcanada.ca/2011/03/great-recession-canada-perception-reality/ accessed 14 August 2020

Boone P and Johnson S, 'The Next Global Problem: Portugal' *The New York Times* (New York 15 April 2010) http://economix.blogs.nytimes.com/2010/04/15/the-next-global-problem-portugal/ accessed 13 October 2016

Bordignon M, 'Fiscal Decentralization: How to Harden the Budget Constraint' in Deroose S, Flores E, Turrini A and Wierts P (eds), *Fiscal Policy Surveillance in Europe* (Palgrave Macmillan 2006)

Bordignon M, Manasse P and Tabellini G, 'Optimal Regional Redistribution Under Asymmetric Information' (2001) 91 Am Econ Rev 709

Bordo MD, Jonung L and Markiewicz A, 'A Fiscal Union for the Euro: Some Lessons from History' (2013) 59 CESifo Economic Studies 449

Borger V, 'The ESM and the European Court's Predicament in *Pringle*' (2013) 14 German LJ 113

Borio C, *Macro-Fiscal Policy Coordination in an EMU* ((6 July 1989) accessible at: www .ecbeuropaeu/ecb/access_to_documents/archives/delors/html/indexenhtml accessed 8 August 2020, 1989)

Bovenberg AL, Kremers J and Maason P, 'Economic and Monetary Union in Europe and Constraints on National Budgetary Policies' (1991) 38 IMF Staff Papers 374

Boyd S, 'BNP Paribas Freezes Funds as Loan Losses Roil Markets' *Bloomberg* (New York 9 August 2007) www.bloomberg.com/apps/news?pid=newsarchiv e&sid=aW1wj5i.vyOg accessed 20 June 2014

Boz E and Mendoza EG, 'Financial Innovation, the Discovery of Risk and the US Credit Crisis' (2014) 62 J Monetary Econ 1

Bradley M and Gulati M, 'Collective Action Clauses for the Eurozone' (2013) 18 Rev Fin 2045

Braun D, 'How to Make German Fiscal Federalism Self-Enforcing: A Comparative Analysis' (2007) 5 ZSE 235

Braun D and Trein P, 'Federal Dynamics in Times of Economic and Financial Crisis' (2014) 53 EJPR 803

Braun D and Trein P, 'How Do Fiscally Decentralized Federations Fare in Times of Crisis? Insights from Switzerland' (2016) 26 Reg Fed Stud 199

Briffault R, 'Courts, Constitutions and Public Finance' in Garret E, Graddy E and Jackson H (eds), *Fiscal Challenges: An Interdisciplinary Approach to Budget Policy* (Cambridge University Press 2008)

Briffault R, 'The Disfavored Constitution: State Fiscal Limits and State Constitutional Law' (2003) 34 Rutgers LJ 956

Briffault R, *Balancing Acts: The Reality Behind State Balanced Budget Requirements* (Twentieth Century Fund Press 1996)

Bris A, Koskinen Y and Nilsson M, 'The Euro and Corporate Valuations' (2009) 22 Rev Financ Stud 3171

Broschek J, 'Historical Institutionalism and the Varieties of Federalism in Germany and Canada' (2011) 42 Publius: The Journal of Federalism 662

Broschek J, 'Pathways of Federal Reform: Australia, Canada, Germany and Switzerland' (2014) 45 Public Choice 51

Broullet E and Ryder B, 'Key Doctrines in Canadian legal Federalism' in Oliver P, Macklem P and Des Rosiers N (eds), *The Oxford Handbook of the Canadian Constitution* (OUP 2017)

Brown D, 'The Financial Crisis and the Future of Federalism in Canada' in Eccleston R and Krever R (eds), *The Future of Federalism* (Elgar 2017)

Brunner K and Meltzer A, 'Money Supply' in Friedman BM and Hahn FH (eds), *Handbook of Monetary Economics* (Elsevier 1990)

Buchheit L and Gulati M, 'Sovereign Debt Restructuring in Europe' (2018) 9 Global Policy 65

Buchheit L, Gulati M and Tirado I, 'Reprofiling Sovereign Debt' (2015) 30 JIBLR 19

Büchs M, *New Governance in European Social Policy: The Open Method of Coordination* (Palgrave Macmillan 2007)

Buiter W, Corsetti G and Roubini N, 'Excessive Deficits: Sense and Nonsense in the Treaty of Maastricht' (1993) 8 Econ Policy 57

Buiter W, Rahbari E and Michels J, 'The Implications of Intra-Euro Area Imbalances in Credit Flows' (2011) CEPS Policy Insight No 57

Buiter WH and Grafe C, 'Reforming EMU's Fiscal Policy Rules: Some Suggestions for Enhancing Fiscal Sustainability and Macroeconomic Stability in an Enlarged European European Union' in Buti M (ed), *Monetary and Fiscal Policies in EMU: Interactions and Coordination* (Cambridge University Press 2003)

Buiter WH, Rahbari E and Michels J, 'The Implications of Intra-Euro Area Imbalances in Credit Flows' (2011) CEPS Policy Insight No 57

Bundesministerium der Finanzen, *The Federal Financial Equalisation System in Germany* (Bunesministerium der Finanzen, 2016)

Burchardt D, 'The Relationship between the Law of the European Union and the Law of Its Member States – A Norm-Based Conceptual Framework' (2019) 15 ECL Rev 73

Burret H and Feld L, '(Un)intended Effects of Fiscal Rules' (2018) 52 Eur J Polit Econ 166

Burret H and Feld L, 'Political Institutions and Fiscal Policies' (2014) 12 DICE Report 3

Burret H, Feld L and Köhler E, '(Un)Sustainability of Public Finances in German Laender: A Panel Time Series Approach' (2016) 53 Econ Model 254

Burret H, Feld L and Köhler E, 'Sustainability of Public Debt in Germany – Historical Considerations and Time Series Evidence' (2013) 233 Jahrbücher f Nationalökonomie u Statistik 291

Buti M, 'Monetary and Fiscal Rules for Public Debt Sustainability' (1990) Economic Papers No 84

Buttonwood, 'The Day After' *The Economist* (23 January 2015) www.economist.com/blogs/buttonwood/2015/01/ecb-and-qe accessed 23 January 2015

Buttonwood, 'The Perils of Planning on the Basis of Economic Forecasts' *The Economist* (26 November 2015) https://www.economist.com/buttonwoods-notebook/2015/11/26/the-perils-of-planning-on-the-basis-of-economic-forecasts accessed 14 June 2021

Byrne J, 'Ireland and the Global Financial Crisis: Growth, Volatility and Financial Development' (2010) 39 JSSISI 166

Caceres C, Guzzo V and Segoviano M, 'Sovereign Spreads: Global Risk Aversion, Contagion or Fundamentals?' (2010) IMF Working Paper No 120

Cahill M, 'Constitutional Exclusion Clauses, Article 29.4.6, and the Constitutional Reception of European Law' (2011) 34 DULJ 74

Cahill M, 'Subverting Sovereignty's Voluntarism: Pluralism and Subsidiarity in Cahoots' in Davies G and Avbelj M (eds), *Research Handbook on Legal Pluralism and EU law* (Elgar Publishing 2018)

Calderón C and Kubota M, 'Gross Capital Inflows Gone Wild: Gross Capital Inflows, Credit Booms and Crises' (2012) World Bank Policy Research Working Papers No 7270

Calleiss C, 'Constitutional Identity in Germany: One for Three or Three in One?' in Calleiss C and Van der Schyff G (eds), *Constitutional Identity in a Europe of Multilevel Constitutionalism* (Cambridge University Press 2019)

Calleiss C, 'From Fiscal Compact to Fiscal Union? New Rules for the Eurozone' (2012) 14 CYELS 101

Calvo G, Leiderman L and Reinhard C, 'Inflows of Capital to Developing Countries in the 1990s' (1996) 10 J Econ Persp 123

Calvo GA, 'Capital Flows and Capital-Market Crises: The Simple Economics of Sudden Stops' (1998) 1 J Appl Econ 35

Cameron D and Simeon R, 'Intergovernmental Relations in Canada: The Emergence of Collaborative Federalism' (2002) 32 Publius 49

Cane P, Kritzer HM (eds), *The Oxford Handbook of Empirical Legal Research* (Oxford University Press 2010)

Canova F and Pappa E, 'The Elusive Cost and the Immaterial Gains of Fiscal Constraints' (2006) 90 JPE 1291

Canova F, Ciccarelli M and Ortega E, 'Similarities and Convergence in G-7 Cycles' (2007) 54 J Monetary Econ 580

Cantor R and Packer F, 'Determinants and Impacts of Sovereign Credit Rankings' (1996) 2 Economic Policy Review 37

Cantor R, Packer F, 'Determinants and Impacts of Sovereign Credit Rankings' (1996) 2 Economic Policy Review 3

Caprio G and Demirgug-Kunt A, 'The Role of Long-term Finance: Theory and Evidence' (1997) 13 World Bank Research Observer 171

Carlin W, 'Heterogeneity in the Euro Area and Why It Matters for the Future of the Currency Union' in Beblavy M, Cobham D and Ódor Lu (eds), *The Euro Area and the Financial Crisis* (Cambridge University Press 2011)

Caruana J and Avdjiev S, 'Sovereign Creditworthiness and Financial Stability: An International Perspective' (2012) Banque de France Financial Stability Review No 16

Castillo de la Torre F, '*Tribunal Constitucional*, Opinion 1/2004 of 13 December 2004, on the Treaty establishing a Constitution for Europe' (2005) 42 CMLR 1169

Central Bank and Financial Services Authority of Ireland, *Financial Stability Review 2004* (FSA Ireland, 2004)

Central Bank and Financial Services Authority of Ireland, *Financial Stability Review 2006* (FSA Ireland, 2006)

Central Statistics Office, 'Information Notice: Classification of Irish Water' (*Central Statistics Office*, 30 July 2015) www.cso.ie/en/nationalaccounts/classifi cationdecisions/classificationofirishwater accessed 18 April 2015

Chalmers D, Davies D and Monti G, *European Union Law* (Cambridge University Press 2010)

Chalmers D, 'Judicial Preferences and the Community Legal Order' (1997) 60 MLR 165

Chalmers D, 'The European Redistributive State and a European Law of Struggle' (2012) 18 ELJ 667

Charlemagne, 'A Grim Take of Judges and Politicians' *The Economist* (4 November 2010) www.economist.com/node/17414379 accessed 25 February 2015

Charlemagne, 'Europe à l'Hollandaise' *The Economist* (London 9 February 2013) 27

Charleton P and Cox A, 'Accepting the Judgements of the Court of Justice of the EU as Authoritative' (2016) 23 MJ 1

Chiti E and Pedro GT, 'The Constitutional Implications of the European Responses to the Financial and Public Debt Crisis' (2013) 50 CMLR 683

Chouliarakis G and Lazaretou S, 'Deja vu? The Greek Crisis Experience, 2010's versus the 1930's. Lessons from History' (2010) Bank of Greece Working Papers No 176

Claes M and Bonelli M, 'Judicial Serendipity: How Portuguese Judges Came to the Rescue of the Polish judiciary' (2018) 14 Eur Const Law Rev 622

Claes M and De Witte B, 'Report on the Netherlands' in JHH Weiler, Anne-Marie Slaughter and Alec Stone Sweet (eds), *The European Courts and National Courts: Doctrine and Jursprudence* (Hart Publishing 1998)

Claes M, 'Constitutionalizing Europe at its Source: The "European Clauses" in the National Constitutions: Evolution and Typology' (2005) 24 YEL 81

Claes M, 'The Primacy of EU Law in European and National Law' in Arnull A and Chalmers D (eds), *The Oxford Handbook of European Union Law* (Oxford University Press 2015)

Claes M, *The National Courts' Mandate in the European Constitution* (Hart Publishing 2006)

Claessens S, Herring RJ, Schoenmaker D and Summe KA, *A Safer World Financial System: Improving the Resolution of Systemic Institutions* (ICMB, Geneva reports on the World Economy, 2012)

Claeys P, Ramos R and Suriñach J, 'Fiscal Sustainability across Government Tiers' (2008) 5 IEEP 139

Cloots E, 'Constitutional Identity in Belgium' in Calleiss C and van der Schyff G (eds), *Constitutional Identity in a Europe of Multilevel Constitutionalism* (Cambridge University Press 2019)

Cloots E, 'Germs of Pluralist Judicial Adjudication: *Advocaten Voor de Wereld* and other references from the Belgian Constitutional Court' (2010) 47 CMLR 645

Cloots E, *National Identity in EU Law* (Oxford University Press 2015)

Cochrane JH, 'The Return of the Liquidity Effect: A Study of the Short-run Relation between Money Growth and Interest Rates' (1989) 7 J Bus Econ Stat 75

Codogno L, Favero C, Missale A, Portes R and Thum M, 'Yield Spreads on EMU Government Bonds' (2008) 18 Econ Policy 505

Cohen BJ, 'Why Can't Europe Save Itself? A Note on a Structural Failure' (2015) 21 Contemporary Politics 220

Cole HL, Dow J and English W, 'Default, Settlement and Signalling: Lending Resumption in a Reputational Model of Sovereign Debt' (1995) 36 Int Econ Rev 365

Columbo C and Eliantonio M, 'Harmonized Technical Standards as Part of EU Law: Juridification with a Number of Unresolved Legitimacy Concerns?' (2017) 24 MJ 323

Commission of the EC, 'Economic and Monetary Union: The Economic Rationale and Design of the System'(Brussels 22 March 1990) http://europa.eu /rapid/press-release_IP-90-231_en.htm accessed 10 February 2014

Commission of the EC, *Intergovernmental Conferences: Contributions by the Commission* (Bulletin of the European Communities, supplement 2/91, 1990)

Commission of the EC, *One Market, One Money* (European Economy No 44, 1990)

Committee of Governors, *Introductory Report to the Draft Statute of ESCB* (19 September, 1990)

Committee of Governors, *Monetary Financing of Budget Deficits in Stage Three* (19 June, 1991)

Committee of Governors, *Report by the Chairmain to the Informal ECOFIN Council Meeting on Economic and Monetary Union Beyond Stage One* (26 March, 1990)

Committee on International Economic Policy and Reform, *Revisiting Sovereign Bankruptcy* (Brookings, 2013)

Constâncio V, 'European Monetary Integration and the Portuguese Case' in Detken C, Gaspar V and Noblet G (eds), *The New EU Member States: Convergence and Stability* (Third ECB Central Banking Conference, ECB 2005)

Contiades X, Papacharalambous C and Papastyliano C, 'The Constitution of Greece: EU Membership Persectives' in Albi A and Bardutzky S (eds), *National Constitutions in European and Global Governance* (Springer 2019)

Cooter R and Ulen T, *Law and Economics* (3rd ed., Addision-Wesley 2000)

Cordon MW and Neary PJ, 'Booming Sector and De-Industrialisation in a Small Open Economy' (1982) 92 Econ J 825

Corsetti G and Roubini N, 'Fiscal Deficits, Public Debt, and Government Solvency: Evidence from OECD Countries' (1991) 5 Jpn Int Econ 364

Corwin E, 'The "Higher Law" Background of American Constitutional Law' (1928) 42 Harv L Rev 1490

Costamanga F, 'The Impact of Stronger Economic Policy Co-ordination on the European Social Dimension: Issues of Legitimacy' in Adams M, Fabbrini F and Larouche P (eds), *The Constitutionalization of European Budgetary Constraints* (Hart Publishing 2014)

Cottarelli C and Guerguil M, *Designing a European Fiscal Union: Lessons from the Experience of Fiscal Federations* (Routledge 2015)

Cottarelli C, 'European Fiscal Union: A Vision for the Long Run' (2013) 149 SSES 167

Cottarelli C, 'Fiscal Federalism – Lessons for the Design of a European Fiscal Union' (ECB-IMF Conference, Frankfurt, 13 December 2012)

Council of the EU, 'EFSM: Council Approves €7bn Bridge Loan to Greece' (*Council of the EU*, 17 July 2015) www.consilium.europa.eu/en/press/press-releases/201 5/07/17-efsm-bridge-loan-greece/ accessed 18 July 2015

Council of the EU, 'Press Release 9696/10: Extraordinary Council Meeting, Economic and Financial Affairs'(Brussels 9–10 May 2010)

Council of the EU, 'Press Release: Statement of the Governing Council on the ECOFIN Council conclusions regarding the correction of excessive deficits in France and Germany' (*ECB*, 25 November 2003) www.ecb.europa.eu/press/pr/ date/2003/html/pr031125.en.html accessed 15 December 2014

Council of the EU, Specifications of the Council of 5 July 2016 on the implementation of the Stability and Growth Pact and Guidelines on the format and content of Stability and Convergence Programmes accessible at: https://ec.europa.eu/economy_finance/economic_governance/sgp/pdf/coc/cod e_of_conduct_en.pdf accessed 8 December 2019

Council of the EU, *Strengthening Economic Governance in the EU: Report of the Task Force to the European council* (15301/10 Brussels, 21 October 2010)

Courchene T, 'A Market Perspective on Regional Disparities' (1981) 7 Can Public Policy 506

Courchene TJ, 'Subnational Budgetary and Stabilization Policies in Canada and Australia' in Poterba JM and Von Hagen J (eds), *Fiscal Institutions and Fiscal Performance* (University of Chicago Press 1999)

Coutinho FP and Piçarra N, 'Portugal: The Impact of European Integration and the Economic Crisis on the Identity of the Constitution' in Albi A and Bardutzky S (eds), *National Constitutions in European and Global Governance* (Springer 2019)

Craig P, 'Constitutional Identity in the United Kingdom: An Evolving Concept' in Calleiss C and Van der Schyff G (eds), *Constitutional Identity in a Europe of Multilevel Constitutionalism* (Cambridge University Press 2019)

Craig P, 'Economic Governance and the Euro Crisis: Constitutional Architecture and Constitutional Implications' in Adams M, Fabbrini F and Larouche P (eds), *The Constitutionalization of European Budgetary Constraints* (Hart Publishing 2014)

Craig P, 'Pringle: Legal Reasoning, Text, Purpose and Teleology' (2013) 20 MJ 3

Craig P, 'The Financial Crisis, the European Union Institutional Order and Constitutional Responsibility' (2015) 22 Ind J Global Legal Stud 243

Craig P, 'The Stability, Coordination and Governance Treaty: Principle, Politics and Pragmatism' (2012) 37 EL Rev 231

Crain M and Millar J, 'Budget Process and Spending Growth' (1990) 31 WMLR 1021

Crawford M, *One Money for Europe? The Economics and Politics of EMU* (Macmillan Press 1996)

Cremer J, Estache A and Seabright P, 'Decentralizing Public Services: What Can We Learn from the Theory of the Firm?' (1996) 106 *Revue d'économie politique* 37

Cruces J and Trebesch C, 'Sovereign Defaults: The Price of Haircuts' (2013) 5 AEJ 85

D'Erasmo P, Mendoza E and Zhang J, 'What is a Sustainable Public Debt?' in Taylor J and Uhlig H (eds), *Handbook of Macroeconomics*, vol 2 (Elsevier 2015)

Dabrowski M, 'Fiscal or Bailout Union: Where is the EU/EMU's Fiscal Integration Heading?' (2013) 2014/1 Revue de l'OFCE No 132

Dabrowski M, 'Monetary Union and Fiscal and Macroeconomic Governance' (2015) European Economy Discussion Papers No 13

Dafflon B and Pujol F, 'Fiscal Preferences and Fiscal Performance: Swiss Cantonal Evidence' (2000) 2 Int Public Manag Rev 54

Dahlby B, 'Reforming the Federal Fiscal Stabilization Program' (2019) 12:18 University of Calgary SPP Briefing Paper 1

Daly E, 'Contitutional Identity in Ireland: National and Popular Sovereignty as Checks on European Integration' in Calleiss C and van der Schyff G (eds), *Constitutional Identity in a Europe of Multilevel Constitutionalism* (Cambridge University Press 2019)

Darvas Z and Leandro Á, *Economic Policy Coordination in the Euro Area under the European Semester* (European Parliament PE 542680, 2015)

Dashwood A, 'The Limits of European Community Powers' (1996) 21 EL Rev 113

Dashwood A, 'The United Kingdom in a Re-formed Union' (2013) 38 EL Rev 737

Dashwood A and others, *Wyatt and Dashwood's European Union Law* (6th ed., Hart 2011)

Davies G and Avbelj M (eds), *Research Handbook on Legal Pluralism and EU Law* (Elgar Publishing 2018)

Davies G, 'Subsidiarity: The Wrong Idea, in the Wrong Place, at the Wrong Time' (2006) 43 CMLR 1

Davies M, 'Legal Pluralism' in Cane P and Kritzer HM (eds), *The Oxford Handbook of Empirical Legal Research* (Oxford University Press 2010)

Dawson M and de Witte F, 'Constitutional Balance in the EU after the Euro-Crisis' (2013) 76 MLR 817

Dawson M, 'The Ambiguity of Social Europe in the Open Method of Coordination' (2009) 34 EL Rev 55

Dawson M, 'The Legal and Political Accountability Structure of "Post-Crisis" EU Economic Governance' (2015) 53 JCMS 976

Dawson M, *New Governance and the Transformation of European Law* (Cambridge University Press 2011)

De Búrca G and Weiler J (eds), *The Worlds of European Constitutionalism* (Cambridge University Press 2012)

De Figueiredo RJ and Weingast BR, 'Self-Enforcing Federalism' (2005) 21 JL Econ & Org 103

De Grauwe P and Ji U, 'How Much Fiscal Discipline in a Monetary Union?' (2014) 39 J Macroecon 348

De Grauwe P, 'Flaws in the Design of the Eurosystem?' (2006) 9 Int Financ 137

De Grauwe P, 'The Greek Crisis and the Future of the Eurozone' (2010) 2 Intereconomics 89

De Grauwe P, *Economics of Monetary Union* (13th ed., Oxford University Press 2020)

De Grauwe, P, 'Flaws in the Design of the Eurosystem?' (2006) 9 Int Financ 137

De Streel A, 'EU Fiscal Governance and the Effectiveness of its Reform' in Adams M, Fabbrini F and Larouche P (eds), *The Constitutionalization of European Budgetary Constraints* (Hart Publishing 2014)

De Streel A, 'The Evolution of the EU Economic Governance since the Treaty of Maastricht: An Unfinished Task' (2013) 20 MJ 336

De Tocqueville A, *Democracy in America*, vol I (Vintage Books, Random House 1945, first published in 1838)

De Witte B, 'Direct Effect, Primacy and the Nature of the Legal Order' in Paul Craig and Búrca Gd (eds), *The Evolution of EU law* (2 ed., Oxford University Press 2011)

De Witte B, 'Sovereignty and European Integration: The Weight of Legal Tradition' in JHH Weiler, Anne-Marie Slaughter and Sweet AS (eds), *The European Courts and National Courts: Doctrine and Jursprudence* (Hart Publishing 1998)

De Witte B, Héritier A and Trechel AH (eds), *The Euro Crisis and the State of European Democracy* (European University Institute 2013)

Debrun X and Kumar MS, 'The Discipline-Enhancing Role of Fiscal Institutions: Theory and Empirical Evidence' (2007) No 171 IMF Working Papers

Debrun X, Gérard M and Harris J, 'Fiscal Watchdogs and Sound Fiscal Policy' in Gaspar V, Gupta S and Mulas-Granads C (eds), *Fiscal Politics* (IMF 2017)

Debrun X, Moulin L, Turrini A and Ayuso-i-Casals J, 'Tied to the Mast? National Fiscal Rules in the European Union' (2008) 54 Econ Policy 299

Dell'Ariccia G and Marquez R, 'Lending Booms and Lending Standards' (2006) 51 J Finance 2511

Dellas H and Tavlas GS, 'An Optimum-Currency-Area Odyssey' (2009) 28 J Int Money Financ 1117

Delledonne G, 'A Legalization of Financial Constitutions in the EU? Reflections on the German, Spanish, Italian and French Experiences' in Adams M,

Fabbrini F and Larouche P (eds), *The Constitutionalization of European Budgetary Constraints* (Hart Publishing 2014)

Delors J, *Report on Economic and Monetary Union in the European Community (The Delors Report)* (Committee for the Study of Economic and Monetary Union 1989)

Dermine P, 'The End of Impunity? The Legal Duties of "Borrowed" EU Institutions under the European Stability Mechanism Framework' (2017) 13 Eur Const Law Rev 369

Deroose S, Moulin L and Wierts P, 'National Expenditure Rules and Expenditure Outcomes: Evidence for EU Member States' (2006) 1 *Wirtschaftspolitische Blätter* 27

Detragiache E and Hamann AJ, 'Exchange Rate-Base Stabilization in Western Europe: Greece, Ireland, Italy and Portugal' (1997) IMF Working Paper 75

Deutsche Bundesbank, 'Monthly Report: August 2011' (2011) 63(8) *Deutsche Bundesbank Monthly Report* 1

Deutsche Bundesbank, 'Approaches to Resolving Sovereign Debt Crises in the Euro Area' in (2011) 42(7) Deutsche Bundebank Monthly Report 41

Dewatripont M and Maskin E, 'Credit and Efficiency in Centralized and Decentralized Economies' (1995) 62 Rev Econ Stud 1843

Dimopoulos A, 'The Use of International Law as a Tool for Enhancing Governance in the Eurozone and its Impact on EU Institutional Integrity' in Adams M, Fabbrini F and Larouche P (eds), *The Constitutionalization of European Budgetary Constraints* (Hart Publishing 2014)

Dobbs M, 'Sovereignty, Article 4 (2)TEU and the Respect of National Identities: Swinging the Balance of Power in Favour of the Member States?' (2014) 33 YEL 320

Dothan M and Thompson F, 'A Better Budget Rule' (2009) 31 J Policy Anal Manag 1021

Doyle M, 'Regional Policy and European Economic Integration', *Collection of papers submitted to the Committee for the Study of Economic and Monetary Union (Delors Committee)* (1989)

Draghi M and Constâncio V, 'Introductory Statements to the Press Conference (with Q&A)' (Frankfurt am Main, 2 August 2012) https://www.ecb.europa.eu/press/pressconf/2012/html/is120802.en.html accessed 15 June 2021

Draghi M, 'Speech by Mario Draghi, President of the European Central Bank at the Global Investment Conference in London 26 July 2012' (*ECB*, 2012) www.ecb.europa.eu/press/key/date/2012/html/sp120726.en.html accessed 28 October 2020

Draghi M, 'The Future of the Euro: Stability through Change' *Die Zeit* (29 August 2012)

Drincóczi T and Bień-Kacała A, 'Illiberal Constitutionalism: The Case of Hungary and Poland' (2019) 20 German LJ 1140

Drincóczi T and Bień-Kacała A, 'Illiberal Constitutionalism: The Case of Hungary and Poland' (2019) 20 German LJ 1140

Dyevre A, 'European Integration and National Courts: Defending Sovereignty under Institutional Constraints?' (2013) 9 EuConst 139

Dyson KH and Featherstone K, *The Road to Maastricht: Negotiating Economic and Monetary Union* (Oxford University Press 1999)

Eaton J and Gerzovitz M, 'Debt with Repudiation: Theoretical and Empirical Analysis' (1981) 48 Rev Econ Stud 289

ECB, 'Fiscal Councils in EU Countries' (2014) ECB Monthly Bulletin June 1996

ECB, 'Monthly Bulletin September 2012' (2012) ECB Monthly Bulletin 7

ECB, 'Press Release: ECB Decides on Measures to Address Severe Tensions in Financial Markets' (*ECB*, 10 May 2010) www.consilium.europa.eu/uedocs/cms Upload/ECB_press_releases.pdf accessed 21 March 2015

ECB, 'Press Release: Governing Council Decision on Emergency Liquidity Assistance Requested by the Central Bank of Cyprus' (*ECB*, 21 March 2013) www.ecb.europa.eu/press/pr/date/2013/html/pr130321.en.html accessed 27 April 2016

ECB, 'Press Release: Technical Features of Outright Monetary Transactions'(Frankfurt 6 September 2012) www.ecb.int/press/pr/date/2012/ html/pr120906_1.en.html accessed 5 March 2015

ECB, 'The Creation of a European Fiscal Board' (2015) 7 ECB Economic Bulletin 48

ECB, 'The Creation of Competitiveness Boards in the Context of Striving towards a Genuine Economic Union' (2015) 7 ECB Economic Bulletin 28

ECB, 'The European Stability Mechanism' (2011) ECB Monthly Bulletin (July) 71

ECB, *ECB Monthly Bulletin October 2012* (ECB 2012)

ECB, *Financial Stability Review 2013* (ECB 2013)

ECB, *Monetary Policy and Inflation Differentials in a Heterogenous Currency Area* (ECB Monthly Bulletin May 2005)

ECOFIN, 'Financial Assistance to Greece' (*ECOFIN*, 20 October 2014) http://ec .europa.eu/economy_finance/assistance_eu_ms/greek_loan_facility/index_en .htm accessed 2 January 2015

Economist, 'Europe's Monetary Opposition' *The Economist* (6 October 2012) www .economist.com/node/21564245/ accessed 11 October 2015.

Economist, 'The PIIGS That Won't Fly' *The Economist* (18 May 2010) www .economist.com/node/15838029 accessed 7 August 2014

ECORYS, CPB and IFO, *A Study on EU Spending* (European Commission 2008)

Editorial, 'Bundesbank President on ECB Bond Purchases: Too Close to State Financing Via the Money Press' *Der Spiegel* (29 August 2012) https://www .spiegel.de/international/europe/spiegel-interview-with-bundesbank- president-jens-weidmann-a-852285.html accessed June 14, 2021

Editorial, 'ECB Shows Its Hand' *Financial Times* (London 10 November 2005) www.ft.com/intl/cms/s/0/9a4c8a78-518e-11 da-ac3b-0000779e2340.html#axz z3VDieCPOQ accessed 23 March 2015

Editorial, 'Endgame for the IMF-EU Feud over Greece's Debt' *Spiegel* (4 March 2016) https://www.spiegel.de/international/europe/op-ed-yanis-varoufakis- imf-eu-quarrel-over-greece-s-debt-a-1085203.html accessed June 14, 2021

Editorial, 'Some Thoughts Concerning the Draft Treaty on a Reinforced Economic Union' (2012) 49 CMLR 1

Editorial, 'Standard & Poor's Raises Greece Rating by Two Notches' *The Irish Times* (22 July 2015) www.irishtimes.com/business/economy/standard-poor-s-raises-greece-rating-by-two-notches-1.2292676 accessed 9 May 2016

Edward DA and Lane RC, *Edward and Lane on European Union Law* (Edward Elgar 2013)

EFB, *Assessment of EU Fiscal Rules* (European Fiscal Board 2019)

EFSF, 'Lending Operations' (*EFSF*, 14 August 2015) www.efsf.europa.eu/about/operations/index.htm accessed 25 February 2015

Efstathiou K and Wolff G, 'EU Policy Recommendations: A Stronger Legal Framework Is Not Enough to Foster National Compliance' (*Vox EU, CEPR*, 17 July 2019) https://voxeu.org/article/stronger-eu-legal-framework-not-enough-foster-national-compliance accessed 20 July 2020

Efstathiou K and Wolff G, 'What Drives National Implementation of EU Policy Recommendations?' (2019) Bruegel Working Paper No 4

Efstathou K and Wolff G, 'Is the European Semester Effective and Useful?' (2018) Bruegel Policy Contribution Issue No 9

Égert B and Kierzenkowski R, 'Exports and Property Prices in France: Are they Connected?' (2014) 37 World Econ 387

Ehrmann M, Fratzscher M, Gürkaynak RS and Swanson ET, 'Convergence and Anchoring of Yield Curves in the Euro Area' (2011) 93 Rev Econ Stat 350

Eichengreen B, 'The Breakup of the Euro Area' in Alesina A and Giavazzi F (eds), *Europe and the Euro* (University of Chicago Press 2010)

Eichengreen B, *Golden Fetters* (Oxford University Press 1992)

Eichengreen B, *The Crisis and the Euro* (Mimeo, University of California Berkeley 2009)

Eichengreen B, *The European Economy since 1945: Coordinated Capitalism and Beyond* (Princeton University Press 2007)

Eisen B and Hill T, 'Canada's Stablization Program Overdue for a Rethink' (*Fraser Institute*, 19 June 2020) www.fraserinstitute.org/blogs/canadas-stabilization-program-overdue-for-a-rethink accessed 6 August 2020

Eleftheriadis P, 'The EU's Relationship to International Law: Lessons from Brexit' in Davies G and Avbelj M (eds), *Research Handbook on Legal Pluralism and EU law* (Edward Elgar 2018)

Enderlein H and Von Müller C, 'German Federalism at the Crossroads' in Peterson PE and Nadler DJ (eds), *The Global Debt Crisis: Haunting US and European Federalism* (Brookings Institution 2014)

English WB, 'Understanding the Costs of Sovereign Default: American State Debts in the 1840's' (1996) 86 Am Econ Rev 259

Ericsson A, 'The Swedish De Bis in Idem Saga – Painting a Multi-Layered Picture' (2014) 17 *Europarättslig tidskrift* 54

Ernits M, Ginter C, Laos S, Allikmes M, Tupay PK, Värk R and Laurand A, 'The Constitution of Estonia: The Unexpected Challenges of Unlimited Primacy of

EU Law' in Albi A and Bardutzky S (eds), *National Constitutions in European and Global Governance* (Springer 2019)

ESM, 'ESM Programme for Greece: Repayment Schedule' (*ESM*, 2014) www.esm.europa.eu/assistance/greece accessed 29 October 2020

ESM, 'Financial Assistance: Greece' (*ESM*, 2020) www.esm.europa.eu/assistance/greece accessed 29 October 2020

Estella A, *Legal Foundations of EU Economic Governance* (Cambridge University Press 2018)

Eurogroup, 'Statement by the Eurogroup' (*Brussels*, 2 May 2010) www.consilium.europa.eu/uedocs/cmsUpload/100502-%20Eurogroup_statement-sn02492.en10.pdf accessed 13 May 2014

European Commission, 'A Stability Pact to Ensure Budgetary Discipline in EMU (Note for the Monetary Committee) II/163/96-EN, 18 March 1996

European Commission, 'Austria' (European E-Justice, 27 February 2020) https://e-justice.europa.eu/content_member_state_law-6-at-en.do?member=1 accessed 28 July 2020

European Commission, 'Building a Strengthened Fiscal Framework in the European Union: A Guide to the Stability and Growth Pact' (2013) European Economy Occasional Papers No 150

European Commission, 'Economic Crisis in Europe: Causes, Consequences and Responses' (2009) European Economy No 7

European Commission, 'Ensuring Budgetary Discipline in Stage Three of EMU' (Note for the Monetary Committee) II/409/96-EN, 19 July 1996

European Commission, 'Fact Sheet Q&A: Country-specific Recommendations 2015' (*European Commission Press Release Database*, 13 May 2014) http://europa.eu/rapid/press-release_MEMO-15-4968_en.htm accessed 27 February 2016

European Commission, 'Fiscal Rules Database' (*DG ECFIN*, 2014) http://ec.europa.eu/economy_finance/db_indicators/fiscal_governance/fiscal_rules/index_en.htm accessed 24 December 2015

European Commission, 'Surveillance of Intra-Euro-Area Competitiveness and Imbalances' (2010) European Economy No 1

European Commission, 'The Economic Adjustment Programme for Greece' (2010) European Economy Occasional Papers No 61

European Commission, 'The EU Economy: 2006 Review' (2006) European Economy No 6

European Commission, 'Towards a Stability Pact' (Note for the Monetary Committee) II/011/96-EN, 10 January 1996

European Commission, 'Vade mecum on the SGP' (2013) European Economy Occasional Papers No 151

European Commission, 'Adding Employment Indicators to the Scoreboard of the Macroeconomic Imbalance Procedure' SWD Ref. Ares (2015) 5426195

European Commission, *EMU@10: Successes and Challenges after Ten Years of Economic and Monetary Union* (European Economy No 2, 2008)

European Commission, *First Alert Mechanism Report on Macroeconomic Imbalances in Member States* (MEMO/12/104, 2012)

European Commission, Letter to Italy of 19 December 2018, Ares (2018) 7351969

European Council, 'European Council Hanover Summit of 27–28 June' (1988) Bull EC 6/1988

European Council, *Statement by the Heads of State or Government of the Euro Area and EU Institutions* (Brussels 25 March 2010)

European Council, *Statement by the Heads of State or Government of the Euro Area and EU Institutions* (Brussels, 21 July 2011)

European Economic Advisory Group (EEAG) *Report on the European Economy* (CESinfo, 2011)

European Fiscal Board, *Annual Report 2019* (European Fiscal Board, 2019)

European Parliament, Briefing: Euro Area Recommendations under the 2016 European Semester [2016] PE542.682

European Parliament Economic Governance Support Unit, *Implementation of the Macroeconomic Imbalance Procedure: State of Play August 2020* (European Parliament PE 497/739, 2020) https://www.europarl.europa.eu/RegData/etude s/IDAN/2016/497739/IPOL_IDA(2016)497739_EN.pdf accessed June 13, 2021

Eurostat, 'EMU Convergence Criterion Series – Monthly Data (online data code irt_lt_mcby_m)' (*Eurostat*, http://epp.eurostat.ec.europa.eu accessed 26 November 2014

Eurostat, 'Government Consolidated Gross Debt (gov_10dd_3dpt1)' (*Eurostat*, 2020) http://epp.eurostat.ec.europa.eu accessed 2 January 2020

Eurostat, 'Government Deficit/Surplus, Debt and Associated Data' (gov_10dd_edpt1)' (*Eurostat*, 2020) http://epp.eurostat.ec.europa.eu accessed 14 September 2020

Eurostat, 'Maastricht Criterion Interest Rates (irt_lt_mcby_a)' (*Eurostat*, 2020) http://epp.eurostat.ec.europa.eu accessed 14 June 2020

Eurostat, 'Money-Market Interest Rates – Annual Data; 3-Month Rates (irt_lt_mcby_a; MAT_M03)' (*Eurostat*, 25 April 2016) http://epp .eurostat.ec.europa.eu accessed 14 September 2016

Evans M, 'Real Rates, Expected Inflation, and Inflation Risk Premia' (1998) 51 J Finance 205

Evas T, 'Judicial Reception of EU law in Estonia' in de Witte B and others (eds), *National Courts and EU Law: New Issues, Theories and Methods* (Edward Elgar Publishing Ltd. 2016) 146

Evas T, *Judicial Application of European Union Law in Post-Communist Countries: The Cases of Estonia and Latvia* (Routledge 2016)

Everaert L, 'Euro Area Sovereign Risk During the Crisis' (2009) IMF Working Paper 222

Everett M and Kelly J, 'Financial Liberalisation and Economic Growth in Ireland' (2004) Central Bank of Ireland Quarterly Bulletin (Autumn), 91

Everson M, 'An Exercise in Legal Honesty: Rewriting the Court of Justice and the Bundesverfassungsgericht' (2015) 21 ELJ 474

Eyraud L and Gomez Sirera R, 'Constraints on Sub-National Fiscal Policy' in Cottarelli C and Guerguil M (eds), *Designing a European Fiscal Union: Lessons from the Experience of Thirteen Federations* (Routledge 2014)

Eyraud L and Lusinyan L, 'Vertical Fiscal Imbalances and Fiscal Performance in Advanced Economies' (2013) 60 J Monetary Econ 571

Eyraud L and Wu T, 'Playing by the Rules: Reforming Fiscal Governance in Europe' (2015) IMF Working Paper 67

Eyraud L, Gaspar V and Poghosyan T, 'Fiscal Politics in the Euro Area' in Gaspar V, Gupta S and Mulas-Granads C (eds), *Fiscal Politics* (IMF 2017)

Fabbrini F, 'The Fiscal Compact, the "Golden Rule" and the Paradox of European Federalism' (2013) 36 BC Intl & Comp L Rev 1

Fabbrini F, *Economic Governance in Europe* (Oxford University Press 2016)

Fagan G and Gaspar V, 'Adjusting to the Euro' (2007) ECB Working Paper Series No 716

Fagan G and Gaspar V, 'Macroeconomic Adjustment to Monetary Union' (2008) ECB Working Paper Series No 946

Fagan G, Gaspar V and Pereira A, 'Macroeconomic Adjustment to Structural Change' in Szapary G and Von Hagen J (eds), *Monetary Strategies for Joining the Euro* (Edward Elgar Publishing Ltd 2004)

Faini R, 'Fiscal Policy and Interest Rates in Europe' (2006) 47 Econ Policy 443

Fama E and Gibbons M, 'Inflation, Real Returns and Capital Investment' (1982) 9 J Monetary Econ 297

Fama E, 'Stock Returns, Real Activity, Inflation and Money' (1981) 71 Am Econ Rev 545

Faruqee H and Lee J, 'Global Dispersion of Current Accounts: Is the Universe Expanding' (2009) 56 IMF Staff Papers 574

Faust F, 'Comparative Law and Economic Analysis of Law' in Reimann M and Zimmerman R (eds), *The Oxford Handbook of Comparative Law* (Oxford University Press 2008)

Favero C, Pagano M and Von Thadden E-L, 'How Does Liquidity Affect Government Bond Yields?' (2010) 45 J Financ Quant Anal 107

Fedelino A and Stehn SJ, 'Fiscal Incentive Effects of the German Equalization System' (2009) IMF Working Paper 124

Feld L and Baskaran T, 'Federalism, Budget Deficits and Public Debt: On the Reform of Germany's Fiscal Constitution' (2010) 6 Rev Law Econ 365

Feld L and Kirchgassner G, 'Public Debt and Budgetary Procedures: Top Down or Bottom Up? Some Evidence from Swiss Municipalities' in Poterba JM and Von Hagen J (eds), *Fiscal Institutions and Fiscal Performance* (University of Chicago Press 1999)

Feld L and Matsusaka J, 'Budget Referendums and Government Spending: Evidence from Swiss Cantons' (2003) 87 JPL 2703

Feld L and Schaltegger C, 'Are Fiscal Adjustments Less Successful in Decentralized Governments?' (2009) 25 Europ J Polit Economy 115

Feld L, Kalb A and Osterloh S, 'Sovereign Bond Market Reactions to Fiscal Rules and No-Bailout Clauses – The Swiss Experience' (2013) 27 Document de treball de l'IEB 1

Feld L, Kalb A, Moessinger M-D and Osterloh S, 'Sovereign Bond Market Reactions to No-Bailout Clauses and Fiscal Rules – The Swiss Experience' (2017) 70 J Int Money Financ 319

Feldstein M, 'The Euro and the Stability Pact' (2005) 27 J Policy Model 421

Fernández-Villaverde J, Garicano L and Santos T, 'Political Credit Cycles: The Case of the Eurozone' (2013) 47 J Econ Persp 145

Feust C and Peichl A, 'European Fiscal Union: What Is It? Does It Work? And Are There Really "No Alternatives"?' (2012) 13 CESifo Forum 3

Fink A and Stratmann T, 'Institutionalized Bailouts and Fiscal Policy: Consequences of Soft Budget Constraints' (2011) 64 KYKLOS 366

Fisher I, *The Rate of Interest* (Macmillan 1907)

Fisher I, *The Theory of Interest* (Macmillan 1930)

Flatters F, Henderson V and Mieszkowski P, 'Public Goods, Efficiency and Regional Fiscal Equalization' (1974) 3 J Public Econ 99

Fleming M, 'Domestic Financial Policies Under Fixed and Under Floating Exchange Rates' (1962) 9 IMF Staff Papers 369

Flemming JM, 'Domestic Financial Policies Under Fixed and Under Floating Exchange Rates' (1962) 9 IMF Staff Papers 269

Flood C, Lahey W and Thomas B, 'Federalism and Health Care in Canada: A Troubled Romance?' in Oliver P, Macklem P and Des Rosiers N (eds), *The Oxford Handbook of the Canadian Constitution* (OUP 2017)

Folkerts-Landau D and Mathieson D, 'The European Monetary System in the Context of the Integration of European Financial Markets' (1989) IMF Occasional Papers No 66

Follette G and Lutz B, 'Fiscal Rules, What Does the American Experience Tell Us?' (2012) US Federal Reserve Board's Finance & Economic Discussion Series, Working Paper No 38

Forbes K and Warnock FE, 'Capital Flow Waves: Surges, Stops, Flight and Retrenchment' (2012) 88 J Int Econ 235

Foremny D, 'Sub-National Deficits in European Countries: The Impact of Fiscal Rules and Tax Autonomy' (2014) 34 Europ J Polit Economy 86

Fornasari F, Webb SB and Zou H-f, 'The Macroeconomic Impact of Decentralized Spending and Deficits: International Evidence' (2000) 1 Ann Econ Fin 403

Foster N, *Austrian Legal System & Laws* (Cavendish Publishing 2003)

Foster N, *Foster on EU Law* (4th ed., Oxford University Press 2013)

Frankel J and Schreger J, 'Over-Optimistic Official Forecasts and Fiscal Rules in the Eurozone' (2013) 149 Rev World Econ 247

Friden G, 'Ratification Processes of the Treaty on European Union: Luxembourg' (1993) 18 EL Rev 241

Friedman BM and Kuttner KN, 'Implementation of Monetary Policy: How Do Central Banks Set Interest Rates?' in Friedman BM and Woodford M (eds), *Handbook of Monetary Economics* (Elsevier 2010)

Friedman M, 'The Demand for Money: Some Theoretical and Empirical Results' (1959) 49 Am Econ Rev 327

Fuentes-Castro D, 'Leverage and Bubbles: A Note on the Spanish Property Market between 1998 and 2006' (2011) 18 Applied Economics Letters 693

Fuest C, 'The European Commission's Proposal for a Common Consolidated Corporate Tax Base' (2008) 24 Oxford Rev Econ Pol 720

Gaillard N, 'How and Why Credit Rating Agencies Missed the Eurozone Debt Crisis' (2014) 9 Cap Mark Law J 1

Galabresi G, *The Future of Law & Economics* (Yale University Press 2016)

Gali J and Monacelli T, 'Optimal Monetary and Fiscal Policy in a Currency Union' (2008) 76 J Int Econ 116

Gali J, 'Notes on the Euro Debt Crisis' (Bernácer Conference, The Euro After the Greek Crisis, Bank of Spain, Barcelona, June 2 2010) https://www.crei.cat/wp-content/uploads/users/pages/debt%20crisis%2003%2006.pdf accessed 14 June 2021

Galligan D, 'Legal Theory and Empirical Research' in Cane P and Kritzer HM (eds), *The Oxford Handbook of Empirical Legal Research* (Oxford University Press 2010)

Gallo D, 'Challenging EU Constitutional Law: The Italian Constitutional Court's New Stance on Direct Effect and the Preliminary Reference Procedure' (2019) 25 Eur Law J 433

Gamkhar S and Shah A, 'The Impact of Intergovernmental Fiscal Transfers: A Synthesis of the Conceptual and Empirical Literature' in Boadway RW and Shah A (eds), *Intergovernmental Fiscal Transfers: Principles and Practice* (The World Bank 2007)

Gandullia L and Leporatti L, 'Subnational Fiscal Balance, Interregional Redistribution and Risk-Sharing in Italy' (2020) 54 Reg Stud 319

Ganelli G, 'The International Effects of Government Spending Composition' (2010) 27 Econ Model 631

Garner O, 'Editorial: The Borders of European Integration on Trial in the Member States: *Dansk Industri, Miller,* and *Taricco*' (2017) 9 Eur J Legal Stud 1

Gaspar V and St Aubyn M, 'Adjusting to the Euro – the Contrast between Portugal and Spain' (10 Years of the Euro Conference, University of Minho, Braga, Portugal, May 2009)

Gaspar V, 'The Making of a Continental Financial System: Lessons for Europe from Early Amerian History' in Gaspar V, Gupta S and Mulas-Granads C (eds), *Fiscal Politics* (IMF 2017)

Gavilán A, Hernández de Cos P, Jimeno JF and Rojas JA, 'The Crisis in Spain: Origins and Developments' in Beblavy M, Cobham D and Ódor Lu (eds), *The Euro Area and the Financial Crisis* (Cambridge University Press 2011)

Gérard P and Verrijdt W, 'Belgian Constitutional Court Adopts National Identity Discourse' (2017) 13 Eur Const Law Rev 182

Gerkrath J, 'The Constitution of Luxembourg in the Context of EU and International Law as "Higher Law"' in Albi A and Bardutzky S (eds), *National Constitutionals in European and Global Governance* (Springer 2019)

Gersdorf M, 'Opinion on the White Paper on the Reform of the Polish Judiciary' (*First President of the Supreme Court of Poland,* 2018) https://archiwumosiatyns

kiego.pl/images/2018/04/Supreme-Court-Opinion-on-the-white-paper-on-the-Reform-of-the-Polish-Judiciary.pdf accessed 12 June 2020

Giavazzi F and Spaventa E, 'The Current Account in a Monetary Union' in Beblavy M, Cobham D and Ódor Lu (eds), *The Euro Area and the Financial Crisis* (Cambridge University Press 2011)

Gibson H, Hall S and Tavlas G, 'The Greek Financial Crisis: Growing Imbalances and Sovereign Spreads' (2012) 31 J Int Money Financ 498

Gibson W, 'Interest Rates and Monetary Policy' (1970) 78 J Polit Econ 431

Gillingham J, *Coal, Steel, and the Rebirth of Europe, 1945-1955: The Germans and French from Ruhr Conflict to Economic Community* (Cambridge University Press 1991)

Gillingham J, *European Integration* (Cambridge University Press 2003)

Giorno C, Hoeller P and De La Maisonneuve C, 'Overheating in Small Euro Area Economies: Should Fiscal Policy React?' (2002) 2 OECD Economics Department Working Papers 323

Giovannini A and Spaventa L, 'Fiscal Rules in the Monetary Union: A No-Entry Clause' in Giovannini A (ed), *The Debate on Money in Europe* (MIT Press 1995)

Goldsmith RW, *Financial Structure and Development* (Yale University Press 1969)

Goldstein M and Woglom G, 'Market-Based Fiscal Discipline in Monetary Unions: Evidence from the US Municipal Bond Market' in Canzoneri M, Grilli V and Masson P (eds), *Market-Based Fiscal Discipline in Monetary Unions: Evidence from the US Municipal Bond Market* (Cambridge University Press 1992)

Goodspeed T, 'Bailouts in a Federation' (2002) 9 Int Tax Pub Finan 409

Goodspeed T, 'Decentralization and Intra-Country Transfers in the Great Recession: The Case of the European Union' (2020) 54 Reg Stud 931

Goodspeed T, 'Soft Budget Constraints in Decentralized Government' (2017) 221 Hacienda Pública Esp 112

Gordon B, 'Tax Competition and Harmonisation under EU Law: Economic Realities and Legal Rules' (2014) 39 EL Rev 790

Gordon M and Dougan M, 'The United Kingdom's European Union Act 2011: "Who Won the Bloody War Anyway?"' (2012) 37 EL Rev 3

Gorton G and He P, 'Bank Credit Cycles' (2008) 75 Rev Econ Stat 118

Gourinchas P-O and Obstfeld M, 'Stories of the Twentieth Century for the Twenty-First' (2012) 4 Am Econ J 227

Government of Canada, 'Backgrounder: The Fiscal Stabilization Program' (*Government of Canada*, 23 February 2016) www.canada.ca/en/department-finance/news/2016/02/backgrounder-the-fiscal-stabilization-program.html accessed 6 December 2019

Government of Canada, *Federal-Provincial Grants and the Spending Power of Parliament* (Queen's Printer 1969)

Grabenwarter C, 'National Constitutional Law Relating to the EU ' in Von Bogdandy A and Bast J (eds), *Principles of European Constitutional Law* (2nd ed., Hart Publishing 2011)

Gregory AW and Watt DG, 'Sources of Variation in International Real Interest Rates' (1995) 28 Can J Econ 120

Griller S, 'Introduction to the Problems in the Austrian, the Finnish and the Swedish Constitutional Order' in Kellermann AE, de Zwaan JW and Czuczai J (eds), *EU Enlargement* (TMC Asser Press 2001)

Grimm D, 'Defending Sovereign Statehood against Transforming the Union into a State' (2009) 5 EuConst 369

Grimm D, 'Does Europe Need a Constitution?' (1995) 1 ELJ 282

Grinath III A and Wallis JJ, 'Debt, Default and Revenue Structure: The American State Debt Crisis in the Early 1840s' (1997) NBER Historical Paper No 97

Grinath III A, Sylla RE and Wallis JJ, 'Sovereign Debt and Repudiation: The Emerging-Market Debt Crisis in the US States' (2004) NBER Working Paper No 10753

Groeteke F and Mause K, 'New Constitutional "Debt Brakes" for Euroland? A Question of Institutional Complementarity' (2012) 23 Const Polit Econ 279

Gros D and Alcidi C, 'The Case of the Disappearing Fiscal Compact' (CEPS Commentary, 5 November 2015)

Gros D and Thygesen N, *European Monetary Integration: from the European Monetary System to Economic and Monetary Union* (Addison Wesley Longman 1992)

Gros D, Mayer T and Ubide A, *The Nine Lives of the Stability Pact: A Special Report of the CEPS Macroeconomic Policy Group* (CEPS, 2004)

Grotewold A, 'West Germany's Economic Growth' (1973) 63 Ann Assoc Am Geogr 353

Groussot X, 'Supr[i]macy à la Française: Another French Exception' (2008) 27 YEL 89

Grund S and Stenström M, 'A Sovereign Debt Restructuring Framework for the Euro Area' (2019) 42 Fordham Int'l LJ 795

Grund S, 'Restructuring Government Debt under Local Law: The Greek Case and Implications for Investor Protection in Europe' (2017) 12 CMLJ 253

Guarascio F and Maltezou R, 'Greece Gets Debt Relief from Euro Zone' *Reuters* (21 June 2018) www.reuters.com/article/us-eurozone-greece/greece-gets-debt-relief-from-euro-zone-idUSKBN1JH3FM accessed 22 June 2018

Guarascio F, 'EU Gives Budget Leeway to France "Because It Is France" – Juncker' *Reuters* (Brussels 31 May 2016) www.reuters.com/article/eu-deficit-france-idUSL8N18S3PL accessed 31 May 2016

Gunlicks A, *The Länder and German Federalism* (Manchester University Press 2003)

Haberler G, 'Economic Aspects of a European Customs Union' (1949) 11 World Politics 431

Habermas J, 'Remarks on Dieter Grimm's "Does Europe Need a Constitution?"' (1995) 1 ELJ 303

Habermas J, *The Crisis of the European Union: A Response* (Polity Press 2012)

Hadfield GK and Weingast BR, 'Law without the State: Legal Attributes and the Coordination of Decentralized Collective Punishment' (2013) 1 JLC 3

Hahn HJ, 'The Stability Pact for European Monetary Union: Compliance with Deficit Limit as a Constant Legal Duty' (1998) 35 CMLR 77

Haket S, 'The Danish Supreme Court's *Ajos* judgment: Rejecting a Consistent Interpretation and Challenging the Effect of a General Principle of EU law in the Danish Legal Order' (2017) 10 Rev Eur Adm Law 135

Hallerberg M, 'Fiscal Federalism Reforms in the European Union and the Greek Crisis' (2010) 12 Eur Union Polit 127

Hallerberg M, Strauch R and Von Hagen J, 'The Design of Fiscal Rules and Forms of Governance in European Union Countries' (2007) 23 Eur J Polit Econ 338

Halmai G, 'Abuse of Constitutional Identity. The Hungarian Constitutional Court on Interpretation of Article E) (2) of the Fundamental Law' (2018) 43 RCEEL 23

Hamilton A, 'Report Relative to a Provision for the Support of Public Credit', *Journal of the House of Representatives of the United States* (National Historical Publications and Records Commission 1826)

Hamilton A, *Report on Public Credit* (Vol 6, 1790)

Hart H, *The Concept of Law* (2 ed., Oxford University Press 1994)

Hartley T, *The Foundations of European Union Law* (8th ed., Oxford University Press 2014)

Hay P, 'The Contribution of the European Communities to International Law' (1969) 59 Proceedings of the American Society of International Law 195

Hayek F, 'The Economic Conditions of Interstate Federalism' in Hayek F (ed), *Individualism & Economic Order* (University of Chicago Press 1948)

Hayek F, *Individualism & Economic Order* (University of Chicago Press 1948)

Hefeker C, 'The Agony of Central Power: Federalism in the German Reich' (2001) 5 Eur Rev Econ Hist 119

Heinemann F, Osterloh S and Kalb A, 'Sovereign Risk Premia: The Link between Fiscal Rules and Stability Culture' (2014) 41 J Int Money Financ 110

Heipertz M and Vedun A, *Ruling Europe: The Politics of the Stablity and Growth Pact* (Cambridge University Press 2010)

Hempell HS and Sørensen CK, 'The Impact of Supply Constraints on Bank Lending in the Euro Area: Crisis Induced Crunching?' (2010) ECB Working Paper Series No 1262

Henning CR and Kessler M, '*Fiscal Federalism: US History for Architects of Europe's Fiscal Union*' (Bruegel Essay and Lecture Series, 2012)

Heppke-Falk K and Wolff G, 'Moral Hazard and Bail-Out in Fiscal Federations: Evidence for the German Länder' (2008) 61 KYKLOS 425

Herdegen MJ, 'Price Stability and Budgetary Restraints in the Economic and Monetary Union: The Law as Guardian of Economic Wisdom' (1998) 35 CMLR 9

Herman F, *Report of the Committee on Economic and Monetary Affairs and Industrial Policy on Economic and Monetary Union* (A3-223/90/A-B, 1990)

Hinarejos A, 'The Court of Justice of the EU and the Legality of the European Stability Mechanism' (2013) 72 CLJ 237

Hinarejos A, 'The Euro Area Crisis and Constitutional Limits to Fiscal Integration' (2014) 14 CYELS 243

Hinarejos A, *The Euro Area Crisis in Constitutional Perspective* (Oxford University Press 2015)

Hines J and Thaler R, 'The Flypaper Effect' (1995) 9 J Econ Persp 217

Hinsely F, *Sovereignty* (2nd ed., Cambridge University Press 1986)

Hirschl R, 'The Question of Case Selection in Comparative Constitutional Law' (2005) 53 AJCL 125

HM Treasury, *An Evolutionary Approach to Economic and Monetary Union* (HM Treasury, 1989)

Hodson D and Maher I, 'Soft Law and Sanctions: Economic Policy Co-ordination and Reform of the Stability and Growth Pact' (2004) 11 J Eur Public Policy 798

Hodson D and Maher I, 'The Open Method as a New Mode of Governance: The Case of Soft Economic Policy Coordination' (2001) 39 JCMS 719

Hodson D, *Governing the Euro Area in Good Times and Bad* (Oxford University Press 2011)

Hoegh K, 'The Danish Maastricht Judgment' (1999) 24 EL Rev 80

Hoffmeister F, 'Constitutional Implications of EU Membership: A View from the Commission' (2007) 3 CYELP 59

Hofman B and Remsperger H, 'Inflation Differentials among the Euro Area Countries: Potential Causes and Consequences' (2005) 16 J Asian Econ 403

Hofmeister H, 'European Monetary Fund – The Commission's Proposal to Establish a European Monetary Fund: A Critical Analysis' (2018) 5 ALJ 139

Hofmeister H, 'From ESM to EMF and Back: A Critical Analysis of the Euro Area Reform Proposals' (2019) 29 Swiss Rev Int'l & Eur L 367

Hogan G and Whelan A, *Ireland and the European Union: Constitutional and Statutory Texts and Commentary* (Sweet & Maxwell 1995)

Hogan G and Whyte G, *JM Kelly: The Irish Constitution* (4th ed., Tottell Publishing 2003)

Hogan G, 'Ireland: The Constitution of Ireland and EU Law' in Albi A and Bardutzky S (eds), *National Constitutions in European and Global Governance* (Springer 2019)

Hogg PW, 'Jurisdiction of the Court of the Supreme Court of Canada' (1980) 3 Canada-US LJ 39

Hogg PW, *Constitutional Law of Canada* (Carswell 2013)

Hoggarth G, Mahadeva L and Martin J, 'Understanding International Bank Capital Flows during the Recent Financial Crisis' (2010) Bank of England Financial Stability Paper No 8

Honohan P, 'Resolving Ireland's Banking Crisis' (2009) 40 Econ Soc Rev 207

Honohan P, 'To What Extent Has Finance Been a Driver of Ireland's Economic Success?' (2006) 4 ESRI Quarterly Economic Commentary 59

Honohan P, *The Irish Banking Crisis: Regulatory and Financial Stability Policy 2003-2008* (Central Bank of Ireland, 2010)

Horvath M, 'EU Independent Fiscal Institutions: An Assessment of Potential Effectiveness' (2018) 56 JCMS 504

House of Lords European Union Committee 6th Report of Session 2003-04: The Future Role of the European Court of Justice (2004 HL 47)

House of Lords European Union Committee, *Amending Article 136 of the Treaty on the Functioning of the European Union* (10th Report of Session 2010-2011)

Huber PM, 'The Rescue of the Euro and Its Constitutionality' in Ringe W-G and Huber PM (eds), *Legal Challenges in the Global Financial Crisis: Bail-outs, the Euro and Regulation* (Hart Publishing 2014)

Hübner K, 'Eurozone: Creeping Decay, Sudden Death or Magical Solution' in Laurson F (ed), *The EU and the Eurozone Crisis* (Ashgate 2013)

Huizinga J and Mishkin F, 'Inflation and Real Interest Rates on Assets with Different Characteristics' (1984) 39 JF 28

Hurst S and Rühl T, 'Swiss Cantons in the Red' (*CreditSuisse*, 5 May 2015) www .credit-suisse.com/us/en/articles/articles/news-and-expertise/2015/05/en/half-of-swiss-cantons-in-th-red.html accessed 14 November 2016

Hylton K, 'Law and Economics versus Economic Analysis of Law' (2019) 48 Eur J Law Econ 77

Iara A and Wolff G, 'Rules and Risks in the Euro Area' (2014) 34 Europe J Polit Economy 222

Illmer A, 'Angela Merkel Rules Out German Bailout for Greece' *Deutsche Welle* (Berlin 1 March 2010) www.dw.com/en/angela-merkel-rules-out-german-bailout-for-greece/a-5299788 accessed 1 September 2013

Imbeau L, '*Deficits and Surpluses in Federated States: A Review of the Public Choice Empirical Literature*' (Annual Conference of the Canadian Political Science Association, Winnipeg, 3 June 2004)

IMF Independent Evaluation Office, *IMF Performance in the Run-Up to the Financial and Economic Crisis: IMF Surveillance in 2004-2007* (IMF, 2011)

IMF, 'Current Account Balance, % GDP' (*IMF WEO Database*, 2020) www.imf.org /external/datamapper/BCA_NGDPD@WEO/OEMDC/ADVEC/WEOWORLD accessed 10 September 2020

IMF, 'General Government Gross Debt (% of GDP)' (*IMF World Economic Outlook*, 2016) www.imf.org/external/pubs/ft/weo/2016/01/weodata/index.aspx accessed 14 September 2016

IMF, 'General Government Net Lending/Borrowing (% of GDP)' (*IMF World Economic Outlook*, April 2016) www.imf.org/external/pubs/ft/weo/2016/01/weo data/weoselser.aspx accessed 14 September 2016

IMF, 'Ireland: Selected Issues' (2015) IMF Country Report No 15/78

IMF, 'Switzerland: 2012 Article IV Consultation' (2012) IMF Country Report No 12/106

IMF, *Euro Area Policies: 2013 Article IV Consultation* (IMF Country Report No 13/232, 2013)

IMF, *Euro Area Policies: Selected Issues* (IMF Country Report No 15/205, 2015)

IMF, *Euro Area: Selected Issues* (IMF, 2013)

IMF, *Executive Board Approves Exceptional Access lending Framework Reforms* (IMF Press Release, 28 January 2016)

IMF, *Financial Sector Assessment Report: Ireland* (IMF, 2006)

IMF, *Fiscal Rules – Anchoring Expectations for Sustainable Public Finances* (IMF, 2009)

IMF, *Initial Lessons of the Crisis* (IMF, 2009)

IMF, *Ireland: Financial System Stability Assessment Update* (IMF Country Report No 06/ 292, 2006)

IMF, Ireland: Letter of Intent, Memorandum of Economic and Financial Policies, and Technical Memorandum of Understanding (3 December 2010) www .imf.org/external/np/loi/2010/irl/120310.pdf accessed 2 January 2014

IMF, *Macro Policy Lessons for a Sound Design of Fiscal Decentralization* (IMF Fiscal Affairs Department, 2009)

IMF, *Staff Report for the 2005 Art IV Consultation: Ireland* (IMF, 2005)

IMF, *Staff Report for the 2006 Article IV Consultation: Ireland* (IMF, 2006)

IMF, *Staff Report for the 2007 Article IV Consultation: Ireland* (IMF, 2007)

IMF, *Staff Report for the 2009 Art IV Consultation (Greece)* (IMF, 2009)

IMF, *Staff Report for the 2014 Article IV Consultation (Euro Area Policies)* (IMF, 2014)

IMF, *Strengthening the Conractual Framework to Address Collective Action Problems in Sovereign Debt Restructuring* (IMF 2014)

Inman R, 'Do Balanced Budget Rules Work? US Experience and Possible Lessons for the EMU' in Siebert H (ed), *Quo Vadis Europe?* (Mohr Siebeck 1997)

Inman R, 'Transfers and Bailouts: Enforcing Local Discipline with Lessons from US Federalism' in Rodden J, Eskeland GS and Litvack J (eds), *Decentralization and the Challenge of Hard Budget Constraints* (MIT Press 2003)

Ioannou D and Stracca L, 'Have the Euro Area and EU Governance Worked? Just the Facts' (2014) 34 1

Ireland (Republic of), Department of Finance, *Ireland's Stability Programme April 2015* (Republic of Ireland, 2015)

Ireland (Republic of), Department of Finance, *Medium-Term Budgetary Framework* (Republic of Ireland, 2014)

Italian Republic, *Italy's Draft Budgetary Plan 2015* (Ministero Dell'Economia e Delle Finanze, 2015)

Jääskinen N, 'The Application of Community Law in Finland: 1995-1998' (1999) 36 CMLR 407

Jabko N, 'Which Economic Governance for the European Union? Facing up to the Problem of Divided Sovereignty' (2011) SIEPS Report No 2

James H, *Making the European Monetary Union* (Princeton University Press 2014)

Jarukaitis I and Švedas G, 'The Constitutional Experience of Lithuania in the Context of European and Global Governance Challenges' in Albi A and Bardutzky S (eds), *National Constitutions in European and Global Governance* (Springer 2019)

Jaumotte F and Sodsriwiboon P, 'Current Account Imbalances in the Southern Euro Area' (2010) IMF Working Paper No 139

Jeffery C, 'Cycles of Conflict: Fiscal Equalization in Germany' (2003) 13 Reg Fed Stud 22

Jenkner E and Lu Z, 'Sub-National Credit Risk and Sovereign Bailouts – Who Pays the Premium?' (2014) IMF Working Paper No 20

Jha PC, 'Theory of Fiscal Federalism: An Analysis' (2015) 17 J Soc Econ Dev 241

Jochimsen B, 'Fiscal Federalism in Germany: Problems, Proposals and Chances for Fundamental Reforms' (2008) 17 German Politics 541

Joerges C, 'The European Economic Constitution and its Transformation through the Financial Crisis' in Patterson D and Söderstn A (eds), *A Companion to European Union Law and International Law* (Wiley-Blackwell 2013)

Joffe M, *Provincial Solvency and Federal Obligations* (Macdonald-Laurier Institute, 2012)

Johnson C and Kriz K, 'Fiscal Institutions, Credit Ratings and Borrowing Costs' (2005) 25 Public Budg Finance 84

Jones E and Kelemen RD, 'The Euro Goes to Court' (2014) 56 Survival 15

Jones ML, 'The Legal Nature of the European Community: A Jurisprudential Analysis Using HLA Hart's Model of Law and a Legal System' (1984) 17 Cornell Int'l LJ 1

Jørgen Mortensen, 'Economic Policy Coordination in the Economic and Monetary Union, from Maastricht via the SGP to the Fiscal Pact' (2013) CEPS Working Document No 381

Joumard I and Kongsrud PM, 'Fiscal Relations across Government Levels' (2003) OECD Economics Department Working Papers No 375

Jovanović M, 'Sovereignty – Out, Constitutional Identity – In: The "Core Areas" of Controversy of EU Membership' (2015) 56 Acta Juridica Hungarica 1588

Jovanović M, *European Economic Integration: Limits and Prospects* (Taylor & Francis 2002)

Juncker J-C, Tusk D, Dijsselbloem J, Draghi M and Schulz M, *Completing Europe's Economic and Monetary Union (Five Presidents' Report)* (European Commission, 2015)

Kaczorowska A, *European Union Law* (3rd ed., Routledge 2013)

Kandel S, Ofer A and Sarig O, 'Real Interest Rates and Inflation: An Ex-Ante Empirical Analysis' (1996) 51 J Finance 205

Kapotas P, 'Greek Council of State Judgment 3470/2011' (2014) 10 Eur Const Law Rev 162

Kawalec S, Pytlarczyk E and Kamiński K, *The Economic Consequences of the Euro* (Routledge 2020)

Kelemen DP, *Eurolegalism: The Transformation of Law and Regulation in the European Union* (Harvard University Press 2011)

Kelemen RD and Teo TK, 'Law, Focal Points, and Fiscal Discipline in the United States and the European Union' (2014) 108 Am Polit Sci Rev 355

Kelemen RD, 'Law, Fiscal Federalism, and Austerity' (2015) 22 Ind J Global Stud 379

Kelemen RD, 'The Uses and Abuses of Constitutional Pluralism: Undermining the Rule of Law in the Name of Constitutional Identity in Hungary and Poland' (2019) 21 CYELS 59

Kellermann AE, De Zwaan J, Cruczi J (eds), *EU Enlargement: The Constitutional Impact at EU and National Level* (TMC Asser Press 2001) 141

Kelly M, 'On the Likely Extent of Falls in Irish House Prices' (2007) Economic Social Research Institute (ESRI) Quarterly Economic Commentary 42

Kelsen H, *Pure Theory of Law* (2nd ed., The Lawbook Exchange Ltd 2002)

Kenan PB, 'Currency Unions and Policy Domains' in Andrews DM, Henning CR and Pauly LW (eds), *Governing the World's Money* (Cornell University Press 2002)

Kenan PB, 'The Theory of Optimum Currency Areas: An Eclectic View' in Mundell R and Swoboda AK (eds), *Monetary Problems of the International Economy* (University of Chicago Press 1969)

Kennedy S and Robbins J, 'The Role of Fiscal Rules in Determining Fiscal Performance' (2001) Department of Finance Working Paper, Government of Canada

Khan M, 'Brussels Avoids Hitting Spain and Portugal with Budget Fine' (*Finantial Times*, 2016) www.ft.com/content/0c1c6dab-5f50-326a-ad92-47ec440d6923 accessed 2 December 2019

Khan M, 'Dutch Question Brussels' Explanation on Italian Budget' *Financial Times* (London 7 March 2019) www.ft.com/content/a389f924-40c5-11e9-9bee-efab61506f44 accessed 12 September 2020

Kiewiet DR and Szakaty K, 'Constitutional Limitations on Borrowing: An Analysis of State Bonded Indebtedness' (1996) 12 JLEO 62

King D, *Fiscal Tiers: The Economics of Multi-Level Government* (Routledge 1984)

King R and Levine R, 'Finance and Growth: Schumpeter Might be Right' (1993) 108 QJ Econ 717

Kirchgässner G, 'Swiss Confederation' in Shah A (ed), *The Practice of Fiscal Federalism: Comparative Perspectives* (McGill-Queen's University Press 2007)

Kirchhof G, 'Debt Limits in Constitutional Law: The "Debt Brake"' in Ringe W-G and Huber PM (eds), *Legal Challenges in the Global Financial Crisis: Bail-outs, the Euro and Regulation* (Hart Publishing 2014)

Kirsch F and Rühmkorf R, 'Sovereign Borrowing, Financial Assistance, and Debt Repudiation' (2017) 64 Econ Theory 777

Kiyotaki N and Moore J, 'Credit Cycles' (1997) 105 J Polit Econ 211

Kneebone R, 'Deficits and Debt in Canada: Some Lessons from Recent History' (1994) 20 Can Pub Pol'y 152

Komárek J, 'Czech Constitutional Court Playing with Matches: The Czech Constitutional Court Declares a Judgment of the Court of Justice of the EU Ultra Vires' (2012) 8 EuConst 323

Kombos C and Shaelou SL, 'The Cypriot Constitution under the Impact of EU Law: An Asymmetrical Formation' in Albi A and Bardutzky S (eds), *National Constitutions in European and Global Governance* (Springer 2019)

Kong H, 'The Spending Power in Canada' in Oliver P, Macklem P and Des Rosiers N (eds), *The Oxford Handbook of the Canadian Constitution* (Cambridge University Press 2017)

Konstitutionsutskottet (Swedish Committee on the Constitution), *Constitutional Amendments before Swedish Membership of the European Union* (Konstitutionsutskottet report 1993/94 KU21 available at: www.riksdagense/sv/dokument-lagar/are nde/betankande/grundlagsandringar-infor-ett-svenskt-medlemskap-i_GH01KU21 1993)

Kopits G and Symansky S, 'Fiscal Rules' (1998) IMF Occasional Paper No 162

Kornai J, '"Hard" and "Soft" Budget Constraint' (1980) 35 Acta Oeconomica 231

Kornai J, 'The Soft Budget Constraint' (1986) 39 Kyklos 3

Kornai J, Maskin P and Roland G, 'Understanding the Soft Budget Constraint' (2003) 41 J Econ Lit 1095

Kosar D and Vyhnánek L, 'Constitutional Identity in the Czech Republic: A New Twist on an Old-Fashioned Idea?' in Calleiss C and Van der Schyff G (eds), *Constitutional Identity in a Europe of Multilevel Constitutionalism* (Cambridge University Press 2019)

Kosta V, 'Case Comment: Michaniki AE v Ethniko' (2009) 5 EUConst 501

Kouretas GP, 'The Greek Debt Crisis: Origins and Implications' (2010) 57 Panoeconomicus 391

Kovács K, 'Changing Constitutional Identity via Amendment' in Blokker P (ed), *Constitutional Acceleration wthin the European Union and Beyond* (Routledge 2018)

Kovács K, 'The Rise of an Ethnocultural Constitutional Identity in the Jurisprudence of the East Central European Courts' (2017) 18 German LJ 1703

Krampf A, 'From the Maastricht Treaty to Post-crisis EMU: The ECB and Germany as Drivers of Change' (2014) 22 Journal of Contemporary European Studies 303

Krüma K and Statkus S, 'The Constitution of Latvia – a Bridge between Traditions and Modernity' in Albi A and Bardutzky S (eds), *National Constitutions in European and Global Governance* (Springer 2019)

Krunke H, 'The Danish Lisbon Judgment' (2014) 10 EuConst 542

Kühn Z, 'The Czech Republic: From a Euro-Friendly Approach of the Constitutional Court to Proclaiming a Court of Justice Judgement *Ultra Vires*' in Albi A and Bardutzky S (eds), *National Consitutions in European and Global Governance* (Springer 2019)

Kumhof M and Laxton D, 'Fiscal Deficit and Current Account Deficits' (2009) IMF Working Paper No 237

Kumm M, 'Rethinking Constitutional Authority: On the Structure and Limits of Constitutional Pluralism' in Avbelj A and Komárek J (eds), *Constitutional Pluralism in the European Union and Beyond* (Hart Publishing 2012)

Kumm M, 'The Jurisprudence of Constitutional Conflict: Constitutional Supremacy in Europe before and after the Constitutional Treaty' (2005) 11 ELJ 262

Kumm M, 'Who Is the Final Arbiter of Constitutionality in Europe? Three Conceptions of the Relationship between the German Federal Constitutional Court and the European Court of Justice' (1999) 36 CMLR 351

Küttel D and Kugler P, 'Explaining Yield Spreads of Swiss Canton Bonds: An Empirical Investigation' (2008) 16 FMPM 208

Lachmayer K, 'The Constitution of Austria in International Constitutional Networks' in Albi A and Bardutzky S (eds), *National Constitutions in European and Global Governance: Democracy, Rights, the Rule of Law* (Springer 2019)

Lago-Peñas S, Martinez-Vazquez J and Sacchi A, 'Fiscal Stability during the Great Recession: Putting Decentralization Design to the Test' (2020) 54 Reg Stud 919

Lamfalussy A, 'Macro-Coordination of Fiscal Policies in an Economic and Monetary Union in Europe', *Collection of papers submitted to the Delors Committee* (1989)

Landon S and Smith CE, 'Government Debt Spillovers and Creditworthiness in a Federation' (2000) 33 Can J Econ 634

Lane PR and McQuade P, 'Domestic Credit Growth and International Capital Flows' (2013) ECB Working Paper Series No 1566

Lane PR and Milesi-Ferretti GM, 'Cross-Country Incidence of the Global Financial Crisis' (2011) 39 IMF Econ Rev 77

Lane PR and Pels B, 'Current Account Imbalances in Europe' (2012) IIIS Discussion Paper No 397

Lane PR, 'Capital Flows in the Euro Area' (2013) European Economy Economic Papers No 497

Lane PR, 'External Imbalances and Fiscal Policy' (2010) IIIS Discussion Paper No 314

Lane PR, 'International Financial Integration and the External Positions of Euro Area Countries' (2010) OECD Economics Department Working Papers No 830

Lane PR, 'The European Sovereign Debt Crisis' (2012) 26 J Econ Persp 49

Lane PR, 'The Irish Crisis' in Beblavy M, Cobham D and Ódor Lu (eds), *The Euro Area and the Financial Crisis* (Cambridge University Press 2011)

Lane PR, 'The Real Effects of European Monetary Union' (2006) 20 J Econ Persp 47

Lane T, 'Market Discipline' (1993) IMF Staff Papers No 53

Lang IG, Durdević Z and Mataija M, 'The Constitution of Croatia in the Perspective of European and Global Governance' in Albi A and Bardutzky S (eds), *National Constitutions in European and Global Governance* (Springer 2019)

Lastra R and Wood G, 'The Crisis of 2007–2009: Nature, Causes, and Reactions' (2010) 13 J Int'l Econ L 531

Lastra RM, 'Systemic Risk, SIFIs and Financial Stability' (2011) 6 CMLJ 197

Lastra RM, *Legal Foundations of International Monetary Stability* (Oxford University Press 2006)

Latané H, 'Cash Balances and the Interest Rate: A Pragmatic Approach' (1954) 36 Rev Econ and Statis 456

Laubach T, 'New Evidence on the Interest Rate Effects of Budget Deficits and Debt' (2009) 7 JEEA 858

Lavapuro J, Ojanen T and Scheinin M, 'Rights-Based Constitutionalism in Finland and the Development of Pluralist Constitutional Review' (2011) 9 I Con 505

Law DS, 'Constitutions' in Cane P and Kritzer HM (eds), *The Oxford Handbook of Empirical Legal Research* (Oxford University Press 2010)

Lebeck C, 'Supranational Law in a Cold Climate: European Law in Scandanavia' (2010) 4 Sant'Anna Legal Studies 2

Leblond P, 'The Political Stability and Growth Pact is Dead: Long Live the Economic Stability and Growth Pact' (2006) 44 JCMS 969

Leeper E and Gordon D, 'In Search of the Liquidity Effect' (1992) 29 J Monetary Econ 341

Legrain P, 'Investors Are Ignoring Eurozone Risks' *Financial Times* (30 April 2014) https://www.ft.com/content/b32c26cc-c627-11e3-ba0e-00144feabdc0 accessed 14 June 2021

Leino P and Salminen J, 'The Euro Crisis and Its Constitutional Consequences for Finland: Is There Room for National Politics in EU Decision-Making?' (2013) 9 Eur Const Law Rev 451

Lenaerts K and Van Nuffel P, *European Union Law* (3rd ed., Sweet & Maxwell 2011)

Lenaerts K, 'Constitutionalism and the Many Faces of Federalism' (1990) 38 Am J Comp L 205

Lenaerts K, 'EMU and the EU's Constitutional Framework' (2014) 39 EL Rev 753

Lenaerts K, 'Federalism and the Rule of Law: Perspectives from the European Court of Justice' (2009) 33 Fortham Int'l LJ 1338

Lenaerts K, 'Federalism: Essential Concepts in Evolution – the Case of the European Union' (1997) 21 Fordham Int'l Law J 746

Lenaerts K, 'How the ECJ Thinks: A Study on Legitimacy' (2013) 36 Forham Int'l LJ 1302

Lenaerts K, 'The Basic Constitutional Charter of a Community Based on the Rule of Law' in Maduro MP and Azoulay L (eds), *The Past and Future of EU Law* (Hart Publishing 2010)

Lenaerts K, 'The Principle of Democracy in the Case Law of the European Court of Justice' (2013) 62 ICLQ 271

Leuthold S, 'Interest Rates, Inflation and Deflation' (1981) 37 FAJ 28

Levine R, 'Finance and Growth: Theory and Evidence' in Aghion P and Durlauf S (eds), *Handbook of Economic Growth* (Elsevier Science 2005)

Lienbacher G and Lukan M, 'Constitutional Identity in Austria' in Calliess C and van der Schyff G (eds), *Constitutional Identity in a Europe of Multilevel Constitutionalism* (Cambridge University Press 2019)

Lindseth PL, 'Power and Legitimacy in the Eurozone: Can Integration and Democracy Be Reconciled?' in Adams M, Fabbrini F and Larouche P (eds), *The Constitutionalization of European Budgetary Constraints* (Hart Publishing 2014)

Liu L and Webb SB, 'Laws for Fiscal Responsibility for Subnational Discipline' (2011) World Bank Policy Research Working Papers No 5587

Lock T, 'Why the European Union Is Not a State' (2010) 5 EuConst 407

Locke J, *Two Treatises on Civil Government* (Routledge 1884)

Lockwood B, 'Distributive Politics and the Costs of Centralization' (2002) 69 Rev Econ Stud 313

Louis J-V, 'Guest Editorial: The No-Bailout Clause and Rescue Packages' (2010) 47 CMLR 971

Ludlow P, '"Reshaping Europe:" The Origins of the Intergovernmental Conferences and the Emergence of a New European Political Architecture', *The Annual Review of European Community Affairs* (CEPS, Brassy's 1991)

MacCormick N, 'Beyond the Sovereign State' (1993) 56 MLR 1

MacCormick N, 'The Maastricht-Urteil: Sovereignty Now' (1995) 1 ELJ 259

MacCormick N, *Questioning Sovereignty* (Oxford University Press 1999)

Machenstein H and Jeffery C, 'Financial Equalization in the 1990s: On the Road Back to Karlsruhe?' in Jeffery C (ed), *Recasting German Federalism: The Legacies of Unification* (Pinter 1999)

Maddaloni A and Peydró J-L, 'Bank Risk-taking, Securitization, Supervision, and Low Interest Rates: Evidence from the Euro-area and the US Lending Standards' (2011) 24 Rev Financ Stud 2121

Maduro MP, 'Contrapunctual Law: Europe's Constitutional Plurlaism in Action' in Walker N (ed), *Sovereignty in Transition* (Hart 2003)

Maduro MP, 'Europe and the Constitution: What If This Is as Good as It Gets?' in JHH Weiler and Wiind M (eds), *European Constitutionalism Beyond the State* (Cambridge University Press 2003)

Maduro MP, 'Three Claims of Constitutional Pluralism' in Avbelj M and Komárek J (eds), *Constitutional Pluralism in the European Union and Beyond* (Hart Publishing 2012)

Majocchi A, 'Stabilisation in the European Monetary Union and Fiscal Federalism' in Fossat A and Panella G (eds), *Fiscal Federalism in the European Union* (Routledge 1999)

Majone G, 'From Regulatory State to a Democratic Default' (2014) 52 JCMS 1216

Maltritz D and Wüste S, 'Determinants of Budget Deficits in Europe' (2014) 48 Econ Model 222

Manasse P, 'Deficit Limits and Fiscal Rules for Dummies' (2007) IMF Staff Papers No 455

Mardell M, 'Stand by for Another Euro Crisis' *BBC News* (21 April 2016) www.bbc.com/news/world-europe-36090188 accessed 12 May 2016

Markakis M and Dermine P, 'Bailouts, the Legal Status of Memoranda of Understanding, and the Scope of Application of the EU Charter: *Florescu*' (2018) 55 CMLR 643

Marshall D, 'Inflation and Asset Returns in a Monetary Economy' (1992) 47 J Finance 1315

Martin-Oliver A, 'Financial Integration and Structural Changes in Spanish Banks during the Pre-Crisis Period' (2012) 24 Establidad Financiera 111

Martinez-Vazquez J and Vulovic V, 'How Well Do Subnational Borrowing Regulations Work?' in Yochino N and Morgan P (eds), *Central and Local Government Relations in Asia: Achieving Fiscal Sustainability* (Edward Elgar 2017)

Martinico G and Repetto G, 'Fundamental Rights and Constitutional Duels in Europe: An Italian Perspective on Case 269/2017 of the Italian Constitutional Court and Its Aftermath' (2019) 15(4) Eur Const Law Rev 731

Maskin P, 'Recent Theoretical Work on the Soft Budget Constraint' (1999) 89 Am Econ Rev 421

Masson P and Melitz J, 'Fiscal Policy Independence in a European Monetary Union' (1991) 2 Open Econ Rev 113

Maxwell J and MacG D, 'The Adjustment of Federal-Provincial Financial Relations' (1936) 2 Can J Econ Polit Sci 374

Mayer C, 'ESM Treaty in Accordance with the Austrian Constitution' (2013) 7 ICL Journal 385

Mayer F, 'Multilevel Constitutional Jurisdiction' in Von Bogdandy A and Bast J (eds), *Principles of European Constitutional Law* (2nd ed., Hart Publishing 2010)

Mayer T, 'Euroland's Hidden Balance-of-Payments Crisis' (2011) Deutsche Bank Research EU Monitor No 88

Mazzucelli C, *France and Germany at Maastricht: Politics and Negotiations to Create the European Union* (Garland Publishing Inc 1997)

McDermot PA, *Contract Law* (Tottel Publishing 2006)

McEldowney J, 'Debt Limits in German Constitutional Law – A UK Perspective' in Ringe W-G and Huber PM (eds), *Legal Challenges in the Global Financial Crisis: Bailouts, the Euro and Regulation* (Hart Publishing 2014)

McGuire P and Wooldridge P, 'The BIS Consolidated Banking Statistics: Structure, Uses and Recent Enhancements' (2005) BIS Quarterly Review (September) https://www.bis.org/publ/qtrpdf/r_qt0509f.htm accessed 14 June 2021

McKinnon R, 'Market-Preserving Fiscal Federalism in the American Monetary Union' in Bleier MI and Ter-Minassian T (eds), *Macroeconomic Dimensions of Public Finance* (Routledge 1997)

McKinnon R, 'Optimum Currency Areas and Key Currencies: Mundel I versus Mundell II' (2004) 42 JCMS 689

McKinnon R, 'Optimum Currency Areas' (1963) 53 Am Econ Rev 717

Meadway J, 'The Euro: Crisis and Collapse?' (2012) 16 Competition and Change 150

Mélitz J and Zumer F, 'Regional Redistribution and Stabilization by the Center in Canada, France, the UK and the US: A Reassesment and New Tests' (2002) 86 J Public Econ 263

Mélitz J, 'How to Save the Euro? Lessons from the US' in Beblavy M, Cobham D and Ódor Lu (eds), *The Euro Area and the Financial Crisis* (Cambridge University Press 2011)

Meltzer A, 'The Demand for Money: The Evidence from the Time Series' (1963) 71 JPE 219

Mendoza E and Terrones M, 'An Anatomy of Credit Booms and their Demise' (2012) 15 Economía Chilena 4

Mendoza E, 'Real Exchange Rate Volatiity and the Price of Nontradable Goods in Economies Prone to Sudden Stups' (2006) 6 Economía 103

Menéndez AJ, 'Editorial: A European Union in Constitutional Mutation' (2014) 20 ELJ 127

Merino AdG, 'Legal Developments in the Economic and Monetary Union During the Debt Crisis: The Mechanisms of Financial Assistance' (2012) 49 CMLR 1613

Michael Gordon and Dougan M, 'The United Kingdon's European Union Act 2011: "Who Won the Bloody War Anyway?"' (2012) 37 EL Rev 3

Milesi-Ferretti GM and Tille C, 'The Great Retrenchment: International Capital Flows During the Global Financial Crisis' (2011) 26 Econ Policy 285

Millar J, 'The Effects of Budget Rules on Fiscal Performance and Macroeconomic Stabilization' (1997) Bank of Canada Working Paper No 15

Miller JC, *The Federalists: 1789-1801* (Harper & Row 1960)

Millet F-X, 'Constitutional Identity in France: Vices and – Above All – Virtues' in Calleiss C and Van der Schyff G (eds), *Constitutional Identity in a Europe of Multilevel Constitutionalism* (Cambridge University Press 2019)

Mishkin F, 'The Real Interest Rate: A Multi-Country Empirical Study' (1984) 17 Can J Econ 283

Miskin F, 'Understanding Real Interest Rates' (1988) 70 Am J Agr Econ 1064

Mitsilegas V, 'Trust' (2020) 21 German LJ 69

Mizuno T, 'Andreas Predöhl's Theory of the Integration of Economic and Political Space' (2014) 7 IJEF 57

Mody A and Sandri D, 'The Eurozone Crisis: How Banks and Sovereigns Came To Be Joined at the Hip' (2012) 27 Econ Policy 199

Monetary Committee of the EC, 'Result of the Discussion in the Committee on 24 April' (Meeting Minutes) [1990] II/185/90-EN

Monetary Committee, 'Economic and Monetary Union Beyond Stage I: Orientations for the Preparation of the Intergovernmental Conference' [1990] Europe Documents No 1609 (3 April 1990)

Monti M, Dāianu D, Fuest C, Georgieva K, Kalfin I, Lamassoure A, Moscovici P, Šimonytė I, Timmermans F and Verhofstadt G, *Future Financing of the EU* (Commission, 2016)

Moody's, 'Greece's Foreign Currency Rating Outlook Changed to Positive' (*Moody's Investors Service*, 10 February 1999) www.moodys.com/research accessed 21 September 2016

Moody 's, 'Moody's Assigns A2 Rating to Drachma Denominated Bond of the Government of Greece' (*Moody's Investors Service*, 28 January 1997) www .moodys.com/research accessed 18 September 2016

Moody's, 'Moody's Assigns Long- and Short-term Sovereign Ceilings' (*Moody's Investors Service*, 2 October 1995) www.moodys.com/research accessed 21 September 2016

Moody's, 'Moody's Raises Greeces Country Ceilings to A2' (*Moody's Investors Service*, 14 July 1999) www.moodys.com/research accessed 21 September 2016

Moody's, 'Moody's will Review for Possible Downgrade to Greece's Long-Term Foreign Currency Country Ceilings' (*Moody's Investors Service*, 20 February 1998) www.moodys.com/research accessed 21 September 2016

Moody's, *Rating Methodology: Sovereign Bond Ratings* (Moody's Investors Service, 2013)

Moody's, 'Moody's Upgrades Sovereign Ceiling Ratings of Greece to Baa1' (*Moody's*, 23 December 1996) www.moodys.com/credit-ratings/Greece-Government-of-credit-rating-348330 accessed 15 August 2020

Moody's, 'Rating Action Moody's Downgrades ESM' (*Moody's Investors Service*, 30 November 2012) www.moodys.com/research/Moodys-downgrades-ESM-to-Aa1-from-Aaa-and-EFSF-to---PR_261114 accessed 15 September 2016

Moravcsik A, *Choice for Europe* (Cornell University 1999)

Morris R, Ongena H and Schuknecht L, 'The Reform and Implementation of the Stability and Growth Pact' (2006) ECB Occasional Paper Series No 47

Mortensen J, 'Economic Policy Coordination in the Econoimc and Monetary Union, from Maastricht via the SGP to the Fiscal Pact' (2013) CEPS Working Document No 381

Moschella M, 'Monitoring Macroeconomic Imbalances: Is EU Surveillance More Effective than IMF Surveillance?' (2014) 52 JCMS 1273

Mueller S and Keil S, 'The Territoriality of Fiscal Solidarity: Comparing Swiss Equalisation with European Union Structural Funding' (2013) 5 Perspect Fed 123

Münchau W, 'Better no Fiscal Union than a Flawed One' *Financial Times* (18 October 2015)

Mundell R, 'A Theory of Optimum Currency Areas' (1961) 51 Am Econ Rev 509

Mundell R, 'Capital Mobility and Stabilization Policy under Fixed and Flexible Exchange Rates' (1963) 29 Can J Econ Polit Sci 475

Mundell R, 'Inflation and Real Interest' (1963) 71 JPE 280

Mundell R, 'The Monetary Dynamics of International Adjustment under Fixed and Flexible Exchange Rates' (1960) 75 Q J Econ 227

Murkens JEK, '"We Want Our Identity Back" – the Review of National Sovereignty in the General Federal Constitutional Court's Decision on the Lisbon Treaty' (2010) 10 PL 530

Murswiek D, 'ECB, ECJ, Democracy and the Federal Constitutional Court' (2014) 15 German LJ 147

National Association of State Budget Officers, *Budget Processes in the States 2015* (NASBO, 2015)

Neergaard U and Sørensen KE, 'Activist Infighting among Courts and Breakdown of Mutual Trust? The Danish Supreme Court, the CJEU, and the *Ajos* Case' (2017) 36 Yearb Eur Law 275

Nergelius J, '2005: The Year When European Law and Its Supremacy was Finally Recognised in Swedish Courts' (2005) 1 SYEL 145

Nergelius J, 'The Constitution of Sweden and European Influences: The Changing Balance Between Democratic and Judicial Power' in Albi A and Bardutzky S (eds), *National Constitutions in European and Global Governance* (Springer 2019)

Nölling W, *Monetary Policy in Europe After Maastricht* (Palgrave Macmillan 1993)

Nuget A, Pearce J and Simeon R, 'The Resilience of Canadian Federalism' in Peterson PE and Nadler D (eds), *The Global Debt Crisis: Haunting US and European Federalism* (Brookings Institution 2014)

Nyberg P, *Misjudging Risk: Causes of the Systemic Banking Crises in Ireland: Report of the Commission of Investigation into the Banking Sector in Ireland* (Stationery Office, 2011)

O'Gorman R, 'Thomas Pringle v Government of Ireland, Ireland and the Attorney General' (2013) 50 Ir Jur 221

O'Rourke KH and Taylor AM, 'Cross of Euros' (2013) 27 Journal of Economic Perspectives 167

O'Donnell R and Honohan P (eds), *Economic and Monetary Union* (Institute of European Affairs 1991)

Oates W, 'An Essay on Fiscal Federalism' (1999) 37 J Econ Lit 49

Oates W, 'On the Evolution of Fiscal Federalism: Theory and Institutions' (2008) 62 Nat Tax J313

Oates W, 'On the Theory and Practice of Fiscal Decentralization' (2006) IFIR Working Paper No 5

Oates W, 'Towards a Second-Generation Theory of Fiscal Federalism' (2005) 12 Int Tax Pub Finan 349

Oates W, *Fiscal Federalism* (Harcourt Brace Jovanovich 1972)

Obstfeld M, 'The Global Capital Market: Benefactor or Menace?' (1998) 12 J Econ Persp 9

Ódor Lu and Kiss G, 'Lost in Complexity' in Ódor Lu (ed), *Rethinking Fiscal Policy after the Crisis* (Cambridge University Press 2017)

OECD, 'Long-Term Interest Rates' (*OECD*, 2020) https://stats.oecd.org accessed 16 November 2020

OECD, 'Quarterly GDP' (*OECD*, 2018) https://data.oecd.org/gdp/quarterly-gdp.htm accessed 12 October 2018

OECD, 'Short-Term Interest Rates, Per Cent Per Annum' (*OECD Monthly Monetary and Financial Statistics (MEI)*, 2016) http://stats.oecd.org accessed 15 September 2016

OECD, *Economic Survey: Ireland* (OECD, 2006)

OECD, *Economic Survey: Ireland* (OECD, 2008)

OECD, *Economic Surveys: Canada 2010* (OECD, 2010)

OECD, *Economic Surveys: Canada 2012* (OECD, 2012)

OECD, *Economic Surveys: Euro Area 2012* (OECD, 2012)

OECD, *Economic Surveys: United States 2010* (OECD, 2012)

OECD, *Regions and Cities at a Glance* (OECD 2018)

OECD, *Revenue Statistics 2014 – Canada* (OECD, 2014)

Ojanen T and Salminen J, 'Finland: European Integration and International Human Rights Treaties as Sources of Domestic Constitutional Change and Dynamism' in Albi A and Bardutzky S (eds), *National Constitutions in European and Global Governance* (Springer 2019)

Ojanen T, 'EU Law and the Response of the Constitutional Law Committee of the Finnish Parliament' (2007) 52 Scan Stud L 204

Olson M, 'The Principle of "Fiscal Equivalence"' (1969) 59 Am Econ Rev 479

Oppenheimer A (ed) *The Relationship between European Community Law and National Law: The Cases*, vol 1 (Cambridge University Press 1994)

Padoa-Schioppa T, 'The European Monetary System: A Long-term View' in Giavazzi F, Micossi S and Miller M (eds), *The European Monetary System* (Cambridge University Press 2003)

Padoa-Schioppa T, *Efficiency, Stability, and Equity: A Strategy for the Evolution of the Economic System of the European Community (Padoa-Schioppa Report)* (Oxford University Press, 1987)

Padoa-Schioppa T, *Proceeding by Steps* (Committee of Governors, 17 November 1988)

Padoa-Schioppa T, *The Road to Monetary Union in Europe* (Clarendon Press 1994)

Padovano F, *The Politics and Economics of Regional Transfers: Decentralization, Interregional Redistribution and Income Convergence* (Edward Elgar 2007)

Palmstorfer R, 'To Bail Out or Not to Bail Out? The Current Framework of Financial Assistance for Euro Area Member States Measured against the Requirements of EU Primary Law' (2012) 37 EL Rev 771

Papadopoulou L, 'Can Constitutional Rules, Even if "Golden", Tame Greek Public Debt?' in Adams M, Fabbrini F and Larouche P (eds), *The Constitutionalization of European Budgetary Constraints* (Hart Publishing 2014)

Patnaik P, 'On Fiscal Deficits and Real Interest Rates' (2001) 36 Econ Polit Weekly 1160

Patomäki H, *The Great Eurozone Disaster* (Zed Books 2013)

Pech L and Scheppele KL, 'Illiberalism Within: Rule of Law Backsliding in the EU' (2017) 19 CYELS 3

Peel Q, 'Germany and Europe: A Very Federal Formula' *Financial Times* (London 9 February 2012) www.ft.com/intl/cms/s/0/31519b4a-5307-11e1-950d-00144fe abdc0.html#axzz3VZyP8kdL accessed 27 March 2015

Peers S, 'The Future of EU Treaty Amendments' (2012) 31 YB Eur L 7

Peers S, 'The Stability Treaty: Permanent Austerity or Gesture Politics' (2012) 8 ECL Review 404

Pérez de Nanclares JMY, 'Constitutional Identity in Spain' in Calleiss C and Van der Schyff G (eds), *Constitutional Identity in a Europe of Multilevel Constitutionalism* (Cambridge University Press 2019)

Pernice I, 'Domestic Courts, Constitutional Constraints and European Democracy: What Solution for the Crisis?' in Adams M, Fabbrini F and Larouche P (eds), *The Constitutionalization of European Budgetary Constraints* (Hart Publishing 2014)

Pernice I, 'Multilevel Constitutionalism and the Treaty of Amsterdam: European Constitution-Making Revisited?' (1999) 36 CMLR 703

Perold A, 'Negative Real Interest Rates: The Conundrum for Investment and Spending Policies' (2012) 69 FAJ 6

Peroni G, 'The Crisis of the Euro and the New Role of the European Central Bank' in de Witte B, Héritier A and Treschel AH (eds), *The Euro Crisis and the State of European Democracy* (European University Institute 2013)

Persson T and Tabellini G, 'Federal Fiscal Constitutions: Risk Sharing and Moral Hazard' (1996) 64 Econometrica 632

Pescatore P, 'International Law and Community Law – A Comparative Analysis' (1970) 7 CMLR 167

Petch T, 'The Compatibility of Outright Monetary Transactions with EU Law' (2013) 7 LFMR 13

Peterson PE and Nadler D (eds), *The Global Debt Crisis: Haunting US and European Federalism* (Brookings Institution Press 2014)

Petter A, 'Federalism and the Myth of the Federal Spending Power' (1989) 60 Can Bar Rev 34

Phelan DR and Whelan A, 'National Constitutional Law and European Integration' (1997) 6 IJEL 24

Phelan DR, *Revolt or Revolution, The Constitutional Boundaries of the European Community* (Sweet and Maxwell 1997)

Phelan W, 'Can Ireland Legislate Contrary to European Community Law?' (2008) 33 EL Rev 530

Piccirilli G, 'The "Taricco Saga": The Italian Constitutional Court Continues Its European Journey' (2018) 14 ECL Rev 814

Pipkorn J, 'Legal Arrangements in the Treaty of Maastricht for the Effectiveness of the Economic and Monetary Union' (1994) 31 CMLR 263

Pisani-Ferry J, *The Euro Crisis and its Aftermath* (Oxford University press 2011)

Poghosyan T, Senhadji A and Cottarelli C, 'The Role of Fiscal Transfers in Smoothing Regional Shocks' in Cottarelli C and Guerguil M (eds), *Designing a European Fiscal Union* (Routledge 2015)

Polten E and Glezl P, *Federalism in Canada and Germany: Overview and Comparison* (Polten & Associates 2014)

Popelier P and Van de heyning C, 'The Belgian Constitution: The Efficacy Approach to European and Global Governance' in Albi A and Bardutzky S (eds), *National Constitutions in European and Global Governance: Democracy, Rights, the Rule of Law* (Springer 2019)

Poterba J, 'Do Budget Rules Work?' in Auerbach AJ (ed), *Fiscal Policy: Lessons from Economic Research* (MIT Press 1997)

Poterba JM and Rueben K, 'State Fiscal Institutions and the US Municipal Bond Market' in Poterba JM and Von Hagen J (eds), *Fiscal Institutions and Fiscal Performance* (University of Chicago Press 1999)

Poterba JM and Rueben KS, 'Fiscal News, State Budget Rules, and Tax-Exempt Bond Yields' (2001) 50 J Urban Econ 537

Poterba JM, 'Balanced Budget Rules and Fiscal Policy: Evidence from the States' (1995) 48 Natl Tax J 329

Poterba JM, 'Budget Institutions and Fiscal Policy in US States' (1996) 86 Am Econ Rev 395

Poulou A, 'The Liability of the EU in the ESM Framework' (2017) 24 MJ 127

Predöhl A, 'The Theory of Location in Its Relation to General Economics' (1928) 36 JPE 371

Preshova D, 'Battleground or Meeting Point? Respect for National Identities in the European Union – Article 4 (2) of the Treaty on European Union' (2012) 8 CYELP 267

Pringle T, 'Written Observations in Case C-370/12 Pringle v Ireland' (*Extempore*, 27 November 2012) www.extempore.ie/2012/10/17/thomas-pringles-written-submissions-to-the-court-of-justice/c-370-12-observations-of-t-pringle-as-filed-2/ accessed 3 May 2017

Protzman F, 'Germany's Top Banker Gives Europe a Warning' *The New York Times* (20 March 1991) www.nytimes.com/1991/03/20/business/germany-s-top-banker-gives-europe-a-warning.html accessed 22 August 2016

Pujol F and Weber L, 'Are Preferences for Fiscal Discipline Endogenous?' (2003) 114 Public Choice 421

Purnhagen KP, 'Voluntary "New Approach" Technical Standards are Subject to Judicial Scrutiny by the CJEU! The Remarkable CJEU Judgment "Elliott" on Private Standards' (2017) 8 Eur J Risk Regul 586

Qian Y and Roland G, 'Federalism and the Soft Budget Constraint' (1998) 88 Am Econ Rev 1143

Qian Y and Weingast BR, 'Federalism as a Commitment to Preserving Market Incentives' (1997) 11 J Econ Persp 83

Rapach DE and Wohar ME, 'Regime Changes in International Real Interest Rates: Are They a Monetary Phenomenon?' (2005) 37 J Money Credit Bank 887

Ratchford B, *American State Debts* (Duke University Press 1941)

Rauchegger C, 'National Constitutional Rights and the Primacy of EU law: *M.A.S.*' (2018) 55 CMLR 1521

Reestman J-H, 'The Franco-German Constitutional Divide: Reflections on National and Constitutional Identity' (2009) 5 EUConst 267

Reestman JH, 'France: Conseil constitutionnel on the Status of (Secondary) Community Law in the French Internal Order. Decision 2004-496' (2005) 1 EuConst 302

Regling K and Watson M, *A Preliminary Report on the Sources of Ireland's Banking Crisis* (Government of Ireland Publications Office, 2010)

Reimann R and Zimmerman R (eds), *The Oxford Handbook of Comparative Law* (Oxford University Press 2008)

Reinhart C and Reinhart V, 'Capital Flow Bonanzas: An Encompassing View of the Past and Present' (2008) NBER Working Paper No. 14321

Reinhart C and Rogoff K, 'From Financial Crash to Debt Crisis' (2011) 101 Am Econ Rev 1676

Reinhart C, Reinhart V and Trebesch C, 'Global Cycles: Capital Flows, Commodities and Sovereign Defaults, 1815–2015' (2016) 106 Am Econ Rev 574

Reinhart V, 'A Year of Living Dangerously: The Management of the Financial Crisis in 2008' (2011) 25 J Econ Persp 71

Reis R, 'The Portuguese Slump and Crash and the Euro Crisis' (2013) 46 Brookings Papers on Economic Activity 143

Repasi R, 'Judicial Protection against Austerity Measures in the Euro Area: Ledra and Mallis' (2017) 54 CMLR 1123

Restuccia D and Rogerson R, 'Misallocation and Productivity' (2013) 16 Rev Econ Dynam 1

Reuter H, 'National Numerical Fiscal Rules: Not Complied With, But Still Effective?' (2015) 39 Europe J Polit Economy 67

Richards C, 'Sarran et Levacher: Ranking Legal Norms in the French Republic' (2000) 25 EL Rev 192

Richards C, 'The Supremacy of Community Law before the French Constitutional Court' (2006) 31 EL Rev 499

Riekmann SP and Wydra D, '"Obligations of Good Faith": On the Difficulties of Building US-Style EU Federalism' (2015) 21 Contemporary Politics 201

Riker WH, *Federalism: Origin, Operation, Significance* (1964)

Ringe, W-G, Huber OM (eds), *Legal Challenges in the Global Financial Crisis: Bail-outs, the Euro and Regulation* (Hart Publishing 2014)

Ritschl A, 'Sustainability of High Public Debt: What the Historical Record Shows' (1996) CEPR Discussion Paper No. 1357

Rodden J and Wibbels E, 'Beyond the Fiction of Federalism: Macroeconomic Management in Multitiered Systems' (2002) 4 World Politics 494

Rodden J, 'Achieving Fiscal Discipline in Federations: Germany and the EMU' in Deroose S, Flores E, Turrini A and Wierts P (eds), *Fiscal Policy Surveillance in Europe* (Palgrave Macmillan 2006)

Rodden J, 'Can Market Discipline Survive in the US Federation?' in Peterson PE and Nadler D (eds), *The Global Debt Crisis: Haunting US and European Federalism* (Brookings Institution Press 2014)

Rodden J, 'Reviving Leviathan: Fiscal Federalism and the Growth of Government' (2003) 57 IO 695

Rodden J, 'Soft Budget Constraints and German Federalism' in Rodden J, Eskeland G and Litvack J (eds), *Discal Decentralization and the Challenge of Hard Budget Constraints* (MIT Press 2003)

Rodden J, 'The Dilemma of Fiscal Federalism: Grants and Fiscal Performance Around the World' (2002) 46 Am J Polit Sci 670

Rodden J, *Hamilton's Paradox: The Promise and Perils of Fiscal Federalism* (Cambridge University Press 2006)

Rodden R, Eskeland G, Jennie Litvack J (eds), *Decentralization and the Challenge of Hard Budget Constraints* (MIT Press 2003)

Rogoff K, 'Can Exchange Rate Predictability Be Acheived without Monetary Convergence: Evidence from the EMS' (1985) 28 Eur Econ Rev 93

Rommerskirchèn C, 'Fiscal Rules, Fiscal Outcomes and Financial Market Behaviour' (2015) 54 Eur J Polit Res 836

Röpke W, *International Order and Economic Integration* (D Reidel Publishing Company 1959)

Röpke W, *The German Question* (George Allen & Unwin Ltd 1946

Rose AK and Spiegel MM, 'Cross-Country Causes and Consequences of the 2008 Crisis: International Linkages and American Exposure' (2010) 15 Pacific Econ Rev 340

Rose AK and Spiegel MM, 'Cross-Country Causes and Consequences of the 2008 Crisis: Early Warning' (2011) 24 Jpn World Econ 1

Rose AK, 'One Money, One Market: The Effect of Common Currencies on Trade' (2000) 15 Econ Policy 9

Rose S, 'Institutions and Fiscal Sustainability' (2010) 63 Nat Tax J 807

Rousseau J-J, *The Social Contract* (Penguin Classics 1968)

Roy-César É, *Canada's Equalization Formula* (Library of Parliament Publication No 2008-20-E, 2008)

Roznai Y, 'Unconstitutional Constitutional Amendments – The Migration and Success of a Constitutional Idea' (2013) 61 Am J Comp L 657

Roznai Y, *Unconstitutional Constitutional Amendments: The Limits of Amendment Powers* (Oxford University Press 2017)

Ruffert M, 'The European Debt Crisis and European Union Law' (2011) 48 CMLR 1777

Ryan C, 'The Euro Crisis and Crisis Management: Big Lessons from a Small Island' (2011) 8 Int Econ Policy 31

Ryvkin B, 'Saving the Euro: Tensions with the European Treaty Law in the European Union's Efforts to Protect the Common Currency' (2012) 45 Cornell Int'l LJ 227

Sadurski W, '"Solange, Chapter 3": Constitutional Courts in Central Europe" (2014) 14 ELJ 1

Sadurski W, 'Polish Constitutional Tribunal under PiS: From an Activist Court, to a Paralysed Tribunal, to a Government Enabler' (2019) 11 Hague J Rule Law 63

Sajo A, 'Learning Co-operative Constitutionalism the Hard Way: The Hungarian Constitutional Court Shying Away from EU Supremacy' (2004) 2 Zeitschrift für Staats-und Europawissenschaften 356

Sandholtz W, 'Monetary Bargains: The Treaty on EMU' in Cafruny A and Rosenthal G (eds), *The State of the European Community: The Maastricht Debates and Beyond* (Lynne Rienner Publishers Inc 1994)

Sankari S and Tuori K, *The Many Constitutions of Europe* (Ashgate 2013)

Sargent TJ, 'Nobel Lecture: United States Then, Europe Now' (2012) 120 J Polit Econ 1

Schaechter A, Kinda T, Budina N and Weber A, 'Fiscal Rules in Response to the Crisis – Towards the "Next-Generation" Rules. A New Dataset' (2012) IMF Working Paper No 187

Schermers H and Waelbroeck D, *Judicial Protection in the European Union* (6th ed., Kluwer Law International 2001)

Schiemann K, 'Europe and the Loss of Sovereignty' (2007) 56 Int'l & Comp LQ 475

Schilling T, 'The Autonomy of the Community Legal Order: An Analysis of Possible Foundations' (1996) 37 Harv Int'l LJ 389

Schmitt C, *Political Theology: Four Chapters on the Concept of Sovereignty* (MIT Press 1985)

Schnabel J, 'Canada' in Braun D, Ruiz-Palmero C and Schnabel J (eds), *Consolidation Policies in Federal States* (Routledge 2016)

Schnabel J, 'Switzerland' in Braun D, Ruiz-Palmero C and Schnabel J (eds), *Consolidation Policies in Federal States* (Routledge 2016)

Schnabel J, 'United States' in Braun D, Ruiz-Palmero C and Schnabel J (eds), *Consolidation Policies in Federal States* (Routledge 2016)

Schnellenbach J, 'German Federalism at the Crossroads: Renegotiating the Allocation of Competencies in a New Financial Environment' in Eccleston R and Krever R (eds), *The Future of Federalism* (Edward Elgar 2017)

Schuknecht L, Von Hagen J and Wolswijk G, 'Government Risk Premiums in the Bond Market: EMU and Canada' (2008) ECB Working Papers No 879

Schularick M and Taylor AM, 'Credit Booms Gone Bust: Monetary Policy, Leverage Cycles and Financial Crises' (2012) 102 Am Econ Rev 1029

Schultz A and Wolff G, 'The German Sub-national Government Bond Market: Structure, Determinants of Yields Spreads and Berlin's Forgone Bail-out' (2009) 229 J Econ Stat 61

Schütze R, *European Union Law* (Cambridge University Press 2018)

Scott FR, 'Centralization and Decentralization in Canadian Federalism' (1951) 29 Can Bar Rev 1095

Scott FR, 'The Constitutional Background of the Taxation Agreements' (1955) 2 McGill LJ 1

Seitz H, 'Fiscal Policy, Deficits and Politics of Subnational Governments: The Case of German Laender' (2000) 102 Public Choice 183

Seitz H, 'Subnational Government Bailouts in Germany' (1999) Zentrum für Europäische Integrationsforschung Working Paper No 20

Seitz H, 'Subnational Government Bailouts in Germany' (2000) IDB Working Papers No 123

Servais D and Ruggeri R, 'The EU Constitution: Its Impact on Economic and Monetary Union and Economic Governance', *Legal Aspects of the European System of Central Banks* (ECB 2005)

Seyad SM, 'A Legal Analysis of the European Financial Stability Mechanism' (2011) 26 JIBLR 421

Sharpston E and Baere GD, 'The Court of Justice as a Constitutional Adjudicator' in Anthony Arnull, Catherine Barnard, Michael Dougan and Spaventa E (eds), *A Constitutional Order of States?* (Hart Publishing 2011)

Shaw J, 'Europe's Constitutional Future' (2005) (Spring) PL 132

Simeon R, *Federal-Provincial Diplomacy: The Making of Recent Policy in Canada* (University of Toronto Press 2006)

Simpson J, 'The Agreement on German External Debts' (1957) 6 ICLQ 472

Simpson W and Wesley J, 'Effective Tool or Effectively Hollow? Balanced Budget Legislation in Western Canada' (2012) 38 Can Public Pol'y 291

Singh R and Plekhanov A, 'How Should Subnational Government Borrowing Be Regulated?' (2007) 53 IMF Staff Papers 426

Sinn H-W, *The Euro Trap: On Bursting Bubbles, Budgets and Beliefs* (Oxford University Press 2014)

Skouras T, 'The Euro Crisis and Its Lessons from a Greek Perspective' (2013) 35 Econ Soc 51

Śledzińska-Simon A and Ziółkowski M, 'Constitutional Identity in Poland: Is the Emperor Putting on the Old Clothes of Sovereignty' in Calleiss C and Van der Schyff G (eds), *Constitutional Identity in a Europe of Multilevel Constitutionalism* (Cambridge University Press 2019)

Smits R, 'The Crisis Response in Europe's Economic and Monetary Union: Overview of Legal Developments' (2015) 38 Fordham Int'l Law J 1135

Smits R, *The European Central Bank: Institutional Aspects* (Kluwer Law International 1997)

Snell J, 'Gauweiler – Some Instituitonal Aspects' (2015) 40 EL Rev 133

Snell J, 'Gauweiler – What Next?' (2015) 40 EL Rev 473

Soguel N, 'The Future of Swiss Federalism: The Challenge of Fiscal Stabilization Policy in the Absence of Coordination' in Eccleston R and Krever R (eds), *The Future of Federalism* (Elgar 2017)

Soros G, 'Remarks at the Festival of Economics' (Festival of Economics, Trento, Italy, 2 June 2012) https://www.georgesoros.com/2012/06/02/remarks_at_the_festival_of_economics_trento_italy/ accessed June 14, 2021

Spiegel P and Wise P, 'Portugal's Anti-Austerity Budget Provokes Brussels Showdown' *Financial Times* (4 February 2016) https://www.ft.com/content/bcfbc34c-cb39-11e5-a8ef-ea66e967dd44 accessed June 14, 2021

Spiegel, 'The Ticking Euro Bomb: How a Good Idea Became a Tragedy' *Spiegel* (5 October 2011) www.spiegel.de/international/europe/the-ticking-euro-bomb-how-a-good-idea-became-a-tragedy-a-790138.html accessed 24 July 2015

Stabilitätsrat, 'Summary of Decisions of the Stability Council for Budgetary Surveillance in Accordance with §3 Stability Council Law' (*10th meeting of the Stability Council on 15 December 2014*, 2014) www.stabilitaetsrat.de/SharedDocs/Downloads/DE/Sitzungen/20141215_10.Sitzung/Beschl%C3%BCsse/20141215_Beschluesse_Haushaltsueberwachung.pdf?__blob=publicationFile accessed 17 June 2015

Stalder K and Röhrs S, *Answers to OECD Questionnaire: Fiscal Rules for Cantons and Communes* (Insitut für Finanzwissenschaft und Finanzrecht, 2005)

Staloff D, *Hamilton, Adams, Jefferson: The Politics of Enlightenment and the American Founding* (Hill & Wang 2005)

Standard and Poor's, *Sovereign Government Rating Methodology and Assumptions* (Standard & Poor's, 2013)

Stanton J, 'The Constitution of Malta: Supremacy, Parliament and the Separation of Powers' (2019) 6 JICL 47

Stark J, 'Lessons from the European Crisis' (2013) 33 Cato J 541

Statistics Canada, 'Revenue and Expenditures' (*Statistics Canada*, 6 January 2016) www.statcan.gc.ca/tables-tableaux/sum-som/l01/cst01/govt02b-eng.htm accessed 10 September 2016

Stegarescu D, *Decentralised Government in an Integrating World*, vol 34 (Physica-Verlag 2006)

Stein E, 'Lawyers, Judges and the Making of a Transnational Constitution' (1981) 75 Am J Comp L 1

Steinberg F and Vermeiren M, 'Germany's Institutional Power and the EMU Regime after the Crisis: Towards a Germanized Euro Area?' (2015) 54 JCMS 388

Stiglitz J, *The Euro: How a Common Currency Threatends the Future of Europe* (Norton 2016)

Streinz R, 'The Limits of Legal Regulation: Will the Treaty on Stability, Coordination and Governance in the Economic and Monetary Union Have a Real Legal Effect?' in Ringe W-G and Huber PM (eds), *Legal Challenges in the Global Financial Crisis: Bail-outs, the Euro and Regulation* (Hart Publishing 2014)

Summers LH, 'International Financial Crises: Causes, Prevention and Cures' (1998) 90 Am Econ Rev 1

Sutherland D, Price R and Joumard I, 'Fiscal Rules for Sub-Central Governments: Design and Impact' (2005) OECD Economics Department Working Papers No 52

Tanchev E, 'Constitutional Amendments Due To Bulgarian Full EU Membership' in Kellermann AE, De Zwaan J, Cruczi J (eds), *EU Enlargement* (TMC Asser Press 2001) 301

Tapp S, 'The Use and Effectiveness of Fiscal Rules in Canadian Provinces' (2013) 39 Can Public Admin 45

Tapp S, *Canadian Experiences with Fiscal Consolidations and Fiscal rules* (Office of the Parliamentary Budget Officer, 2010)

Taylor C, 'CSO Provisionally Puts Irish Water on State Books' *The Irish Times* (3 April 2015) www.irishtimes.com/news/politics/cso-provisionally-puts-irish-water-on-state-books-1.2164485 accessed 18 April 2016

Taylor J, 'Discretion versus Policy Rules in Practice' (1993) 39 Carnegie-Rochester Conference Series on Public Policy 195

Taylor J, 'The Financial Crisis and the Policy Responses: An Empirical Analysis of What Went Wrong' (2009) NBER Working Papers No 14631

Tellier G and Imbeau L, 'Budget Deficits and Surpluses in the Canadian Provinces: A Pooled Analysis' (European Public Choice Society Annual Conference, Berlin, April 2004)

Ter-Minassian T and Craig J, 'Control of Subnational Government Borrowing' in Ter-Minassian T (ed), *Fiscal Federalism in Theory and Practice* (IMF 1997)

Ter-Minassian T, 'Fiscal Rules for Subnational Governments: Can they Promote Fiscal Discipline?' (2007) 6 *OECD Journal on Budgeting* 1

The Economist, 'The Euro Crisis Was Not a Government Debt Crisis' *The Economist* (23 November 2015) 12 https://www.economist.com/free-exchange/2015/11/23/the-euro-crisis-was-not-a-government-debt-crisis accessed 14 June 2021

The Economist, 'The Mundell-Fleming Trilemma' (*The Economist*, 27 August 2016) www.economist.com/schools-brief/2016/08/27/two-out-of-three-aint-bad accessed 22 November 2020

Theil S, 'What Red Lines, If Any, Do the Lisbon Judgments of the European Constitutional Courts draw for Future EU Integration?' (2014) 15 German LJ 599

Tholoniat L, 'The Career of the Open Method of Coordination: Lessons from a "Soft" EU Instrument' (2010) 33 West Eur Polit 93

Thygesen N, 'The Delors Report and EMU 1989' (1989) 65 International Affairs 637

Timmermans C, 'Publication Review: The Worlds of European
    Constitutionalism' (2014) 10 EuConst 349
Tobin J, 'Liquidity Preference and Monetary Policy' (1947) 29 Rev Econ and
    Statis 124
Tobin J, 'Money and Economic Growth' (1965) 33 Econometrica 671
Tombe T, 'An (Overdue) Review of Canada's Fiscal Stabilization Program' (2020)
    IRRP Insight No 31
Tomkin J, 'Contradiction, Circumvention and Conceptual Gymnastics: The
    Impact of the Adoption of the ESM Treaty on the State of European
    Democracy' (2013) 14 German LJ 169
Tommasi M and Weinschelbaum F, 'Centralization vs Decentralization: A
    Principal-Agent Analysis' (2007) 9 J Public Econ Theory 369
Toplak J and Gardasevic D, 'Concepts of National and Constitutional Identity in
    Croatian Constitutional Law' (2017) 42 RCEEL 263
Traclet V, 'Monetary and Fiscal Policies in Canada: Some Interesting Principles
    for EMU?' (2004) Bank of Canada Working Paper No 28
Treisman D, 'Political Decentralization and Economic Reform: A
    Game-Theoretic Analysis' (1999) 43 Am J Polit Sci 488
Trichet J-C, 'International Policy Coordination in the Euro Area: Toward an
    Economic and Fiscal Federation by Exception' (2013) 35 J Policy Model 473
Trichet J-C, 'The ECB's Response to the Recent Tensions in Financial Markets'
    (38th Economic Conference of the *Oesterreichische Nationalbank*, Vienna, 31 May
    2010)
Triffin R, *Gold and the Dollar Crisis: The Future of Convertibility* (Yale University Press
    1960
Tsoukalis L, *The Politics and Economics of European Monetary Integration* (George
    Allen & Unwin 1977)
Tuori K and Tuori K, *The Eurozone Crisis: A Constitutional Anlysis* (Cambridge
    University Press 2014)
Tushnet M, 'Comparative Constitutional Law' in Reimann M and
    Zimmerman R (eds), *The Oxford Handbook of Comparative Law* (Oxford
    University Press 2008)
Umbach M, *German Federalism: Past, Present, Future* (Palgrave Macmillan 2002)
Ungerer, *A Concise History of European Monetary Ingegration: From EPU to EMU*
    (Quorum Books 1997)
Unicredit, *Handbook of German States* (Unicredit 2012)
US General Accounting Office, *Balanced Budget Requirements: State Experiences and
    Implications for the Federal Government* (GAO/AFMD-93-58BR, 1993)
Ušacka A, 'The Impact of the European Integration Process on the Constituton of
    Latvia' in Kellermann AE, De Zwaan J, Cruczi J (eds), *EU Enlargement* (TMC Asser
    Press 2001) 337
Vadapalas V, 'Lithuania: the Constitutional Impact of the Enlargement at
    National Level' in Kellermann AE, de Zwaan JW and Czuczai J (eds), *EU
    Enlargement* (TMC Asser Press 2001)

Valero J, 'EU Puts "Ever Closer Union" on Hold' *EurActivcom* (11 October 2016) www.euractiv.com/section/future-eu/news/eu-puts-ever-closer-union-on-hold/ accessed 11 October 2016

Van Aken W and Artige L, 'A Comparative Analysis of Reverse Majority Voting' in De Witte B, Heritier A and Treschsel AH (eds), *The Euro Crisis and the State of European Democracy* (European University Institute 2013)

Van Malleghem P-A, '(Un)Balanced Budget Rules in Europe and America' in Adams M, Fabbrini F and Larouche P (eds), *The Constitutionalization of European Budgetary Constraints* (Hart Publishing 2014)

Van Rompuy H, *Towards a Genuine Economic and Monetary Union* (EUCO 120/12, 2012)

Van Ypersele J and Koeune J-C, *The European Monetary System: Origins, Operation and Outlook* (European Communities 1985)

Vatter A, *Swiss Federalism: The Transformation of a Federal Model* (Routledge 2018)

Velkouleskou D, Thomsen P and Petrova I, 'Transcript of 9 March 2016 IMF Teleconference on Greece' (Wikileaks Release: 2 April 2016)

Verfassungsgerichtshof Österreichischer, 'European Fiscal Compact Not Held To Be Unconstitutional' (*Verfassungsgerichtshof Österreichischer*, 5 November 2013) www.verfassungsgerichtshof.ataccessed 28 October 2016

Viganò F, '*Melloni* Overruled? Considerations on the *"Taricco II"* Judgment of the Court of Justice' (2018) 9 NJECL 18

Vikarská Z and Bobek M, 'Slovakia: Between Euro-Optimism and Euro-Concerns' in Albi A and Bardutzky S (eds), *National Constitutions in European and Global Governance* (Springer 2019)

Vita V, 'The Romanian Constitutional Court and the Principle of Primacy: To Refer or Not to Refer?' (2019) 16 German LJ 1623

Volpato A, 'The Harmonized Standards before the ECJ: *James Elliott Construction*' (2017) 54 CMLR 591

Von Bogdandy A and Bast J (eds), *Principles of European Constitutional Law* (2nd ed., Hart Publishing 2011)

Von Bogdandy A and Schill S, 'Overcoming Absolute Primacy: Respect for National Identity under the Lisbon Treaty' (2011) 48 CMLR 1417

Von Hagen J and Eichengreen B, 'Federalism, Fiscal Restraints and European Monetary Union' (1995) 48 Am Econ Rev 134

Von Hagen J and Harden I, 'National Budget Processes and Fiscal Performance' (1994) 3 European Economy 311

Von Hagen J and Hofman B, 'Macroeconomic Implications of Low Inflation in the Euro Area' (2004) 15 N Amer J Econ Financ 5

Von Hagen J, 'A Note on the Empirical Effectiveness of Formal Fiscal Restraints' (1991) 44 J Public Econ 199

Von Hagen J, 'Budgeting Procedures and Fiscal Performance in the European Communities' (1992) 96 European Economy 1

Von Hagen J, 'Fiscal Arrangements in a Monetary Union: Some Evidence from the US' in Fair D, De Boissieu C and Alworth J (eds), *Fiscal Policy, Taxation and the Financial System in an Increasingly Integrated Europe* (Kluwer 1992)

Von Hagen J, 'Fiscal Rules and Fiscal Performance in the EU and Japan' (2005) CEPR Discussion Paper No 5330

Von Hagen J, Schuknecht L and Wolswijk G, 'Government Bond Risk Premiums in the EU Revisited: The Impact of the Financial Crisis' (2011) 27 Eur J Polit Econ 36

Walker N, 'The Idea of Constitutional Pluralism' (2002) 65 MLR 317

Wallis JJ and Wieingast BR, 'Dysfunctional or Optimal Institutions?' in Garrett E, Graddy EA and Jackson HE (eds), *Fiscal Challenges: An Interdisciplinary Approach to Budget Policy* (Cambridge University press 2009)

Wallis JJ, 'Constitutions, Corporations and Corruption: American States and Constitutional Change, 1842 to 1852' (2005) 65 J Econ Hist 211

Walters AA, *Sterling in Danger: The Economic Consequences of Pegged Exchange Rates* (Institute of Economic Affairs 1990)

Watts RL, 'German Federalism in Comparative Perspective' in Jeffery C (ed), *Recasting German Federalism: The Legacies of Unification* (Pinter 1999)

Weatherill S, *Law and Integration in the European Union* (Oxford University Press 1995)

Webley L, 'Qualitative Approaches to Empirical Legal Research' in Cane P and Kritzer HM (eds), *The Oxford Handbook of Empirical Legal Research* (Oxford University Press 2010)

Weder di Mauro B and Zettelmeyer J, *The New Global Financial Safety Net*, vol 4 (Centre for International Governance Innovation 2017)

Weidmann J, 'Crisis Management' (Walter Eucken Lecture, Freiburg, 2 November 2013)

Weiler J, 'Does Europe Need a Constitution? Demos, Telos and the German Maastricht Decision' (1995) 1 ELJ 219

Weiler J, 'In Defence of the Status Quo: Europe's Constitutional *Sonderweg*' in JHH Weiler and Wind M (eds), *European Constitutionalism Beyond the State* (Cambridge University Press 2003)

Weiler J, 'The Transformation of Europe' (1990-1991) 100 Yale LJ 2403

Weiler JHH, Wind M (eds), *European Constitutionalism Beyond the State* (Cambridge University Press 2003)

Weingast BR, 'Second Generation Fiscal Federalism: The Implications of Fiscal Incentives' (2009) 65 J Urban Econ 279

Weingast BR, 'The Economic Role of Political Institutions: Market-Preserving Federalism and Economic Development' (1995) 10 JL Econ & Org 1

Weiss L, 'The Effects of Money Supply on Economic Welfare in the Steady State' (1980) 48 Econometrica 565

Wendel M, 'Exceeding Judicial Competence in the Name of Democracy: The German Federal Constitutional Court's OMT Reference' (2014) 10 EuConst 263.

Werner P, *Report to the Council and the Commission on the Realisation by Stages of Economic and Monetary Union in the Community (Werner Report)* (1970, EC Bulletin 11 supplement)

Wheare K, *Federal Government* (Oxford University Press 1987)

Wibbels E, 'Bailouts, Budget Constraints and Leviathans: Comparative Federalism and Lessons from the Early States' (2003) 36 Comp Polit Stud 475

Wibbels E, *Federalism and the Market* (Cambridge University Press 2005)

Wildasin DE, 'Externalities and Bailouts: Hard and Soft Budget Constraints in Intergovernmental Fiscal Relations' (1997) World Bank Policy Research Working Papers No 1843

Wolff G, 'A Budget for Europe's Monetary Union' (2012) 22 Breugel Policy Contribution 1

Woods L and Watson P, *Steiner & Woods EU Law* (12th ed., Oxford University Press 2012)

World Bank, 'Domestic Credit to Private Sector (% of GDP) (FS.AST.PRVT.GD.ZS)' (*World Bank*, 2014) www.data.worldbank.org accessed 26 November 2014

World Bank, 'GDP Per Capita (Current LCU)' (*World Bank*, 2014) www .data.worldbank.org accessed 26 November 2014

World Bank, 'Inflation by GDP Deflator (NY.GDP.DEFL.KD.ZG)' (*World Bank*, 2016) www.data.worldbank.org accessed 15 September 2016

World Bank, 'Interest Payments as a % of Revenue (GC.XPN.INTP.RV.ZS)' (*World Bank*, 2015) www.data.worldbank.org accessed 26 November 2015

World Bank, 'Real Effective Exchange Rate (PX.REX.REER)' (*World Bank*, 2014) www.data.worldbank.org accessed 26 November 2014

World Bank, 'Surplus/Deficit (% of GDP) (GC.BAL.CASH.GD.ZS)' (*World Bank*, 2016) www.data.worldbank.org accessed 13 September 2016

Wurgler J, 'Financial Markets and the Allocation of Capital' (2000) 58 J Financ Econ 187

Wyatt D, 'Is the European Union an Organisation of Limited Powers?' in Arnull A, Barnard C, Dougan M and Spaventa E (eds), *A Constitutional Order of States?* (Hart Publishing 2011)

in C, 'EMU: Why and How It Might Happen' (1997) 11 J Econ Persp 3

Wyplosz C, 'European Monetary Union: The Dark Sides of a Major Success' (2006) 21 Econ Policy 208

Wyplosz C, 'Fiscal Discipline in a Monetary Union without Fiscal Union' in Ódor Lu (ed), *Rethinking Fiscal Policy after the Crisis* (Cambridge University Press 2017)

Wyplosz C, 'Monetary Union and Fiscal Policy Discipline' (1991) European Economy Special Edition No 1 165

Wyplosz C, 'The Centralization-Decentralization Issue' (2015) European Economy Discussion Papers No 14

Wyplosz C, 'The Common Currency: More Complicated Than It Seems' in Badinger H and Nitsch V (eds), *Routledge Handbook of the Economics of European Integration* (Routledge 2015)

Wyplosz C, 'Theory to Practice', *European Fiscal Board Workshop 2019: Independent Fiscal Institutions in the EU Fiscal Framework* (European Union 2019)

Xafa M, 'EMU and Greece: Issues and Prospects for Membership' in Baldassarri M and Mundell R (eds), *Building the New Europe Volume I: The Single Market and Monetary Unification* (Palgrave Macmillan 1990)

Xenophon Contiades and Tassopoulos IA, 'The Impact of the Financial Crisis on the Greek Constitution' in Contiades X (ed) *Constitutions in the Global Financial Crisis* (Ashgate Publishing 2013) 195

Xuereb PG, 'The Constitution of Malta: Reflections on New Mechanisms for Synchrony of Values in Different Levels of Governance' in Albi A and Bardutzky S (eds), *National Constitutions in European and Global Governance* (Springer 2019)

Zeitler F-C, 'The European Public Debt Crisis and the Institutional Framework of the Monetary Union: Experience and Adjustments' in Ringe W-G and Huber PM (eds), *Legal Challenges in the Global Financial Crisis: Bail-outs, the Euro and Regulation* (Hart Publishing 2014)

Ziblatt D, 'Between Centralization and Federalism in the European Union' in Peterson P and Nadler D (eds), *The Global Debt Crisis: Haunting US and European Federalism* (Brookings Institution Press 2014)

Index

Printed by Printforce, the Netherlands